P9-EGL-307

How to Cook *Everything*®

fast

OTHER BOOKS BY MARK BITTMAN

How to Cook Everything

How to Cook Everything Vegetarian

How to Cook Everything The Basics

VB6: Eat Vegan Before 6:00

The VB6 Cookbook

Food Matters

The Food Matters Cookbook

The Best Recipes in the World

Fish: The Complete Guide to Buying and Cooking

Leafy Greens

Mark Bittman's Kitchen Express

Mark Bittman's Quick and Easy Recipes from The New York Times

The Mini Minimalist

Jean-Georges: Cooking at Home with a Four-Star Chef

Simple to Spectacular

How to Cook *Everything*® *fast*

A BETTER WAY TO COOK GREAT FOOD

Mark Bittman

Illustrations by Olivia de Salve Villedieu

Houghton Mifflin Harcourt
Boston New York
2014

Design by MGMT. design

Illustrations by Olivia de Salve Villedieu.

www.hmhco.com

Library of Congress Cataloging-in-Publication Data is available.

ISBN 978-0-470-93630-6 (cloth); ISBN 978-0-544-33340-6 (ebk)

Printed in the United States of America

DOC 10 9 8 7 6 5 4 3 2 1

To my fabulous women-children, Kate and Emma, who have always been there for me.

Acknowledgments

How to Cook Everything Fast—let's just call it *Fast*—has been, like all the books in this series, a massive undertaking (do you feel how heavy it is?), a huge and (for those of us involved in it) hugely important project, many years in conception and quite a few in the making. It's not just a big book, and it's not just a good recipe collection: It's a collection of recipes in a style we've devised to teach you how to cook in the way people who really know how do all the time.

It wasn't easy, and I didn't do it by myself. In fact, like all the How to Cook Everything books, this was a team effort. Kerri Conan and I have now worked on something like ten books together, and none of them would've happened without her. On this one, our efforts were eased by those of Daniel Meyer, who bore the lion's share of recipe conception, writing, and testing; and Jennifer Griffin, who was the editor of the original *How to Cook Everything* (1997!) and has joined us in getting things ready for our current editors at HMH, chief among them the stellar Adam Kowit.

Others who deserve credit on "our" side include my agent of 25-plus years, Angela Miller; the great Chris Benton; and Megan Gourley, Eve Turow, Elena Goldblatt, Maria Fantaci, and David Bowers. At HMH, we are lucky enough to have been working under the steady hands of Bruce Nichols and Natalie Chapman, and we owe gratitude to the amazing Rebecca Liss, the steadfast Linda Ingroia, and to Molly Aronica, Brad Parsons, Jessica Gilo, Marina Padakis Lowry, Jamie Selzer, David Futato, Tom Hyland, Kevin Watt, Michaela Sullivan, Melissa Lotfy, and of course the wonderful Laurie Brown.

We talk a lot about text and recipes, because we—most of the people mentioned above—work in words. But designing *Fast* took about 30,000 iterations (okay, an exaggeration; 20,000) until it reached what we believe is the gorgeous, accessible, well-organized book you're holding. That design is thanks to MGMT. Design: Alicia Cheng, Pilar Torcal, and Olivia de Salve Villedieu, who also did the helpful illustrations scattered throughout.

Some people's roles cannot be easily defined but were critical nevertheless. These folks include Sean Santoro, Wendy and Kim Marcus, John Willoughby, and Trish Hall. Other friends and family will presumably forgive me for not singling them out—you know who you are.

Finally, the amount contributed here by Kelly Doe can't be overestimated. The imprints of her index finger are everywhere.

Mark Bittman
New York City, Summer 2014

Contents

TIME TO COOK 8

THE FAST KITCHEN 10

MAIN DISHES

Salads 40

Sandwiches 128

Soups and Stews 198

Pasta and Noodles 274

Rice and Grains 346

Vegetables 410

Beans and Tofu 472

Seafood 532

Chicken 606

Meat 704

Breakfast 802

ACCOMPANIMENTS

Appetizers 872

Sides 902

Dessert 966

FAST NAVIGATION 1004

VEGETARIAN MAIN DISHES 1008

KITCHEN NOTES 1010

INDEX 1012

Time to Cook

Cooking is an essential human activity. It can relax us after long, stressful days, bring us closer to our families, and put a lifetime of nourishment and endless eating possibilities right at our fingertips. Then why do we avoid it? Many of us claim we just don't have time to cook, and given the abundance of restaurants and food companies jockeying to feed us, that has become a perfectly acceptable position.

In the last 50 years, the way we feed ourselves has changed, and with reason. More women are in the workforce than ever before; kids rush between activities and sports and often arrive home as late as their parents. Even people without children have less time to spend planning, shopping, and cooking, as we work more hours than we used to.

Yet as eaters we've become more sophisticated; we understand and experience and appreciate flavors that were once foreign, and we care more than ever about the quality of the ingredients we buy. We know what eating well is but often don't have the time to do it, so we settle for eating fast.

Over the years, I've found easy ways to put real meals on the table. Life may have become more complicated, but cooking can become simpler.

The fact is that you do have time to cook: You just need better recipes. Imagine a road map that captures the rhythm of the kitchen, where preparation and cooking happen seamlessly. Soup begins to simmer while you prepare more vegetables for the pot; oil shimmers in a skillet as you chop an onion; broiled meat rests while rice steams. This is naturally fast cooking, the kind experienced cooks do intuitively.

Fast cooking involves strategy, not compromise. Here I take seemingly complicated dishes like wonton soup and spanakopita and reduce them to their essentials, taking them apart and reconstructing them with all the flavors and textures you love about the originals. Smart, easy techniques, like cutting meat into smaller pieces for lightning-quick braises and harnessing the power of the broiler, give you all the pleasure of eating homemade meals with minimal work and—perhaps more important—*time.*

The result is delicious food prepared from real ingredients—and quickly. There are plenty of shortcuts here, and for the most part they don't compromise flavor or texture. (When they do, they're worth it.) As a practical purist, I open cans and boxes like everyone else, provided what's inside is nutritious and minimally processed. (There's a checklist of what qualifies as convenience food in this book on page 20; if you're already a *How to Cook Everything* fan, there won't be any surprises.)

In short, *How to Cook Everything Fast* is both a series of strategies and a collection of all-new recipes that do the thinking for you. Whether you're a beginner hoping to learn how to weave homemade meals into your regular routine or an experienced cook looking to become more efficient, I can help you get where you want to be, while giving you all the time you need.

The Fast Kitchen

FASTER IS BETTER 12

Real-Time Cooking 12

Helping Hands 12

Rethinking the Meal 13

Make Room for Dessert 13

The Myth of *Mise en Place* 13

FAST INGREDIENTS 14

Shopping for Speed 14

Pantry Staples 15

Fridge Staples 18

Freezer Staples 19

Shortcut Cheat Sheet 20

Interchangeable Ingredients 21

FAST EQUIPMENT 22

Key Tools 22

SETUP FOR SPEED 24

FAST STRATEGIES 26

Rinse, Don't Repeat 26

Consolidate Mincing 26

Thinner (and Smaller) = Faster 26

Grate for Puréeing 26

Start with Heat 26

Adjust the Heat 27

Don't Wait for the Oven 27

Heat Oil in the Oven 27

Embrace the Broiler 27

Take Advantage of Steam 27

Use Less Liquid for Braising 27

Clean as You Go 27

PREP SHORTCUTS 28

A NEW KIND OF RECIPE 36

HOW TO USE THIS BOOK 38

Gathering Ingredients 38

"Do the Blue" 38

Make-Ahead Master Recipes 38

Recipe-Free Cooking 38

Ingredients at a Glance 39

New Techniques 39

A Word About Food Safety 39

Faster Is Better

Fast doesn't mean frantic. In fact, if you use your head, fast cooking can be pleasurable. As with many skills, learning to be efficient, comfortable, and confident in the kitchen comes with practice. Here the lessons are built into the recipes, so you can just dive in, and, without realizing it, you'll hone your skills and become naturally more efficient whenever you cook.

Real-Time Cooking

The process of getting a home-cooked meal on the table involves four tasks: shopping, preparation, cooking, and cleaning up. Common "wisdom" would have you complete these steps linearly, finishing one before beginning the next. Shop. Unpack the groceries. Wash, trim, chop, slice, dice. Stand at the stove. Serve. Eat. Tackle the dishes.

But that approach ignores the natural rhythm of experienced cooks. In reality, the action ebbs and flows within a span of time rather than to the beat of a ticking clock. While something simmers, roasts, or sautés, you have the flexibility to make a loop between counter, fridge, and stove, pause at the sink to wash some dishes, or work on making a salad. Efficiency comes when you put time on your side and maximize every minute.

This is real-time cooking, where gathering, preparing, and combining ingredients become one seamless endeavor. It's both faster and easier than the more common step-by-step process and embodies concepts that are not only fundamental to these recipes but applicable to all others. Embrace real-time cooking and you'll be looking at the components of cooking—food, tools, and techniques—from a completely different perspective.

Helping Hands

Actually, too many cooks don't spoil the broth; some of the best moments in the kitchen involve sharing a countertop with family and friends. Even one extra set of hands can be a huge help. (If there's a youngster around who's willing and able, you'll be spreading the joy into the next generation.) In fact these recipes are perfect for divvying up tasks among all your helpers; see "Do the Blue" on page 38.

Rethinking the Meal

It's not a new concept, but you can cook one dish and call it dinner; it helps, of course, if you serve it with a couple of *very* simply executed appetizers, sides, and desserts. So the bulk of the recipes in *Fast* are for main courses that eat like meals, dishes that bring several components (like meat, vegetables, and starches) together on one plate in ways that both retain their distinction and integrity and create a whole that's more than the sum of its parts. Of course if you have the inclination, you can make a starter or try a salad, vegetable, noodle, rice, or grain dish from Sides, which are easy to prepare while you're cooking the mains (you'll find specific suggestions after each recipe). These strategies provide plenty of options in this book for assembling all kinds of fast meals, from everyday kitchen-table lunches and dinners to breakfasts, parties, and celebrations. (For a tutorial on other recipe features, see A New Kind of Recipe on page 36.)

Make Room for Dessert

For many of us, finishing the meal with a little something sweet isn't a luxury but a necessity. I've always favored simpler desserts so it seems natural to include a chapter of mostly familiar favorites, now streamlined to the point where they become easy enough for typical weeknights. Most, in fact, can be pulled together in the few minutes before you get started on the main dish and sides; you can prepare many of them up to several hours in advance. And some are so fast you can whip them up while someone else gets a head start on cleanup.

The Myth of *Mise en Place*

Although many terrific ideas have moved from restaurants to home kitchens, *mise en place*—prepping all the ingredients ahead of time—isn't one of them. The term—it means, roughly, "put in place"—is great if you have an assistant who can work through the recipe's ingredient list and get each item ready to cook. At that point, you just cook. It's undeniably handy to have food chopped, measured, neatly arranged in cups on a tray, and put within arm's reach of the stove before turning it on, but it's also completely impractical when you're working alone or even have a little help. Doing all the prep ahead of time often leaves you twiddling your thumbs, waiting for food to cook. (Unless, of course, you're in a restaurant, cooking ten things at once.)

Fast Ingredients

A well-stocked kitchen is the backbone of fast cooking; this section lists the staples to keep in your pantry, fridge, and freezer and provides a quick rundown of which time-saving ingredients are worth buying. I've also included two charts to inspire improvisation: a substitution chart for those times when you don't have (or don't fancy) a particular ingredient; and a flavor profile chart that groups the seasonings and key ingredients of various cuisines so you can see how to vary recipes easily. But before you can cook, you've got to shop.

Every kitchen should have the ingredients in the charts that follow. Some are no-brainers, like salt and pepper, while others are the kinds of instant flavor boosters that are essential for fast cooking, like soy sauce and real Parmesan cheese. Other flavor-packed ingredients (not absolute essentials, but nice to have around) include olives, capers, anchovies, sun-dried tomatoes, tahini, miso, and (of course) bacon.

Shopping for Speed

The faster you shop, the sooner you get into the kitchen. Making a shopping list is an obvious advantage and worth reminding you about here; it's easier to keep one perpetually going on your smart phone or an old-fashioned notepad than to try to create one from scratch. Then try to strike a balance between spontaneous, impromptu shopping—like stopping after work for fresh vegetables and meat—and weekly or even biweekly stocking up. Since the most efficient scenario is to cook from what you already have at home as often as possible, the goal is to get in the habit of using short-storing foods first. The lists here will help you do that.

Pantry Staples

Consider these the essentials. (Some actually keep better in the fridge but are considered pantry items.) As you explore the recipes you'll customize this list.

Ingredient	Details	Storage
EXTRA VIRGIN OLIVE OIL	What I mean when I write *olive oil*. It doesn't have to be expensive (and don't let anyone tell you it doesn't work for frying).	Keep a small bottle on the counter, to be refilled from a big bottle or can you keep in the fridge.
VEGETABLE OILS	Use oil pressed from a particular seed, not the generic stuff labeled *vegetable oil*. Best are grapeseed, safflower, sunflower, canola, and peanut oils. Use them when you want a more neutral flavor than olive oil (although peanut oil is pretty distinctive). Sesame oil—use the dark, toasted kind—is a special case and used more as a flavorful condiment and less for cooking.	Best refrigerated; keep a small jar on the counter or in a cabinet for immediate use.
VINEGARS	Sherry vinegar is my favorite; other wine vinegars are also good; balsamic and rice vinegars are lower in acidity and useful.	Vinegar keeps for at least a year at room temperature. A cloudy sediment might settle at the bottom of the bottle; don't worry about it.
SALT & BLACK PEPPER	I use coarse kosher or sea salt for almost everything. Good quality preground pepper is fine, but grinding your own is preferable and easy.	Keep a small bowl or jar of salt and a pepper mill (or preground pepper in a small jar) on the counter.
SPICES AND DRIED HERBS	The essentials: chili and curry powders (page 758), cayenne, smoked paprika, cumin, ground ginger, and coriander. Dried oregano, sage, rosemary, tarragon, dill, and thyme are acceptable substitutes for fresh and are options given in most recipes.	Keep in a cool, dark (and handy) place. Replace what you don't use within a year. (Scrawl the date on the label when it goes in and you'll know when the time's up.)

Ingredient	Details	Storage
GARLIC, ONIONS, AND GINGER	Loads of recipes in this book, and everywhere else, start with garlic, onions, or both, while ginger is essential to Asian cooking.	Keep garlic and onions in a basket or bowl on the counter; they'll last for weeks. (Refrigerate for longer storage.) Once you slice into a knob of ginger, store it loosely wrapped in the fridge until it starts to look funky—usually a couple of weeks.
RICE AND OTHER GRAINS	The quickest-cooking, and therefore most used here, are white rice (short or long grain), couscous, bulgur, and quinoa. There are other options if you can work ahead or have a little more time; see page 352.	A cabinet is fine, but if you have room, they'll keep better and longer in the freezer. (Cooked grains freeze well for several months too. See the recipe on page 355.)
DRIED PASTA AND NOODLES	There are plenty of different shapes to choose from in both white and whole wheat varieties. Italian pastas are usually best, and the shapes are mostly interchangeable. See page 332 for a rundown of Asian noodles.	These will keep indefinitely.
DRIED BEANS	Cheap, delicious, and easy to cook (see page 496 for an all-purpose recipe) but time-consuming. Except for lentils, the recipes in this book call for canned or frozen beans (or your own precooked beans—whenever you have some handy).	The longer you keep these, the longer they'll take to cook. So don't buy more than you'll use within a few months.
CANNED TOMATOES AND TOMATO PASTE	I use whole peeled, diced, and crushed tomatoes (see page 294). Tomato paste in a tube (like toothpaste) is more convenient than canned.	Canned, jarred, and boxed tomatoes are all dated, as is paste. If you don't use all of the can, put leftovers in an airtight bag, squeeze the air out, and freeze. Next time, just defrost or cut off a chunk.

Ingredient	Details	Storage
PEANUT BUTTER	Should contain peanuts and salt, nothing else.	Keep in the fridge after opening.
COCONUT MILK	You'll use it more than you think. In cans; full- and reduced-fat coconut milk will both work fine in the recipes here.	It keeps in the fridge for several days after opening, or freezes well for months.
SOY SAUCE (AND FISH SAUCE)	Soy sauce is essential; fish sauce (nam pla) is less so but great to have around.	Both last a long time, but fish sauce stays fresher longer when stored in the fridge.
SUGAR, HONEY, AND MAPLE SYRUP	Sugar is sugar. Honey and maple syrup should be real, meaning free of additives or additional sweeteners.	Honey never goes bad; maple syrup is best refrigerated after opening.
FLOUR, CORNMEAL, BAKING POWDER, AND BAKING SODA	Unbleached flour, please (I like having both white and whole wheat), and stone-ground cornmeal.	Baking powder and soda have expiration dates; flour and cornmeal keep for a year or so, longer if you freeze them.
CONDIMENTS	Ketchup, mayonnaise, Dijon mustard, hot sauce, and whatever else you crave. To make your own mayonnaise, barbecue sauce, and salsa, see page 144.	Put mayonnaise, mustard, and ketchup in the fridge after opening. Hot sauce can go in the pantry (it will taste better but won't keep indefinitely).
NUTS AND SEEDS	As big a variety as you think you'll use. Walnuts, almonds, and peanuts are most essential, though they're virtually interchangeable.	Use within a few months or store in the freezer.

Fridge Staples

For the most part, these are the least perishable of the perishables.

Ingredient	Details	Storage
BUTTER, MILK, AND YOGURT	Butter should be unsalted; milk and yogurt, preferably full fat.	Keep a little butter in the fridge and the rest in the freezer. Yogurt and milk are dated.
EGGS	From real free-ranging birds if possible. For lots more info, see page 828.	Supermarket eggs are dated but generally keep much longer. Recently laid eggs (like those you find at a farmers' market) are best when still fresh but will also last for weeks or months.
PARMESAN CHEESE	Real Parmesan from Italy (get it in a chunk) is worth the price; Grana Padano is nearly as good. Everything else is an imitation.	Wrap a chunk in wax paper and it will keep for months. (It is virtually indestructible; if it gets a spot of mold, just cut it off.)
FRESH HERBS	Parsley, cilantro, basil, rosemary, sage, thyme, tarragon, and oregano should all be in the rotation. The flavor boost that fresh herbs give is unmatched.	Thyme, rosemary, oregano, and sage can simply be wrapped in plastic. Others will live longer if you trim the bottoms and set in a jar of water with a plastic bag on top. Easier just to use quickly, within a couple of days.
LEMONS, LIMES, AND ORANGES	You'll want both juice and zest, so get real fruit, not bottles of juice.	These will keep for a few weeks in the fridge; use before they get moldy or shrivel and dry.

Ingredient	Details	Storage
FRESH CHILES	Jalapeños strike a good balance of availability and moderate but real heat; all are useful (see page 456 for more info).	Most will last for several weeks in the fridge.
APPLES, PEARS, CABBAGE, SQUASHES, POTATOES, AND OTHER ROOT VEGETABLES	Long keeping and always useful.	These all tend to keep best in the fridge—often up to several weeks. Store on the counter if there's no room.

Freezer Staples

I treat the freezer like the pantry on ice. Lucky you if you've got space for a big one.

Ingredient	Details	Storage
HOMEMADE STOCK	When I don't have homemade stock, I use water; the canned stuff just doesn't taste right. All the stock recipes you'll need are on page 212.	Refrigerate for several days or freeze in airtight containers, ice cube trays, or resealable plastic bags.
FROZEN VEGETABLES	Convenient and often better tasting and more nutritious than out-of-season "fresh" produce. Corn, peas, spinach and other greens, and edamame and other beans are best; others can be valuable.	Don't overbuy, but these will last for months, although sooner is better.
FROZEN FRUIT	Essential for making fast smoothies and sorbets. I always try to keep at least one or two from this list in the freezer: strawberries, raspberries, peaches, and mangoes.	Best within weeks; will last for months.
COOKED BEANS	The perfect setup for fast—and excellent—cooking. See page 496 for a big-batch beans recipe.	Freeze beans (in containers covered with their cooking liquid) for up to a few months. Thaw in the fridge, microwave, or during cooking.

Ingredient	Details	Storage
COOKED GRAINS	Just like beans; indispensible for fast, spontaneous meals. See the master recipe on page 355.	Store grains in resealable bags with all air squeezed out. Thaw in the fridge, microwave, or during cooking.
HOMEMADE TOMATO SAUCE	Infinitely better than store-bought.	Refrigerate for days or cook a big batch, divide it among freezer containers in sizes you'll use, and freeze for months—or longer. Thaw in the microwave.

Shortcut Cheat Sheet

Many will tell you that the key to fast cooking is to stock your kitchen with foods that have been prepared so that you're left with very little work to do once you get home. While some of these foods are useful, others sacrifice too much in the way of quality and are better skipped in lieu of versions you make yourself (see the page references for recipes and information). Here's the breakdown:

Worth It

Canned tomatoes
Canned beans
Canned tuna (preferably packed in olive oil but water-packed is fine too)
Frozen fruits and vegetables
Panko bread crumbs (sort of; see page 71)
Deli meat (or see page 774)
Many condiments (for others, see page 144)

Not Worth It

Canned or packaged stock (page 212)
Jarred tomato sauce and salsa (page 296; page 145)
Packaged hummus (page 939)
Rotisserie chicken (page 688)
Prechopped vegetables
Pregrated Parmesan
Prewashed salad greens
Just about any other shortcut ingredient

Interchangeable Ingredients

Whenever a recipe calls for something you don't have, use this chart for Plan B. The ingredients in the right column can be substituted for those in the left and vice versa. (Cooking times may vary a bit.)

STOCK	Water, wine, beer, apple cider (to taste, of course)
FRESH TOMATOES	Canned tomatoes (drained diced canned tomatoes can even work in some salads).
NUTS AND DRIED FRUIT	Any nut or dried fruit can be substituted for another.
VINEGAR	Any type will work; lemon and lime juice too.
FISH SAUCE	Soy sauce
DRIED OR FRESH RED CHILES	Red chile flakes or cayenne
COOKED/CANNED BEANS	Totally interchangeable
CILANTRO	Parsley, basil
TARRAGON	Dill, mint, chives, chervil
ROSEMARY	Thyme, sage, oregano
SHALLOTS	Onions, leeks
LEMONGRASS	Lemon zest
SALAD GREENS	Totally interchangeable
KALE	Collards, chard, spinach, escarole, bok choy
CAULIFLOWER	Broccoli
FENNEL	Celery
ASPARAGUS	Green beans or snap peas
FRESH PEAS, SNAP PEAS, OR SNOW PEAS	Frozen shelled peas
JÍCAMA	Radishes, kohlrabi
PARSNIPS (COOKED)	Carrots (cooked)
PEARS	Apples
SWEET POTATOES	Carrots, parsnips, or winter squash
SOUR CREAM	Yogurt
HEAVY CREAM (CALLED "CREAM")	Half-and-half (unless you're whipping it)
SCALLOPS	Shrimp, squid
MUSSELS	Clams
FISH FILLETS	More interchangeable than you think (see page 542)
BONELESS, SKINLESS CHICKEN BREASTS	Boneless, skinless chicken thighs

Fast Equipment

A cluttered kitchen is a slow kitchen. Here's a list of all you need.

Key Tools

I've grouped all the equipment you'll need to cook from this book according to how it will be used, loosely in order of importance and frequency. Remember: Less can be more, especially when it comes to speed.

Type of Equipment	What You Need	Kitchen Notes
STOVEWARE	Large skillets; large pot (1 gallon); medium skillet (8 to 10 inches); stockpot (2 gallons); 1- to 2-quart saucepans. All of these should have lids.	I use large skillets (often several at the same time) for everything. So get two: maybe one cast iron and one nonstick or stainless. 12 inches is fine; 13 or 14 inches is even better. (The more food you can comfortably fit in a skillet without crowding, the better it will brown—in fewer batches.)
OVENWARE	18 × 13-inch rimmed baking sheets; metal roasting pan; 9 × 13-inch baking pan or dish; 9-inch square baking pan; wire racks; muffin tin; 9-inch pie plate; 9-inch round cake pan (springform is ideal).	You can never have enough rimmed baking sheets; some recipes here use two at the same time, so stock up (they're cheap, and you can stack them). Baking dishes should be metal, glass, ceramic, or enameled cast iron. Muffin tins, pie plates, and cake pans don't get much action in this book but have some uses beyond baking.
SMALL APPLIANCES	Food processor; blender; microwave oven; electric mixer. (Maybe an immersion blender.)	If you don't have a food processor, buy one; it will change your life. (Used ones are really inexpensive.) An electric mixer is less critical but will make desserts easier; the handhelds are great. You can live without a microwave, but there are recipes in this book that use one. And a blender makes smoother purées than anything else; not critical, but nice—consider at least an immersion blender.

Type of Equipment	What You Need	Kitchen Notes
KNIVES	Chef's knife; long serrated knife; paring knife.	You'll rely on a chef's knife (8 to 10 inches is best for most people) to make quick work of prep; it should feel as comfortable in your hand as possible. You'll use the serrated knife for bread and fine slicing. I keep a half dozen cheap paring knives on hand all the time.
UTENSILS	Large spoons; spatulas; tongs; peeler; box grater (and/or fine grater); kitchen scissors; can opener; liquid and dry measuring cups and spoons; quick-read thermometer; whisk; ladle; brushes; potato masher; rolling pin; mandoline (nice, and there are cheap but good ones out there).	You should have a few wooden spoons and two metal: one slotted, one not. You'll need one flexible metal spatula for flipping and a rubber or silicone version for scraping. A rolling pin is handy but used sparingly in this book; a wine bottle does the trick in a pinch (especially if you've already consumed its contents). And truth be told, I probably use a fork for "whisking" much more often than I use an actual whisk; it's just as fast, although you've got to work a little harder.
ACCESSORIES	Cutting boards (wood and plastic if you'd like); kitchen towels; pot holders; kitchen timer; pepper mill; parchment paper.	I like a big, sturdy wooden cutting board that lives on the counter and a smaller plastic one that I stash somewhere else. A clean kitchen is a fast kitchen, so keep lots of kitchen towels on hand. A kitchen timer is a bit of a relic in a smart phone world, but it's at the very least a hilarious way to show off how fast you're cooking.
BOWLS/STORAGE	Mixing bowls; large colander; mesh strainers; salad spinner; glass jars; plastic storage containers; resealable plastic bags, foil, wax, or parchment paper and plastic wrap.	A salad spinner is by far the most efficient way to clean, dry, and store greens. I store vinaigrettes and homemade condiments in glass jars in the fridge and always keep plenty of plastic containers and freezer bags for storing big batches of cooked beans, grains, and leftovers. (I can't say it enough: There's no faster way to cook than eating something that's already been made.)

Setup for Speed

There's no "right" way to organize a kitchen. But this diagram illustrates a few features that can make yours as efficient as possible.

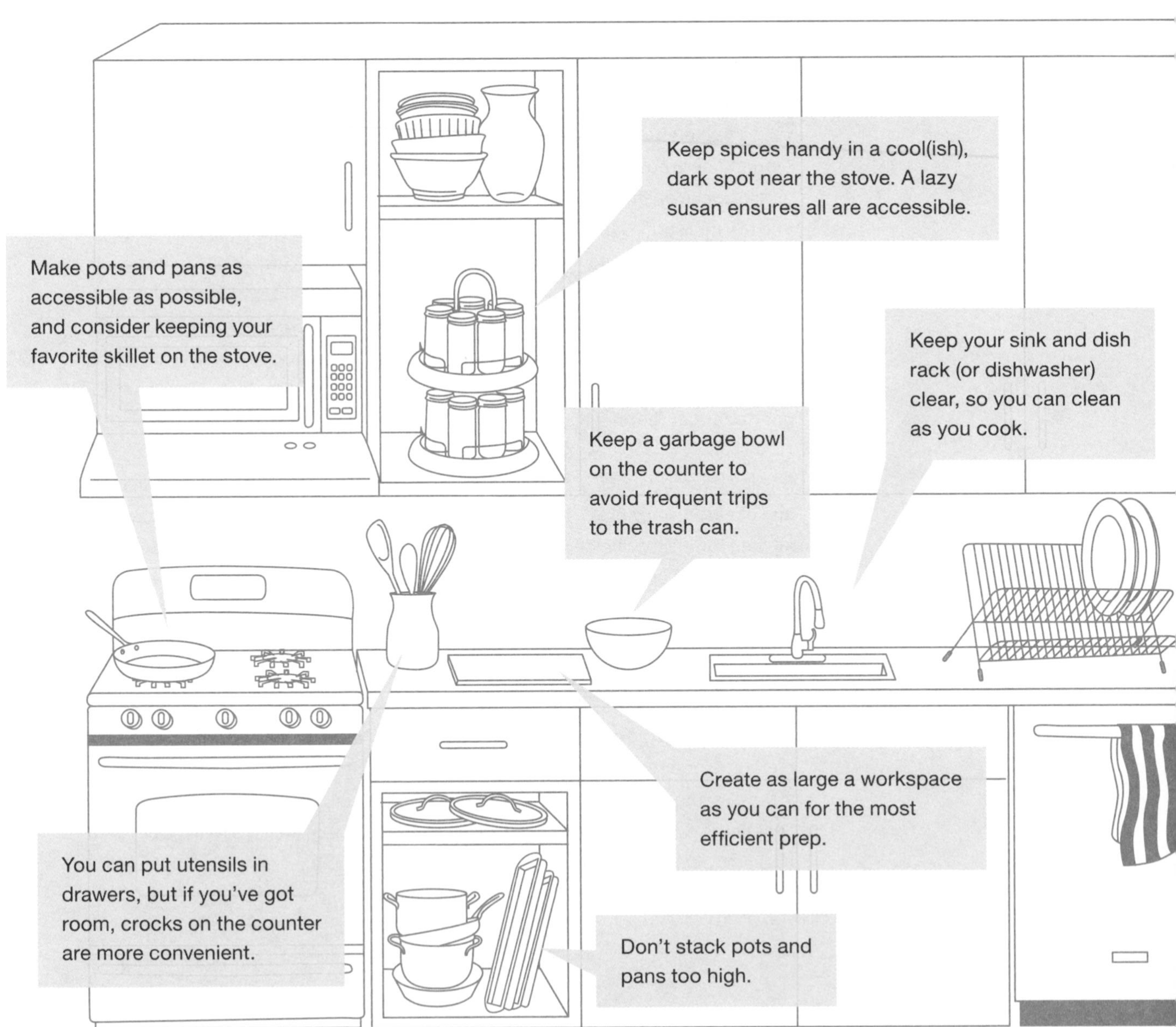

Keep spices handy in a cool(ish), dark spot near the stove. A lazy susan ensures all are accessible.
Make pots and pans as accessible as possible, and consider keeping your favorite skillet on the stove.
Keep your sink and dish rack (or dishwasher) clear, so you can clean as you cook.
Keep a garbage bowl on the counter to avoid frequent trips to the trash can.
Create as large a workspace as you can for the most efficient prep.
You can put utensils in drawers, but if you've got room, crocks on the counter are more convenient.
Don't stack pots and pans too high.

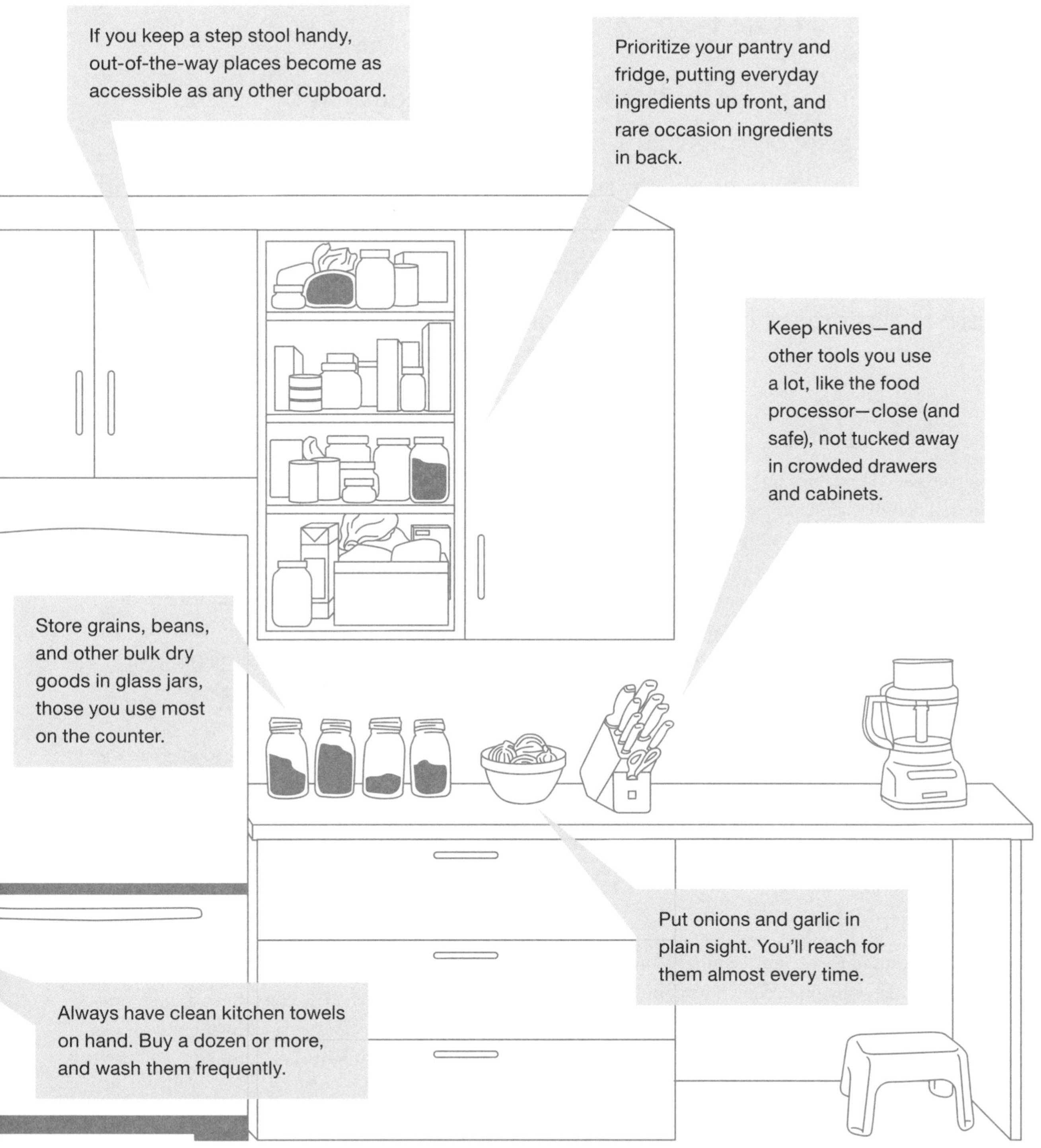
If you keep a step stool handy, out-of-the-way places become as accessible as any other cupboard.
Prioritize your pantry and fridge, putting everyday ingredients up front, and rare occasion ingredients in back.
Keep knives—and other tools you use a lot, like the food processor—close (and safe), not tucked away in crowded drawers and cabinets.
Store grains, beans, and other bulk dry goods in glass jars, those you use most on the counter.
Put onions and garlic in plain sight. You'll reach for them almost every time.
Always have clean kitchen towels on hand. Buy a dozen or more, and wash them frequently.

Fast Strategies

The practice of prepping and cooking simultaneously is by far the biggest key to fast cooking that I have to offer here; it can be applied to boiling, steaming, pan-cooking, roasting, baking, broiling, grilling, and even braising and frying. But I'm always thinking about ways to be more efficient in the kitchen, so here is a preview of the other time-saving tips that are incorporated into recipes throughout the book.

Rinse, Don't Repeat

Washing fruits and vegetables isn't included in recipe Prep directions because I assume you will do it how and when you see fit (or not). But here are a few efficient ways to work it into the flow: If you have a bunch of produce, consider putting it all in a colander together and rinsing under cold running water all at once. If you run out of room in the colander, do them in batches and put what's done on towels. If vegetables are going to be used toward the end of a recipe, wash while you have downtime while other things cook. Sometimes it's easiest to run water over foods like carrots or cabbage after they've been trimmed or peeled. (For more about food safety, see page 39.)

Consolidate Mincing

If a recipe uses minced garlic, minced ginger, and/or minced chiles at the same time, don't mince those things one at a time. Instead, peel the garlic and ginger, trim the chiles, put them all in a pile, then start chopping and mince them all together using a rocking motion.

Thinner (and Smaller) = Faster

This is obvious but worth remembering: Big, thick pieces take longer to cook through than foods cut small or sliced thin. That's as true of vegetables as it is of meat, and with a knife in your hand you have quite a bit of control over the size and shape of the ingredients before they hit the pan. (And grated vegetables cook the fastest of all; see the next one.)

Grate for Puréeing

If you're making a puréed vegetable soup, grate the vegetables so that they become tender as quickly as possible. After all, it makes no difference what they look like at the beginning.

Start with Heat

Appliances, pots, pans, water, and fat take time to get hot. So before doing anything else, turn on the oven, heat the broiler, and/or set water to boil. And since many of the recipes start with sautéing (or pan-cooking), you can preheat skillets too.

Adjust the Heat

While I've tried my best to balance the simultaneous flows of cooking and prepping, there may be times when you get slightly out of sync. Don't worry! You can always raise, lower, or turn off the heat on the stove to accommodate the speed of your prep work. So, if the oil in a skillet is hot but you haven't finished chopping the onion that's supposed to go in it, lower or turn off the heat until you're ready.

Don't Wait for the Oven

Unless you're baking—or roasting something that requires an initial blast of very high heat—you don't have to wait for the oven to reach its final temperature before adding food. Vegetables are the best examples, but slow-roasted or braised meat and chicken can work too. Remember that if you do this, cooking times will differ from those in the recipes.

Heat Oil in the Oven

Put a baking sheet or roasting pan with a little oil in the oven as it heats. When you add whatever you're roasting to the pan, you'll immediately get the sizzle and sear that you're looking for on the bottom.

Embrace the Broiler

Many of the recipes take advantage of broiling as a useful way to provide quick blasts of heat and a means of diverting food from the often crowded stovetop. With the rack farther away from the heat, the broiler can also be used for thicker cuts of meat or firmer vegetables that need a little more time to cook through. (See page 720 for the details.)

Take Advantage of Steam

More efficient than using a real steamer is employing the steam that occurs naturally when you sauté or simmer something with moisture in it—usually vegetables or starches—to cook something else, especially proteins like fish, chicken, or eggs. A skillet of beans simmering with a splash of stock gives off steam, as does bubbling tomato sauce or zucchini cooking with olive oil. Put a lid on any of those pans and you've got yourself a steamer for whatever you might lay on top of the cooking food. (For more details about this process, see the recipe on page 684. Or see page 685 for how to rig a steamer.)

Use Less Liquid for Braising

The amount of liquid that we normally use for braising can take a while to come to an initial boil and a long time at the end to reduce into a sauce. Start with submerging your braising ingredients in about 1 inch of liquid, cover the pot, and cook, turning occasionally, adding a little more liquid as necessary.

Clean as You Go

A delicious meal is less enjoyable when there's a messy kitchen waiting for you. Just like you use some natural breaks in the cooking process to prep, use other bits of downtime to clean dishes you're done using, wipe down counters and cutting boards—that sort of thing.

Prep Shortcuts

The prep steps in the recipes tell when—and, in most cases, how—to get food ready for cooking. This visual guide demonstrates the most efficient ways to slice, chop, snip, and grate.

Vegetables and Fruits

APPLES AND PEARS

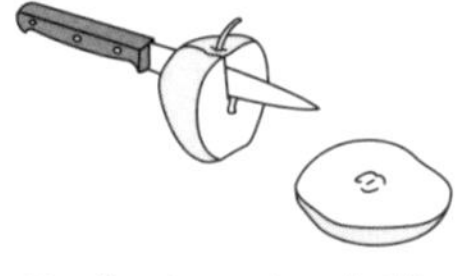

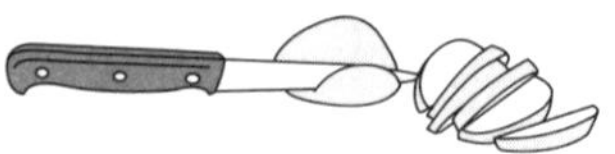

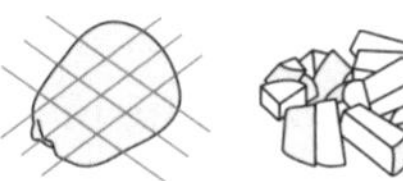

1. Peeling is optional. Slice downward around the core, removing flesh in pieces.
2. Cut the pieces into slices or wedges.
3. Or cut the pieces in a crosshatch pattern to chop.

AVOCADO

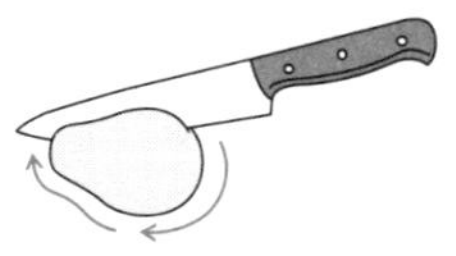

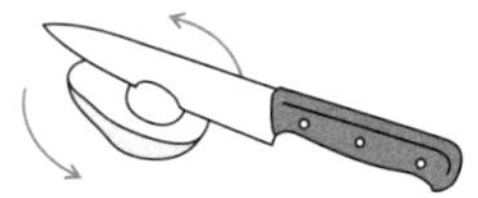

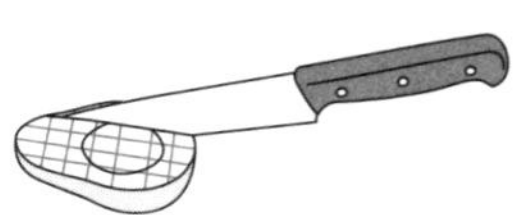

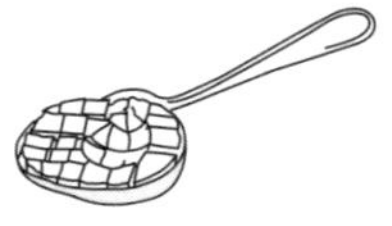

1. Insert the knife to the pit; rotate to cut all the way around, and twist to separate.
2. Firmly but carefully, whack the base of the knife into the pit and twist to remove it.
3. For slices or cubes, hold half and cut only the flesh.
4. Scoop out the chunks of flesh with a spoon.

BELL PEPPERS

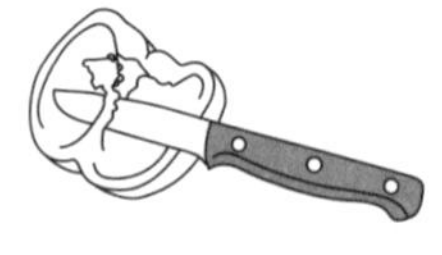

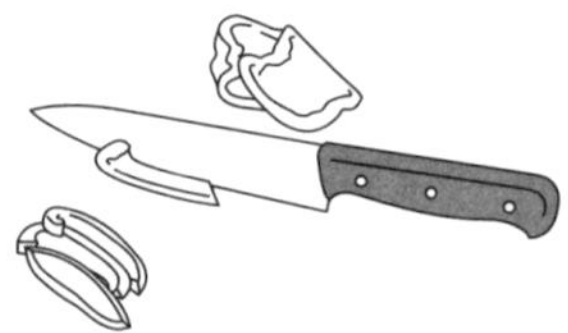

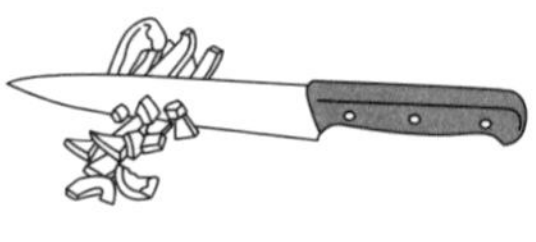

1. Cut downward around the core; turn and repeat all around.
2. Remove any remaining white pith with a paring knife (or not).
3. Cut the pepper into strips.
4. Gather the strips and cut them crosswise to chop.

BROCCOLI

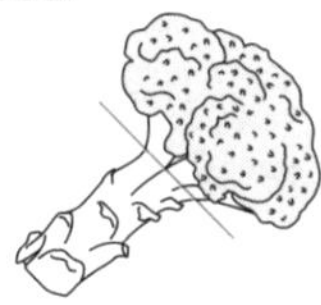

1. Trim away the tough end, then cut off and save the stalk.

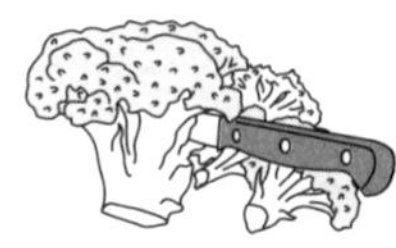

2. Cut downwards to remove the florets (or break them off), rotating the head as you go.

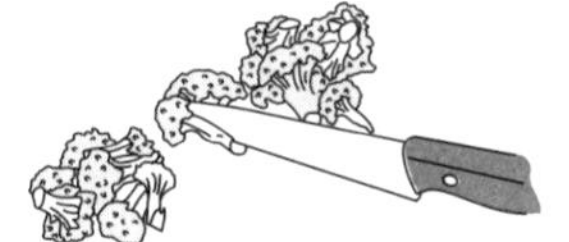

3. Chop the florets into smaller pieces if you like.

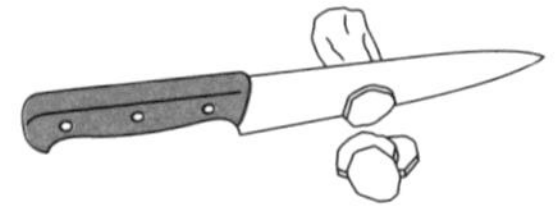

4. Peel the stalk and slice into coins or chop in bits.

BUTTERNUT (OR WINTER) SQUASH

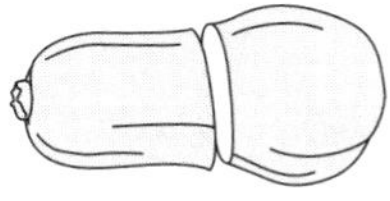

1. Cut crosswise into two halves and put flat-side down.

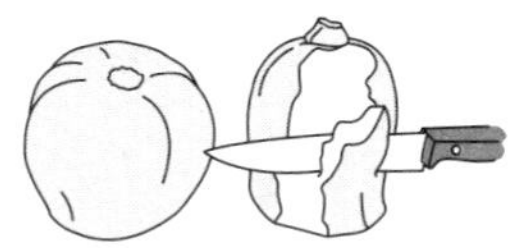

2. Cut downward to remove the skin; trim off the ends.

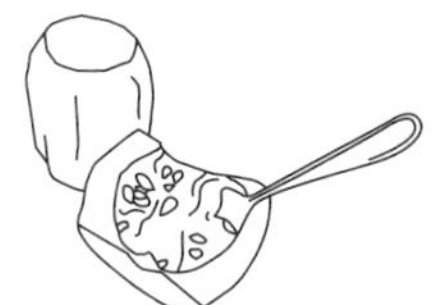

3. Halve again to access the seeds and remove them.

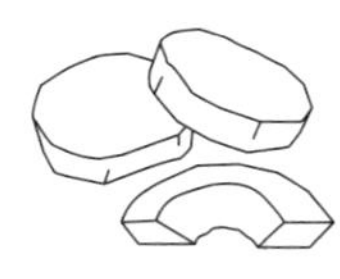

4. Slice into manageable pieces of relatively equal thickness.

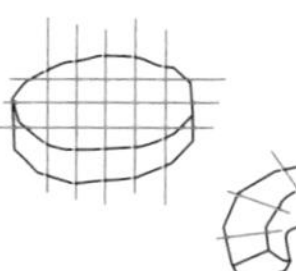

5. Following the contours of the squash, cut into cubes.

CABBAGE

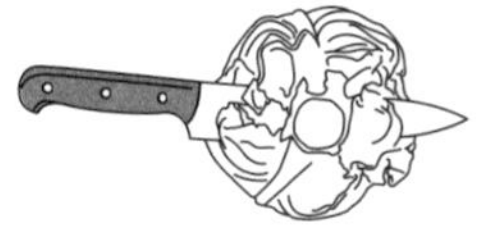

1. If the core isn't flat, trim some off so it is.

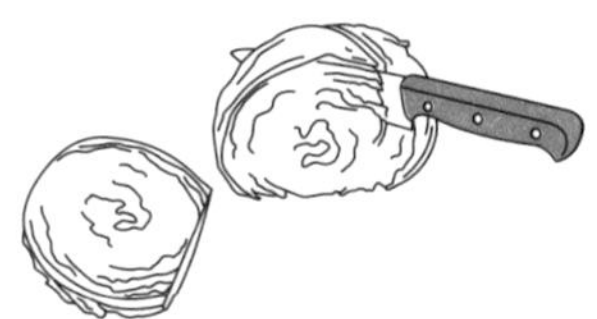

2. Slice downward at a slight angle around the core to remove the leaves.

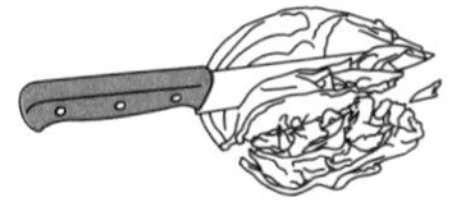

3. Slice into thin shreds (or cut in a crosshatch pattern to chop).

CARROTS

1. Peeling is optional, depending on how they look and will be used.

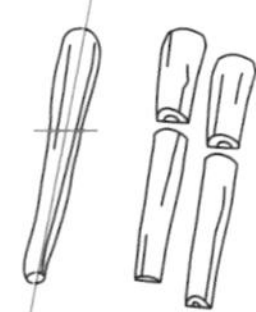

2. Slice carrots crosswise into manageable chunks; halve thick pieces lengthwise.

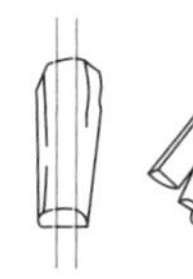

3. Slice the carrots lengthwise into sticks.

4. Gather the carrot sticks together, and slice across to chop.

Vegetables and Fruits *Continued*

CAULIFLOWER

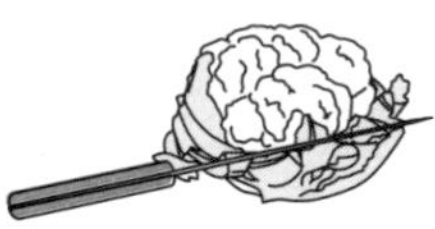

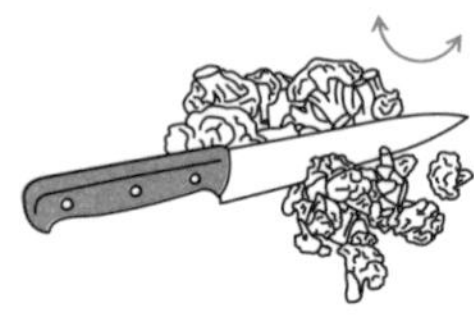

1. If the core isn't flat trim some off so it is.
2. Slice downward to cut the head in half; remove any leaves.
3. Cut around the core to make florets (or break them off).
4. It's even faster to cut florets from an upside-down cauliflower.
5. For chopped cauliflower, rock the knife over the florets.

CHILES

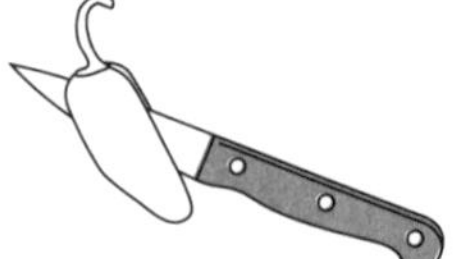

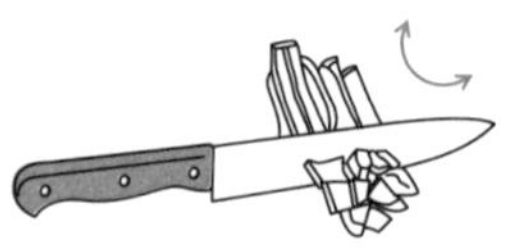

1. To quickly mince, remove the stem and rock a knife over the whole chile.
2. For less heat, hold the stem and cut off a piece of flesh.
3. Roll the chile over and repeat until cored.
4. Then rock a knife over the slices until minced.

CITRUS

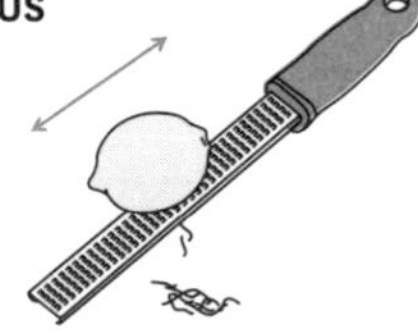
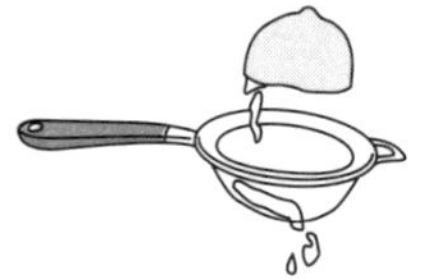
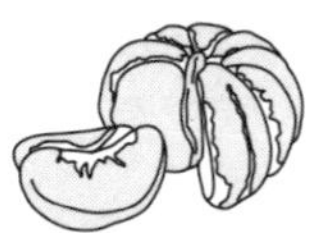
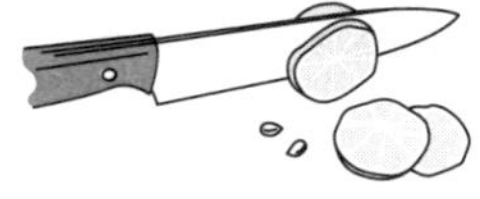

1. For zest, run the fruit back and forth along a fine grater.
2. For juice, squeeze a half over a strainer (or your loosely cupped hand).
3. For segments, peel; then break the fruit apart and remove the seeds.
4. Or cut peeled fruit crosswise into attractive wheels.

CORN

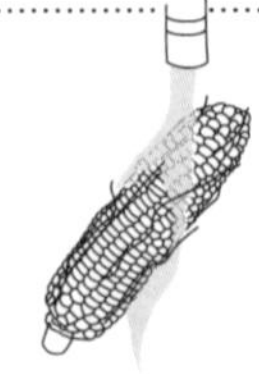

1. Grab the husk and pull down; repeat to reveal as much of the cob as you can.
2. Run the ear under water and pull off the remaining threads of silk.
3. Trim off any rough-looking tops or bottoms if necessary.
4. To remove the kernels, stand up the ear, cut downward, turn, and repeat.

CUCUMBER

1. Trim the ends. Then peel only if the skin is thick or waxy.

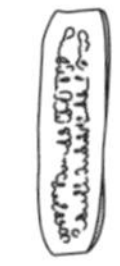

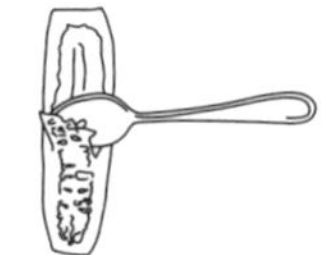

2. Cut lengthwise, then spoon out the seeds if you'd like.

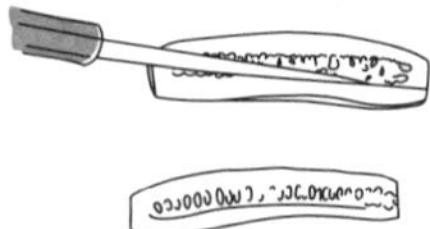

3. Or cut around the seeds to remove the flesh in pieces.

4. Cut lengthwise into spears.

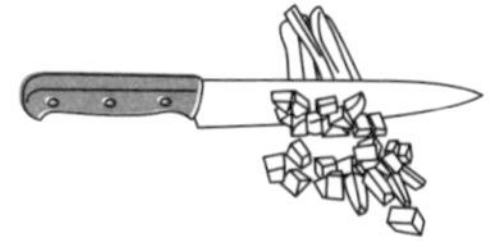

5. To chop, cut the spears crosswise.

GARLIC

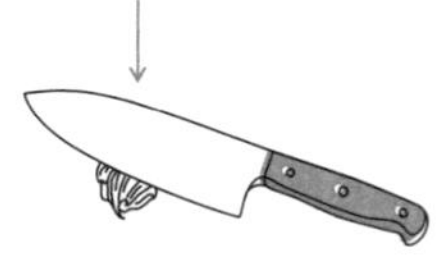

1. Lightly crush with the flat side of a knife, pressing it down with your hand.

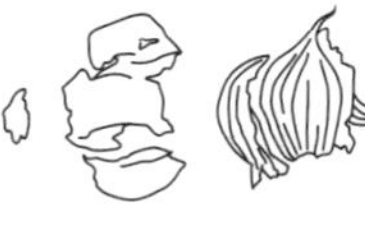

2. Peel and trim or pinch off the stem end. (Or not.)

3. Rock the knife over the cloves until minced.

GINGER

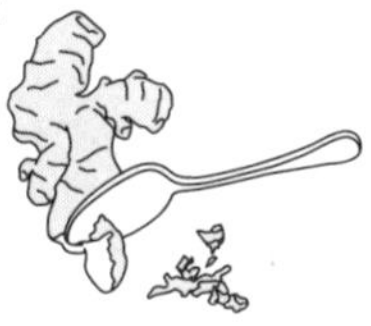

1. Scrape off most of the skin with a spoon or remove it all with a paring knife.

2. Cut lengthwise into thin slices.

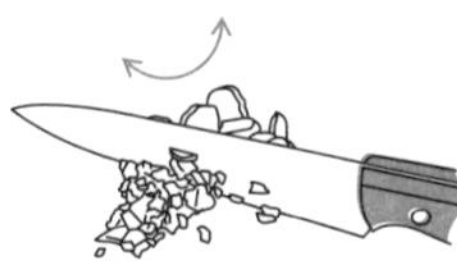

3. Rock the knife over the slices until minced.

HERBS

1. Most of the cilantro sprig is edible; for other herbs discard any tough stems.

2. Cut to remove the leaves and most tender stems.

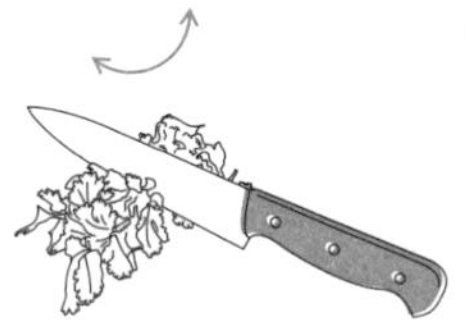

3. Rock the knife over a pile of leaves and tender stems to chop.

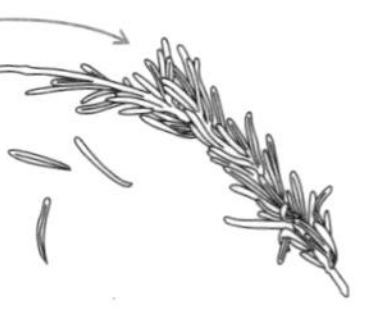

4. Or hold a sturdy herb sprig and pull down to strip it.

5. Then rock the knife over the leaves to chop.

Vegetables and Fruits *Continued*

MANGOES

1. Cut downward around both flat sides of the pit.

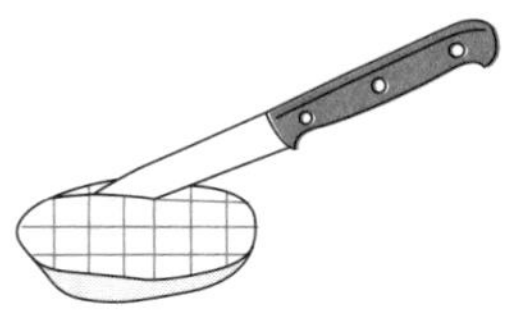

2. Hold the mango half; slice or crosshatch through only the flesh.

3. Turn the mango inside out; cut the flesh from the skin.

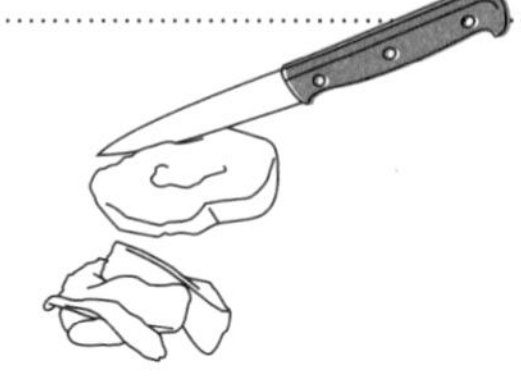

4. Slice off whatever remaining flesh you can from the pit.

MELONS

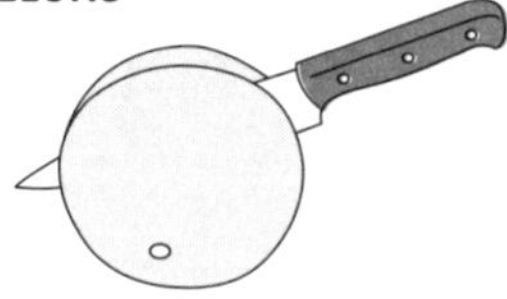

1. Carefully halve the melon through its equator.

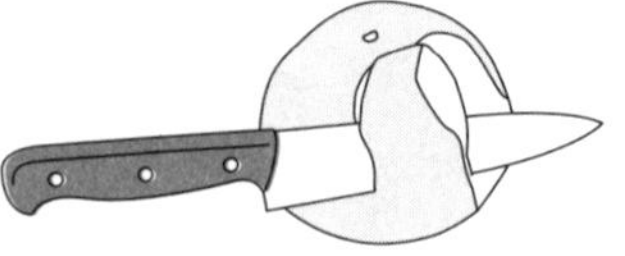

2. Put the melon on its flat side; cut downward, turning, to remove the rind.

3. Cut off the ends (slicing away from you). Remove the seeds if they're in the interior cavity.

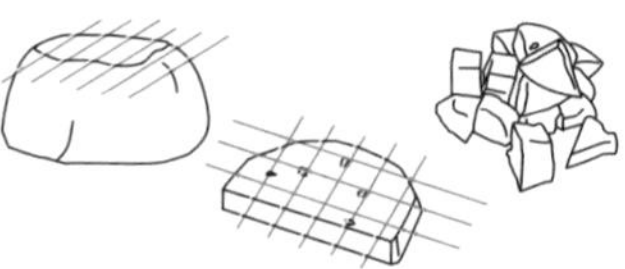

4. Chop into chunks or slice (removing watermelon seeds as you go).

ONIONS

1. Cut off both ends.

2. Slit through the skin and first layer, then remove them.

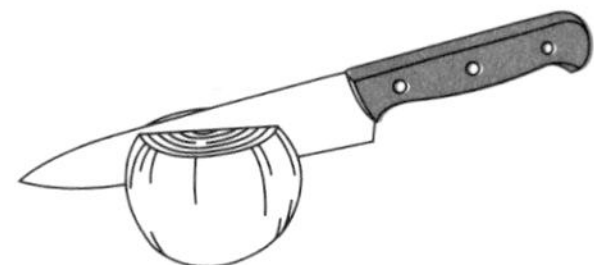

3. Cut the onion in half from top to bottom.

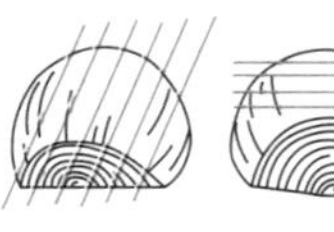

4. For slices, cut from top to bottom or crosswise in any thickness.

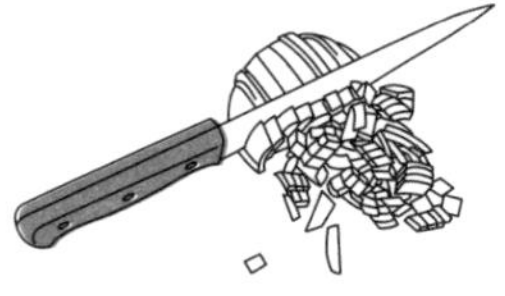

5. To chop, bundle slices and cut across them.

PINEAPPLE

1. Slice off of the top and bottom.

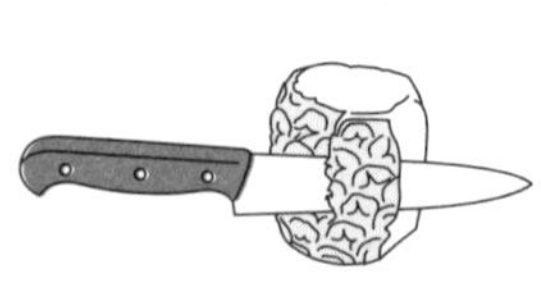

2. Stand the pineapple up and cut following the contours to remove the skin.

3. Cut downward around the core, removing the flesh in 3 or 4 large pieces.

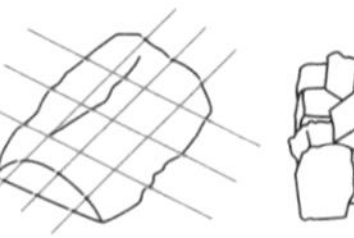

4. Cut the pieces lengthwise, then crosswise to make cubes.

SCALLIONS

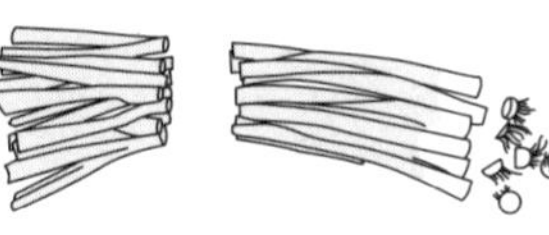

1. Trim off the darkest part of the tops and the root ends.

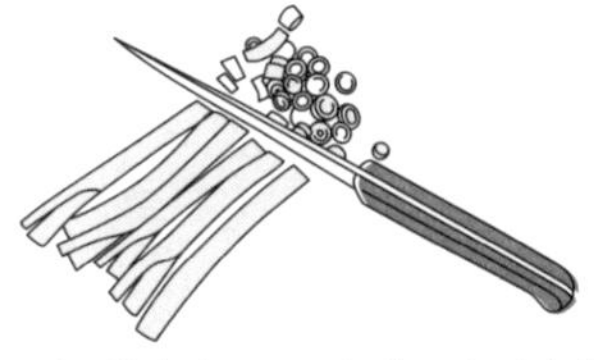

2. Cut at an angle (or straight) across all the scallions at once for slices.

3. For chopped scallions, rock the knife over them.

STONE FRUIT

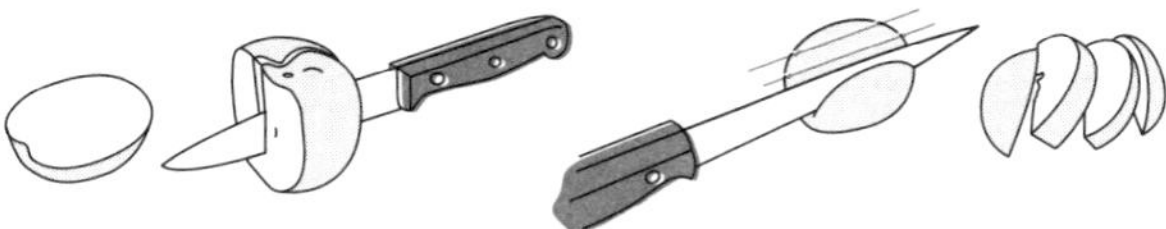

1. Slice downward around the pit, removing flesh in 3 or 4 pieces.

2. Cut the pieces into slices.

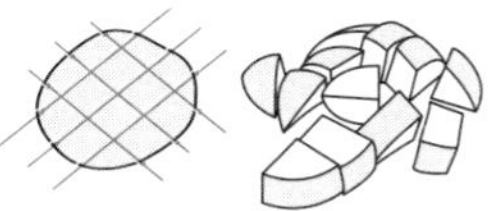

3. Or cut the pieces in a crosshatch pattern to chop.

STURDY GREENS

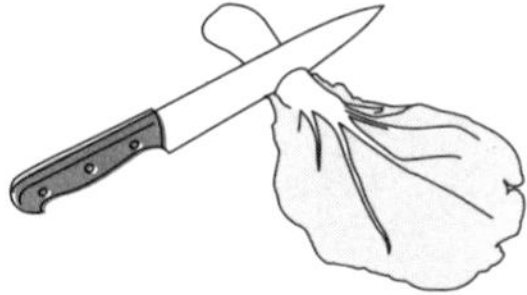

1. Trim the ends. Separate the leaves from the stems (if you like).

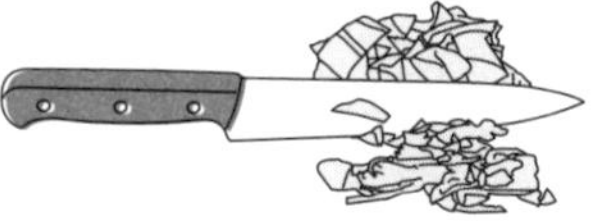

2. Gather the leaves into a bunch, and cut crosswise into "ribbons."

3. For smaller pieces, rock your knife over the slices a few times to chop.

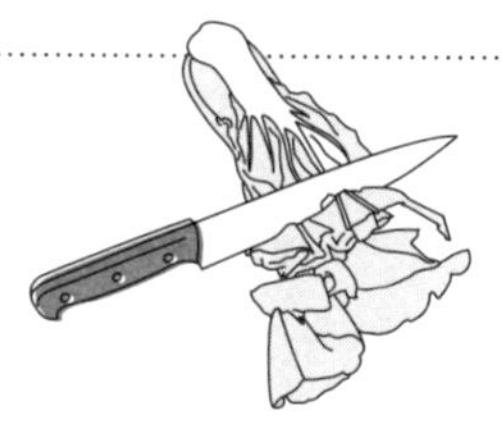

4. For fast stems and leaves together: cut crosswise from the top.

TOMATOES

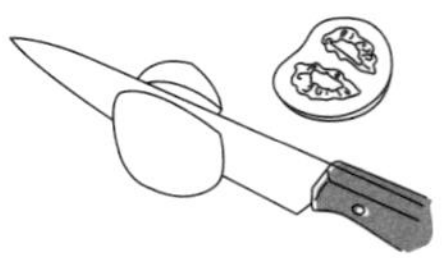

1. Put the fruit upside-down and slice downward at an angle to remove the core.

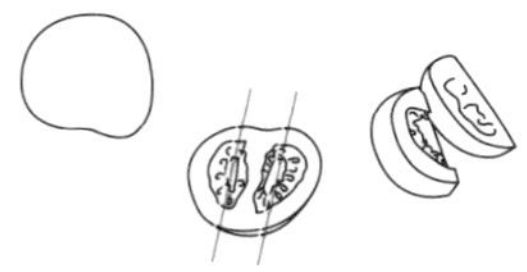

2. Slice each piece lengthwise into wedges.

3. Slice the wedges crosswise into chunks if you'd like.

4. Make sure to capture the juice.

Techniques

CHOPPING WITH SCISSORS

1. It's super-fast to chop cooked or tender raw vegetables with scissors.

2. Keep working the scissors through the vegetables as you turn the bowl.

GRATING BY HAND

1. For faster chopping and cooking: Stand the box grater up on a cutting board.

2. Push the vegetable up and down over the largest holes on the grater; be assertive.

3. As they accumulate inside the grater, empty the pieces onto the board.

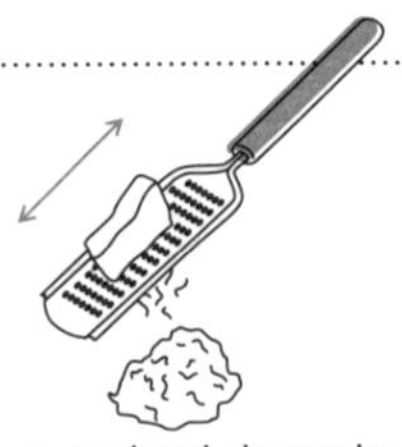

4. To grate hard cheese by hand, run it back and forth along a fine grater.

GRATING BY MACHINE

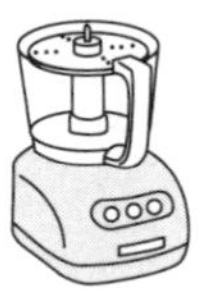

1. A grating attachment will tackle many foods efficiently.

2. Cut pieces that will fit easily through the feed tube.

3. Push the vegetables through with the cylinder.

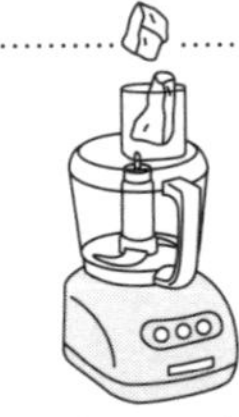

4. Use the metal blade on hard cheese and vegetables for a fine texture.

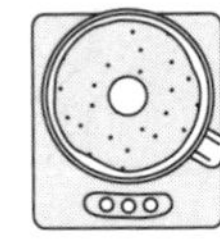

5. Pulse a few times, careful not to overdo it.

MAKING CHICKEN CUTLETS

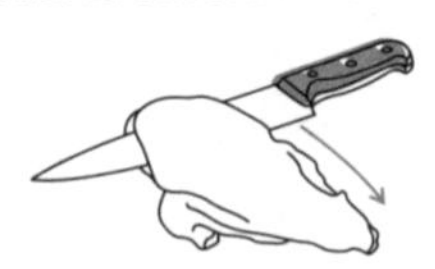

1. With the knife parallel to the cutting board, halve the breast into flat cutlets.

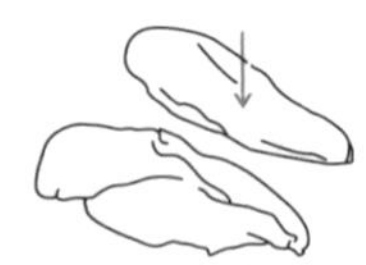

2. If you want them more even, flatten out each cutlet with the palm of your hand.

MAKING THIN RIBBONS

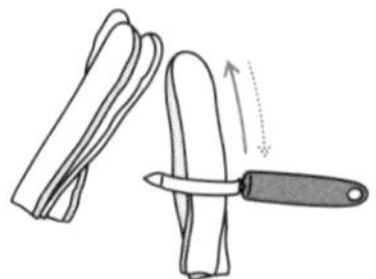

1. Work in either direction to make ribbons of vegetables or cheese with a vegetable peeler.

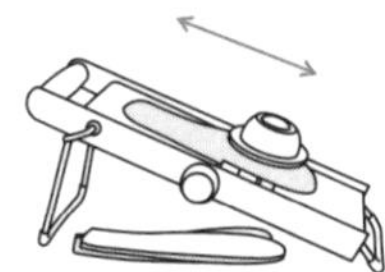

2. Or make the ribbons on a mandolin if you've got one.

PREPARING MEAT

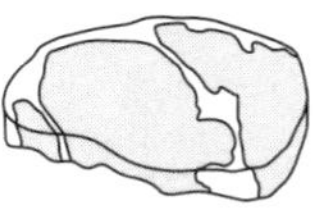

1. Trimming fat from meat takes time; I don't usually bother.

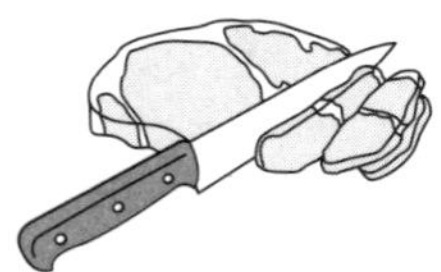

2. Slice thinly against the grain; it's easier if you freeze the meat for a few minutes.

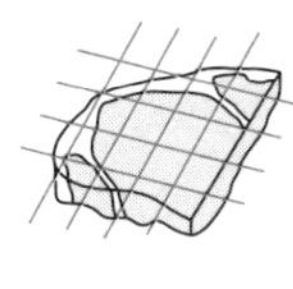

3. Or cut into chunks. The smaller the piece, the faster it cooks.

A New Kind of Recipe

This icon tells you how fast your recipe is:

- ◔ 0 to 15 minutes
- ◑ 16 to 30 minutes
- ◕ 31 to 45 minutes

Almost every recipe in this book is a main dish.

A shopping list. You don't prep the food here; you'll do that later.

SPEED ◑ SERVES 4

White Beans with Sausage, Greens, and Garlic

All ingredient preparation happens here. Prep steps appear in blue, Cook in black.

White beans, greens, and Italian sausage make one of th… this quickly if you want the beans to remain intact or long and slow if you've got the time and want the beans to fall apart a bit. See the Notes on the opposite page.

Ingredients

2 tablespoons olive oil

12 ounces sweet or hot Italian sausage

1 ½ pounds spinach, kale, collards, escarole, chard, or broccoli rabe

2 garlic cloves

4 cups cooked or canned white beans (two 15-ounce cans)

½ cup chicken stock or water

4 ounces Parmesan cheese (1 cup grated)

Salt and pepper

Prep | Cook

1. Put 2 tablespoons olive oil in a large skillet or large pot over medium-high heat.

   Cut the sausage into slices.

2. Add the sausage to the skillet and cook, stirring occasionally until lightly browned, 5 or 6 minutes.

   Trim and chop the greens, keeping any thick stems separate (discard thick spinach stems).

3. When the sausage is lightly browned, add any chopped stems to the skillet and cook until they begin to soften, 3 or 4 minutes.

   Peel and mince 2 garlic cloves.

   If you're using canned beans, rinse and drain them.

4. When the stems begin to soften, add the leaves, a handful at a time if necessary to fit them in, along with the garlic, beans, and ½ cup chicken stock or water.

A Prep step often takes place *while* other cooking is happening to take advantage of downtime. Here, you prep the greens while the sausage browns.

Note that I repeat ingredient quantities. That way you don't have to look back at the ingredients list.

You could buy these, but sometimes making your own pays off—and adds no time if you've got it stored in your refrigerator or freezer. The foods worth making yourself are called out here.

5. Cook, stirring occasionally until the beans are warmed through and the greens are just wilted—3 or 4 minutes for spinach; 4 or 5 minutes for escarole, chard, and broccoli rabe; 5 or 6 minutes for kale and collards.

   Grate 1 cup Parmesan.

6. Add the Parmesan to the skillet and stir. Season with salt and pepper. Taste and adjust the seasoning and serve.

VARIATIONS

White Beans with Bacon, Greens, and Garlic
Substitute chopped bacon for the sausage. Cook until crisp and drain the excess fat before adding the stems.

Black Beans with Chorizo, Greens, and Garlic
Substitute fresh Mexican-style chorizo for the Italian sausage and black beans for white. Omit the Parmesan.

Kidney Beans with Ham, Greens, and Garlic
Substitute chopped smoked ham for the Italian sausage and kidney beans for the white beans. Omit the Parmesan and add a dash of hot sauce instead if you like.

NOTES

MAKE YOUR OWN

Cooked Beans 496

Chicken Stock 213

IF YOU HAVE MORE TIME
If you want a soft stewy mixture, let the beans and greens bubble gently, adding more stock or water if the pan gets too dry, until the greens are very tender and the beans begin to break apart, up to 45 minutes.

SIDES

Garlic Bread 90[illegible]

Bruschetta 909

Caprese Salad 922

These are my favorite accompaniments for this dish. They're optional, of course.

If you want to avoid shortcuts, check here. If you want *additional* shortcuts, look for Even Faster notes.

Variations are sometimes tweaks and at other times are all-new recipes.

How to Use This Book

The diagram on the previous page is designed to be a handy reference for what's included in the recipes. Some of the book's unique features are worth further explanation.

Gathering Ingredients

To save valuable prep time I always focus on streamlining ingredients to what's absolutely necessary. And since these ingredients lists are essentially shopping lists, all you need to do before you start cooking is to put the required items on the kitchen counter, or at least make sure that you have everything you need handy. You should use the ingredients list to give you an accurate idea of how much you need of each item; the recipe directions tell you how to prepare and cook them.

"Do the Blue"

All recipe directions are coded in blue and black numbered steps that reflect the most efficient order and timing of tasks. They might look longer than traditional recipes, but all activity—preparation and cooking—is included in the detail. Believe me, they're faster.

And the recipes can accommodate those who feel more comfortable prepping ingredients ahead of time, as well as those who are lucky enough to have a helper in the kitchen. Since prep steps are highlighted in blue, you can easily identify them when you first look at a recipe and do all the necessary chopping and slicing before you start cooking. Or you can simply say to your helper, "You do the blue steps while I do the black" (or vice versa). This, I think, is really cool.

Make-Ahead Master Recipes

How much faster could you cook if some of the work was already done when you started? A lot. So in addition to the hundreds of recipes and variations in this book, I've included a handful of Master Recipe features: basic homemade staples that I like to keep stocked in my fridge, freezer, or pantry at all times—things like vinaigrette, cooked beans, stock, tomato sauce, or spice blends. You can buy these, of course, but they're significantly better if you make them yourself.

The Make Your Own section that follows many recipe directions points you to these homemade versions whenever you can use them.

Recipe-Free Cooking

The fastest way to cook is to improvise—or at least be flexible. That's why many chapters include Recipe-Free features. Each illustrates a cooking technique (like stir-frying) or kind of dish (like soup) boiled down to its essential process.

Think of these as a bird's-eye road map rather than turn-by-turn directions: They show you how to get from point A to point B, but what you do in between is up to you. So building a soup outlines how you add different kinds of ingredients in consecutive stages. Once you become comfortable with the basic framework of a technique or dish, you can plug in all sorts of ingredients of your choosing, endlessly varying the flavors of the dish. Teach a cook a recipe and he'll cook for a night; teach a cook a technique and she'll improvise for a lifetime.

Ingredients at a Glance

All How to Cook Everything books include detailed information about buying and preparing key ingredients, and this latest addition to the family works the same way. The difference here is that these features focus on precisely what you need to know in order to cook *fast* from scratch—without compromising texture or flavor. A list of all of these—arranged by chapter—starts on page 15 so you can find them easily.

New Techniques

In addition to the Recipe-Free illustrated guides for fast preparation and cooking methods described earlier, I've tucked two-page features and other shortcut techniques among the recipes. From general topics like maximizing your grill and broiler, to ingredient-specific topics like pressing tofu or shaving hard cheese, these tips will help you cook both better *and* faster—and eat while you learn.

A Word About Food Safety

I know . . . fussing over kitchen hygiene while you're trying to cook isn't particularly fast. But neither is getting sidelined with a food-borne illness, so it's well worth your time to practice the most basic food safety habits. This means washing your hands before, during, and after handling food, especially when going from raw meats to anything else. Keep all of your work surfaces, sinks, and utensils clean the same way. (Soap and hot water will do the trick; antimicrobial concoctions can promote germ resistance. Use a weak bleach solution once in a while for deep cleaning.) Your refrigerator should always be between 35°F and 40°F and your freezer around 0°F (this temperature also helps minimize freezer burn).

Washing fruits and vegetables is really a matter of personal choice. At one end of the spectrum are people who use soapy water, especially on produce that's visibly dirty or has been known to have problems—like melons, greens, and squash; other folks wash virtually nothing. I usually come down somewhere in the middle and decide case by case based on what it looks like and whether I'm going to eat it raw or cooked; I tend to be quite blasé about food that I'm cooking, for better or worse.

All of those rules are easy enough to follow. But things do get a little more complicated when we talk about bacteria and cooking temperatures. Sometimes meat, poultry, fish, or eggs contain disease-causing bacteria. There are two ways to minimize the risk. The first is to cook thoroughly, which can result in dry food that isn't ideal from your palate's perspective; I don't do that myself, and my recipes don't recommend doing it either, but it's a judgment call. The second way to minimize the risk of harmful bacteria is to buy the best-quality products you can, from sources you trust the most. This I do recommend. It's not a failsafe, but it's much less of a sacrifice than a life of eating well-done steak.

Salads

Watercress with Peaches, Pecans, and Blue Cheese 44

Tomato Salad with Strawberries, Feta, and Balsamic 46

Arugula with Fried Eggs and Shaved Parmesan 50

Endive and Radicchio with Bacon Vinaigrette 52

Steakhouse Salad 54

Grated Beet and Carrot Salad with Toasted Cashews 56

Puffed Rice Salad with Dates and Almonds 60

White Bean and Cucumber Salad with Yogurt and Dill 62

Chickpea and Carrot Salad with Warm Cumin Oil 64

Crab and Celery Root Rémoulade 66

Poached Shrimp Salad with Herby Tartar Sauce 68

Cucumber and Salmon Salad with Caper and Mustard Dressing 72

Fresh Tuna, Avocado, and Green Bean Salad 74

Asparagus and Kale Caesar Salad 76

Seared Scallops with Grilled or Broiled Romaine 78

Warm Kale Salad with Pine Nuts and Balsamic Currants 80

Warm Pickled Cauliflower Salad with Roasted Red Peppers 82

Green Bean Salad with Caramelized Onions and Toasted Almonds 84

Broiled Eggplant and Zucchini Salad with Tahini Dressing 86

Cabbage with Crisp Tofu and Peanut-Lime Dressing 88

Pressed Tofu and Cucumber Salad with Hoisin Vinaigrette 90

Curried Tofu Salad with Pecans and Golden Raisins 92

Bulgur, Apple, and Fennel Salad 94

Veggie Fajita Salad 96

Warm Escarole and White Bean Salad with Poached Eggs 98

Raw Butternut Squash Salad with Warm Edamame 100

Warm Three-Bean Potato Salad 102

Tuna and Egg Salad with Radishes and Dill 104

Zucchini Slaw with Chopped Spicy Chicken 106

Corn and Black Bean Salad with Garlic Chicken 108

Greek Salad with Orzo and Shrimp 110

Hot and Sour Bok Choy with Mussels 112

Tomato and Chicken Salad with Basil Vinaigrette 114

Warm Spinach and Chicken Salad with Parmesan Dressing 116

Middle Eastern Chicken and Bread Salad 118

BLT Salad with Rosemary-Mayo Dressing 120

Kimchi and Snow Pea Salad with Grilled or Broiled Beef 122

Broccoli Tabbouleh with Charred Tomato and Lemon 124

Charred Brussels Sprout Salad with Walnuts and Gorgonzola 126

Salads

For a long time our salads were small piles of raw vegetables—iceberg lettuce and tomatoes, primarily—that you ate before dinner. Or, worse, something whose main function was to make your steak look that much better. These were absolute afterthoughts, something that you ate reluctantly but never with relish.

Salad has come a long way in both variety and reputation. It is now totally acceptable—and even increasingly popular—to eat a salad and piece of bread and call it a meal. (Many people skip the bread.) The key is having a broad enough repertoire to keep you interested and enough ingredients to keep you satisfied. (After all, how useful is a salad if all it does is make you want a steak?)

Fortunately for us, salads are among the easiest, most versatile, and fastest dishes to make: Many of the components can be left raw and prepared in advance, while leftovers can readily become part of the routine. At their simplest, of course, salads are greens and raw vegetables tossed with vinaigrette.

But they can be expanded, and are limited only by your imagination: Adding cooked vegetables, beans, noodles, grains, and breads, or tofu, fish, chicken, or meat to the bowl increases the possibilities exponentially, and guarantees that you won't be left hungry. And, of course, you'll find all different types of dressing throughout this chapter.

Chapter Highlights

One Bowl, Endless Salads Make dressing, add stuff, and toss: a blueprint for easy, one-bowl salad. Recipe-Free Salads (page 58).

Warm Vinaigrettes Warm dressings add intense flavor and a cozy vibe. Endive and Radicchio with Bacon Vinaigrette (page 52).

Cooking, Once Removed Sometimes the magic is in the mingling of raw ingredients with hot cooked ones. Warm Spinach and Chicken Salad with Parmesan Dressing (page 116).

Root Vegetables, Raw Root vegetables take the longest to cook. The fastest solution? Don't cook them at all. Grated Beet and Carrot Salad with Toasted Cashews (page 56); Raw Butternut Squash Salad with Warm Edamame (page 100).

Salt and Let Sit Sprinkle raw vegetables with salt, then leave them alone while you prepare something else. Pressed Tofu and Cucumber Salad with Hoisin Vinaigrette (page 90).

Loving Tofu If you're still skeptical about tofu, these will make you a believer. Cabbage with Crisp Tofu and Peanut-Lime Dressing (page 88), Pressed Tofu and Cucumber Salad with Hoisin Vinaigrette (page 90), Curried Tofu Salad with Pecans and Golden Raisins (page 92).

Egg Salad It's no longer mayonnaise and white bread. Arugula with Fried Eggs and Shaved Parmesan (page 50), Warm Escarole and White Bean Salad with Poached Eggs (page 98), Tuna and Egg Salad with Radishes and Dill (page 104).

Broiled Bits Why you want to pulse vegetables in the food processor and then stick them in the broiler. Charred Brussels Sprout Salad with Walnuts and Gorgonzola (page 126).

Two Vegetables, One Pot One pot doesn't mean one vegetable. Warm Three-Bean Potato Salad (page 102).

Bread Salad Where croutons started. Middle Eastern Chicken and Bread Salad (page 118).

Kimchi Kimchi makes a surprising and sensational salad base. Kimchi and Snow Pea Salad with Grilled or Broiled Beef (page 122).

SPEED ◔ SERVES 4

Watercress with Peaches, Pecans, and Blue Cheese

Perfect during summer with the juiciest peaches you can find, this salad also lets you experiment with other fruit, nut, cheese, and greens combinations based on whatever looks good or what you have on hand—even in winter.

Ingredients

1 cup pecans

2 bunches watercress (1 pound)

3 large peaches (about 1 pound)

⅓ cup olive oil

2 tablespoons balsamic vinegar

Salt and pepper

4 ounces blue cheese (1 cup crumbled)

Prep | Cook

1. Put 1 cup pecans in a large skillet over medium-high heat. Cook, shaking the pan occasionally and adjusting the heat so they don't burn, until the pecans are lightly browned and fragrant, 3 to 5 minutes.

   Trim the watercress, cutting off any thick stems, and put it in a large bowl.

   Pit and slice the peaches. Add them to the bowl.

2. Drizzle the watercress and peaches with ⅓ cup olive oil and 2 tablespoons balsamic vinegar and sprinkle with salt and pepper. Toss, lifting gently from the bottom to coat with the dressing.

3. Add the pecans. Crumble 1 cup blue cheese and add. Toss again, taste and adjust the seasoning, and serve.

VARIATIONS

Arugula with Apricots, Marcona Almonds, and Manchego
Substitute Marcona almonds (no need to toast them) for the pecans, fresh apricots for the peaches, arugula for the watercress, sherry vinegar for balsamic, and shaved manchego cheese for the blue cheese. If you like, add a pinch of smoked paprika when you mix in the dressing.

Spinach with Apples, Walnuts, and Goat Cheese
Instead of pecans, peaches, watercress, and blue cheese, use walnuts, apples, spinach, and goat cheese.

Kale with Tomatoes, Pine Nuts, and Parmesan
Substitute ½ cup pine nuts for the pecans, halved cherry tomatoes for the peaches, kale for the watercress, and shaved Parmesan for the blue cheese. I love lacinato kale for raw salads, but you can use any kale. Whichever you choose, chop the leaves into bite-sized pieces.

NOTES

DRESSING SALAD ON THE FLY
If you are making a big batch of vinaigrette, I highly recommend combining all the ingredients in a jar and shaking it until they all come together. But if you're shooting for speed, or just want enough vinaigrette for one batch of salad, by all means simply pour oil and vinegar and sprinkle salt and pepper right onto the salad; as you toss they will mix together perfectly. No shaking required.

SIDES

Bruschetta 909

Warm Buttery Bread 906

Crisp Roasted Potatoes 965

SPEED ◔ SERVES 4

Tomato Salad with Strawberries, Feta, and Balsamic

There's a reason pairing tomatoes with fruits like strawberries and watermelon has become more common: The combination of sweet fruit and sweet-tart tomatoes is unbelievable, especially when you add the salty kick of feta.

Ingredients

5 or 6 medium ripe tomatoes (2 pounds)

3 cups strawberries

1 tablespoon olive oil

1 tablespoon balsamic vinegar

Salt and pepper

4 ounces feta cheese (1 cup crumbled)

Prep | Cook

Core the tomatoes and cut into wedges or large chunks; put them in a large bowl.

Hull the strawberries and cut them into halves or quarters; add them to the bowl.

1. Add 1 tablespoon olive oil, 1 tablespoon balsamic vinegar, and a sprinkle of salt and pepper to the bowl; toss.
2. Crumble 1 cup feta over the top and serve.

VARIATIONS

Tomato Salad with Watermelon, Feta, and Balsamic
Instead of the strawberries, use 3 cups of watermelon cut into 1-inch chunks.

Tomato and Strawberry Panzanella
Substitute chunks of fresh mozzarella for the feta. Add a handful of bread cubes lightly toasted in olive oil and some torn fresh basil leaves.

Tomato Salad with Tomatillos and Queso Fresco
Use 8 ounces of tomatillos instead of the strawberries and queso fresco and lime juice instead of the feta and balsamic.

NOTES

IF YOU HAVE MORE TIME
Let the tomatoes and strawberries marinate in the oil, vinegar, salt, and pepper for 15 to 20 minutes before adding the feta.

SIDES

Garlic Bread 906

Bruschetta 909

Crisp Seasoned Pita 908

Salad Greens

The following chart includes both head lettuce, which grows from a core that needs to be removed along with the outermost leaves, and loose-leaf greens, which are grown in small, loose bunches whose stems often need to be trimmed.

Greens	Description
ROMAINE	Long crunchy leaves, slightly bitter and still moist. Essential for Caesar salad, and because the tight inner leaves are protected by the ones on the outside, romaine will keep in the refrigerator literally for weeks.
ICEBERG	The familiar tightly packed heads that are incredibly crisp and, some might say, watery. Iceberg doesn't have a lot of flavor, so it's best to mix it with other greens, cut it into wedges and use it as a canvas for very flavorful dressings, or shred to use as a crunchy, refreshing garnish. Like romaine, it will keep in the fridge for weeks.
BOSTON (OR BUTTER)	Small, loose heads with a trace of bitterness and a soft, buttery texture. Dress the tender leaves at the very last moment and will keep in the fridge for only a few days.
BELGIAN ENDIVE	Long and slender with firm, crunchy, and very bitter leaves. The concave leaves are perfect for stuffing and firm enough for dipping. Cooking endive mellows its bitterness and brings out its sweetness, which can be profound.
RADICCHIO	Small, tight heads, with beautiful white and purple leaves. It looks and acts like a cabbage but has the same striking bitterness as endive.
GREEN- AND RED-LEAF LETTUCE	Easy to find in supermarkets and farmers' markets everywhere. Not loaded with flavor but a good choice for a basic green salad.
SPINACH	Baby spinach in packages is certainly easier to deal with, but opt for the big leaves when you can; they have more flavor. Whichever kind you use, remember that spinach shrinks down tremendously when cooked. The sooner you use it after buying, the better.

Greens	Description
ARUGULA	Like spinach, the larger bunches have more flavor than the packaged baby variety. And that flavor, spicy like mustard, is remarkable. Use ASAP.
WATERCRESS	Intensely peppery and often unjustly used as a garnish rather than as a main component. Use as you would arugula, keeping in mind that it has an even more aggressive flavor.
DANDELION GREENS	These vitamin-packed greens are mild when young and bracingly bitter (and tougher) when mature. You always can buy them at farmers' markets in the spring, although they're popping up more in supermarkets now too.
ESCAROLE	Curly leaves that go from white at the center to dark green at the edges. Raw, they're distinctly bitter. Cooked, they're wonderfully mild.
FRISÉE	These wispy, crinkly leaves are white and light green, crisp, and very bitter. They can handle a rich dressing—they're classic with bacon and poached eggs—as long as you don't drench them and make them soggy.
MESCLUN	Describes a "mixture" (that's what the word means) of different types of greens, herbs, and sometimes even edible flowers. It's sold premixed in all supermarkets, but the best kind of mesclun is the one you mix yourself, especially if you're a gardener or have access to an interesting assortment of greens.

Preparing Salad Greens

If you have a salad spinner, put the torn leaves or loose-leaf greens in the insert, fill the bowl with water, swirl the leaves around, discard the water, and repeat until you don't see dirt in the water. If you don't have a spinner, set a colander inside a stockpot. To dry the leaves either give them a spin or gently shake and toss them with a clean kitchen towel. Do a big batch and store what you don't use: Put the dried greens in the fridge in the covered salad spinner or loosely wrap them in paper towels, set them inside a plastic bag, and seal it loosely. They'll keep for 2 to 4 days.

Washing Prewashed Greens

To cut down on prep time, you may be inclined to buy greens that come ready to go in plastic tubs or bags; after all, they eliminate the need for trimming and chopping. But even though these greens are theoretically prewashed, I wash them again just to be safe.

SPEED SERVES 4

Arugula with Fried Eggs and Shaved Parmesan

Sharp, peppery arugula dressed with tart lemon juice and olive oil is an ideal bed for an oozing fried egg. Not only does the egg white add some heft to the salad, but as you eat, the yolk mixes with the olive oil, lemon, and Parmesan to form an irresistibly creamy and rich dressing.

Ingredients

1 tablespoon butter

4 eggs

1 large bunch arugula (12 ounces)

Salt and pepper

1 lemon

3 tablespoons olive oil

4 ounces Parmesan cheese (1 cup shaved)

Prep | Cook

1. Put a large skillet over medium heat. After about 1 minute, add 1 tablespoon butter and swirl it around. Once the butter foam subsides, crack the eggs into the skillet and cook until the whites are no longer translucent, 2 or 3 minutes.

   Trim the arugula and put it in a large bowl.

2. When the egg whites are no longer translucent, turn the heat to low and sprinkle the eggs with salt and pepper. Cook, undisturbed, until the whites are firm and the yolks are as runny as you like, just a few more minutes. If the eggs are ready before you've finished the dressing, move the skillet to a cool surface.

3. Halve the lemon and squeeze the juice into the bowl. Add 3 tablespoons oil and a sprinkle of salt and pepper. Shave about 1 cup of Parmesan with a vegetable peeler, add to the bowl, and toss. Taste and adjust the seasoning and divide the salad among 4 plates.

4. When the eggs are done as you like, remove them from the skillet and put one on top of each salad. Serve immediately.

VARIATIONS

Spinach with Fried Eggs and Feta

Substitute spinach for the arugula and 1 cup crumbled feta for the Parmesan.

Endive with Fried Eggs and Blue Cheese

A little more intense, and crunchier too. Use about 8 cups chopped endive (or frisée) instead of the arugula and substitute 1 cup crumbled blue cheese for the Parmesan.

NOTES

SHAVING PARMESAN

Parmesan has fantastic texture: firm, but not opposed to melting on your tongue. While 90 percent of the time I grate Parmesan in cooking, sometimes it's more appealing to make thin shavings or shreds to preserve some of that texture. Just take a chunk, find a side that's fairly smooth, and start shaving it with a vegetable peeler. (It's easiest to work toward you, controlling the blade with short strokes and anchoring the cheese with your thumb.) If you prefer smaller shreds, grate the cheese over the biggest holes of a box grater.

SIDES

Bruschetta 909

Warm Buttery Bread 906

Garlic Bread 906

SPEED SERVES 4

Endive and Radicchio with Bacon Vinaigrette

Bacon vinaigrette? That got your attention! Many salads have pieces of bacon sprinkled over them, and that's fine. This one features the bacon cooking fat as well, which becomes the basis of a warm dressing. Its smoky, salty flavor takes the edge off the bitter endive and radicchio. There's no subtlety here; this salad is a knockout.

Ingredients

8 slices bacon

6 heads endive (1 ½ to 2 pounds)

1 small head radicchio

1 large shallot

1 teaspoon Dijon mustard

¼ cup olive oil

3 tablespoons balsamic vinegar

Salt and pepper

Prep | Cook

1. Put a large skillet over medium-high heat.

   Chop 8 slices bacon. Line a plate with paper towels.

2. Add the bacon to the skillet and cook, stirring occasionally until crisp, 5 to 10 minutes.

   Trim and chop the endive and radicchio and put them in a large bowl.

   Trim, peel, and mince the shallot.

3. When the bacon is crisp, transfer it to the paper towels with a slotted spoon. Pour off all but 2 tablespoons of the fat and turn off the heat.

4. Add the shallot to the skillet, then whisk in 1 teaspoon Dijon, ¼ cup olive oil, 3 tablespoons balsamic vinegar, and a sprinkle of salt and pepper.

5. Pour the dressing over the endive and radicchio, add the cooked bacon, and toss. Taste and adjust the seasoning and serve.

VARIATIONS

7 Other Bases for Warm Vinaigrette

Sauté any of the following in about ¼ cup olive oil instead of using the bacon. No need to add more oil when you add the remaining vinaigrette ingredients:

1. 4 to 6 ounces prosciutto
2. 4 to 6 ounces smoked Spanish chorizo or fresh Italian sausage
3. ⅓ cup chopped nuts
4. ¼ cup chopped olives, dried tomatoes, whole capers, or a few chopped anchovies
5. 1 tablespoon minced or slivered garlic
6. 1 tablespoon minced fresh ginger or chile
7. 2 teaspoons cumin or coriander seeds

NOTES

IF YOU HAVE MORE TIME

Endive and Radicchio with Creamy Bacon Vinaigrette

The blender is an incomparable tool for making thick, smooth vinaigrettes. Pour the 2 tablespoons bacon fat, mustard, olive oil, vinegar, and a sprinkle of salt and pepper into a blender and turn it on. Once a creamy emulsion forms, turn off the blender and stir in the shallots. (Or just blend the shallots with the other ingredients.) Proceed with the recipe.

MORE USES FOR WARM VINAIGRETTE

It may not be as versatile as regular vinaigrette, but the warm version can be used in all sorts of dishes. As a salad dressing, its residual heat will gently wilt greens, and takes a bit of the raw edge off other vegetables. I love tossing it with bean or grain salads, and you can even consider it among the simplest possible sauces for pasta, rice, cooked vegetables, meat, or fish.

SIDES

Warm Buttery Bread 906

Bruschetta 909

Garlic Bread 906

SPEED ◔ SERVES 4

Steakhouse Salad

The "wedge" salad is a steakhouse classic made with iceberg lettuce, tomatoes, crisp bacon, and blue cheese dressing. This Italian-style version uses romaine instead of iceberg, cherry tomatoes, sliced radicchio, Gorgonzola dressing, and crisp salami. It's more flavorful than the original and can be prepared in little more time than it takes to crisp the salami.

Ingredients

1 tablespoon olive oil

4 ounces salami

1 large head romaine lettuce

1 small head radicchio

1 lemon

½ cup sour cream

½ cup yogurt

Salt and pepper

4 ounces Gorgonzola cheese (1 cup crumbled)

1 pint cherry tomatoes

Prep | Cook

1. Put 1 tablespoon olive oil in a large skillet over medium-high heat.

   Chop the salami.

2. When the oil is hot, add the salami to the skillet and cook, stirring occasionally until crisp, 5 to 10 minutes.

   Carefully trim the lettuce, leaving the leaves attached at the stem end. Cut the head lengthwise into quarters.

   Trim and thinly slice the radicchio.

   Halve the lemon; refrigerate 1 half for another use.

   Put ½ cup sour cream, ½ cup yogurt, the juice of ½ lemon, and a sprinkle of salt and pepper in a small bowl. Crumble 1 cup Gorgonzola, add it to the bowl, and stir to combine. Taste and adjust the seasoning.

   Halve the cherry tomatoes.

3. Put each romaine quarter cut side up on a plate and top with the radicchio, cherry tomatoes, and Gorgonzola dressing. Sprinkle the salami over the top and serve.

VARIATIONS

Spanish Steakhouse Salad
Use 4 ounces chopped smoked Spanish chorizo instead of the salami. Use any blue cheese (use Cabrales if you want to be particularly Spanish about it) and stir a little smoked paprika into the dressing.

Bacon Steakhouse Salad
Substitute bacon for the salami and lower the heat to medium in Step 1. It will take 10 to 15 minutes to cook. Use a good American blue cheese instead of the Gorgonzola.

NOTES

EVEN FASTER
Don't bother cutting the cherry tomatoes in half.

SIDES

Bruschetta 909

Warm Buttery Bread 906

Garlic Bread 906

SPEED ◔ SERVES 4

Grated Beet and Carrot Salad with Toasted Cashews

Beets take a long time to cook, but that doesn't mean they need to be excluded from your fast repertoire: Just grate them and serve them raw; they're so earthy and delicious you may never cook them again. With carrots and scallions, the colors in this dish are stunning.

Ingredients

1 cup cashews

2 large or 3 small beets (1 pound)

5 medium carrots (1 pound)

Salt

3 scallions

2 limes

2 tablespoons sesame oil

Prep | Cook

1. Put 1 cup cashews in a medium skillet over medium heat. Cook, shaking the skillet occasionally and adjusting the heat so they don't burn, until the cashews are lightly browned and fragrant, 3 to 5 minutes.

   Trim and peel the beets and carrots. If you're using a food processor for grating, cut the beets into chunks that will fit through the feed tube.

2. When the cashews are toasted, turn off the heat. Shred the beets and carrots in a food processor with a grating disk or by hand with a box grater. Put them in a large bowl and sprinkle with salt.

   Trim and slice the scallions.

   Halve the limes.

3. Add the scallions and cashews to the bowl. Squeeze in the lime juice and add 2 tablespoons sesame oil. Toss, taste and adjust the seasoning, and serve.

VARIATIONS

Grated Beet and Carrot Salad with Olives, Mint, and Lemon
Use 1 cup chopped pitted olives instead of cashews (no need to cook them). Replace the scallions with 1/4 cup chopped fresh mint, the limes with 1 lemon, and the sesame oil with olive oil.

Grated Beet and Cabbage Salad with Rye Croutons, Yogurt, and Dill
Substitute 1 cup rye bread cubes for the cashews; sauté them in 1 tablespoon butter until golden and crisp. Substitute 1 pound red cabbage for the carrots, 1/4 cup chopped fresh dill for the scallions, 1 lemon for the limes, and 1/2 cup Greek yogurt or sour cream for the sesame oil.

NOTES

IF YOU HAVE MORE TIME
To intensify the flavor of the beets and carrots and soften them up a bit, toss the grated vegetables with the lime juice and sesame oil and let sit for at least 15 minutes.

RAW ROOT VEGETABLES
We usually think of root vegetables — squash, parsnips, beets, celery root, and so on — as wintry foods meant for roasting, braising, or other long-cooking methods. They are wonderful for that, indeed, but you can also eat almost all of them raw. Eating roots raw gives you a satisfying crunch and a sense of the freshness of spring, even if it's still the dead of winter outside. Since root vegetables are sturdy, it's best to grate them, as done here. You can also shave or julienne them, which takes longer.

If the grated vegetable still seems too crispy for comfort, let it marinate for a half an hour or longer in a vinaigrette (or, better yet, a warm vinaigrette; see page 52). It will "cook" them a bit similar to the way a ceviche "cooks" raw seafood. Note that not all roots should be eaten raw. Stick to low-starch choices like the ones mentioned and avoid things like potato and taro root.

SIDES

Warm Flour Tortillas 907

White Rice 941

Scallion Pancakes 940

RECIPE-FREE

Salads

1 Start cooking (or don't).

If you're making a salad in which something needs to be cooked or heated—think roasted vegetables or cooked bacon—start there. Heat a pan or turn on the oven, broiler, or grill. Get those ingredients cooking and turn your attention to the dressing.

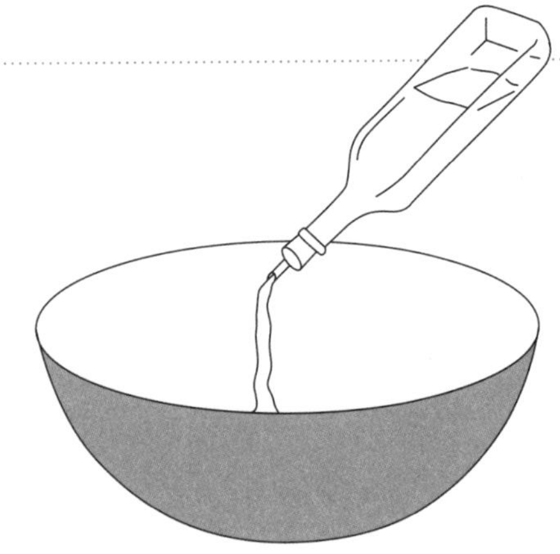

2 Choose your oil.

Ninety percent of the time it will be olive oil. For dressings with soy sauce I'll sometimes use a combination of sesame oil and a vegetable oil. Pour about ⅓ cup into a large, wide bowl big enough to hold the salad—and ideally with a little room to spare for tossing.

3 Choose your acid.

Add about 2 tablespoons vinegar or lemon or lime juice to the bowl. For any salads inspired by Asian cuisines, rice vinegar is a good option too.

4 Choose your seasonings.

Some ideas beyond salt and pepper: chopped fresh herbs; dried herbs or spices; minced garlic, ginger, or chiles; chopped olives; honey; soy sauce; citrus zest; chopped nuts; or crumbled cooked bacon.

5 Make it creamy (if you like).

A tablespoon or 2 of ingredients like mayonnaise, yogurt, crème fraîche, mustard, ketchup, hoisin, miso, peanut butter, hummus, pesto, or Parmesan to add creaminess and thicken the dressing a bit.

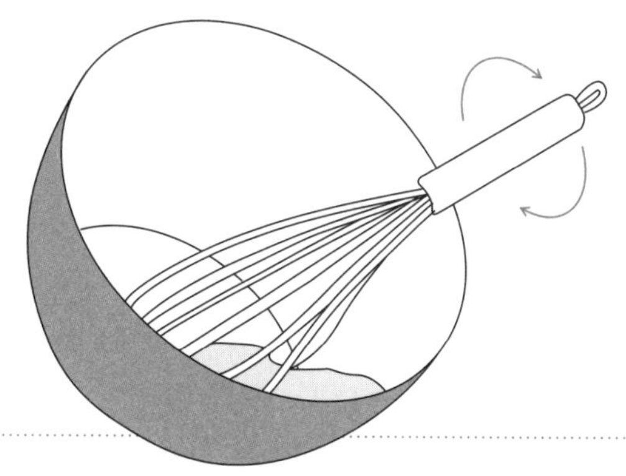

6 Whisk, but don't go crazy.

Whisk until well combined (if you want a super-emulsion, use a blender). Taste and adjust the seasoning; you'll have a final chance to make adjustments once you add the rest of the ingredients.

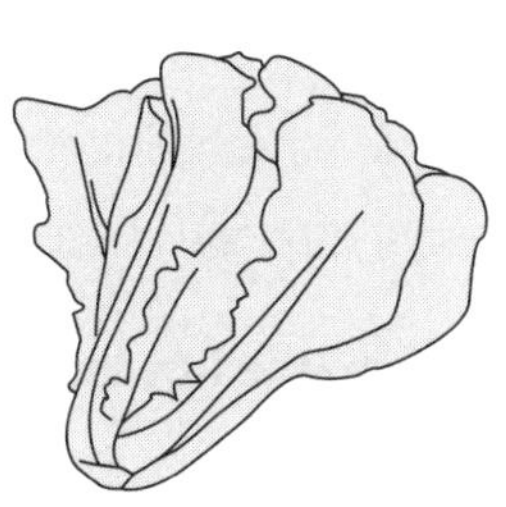

7 Chop and drop.

Prep and pile the salad ingredients in the bowl as you go. The ones that you add first sit in the dressing the longest, so start with harder vegetables like carrots and onions. Save things like tomatoes and especially tender salad greens for the end.

8 Toss, taste, and serve.

Gently toss everything together using tongs, 2 spoons, or a clean pair of hands: Scoop under the greens along the inside of the bowl, then up through the center; repeat until everything is coated evenly. Taste again. Add more salt or pepper, or any of the individual components of the dressing.

SPEED SERVES 4

Puffed Rice Salad with Dates and Almonds

Puffed rice makes for a quick, unusual, and wonderfully crunchy salad. Here it's softened ever so slightly by chopped dates marinated in orange juice, olive oil, ginger, and herbs. I like puffed basmati rice, which you can find at some supermarkets and most Indian markets, but you can also use regular puffed rice cereal if that's all you can find.

Ingredients

2 cups dried dates

1 bunch fresh mint

1 bunch fresh cilantro

½ inch fresh ginger

1 orange

½ cup almonds

¼ cup olive oil

Salt and pepper

6 cups puffed basmati rice or puffed rice cereal

Prep | Cook

Pit 2 cups dried dates if necessary and chop them; put in a large bowl.

Chop ½ cup each of mint leaves and cilantro and add them to the bowl.

Peel and mince ½ inch fresh ginger; add it to the bowl.

Zest the orange right into the bowl, then cut it in half.

1. Add ½ cup almonds to the bowl. Squeeze in the orange juice, add ¼ cup olive oil, sprinkle with salt and pepper, and toss; let sit for about 10 minutes.
2. Add 6 cups puffed rice and toss. Taste and adjust the seasoning and serve.

VARIATIONS

Puffed Rice Salad with Dried Tomatoes and Olives
Use dried tomatoes instead of the dates, basil and parsley instead of the mint and cilantro, 1 garlic clove in place of the ginger, and ½ cup chopped pitted olives instead of the almonds.

Red Beans and Puffed Rice
Skip the almonds. Substitute 2 cups cooked or drained canned red beans for the dates, 1 cup chopped parsley for the mint and cilantro, 1 small red onion, chopped, for the ginger, and a lime for the orange.

Puffed Wheat Salad with Dried Apricots and Pistachios
Use dried apricots instead of the dates and pistachios instead of almonds. Substitute puffed wheat cereal for the rice.

NOTES

EVEN FASTER
Don't wait for the dates to marinate; just add the puffed rice right away and serve.

IF YOU HAVE MORE TIME
To soften up the dates and almonds, marinate for another 10 to 15 minutes in the dressing before adding the puffed rice.

SIDES

Crisp Seasoned Pita 908

Green Salad 911

Cucumber Raita 916

SPEED SERVES 4

White Bean and Cucumber Salad with Yogurt and Dill

Dressing white beans in a light yogurt sauce enhances their natural creaminess and adds a refreshing tang. Lemon and dill brighten things even further, while cucumbers and red onion provide the necessary crunch.

Ingredients

¾ cup Greek yogurt

3 tablespoons olive oil

1 lemon

1 bunch fresh dill

Salt and pepper

4 cups cooked or canned white beans (two 15-ounce cans)

3 medium cucumbers

1 small red onion

Prep | Cook

1. Put ¾ cup yogurt and 3 tablespoons olive oil in a large bowl and whisk to combine.

   Halve the lemon; squeeze the juice into the bowl.

   Strip ¼ cup dill leaves from the stems and chop; add them to the bowl.

2. Add a sprinkle of salt and pepper to the yogurt sauce and whisk until smooth, adding a splash of water if necessary to make it the consistency of a thick dressing.

   If you're using canned beans, rinse and drain them; add the beans to the bowl.

   Trim and peel the cucumbers; cut them in half lengthwise and scoop out the seeds with a spoon. Chop them and add them to the bowl.

   Trim, peel, halve, and slice the red onion; add it to the bowl.

3. Toss the beans and vegetables with the dressing until coated. Taste and adjust the seasoning and serve.

VARIATIONS

Black Bean and Cabbage Salad with Sour Cream and Cilantro

Use ½ cup sour cream instead of ½ cup of the yogurt, 2 limes instead of the lemon, cilantro in place of dill, black beans instead of white, and 4 cups shredded red or green cabbage in place of the cucumbers.

Chickpea and Cucumber Salad with Tahini and Parsley

Replace ¼ cup of the yogurt with ¼ cup tahini, the dill with parsley, and the white beans with chickpeas. If you like, add 1 teaspoon cumin to the dressing.

NOTES

MAKE YOUR OWN

Cooked Beans 496

VERSATILE DILL

Dill is an underrated herb; its uniquely grassy flavor lends itself to all sorts of uses, from brightening rich stews to freshening up sauces and giving run-of-the-mill salad greens an unexpected kick. As an added bonus, dill is less fragile than cilantro and basil, which means it keeps longer in the fridge.

SIDES

Bruschetta 909

Crisp Seasoned Pita 908

Green Salad 911

Fennel Salad 917

SPEED SERVES 4

Chickpea and Carrot Salad with Warm Cumin Oil

Slowly infusing olive oil with seasonings is a wonderful way to make a complex dressing without paying much attention to it. Whole cumin seeds, lemon zest, and garlic flavor the olive oil, which graces chickpeas and sliced carrots. Cumin seeds add crunch, but if you like things smooth, just pour the oil through a strainer into the bowl.

Ingredients

½ cup olive oil

1 garlic clove

1 lemon

2 tablespoons cumin seeds

5 to 7 medium carrots (1 pound)

4 cups cooked or canned chickpeas (two 15-ounce cans)

1 bunch fresh mint

Salt and pepper

Prep | Cook

1. Put ½ cup olive oil in a small saucepan over low heat.

   Smash and peel 1 garlic clove; add it to the oil.

   Zest the lemon directly into the oil. Refrigerate the fruit for another use.

2. Stir 2 tablespoons cumin seeds into the oil. Let the oil warm up slowly, undisturbed, until it starts to bubble steadily, about 10 minutes.

   Trim and peel the carrots; slice them into thin coins or half-moons. Put them in a large bowl.

   If you're using canned chickpeas, rinse and drain them; add the beans to the bowl.

   Chop ½ cup mint leaves and add to the bowl.

3. When the olive oil is warm and slightly bubbly, discard the garlic clove and pour the oil over the chickpeas and carrots; stir to coat well.

4. Sprinkle the mixture with salt and pepper and toss. Taste and adjust the seasoning and serve.

VARIATIONS

Chickpea and Roasted Red Pepper Salad with Warm Paprika Dressing
Substitute 1 tablespoon smoked paprika for the cumin seeds. Instead of carrots, use 12 ounces sliced roasted red peppers. Use parsley instead of mint.

Edamame and Cucumber Salad with Warm Ginger Dressing
Use edamame instead of chickpeas. (Defrost if frozen.) Substitute half sesame oil/half vegetable oil for the olive oil, lime zest for lemon, 1 tablespoon minced fresh ginger for the cumin seeds, 2 cucumbers for the carrots, and scallions for the mint. Garnish with sesame seeds if you like.

NOTES

MAKE YOUR OWN

Cooked Beans 496

EVEN FASTER

Don't warm the oil. Instead, just whisk together the oil, lemon zest, garlic (mince it), and cumin seeds, and toss the cold dressing with the chickpeas and carrots.

SIDES

Crisp Seasoned Pita 908

Cucumber Salad 915

Seared Broccoli or Cauliflower 925

Couscous 910

SPEED SERVES 4

Crab and Celery Root Rémoulade

Easier and better than classic celery root rémoulade. In fact, I like this better than classic crab cakes too. And the variations open the door to all sorts of ingredient combinations.

Ingredients

1 cup mayonnaise

1 tablespoon Dijon mustard

1 garlic clove

2 tablespoons capers

2 anchovy fillets

1 bunch fresh parsley

¼ teaspoon cayenne

Salt and pepper

1 pound cooked lump crabmeat

1 large or 2 medium celery roots (1 ½ pounds)

Prep | Cook

1. Put 1 cup mayonnaise and 1 tablespoon Dijon mustard in a large bowl.

   Peel and mince 1 garlic clove; add to the bowl.

   Chop 2 tablespoons capers and 2 anchovy fillets; add them to the bowl.

   Chop ¼ cup parsley and add it to the bowl.

2. Add ¼ teaspoon cayenne and a sprinkle of salt and pepper to the bowl and stir.

   Pick through the crabmeat, discarding pieces of shell or cartilage. Add the meat to the bowl.

   Trim and peel the celery root. If you're using a food processor for grating, cut them into chunks that will fit through the feed tube.

   Shred the celery root in a food processor with a grating disk or by hand with a box grater.

3. Add the celery root to the bowl and toss to combine. Taste and adjust the seasoning and serve.

VARIATIONS

Celery Root Rémoulade with Hard-Boiled Eggs
Trade 8 hard-boiled eggs, chopped, for the crabmeat.

Shrimp and Celery Root Rémoulade
Use 1 pound chopped cooked shrimp in place of the crabmeat.

Tuna and Celery Root Rémoulade
Substitute 12 ounces canned tuna, drained, for the crabmeat.

Chicken and Celery Root Rémoulade
Instead of crabmeat, use 1 pound shredded or chopped cooked chicken.

NOTES

MAKE YOUR OWN
Mayonnaise 144

IF YOU HAVE MORE TIME
If you really want to practice your knife skills, after trimming and peeling the celery root, cut it into matchsticks ¼ inch thick by 1 ½ inches long.

SIDES

Warm Buttery Bread 906

Green Salad 911

Chopped Salad 912

SPEED SERVES 4

Poached Shrimp Salad with Herby Tartar Sauce

Poaching shrimp is effortless and frees you up to do so many things. Here the shrimp steep in just-boiled water off the heat, which gives time to put together a tartar sauce. This technique also works for scallops and small chunks of fish.

Ingredients

Salt

1 medium head Boston lettuce

½ cup mayonnaise

2 teaspoons Dijon mustard

1 ½ pounds medium peeled shrimp

1 bunch fresh dill

3 sprigs fresh tarragon

2 sweet pickles or ¼ cup capers

1 lemon

Salt and pepper

Prep | Cook

1. Bring a medium saucepan of water to a boil and salt it.

   Trim the lettuce and tear off the leaves whole.

2. Put the lettuce leaves overlapping on a platter.

3. Put ½ cup mayonnaise and 2 teaspoons Dijon mustard in a medium bowl.

4. When the water comes to a boil, add the shrimp, cover, and turn off the heat. Let it sit for 10 minutes.

   Strip ¼ cup dill leaves from the stems and chop; add them to the bowl.

   Strip the leaves from 3 sprigs tarragon, chop, and add them to the bowl.

   Chop 2 sweet pickles or ¼ cup capers; add to the bowl.

   Halve the lemon; squeeze the juice of 1 half into the bowl. Refrigerate the remaining half for another use.

5. Add a sprinkle of salt and pepper to the bowl, stir to combine, taste, and adjust the seasoning.

6. When the shrimp are cooked through, drain them and run them under cold water to cool.

7. Add the shrimp to the bowl with the tartar sauce and toss to coat. Spoon the shrimp over the lettuce leaves and serve.

VARIATIONS

Poached Shrimp Salad with Curried Tartar Sauce
Skip the tarragon. Substitute 2 teaspoons curry powder for the mustard, cilantro for the dill, 1/4 cup chopped cucumber for the pickles, and lime for the lemon.

Poached Scallop Salad with Herby Tartar Sauce
Use large sea scallops, cut into quarters, or smaller bay scallops instead of the shrimp.

Poached Salmon Salad with Herby Tartar Sauce
Use salmon fillet instead of the shrimp; cut it into 1-inch chunks.

NOTES

MAKE YOUR OWN

Mayonnaise 144

THE CITRUS CYCLE

If you were to open my refrigerator at any given time you'd be likely to find halves of lemons and limes scattered all over the place and the occasional fruit with some or all of its zest scraped off. That's because you don't always use entire lemons or limes at once.

Sometimes you'll just want the zest, in which case you can refrigerate the rest of the fruit easily for another week without having to wrap it up. To store citrus halves, put the whole piece in a sealed plastic bag, wrap the cut side in aluminum foil or plastic wrap, or lay a paper towel in the fridge and put the fruit cut side down on the towel.

To get the most out of citrus I make it a point to use the zest first, since once you cut the fruit and squeeze out the juice it's a lot harder to get the zest.

SIDES

Warm Buttery Bread 906

Bruschetta 909

Celery Salad 917

Avocado with Lemon and Salt 920

Vinaigrette and Croutons

Since vinaigrette is the most useful sauce in existence, there are versions all over this book. Most are whisked together in a salad bowl before the main ingredients are added, others involve pouring oil and vinegar over vegetables before serving, and a few are even concocted right in a hot skillet to make a warm dressing that gently wilts greens.

But if I'm making a bigger batch of vinaigrette that I want to use over a few days, I use the blender. It obviously adds a big piece of equipment to clean, but it makes the creamiest vinaigrette. The recipe here makes a bit more than a cup, and there are plenty of variations to follow.

Then there are croutons, the crisp hunks of bread that make salads—and other things—so much better. And bread crumbs, which are shockingly good on salads and also used throughout the book.

Vinaigrette

1 Combine and Blend

Put 1 cup olive oil, 6 tablespoons wine vinegar (sherry, red wine, white wine, or balsamic), 2 teaspoons Dijon mustard, and a sprinkle of salt and pepper in a blender. Turn the machine on and wait until a creamy emulsion forms, about 30 seconds.

2 Adjust the Flavor Balance

Taste the vinaigrette and see what it needs. You may want to add more vinegar, a teaspoon at a time, until the balance tastes right or a bit of honey or sugar to balance out the sharpness of the mustard.

3 Add the Shallot

Add 1 large shallot, cut into chunks, and turn the blender on and off a few times to mince it. Taste and adjust the seasoning. Use immediately or store in the refrigerator for a few days; bring it back to room temperature and whisk it before using.

VARIATIONS

15 Additions to Vinaigrette

1. Any dried herb or spice: The specific quantities will vary, but start with as little as a pinch—1/8 teaspoon or so.
2. Minced fresh garlic: Start with a *very* small clove or a piece of a big one. For a milder flavor, let a crushed clove sit in the vinaigrette for a few minutes, then fish it out. Or wipe your salad bowl with a crushed clove and discard.
3. Minced red onion, scallion, shallot, mild white onion, leek, etc.: Start with a tablespoon or so.
4. Honey, maple syrup, or other sweeteners, within reason: no more than a tablespoon or so.
5. Freshly grated Parmesan or crumbled blue cheese, feta, or goat cheese: from a tablespoon to 1/4 cup.
6. Minced pickles, preferably cornichons: from a tablespoon to 1/4 cup.
7. An egg or a couple of tablespoons fresh or sour cream or yogurt or puréed soft tofu, any of which will add incredible creaminess to your vinaigrette.
8. Prepared or freshly grated horseradish: at least 1 teaspoon.
9. Minced tomato, seeded and, preferably, peeled, or bits of reconstituted dried tomato.
10. A tablespoon or two of any stock, juice, wine, beer, or booze.
11. A small handful of seeds, like sesame, poppy, sunflower, or minced pumpkin seeds.
12. Canned chipotle: 1 pepper is plenty, with just a tiny bit of its adobo.
13. 1 small slice of day-old bread (crust removed).
14. 1 small peach, pear, or apple, peeled, pitted or cored, and cut into chunks.
15. 1/4 cup salsa or chutney.

Croutons

1 Heat the Oil and Cut the Bread

Put about 1/4 cup olive oil in a large skillet over medium heat. You want the skillet to be big enough to accommodate the bread in one layer. Cut 4 large or 12 small slices of bread into 1/2- to 1-inch cubes.

2 Brown the Bread

Add the bread to the skillet and sprinkle with salt and pepper. Toss the bread to coat with the oil and cook, tossing occasionally and adding more oil if the pan dries out (it likely will), until the bread is lightly browned all over. Use immediately or cool and store in a tin or wax paper for a few days.

VARIATIONS

Garlic Croutons

Add a smashed garlic clove to the skillet along with the oil.

Herbed Croutons

As the bread cubes brown, stir in about 1/4 cup minced fresh parsley, dill, or basil or 1 or 2 tablespoons minced fresh rosemary, sage, thyme, or oregano.

Spiced Croutons

Add about 1 teaspoon chili powder or curry powder (page 758) or other spice blends that you like.

Bread Crumbs

Skip the oil and toasting. Cut or tear the bread into 2-inch pieces and put them in a food processor. Pulse a few times to break up the bread, then continue pulsing until they reach the consistency you want: coarse (pea-sized), fine (like coarse grain), or somewhere in between. Use right away or store in an airtight container in the pantry for up to 1 month or in the freezer for up to 3 months.

SPEED SERVES 4

Cucumber and Salmon Salad with Caper and Mustard Dressing

Poached salmon with mustard sauce is a classic. Add chopped cucumbers, capers, and fresh dill—all good friends of salmon—and it becomes a fantastic salad.

Ingredients

1 pound salmon fillet

Salt

1 lemon

1 bunch fresh dill

½ cup mayonnaise

2 tablespoons Dijon mustard

¼ cup capers

Pepper

4 medium cucumbers

1 small red onion

Prep | Cook

1. Put the salmon in a skillet big enough to hold it (cut it into pieces if you need to) and cover with cold water. Add a pinch of salt, put over high heat, and cover.

   Halve the lemon; squeeze the juice into a large bowl.

   Strip ¼ cup dill leaves from the stems and chop; add to the bowl.

   Add ½ cup mayonnaise, 2 tablespoons Dijon mustard, ¼ cup capers, and a sprinkle of salt and pepper to the bowl. Stir to combine, taste, and adjust the seasoning.

2. When the water comes to a boil, turn off the heat and let the salmon sit, covered, for 3 or 4 minutes for rare, 6 or 7 minutes for medium.

   Trim and peel the cucumbers; cut them in half lengthwise and scoop out the seeds with a spoon.

   Thinly slice the cucumbers; add them to the bowl.

   Trim, peel, halve, and thinly slice the onion; add it to the bowl.

3. When the salmon is cooked to your liking, remove it from the water, pull off and discard the skin, and cut the fish into chunks or break it into large flakes.

4. Add the salmon to the bowl and toss gently. Taste and adjust the seasoning and serve.

VARIATIONS

Cucumber and Salmon Salad with Ginger-Peanut Dressing
Substitute a lime for the lemon; mint for the dill; 1/4 cup sesame oil, 1/4 cup vegetable oil, and 2 tablespoons soy sauce for the mayonnaise; peanut butter for the mustard; and 1 teaspoon minced fresh ginger for the capers.

Fish and White Bean Salad with Tomato Vinaigrette
An even heartier dish. Use a thick white fish fillet instead of the salmon and cook through; unlike salmon, you don't want to leave it rare in the middle. Swap 1 tablespoon chopped fresh rosemary for the dill, 1/3 cup olive oil for the mayonnaise, 1 ripe tomato, finely chopped, for the mustard, and 1/4 cup chopped pitted olives for the capers. Use 4 cups cooked or canned white beans instead of the cucumbers.

NOTES

MAKE YOUR OWN

Mayonnaise 144

EVEN FASTER

If you can find super-fresh wild salmon and like to eat it raw, skip the poaching, remove the skin, cut the salmon into cubes, and toss it with the cucumbers, capers, and dressing.

If you have a mandoline, use it to the slice the cucumbers and onion.

SIDES

Warm Buttery Bread 906

Green Salad 911

Tomatoes with Fried Bread Crumbs 930

SPEED SERVES 4

Fresh Tuna, Avocado, and Green Bean Salad

Searing tuna delivers a browned crust and a rare interior. The soft flesh of the tuna and the creaminess of avocado play nicely against crisp-tender green beans and crunchy red onions. If you prefer your tuna more well done, cook it for a few extra minutes on each side, lowering the heat if necessary to prevent burning.

Ingredients

Salt

1 pound green beans

1 lime

⅓ cup olive oil, plus more as needed

1 tablespoon soy sauce

1 small red onion

Ice cubes

1 pound fresh tuna

1 teaspoon vegetable oil

2 avocados

Prep | Cook

1. Bring a medium pot of water to a boil and salt it.

   Trim the green beans; cut them into 2-inch pieces.

   Halve the lime; squeeze the juice into a large bowl.

2. Add ⅓ cup olive oil and 1 tablespoon soy sauce to the bowl and whisk.

   Trim, peel, halve, and thinly slice the onion; add it to the bowl.

3. When the water comes to a boil, add the green beans and cook until they're just tender, 2 or 3 minutes. Put a large skillet over high heat.

   Prepare a bowl of ice water for the green beans.

4. When the green beans are just tender, drain and transfer them to the ice bath.

5. When the skillet is very hot, rub the tuna all over with 1 teaspoon vegetable oil, sprinkle with salt, and put it in the skillet. Cook, turning once, until it's browned on both sides but still raw in the center, 3 or 4 minutes per side.

Pit the avocados, scoop out the flesh, and cut into small chunks; add them to the bowl with the dressing.

Drain the green beans well, and add them to the bowl.

6. Cut the tuna into 1-inch chunks and add it to the bowl. Toss gently, adding more olive oil if the salad looks too dry. Taste and adjust the seasoning and serve.

VARIATIONS

Fresh Tuna Salad, Niçoise Style

Substitute 2 tablespoons red wine vinegar for the lime juice, 1 teaspoon Dijon mustard for the soy sauce, and 2 cups cherry tomatoes for the avocados. Add ½ cup pitted olives (preferably Niçoise) to the bowl before tossing.

Tofu, Avocado, and Green Bean Salad

Replace the olive oil with half sesame oil and half vegetable oil. Use 1 brick firm tofu (12 to 14 ounces) instead of the tuna. Cut the tofu into cubes and gently toss it with the rest of the salad (no need to cook it).

Fresh Tuna, Mango, and Green Bean Salad with Thai Vinaigrette

Use fish sauce instead of soy sauce and 2 cups chopped fresh mango in place of the avocados.

NOTES

EVEN FASTER

If you can find perfectly fresh tuna and like to eat it completely raw, cut the uncooked tuna into cubes and toss it into the salad.

SIDES

White Rice 941

Warm Flour Tortillas 907

Tomato Salad with Sesame and Soy 913

Scallion Pancakes 940

SPEED ◑ SERVES 4

Asparagus and Kale Caesar Salad

Caesar salad is ubiquitous because everybody loves it—that garlic bite, the snap of fresh romaine, and the unctuous dressing. But even old favorites can use makeovers; this exciting riff uses the star ingredients of Caesar dressing with asparagus. Swap the traditional romaine for sturdy kale and an old friend becomes a new flame.

Ingredients

1 large bunch asparagus (1 pound)

¾ cup olive oil

Salt and pepper

4 thick slices any rustic bread (a little stale is fine)

1 bunch kale, preferably lacinato (1 pound)

1 garlic clove

1 lemon

4 anchovy fillets or 2 teaspoons anchovy paste

1 egg

Worcestershire sauce

4 ounces Parmesan cheese (1 cup grated)

Prep | Cook

1. Turn the broiler to high; put the rack 4 inches from the heat.

   Trim the asparagus.

2. Put the asparagus on a rimmed baking sheet. Drizzle with 2 tablespoons olive oil, sprinkle with salt and pepper, and toss. Put them on 1 side of the sheet and broil, turning as necessary, until tender and slightly charred, 5 to 10 minutes.

   Cut 4 thick slices bread into cubes. Toss with 2 tablespoons olive oil and a sprinkle of salt and pepper.

3. When the asparagus has cooked for a few minutes, add the bread to the pan and broil, shaking the pan once or twice so the bread browns all over, 2 to 5 minutes.

   Trim and slice the kale into thin ribbons.

4. Check on the asparagus and bread. If the bread is done before the asparagus (or vice versa), transfer it to a plate and return the pan to the broiler until everything is done.

   Peel and halve 1 garlic clove. Rub the cut sides all over the inside of a large bowl, then mince it and add it to the bowl.

Halve the lemon. Chop 4 anchovy fillets or measure 2 teaspoons anchovy paste and add to the bowl.

5. Lightly mash together the anchovies and garlic in the bottom of the bowl with a fork. Separate the egg; add the yolk to the bowl and discard the white or refrigerate it for another use. Squeeze in the lemon juice; add a dash of Worcestershire and plenty of pepper.

6. Whisk, streaming in ½ cup olive oil as you go, until it forms a creamy dressing. Grate 1 cup Parmesan cheese, add, and whisk again. Taste and adjust the seasoning.

7. Cut the asparagus into 2-inch pieces and add to the bowl along with the kale and croutons. Toss to coat with the dressing and serve.

VARIATIONS

Classic Caesar Salad

Use 2 heads romaine lettuce, chopped and raw, instead of the asparagus and kale.

NOTES

EVEN FASTER

If you find pencil-thin asparagus — easy enough in the spring — you can eat them raw. Just cut them into 2-inch pieces and proceed directly to toasting the croutons and making the dressing.

SNAPPING ASPARAGUS

Before cooking asparagus you'll want to trim off the thick, tough bottoms. To do this, take 1 stalk and snap off the bottom with your fingers; this will naturally happen in the right place. Now that you know how much of the bottom to take off, trim the remaining stalks with a knife. If the asparagus are especially thick, you can also peel the lower part of the stalks with a vegetable peeler.

SIDES

Fennel Salad 917

Tomato Salad 913

Broiled Cherry Tomatoes 931

SPEED ◐ SERVES 4

Seared Scallops with Grilled or Broiled Romaine

Seared scallops are pretty perfect on their own, but the pan sauce built from their juices makes a wonderful dressing for grilled or broiled romaine. The sweetness of the scallops and acidity in the sauce are a great match for the smoky lettuce. If you can't find hearts of romaine, you can make them yourself. Buy big heads of romaine lettuce and remove the outer leaves until you get to the tidy, smaller leaves in the center. Reserve the outer leaves for another salad.

Ingredients

4 hearts romaine lettuce

6 tablespoons olive oil

Salt and pepper

1 garlic clove

1 lemon

2 tablespoons butter

1 pound sea scallops

1 small red bell pepper

½ cup white wine

Prep | Cook

1. Prepare a grill or turn the broiler to high; put the rack 4 inches from the heat.

   Halve the hearts of romaine lengthwise, leaving them attached at the stem end.

2. Drizzle the romaine with 4 tablespoons olive oil and sprinkle with salt and pepper. Grill or broil (cut side toward the heat), until the cut side is lightly charred, 2 to 5 minutes.

3. When the romaine is lightly charred, put 2 pieces cut sides up on 4 plates.

4. Put a large skillet over medium-high heat.

   Peel and mince 1 garlic clove.

   Halve the lemon.

5. Add 2 tablespoons butter, 2 tablespoons oil, and the garlic to the skillet; 30 seconds later, add the scallops and sprinkle with salt and pepper.

6. Cook, turning once, until the scallops are nicely browned on both sides, about 2 minutes per side; transfer to a plate.

   Core, seed, and chop the bell pepper.

7. Squeeze the lemon juice into the skillet; add ½ cup white wine and the bell pepper. Cook until the liquid reduces slightly, a minute or 2.

8. Add the scallops (and any juices) back to the skillet and stir to coat with the sauce. Spoon the scallops and the sauce over the romaine and serve immediately.

VARIATIONS

Seared Scallops with Grilled or Broiled Bok Choy and Ginger Dressing

Use 4 or more heads baby bok choy (depending on their size) instead of the romaine. Substitute 1 fresh hot green chile for the bell pepper, 2 limes for the lemon, 1 inch fresh ginger, minced, for the garlic, and sake or a bit of mirin for the white wine.

Seared Scallops with Arugula and Orange Dressing

Replace the romaine with 1 large bunch (12 ounces) arugula; divide it (raw) among 4 plates and drizzle with a few tablespoons olive oil. Use 1 large shallot, minced, instead of the red bell pepper and an orange in place of the lemon.

NOTES

EVEN FASTER

Leave the lettuce raw (less flavor, but less work).

GRILLING GREENS

In recent years, cooks have discovered that a quick blast of heat adds some color and smoky flavor to the outside of lettuce and other greens without cooking the inside. That gives us the best of both worlds: the flavor of the fire mixed with the crisp freshness of the greens.

Just make sure to choose greens that can stand up to the heat. Romaine, iceberg, cabbage, and bok choy all do wonderfully; very tender greens like arugula, Boston lettuce, and Bibb lettuce will wilt too quickly. For greens that come in bunches it can be nice to keep them all together, tied with string, so that they're easy to turn, and the outside leaves char while the inside leaves are protected.

SIDES

Warm Buttery Bread 906

Bruschetta 909

Tomato Salad 913

Quinoa 945

SPEED ◐ SERVES 4

Warm Kale Salad with Pine Nuts and Balsamic Currants

I love the taste and the sturdy texture of kale—it holds up to almost any treatment—and it's so good for you I feel virtuous every time I eat it. This salad is every bit as good raw as it is cooked, so use the Even Faster variation at the end of the recipe some night when you just can't be bothered to turn on the stove.

Ingredients

1 large or 2 medium bunches kale, preferably lacinato (1 ½ pounds)

2 tablespoons olive oil

¼ cup balsamic vinegar

¼ cup dried currants or raisins

2 garlic cloves

¼ cup pine nuts

Salt and pepper

2 ounces Parmesan cheese (½ cup shaved)

Prep | Cook

Trim and chop the kale.

1. Put 2 tablespoons olive oil in a large skillet over high heat.

   Put ¼ cup balsamic vinegar and ¼ cup currants or raisins in a large bowl; toss to coat.

2. When the oil is hot, add the kale and cook, stirring occasionally until it begins to wilt, 2 or 3 minutes.

   Peel and mince 2 garlic cloves.

3. When the kale is mostly wilted, add the garlic, ¼ cup pine nuts, and a sprinkle of salt and pepper. Cook, stirring occasionally until the liquid evaporates and the kale begins to brown, another 2 or 3 minutes.

   Shave ½ cup Parmesan with a vegetable peeler.

4. When the kale is done, add it to the bowl with the currants. Add the Parmesan and toss. Taste and adjust the seasoning and serve hot or warm.

VARIATIONS

Warm Kale with Cashews, Scallions, and Soy Currants or Raisins

Replace the olive oil with vegetable, the balsamic with soy sauce, the pine nuts with ½ cup cashews, and the Parmesan with ½ cup chopped scallions. Since you're using soy sauce, go easy on the salt.

Warm Collards with Peaches and Ham

Use collards greens, sliced into wide ribbons, instead of the kale. They will take an additional 5 minutes to cook. Instead of currants and balsamic, soak about 1 cup chopped fresh peaches in ¼ cup cider vinegar. Use ½ cup chopped pecans instead of pine nuts and a little chopped cooked ham in place of the Parmesan.

NOTES

EVEN FASTER

Raw Kale Salad with Pine Nuts and Balsamic Currants

Chop the kale into smaller pieces than you might if you were cooking it. Instead of mincing the garlic, just take 1 peeled clove, rub it around the inside of the bowl, and discard it or save for another use. Let the currants soak in the balsamic until they plump up slightly, a few minutes, then add the raw kale along with the rest of the ingredients. Toss and serve.

IF YOU HAVE MORE TIME

Toast the pine nuts in a skillet over medium heat for 3 to 5 minutes.

SIDES

Bruschetta 909

Creamy Polenta 947

Skin-On Mashed Potatoes 961

SPEED ◐ SERVES 4

Warm Pickled Cauliflower Salad with Roasted Red Peppers

Boiling cauliflower in a vinegar-based brine infuses a ton of pickly flavor into the vegetable as it cooks. It'll be just tender, but still with plenty of crunch. This is a wonderful excuse to serve pickled vegetables warm, which is a rare and underrated treat. To make the salad even more substantial, serve it with a side of thinly sliced prosciutto.

Ingredients

½ cup red wine vinegar

1 bay leaf

2 teaspoons salt

1 teaspoon dried oregano

1 large or 2 small heads cauliflower (about 2 pounds)

4 celery stalks

8 roasted red peppers

⅔ cup green olives

¼ cup olive oil

Pepper

Prep | Cook

1. In a large pot, combine ½ cup red wine vinegar, 4 cups water, 1 bay leaf, 2 teaspoons salt, and 1 teaspoon dried oregano; turn the heat to high.

   Break or chop the cauliflower into florets.

2. When the liquid comes to a boil, add the cauliflower, cover the pot, and cook until the cauliflower is just tender, 8 to 10 minutes.

   Trim and chop the celery; put in a large bowl.

   Slice 8 roasted red peppers; add them to the bowl.

   Pit ⅔ cup green olives if necessary and chop them up a bit; add them to the bowl.

3. When the cauliflower is just tender, drain it, reserving about ½ cup of the brine.

4. Add the cauliflower to the bowl along with ¼ cup olive oil, a splash of the brine, and a sprinkle of pepper. Toss, taste, and adjust the seasoning, adding more brine if it needs it; serve hot or warm.

VARIATIONS

Warm Pickled Cauliflower Salad with Prosciutto

If you don't like your prosciutto on the side, add it to the dish: Use 4 ounces chopped prosciutto instead of, or in addition to, the celery.

Warm Pickled Broccoli Salad

Balsamic vinegar makes the brine darker and sweeter. Substitute balsamic vinegar for half of the red wine vinegar, broccoli for the cauliflower, and 1/4 cup pine nuts and 1/4 cup raisins for the celery. Use black olives (oil-cured are my favorite here) instead of green and add up to a cup of grated Parmesan before tossing. Broccoli cooks faster than cauliflower, so start checking on it after 5 minutes.

NOTES

MAKE YOUR OWN

Roasted Red (or Other Large) Peppers 417

EVEN FASTER

Using Jarred Roasted Peppers

While it's hard to beat the smoky flavor of homemade roasted red peppers, jarred peppers are undeniably convenient. Most of those available at the supermarket are packed in an acidic brine, which detracts from the charred flavor of the peppers themselves. Rinse these off in a bowl of water to remove the brine, then carefully pat them dry with paper towels (they're delicate); leaving them wet will water down whatever you add them to, especially salads. If you can find peppers packed in olive oil, use them right out of the jar. And be sure to put that pepper-flavored oil to use in dressings and sauces.

SIDES

Warm Buttery Bread 906

Bruschetta 909

Quinoa 945

Skin-On Mashed Potatoes 961

SPEED ◐ SERVES 4

Green Bean Salad with Caramelized Onions and Toasted Almonds

Caramelized onions are one of those miracle preparations that seem to go with everything and improve whatever they're with. But they take about an hour to cook, and when I don't have that time I use this shortcut. For the more traditional—and time-consuming—way to caramelize onions, see If You Have More Time. Note that this recipe calls for thin green beans—also called *haricots verts*. If you only have access to thick green beans, blanch them in boiling water for a few minutes before adding to the salad.

Ingredients

3 medium onions

1 pound thin green beans

1 bunch spinach (1 pound)

1 lemon

½ cup slivered almonds

¼ cup olive oil, or more as needed

1 teaspoon sugar

Salt and pepper

Prep | Cook

Trim, peel, halve, and thinly slice the onions.

1. Put the onions in a large skillet over medium heat. Cover and cook, stirring infrequently until the onions are dry and almost sticking to the pan, 15 to 20 minutes. If they look like they are burning at any point, add a couple tablespoons water or oil.

   Trim the green beans and cut into 2-inch pieces; put them in a large bowl.

   Trim the thick stems from the spinach and chop the leaves; add to the bowl.

   Cut the lemon in half.

2. Put ½ cup slivered almonds in a small skillet over medium heat. Cook, shaking the skillet occasionally and adjusting the heat so they don't burn, until the almonds are lightly browned and fragrant, 3 to 5 minutes. Add them to the bowl with the green beans and spinach.

3. When the onions are dry and almost sticking to the pan, stir in 1/4 cup olive oil, 1 teaspoon sugar, and a sprinkle of salt and pepper and reduce the heat to medium-low.

4. Cook, stirring occasionally, for another 5 minutes or so. Squeeze in the lemon juice, scrape any browned bits off the bottom of the skillet, and turn off the heat.

5. Pour the onions and all the oil and juices over the green beans and spinach and toss. Taste and adjust the seasoning and serve.

VARIATIONS

Snow Pea Salad with Soy-Caramelized Onions and Toasted Peanuts
Substitute snow peas for the green beans, a lime for the lemon, half sesame oil/half vegetable oil for the olive oil, and peanuts for the almonds. Instead of adding salt to the onions in Step 3, add 1 tablespoon soy sauce.

NOTES

IF YOU HAVE MORE TIME
After adding the olive oil, salt, and pepper (omit the sugar), cook the onions for another 30 to 40 minutes over medium-low heat. When they are almost jamlike, stir in the lemon juice and a little extra oil or warm water if needed to create a dressing.

SIDES

Warm Buttery Bread 906

Quinoa 945

Skin-On Mashed Potatoes 961

SPEED ◐ SERVES 4

Broiled Eggplant and Zucchini Salad with Tahini Dressing

Broiled vegetables cook quickly and acquire a nice smoky char. You can dress broiled eggplant and zucchini with just olive oil and parsley if you like, but here a rich, tangy dressing of tahini, yogurt, and lemon juice is especially nice. Sprinkle some crumbled feta on top if you have it.

Ingredients

1 large or 2 medium eggplants (about 2 pounds)

2 medium zucchini (about 1 pound)

½ cup olive oil, or more as needed

Salt and pepper

1 garlic clove

1 lemon

¼ cup tahini

¼ cup Greek yogurt

¼ teaspoon cumin

1 small red onion

Several sprigs fresh parsley for garnish

Prep | Cook

1. Turn the broiler to high; put the rack 4 inches from the heat.

   Trim and cut the eggplant on the diagonal into 1-inch-thick slices. Trim and slice the zucchini in half lengthwise.

2. Put the eggplant slices and zucchini halves (cut side up) on a rimmed baking sheet, brush both sides with a little olive oil, brushing a bit extra on the eggplant, and sprinkle with salt and pepper.

3. Broil, turning the eggplant slices once and leaving the zucchini cut side up, until they're tender and nicely browned all over, 8 to 15 minutes.

   Peel and mince 1 garlic clove.

   Cut a lemon in half; refrigerate 1 half for another use.

   Stir ¼ cup tahini, ¼ cup Greek yogurt, ¼ teaspoon cumin, the garlic, the juice of ½ lemon, 2 tablespoons olive oil, and a sprinkle of salt and pepper together in a large bowl.

   Trim, peel, and halve the onion; chop 1 half and refrigerate the other for another use.

4. When the eggplant and zucchini are tender and browned, transfer them to a platter and spread with the dressing. Sprinkle with chopped onion.

   Chop several sprigs parsley and sprinkle on top of the eggplant and zucchini.

5. Taste and adjust the seasoning and serve.

VARIATIONS

Broiled Eggplant and Zucchini Salad with Mustard Dressing
Substitute 1 tablespoon red wine vinegar for the lemon juice, ¼ cup Dijon for the tahini, and 1 tablespoon chopped fresh tarragon for the cumin.

Broiled Eggplant and Tomato Salad with Peanut-Soy Dressing
Instead of zucchini, use 3 large tomatoes; you can cut them into chunks and broil them if you like, but I prefer them raw here. Use 1 whole lime instead of lemon, ½ cup peanut butter in place of tahini, 2 tablespoons soy sauce instead of yogurt, 1 minced fresh hot chile instead of cumin, and cilantro in place of parsley. No need for any additional salt in the dressing.

NOTES

IF YOU HAVE MORE TIME
Salting the eggplant before cooking helps draw out some moisture and tenderize the flesh. Sprinkle the eggplant slices liberally with salt and let it rest in a colander in the sink for up to an hour; then rinse and pat dry. Proceed with the recipe, omitting any additional salt.

SIDES

Rice Pilaf 944

Crisp Seasoned Pita 908

Couscous 910

SPEED ◐ SERVES 4

Cabbage with Crisp Tofu and Peanut-Lime Dressing

This salad is a dream if you like a lot of crunch: There's shredded cabbage, thinly sliced red onion, peanuts, and crisp crumbled tofu. Broiling the tofu away from the flame allows it to crisp quickly without burning; tossed with some salt and red chile flakes, the crumbles make an irresistible stir-in or garnish. Try them on other salads, cooked vegetables, grains, or noodles and see the variations for more ways to season them.

Ingredients

2 bricks firm tofu (12 to 14 ounces each)

⅓ cup plus 1 tablespoon vegetable oil

1 teaspoon red chile flakes

Salt

1 lime

3 tablespoons peanut butter

Hot sauce (optional)

1 small head Savoy or green cabbage (1 pound)

1 small red onion

½ cup peanuts

Prep | Cook

1. Turn the broiler to high; put the rack 6 inches from the heat.
2. Squeeze as much water as you can out of the tofu. Crumble the tofu onto a rimmed baking sheet and toss with 1 tablespoon vegetable oil, 1 teaspoon red chile flakes, and a sprinkle of salt. Broil, checking and stirring occasionally until the tofu crumbles are brown and crisp, 20 to 25 minutes.

   Halve the lime.
3. In a large bowl, whisk together ⅓ cup vegetable oil, the juice of the lime, 3 tablespoons peanut butter, 3 tablespoons hot water, some salt, and a dash of hot sauce if you're using it.

   Trim, core, and quarter the cabbage. Cut each quarter crosswise into thin ribbons; add to the bowl.

Trim, peel, halve, and thinly slice the red onion; add to the bowl. Chop ½ cup peanuts; add them to the bowl.

4. When the tofu is crisp, add it to the bowl. Toss, taste and adjust the seasoning, and serve.

VARIATIONS

Shredded Cabbage with Crisp Curried Tofu and Coconut-Lime Dressing

Use ¼ cup coconut milk instead of the peanut butter; no need to thin it with the hot water. Swap curry powder for the red chile flakes.

Shredded Cabbage with Crisp Pork and Tahini-Lemon Dressing

Use 12 ounces ground pork in place of the tofu and olive oil instead of vegetable. Broil the pork, stirring occasionally and breaking it up as you go, until it's crisp, 15 to 20 minutes. Drain off most of the fat when it's done. Omit the water from the dressing. Substitute a lemon for the lime, tahini for the peanut butter, cumin for the red chile flakes, and 1 tablespoon sesame seeds (no need to chop them, of course) for the peanuts.

7 Ways to Season Crumbled Tofu

Toss any of the following with the tofu instead of the red chile flakes:

1. 1 teaspoon chili powder or smoked paprika
2. 1 tablespoon minced garlic or fresh ginger (stir into the tofu a few minutes before it's done)
3. 2 teaspoons chopped fresh rosemary, sage, thyme, or oregano
4. ¼ cup chopped fresh cilantro or parsley
5. ½ cup grated Parmesan cheese
6. 1 tablespoon grated citrus zest
7. ¼ cup shredded unsweetened coconut or chopped nuts (stir into the tofu a few minutes before it's done)

NOTES

IF YOU HAVE MORE TIME

For a thicker, creamier dressing, make it in the blender.

SIDES

White Rice 941

Quick Brown Rice 941

Scallion Pancakes 940

Sesame Noodles 949

SPEED ◑ SERVES 4

Pressed Tofu and Cucumber Salad with Hoisin Vinaigrette

Pressing a brick of tofu rids it of excess moisture and firms up the texture; salting cucumbers also pulls out moisture but makes them softer. Both techniques are nice hands-off ways to improve ingredients while you work on something else.

Ingredients

2 bricks firm tofu (12 to 14 ounces each)

2 medium cucumbers

Salt

¼ cup vegetable oil

2 tablespoons hoisin

1 tablespoon rice vinegar

3 scallions

Prep | Cook

1. Cut each brick of tofu in half through its equator and put the pieces on 4 layers of paper towel. Cover with 4 more paper towels and put something heavy (like a baking sheet with a few cans of beans on it) on top so the tofu bulges slightly at the sides but doesn't crack.

   Trim the cucumbers and peel if necessary; cut them in half lengthwise, scoop out the seeds with a spoon, and chop.

   Put the cucumbers in a colander, sprinkle lightly with salt, and toss. Let them sit for about 10 minutes.

2. Whisk together ¼ cup vegetable oil, 2 tablespoons hoisin, and 1 tablespoon rice vinegar in a large bowl.

   Chop the scallions.

3. After the cucumbers have been in the colander for about 10 minutes, add them and the scallions to the bowl with the dressing.

4. Cut the tofu into cubes and add it to the bowl. Toss, taste and adjust the seasoning, and serve.

VARIATIONS

Pressed Tofu and Tomato Salad with Soy Vinaigrette
Replace the cucumbers with 2 pints cherry tomatoes, halved, and the hoisin with soy sauce. Since the soy sauce is salty, you might want to salt the tomatoes a little less or rinse off the salt before adding them to the bowl.

Pressed Tofu and Celery Salad with Sesame-Chile Vinaigrette
Use 12 celery stalks, sliced or cut into matchsticks, instead of the cucumbers. Substitute 2 tablespoons sesame oil for half of the vegetable oil and 1 tablespoon sesame seeds plus 1 teaspoon red chile flakes for the hoisin.

NOTES

EVEN FASTER
If you skip pressing the tofu and salting the cucumbers (just cut them both into chunks at the beginning), this salad comes together in fewer than 10 minutes.

IF YOU HAVE MORE TIME
Press the tofu in the refrigerator for a few hours or even overnight. It will become firmer and develop a chewy, almost meaty texture.

SALTING VEGETABLES
Sprinkling raw vegetables with salt and letting them sit for a while intensifies their flavor and tenderizes them a bit; you're essentially making the simplest possible pickle. Remember, one of the major advantages of this process is that the vegetable takes care of itself while you cook — or do — something else.

SIDES

White Rice 941

Quick Brown Rice 941

Sesame Noodles 949

SPEED ◐ SERVES 4

Curried Tofu Salad with Pecans and Golden Raisins

Sometimes chicken is an irreplaceable ingredient in a dish; other times it's not. In curried "chicken" salad, for instance, all I want is something with a firm texture and a mild flavor to soak up the dressing, and extra-firm tofu fits the bill perfectly, without cooking. The best parts of the classic remain in place: crunchy chopped nuts, celery, onions, soft-sweet raisins, and the rich curry dressing.

Ingredients

1 small head romaine or red leaf lettuce

½ cup mayonnaise

½ cup Greek yogurt

1 tablespoon curry powder

Salt and pepper

1 brick extra-firm tofu (12 to 14 ounces)

2 large apples

3 celery stalks

1 small red onion

1 bunch fresh cilantro

½ cup pecans

½ cup golden raisins

Prep | Cook

Trim the lettuce and tear the leaves off whole.

1. Put the lettuce leaves, overlapping, on a platter.
2. Put ½ cup mayonnaise, ½ cup Greek yogurt, 1 tablespoon curry powder, and a sprinkle of salt and pepper in a large bowl. Stir until smooth and evenly colored.
3. Drain the tofu well and crumble it into the bowl.

   Core and chop the apples; trim and chop the celery, including any leaves. Add both to the bowl.

   Trim, peel, and chop the onion; add to the bowl.

   Chop ½ cup cilantro and add it to the bowl.

   Chop ½ cup pecans; add to the bowl.
4. Add ½ cup golden raisins to the bowl. Stir to combine, taste, and adjust the seasoning. Spoon the salad over the lettuce leaves and serve.

VARIATIONS

Chipotle Tofu Salad with Pepitas and Raisins
Substitute 1 tablespoon chopped chipotle in adobo for the curry powder, 1 small jícama, peeled and chopped, for the apples, and shelled pumpkin seeds (no need to chop them) for the pecans.

Curried Crab Salad with Coconut and Cherry Tomatoes
Use 1 pound cooked lump crabmeat instead of the tofu. Substitute 3 cups halved cherry tomatoes for the apples, 1/4 cup shredded unsweetened coconut for the pecans, and 1/2 cup halved red or green grapes for the golden raisins. Keep the curry powder; it goes great with crab.

Curried Chicken Salad
Put 1 1/2 pounds boneless, skinless chicken breasts in a pot over high heat with water to cover. Bring to a boil, reduce the heat so the water bubbles gently, cover, and cook until the chicken is just cooked through, 10 to 15 minutes. To check for doneness, cut the breast in half; the chicken should be white and opaque all the way through. Chop or shred the chicken and use it instead of the tofu.

NOTES

MAKE YOUR OWN

Mayonnaise 144

Curry Powder 758

TOFU FOR CHICKEN
As I said, there are times when it's reasonable to use tofu in place of chicken and get similar flavor and texture. Obviously, you'd never try to replace a roast chicken with roast tofu, but in recipes where you end up cutting or shredding cooked chicken into small pieces and coating it in flavorful sauces, extra-firm tofu, which has a comparable chewiness and neutral flavor, stands in quite well.

In addition to salads with rich, creamy dressings, you might consider replacing chicken with tofu in enchiladas, tacos, or burritos; stir-fries; and any chilies, soups, or sauces that call for ground chicken or turkey.

SIDES

Warm Buttery Bread 906

Crisp Seasoned Pita 908

Warm Flour Tortillas 907

SPEED ◑ SERVES 4

Bulgur, Apple, and Fennel Salad

Chewy, hearty bulgur is a great match for crisp slices of apple and fennel. If you have a mandoline, good knife skills, or you just don't mind eating the core, you can thinly slice the fennel, core and all. For more details about preparing fennel, see page 446.

Ingredients

3 medium apples

2 medium fennel bulbs

1 lemon

½ cup shelled pistachios

¼ cup olive oil

Salt and pepper

1 cup bulgur

Prep | Cook

1. Bring 2 ½ cups water to a boil in a small saucepan.
   Core and slice the apples; put in a large bowl.
   Trim the fennel and thinly slice crosswise to get a pile of crescent-shaped pieces (pull apart any that are stuck together). Discard any hard center pieces. Add to the bowl.
   Halve the lemon; squeeze the juice into the bowl.
2. Add ½ cup pistachios to the bowl with the apples and fennel. Add ¼ cup olive oil, sprinkle with salt and pepper, and toss.
3. Put 1 cup bulgur in another large bowl with a large pinch of salt. Pour the boiling water over all and cover with a plate. Finely ground bulgur will take 10 to 15 minutes to become tender, medium 15 to 20, and coarse 20 to 25.
4. When the bulgur is tender, drain off any excess water through a strainer and add the bulgur to the bowl with the apples and fennel. Toss, taste and adjust the seasoning, and serve.

VARIATIONS

Couscous, Fennel, and Orange Salad with Olives
Instead of the apples, peel 3 oranges, separate them into segments, and chop them. Make couscous instead of bulgur, following the package directions, substitute ½ cup chopped pitted olives for the pistachios, and leave out the lemon.

Bulgur, Apple, and Fennel Salad with Crisp Ham
Instead of, or in addition to, the pistachios, cook 4 ounces sliced ham, chopped, in olive oil in a skillet over medium-high heat until browned and slightly crisp, 5 or 6 minutes. Toss the ham and any rendered fat with the rest of the ingredients.

NOTES

TYPES OF APPLES
There are literally thousands of apple varieties, often divided—including by me—into three categories: eating, cooking, and all-purpose. Any apple that tastes delicious to you will work in salads, but for cooking, the division isn't arbitrary. So if you want a little more to go on, here's a quick list: For eating raw try Macoun or Gala. Ida Red and Rome are good choices for cooking. And to keep handy as all-purpose apples, you can't go wrong with Cortland, Jonagold, Golden Delicious, Granny Smith, or McIntosh.

SIDES

Warm Buttery Bread 906

Crisp Seasoned Pita 908

Carrot Salad with Raisins 914

Hummus 939

SPEED ◐ SERVES 4

Veggie Fajita Salad

Here's a salad with most of the components of a traditional fajita, minus the steak. Mushrooms and zucchini get a run under the broiler, while peppers and onions sizzle away in a skillet. All are tossed with a salsa of sorts—fresh corn, tomatoes, cilantro, lime—and sour cream. Serve with flour tortillas if you like.

Ingredients

3 portobello mushrooms

2 medium zucchini

¼ cup vegetable oil

Salt and pepper

2 bell peppers (any color)

1 medium onion

2 ears corn

1 large ripe tomato

1 bunch fresh cilantro

1 lime

Sour cream for garnish

Prep | Cook

1. Turn the broiler to high; put the rack 4 inches from the heat.

   Trim the mushrooms and zucchini. Halve the zucchini lengthwise.

2. Put the mushrooms and zucchini, cut side up, on a rimmed baking sheet, rub with 2 tablespoons vegetable oil, and sprinkle with salt and pepper.

3. Broil, turning the mushrooms once and leaving the zucchini cut side up, until they're tender and nicely browned all over, 10 to 15 minutes.

4. Put 2 tablespoons vegetable oil in a large skillet over medium-high heat.

   Core, seed, and slice the bell peppers.

   Trim, peel, halve, and slice the onion.

5. When the oil is hot, add the peppers and onion and sprinkle with salt and pepper. Cook, stirring occasionally, until they're tender and browned, 8 to 12 minutes.

   Husk the corn, trim, and strip the kernels off the cob; put them in a large bowl.

   Core and chop the tomato; add it to the bowl.

   Chop ½ cup cilantro and add it to the bowl.

Halve the lime; squeeze the juice into the bowl. Sprinkle with salt and pepper.

6. When the mushrooms and zucchini are tender and browned, slice or chop them as you like and add them to the bowl.

7. When the peppers and onions are tender and browned, add them to the bowl.

8. Toss, taste and adjust the seasoning, and serve with sour cream.

VARIATIONS

Steak Fajita Salad
Substitute 1 pound skirt steak for the peppers and onions. To cook the steak, put a large skillet over high heat, pat the steak dry with a paper towel, and sprinkle both sides with salt and pepper. Cut the steak in half if needed to fit it into the skillet. When the skillet is very hot, add the steak and cook, turning once, until browned on both sides but still a bit pinker inside than you like it, 3 to 5 minutes per side. Let the steak rest on a cutting board covered loosely with aluminum foil until the mushrooms and zucchini are done. Slice the steak thinly across the grain and toss it with the vegetables and salsa.

Veggie and Black Bean Fajita Salad
Add a cup of cooked or drained canned black beans to the corn, tomato, and cilantro mixture.

Broiled Vegetable Salad with White Bean Dressing
Skip the cilantro, lime, and sour cream. In a food processor, combine 1 cup cooked or canned white beans, 1 small garlic clove, the juice of a lemon, ⅓ cup olive oil, and a sprinkle of salt and pepper. Process until the mixture is smooth and thin enough to pour; add a splash of water to thin the dressing if necessary. Taste and adjust the seasoning. Toss half of the dressing with the corn and tomato mixture and save the other half to drizzle over the broiled vegetables. Garnish with chopped fresh parsley.

NOTES

EVEN FASTER
Instead of cooking the mushrooms, zucchini, peppers, and onion, use Roasted Vegetables (page 417) that you already have.

IF YOU HAVE MORE TIME
Make Avocado with Lime and Chili Salt (page 920) and serve it on top of the salad.

SIDES

Warm Flour Tortillas 907

Chile-Cumin Black Beans 937

Refried Beans 938

SPEED ◐ SERVES 4

Warm Escarole and White Bean Salad with Poached Eggs

This cousin to the classic *frisée au lardons*—with its luscious poached egg on top—substitutes white beans and Parmesan for bacon, and, believe me, it's a fair trade.

Ingredients

¼ cup olive oil, plus more for garnish

2 garlic cloves

½ teaspoon red chile flakes (optional)

1 large bunch escarole (1 to 1 ½ pounds)

4 cups cooked or canned white beans (two 15-ounce cans)

Salt and pepper

2 teaspoons white vinegar

4 eggs

4 ounces Parmesan cheese (1 cup grated)

Prep | Cook

1. Put ¼ cup olive oil in a large skillet over medium-low heat.

   Peel and mince 2 garlic cloves.

2. Add the garlic to the skillet, along with a pinch of red chile flakes if you're using them. Cook so that the garlic flavors the oil but doesn't brown.

   Trim and chop the escarole.

3. Add the escarole to the skillet and raise the heat to medium. Cook, tossing occasionally until it's wilted, 4 or 5 minutes.

4. Put about an inch of water in a medium skillet over high heat.

   If you're using canned beans, rinse and drain them.

5. When the escarole is mostly wilted, stir in the beans, sprinkle with salt and pepper, cover the skillet, and turn the heat to low to warm the beans through.

6. When the water in the skillet comes to a boil, add 2 teaspoons white vinegar and a sprinkle of salt and lower the heat so the water barely bubbles.

7. One at a time, crack the eggs into a shallow bowl and slide them into the water. Cook just until the whites are set and the yolks have filmed over, 3 to 5 minutes.

   Divide the escarole and bean mixture among 4 bowls.

8. When the eggs are done, remove them one at a time with a slotted spoon, allow the water to drain off for a few seconds, then put them on top of the escarole and beans. Grate 1/4 cup Parmesan over the top of each, garnish with a drizzle of olive oil, and serve immediately.

VARIATIONS

Warm Escarole and White Bean Salad with Squid

Skip the eggs. Once the escarole and white bean mixture is warm, divide it among 4 bowls and wipe out the skillet. Put 2 tablespoons olive oil in the skillet and turn the heat to high. When the oil is hot, add 8 to 12 ounces sliced squid and sprinkle with salt and pepper. Cook, stirring occasionally until the squid is tender and lightly browned, 1 to 2 minutes. Serve it on top of the escarole and beans, with or without the Parmesan.

NOTES

MAKE YOUR OWN

Cooked Beans 496

POACHING EGGS

Poached eggs have a reputation as being tricky; they're not. They take a little practice, maybe, but the same is true of pancakes. For breakfast, they're a welcome change from fried and scrambled eggs (try the Fast Florentine, page 850), but I eat them more often for lunch on a salad, a plate of beans, or a serving of roasted vegetables. You puncture the yolk and it oozes all over the dish, contributing to an irresistible sauce.

A few simple tricks will really put you ahead of the game: Add a splash of vinegar to the poaching water to help the egg white gather around the yolk instead of flying off in every direction. Another headache saver is to crack the eggs into small shallow bowls before sliding them into the water; if you crack an egg right into the water, even from close above, the chances are that the yolk will break up.

Poached eggs don't benefit from being poked and prodded during cooking; once they're in the water, don't hover. They'll invariably have ragged edges when they come out of the water; I like that look, but if you want something neater, trim away the edges with a knife or scissors.

SIDES

Bruschetta 909

Warm Buttery Bread 906

Garlic Bread 906

SPEED ◐ SERVES 4

Raw Butternut Squash Salad with Warm Edamame

I sometimes eat butternut squash raw. People are shocked by this, but once you've tried it, it's hard to go back to roasting. This method is so easy, quick, and unexpected. And then there's the taste: Raw butternut has an earthy flavor and a wonderful crunch that comes alive when you toss it with something warm. Here, edamame are warmed up in a mixture of olive oil and sherry vinegar flavored with leeks and sage.

Ingredients

½ cup olive oil

1 medium leek

3 sprigs fresh sage

4 cups frozen edamame

2 tablespoons sherry vinegar

Salt and pepper

1 small butternut squash (1 ½ pounds)

Prep | Cook

1. Put ½ cup olive oil in a large skillet over medium heat.

   Trim the leek and slice the white and light green parts only.

2. When the oil is warm, add the leek. Cook, stirring occasionally until soft, 3 to 5 minutes.

   Strip the sage leaves from 3 sprigs and chop.

3. When the leek is soft, add the sage, 4 cups edamame, 2 tablespoons sherry vinegar, a sprinkle of salt and pepper, and ½ cup water. Reduce the heat to medium-low and cook, stirring occasionally until the edamame are warmed through, 6 to 8 minutes.

   Cut the squash in half crosswise; peel and trim it, and scoop out the seeds. Cut the squash into chunks that will fit through the feed tube of a food processor. Shred the squash in a food processor with a grating disk; put it in a large bowl.

4. Pour the edamame and leek mixture over the squash and toss. Taste and adjust the seasoning and serve warm.

VARIATIONS

Raw Butternut Squash Salad with Warm Red Beans
Use 1 small red onion, sliced, instead of the leek, fresh oregano instead of the sage, cooked or canned red beans (two 15-ounce cans) for the edamame, and the juice of 1 lime in place of the vinegar.

Raw Zucchini Salad with Warm Lima Beans
Substitute 1/4 cup fresh dill leaves for the sage, frozen lima beans for the edamame, and the juice of 1 lemon for the vinegar. Instead of squash, use 1 pound zucchini (grated the same way).

Sautéed Butternut Squash with Warm Edamame
If I can't convince you to try raw butternut squash, cook the grated squash with some olive oil and a sprinkle of salt and pepper in a skillet over medium-high heat until soft and lightly browned, 6 to 10 minutes. Toss with the edamame and warm dressing and serve.

NOTES

IF YOU HAVE MORE TIME
To soften the squash a bit more, let it sit in the warm dressing for 10 or 15 minutes before serving.

SIDES

Warm Buttery Bread 906

Crisp Seasoned Pita 908

Whole Wheat Couscous 910

SPEED ◐ SERVES 4

Warm Three-Bean Potato Salad

Typical three-bean salads feature a sickly sweet vinegar dressing. I use just a touch of honey for sweetness and add potatoes for extra body. Boiling the green beans and potatoes in the same pot as the potatoes saves time and extra dishes.

Ingredients

Salt

2 or 3 medium russet or Yukon Gold potatoes (1 pound)

½ cup olive oil

3 tablespoons red wine vinegar

2 teaspoons Dijon mustard

1 teaspoon honey

Pepper

1 small red onion

8 ounces green beans

2 cups cooked or canned kidney beans (one 15-ounce can)

2 cups cooked or canned chickpeas (one 15-ounce can)

1 bunch fresh parsley

Prep | Cook

1. Put 1 ½ inches of water and a large pinch of salt in a medium pot; turn the heat to high.

   Peel the potatoes if you like. Cut them into ½-inch chunks and add them to the pot.

   Whisk ½ cup olive oil, 3 tablespoons red wine vinegar, 2 teaspoons Dijon mustard, 1 teaspoon honey, and a sprinkle of salt and pepper together in a large bowl.

   Trim, peel, halve, and thinly slice the onion; add it to the bowl with the dressing.

   Trim and chop 8 ounces green beans.

2. When the water comes to a boil, cover the pot and continue to boil until the potatoes are a little short of tender, 4 to 6 minutes.

   If you're using canned beans, rinse and drain them; add the kidney beans and chickpeas to the bowl.

3. When the potatoes are nearly tender, add the green beans to the pot. Cook until the potatoes and green beans are tender, 2 to 5 minutes.

   Chop ½ cup parsley and add it to the bowl.

4. When the potatoes and green beans are tender, drain and add them to the bowl. Toss, taste and adjust the seasoning, and serve.

VARIATIONS

Warm Three-Bean and Sweet Potato Salad
Use sweet potatoes instead of russet or Yukon Gold. Substitute cider vinegar for the red wine vinegar, 1 teaspoon cumin for the Dijon mustard, pinto beans and black beans for the kidney beans and chickpeas, and cilantro for the parsley.

Warm Greens and Chickpea Potato Salad
Instead of the green beans, use 1 pound chopped escarole. Substitute more chickpeas for the kidney beans. Serve with a sprinkling of grated Parmesan, if you'd like.

NOTES

MAKE YOUR OWN
Cooked Beans 496

TWO VEGETABLES, ONE POT
Sometimes it just doesn't make sense to boil different vegetables in separate pots of water, so once I've got my water boiling I use it for everything. Often, as in this recipe, I boil multiple vegetables at the same time, letting firmer ones cook on their own for a bit, then adding tender ones for the last few minutes so they finish together. It's a great way to save time and space, and, as long as one ingredient doesn't ruin the water for the other — beets, for example, would turn the whole thing pink — it's just as good as using 2 pots.

SIDES

Green Salad 911

Celery Salad 917

Tomato Salad 913

SPEED ◑ SERVES 4

Tuna and Egg Salad with Radishes and Dill

Sometimes it's hard to decide between two lunch-box classics: tuna salad and egg salad. That's why I mix them together, adding chopped radishes and pickles for crunch.

Ingredients

4 large eggs

Ice cubes

1 small head Boston or Bibb lettuce

4 large radishes

1 bunch fresh dill

2 pickles, any kind you like

Two 6-ounce cans tuna, preferably packed in olive oil

½ cup mayonnaise

2 teaspoons Dijon mustard

Salt and pepper

Prep | Cook

1. Fill a medium saucepan about two-thirds with water and gently submerge the eggs. Bring to a boil, turn off the heat, and cover. Set a timer: Large to extra-large eggs will cook in 9 minutes.

   Fill a large bowl with ice water.

   Trim the lettuce, tear the leaves off whole, and put them, overlapping, on a platter.

   Trim and chop 4 large radishes; put in a large bowl.

   Strip 2 tablespoons dill leaves from the stems and chop; add to the bowl.

   Chop the pickles; add to the bowl.

   Drain the tuna; add to the bowl.

2. Add ½ cup mayonnaise and 2 teaspoons mustard to the bowl.
3. When the eggs are done, transfer them to the ice water with a slotted spoon. Leave them submerged for at least 1 minute.
4. Crack, peel, and chop the eggs.
5. Add the eggs to the bowl along with a sprinkle of salt and pepper and stir to combine. Taste and adjust the seasoning. Spoon the salad over the lettuce leaves and serve.

VARIATIONS

Shrimp or Lobster and Egg Salad with Cucumber and Tarragon

Swap 1 cup chopped peeled and seeded cucumbers for the radishes and tarragon for the dill. Instead of tuna, use 12 ounces chopped cooked shrimp or lobster.

Smoked Salmon and Egg Salad with Celery Hearts and Leaves

Use 1 cup chopped celery hearts and leaves instead of radishes and 12 ounces chopped smoked salmon in place of the tuna.

Spicy Crab and Egg Salad with Bell Pepper

Substitute crab for the tuna, 1 cup chopped red bell pepper for the radishes, and parsley for the dill. Add 1 teaspoon cayenne to the mix and a pinch of Old Bay seasoning if you have it.

NOTES

MAKE YOUR OWN

Mayonnaise 144

TYPES OF RADISHES

Radishes don't get much love, perhaps because they're ubiquitous year-round in every supermarket across the country, or maybe because they're "too spicy," though that's a plus when you're looking for flavor in a hurry. I love radishes and in recipes they're interchangeable, though some are hotter than others: Common red varieties are sharp without being too hot, and in peak season you'll find other similar radishes in an array of colors—pink, crimson, purple, and white. Harder to find are super-spicy black radishes (the flesh is white) and ultra-mild, gorgeous watermelon radishes, green outside and pink inside. Daikon radishes—common in Japanese and Korean cuisines—are white, quite mild, and sometimes as big as your arm. Jícama aren't technically radishes but make a fine substitute. All keep in the fridge for at least a week and can be prepared in advance and chilled for up to a day in a bowl of cold water.

SIDES

Warm Buttery Bread 906

Cucumber Salad 915

Fennel Salad 917

Tomato Salad 913

SPEED ◐ SERVES 4

Zucchini Slaw with Chopped Spicy Chicken

Grating and salting zucchini softens it up but doesn't take away its wonderful crunch.

Ingredients

3 or 4 large zucchini (1 ½ pounds)

Salt

1 small red onion

1 bunch fresh parsley

6 tablespoons olive oil

2 garlic cloves

1 fresh hot green chile (like serrano)

1 ½ pounds boneless, skinless chicken breasts or thighs

Pepper

1 lemon

Prep | Cook

Trim the zucchini. If you're using a food processor for grating, cut them into chunks that will fit through the feed tube.

1. Shred the zucchini in a food processor with a grating disk or by hand with a box grater.

2. Put the zucchini in a colander, sprinkle lightly with salt, and toss. Let it sit for 10 to 15 minutes.

   Trim, peel, halve, and thinly slice the onion; put it in a large bowl.

   Chop ½ cup parsley and add it to the bowl.

3. Put 2 tablespoons olive oil in a medium skillet over low heat.

   Peel 2 garlic cloves; trim the chile. Mince them both together.

4. Put the garlic and chile in the skillet.

   Chop the chicken into small pieces.

5. Add the chicken to the skillet, sprinkle with salt and pepper, and raise the heat to medium-high. Cook, stirring occasionally, until the chicken loses its pink color and is cooked through, 5 to 10 minutes.

   Halve the lemon.

6. While the chicken cooks, squeeze the water out of the zucchini and transfer the zucchini to the bowl. Squeeze in the lemon juice and add 4 tablespoons oil.

7. When the chicken is cooked, add the mixture to the bowl and toss. Taste and adjust the seasoning and serve.

VARIATIONS

Zucchini Slaw with Chopped Spicy Shrimp
Instead of the chicken, use 1 ½ pounds peeled shrimp. You'll need to cook them for only 3 to 5 minutes.

Jícama Slaw with Chopped Spicy Chicken
Use peeled jícama instead of the zucchini. Substitute cilantro for the parsley and 2 limes for the lemon. If you like, add 1 teaspoon chili powder to the chicken as you cook it in the skillet.

Zucchini Slaw with Crisp Ground Lamb
Substitute 12 ounces ground lamb for the chicken and 1 tablespoon cumin for the green chile. Cook the lamb in the skillet by itself until it browns, then add the garlic and cumin; cook until the lamb is slightly crisp.

NOTES

IF YOU HAVE MORE TIME
Leave the salted zucchini in the colander for about 30 minutes for a more tender slaw.

CHOPPING CHICKEN
Chopping boneless, skinless chicken breasts or thighs into small bits helps chicken cook quickly and adds texture throughout a dish. You can always use the food processor to pulse the chicken into small pieces, but when you factor in the time it takes to clean the food processor, chopping by hand is probably just as fast. I like to cut the chicken into long, thin strips, then rock the knife back and forth crosswise to cut the strips into little pieces. It doesn't matter if the pieces aren't exactly the same size, so you can chop quickly, almost as if you're mincing garlic.

SIDES

Warm Flour Tortillas 907

Bruschetta 909

Quinoa 945

SPEED ◑ SERVES 4

Corn and Black Bean Salad with Garlic Chicken

Charred corn kernels add a smoky dimension to black bean salad. Broiled chicken cutlets, sprinkled with spices and rubbed with garlic, make it a meal. (For the best way to strip corn kernels from the cob, see page 32.)

Ingredients

4 ears fresh corn

Salt

2 garlic cloves

4 boneless, skinless chicken thighs (about 12 ounces)

2 tablespoons vegetable oil

¼ teaspoon cayenne

1 teaspoon cumin

Pepper

4 large or 8 small radishes

4 cups cooked or canned black beans (two 15-ounce cans)

1 bunch fresh cilantro

2 limes

Sour cream for garnish (optional)

Prep | Cook

1. Put a large skillet over medium-high heat. Turn the broiler to high; put the rack 4 inches from the heat.
   Husk the corn, trim, and cut the kernels off the cob.
2. Put the corn in the skillet and sprinkle with salt. Cook, stirring occasionally, until the corn chars lightly, 5 to 10 minutes.
   Peel and halve 2 garlic cloves.
3. Put the chicken on a rimmed baking sheet; rub with 2 tablespoons vegetable oil and sprinkle with ¼ teaspoon cayenne, 1 teaspoon cumin, salt, and pepper.
4. Broil, turning once, until lightly browned on both sides and just cooked through, 2 to 5 minutes per side.
5. When the corn is lightly charred, put it in a large bowl.
   Trim and chop 4 large or 8 small radishes; add them to the bowl.
   If you're using canned beans, rinse and drain them; add the beans to the bowl.
   Chop ½ cup cilantro and add it to the bowl.
   Halve the limes; squeeze the juice into the bowl.

6. When the chicken is done, remove it from the broiler and rub all over with the raw garlic.

7. Toss the corn and black bean mixture together, taste and adjust the seasoning, and divide among 4 plates or bowls.

8. Slice the chicken, lay the slices over the top of the corn and black beans, garnish with a dollop of sour cream if you like, and serve.

VARIATIONS

Corn and Edamame Salad with Ginger Chicken
Skip the cayenne and cumin. Instead of the rubbing the chicken cutlets with garlic cloves, rub them with a piece of peeled fresh ginger. Substitute sesame oil for vegetable, 1 cup chopped daikon radish for the red radishes, and edamame for the black beans.

Corn and White Bean Salad with Garlic Chicken
Omit the cumin. Use olive oil instead of vegetable, red chile flakes instead of cayenne, 1 cup halved cherry tomatoes in place of radishes, white beans instead of black, basil instead of cilantro, and 1 lemon in place of the limes.

Corn and Black Bean Salad with Shrimp
Use 1 pound peeled shrimp in place of the chicken. Rather than rubbing all those shrimp with garlic cloves, mince the garlic and toss it with the shrimp before broiling for 2 or 3 minutes per side.

NOTES

MAKE YOUR OWN

Cooked Beans 496

CHICKEN AS BRUSCHETTA
The way you make bruschetta is by rubbing grilled or broiled toast with a cut clove of raw garlic, which cooks very gently on the surface of the hot bread. The same technique works wonderfully for chicken and even steak. Plus, it eliminates the possibility of minced garlic burning during cooking.

SIDES

White Rice 941

Warm Corn Tortillas 907

Mango Chutney 194

SPEED ◑ SERVES 4

Greek Salad with Orzo and Shrimp

Add warm orzo and shrimp to a classic Greek salad and you turn it into, well, an even better Greek salad, as well as a satisfying main course. If you wanted to make this vegetarian, you could just as easily leave out the shrimp, and the salad would still be plenty substantial.

Ingredients

Salt

2 medium cucumbers

4 medium ripe tomatoes (1 ½ pounds)

1 cup orzo

1 small red onion

1 bunch fresh mint

½ cup kalamata olives

1 lemon

1 pound peeled shrimp

Pepper

4 ounces feta cheese (1 cup cubed)

⅓ cup olive oil

Prep | Cook

1. Bring a small saucepan of water to a boil and salt it.
2. Prepare a grill or turn the broiler to high; put the rack 4 inches from the heat.

   Trim the cucumbers and peel if necessary; cut them in half lengthwise and scoop out the seeds with a spoon. Chop them and put them in a large bowl.

   Core and chop the tomatoes; add to the bowl.
3. When the water comes to a boil, add 1 cup orzo; start tasting after 5 minutes.

   Trim, peel, halve, and thinly slice the red onion; add to the bowl.

   Chop ¼ cup mint leaves and add to the bowl.

   Pit ½ cup olives if necessary; add them to the bowl.

   Halve the lemon; squeeze the juice into the bowl.
4. When the orzo is tender but not mushy, drain; add to the bowl.
5. When the grill or broiler is hot, sprinkle the shrimp with salt and pepper, and cook, turning once, until they're lightly browned on the outside and just cooked through, 2 to 3 minutes per side.

   Cut 4 ounces feta into small chunks; add them to the bowl.

6. When the shrimp are done, add to the bowl. Add ⅓ cup olive oil and a sprinkle of salt and pepper. Toss, taste and adjust the seasoning, and serve immediately.

VARIATIONS

Green Salad with Orzo and Steak

Instead of shrimp, use 1 pound skirt or flank steak. Grill or broil until it's a bit pinker in the middle than you might like, 3 to 5 minutes per side for medium rare. Let the steak rest for 5 minutes, slice thinly, and lay over the top of the salad.

Greek Salad with Orzo and Squid

Substitute 1 pound whole cleaned squid for the shrimp. Grill or broil until lightly charred all over, just a minute or 2 per side. If you're not getting much browning on the squid in the broiler, just take it out after a few minutes. It's way better to have tender, uncharred squid than nicely browned rubber bands, which is what the squid will feel like if you cook it for too long.

NOTES

PITTING OLIVES

Pitting olives is one of those laborious kitchen tasks that sometimes (if you can't find good pitted olives) you just have to put up with. If you don't have a pitter (I don't), the fastest way is to crush the olive with the side of a chef's knife and pick out the pit. If that doesn't work (some olives refuse to crush), slice down the length of the flesh with a paring knife and pick the pit out with your fingers.

SIDES

Crisp Seasoned Pita 908

Cucumber Salad 915

Fennel Salad 917

Hummus 939

SPEED ◐ SERVES 4

Hot and Sour Bok Choy with Mussels

The mixture of steamed greens and mussels is hardly a conventional salad, but it's a good one. The juice from the mussels mixes into the hot and sour steaming liquid to create an intense and intoxicating dressing. Plus, cooking the shellfish directly on top of the bok choy at the same time saves time and dishes.

Ingredients

2 pounds mussels

1 head bok choy (about 1 ½ pounds)

1 inch fresh ginger

1 fresh hot green chile (like Thai)

Several sprigs fresh cilantro

1 tablespoon sesame oil

1 tablespoon vegetable oil

1 tablespoon rice vinegar

2 tablespoons soy sauce

Prep | Cook

Scrub and debeard the mussels; discard any that don't close when you press the shell together.

Trim the bok choy and cut (or pull) the leaves from the ribs. Slice the stems and cut the leaves into thin ribbons.

1. Put a medium pot over medium-high heat.

   Peel 1 inch fresh ginger; trim the chile. Mince them together.

   Chop several sprigs cilantro.

2. Put 1 tablespoon sesame oil and 1 tablespoon vegetable oil in the pot. Put the bok choy stems on the bottom, then add the leaves, followed by the mussels.

3. Add the ginger and chile, 1 tablespoon rice vinegar, 2 tablespoons soy sauce, and about ¼ cup water. Cover the pot.

4. Cook until all the mussels open, 5 to 10 minutes.

5. Sprinkle with the cilantro, toss, and serve.

VARIATIONS

Hot and Sour Cabbage with Salmon
Instead of the mussels, use 1 ½ pounds salmon fillets. Use 1 ½ pounds chopped Napa cabbage instead of the bok choy. Cut the salmon into 4 pieces before or after steaming. Instead of tossing it with the cabbage, divide the cabbage among 4 plates or bowls and serve the salmon on top.

Steamed Broccoli Rabe with Shrimp
Use 1 pound peeled shrimp instead of the mussels and chopped broccoli rabe instead of the bok choy. Substitute 2 garlic cloves for the ginger, ¼ teaspoon red chile flakes for the green chile, parsley for the cilantro, butter and olive oil for the sesame and vegetable oils, and the juice of 1 lemon for the rice vinegar. Skip the soy sauce and steam until the shrimp are pink all over and just cooked through, 3 to 5 minutes.

SIDES

White Rice 941

Sesame Noodles 949

Scallion Pancakes 940

SPEED ◐ SERVES 4

Tomato and Chicken Salad with Basil Vinaigrette

Ripe tomatoes and fresh basil are one of those summer combinations that are nearly impossible to beat. Add some simply cooked chicken and you've got a salad that's refreshing, satisfying, and ready in only a little more time than it takes to pull together a tomato salad.

Ingredients

5 or 6 medium ripe tomatoes (2 pounds)

Salt and pepper

4 boneless, skinless chicken thighs (about 12 ounces)

⅓ cup plus 2 tablespoons olive oil

1 lemon

1 bunch fresh basil

Prep | Cook

1. Prepare a grill or turn the broiler to high; put the rack 4 inches from the heat.

   Core and slice the tomatoes; spread them out on a platter and sprinkle with salt and pepper.

2. Put the chicken on a rimmed baking sheet, drizzle with 2 tablespoons olive oil, and sprinkle with salt and pepper.

3. When the grill or broiler is hot, cook the chicken, turning once, until lightly browned on both sides and just cooked through, 2 to 5 minutes per side.

   Cut the lemon in half and squeeze the juice into a medium bowl. Strip ½ cup basil leaves from the stems and chop; add to the bowl.

4. Add ⅓ cup olive oil and a sprinkle of salt and pepper to the bowl and whisk the vinaigrette.

5. When the chicken is just cooked through, transfer it to a cutting board and cut it on the diagonal into wide slices. Nestle them in with the tomatoes, drizzle the vinaigrette over the top, and serve.

VARIATIONS

Peach and Chicken Salad with Tarragon Vinaigrette Substitute 8 ripe peaches, cut into wedges, for the tomatoes and 2 tablespoons chopped fresh tarragon for the basil.

Pear and Chicken Salad with Mustard Vinaigrette Substitute 6 pears for the tomatoes and 2 teaspoons Dijon mustard for the basil.

Cucumber and Chicken Salad with Dill Vinaigrette Use 3 medium cucumbers in place of the tomatoes and 2 tablespoons chopped fresh dill instead of the basil.

NOTES

IF YOU HAVE MORE TIME You can use chicken breasts instead of thighs. Set the rack 6 inches away from the heat and cook for closer to 6 to 8 minutes per side.

SIDES

Warm Buttery Bread 906

Bruschetta 909

Pasta, Plain and Simple 948

SPEED ◐ SERVES 4

Warm Spinach and Chicken Salad with Parmesan Dressing

Walnuts and a Parmesan dressing make this chicken salad nutty and rich, while barely wilted spinach adds earthiness and freshness.

Ingredients

3 or 4 boneless, skinless chicken breasts (about 1 ½ pounds)

1 cup white wine or water

1 bay leaf

3 sprigs fresh thyme

⅓ cup olive oil

2 tablespoons red wine vinegar

Salt and pepper

4 ounces Parmesan cheese (1 cup grated)

8 ounces baby spinach

½ cup walnuts

Prep | Cook

1. Put the chicken, 1 cup white wine or water, 1 bay leaf, and 3 sprigs fresh thyme in a medium skillet over high heat.

2. When the liquid boils, lower the heat so it bubbles gently. Cover and cook until the chicken is opaque and just cooked through, 10 to 15 minutes.

3. Combine ⅓ cup olive oil, 2 tablespoons red wine vinegar, and a sprinkle of salt and pepper in a large bowl.
   Grate 1 cup Parmesan, add to the bowl, and whisk to combine.
   Add 8 ounces baby spinach to the bowl.
   Add ½ cup walnuts to the bowl.

4. When the chicken is just cooked through, transfer it to a cutting board and chop it while it's still hot.

5. Add the warm chicken to the bowl and toss well so that it begins to wilt the spinach. Taste and adjust the seasoning and serve.

VARIATIONS

Warm Tomato and Chicken Salad with Parmesan Dressing
Use 5 or 6 medium ripe tomatoes, chopped, instead of the spinach. They won't wilt, of course, but the heat from the chicken will warm them a bit and pull out some of their juice.

Warm Spinach and Chicken Salad with Curry Dressing
Substitute coconut milk for the white wine or water, cilantro for the thyme, and 1 teaspoon curry powder for the Parmesan.

NOTES

EVEN FASTER
Use boneless chicken thighs instead of chicken breasts; start checking them after 5 minutes.

COOKING, ONCE REMOVED
One of my favorite fast techniques — if you can really even call it a technique — is gently wilting greens by tossing them with something that has just been cooked. The residual warmth — here, from poached chicken — softens the greens ever so slightly and boosts their flavor without eliminating their crunch. Some of the greens that take well to this treatment are spinach, arugula, watercress, kale, escarole, endive, radicchio (not green, I know), and cabbage.

Pretty much any warm food is fair game to toss them with, including sautéed or roasted vegetables, warm sauces or dressings, toasted croutons, and crisp bacon.

SIDES

Warm Buttery Bread 906

Bruschetta 909

Tomato Salad 913

Pasta, Plain and Simple 948

Bulgur with Lemon and Parsley 946

SPEED ◐ SERVES 4

Middle Eastern Chicken and Bread Salad

This is essentially a classic Middle Eastern bread salad (fattoush) with grilled or broiled chicken added in. The pita—also grilled or broiled—soaks up the flavor like a sponge.

Ingredients

3 or 4 medium ripe tomatoes (1 pound)

1 medium cucumber

1 small red onion

4 boneless, skinless chicken thighs (about 12 ounces)

⅓ cup plus 3 tablespoons olive oil

Salt and pepper

2 pitas

1 bunch fresh parsley

1 lemon

Prep | Cook

1. Prepare a grill or turn the broiler to high; put the rack 4 inches from the heat.

   Core the tomatoes, cut them into chunks, and put them in a large bowl.

   Trim the cucumber and peel if necessary; cut it in half lengthwise and scoop out the seeds with a spoon. Chop and add to the bowl.

   Trim, peel, halve, and thinly slice the onion; add it to the bowl.

2. Drizzle the chicken with 2 tablespoons olive oil and sprinkle with salt and pepper.

3. When the grill or broiler is hot, cook the chicken, turning once, until browned on both sides and just cooked through, 6 to 8 minutes per side.

   Brush the pita with 1 tablespoon olive oil and sprinkle with salt and pepper.

   Chop ½ cup parsley and add it to the bowl.

   Halve the lemon; squeeze the juice into the bowl.

4. When the chicken is just cooked through, transfer it to a cutting board.

5. Grill or broil the pita, turning once, until lightly charred, a minute or 2 per side.

6. When the pita is lightly charred, transfer it to the cutting board. Chop the pita and the chicken; add them to the bowl.

7. Add ⅓ cup olive oil and a sprinkle of salt and pepper. Toss, taste and adjust the seasoning, and serve.

VARIATIONS

Chicken and Tortilla Salad

Substitute 1 ½ cups sliced radishes for the cucumber, cilantro for the parsley, and 2 limes for the lemon. Instead of pitas, use 2 large flour tortillas. Add a few dashes of hot sauce and some crumbled queso fresco — or even feta — if you like.

Shrimp Panzanella

Use 12 ounces peeled shrimp instead of the chicken; grill or broil until they're pink all over and cooked through, 2 or 3 minutes per side. Swap 4 slices of crusty bread for the pita and 2 tablespoons balsamic vinegar for the lemon juice. Add a handful of chopped pitted olives and some shaved Parmesan to the salad as well.

NOTES

TOASTED BREAD SALAD

It's nothing new to adorn salads with croutons, but the peasant trick of making toasted bread the foundation of the salad is a bit underused, I think. Grilled, broiled, or simply toasted pieces of bread instantly add crunch, chewiness, and heft to a salad; they soak up dressings perfectly, and they're a convenient way to use up any leftover bread.

Any bread will work, from rustic loaves to baguettes, pita, corn and flour tortillas, even regular sandwich bread, or hamburger or hot dog buns. Just brush the bread with a little oil or butter, cut it into chunks (leave flatbreads whole until after cooking), and cook until crisp on the outside but still a bit chewy in the middle.

SIDES

Rice Pilaf 944

Bulgur with Lemon and Parsley 946

Hummus 939

SPEED ◐ SERVES 4

BLT Salad with Rosemary-Mayo Dressing

This salad is exactly what it sounds like: the makings of a classic BLT chopped up in a bowl. Cutting the bacon into pieces lets you cook a lot of it at once without paying too much attention to it, especially if you cook it in the microwave as described on the opposite page. I've omitted the bread here, so if you want the full-on BLT experience, make some Warm Buttery Bread (page 906) on the side or toss pieces of toast in with the other ingredients.

Ingredients

8 slices bacon

3 or 4 sprigs fresh rosemary

½ cup mayonnaise

Salt and pepper

5 or 6 medium ripe tomatoes (2 pounds)

1 head Boston lettuce

Prep | Cook

1. Put a large skillet over medium heat.

   Chop 8 slices bacon into 1-inch pieces. Line a plate with paper towels.

2. Add the bacon to the skillet. Cook, stirring occasionally until crisp, 5 to 10 minutes.

   Strip the rosemary leaves from 3 or 4 sprigs and chop. Put them in a large bowl.

3. Add ½ cup mayonnaise and a sprinkle of salt and pepper to the bowl; stir, adding a tablespoon or 2 of water, until smooth and slightly thinned.

   Core the tomatoes; cut them into wedges and add them to the bowl.

4. When the bacon is crisp, transfer it to the paper towels with a slotted spoon.

   Trim the lettuce; tear the leaves a bit and add them to the bowl.

5. Toss the lettuce and tomatoes with the dressing and divide the salad among 4 plates or bowls. Sprinkle the bacon on top and serve.

VARIATIONS

Sausage and Pepper Salad with Mustard Dressing
Another classic sandwich turned salad. Instead of bacon, cook 8 to 12 ounces crumbled Italian sausage in 2 tablespoons olive oil until browned and slightly crisp, 5 to 10 minutes. Use 4 large bell peppers — a combination of red and yellow is nice — and 1 small onion instead of the tomatoes. Slice both thinly, since you're eating them raw. Use 1 teaspoon dried oregano instead of rosemary and ⅓ cup olive oil, 1 tablespoon brown mustard, and 2 tablespoons red wine vinegar instead of the mayonnaise.

NOTES

MAKE YOUR OWN

Mayonnaise 144

BACON IN THE MICROWAVE
Fast, easy, and effective, as long as you don't need much. Here's how: Line a microwave-safe dish with 3 or 4 layers of paper towels to absorb the grease. Put the slices on top; close together is fine, but ideally not touching. Cover with more paper towels; if you want, add another layer of bacon on top, and cover with more paper towels. Microwave on high for about 1 minute per slice of bacon up to 5, cooking for additional time as necessary. Remove the bacon just before it's done to your liking (it will continue to crisp for a few seconds), and immediately transfer it to another new plate, or it may stick to the towels.

SIDES

Warm Buttery Bread 906

French Fries 963

Cucumber Salad 915

Fennel Salad 917

SPEED ◐ SERVES 4

Kimchi and Snow Pea Salad with Grilled or Broiled Beef

Sliced raw snow peas and kimchi make a wonderfully crunchy and bright foil for tender grilled or broiled beef. (For more about kimchi, see the Notes.)

Ingredients

1 pound snow peas

3 cups kimchi

1 pound boneless beef sirloin or rib-eye steak

Salt and pepper

Several sprigs fresh mint

1 tablespoon sesame oil

Prep | Cook

1. Prepare a grill or turn the broiler to high; put the rack 4 inches from the heat.

   Slice the snow peas on a diagonal and put them in a large bowl.

2. Add 3 cups kimchi to the bowl along with some of its juice. Toss to combine.

3. When the grill or broiler is hot, sprinkle the steak all over with salt and pepper. Cook, turning once, until charred on both sides but still one shade pinker inside than you like. Figure 2 to 5 minutes per side, depending on your grill or broiler; use a knife to nick and peek.

4. Transfer the meat to a cutting board to let it rest.

   Strip the mint leaves from several sprigs, chop, and add them to the bowl.

5. Slice the steak thinly against the grain; add it to the bowl. Add 1 tablespoon sesame oil to the bowl and toss. Taste and adjust the seasoning and serve.

VARIATIONS

Sauerkraut and Apple Salad with Grilled or Broiled Pork
Use 3 apples, sliced, instead of the snow peas and sauerkraut instead of the kimchi. Instead of beef, use a pork tenderloin; grill or broil it until browned on both sides and just slightly pink in the middle, 10 to 15 minutes, and chop into pieces. Swap 4 fresh sage leaves for the mint.

NOTES

EVEN FASTER
If you don't mind, just leave the snow peas whole.

KIMCHI
Kimchi, the spicy fermented cabbage from Korea, packs a huge punch of flavor and texture. It's both tangy and hot, and even though it's fermented for a long time, it retains a vibrant crunch.

Like sauerkraut, kimchi is something that you can make on your own — by combining cabbage, salt, vinegar, and Korean chile paste — but it isn't fast. Luckily, high-quality kimchi is easy to find, certainly at Asian grocery stores and increasingly at mainstream supermarkets. Don't hesitate to buy a big jar if you find one; it will keep for a few months in your fridge, and there are a number of ways to use it, from mixing it with plain rice or Asian noodles to stirring it into soup to stir-frying it. Or eat it straight.

For a quick, impromptu kimchi, see Stir-Fried Beef with Skillet "Kimchi" (page 712).

SIDES

White Rice 941

Scallion Pancakes 940

Sesame Noodles 949

Fire and Ice Noodles 950

Broccoli Tabbouleh with Charred Tomato and Lemon

Tabbouleh is a classic Middle Eastern salad of bulgur, tomatoes, herbs, lemon, and olive oil. If you pulse raw broccoli in the food processor, you wind up with crunchy bits that make a fine addition. Charring the tomatoes and lemon is gilding the lily, but you do it while the bulgur cooks, and it only takes a little extra work.

Ingredients

1 lemon

1 pint cherry tomatoes

1 cup bulgur

Salt

4 tablespoons olive oil

Pepper

1 small head broccoli (about 1 pound)

1 bunch fresh mint

1 bunch fresh parsley

1 garlic clove

Prep | Cook

1. Bring 2 ½ cups water to a boil in a small saucepan.
2. Turn the broiler to high; put the rack 4 inches from the heat.

   Halve the lemon crosswise and trim off a small piece from each end so it can stand cut side up.

   Put the cherry tomatoes on a rimmed baking sheet along with the lemon halves, facing up.
3. Put 1 cup bulgur in a large bowl with a large pinch of salt. Pour the boiling water over the grains and cover with a plate. Finely ground bulgur will take 10 to 15 minutes to become tender, medium 15 to 20, and coarse 20 to 25.
4. Drizzle the lemon halves and cherry tomatoes with 2 tablespoons olive oil and sprinkle with salt and pepper.
5. Broil, stirring the tomatoes every few minutes, until the tomato skins brown, blister, and crack and the lemon halves are slightly charred, 4 to 10 minutes, depending on your broiler.

   Break or chop the broccoli into florets (include the floret stems), and put everything in a food processor.

Chop ½ cup each mint and parsley leaves and add them to the food processor.

Peel 1 garlic clove; add it to the food processor.

6. When the tomatoes and lemons are done, put the tomatoes in a large bowl. Set the lemon aside.
7. Pulse the broccoli mixture in the food processor until it's chopped into little bits, bigger than bulgur but smaller than peas. Add the mixture to the bowl with the tomatoes.
8. When the bulgur is tender, drain off any excess water through a strainer and add the bulgur to the bowl.
9. Add 2 tablespoons olive oil, squeeze in the juice from the charred lemon, and sprinkle with salt and pepper. Toss, taste and adjust the seasoning, and serve.

VARIATIONS

Cauliflower Tabbouleh with Charred Tomato and Lemon
Use 1 small head cauliflower, trimmed, instead of broccoli.

Fennel and Radish Tabbouleh with Charred Tomato and Lime
A little spicy from the radishes. Use 1 medium fennel bulb and 2 cups chopped radishes instead of the broccoli. Substitute 3 limes for the lemon and cilantro for the parsley.

NOTES

EVEN FASTER
Forget about charring the tomatoes and lemons. Just halve the cherry tomatoes and use both the tomatoes and lemons raw.

TIMING BULGUR
Remember: Steep finely ground bulgur for 10 to 15 minutes, medium for 15 to 20, and coarse for 20 to 25. (See pages 352 to 353 for more about grains.)

SIDES

Crisp Seasoned Pita 908

Fennel Salad with Olives 917

Hummus 939

Roasted Red Pepper Hummus 939

SPEED SERVES 4

Charred Brussels Sprout Salad with Walnuts and Gorgonzola

Crunchy charred Brussels sprouts and walnuts with creamy Gorgonzola is a decadent combination. Chopping the Brussels sprouts and tossing them with olive oil, salt, and pepper is all reduced to one quick step in the food processor.

Ingredients

2 pounds Brussels sprouts

1 garlic clove

3 tablespoons olive oil

Salt and pepper

1 cup walnuts

4 ounces Gorgonzola cheese (1 cup crumbled)

2 tablespoons balsamic vinegar

Prep | Cook

1. Turn the broiler to high; put the rack 6 inches from the heat.
   Trim the Brussels sprouts.
   Peel 1 garlic clove.
2. Put the Brussels sprouts, garlic, 3 tablespoons olive oil, and a sprinkle of salt and pepper in a food processor.
3. Pulse until the Brussels sprouts are roughly chopped. They will be a bit uneven, but that's okay.
4. Put the Brussels sprouts on a rimmed baking sheet and broil, stirring and checking occasionally until they're browned and just tender, 10 to 15 minutes.
5. Put 1 cup walnuts in a large skillet over medium heat. Cook, shaking the pan occasionally until the nuts darken and are fragrant, 3 to 5 minutes. Transfer the walnuts to a large bowl.
6. When the Brussels sprouts are browned and just tender, add them to the bowl. Crumble 1 cup Gorgonzola, add to the bowl, and drizzle with 2 tablespoons balsamic vinegar.
7. Toss, taste and adjust the seasoning, and serve.

VARIATIONS

Charred Brussels Sprout and Fig Salad with Walnuts
Instead of the Gorgonzola—or in addition to it—add a handful of chopped fresh or dried figs.

Charred Brussels Sprouts and Apple or Pear Salad
Substitute pecans for the walnuts and use chopped apples or pears instead of, or in addition to, the Gorgonzola.

Charred Broccoli Salad with Almonds and Ricotta Salata
Use broccoli instead of Brussels sprouts. Since it won't take as long to cook, put the broiler rack closer to the heat (about 4 inches) and cook for 5 to 10 minutes. Replace the walnuts with almonds and the Gorgonzola with grated ricotta salata.

NOTES

IF YOU HAVE MORE TIME
If you prefer larger pieces of Brussels sprouts, heat the oven to 425°F; halve or quarter the Brussels sprouts; toss them with the olive oil, minced garlic, salt, and pepper; and roast, stirring occasionally until they are tender and well browned, 30 to 45 minutes.

BROILED BITS
It may seem strange to buzz Brussels sprouts in the food processor and then broil them. But once you try it you'll be loath to go back to the laborious task of halving them by hand and then waiting for the large pieces to roast thoroughly. This way is much faster: The machine does the chopping in a couple of pulses, and the small pieces broil in about half the time. The best thing of all could be the flavor: Because there's so much surface area on small pieces, you get more of the delicious crispy bits than you would otherwise.

SIDES

Bruschetta 909

Warm Buttery Bread 906

Creamy Polenta 947

Sandwiches

Radish and Herb Butter Baguette 132

Broiled Cheese 134

Peanut Butter and Banana Sandwich with Honey and Raisins 138

Hummus and Vegetable Pita Pockets 140

Tofu Sandwich with Cucumber and Hoisin Mayo 142

Tuna Sandwich with Pickles and Mustard 146

Crab Salad Sandwich 148

Broiled Ham and Gruyère with Apples 150

Smoky Black Bean and Carrot Burgers 152

Egg Salad Sandwich with Lots of Vegetables 154

Eggplant Parmesan Sub 156

Salmon Sandwich with Peanut Vinaigrette 158

Sriracha Shrimp Salad Roll 160

Seared Tuna Sandwich with Wilted Bok Choy and Soy Mayo 162

Chicken Salad Sandwich with Grapes and Rosemary 164

Chicken, Bacon, Avocado, and Tomato Wrap 166

Blackened Chicken Sandwich with Pickled Red Onions 168

Chicken and Black Bean Burrito 170

Turkey and Broccoli Rabe Hero 172

Open-Face Lyonnaise Sandwich 174

Spanish Dip 176

Sausage and Pepper Sub 178

Bánh Mì 180

Steak Tacos with Lots of Options 182

Crisp Pork and Watermelon Tacos 184

Reuben with All the Trimmings 186

Big T's Meat Sauce Sub 188

Steak Sandwich with Charred Onions 192

Curried Chicken Sandwich with Mango Chutney 194

BBQ Chopped Pork and Slaw Sandwich 196

Sandwiches

You already know how to make a sandwich. But do you venture beyond grilled cheese and sliced turkey or ham?

Like most staples of the American diet, sandwiches have progressed a long way since PB & J and bologna on Wonder Bread were the gold standard. The varieties and options continue to increase exponentially, and the expectations for creativity and execution have grown with them. All of that is to the good.

A few of the sandwiches in this chapter—especially those toward the beginning—are light enough to be considered snacks; to make them a meal you might want to include a similarly easy soup or side. Others are slightly more substantial, although no more effort than making grilled cheese or tuna on toast. The bulk are what I think of as main-course sandwiches and will take a few more minutes to pull off but are worth the extra effort.

Like all the recipes in this book, these sandwiches require—and benefit from—a certain degree of multitasking. Though never complicated or arduous, the process usually goes beyond taking the butter out of the fridge while you're making toast.

This chapter will give you a feel for what should happen when—it's often the same from one sandwich to the next—and open up a new world of possibilities for satisfying sandwich-based meals that you can make quickly and easily.

Chapter Highlights

One Sandwich Is Faster than Four The fastest way to make a sandwich is on a baguette. Radish and Herb Butter Baguette (page 132).

All Things Bread How I choose, store, and toast bread. Good Bread (page 136).

Where Your Bread Is Buttered Why brushing melted butter onto soft bread solves problems. Brushing vs. Spreading Butter (page 149).

Make Your Own Condiments Recipes (and variations) for mayonnaise, salsa, and barbecue sauce (page 144).

What About Fruit Condiments? Yes, there's time to make savory fruit condiments for sandwiches from scratch. Curried Chicken Sandwich with Mango Chutney (page 194).

Is Vinaigrette the New Mayo? Not quite, but it's a wonderful way to moisten and flavor a sandwich. Salmon Sandwich with Peanut Vinaigrette (page 158).

Wide Open Why open-face sandwiches are so great. Open Your Mind to Opening Your Sandwich (page 175).

Better than Deli Turkey Do away with deli turkey for good. Turkey and Broccoli Rabe Hero (page 172).

Taco Time When a taco isn't Mexican. Anything Tacos (page 183).

Fast Pizza (Sort Of) With premade pizza dough, homemade pizza is quick and delicious. Cheat-a-Little Pizza (page 190).

If You're Looking for a Meatball Sub A terrific deconstructed version. Big T's Meat Sauce Sub (page 188).

The Reuben Miracle A fantastic spin on a corned beef or pastrami Reuben. Reuben with All the Trimmings (page 186).

SPEED SERVES 4

Radish and Herb Butter Baguette

Radish, butter, and salt on a baguette is a rite of spring in France and elsewhere. The combination gets even better with a little tarragon and mint added to the butter and a handful of arugula complementing the peppery bite of the radish.

Ingredients

4 tablespoons (½ stick) butter

3 sprigs fresh mint

2 sprigs fresh tarragon

4 to 6 radishes

1 baguette

Salt and pepper

2 cups arugula

Prep | Cook

Put 4 tablespoons butter in a medium bowl.

Strip the mint leaves from 3 sprigs and the tarragon leaves from 2 sprigs and chop; add to the bowl.

Trim and thinly slice the radishes.

Halve the baguette lengthwise.

1. Add a sprinkle of salt and pepper to the butter and herb mixture and mash to combine; you want it to be spreadable.
2. Spread the butter onto one side of the baguette and lay the radish slices on top.

   Trim 2 cups arugula.
3. Put the arugula on top of the radishes and top with the other half of the baguette. Cut the baguette into 4 sections and serve.

VARIATIONS

Jícama and Chile Mayo Baguette
Substitute ½ cup mayonnaise for the butter, 2 fresh hot green chiles (like jalapeño), minced, for the mint, and cilantro for the tarragon. Add some grated lime zest to the mayo if you like. Instead of the radishes, use 8 ounces jícama, thinly sliced.

Apple and Honey-Mustard Baguette
Use ⅓ cup Dijon mustard instead of the butter, 2 tablespoons honey instead of the mint, and fresh rosemary in place of the tarragon. Instead of the radishes, use 1 or 2 apples, thinly sliced.

Fennel and Garlic Butter Baguette
Substitute 2 tablespoons olive oil for 2 tablespoons of the butter, 1 minced garlic clove for the mint, and parsley for the tarragon. Add some red chile flakes and 1 teaspoon grated lemon zest as well. Instead of the radishes, use 1 large fennel bulb, thinly sliced.

Ricotta and Olive Baguette
Instead of butter, use ¾ cup good ricotta cheese and a drizzle of olive oil. Swap 1 teaspoon grated lemon zest for the parsley and mint. Instead of radishes, use 1 cup chopped pitted olives; a mix is nice.

Goat Cheese, Peach, and Pecan Baguette
Instead of butter, use 8 ounces goat cheese. Keep the mint, but skip the tarragon. Instead of radishes, use 1 or 2 thinly sliced peaches. Before adding the peaches, chop ½ cup pecans and toast them in a dry skillet over medium heat for 3 to 5 minutes. Press them gently on top of the goat cheese so they stick, then lay the peach slices on top.

NOTES

IF YOU HAVE MORE TIME
Toast the baguette.

ONE SANDWICH IS FASTER THAN FOUR
This probably sounds obvious, but I've seen enough people do the opposite that it seems worth mentioning: If you're making a sandwich on a baguette or any other long loaf of bread, instead of cutting the bread into sections and assembling individual sandwiches, cut it in half the long way, assemble one giant sandwich, then cut it into as many pieces as you like.

SIDES

Green Salad 911

Seared Broccoli or Cauliflower 925

Succotash 933

Tender Vegetables 954

SPEED ◔ SERVES 4

Broiled Cheese

Have you made grilled cheese in the broiler? Faster, better, more efficient.

Ingredients

4 tablespoons (½ stick) butter

8 ounces cheddar cheese (2 cups grated)

8 slices sandwich bread

Prep | Cook

1. Turn the broiler to high; put the rack 6 inches from the heat.

   Melt 4 tablespoons butter in the microwave or in a small pot over medium-low heat.

   Slice 8 ounces cheddar cheese or grate 2 cups.

2. Brush the melted butter on 1 side of each of 8 slices bread. Assemble 4 cheese sandwiches so that the buttered sides are facing out.

3. Put the sandwiches on a rimmed baking sheet and broil, turning once, until the bread is toasted on both sides and the cheese is melted, 2 or 3 minutes per side. Serve immediately.

VARIATIONS

8 Other Cheeses to Use

1. Mozzarella
2. Provolone
3. Jack cheese
4. American
5. Gruyère
6. Brie
7. Goat cheese
8. Manchego

10 Additions to Broiled Cheese

Add any of the following, alone or in combination, when you assemble the sandwiches:

1. Sliced tomato
2. Sliced onion or fennel
3. Sliced apple or pear
4. Cooked bacon or sausage
5. Prosciutto, ham, or salami
6. Sliced green chiles
7. Mustard
8. Chipotles in adobo
9. Maple syrup or honey
10. Jelly

NOTES

IF YOU HAVE MORE TIME

Thin-sliced sandwich bread is the most traditional and fastest for grilled cheese, but try experimenting with loaves of bread that you cut yourself, which are generally more interesting, more substantial, and tastier than presliced sandwich bread. Since the slices you cut are likely to be a little thicker than the ones cut by a machine, it takes another minute or two for the heat to penetrate the bread and melt the cheese.

SIDES

Green Salad 911

Tomato Salad 913

French Fries 963

Sautéed Greens with Garlic 924

Coleslaw 923

Good Bread

Good (or at least acceptable) bread has become common enough in grocery stores that there's no reason to settle for a lousy loaf. Skip the bagged bread aisle and head straight for the bakery section or, even better, go to an actual bakery. Look for loaves with a real crust—it should be quite hard and make a bit of a crackling sound when squeezed. If you you're planning to make sandwiches, you might ask the baker for the loaf to be sliced, saving yourself some time.

Type of Bread	Why I Like It
BAGUETTE	You can find real baguettes at many supermarkets these days. They're crisp on the outside, tender in the middle, and great for sandwiches where you want the bread to star. Typical baguettes are around 2 feet long.
CIABATTA AND FOCACCIA	Ciabatta and often focaccia are sold as individual pieces that are perfect for sandwiches, with a large surface area for laying out ingredients.
CHALLAH AND BRIOCHE	Soft, golden egg breads with glossy crusts; flavorful, rich, and wonderful toasted. They're also ideal for French toast, so you'll never waste leftovers.
WHOLE WHEAT, MULTIGRAIN, AND RYE	Often available as whole loaves at bakeries (ask the baker to slice them for you), but there are good bagged versions as well. Hearty enough to be eaten as is and even to stand up to grilling.
PITA	The ones with pockets are ideal for stuffing, while the pocketless version makes a great wrap. Toast them or at least warm them up.
HAMBURGER BUNS	Sometimes a soft bun is exactly what you want, and these are available in white, whole wheat, and potato or egg dough (both of which are superior).

Type of Bread	Why I Like It
SANDWICH BREAD	While there are certainly some decent sandwich breads that come presliced in plastic bags, in general bread that you can buy in whole loaves is better. (There is, however, charm in self-sliced bread.)

Toasting Bread, Toasting Sandwiches

Toast is often a better choice than plain bread; it's different in texture and taste. It can deepen the flavor of a sandwich and turn a snack into a meal. Throughout this chapter I suggest my preferences, but almost any sandwich can be made with toasted bread, and it's up to you to choose. Generally, toasting is best for sandwiches that are going to be eaten right away; packed toasted sandwiches quickly become soggy. If you must, let the toasted bread cool completely before you assemble and pack the sandwiches.

How to make toast? For a crowd, the best tool is the broiler. Just lay the slices of bread on a baking sheet and broil about 6 inches from the heat, turning once until they're as dark on both sides as you like. You can toast a lot of bread this way very easily. And you'll get some nicely charred bits, especially if the bread you use is rough, like baguette. If you're making just a sandwich or two, revert to the toaster.

Sometimes it's best to toast the sandwich as a whole: The outsides become crisp and golden and the insides nice and hot or possibly melted, as in the case of Broiled Cheese (page 134). Again, if you're cooking for more than two, use the broiler: set the sandwiches on a rack away from the heat (again about 6 inches). If the bread is toasting faster than the inside is getting hot, either turn off the broiler and continue cooking the sandwiches in a 400°F oven until the insides heat through or lay a couple of sheets of aluminum foil over the tops of the sandwiches so the bread isn't directly exposed to the heat. If you're making only one or two sandwiches, stick with the traditional buttered or oiled skillet. Use either method with the sandwiches in this chapter and you'll end up with a crisp golden brown outside and a hot, melty interior.

Storing Bread

Presliced sandwich bread and buns sold at supermarkets are easy to store, because they contain preservatives that make them last. Store in their bags, in a bread box, or on the counter for at least a few days, in the refrigerator for a week or two, or in the freezer, wrapped as tightly as possible, for a month or two.

Freshly baked bread without the preservatives doesn't keep nearly as long. Wrap it in wax paper—plastic makes the crust soggy—and store it in a bread box or on the counter for one to several days, depending on the bread. Otherwise, the best option is the freezer; wrap the bread tightly in aluminum foil or heavy plastic bags and keep in the freezer for up to a month or two. You'll need to recrisp it once it thaws. If your fresh bread is getting stale, just toast it before making your sandwich. You won't notice much, if at all.

SPEED SERVES 4

Peanut Butter and Banana Sandwich with Honey and Raisins

One of the few dishes that is equally appropriate for breakfast, lunch, or a snack. Okay, maybe dinner too. The raisins add a chewiness, along with flavor that's as intense as any jelly.

Ingredients

3 tablespoons butter

¾ cup peanut butter

8 slices sandwich bread

4 teaspoons honey

4 tablespoons raisins

2 bananas

Salt

Prep | Cook

1. Turn the broiler to high; put the rack 6 inches from the heat.

   Melt 3 tablespoons butter in the microwave or in a small pot over medium-low heat.

2. Spread ¾ cup peanut butter on 4 slices bread; drizzle about a teaspoon of honey over each. Sprinkle 1 tablespoon raisins over each, pressing them down a bit so they stick in the peanut butter.

   Peel and slice the bananas.

3. Lay the banana slices on top of the raisins, sprinkle with salt, and close the sandwiches.

4. Brush both sides of each sandwich with melted butter and put them on a rimmed baking sheet.

5. Broil, turning once, until the bread is toasted on both sides, 2 or 3 minutes per side. Serve hot or warm.

VARIATIONS

Peanut Butter and Tomato Sandwich with Soy Sauce
This may sound weird, but it's common to use peanut sauce on tomatoes in many parts of the world. Substitute soy sauce and a drizzle of Sriracha for the honey and sliced tomatoes for the bananas. Skip the raisins and the salt (the soy sauce has plenty) and add a sprinkle of chopped fresh cilantro if you like.

Peanut Butter and Pickle Sandwich
There's no explanation for why this is so good: Use sliced pickles instead of the bananas and skip the honey and raisins.

Almond Butter and Apple Sandwich
Replace the peanut butter with almond butter and the bananas with sliced apples.

NOTES

DIY NUT BUTTER
All you need to make your own nut butter are nuts, salt, water, and a food processor. Toast the nuts if you like, then put them in the processor's work bowl with a sprinkle of salt; pulse to grind into a coarse paste. Add 2 tablespoons water for every 1 cup nuts, and let the machine run until the mixture is creamy, 1 or 2 minutes, adding more water a tablespoon at a time if necessary. You can also add spices (like cinnamon, or even cayenne) or a little fresh fruit. Either way it keeps in the fridge for weeks. Some good combos:

1. Peanut, grape, vanilla
2. Walnut, apple, cinnamon
3. Pecan, peach, cayenne
4. Hazelnut, strawberry, black pepper
5. Cashew, mango, nutmeg
6. Almond, apricot, cardamom
7. Pistachio, pear, clove

SIDES

Pick-a-Fruit Salad 921

French Fries 963

Sweet Potato Fries 963

SPEED ◔ SERVES 4

Hummus and Vegetable Pita Pockets

This sandwich is one of the best reasons to make hummus. Spread it thickly inside the crisp, toasted pita pocket and fill with cucumbers, tomatoes, and feta. The hummus you'll make in this recipe amounts to about 2 cups, so ½ cup for each pita. To make the sandwiches lighter, halve the amount of hummus and double the vegetables.

Ingredients

Four 8-inch pitas with pockets

¼ cup olive oil, plus more for drizzling

Salt and pepper

1 lemon

2 garlic cloves

2 cups cooked or canned chickpeas (one 15-ounce can)

½ cup tahini

1 tablespoon cumin or paprika

2 or 3 medium tomatoes (1 pound)

1 large cucumber

4 ounces feta cheese (1 cup crumbled)

Prep | Cook

1. Prepare a grill or turn the broiler to high; put the rack 4 inches from the heat.

   Drizzle the pitas with olive oil (about ½ teaspoon per side) and rub them all over with your fingers. Sprinkle salt and pepper over all and spread them out on a baking sheet.

   Halve the lemon; squeeze the juice into a food processor or blender.

   Peel and chop 2 garlic cloves.

   If you're using canned chickpeas, rinse and drain them.

2. Add the garlic, chickpeas, ½ cup tahini, ¼ cup olive oil, 1 tablespoon cumin or paprika, and a sprinkle of salt and pepper to the food processor or blender.

3. Let the machine run, adding water, chickpea-cooking liquid, or olive oil as necessary, until the purée is as smooth as you like. Taste and adjust the seasoning.

   Core the tomatoes and cut them into chunks; put them in a medium bowl.

Peel the cucumber if necessary, cut it in half lengthwise, and scoop out the seeds with a spoon. Chop and add to the bowl.

4. Grill or broil the pitas, turning once, until browned (even slightly charred) on both sides, 2 to 5 minutes total.

   Crumble 1 cup feta and add to the bowl; sprinkle with salt and pepper, drizzle with a little olive oil, and toss.

5. When the pitas are browned, cut each one in half, spreading them apart a bit to widen the pocket.

6. Spoon some hummus into each pocket, spreading it along the inner walls. Then spoon in the vegetable and feta mixture, top with a little more hummus if you like, and serve.

VARIATIONS

7 Additions to Hummus and Vegetable Pita Pockets

Add any of the following, alone or in combination, to the tomato, cucumber, and feta mixture:

1. Sliced red onions
2. Sliced roasted red peppers (page 417)
3. Chopped pitted olives
4. Chopped fresh parsley, dill, or mint
5. Cooked bulgur (page 125)
6. Browned ground lamb
7. Avocado slices

NOTES

EVEN FASTER

Don't toast the pita.

Instead of making the hummus as described in Steps 1 through 3, use hummus you've already made (page 939).

SIDES

Green Salad 911

Chopped Salad 912

Sautéed Greens with Garlic 924

Seared Broccoli or Cauliflower 925

Tofu Sandwich with Cucumber and Hoisin Mayo

I'm crazy about cucumber sandwiches. Not the dainty English teatime fare, although those are good too, but big-flavored ones, like those with goat cheese, hummus, and, yes, tofu.

Ingredients

3 tablespoons vegetable oil, plus more for brushing the bread

1 brick firm tofu (12 to 14 ounces)

4 hamburger buns

⅓ cup mayonnaise

1 tablespoon hoisin

1 medium cucumber

Prep | Cook

1. Turn the broiler to high; put the rack 6 inches from the heat. Put 3 tablespoons vegetable oil in a large skillet (preferably nonstick) over medium-high heat.

   Cut the tofu into 8 slices and pat them dry with a paper towel.

2. Add the tofu to the skillet and cook, turning once, until it's golden and crisp on both sides, 3 or 4 minutes per side.

3. Split the buns in half, brush the insides with a little oil, and broil until lightly toasted, 2 to 5 minutes.

   Put ⅓ cup mayonnaise and 1 tablespoon hoisin in a small bowl; stir to combine.

   Peel the cucumber if necessary and cut into thin slices.

4. When the tofu and buns are done, remove both from the heat. Spread the hoisin mayonnaise on the buns and top with the cucumber slices. Lay 2 slices tofu on top of each, close the sandwiches, and serve.

VARIATIONS

Buffalo Tofu Sandwich
Use half mayonnaise, half sour cream, and substitute ¼ cup crumbled blue cheese for the hoisin. Instead of the cucumber, slice 2 celery stalks into matchsticks. After you lay the tofu on top of the sandwiches, drizzle with hot sauce.

Tofu Sandwich with Pickles and Dijon Mayo
Replace the hoisin with Dijon mustard and the cucumber with 2 dill pickles.

Tofu Sandwich with Red Onions and Chipotle Mayo
Substitute 1 tablespoon chopped chipotles in adobo for the hoisin and 1 small red onion, thinly sliced, for the cucumber.

NOTES

MAKE YOUR OWN

Mayonnaise 144

IF YOU HAVE MORE TIME
For crunchier tofu, dredge the slices in flour, then beaten eggs, then panko bread crumbs before cooking. Panfry over medium heat until the panko coating is golden and crisp, 3 or 4 minutes per side.

SIDES

Green Salad with Sesame-Soy Dressing 911

Avocado with Lemon and Salt 920

Carrot Salad with Soy Sauce and Scallions 914

MASTER RECIPE

Make Your Own Condiments

Needless to say, condiments are an integral part of fast cooking. Given how often we reach for them, it pays to use quality products and even make some yourself. Three of the most common and beloved—mayonnaise, salsa, and barbecue sauce—are fast and simple to prepare, and the taste is in a different league from the processed stuff typically found in stores. Here's how to make them.

Mayonnaise

Takes 10 minutes and makes 1 cup.

1 Combine an Egg Yolk and Mustard

Put 1 egg yolk and 2 teaspoons Dijon in a food processor or blender. Turn the machine on.

2 Stream in Oil

With the machine running, add 1 cup vegetable oil in a slow, steady stream. Once an emulsion forms you can start to add the oil a little faster, until it's all incorporated and the mayonnaise is thick and creamy.

3 Season and Store

Sprinkle with salt and pepper, add 1 tablespoon sherry vinegar or lemon juice, and blend or process once more to combine. Use right away or store in the refrigerator for about 1 week.

VARIATIONS

7 Ways to Flavor Mayonnaise

Add any of the following, alone or in combination, in Step 3:

1. 1 tablespoon minced garlic, ginger, or chile
2. 1/4 cup chopped fresh basil, cilantro, parsley, or chives
3. 1 tablespoon chopped fresh rosemary, oregano, or thyme
4. 2 tablespoons soy sauce
5. 1 or 2 teaspoons grated citrus zest
6. 1 teaspoon prepared horseradish, hot sauce, or Worcestershire
7. 1 or 2 tablespoons any dried spice blend, like curry powder or chili powder

Fresh Tomato Salsa

Takes 15 minutes and makes 2 cups.

1 Combine the Ingredients

In a large bowl, combine 2 large ripe tomatoes, chopped, 1 medium white onion, chopped, 1 fresh hot green chile (like serrano), minced, 1 garlic clove, minced, ½ cup chopped fresh cilantro, the juice of 1 or 2 limes, and a sprinkle of salt and pepper.

2 Let the Flavors Develop

If possible, let the salsa sit for about 15 minutes before serving so the flavors have a chance to develop. Use right away or store in the refrigerator for 3 or 4 days.

VARIATIONS

Puréed Tomato Salsa

For a smoother version, pulse the salsa in the food processor or blend it in the blender until it reaches the consistency you like.

Black Bean Salsa

Add 1 cup cooked black beans and 1 teaspoon cumin in Step 1. Let the salsa sit for 30 minutes if you have time.

8 Ingredients to Use in Salsa Instead of Tomatoes

1. Tomatillos
2. Any melon
3. Peaches, plums, or nectarines
4. Corn kernels
5. Radishes
6. Pineapple
7. Mango
8. Black beans

Barbecue Sauce

Takes 20 minutes and makes 2 cups.

1 Combine the Ingredients

In a small saucepan over medium-low heat, combine 2 cups ketchup; ¼ cup red wine, rice, or apple cider vinegar; ½ cup dry red wine or water; 1 tablespoon Worcestershire or soy sauce; 1 tablespoon minced onion; 1 garlic clove, minced; and 1 tablespoon chili powder.

2 Simmer

Cook the sauce, stirring occasionally until the flavors blend together, about 10 minutes. Taste and adjust the seasoning, adding salt and pepper if necessary. Use right away or let cool, then cover and store in the refrigerator for about 1 week.

VARIATIONS

Dijon Barbecue Sauce

Reduce the vinegar to 2 tablespoons and add ¼ cup Dijon mustard in Step 1.

Chipotle Barbecue Sauce

Add 1 or 2 mashed chipotles with some of their adobo sauce in Step 1.

Chinese-Style Barbecue Sauce

Substitute 1 cup hoisin for 1 cup of the ketchup. Use rice vinegar and soy sauce and add 1 tablespoon minced fresh ginger in Step 1.

Tuna Sandwich with Pickles and Mustard

Everybody has a favorite spin on a tuna salad sandwich. (Some people make it with peanut butter.) This one uses olive oil and Dijon instead of mayonnaise and spikes the tuna with chopped pickles to add tanginess and crunch and parsley to lighten it up. It's super and different, especially when you try the variations.

Ingredients

Two 6-ounce cans tuna, preferably packed in olive oil

2 dill pickles

1 bunch fresh parsley

8 slices sandwich bread

¼ cup olive oil

2 teaspoons Dijon mustard

Salt and pepper

Prep | Cook

1. Turn the broiler to high; put the rack 6 inches from the heat.

   Drain the tuna; put it in a medium bowl.

   Chop 2 pickles; add them to the bowl.

   Chop ¼ cup parsley and add it to the bowl.

   Put 8 slices bread on a rimmed baking sheet.

2. Broil the bread, turning once, until lightly browned on both sides, 2 to 5 minutes total.

3. Add ¼ cup olive oil, 2 teaspoons Dijon, and a sprinkle of salt and pepper to the bowl. Stir to combine, taste, and adjust the seasoning.

4. When the bread is lightly toasted, remove it from the broiler; assemble the sandwiches and serve.

VARIATIONS

Tuna Sandwich with Olives

Substitute ½ cup chopped pitted olives for the pickles and ¼ cup mayonnaise for the olive oil. Keep the Dijon if you like.

Tuna Pita with Cucumbers and Feta

Substitute 1 medium cucumber, peeled, seeded, and chopped, for the pickles. Instead of sandwich bread, use pita pockets. Substitute at least ¼ cup crumbled feta for the Dijon and add the juice of a lemon along with the olive oil.

Tuna Sandwich with Fennel, Capers, and Lemon

I particularly like this version on a baguette, but use whatever bread you like. Replace the pickles with 1 small fennel bulb, chopped, and the Dijon with 2 tablespoons capers. Add the juice of a lemon along with the olive oil.

Tuna Sandwich with Avocado and Cilantro

Extra creamy. Use 1 avocado, chopped, instead of the pickles, cilantro instead of the parsley, and 1 small red onion, chopped, instead of the Dijon. Stir the tuna a little more so that the avocado mashes up and turns the mixture creamy and light green.

NOTES

IF YOU HAVE MORE TIME

Tuna Melt with Pickles and Mustard

After you flip the bread, put a slice or 2 of cheese on top of 4 pieces. Continue broiling until the cheese melts.

SIDES

Green Salad 911

Fennel Salad 917

Cucumber Salad 915

SPEED SERVES 4

Crab Salad Sandwich

This is no-frills, old-school crab salad on toast. Some lettuce and tomato on top and a cold beer on the side and you're good to go. For some newfangled crab salads, see the Variations.

Ingredients

2 tablespoons butter

1 pound cooked lump crabmeat

½ cup mayonnaise

Salt and pepper

8 slices sandwich bread

1 large ripe tomato

1 small head Boston or Bibb lettuce

Prep | Cook

1. Turn the broiler to high; put the rack 6 inches from the heat.

   Melt 2 tablespoons butter in the microwave or in a small pot over medium-low heat.

   Pick through the crabmeat, discarding any pieces of shell or cartilage. Put the meat in a large bowl.

2. Add ½ cup mayonnaise and a sprinkle of salt and pepper to the bowl; stir to combine, taste, and adjust the seasoning.

3. Put 8 slices bread on a rimmed baking sheet and brush both sides with the butter. Broil the bread, turning once, until lightly browned on both sides, 2 to 5 minutes total.

   Core and slice the tomato.

   Tear off 4 to 8 whole lettuce leaves. (Refrigerate the remaining lettuce for another use.)

4. When the bread is lightly toasted, remove it from the broiler. Spoon some crab salad onto the bread, top with the lettuce and tomatoes, close the sandwiches, and serve.

VARIATIONS

Creole Crab Salad Sandwich
Add 2 teaspoons Dijon mustard, 1 cup corn kernels, 1 chopped red bell pepper, and 2 teaspoons Old Bay seasoning to the crab mixture.

Buttery Crab Salad Sandwich
Use 4 tablespoons (½ stick) butter, melted, instead of mayonnaise. Add ½ cup chopped radishes and 1 tablespoon chopped fresh tarragon to the crab mixture.

Soy-Spiked Crab Salad Sandwich
Reduce the mayonnaise to ¼ cup. Add 1 tablespoon soy sauce, 2 teaspoons sesame oil, ½ cup chopped scallions, and ¼ cup toasted sesame seeds to the crab mixture.

NOTES

MAKE YOUR OWN

Mayonnaise 144

BRUSHING VS. SPREADING BUTTER
We've all had the experience of trying to spread hard-from-the-fridge butter onto slices of soft bread: The butter stays in a clump, and sometimes your knife rips right through the bread. If you don't think ahead and soften butter on the counter, just melt it in the microwave or in a small pot on the stove while you do something else; then use a brush to apply it to the bread. Even if you have softened butter, brushing will get you a thinner, more even coating than spreading could.

SIDES

Cucumber Salad 915

French Fries 963

Sweet Potato Fries 963

Avocado with Lemon and Salt 920

No-Mayo Slaw 923

Broiled Ham and Gruyère with Apples

A variation on the Parisian classic Croque Monsieur. *Croque* means "crunch," and, thanks to the apple, this sandwich crunches even more than usual.

Ingredients

4 tablespoons (½ stick) butter

8 ounces Gruyère cheese (2 cups grated)

1 large apple

8 slices sandwich bread

2 tablespoons Dijon mustard

4 slices ham

Prep | Cook

1. Turn the broiler to high; put the rack 6 inches from the heat.

   Melt 4 tablespoons butter in the microwave or in a small pot over medium-low heat.

   Slice 8 ounces Gruyère or grate 2 cups.

   Core and slice the apple.

2. Brush the melted butter on 1 side of 8 slices bread and 2 tablespoons Dijon on the other side. Assemble 4 ham, cheese, and apple sandwiches so that the buttered sides are facing out.

3. Put the sandwiches on a rimmed baking sheet and broil, turning once, until the bread is toasted on both sides and the cheese is melted, 2 or 3 minutes per side. Serve immediately.

VARIATIONS

Broiled Turkey and Brie with Tomatoes
Substitute Brie for the Gruyère, turkey for the ham, and 1 or 2 tomatoes for the apple. Keep the Dijon if you like. Alternatively, pesto is fantastic here.

Broiled Salami and Provolone with Roasted Red Peppers
Substitute provolone for the Gruyère, salami for the ham (you might want a few extra slices if they're small), and sliced roasted red peppers (page 417) for the apple.

Broiled Prosciutto and Mozzarella with Melon
Use fresh mozzarella instead of the Gruyère, prosciutto instead of the ham, and some thin slices of cantaloupe in place of the apples.

NOTES

IF YOU HAVE MORE TIME
Cook the sandwiches 2 at a time in a large skillet, flipping each once the bread becomes crisp and golden. Keep them warm in a 200°F oven while you cook the second batch.

SIDES

Green Salad 911

Tomato Salad 913

French Fries 963

Sautéed Greens with Garlic 924

Frozen Vegetable Soup 214

Coleslaw 923

SPEED  SERVES 4

Smoky Black Bean and Carrot Burgers

Patties made out of black beans and oats not only look astonishingly like a real hamburger; the taste and texture are better than in any vegetarian burger you've ever tried. Here I add a carrot for a little crunch and chipotles and cumin for smokiness.

Ingredients

1 large carrot

1 garlic clove

2 cups canned black beans (one 15-ounce can)

¾ cup rolled oats, plus more if needed

2 chipotles in adobo

2 teaspoons cumin

Salt and pepper

2 tablespoons olive oil, plus more for brushing the buns

4 hamburger buns

1 small red onion

Several sprigs fresh cilantro

⅓ cup mayonnaise

Prep | Cook

Trim, peel, and cut the carrot into small chunks; put it in a food processor and pulse it into small bits.

Peel and mince 1 garlic clove; add it to the food processor.

Rinse the beans in a colander and drain them; add them to the food processor.

1. Add ¾ cup oats, 2 chipotles in adobo, 2 teaspoons cumin, and a sprinkle of salt and pepper to the food processor.
2. Process until the mixture is combined but not puréed, about 30 seconds. If the mixture is too thin, pulse in a few more oats; if it's too thick (unlikely), pulse in a splash of water.
3. Put 2 tablespoons olive oil in a large skillet over medium heat. Turn the broiler to high; put the rack 6 inches from the heat.
4. Shape the bean mixture into 4 patties (about ½ inch thick). When the oil is hot, cook the burgers, turning once, until crisp on both sides, 4 or 5 minutes per side, adding more oil if the pan is dry.

5. Split the buns in half, brush with a little oil, and broil until lightly toasted, 2 or 3 minutes.

   Trim, peel, halve, and thinly slice the onion.

   Strip the cilantro leaves from several sprigs.

6. When the buns are toasted, remove them from the broiler; spread ⅓ cup mayonnaise on the buns. Add the onion, cilantro leaves, and burgers. Close the sandwiches and serve.

VARIATIONS

White Bean and Zucchini Burgers
Substitute 1 small zucchini for the carrot, white beans for black, 1 tablespoon grated lemon zest for the chipotles, 2 teaspoons chopped fresh rosemary for the cumin, and basil for the cilantro.

BBQ Black-Eyed Pea and Sweet Potato Burgers
Replace the carrot with ½ small sweet potato, the black beans with black-eyed peas, and the chipotles with barbecue sauce.

NOTES

MAKE YOUR OWN
Cooked Beans (cooked until they fall apart) 496

Mayonnaise 144

SIDES

French Fries 963

Green Salad 911

Avocado with Lemon and Salt 920

SPEED ◐ SERVES 4

Egg Salad Sandwich with Lots of Vegetables

Loaded with fresh cucumbers and tomatoes and dressed with olive oil and lemon, this sandwich puts the "salad" back in egg salad.

Ingredients

4 eggs

1 medium cucumber

2 medium ripe tomatoes

1 small red onion

1 bunch fresh parsley

8 slices sandwich bread

1 lemon

¼ cup olive oil

Salt and pepper

Prep | Cook

1. Turn the broiler to high; put the rack 6 inches from the heat.
2. Fill a medium saucepan about two-thirds with water and gently submerge the eggs. Bring to a boil, turn off the heat, and cover. Set a timer for 9 minutes.

   Fill a large bowl with ice water.

   Peel the cucumber if necessary, cut it in half lengthwise, scoop out the seeds with a spoon, and chop. Put it in a large bowl.

   Core and chop the tomatoes; add to the bowl.

   Trim, peel, and chop the onion; add to the bowl.

   Chop ¼ cup parsley and add to the bowl.

   Put 8 slices bread on a rimmed baking sheet.
3. Broil the bread, turning once, until lightly browned on both sides, 2 to 5 minutes total.

   Grate the lemon zest into the bowl; refrigerate the remaining fruit for another use.
4. When the eggs are done, transfer them to the ice water with a slotted spoon. Leave them submerged for at least 1 minute.

5. Crack and peel the eggs, transfer them to a cutting board, and chop. Add them to the bowl.

6. Add 1/4 cup olive oil and a sprinkle of salt and pepper to the bowl; toss, taste, and adjust the seasoning. Assemble the sandwiches and serve.

VARIATIONS

Curried Egg Salad Sandwich with Lots of Vegetables
Use cilantro instead of parsley and lime zest instead of lemon. Add 1 teaspoon curry powder along with the olive oil.

Egg and Arugula Salad Sandwich
Instead of the cucumber, use 2 cups arugula. If you chop the leaves up slightly, the sandwiches will be easier to assemble and eat.

"Classic" Egg Salad Sandwich with Lots of Vegetables
Substitute 1/4 cup mayonnaise and 2 teaspoons Dijon mustard for the olive oil.

SIDES

Green Salad 911

Celery Salad 917

No-Mayo Slaw 923

SPEED ◐ SERVES 4

Eggplant Parmesan Sub

Easy to cook, easy to assemble. Traditionally slices of eggplant for "parm" are dredged in flour and fried, but you don't need to bother with that; just brown chunks of eggplant and combine them with the tomato sauce. If you crave the fried taste of the classic coating, see If You Have More Time for instructions.

Ingredients

3 tablespoons olive oil

1 medium eggplant (1 to 1 ½ pounds)

Salt and pepper

4 sub rolls

4 ounces mozzarella cheese (1 cup grated)

4 ounces Parmesan cheese (1 cup grated)

One 14-ounce can crushed tomatoes

Several sprigs fresh basil

Prep | Cook

1. Turn the broiler to high; put the rack 6 inches from the heat. Put 3 tablespoons oil in a large skillet over medium heat.
   Trim the eggplant and cut it into ½-inch cubes.

2. Add the eggplant to the skillet, sprinkle with salt and pepper, and raise the heat to medium-high. Cook, stirring occasionally until lightly browned all over, 6 to 8 minutes.

3. Put the sub rolls on a rimmed baking sheet and broil until lightly toasted, 1 to 3 minutes.
   Grate 1 cup each mozzarella and Parmesan.

4. Remove the toasted rolls from the broiler; leave the broiler on.

5. When the eggplant is lightly browned, add the crushed tomatoes, stir to combine, and cook until the eggplant is tender, another 2 or 3 minutes.
   Strip the basil leaves from several sprigs.

6. When the eggplant is tender, spoon the eggplant and tomato mixture into each roll; top with the basil leaves and then cheese.

7. Return the sandwiches to the broiler and cook until the cheese is bubbly and brown. Top the sandwiches with the other side of the roll. Serve immediately.

VARIATIONS

Chicken Parm Sub
Instead of the eggplant, use 1 ½ pounds boneless chicken breast, cut into 1-inch chunks. Sauté them in the oil until lightly browned, 5 or 6 minutes, then add the tomatoes and cook until the chicken is just cooked through, 2 or 3 minutes more.

NOTES

EVEN FASTER
Instead of the crushed tomatoes, use about 2 cups Tomato Sauce (page 296).

IF YOU HAVE MORE TIME
Classic Eggplant Parm Sub
Slice the eggplant into ¼-inch rounds. Dredge them in flour, then beaten egg, then bread crumbs, stacking them between paper towels as you go. Working in batches, fry the slices in ¼ inch of olive oil over medium-high heat, turning once, until golden and crisp on both sides and tender in the middle, 4 to 6 minutes total. Drain on paper towels. When you're done, assemble the subs, eggplant on the bottom, then tomato sauce and basil, then the cheese. Broil, or bake at 450°F, until the cheese is bubbly and brown.

SIDES

Green Salad 911

Caprese Salad 922

Fennel Salad with Olives 917

Sautéed Greens with Garlic 924

Seared Broccoli or Cauliflower 925

SPEED SERVES 4

Salmon Sandwich with Peanut Vinaigrette

If you want a fast salmon sandwich that really tastes like salmon, try this. It's a light treatment that lets the salmon stand on its own.

Ingredients

1 ½ pounds salmon fillet

1 tablespoon vegetable oil

Salt and pepper

¼ cup peanuts

1 lime

1 tablespoon soy sauce

1 tablespoon sesame oil

3 scallions

Several sprigs fresh cilantro

4 hamburger buns

Prep | Cook

1. Prepare a grill or turn on the broiler; put the rack 4 inches from the heat.

   Put the salmon on a rimmed baking sheet, rub with 1 tablespoon vegetable oil, and sprinkle with salt and pepper.

   Chop ¼ cup peanuts; put them in a small bowl.

   Halve the lime and squeeze the juice into the bowl.

2. Add 1 tablespoon soy sauce and 1 tablespoon sesame oil to the bowl. Stir to combine.

3. When the grill or broiler is hot, cook the salmon, turning once, until browned on both sides and cooked as you like, 3 or 4 minutes per side if you like it a little soft in the middle, another minute or 2 if you like it firmer.

   Trim and slice the scallions.

   Strip the cilantro leaves from several sprigs.

4. When the salmon is done, remove it from the grill or broiler.

5. Split the buns in half and grill or broil until lightly toasted, a minute or 2.

6. Using a knife or metal spatula, cut the salmon into 4 equal pieces and put them in the buns. Drizzle the peanut vinaigrette onto the salmon and top with the scallions and cilantro. Close the sandwiches and serve.

VARIATIONS

Salmon Sandwich with Tarragon Mayo

Rub the salmon with olive oil instead of vegetable. Instead of the vinaigrette, combine ⅓ cup mayonnaise, the juice of a lemon, 1 tablespoon chopped fresh tarragon, salt, and pepper. Spread the mixture on the toasted buns before adding the salmon. Top with sliced tomatoes instead of the scallions and cilantro.

Salmon Sandwich with Chipotle-Avocado Spread

Instead of the vinaigrette, put 1 ripe avocado in a bowl and mash it with a chopped chipotle in adobo, the juice of a lime, salt, and pepper; you want to mash it up enough so the mixture is smooth and spreadable. Spread it on the toasted buns before adding the salmon. Top with cilantro and sliced red onions.

NOTES

EVEN FASTER

If you have room, grill or broil the salmon and the buns at the same time.

SIDES

Green Salad 911

Cucumber Salad with Soy Sauce and Mirin 915

Ginger-Orange Bean Sprouts 919

Avocado with Lime and Chili Salt 920

SPEED ◐ SERVES 4

Sriracha Shrimp Salad Roll

Grilling or broiling puts a nice smoky edge on normally tame shrimp salad, while a Sriracha-spiked riff on tartar sauce adds heat.

Ingredients

2 tablespoons butter

1 lime

1 small cucumber

Several sprigs fresh cilantro

⅓ cup mayonnaise

2 teaspoons Sriracha (or more to taste)

1 pound peeled shrimp

Salt and pepper

4 hot dog buns

Prep | Cook

1. Prepare a grill or turn the broiler to high; put the rack 4 inches from the heat.

   Melt 2 tablespoons butter in the microwave or in a small pot over medium-low heat.

   Halve the lime and squeeze the juice into a large bowl.

   Peel the cucumber if necessary; cut it in half lengthwise and scoop out the seeds with a spoon. Finely chop and add it to the bowl.

   Chop several sprigs cilantro and add to the bowl.

2. Add ⅓ cup mayonnaise and 2 teaspoons Sriracha to the bowl; stir to combine.

3. When the grill or broiler is hot, place the shrimp on a baking sheet or grill pan and sprinkle with salt and pepper. Cook, turning once, until they're lightly browned on the outside and just cooked through, 2 or 3 minutes per side.

   Brush the insides of the buns with the melted butter.

4. When the shrimp are done, remove them from the grill or broiler. Grill or broil the buns, turning as necessary, until lightly toasted inside and out, 2 to 5 minutes total.

5. While the buns toast, chop the shrimp and add them to the bowl; toss, taste, and adjust the seasoning, adding more Sriracha if you like it hotter.

6. Spoon the shrimp into the toasted buns and serve.

VARIATIONS

Shrimp Salad Roll with Tomato-Paprika Mayo
Replace the lime with lemon, the cucumber with 1 medium tomato, the cilantro with parsley, and the Sriracha with 1 teaspoon smoked paprika.

Curried Shrimp Salad Roll
Use 1 teaspoon curry powder instead of the Sriracha.

Scallop Roll with Lemon-Tarragon Aïoli
Substitute a lemon for the lime, 1 tablespoon chopped tarragon for the cilantro, and 1 teaspoon minced garlic for the Sriracha. Skip the cucumber. Use sea scallops instead of shrimp: Grill or broil them, turning once, until they're browned on both sides and opaque all the way through, about 5 minutes total.

Fish Sandwich
Substitute a lemon for the lime, 2 pickles for the cucumber, parsley for the cilantro, and 2 tablespoons chopped capers for the Sriracha. Use 1 ½ pounds thick white fish fillets instead of the shrimp. Grill or broil, turning once, until browned on both sides and just cooked through in the middle, 5 or 6 minutes per side. Divide the fish among 4 toasted hamburger buns or sandwich bread; top with tartar sauce and a little lettuce.

NOTES

MAKE YOUR OWN
Mayonnaise 144

EVEN FASTER
If you have room, grill or broil the shrimp and the buns at the same time.

SIDES

Green Salad 911

Soy Slaw 923

Carrot Salad with Soy Sauce and Scallions 914

SPEED ◐ SERVES 4

Seared Tuna Sandwich with Wilted Bok Choy and Soy Mayo

The combination of soy sauce and mayo is unusual and fantastic; add seared tuna, crisp on the outside and rare in the middle, and you have a keeper. I skip the bok choy stems in this recipe and just quickly wilt the leaves.

Ingredients

1 ½ pounds fresh tuna

2 teaspoons vegetable oil

Salt and pepper

1 head bok choy

8 slices sandwich bread

½ inch fresh ginger

⅓ cup mayonnaise

1 tablespoon soy sauce

2 tablespoons sesame seeds

Prep | Cook

1. Turn the broiler to high; put the rack 6 inches from the heat. Put a large skillet over high heat.

   Rub the tuna all over with 1 teaspoon vegetable oil; sprinkle with salt and pepper.

2. When the skillet is very hot, add the tuna and cook, turning once, until it's browned on both sides but still raw in the center, 3 or 4 minutes per side.

   Slice off 2 cups bok choy leaves; refrigerate the rest of the head for another use.

   Put 8 slices bread on a rimmed baking sheet.

3. Broil the bread, turning once, until lightly toasted on both sides, 2 to 5 minutes total.

   Peel and mince ½ inch ginger; put it in a small bowl.

4. When the tuna is done, remove it from the skillet. Add 1 teaspoon oil to the skillet, followed immediately by the bok choy and a sprinkle of salt and pepper.

5. Cook the bok choy, stirring occasionally, until just wilted, no more than a minute, then remove from the heat.

6. When the bread is toasted, remove it from the broiler.
   Add ⅓ cup mayonnaise and 1 tablespoon soy sauce to the ginger; stir to combine.

7. Spread the mayonnaise mixture on 4 slices of the bread, sprinkle with 2 tablespoons sesame seeds, and top with the bok choy.

8. Cut the tuna into slices and lay them on top of the bok choy. Close the sandwiches and serve.

VARIATIONS

Seared Tuna Niçoise Sandwich
Instead of the bok choy leaves, use 8 ounces green beans: Stir-fry them until lightly browned and just tender (but still with some crunch), 3 to 5 minutes. Substitute ¼ cup chopped pitted Niçoise olives for the ginger and ¼ cup chopped cornichons for the soy sauce. Top the sandwiches with sliced tomatoes.

NOTES

MAKE YOUR OWN
Mayonnaise 144

EVEN FASTER
If you like to eat tuna raw, just cut the fresh tuna into slices and don't bother searing it.

SIDES

Tomato Salad with Sesame and Soy 913

Cucumber Salad with Soy Sauce and Mirin 915

Soy Slaw 923

Edamame Succotash 933

SPEED ◑ SERVES 4

Chicken Salad Sandwich with Grapes and Rosemary

Chicken salad with grapes has been around since I was a kid. Some mothers in the sixties made it with powdered Italian dressing and Sweet'N Low. I've replaced that junk with real ingredients and kept the tangy-sweet spirit of the sandwich.

Ingredients

1 ½ pounds boneless, skinless chicken breasts

1 cup white wine or water

1 bay leaf

3 sprigs fresh rosemary

⅓ cup mayonnaise

2 teaspoons Dijon mustard

Salt and pepper

1 bunch red or green grapes

1 baguette

Prep | Cook

1. Put the chicken, 1 cup wine or water, and 1 bay leaf in a medium skillet over high heat.
2. When the liquid boils, lower the heat so it bubbles gently. Cover and cook until the chicken is opaque and just cooked through, 10 to 15 minutes.
   - Strip the leaves from 3 rosemary sprigs, chop, and put them in a large bowl.
   - Add ⅓ cup mayonnaise, 2 teaspoons Dijon, and a sprinkle of salt and pepper to the bowl; stir to combine.
   - Pick off 1 cup grapes from the bunch, slice each grape in half, and add them to the bowl.
   - Have the baguette lengthwise.
3. When the chicken is cooked, transfer it to a cutting board. Chop or shred it and add it to the bowl. Stir to coat the chicken and grapes in the dressing. Taste and adjust the seasoning.
4. Spoon the chicken salad onto 1 half of the baguette, top with the other half, cut the sandwich into 4 sections, and serve.

VARIATIONS

Chicken Salad Sandwich with Grapes and Curry
Substitute 2 teaspoons curry powder for the rosemary. For extra crunch, add some chopped celery, red onion, and/or walnuts.

Chicken Salad Sandwich with Olives and Thyme
Replace the rosemary with thyme and the grapes with pitted olives. Substitute olive oil for the mayonnaise, keep the Dijon, and add the juice of a lemon.

Turkey Salad Sandwich with Apples and Sage
Substitute 2 turkey tenderloins or turkey breast cutlets for the chicken. Up the poaching water to 2 cups and cook the turkey for closer to 20 to 25 minutes. Substitute sage for the rosemary and 1 cup chopped apples for the grapes.

NOTES

MAKE YOUR OWN

Mayonnaise 144

EVEN FASTER
Use chicken tenders instead of chicken breasts; they'll take 5 to 10 minutes.

Instead of cooking chicken breasts as described in Steps 1 and 2, use a Whole Roast Chicken (page 688).

IF YOU HAVE MORE TIME
Toast the baguette.

Chill the chicken salad in the refrigerator before assembling the sandwich.

SIDES

Green Salad 911

Tomato Salad 913

Fennel Salad 917

Sautéed Greens with Garlic 924

SPEED ◐ SERVES 4

Chicken, Bacon, Avocado, and Tomato Wrap

Smoky chicken, crisp bacon, creamy avocado, juicy tomatoes, wrapped in a perfect package.

Ingredients

4 slices bacon

2 boneless, skinless chicken breasts (about 1 pound)

1 tablespoon olive oil

Salt and pepper

2 medium ripe tomatoes

1 small red onion

1 avocado

1 lime

4 sandwich wraps

Prep | Cook

1. Prepare a grill or turn the broiler to high; put the rack 4 inches from the heat.

2. Put the bacon in a large skillet over medium heat. Cook, turning as necessary until crisp, 5 to 10 minutes.

   Line a plate with paper towels.

   Cut the chicken breasts in half horizontally so you end up with 2 flat cutlets for each breast. Press down on each cutlet a bit to flatten, then rub the chicken with 1 tablespoon oil and sprinkle with salt and pepper.

3. When the grill or broiler is hot, cook the chicken, turning once, until lightly browned on both sides and just cooked through, 2 to 5 minutes per side.

   Core the tomatoes; halve them and then slice.

   Trim, peel, halve, and slice the onion.

4. When the bacon is crisp, transfer it to the paper towels (save the rendered fat in case you want to drizzle it into your wrap).

   Halve and pit the avocado; scoop out the flesh and slice it.

   Halve the lime.

   Lay the wraps out on the counter.

5. When the chicken is done, transfer it to a cutting board and slice it.

6. Lay the chicken in the wraps, followed by the bacon, tomatoes, avocado, and red onion. Squeeze some lime juice over the top, sprinkle with salt and pepper, and drizzle on bacon fat if you like.

7. Wrap them all up like a burrito and serve.

VARIATIONS

Chicken, Bacon, Tomato, and Blue Cheese Wrap
Skip the lime juice. Instead of (or in addition to) the avocado, crumble some blue cheese into the wrap.

Greek Chicken Wrap
For saltiness I like to use a handful of chopped kalamata olives instead of the bacon. Substitute 1 small cucumber, sliced, for the avocado, and lemon for the lime. Sprinkle on some feta, and, since there's no bacon fat, drizzle on olive oil instead.

Chipotle BLT Wrap
Skip the chicken and double the bacon. Stuff the wrap with some chopped romaine lettuce in addition to the tomato, red onion, and avocado. Stir together rendered bacon fat, 2 chopped chipotles in adobo, and the lime juice. Drizzle it over the top before wrapping.

NOTES

EVEN FASTER
Stir-fry the chicken and the bacon together: Cut the bacon into 1-inch pieces and start cooking them in the skillet over medium heat. Slice the raw chicken cutlets and add them to the skillet. Cook, stirring occasionally until the bacon is crisp and the chicken is cooked through, 5 to 10 minutes. Spoon the mixture into the wraps and proceed as directed.

Instead of cooking chicken breasts as described in Step 3, use a Whole Roast Chicken (page 688).

IF YOU HAVE MORE TIME
After turning the chicken cutlets, lay a slice or 2 of cheddar cheese on top of each one. Cook until the cheese is melted. Slice the chicken as directed.

WRAP IT UP
While "wraps" are marketed as their own distinct product in supermarkets, it's good to remember that any thin, flexible piece of bread can be used as a wrap. Of course, flour tortillas — plain, whole wheat, or any number of flavors that they now come in — are the most common, but lavash, naan, and the pocketless pitas used for gyros are equally appealing. You can even use corn tortillas if you'd rather have a few smaller wraps than one big one.

SIDES

Green Salad 911

Tomato Salad with Olive Oil and Yogurt 913

Chile-Cumin Black Beans 937

SPEED ◑ SERVES 4

Blackened Chicken Sandwich with Pickled Red Onions

Chicken breasts layered with a powerful spice mixture and blackened in a skillet make a terrific sandwich. And since the onions need nothing more than to be left alone as they pickle, you have the time to make this classic condiment.

Ingredients

½ cup red wine vinegar

1 tablespoon sugar

Salt

1 medium red onion

2 tablespoons vegetable oil, plus more if needed

1 teaspoon chili powder

1 teaspoon cumin

1 teaspoon coriander

2 boneless, skinless chicken breasts (about 1 pound)

1 avocado

Several sprigs fresh cilantro

4 soft sandwich rolls

2 ounces queso fresco (½ cup crumbled; optional)

Prep | Cook

1. Put ½ cup vinegar, ½ cup water, 1 tablespoon sugar, and a sprinkle of salt in a small saucepan over high heat.
   Trim, peel, halve, and slice the onion.

2. When the liquid comes to a boil, add the onion slices, submerge them as much as you can in the liquid, cover, and turn off the heat. Just leave them there until you're ready to make the sandwiches.

3. Put 2 tablespoons vegetable oil in a large skillet over medium-low heat.
   Combine 1 teaspoon each chili powder, cumin, coriander, and salt in a small bowl.
   Cut the chicken breasts in half horizontally so you end up with 2 flat cutlets for each breast. Press down on each cutlet a bit to flatten, then sprinkle the spice rub all over the chicken, pressing it in.

4. Raise the heat under the skillet to medium and add the chicken, working in 2 batches if necessary to avoid crowding the pan. Cook, turning once, until the spice rub is well browned (or even blackened) and the chicken is cooked through, 3 or 4 minutes per side.

   Halve and pit the avocado; scoop out the flesh and slice it.

   Strip the cilantro leaves from several sprigs.

   Slice the sandwich rolls in half.

   Crumble ½ cup queso fresco if you're using it.

5. When the chicken is done, put 1 cutlet on each bun. Lay the avocado slices on top, then use tongs to add the pickled onions (it's more than okay if some of the pickling liquid splashes onto the sandwich).

6. Top with the cilantro leaves and queso fresco if you're using it. Close the sandwiches and serve.

VARIATIONS

BBQ Blackened Chicken Sandwich with Pickled Cucumbers
Use 1 small cucumber, very thinly sliced, instead of the red onion. For the spice rub, use 1 teaspoon each paprika, chili powder, brown sugar, and salt. Skip the avocado, cilantro, and queso fresco and go for a squirt of your favorite barbecue sauce instead.

NOTES

MAKE YOUR OWN
Chili Powder 758

IF YOU HAVE MORE TIME
Toast the rolls.

Let the onions pickle for at least 30 minutes or up to a few hours. They'll get softer and more acidic as you go.

SIDES

Jícama and Radish Salad 918

Cucumber Salad with Hot Sauce and Lime Juice 915

Mexican Street Corn 932

SPEED ◐ SERVES 4

Chicken and Black Bean Burrito

If you have a great burrito spot, I envy you, because most store-bought burritos are mushy and flavorless.

Ingredients

1 cup long-grain rice

Salt

3 medium ripe tomatoes (about 1 pound)

1 small onion

1 fresh hot green chile (like jalapeño)

1 bunch fresh cilantro

2 limes

Pepper

2 tablespoons vegetable oil

6 boneless, skinless chicken thighs (about 1 pound)

2 cups cooked or canned black beans (one 15-ounce can)

2 garlic cloves

1 teaspoon chili powder

1 teaspoon cumin

4 large flour tortillas

Sour cream

Prep | Cook

1. Put 1 cup rice in a medium saucepan; add a big pinch of salt and 2 cups water to cover. Bring to a boil, then adjust the heat so the mixture bubbles steadily but not vigorously; cover. Cook, undisturbed, until small craters appear on the surface, 10 to 15 minutes.

   Core and chop the tomatoes; put them in a medium bowl.

   Trim, peel, and chop the onion; add it to the bowl.

   Trim and mince the chile; add it to the bowl.

   Chop ½ cup cilantro and add it to the bowl.

   Halve the limes; squeeze the juice into the bowl. Sprinkle with salt and pepper and stir.

2. Put 2 tablespoons vegetable oil in a large skillet over medium-high heat.

   Chop the chicken into ½-inch chunks.

3. When the oil is hot, add the chicken to the skillet, sprinkle with salt and pepper, and cook, stirring occasionally until it loses its pink color, 3 or 4 minutes.

4. When craters appear on the surface of the rice, tip the pot to see if any liquid remains. If so, cover and keep cooking until the rice is dry, checking every minute or 2 until the liquid is gone. Turn off the heat and cover.

   If you're using canned beans, rinse and drain them.

   Peel and mince 2 garlic cloves.

5. When the chicken is no longer pink, add the beans and garlic, along with 1 teaspoon chili powder, 1 teaspoon cumin, and a sprinkle of salt and pepper. Cook, stirring occasionally until the beans are hot and the chicken is cooked through, 3 to 5 minutes.

6. Put the tortillas in the microwave for 15 seconds or so to warm them up. Lay them out and top them with the rice.

7. When the chicken and beans are done, spoon the mixture over the rice. Top with the salsa and a few dollops of sour cream if you like. Wrap the burritos tightly and serve.

VARIATIONS

Steak and Black Bean Burrito with Fresh Salsa

Use 1 pound sliced skirt steak instead of the chicken; you can get away with cooking it a little less.

Shrimp and White Bean Burrito with Corn Salsa

Substitute 2 cups fresh or thawed frozen corn kernels for the tomatoes and 1 pound peeled shrimp for the chicken. Replace the black beans with white and add them at the same time as the shrimp; by the time the beans are hot, the shrimp will be cooked.

NOTES

MAKE YOUR OWN

Cooked Beans 496

Chili Powder 758

EVEN FASTER

Skip the salsa; just top with your favorite hot sauce instead. Or, instead of making the salsa as described in the Prep after Step 1, use Fresh Tomato Salsa (page 145).

Instead of cooking chicken thighs as described in Step 3, use a Whole Roast Chicken (page 688).

SIDES

Mexican Street Corn 932

Ripe Plantains 960

SPEED ◐ SERVES 4

Turkey and Broccoli Rabe Hero

The combination of sautéed broccoli rabe, melted mozzarella, and lemon zest is so good that you can skip the meat and not miss it a bit. But tucking some quickly braised sliced turkey into the bottom of the sandwich is a treat.

Ingredients

4 tablespoons olive oil

2 turkey tenderloins or turkey breast cutlets (1 to 1 ½ pounds total)

Salt and pepper

12 ounces broccoli rabe

2 garlic cloves

8 ounces fresh mozzarella cheese

4 sub rolls

½ cup chicken stock or water

½ teaspoon red chile flakes

1 lemon

Prep | Cook

1. Turn the broiler to high; put the rack 6 inches from the heat. Put 2 tablespoons olive oil in a large skillet over medium-high heat.
   Sprinkle the turkey with salt and pepper.
2. When the oil is hot, put the turkey in the skillet and cook, turning once, until browned on both sides, 5 or 6 minutes per side.
   Trim and chop the broccoli rabe, separating any thick stems if necessary.
   Peel 2 garlic cloves; cut them into slivers.
   Slice 8 ounces mozzarella.
3. Put the sub rolls on a rimmed baking sheet and broil until lightly toasted, 2 to 5 minutes.
4. When the turkey is browned, add ½ cup stock or water to the skillet and partially cover the pan. Adjust the heat so the mixture bubbles gently but steadily and cook until the turkey is cooked through, 5 to 10 minutes.
5. Add 2 tablespoons olive oil to the skillet. Add any thick broccoli rabe stems and cook until they begin to soften, 3 or 4 minutes.
6. When the rolls are toasted, remove them from the broiler. Leave the broiler on.

7. When the stems begin to soften, add the broccoli rabe leaves, a handful at a time if necessary, the garlic slivers, ½ teaspoon red chile flakes, and a sprinkle of salt and pepper. Cook until the leaves are just wilted, 3 or 4 minutes.
8. When the turkey is cooked through, thinly slice it; divide it among the sub rolls.
9. When the broccoli rabe is just wilted, lay it on top of the turkey. Lay the slices of mozzarella on top.
10. Return the sandwiches to the broiler and cook until the cheese is bubbly and brown. Grate some lemon zest over the top (refrigerate the remaining fruit for another use) and serve immediately.

VARIATIONS

Turkey and Spinach Hero with Fontina and Lemon Zest
Substitute spinach leaves for the broccoli rabe and fontina cheese for the mozzarella. Cook the spinach for a just a couple minutes.

Turkey and Kale Hero with Gruyère
Substitute kale for the broccoli rabe and Gruyère for the mozzarella. Skip the lemon. Cook the kale for a minute or 2 longer than the broccoli rabe.

Tomato and Broccoli Rabe Hero with Mozzarella and Lemon Zest
Skip the turkey and start by sautéing the broccoli rabe. Cut 2 large ripe tomatoes into thick slices and lay them in the bottom of the toasted sub rolls instead of the turkey.

NOTES

MAKE YOUR OWN
Chicken Stock 212

EVEN FASTER
Use deli turkey instead of homemade.

IF YOU HAVE MORE TIME
Ladle some tomato sauce over the turkey and broccoli rabe before topping with the mozzarella and broiling.

SIDES

Tomato Salad 913

Carrot Salad with Raisins 914

Broiled Cherry Tomatoes 931

SPEED ◐ SERVES 4

Open-Face Lyonnaise Sandwich

How do you make one of the world's great sandwiches? Take one of the world's great salads and put it on a piece of toast. *Salade Lyonnaise*—a sublime mixture of frisée, bacon, soft-cooked egg, and Dijon vinaigrette—needs no embellishment.

Ingredients

8 slices bacon

1 head frisée

1 shallot

4 thick slices any rustic bread

1 tablespoon red wine vinegar

2 teaspoons Dijon mustard

Salt and pepper

2 tablespoons butter

4 eggs

Prep | Cook

1. Turn the broiler to high; put the rack 6 inches from the heat.
2. Put 8 slices bacon in a large skillet over medium heat. Cook, turning as necessary until crisp, 5 to 10 minutes.

   Line a plate with paper towels.

   Trim the frisée and separate the leaves; put them in a bowl.

   Trim, peel, and mince the shallot.
3. Broil 4 slices bread, turning once, until lightly toasted on both sides, 2 to 5 minutes total.
4. When the bacon is crisp, transfer it to the paper towels; leave the fat in the skillet. Add the shallot, 1 tablespoon red wine vinegar, and 2 teaspoons Dijon to the skillet. Stir to combine and pour the dressing over the frisée. Sprinkle with salt and pepper and toss.
5. Return the skillet to medium heat and add 2 tablespoons butter. When the foam subsides, crack the eggs into the skillet and cook until the whites are no longer translucent, 2 or 3 minutes.
6. When the egg whites are no longer translucent, turn the heat to low and sprinkle with salt and pepper.

   Put 2 slices bacon on each piece of bread and pile the frisée on top.

7. When the egg whites are completely firm and the yolks are as runny as you like, remove the eggs from the skillet and put 1 on top of each sandwich. Serve immediately.

VARIATIONS

Open-Face Cobb Sandwich
Use romaine, Boston, or Bibb lettuce instead of the frisée; add some halved cherry tomatoes and crumbled blue cheese to the mix as well. Hard-boiled eggs are classic in Cobb salad; if you have any, chop a few and toss them with the salad. Or just stick with the sunny-side-up eggs.

NOTES

EVEN FASTER
Instead of using the shallot, vinegar, and Dijon as described in Step 4, add a couple tablespoons Vinaigrette (page 70) to the pan.

IF YOU HAVE MORE TIME
If you prefer, poach the eggs instead of frying them. See page 99.

OPEN YOUR MIND TO OPENING YOUR SANDWICH
Most of the sandwiches sold in delis and restaurants in this country (and maybe the world) have too much bread. It throws the entire balance of a sandwich out of whack and leaves you feeling much fuller than you'd like to be. Of course, in your own kitchen you are in total control of the bread situation, but one foolproof way to ensure that your sandwiches aren't too bready is to take away an entire slice. Open-face sandwiches are just as enjoyable as regular sandwiches, but a whole slice of carbs lighter. They are great vehicles for salady mixtures, like the one here, cold cuts, and tuna melts. And honestly, anything you can put between 2 slices of bread you can probably figure out how to put on top of just one.

SIDES

Tomato Salad 913

Fennel Salad 917

French Fries 963

SPEED  SERVES 4

Spanish Dip

This sandwich is a riff on the classic French dip in concept but not ingredients. It's a chorizo and manchego grilled cheese with a tomato dipping sauce called *salmorejo*—kind of like a thick gazpacho. Traditional? Maybe not. Delicious? *¡Sí!*

Ingredients

2 medium ripe tomatoes

1 garlic clove

9 slices rustic white bread

¾ cup olive oil

¼ cup sherry vinegar

Salt and pepper

8 ounces manchego cheese (2 cups grated)

8 ounces smoked Spanish chorizo

Prep | Cook

1. Turn the broiler to high; put the rack 6 inches from the heat.

   Core and cut the tomatoes into chunks; put them in a blender.

   Peel 1 garlic clove; add it to the blender.

   Tear 1 slice bread into pieces and add them to the blender.

2. Add ½ cup olive oil, ¼ cup sherry vinegar, and a sprinkle of salt and pepper to the blender. Turn the machine on and purée until the mixture is smooth and thick, adding a splash of water if necessary. Taste and adjust the seasoning.

3. Pour the mixture into 4 individual bowls for dipping.

   Slice 8 ounces manchego or grate 2 cups.

   Thinly slice the chorizo.

4. Drizzle ¼ cup oil on 8 slices bread. Assemble 4 chorizo and manchego sandwiches so that the oiled sides of the bread are facing out.

5. Put the sandwiches on a rimmed baking sheet and broil, turning once, until the bread is toasted on both sides and the cheese is melted, 2 or 3 minutes per side. Serve immediately, with the tomato dip on the side.

VARIATIONS

Italian Dip

Instead of making the salmorejo, use pesto (page 284). Substitute mozzarella for the manchego and sliced tomatoes for the chorizo.

NOTES

EVEN FASTER

Skip the salmorejo. When assembling the sandwiches, top each one with sliced tomatoes, a drizzle of sherry vinegar, and a sprinkle of salt and pepper.

IF YOU HAVE MORE TIME

Cook the sandwiches 2 at a time in a large skillet. Keep them warm in a 200°F oven.

SIDES

Green Salad 911

Chopped Salad 912

Fennel Salad 917

Broiled Cherry Tomatoes 931

Plum, Manchego, and Parsley Salad 922

SPEED ◐ SERVES 4

Sausage and Pepper Sub

Cooking the sausages and vegetables together not only makes both taste better but also saves time and dishes. Besides, this is how my mother did it, so enough said.

Ingredients

2 tablespoons olive oil, plus more for drizzling

4 Italian sausages (1 pound)

2 medium red or yellow bell peppers

1 large onion

Salt and pepper

4 hard sub rolls

Prep | Cook

1. Put 2 tablespoons olive oil in a large skillet over medium heat.

   Split the sausages in half lengthwise, but don't cut all the way through; they should open flat like a book.

2. When the oil is hot, add the sausages face down and cook, turning once, until lightly browned on both sides, about 5 minutes.

   Core, seed, and slice the peppers; add them to the skillet.

   Trim, peel, halve, and slice the onion; add it to the skillet.

3. Sprinkle everything with salt and pepper and cook, stirring occasionally until the vegetables are very tender, 15 to 20 minutes.

4. Drizzle the sub rolls with olive oil and lay a sausage in each one. Pile the vegetables on top and serve.

VARIATIONS

Bratwurst and Onion Sub
Substitute bratwurst for the Italian sausage, skip the peppers, and use 2 large onions. Cook them in butter instead of olive oil and, if you like, add a splash of beer (about ½ cup) to the skillet during cooking. Make sure the beer is evaporated before you assemble the sandwiches; its flavor will infuse the brats and onions as everything cooks down.

Sausage and Broccoli Rabe Sub
Use 1 small head broccoli rabe, chopped, and 3 garlic cloves, slivered, instead of the peppers and onions. The rabe will be tender in 10 to 15 minutes.

Sausage and Pepper Sub with Melted Mozzarella
After you've assembled the subs, put them on a rimmed baking sheet and lay some sliced mozzarella over the top. Broil until the cheese is bubbly and brown.

NOTES

EVEN FASTER
To speed up the cooking process slightly, cook the sausage and vegetables over medium-high heat. The sausage and peppers might end up a bit less tender but not much.

IF YOU HAVE MORE TIME
Toast the sub rolls under the broiler if you like. Doesn't take more time, only slightly more effort.

SIDES

Chopped Salad 912

Caprese Salad 922

Sautéed Greens with Garlic 924

Seared Broccoli or Cauliflower 925

SPEED ◑ SERVES 4

Bánh Mì

Bánh mì—a Vietnamese-style hoagie—is often a complicated affair with a number of different components. Here it's pared down to the absolute essentials: pork and pickled vegetables. Pretty cool for 30 minutes.

Ingredients

1 small daikon radish or 4 small regular red radishes

1 large carrot

1 small cucumber

Salt

3 tablespoons sugar

1 inch fresh ginger

1 garlic clove

1 tablespoon peanut oil

1 pound ground pork

½ cup mayonnaise

2 teaspoons Sriracha, or more to taste

1 tablespoon fish sauce

1 tablespoon soy sauce

4 hard sub rolls

Several sprigs fresh cilantro

Prep | Cook

Trim and peel the daikon or 4 small radishes, carrot, and cucumber. Cut the cucumber in half lengthwise and scoop out the seeds with a spoon.

If you're using a food processor for grating, cut the vegetables into chunks that will fit through the feed tube. Shred them by machine or by hand on a box grater.

Put the vegetables in a colander in the sink; sprinkle with 1 tablespoon salt and 3 tablespoons sugar and toss. Let sit.

1. Put a large skillet over medium-high heat.

   Peel and mince 1 inch ginger and 1 garlic clove.

2. Add 1 tablespoon peanut oil to the skillet along with the ginger and garlic. After a quick stir, add the ground pork; let it brown in the pan, 2 or 3 minutes.

3. Turn the broiler to high; put the rack 6 inches from the heat.

   Stir together ½ cup mayonnaise and 2 teaspoons Sriracha in a small bowl.

4. Add 1 tablespoon each fish sauce and soy sauce to the pork. Stir and cook until most of the liquid has evaporated, 3 to 5 minutes.

5. Split the sub rolls open and broil them until lightly toasted, 1 to 3 minutes.
6. When the pork is fully cooked, remove the pan from the heat.
7. When the sub rolls are toasted, remove them from the broiler; spread with Sriracha mayonnaise.
8. By now the shredded vegetables will have released some water; squeeze out the water through the colander. Divide the vegetables among the sub rolls.
9. Lay the pork on top of the shredded vegetables. Top with several cilantro sprigs (stems and all) and serve.

VARIATIONS

Shrimp Bánh Mì
Use 1 pound peeled shrimp instead of the pork. Add it to the skillet in Step 4 along with the fish sauce.

Beef Bánh Mì
Substitute 1 pound ground beef for the pork.

3 Additions to Bánh Mì
Add any of the following, alone, to the sandwiches:

1. 1 tomato, cut into 8 to 10 wedges
2. 1 fried egg per sandwich
3. Pâté, spread on the bread before adding toppings

NOTES

MAKE YOUR OWN
Mayonnaise 144

IF YOU HAVE MORE TIME
Let the shredded vegetables sit in the colander for up to an hour.

SIDES

Ginger-Orange Bean Sprouts 919

Avocado with Rice Vinegar and Peanuts 920

Stir-Fried Bok Choy 927

SPEED ◐ SERVES 4

Steak Tacos with Lots of Options

Grill or broil skirt steak and warm a pile of corn tortillas; from there you're limited only by your imagination. We start with the traditional route—radishes, cilantro, and lime—but see the list for all sorts of other fillings.

Ingredients

4 large radishes

2 limes

Several sprigs fresh cilantro

1 pound skirt steak

Salt and pepper

8 corn tortillas

Prep | Cook

1. Prepare a grill or turn the broiler to high; put the rack 4 inches from the heat.

   Trim and chop 4 large radishes.

   Halve the limes.

   Strip the cilantro leaves from several sprigs.

2. When the grill or broiler is hot, sprinkle the steak all over with salt and pepper. Cook, turning once, until charred on both sides but still one shade pinker inside than you like it. Figure 2 to 5 minutes per side, depending on your grill or broiler; use a knife to nick and peek.

3. Transfer the meat to a cutting board to let it rest.

4. Wrap 8 tortillas in a damp paper towel and microwave for 15 seconds.

5. Slice the steak thinly against the grain. Assemble the tacos: steak first, then radishes and cilantro, then a squeeze of lime. Serve immediately.

VARIATIONS

14 Other Taco Fillings from Elsewhere in the Book

1. Broiled shrimp (page 110)
2. Broiled chicken (page 612)
3. Broiled fish (page 536)
4. Stir-fried tofu (page 636)
5. Fajita Peppers and Onions (page 928)
6. Jícama and Radish Salad (page 918)
7. Chile-Cumin Black Beans (page 973)
8. Avocado with Lemon and Salt (page 920)
9. Caprese Salad (page 922)
10. Sautéed Greens with Garlic (page 924)
11. Succotash (page 933)
12. Charred Brussels Sprout Salad with Walnuts and Gorgonzola (page 126)
13. Kimchi and Snow Pea Salad with Grilled or Broiled Beef (page 122)
14. Tortilla Scramble (page 842)

NOTES

IF YOU HAVE MORE TIME

Instead of microwaving the tortillas, put them, one at a time, directly on the gas burners on your stove. Cook until lightly charred on both sides, about 30 seconds total. Or, since you already have the grill or broiler going for the steak, char the tortillas on the grill or under the broiler.

ANYTHING TACOS

As you can see from the list—which could have been 10 times longer than it is—there are really no rules to what you can put in a taco. We think tacos should have Mexican flavors, because that's where they come from and that's what we're used to, but a tortilla is a blank canvas, one that accommodates any ingredients.

You might keep a stack of corn tortillas in your fridge all the time, because they're the perfect vehicle for all kinds of leftovers: cooked meat and fish, cooked vegetables and greens, raw salads, and bean dishes too. You've already put all of the work into the leftovers, so all you need to do is warm the tortillas and the filling, assemble the tacos, and maybe freshen them up a bit with some herbs or a drizzle of your favorite condiment on top. This way, tacos are never more than 5 minutes away.

SIDES

Ripe Plantains 960

White Rice 941

Jícama and Radish Salad 918

Chile-Cumin Black Beans 937

Avocado with Lime and Chili Salt 920

SPEED ◐ SERVES 4

Crisp Pork and Watermelon Tacos

The combination of crisp fatty pork and cool juicy watermelon needs nothing beyond a squeeze of lime for a garnish and a tortilla to wrap it all up. Crumbled queso fresco is a nice addition if you have it, as is a cold beer.

Ingredients

2 tablespoons vegetable oil

1 pound boneless pork shoulder

Salt and pepper

1 small seedless watermelon (you'll need only 2 cups)

1 garlic clove

1 teaspoon cumin

1 teaspoon chili powder

2 limes

Several sprigs fresh cilantro

8 corn tortillas

2 ounces queso fresco (½ cup crumbled; optional)

Prep | Cook

1. Put 2 tablespoons vegetable oil in a large skillet over medium-high heat.

   Cut the pork into thin strips about 2 inches long.

2. Add the pork to the skillet, sprinkle with salt and pepper, and cook, stirring occasionally until it begins to crisp, 6 to 8 minutes.

   Halve and peel the watermelon; chop the flesh into ½-inch chunks. Save 2 cups for the tacos and refrigerate the rest for another use.

   Peel and mince 1 garlic clove.

3. When the pork begins to crisp, stir in the garlic, 1 teaspoon cumin, and 1 teaspoon chili powder. Continue cooking, stirring occasionally until the spices are fragrant and the pork is crisp, 2 or 3 minutes.

   Halve the limes.

   Strip the cilantro leaves from several sprigs.

   Wrap 8 tortillas in a damp paper towel and microwave for 15 seconds.

   Crumble ½ cup queso fresco if you're using it.

4. When the pork is crisp all over, assemble the tacos: Put the pork in a tortilla, top with the watermelon and cilantro, and squeeze the lime juice over the top. Add queso fresco if you're using it and serve.

VARIATIONS

Crisp Pork and Peach Tacos
Substitute 2 cups chopped peaches (about 3) for the watermelon, smoked paprika for the cumin, and basil for the cilantro.

Crisp Pork and Apple Tacos
Use 2 cups chopped apples instead of the watermelon, 1 teaspoon chopped fresh sage instead of the cumin, and 1 teaspoon Dijon mustard instead of the chili powder. Use 1 lemon in place of the limes; skip the cilantro and queso fresco.

Crisp Chicken and Watermelon Tacos
Substitute 1 pound boneless, skinless chicken thighs for the pork.

NOTES

MAKE YOUR OWN

Chili Powder 758

EVEN FASTER
Use 8 slices bacon, chopped into 1-inch pieces, instead of the pork shoulder. It will begin to crisp a bit faster than the pork shoulder; when it does, add the garlic and just ½ teaspoon each of cumin and chili powder and continue until done. Drain the bacon on paper towels before assembling the tacos. The flavor will be different, smoky and unmistakably bacony, which is never a bad thing.

SIDES

White Rice 941

Mexican Street Corn 932

Chile-Cumin Black Beans 937

SPEED ◐ SERVES 4

Reuben with All the Trimmings

To make a Reuben from scratch without buying corned beef or pastrami at the deli or curing meat for days, you have to cheat. Cook some cabbage with vinegar for a kind of instant sauerkraut, then crisp thinly sliced beef in a skillet with lots of black pepper and coriander—the pastrami spices. Homemade Russian dressing makes it all work.

Ingredients

1 pound beef sirloin or rib-eye

4 tablespoons (½ stick) butter

1 small head green cabbage (you'll need only 2 cups shredded)

¼ cup cider vinegar

1 teaspoon sugar

Salt and pepper

2 tablespoons olive oil

8 ounces Swiss cheese (2 cups grated)

8 slices rye bread

1 teaspoon coriander

1 dill pickle

⅓ cup mayonnaise

2 tablespoons ketchup

Prep | Cook

Put the beef in the freezer. Take 4 tablespoons butter out of the refrigerator.

1. Put a large skillet over medium heat.

Cut the cabbage in half; trim and core 1 half; cut into shreds. You should end up with about 2 cups of shredded cabbage. Refrigerate the rest of the cabbage for another use.

2. Put the cabbage in the skillet with ¼ cup cider vinegar, ¼ cup water, 1 teaspoon sugar, and a sprinkle of salt and pepper.

3. Raise the heat to medium-high, cover, and cook, stirring once or twice until the cabbage is tender and the liquid is evaporated, 4 or 5 minutes.

Remove the beef from the freezer; slice it as thinly as you can.

4. When the cabbage is tender, transfer it to a bowl; wipe out the skillet and return it to medium-high heat.

5. Add 2 tablespoons olive oil and the beef to the skillet; sprinkle with salt and lots of pepper. Cook, stirring occasionally until it begins to brown, 4 or 5 minutes.

6. Turn the broiler to high; put the rack 6 inches from the heat.
   Slice 8 ounces Swiss cheese or grate 2 cups.
   Spread the butter on 8 slices rye bread.

7. When the beef begins to brown, stir in 1 teaspoon coriander and cook until it's fragrant, another minute or 2.

8. Assemble the sandwiches — first the cheese, then the beef, then the cabbage — so the buttered sides of the bread are facing out.

9. Put the sandwiches on a rimmed baking sheet and broil, turning once, until the bread is toasted on both sides and the cheese is melted, 2 or 3 minutes per side.
   Chop the pickle and put it in a small bowl. Add 1/3 cup mayonnaise, 2 tablespoons ketchup, and a sprinkle of salt and pepper. Stir to combine, taste, and adjust the seasoning.

10. When the sandwiches are toasted, remove them from the broiler and either open them up and spread the Russian dressing inside or serve it on the side for dipping.

VARIATIONS

Fast Rachel

With coleslaw instead of "sauerkraut." Instead of cooking the cabbage, combine it in a bowl with the vinegar, sugar, and Russian dressing ingredients. Toss to coat and let it sit while you do the rest of the cooking. You can broil it in the sandwiches if you like or put it on at the end.

NOTES

MAKE YOUR OWN

Mayonnaise 144

EVEN FASTER

With deli corned beef or pastrami and store-bought sauerkraut, this sandwich is a breeze.

SIDES

French Fries 963

Cucumber Salad 915

Tomato Salad 913

SPEED ◐ SERVES 4

Big T's Meat Sauce Sub

The long-gone much-missed Big T's sub shop in Cambridge, Massachusetts, sold this sub, which contained only the sauce used to bathe its meatballs, for a dollar back in the 1990s. It was brilliant and beloved and, strangely, better than Big T's sub with meatballs.

Ingredients

2 tablespoons olive oil

6 ounces ground beef

6 ounces ground pork

Salt and pepper

1 bunch fresh parsley

1 ounce Parmesan cheese (¼ cup grated)

8 ounces provolone cheese (2 cups grated)

One 14-ounce can crushed tomatoes

4 sub rolls

Prep | Cook

1. Put 2 tablespoons olive oil in a medium skillet over medium heat. Turn the broiler to high; put the rack 6 inches from the heat.
2. Put the ground beef and pork in the skillet and sprinkle with salt and pepper.

   Chop ¼ cup parsley and add it to the skillet.

   Grate ¼ cup Parmesan and add to the skillet.
3. Stir the meat to break it up a bit and combine all the ingredients. Cook, stirring once or twice, until the meat loses its pink color, 3 or 4 minutes.

   Slice 8 ounces provolone or grate 2 cups.
4. When the meat loses its pink color, add the crushed tomatoes and stir to combine. Adjust the heat so the mixture bubbles gently but steadily and simmer for 5 minutes, adding a splash of water if the mixture gets too thick.
5. Put the sub rolls on a rimmed baking sheet and broil until lightly toasted, 1 to 3 minutes.

   Remove them; leave the broiler on.

6. Once the sauce has simmered for 5 minutes, spoon it into the rolls. Top with the provolone, return the sandwiches to the broiler, and broil until the cheese is bubbly and brown. Serve immediately.

VARIATIONS

Vegetarian Sauce Sub

Substitute 1 medium onion and 1 large bell pepper, both chopped, for the beef and pork. Sauté the vegetables until they begin to soften, then add the tomatoes, parsley, and Parmesan and simmer until the vegetables are tender.

NOTES

EVEN FASTER

Skip browning the meat; add the crushed tomatoes to the skillet at the beginning, bring the sauce to a bubble, and let it simmer for 5 minutes.

Instead of using crushed tomatoes as described in Step 4, add about 2 cups Tomato Sauce (page 296).

IF YOU HAVE MORE TIME

Let the sauce simmer for 20 to 30 minutes; it will pick up a richer, meatier flavor in that time.

SIDES

Caprese Salad 922

Sautéed Greens with Garlic 924

Seared Broccoli or Cauliflower 925

Tender Vegetables 954

Cheat-a-Little Pizza

We associate pizza with being "fast" because it's most often delivered to our houses 30 minutes after we call to order it. Of course, making your own pizza dough from scratch is another story. It's not a particularly arduous process, but the dough does need time to rise.

I'm obviously a big proponent of making everything that you can at home, but the truth is that pizza dough is one of those things that you can buy at the store without sacrificing much quality. Look for dough that appears as if it's been made by a person. It's often sold in clear plastic bags or containers, already shaped into a ball, or frozen. Avoid the kind that comes in metal canisters. Or just ask your favorite pizza place if it will sell you some dough. I figure that 36 ounces serves 4 people generously. And leftovers are always welcome with homemade pizza.

Once you've got dough in hand, making pizza is fast; the slowest part is waiting for your oven to heat as high as it will go. While that's happening you shape the dough and prepare the toppings (see the list below for lots of ideas). As tempting as it may be, don't overload the pizza; if there's too much on top, the crust will not get crisp.

Since most people don't have pizza peels and pizza stones, the recipe here uses a rimmed baking sheet, but if you've got those things, use them.

Pizza

① Heat the Oven.

Heat the oven as high as it will go (at least 500°F is ideal). Grease a rimmed baking sheet with a little olive oil.

② Roll and Top the Crust.

Roll out 1 ball of premade pizza dough on a lightly floured surface and transfer it to the oiled baking sheet. Pizza dough is very springy. If it won't roll out, you can press it out with your fingers. Drizzle the top with a little olive oil (not too much) and sprinkle with salt and pepper. Spread about 2 cups tomato sauce almost all the way out to the edges. The crust can be as big as you want it to be, and don't worry if it's blob shaped; home cooks rarely get a pure rectangle or circle. Sprinkle 2 cups grated mozzarella over the top.

③ Bake the Pizza.

Put the baking sheet in the oven and cook until the crust is crisp and the cheese is bubbly and brown, 8 to 12 minutes, depending on the heat of your oven. Let the pizza rest for a minute or 2 before slicing, so you can cut through the cheese without its oozing off the pizza. Serve hot.

VARIATIONS

13 Pizza Toppings

Use any of the following, alone or in combination, in Step 2:

1. Torn basil leaves or any chopped fresh herbs
2. Minced garlic or chiles
3. Sliced raw onions, mushrooms, or peppers
4. Roasted red peppers (page 417)
5. Chopped pitted olives
6. Cooked bacon, sausage, ham, prosciutto, or salami
7. Pesto (page 285)
8. Caramelized onions (page 84)
9. Anchovies, capers, or dried tomatoes
10. Rinsed and dried tender greens, like arugula or spinach
11. Grated cheddar, provolone, Jack, or Parmesan cheese
12. Dollops of goat cheese or ricotta
13. Crumbled blue cheese or feta

SPEED ◐ SERVES 4

Steak Sandwich with Charred Onions

Charring onions doesn't require nearly as much time or finesse as caramelizing them, and with their smokiness and crunch they're actually preferable on a steak sandwich. Both the steak and onions cook over high heat, so now's the time to turn on your hood or open the windows, because it'll get a bit smoky.

Ingredients

1 tablespoon vegetable oil

1 pound beef sirloin or rib-eye

Salt and pepper

1 large onion

4 ciabatta rolls

⅓ cup mayonnaise

2 cups arugula

Prep | Cook

1. Turn the broiler to high; put the rack 6 inches from the heat. Put 1 tablespoon vegetable oil in a large skillet over high heat.

   Sprinkle the steak with salt and pepper.

2. When the oil is hot (nearly smoking), add the steak. Cook, turning once until charred on both sides but still a bit pinker inside than you like it. Figure 2 to 5 minutes per side; use a knife to nick and peek.

   Trim, peel, halve, and slice the onion.

3. When the steak is done, transfer it to a cutting board to rest.

4. Add the onion to the skillet and cook, stirring occasionally until it is soft and starting to blacken around the edges, 6 to 10 minutes.

5. Split the ciabatta rolls in half and broil until lightly toasted, 1 to 3 minutes.

6. When the rolls are toasted, remove them from the broiler. Spread ⅓ cup mayonnaise on the rolls; lay the arugula on top.
7. When the onions are starting to blacken around the edges, pile them onto the sandwiches.
8. Slice the steak across the grain and lay the slices on top of the onions. Sprinkle the steak with a little more salt and pepper if you like, close the sandwiches, and serve.

VARIATIONS

Steak Sandwich with Charred Scallions and Soy Mayo
Substitute 1 bunch scallions, cut into 2-inch pieces, for the onion. Mix 1 tablespoon soy sauce into the mayonnaise before spreading it on the bread.

Steak Sandwich with Warm Horseradish Mayo
Skip the charred onions. Combine the mayonnaise with 2 tablespoons prepared horseradish and spread it on the ciabatta before you toast it. Broil until the mayo starts to bubble and brown. Top with the arugula, steak, thinly sliced raw red onions, and sliced tomatoes.

NOTES

MAKE YOUR OWN
Mayonnaise 144

EVEN FASTER
Use a thin, quick-cooking cut of beef like skirt steak.

Use deli roast beef instead of steak.

SIDES

Green Salad 911

Creamed Spinach 936

French Fries 963

Broiled Cherry Tomatoes 931

SPEED SERVES 4

Curried Chicken Sandwich with Mango Chutney

Some chutneys take forever, but here you need only cook a little of the water out of the chopped mango to make it soft and luscious. While that's happening, boneless chicken thighs take a ride under the broiler.

Ingredients

¼ cup red wine vinegar

1 tablespoon honey

Salt

1 mango

1 small red onion

6 boneless, skinless chicken thighs (about 1 pound)

1 tablespoon vegetable oil

1 tablespoon curry powder

Pepper

Several sprigs fresh cilantro

Several sprigs fresh mint

½ cup Greek yogurt

Two 8-inch pitas with pockets

Olive oil for drizzling

Prep | Cook

1. Turn the broiler to high; put the rack 6 inches from the heat.
2. Put ¼ cup red wine vinegar, ¼ cup water, 1 tablespoon honey, and a sprinkle of salt in a small saucepan over medium-low heat.

   Cut the mango away from the pit; crosshatch through the flesh; turn each piece inside out; cut the pieces away from the skin.

   Trim, peel, and chop the onion.
3. Add the mango and onion to the liquid and adjust the heat so that it bubbles steadily but not rapidly. Cook, stirring occasionally, until the mango breaks down and the mixture turns into a thick sauce, 10 to 15 minutes.
4. Put the chicken thighs on a rimmed baking sheet; rub with 1 tablespoon vegetable oil and sprinkle all over with 1 tablespoon curry powder, salt, and pepper.
5. Broil the chicken, turning once, until lightly browned on both sides and just cooked through, 6 to 8 minutes per side.
6. Check on the chutney; if the mango hasn't broken down yet and the mixture looks too dry, add a splash of water.

Chop several sprigs cilantro; strip the mint leaves from several stems and chop; put them all in a small bowl.

Add ½ cup yogurt and a sprinkle of salt and pepper to the bowl; stir to combine, taste, and adjust the seasoning.

7. When the chicken is done, transfer it to a cutting board. Leave the broiler on.

8. Drizzle the pitas with olive oil (about ½ teaspoon per side) and rub them all over with your fingers. Sprinkle salt and pepper over all.

9. Broil the pitas, turning once, until browned (even slightly charred) on both sides, 2 to 5 minutes total.

   Cut the chicken into thick slices.

10. When the pitas are toasted, remove them from the broiler and spread the yogurt sauce inside the pockets. Lay the chicken slices on top, spoon the chutney over the chicken, and serve.

VARIATIONS

BBQ Chicken Sandwich with Peach Chutney
Substitute cider vinegar for the red wine vinegar and 2 peaches for the mango. Use paprika instead of the curry powder and your favorite barbecue sauce instead of the yogurt sauce.

Miso Chicken Sandwich with Pineapple Chutney
Swap 2 tablespoons fish sauce and the juice of 1 lime for the vinegar and 1 ½ cups chopped pineapple for the mango. Rub the chicken with miso paste instead of curry powder. Use ⅓ cup mayonnaise instead of the yogurt. Skip the mint and add a teaspoon or 2 of soy sauce (no need for salt).

NOTES

MAKE YOUR OWN
Curry Powder 758

EVEN FASTER
If you have room, broil the chicken and the pitas at the same time.

Instead of the chutney, just top the sandwich with thin slices of raw mango and red onion.

SIDES

Green Salad 911

Grape Salad with Mint 913

Peas with Ginger 934

SPEED SERVES 4

BBQ Chopped Pork and Slaw Sandwich

The process of making real pulled pork is "low and slow," where the meat is cooked at a very low temperature for a very long time. Consider this approach—chopped, spiced, seared, and quick-simmered—"high and fast." And here is one case where squishy white hamburger buns are really what you want.

Ingredients

1 small head green cabbage (you'll need 2 cups shredded)

2 tablespoons mayonnaise

3 tablespoons cider vinegar

1 teaspoon sugar

Salt and pepper

2 tablespoons vegetable oil

12 ounces pork shoulder

2 teaspoons chili powder

1 teaspoon paprika

1 teaspoon brown sugar

⅓ cup ketchup

2 teaspoons yellow mustard

1 tablespoon honey

4 hamburger buns

Prep | Cook

Cut the cabbage in half; trim and core 1 half; cut into shreds. You should end up with about 2 cups of shredded cabbage. Refrigerate the rest of the cabbage for another use.

1. Put the shredded cabbage in a medium bowl with 2 tablespoons mayonnaise, 2 tablespoons cider vinegar, 1 teaspoon sugar, and a sprinkle of salt and pepper. Toss and set aside.

2. Put 2 tablespoons vegetable oil in a large skillet over low heat.
   Cut the pork into roughly ¼-inch pieces.

3. Add the pork to the skillet and turn the heat to medium-high. Add 2 teaspoons chili powder, 1 teaspoon each paprika, brown sugar, and salt, and ½ teaspoon pepper. Cook, stirring occasionally until nicely browned, 6 to 10 minutes.

4. Turn the broiler to high; put the rack 6 inches from the heat.

5. When the pork is nicely browned, stir in ⅓ cup ketchup, 2 teaspoons mustard, 1 tablespoon honey, 1 tablespoon cider vinegar, and ½ cup water. Adjust the heat so the mixture simmers gently.

6. Cook, stirring occasionally until the pork is tender and the sauce reduces and just coats the meat (you don't want it too wet), about 10 minutes. Taste and adjust the seasoning, adding more salt or spices as you like.

7. While the pork cooks, split the buns in half and broil until lightly toasted, 1 to 3 minutes.

8. Pile the pork onto the toasted buns, top with the cabbage slaw, close the sandwiches, and serve.

NOTES

MAKE YOUR OWN

Mayonnaise 144

Chili Powder 758

EVEN FASTER

Instead of making the sauce as described in Step 5, add about ¾ cup Barbecue Sauce (page 145).

IF YOU HAVE MORE TIME

Let the pork simmer slowly in the sauce until it's very tender, up to an hour.

Let the cabbage marinate in the dressing in the refrigerator until it loses some of its crunch, up to a few hours.

SIDES

Mexican Street Corn 932

French Fries 963

Chile-Cumin Black Beans 937

Soups and Stews

Melon Gazpacho with Crisp Prosciutto 202

Green Gazpacho 204

Avocado Soup with Crab and Corn 206

Spicy Black Bean Soup 208

Bacon and Egg Drop Soup 210

Frozen Vegetable Soup 214

Provençal Tomato Soup with Fennel 216

Creamy Parsnip Soup with Parsley Pesto 218

Butternut Squash Soup with Apples and Bacon 220

Sweet Pea Soup with Crisp Ham 222

Tomato and Bread Soup with White Beans 224

Pasta e Fagioli 226

Chickpea and Couscous Stew with Moroccan Spices 228

Seafood Chowder 230

Miso Soup with Scallops, Soba, and Spinach 234

Fast Pho 236

Homemade Chicken Ramen 238

Chicken Tamale Soup 240

Spicy Peanut Soup with Chicken and Collards 242

Cabbage Soup with Smoked Sausage 244

Sausage, Cannellini, and Kale Soup 246

Broken Wonton Soup 248

Korean-Style Beef Soup with Rice 250

Thai Coconut Soup with Carrots and Beef 252

Lamb Stew with Green Beans and Tomatoes 254

Bone-In Chicken Noodle Soup 256

American Onion Soup 258

Shrimp Gumbo 260

Curried Chicken and Vegetable Soup with Rice 262

Mushroom and Chicken Stew with Dill and Paprika 264

Lentil Soup, with or Without Ham 266

Collard Greens Stewed with Smoked Pork 268

Hot and Sour Soup with Bok Choy and Pork 270

Beef and Butter Bean Chili 272

Soups and Stews

Soups and stews are fast and foolproof, the most basic of foods: You chop up some ingredients, maybe get them going in oil, chop up more stuff, add that, pour liquid over everything, crank the heat, and suddenly you have a pot of soup going. Really.

In fact the concept of cooking and prepping simultaneously is best illustrated with soups and stews. Whenever you have downtime you can turn your attention to prepping more food to drop into the pot. Or you can do something else: start a side dish, assemble a salad, make dessert.

Soups and stews give you plenty of leeway and put you in complete control of pacing. If you need more time to get other food ready, simmer slowly or even stop the cooking. If you're in a hurry, cook steadily. Your soup or stew will wait for you, and unlike cooking a perfect steak, there are few moments along the way in which the fate of the dish hangs in the balance of a few seconds or even a few minutes.

It gets even better: Want to vary textures and flavors? Wait until the last minute to stir in some vegetables, herbs, or seasonings. You added too much salt? Add more liquid. You overcooked the vegetables? Oh well: The soup is thicker. It's hard to make a "bad" soup or stew, but this chapter will show you that even great ones are easy to come by.

Chapter Highlights

Egg-Enriched Soup. Cooking eggs in broth is one of the best ways to turn soup into a hearty meal. Bacon and Egg Drop Soup (page 210).

Cold Vegetables, Hot Soup. Frozen vegetables are tailor-made for fast soups. Frozen Vegetable Soup (page 214).

Stocking Up. Store-bought stocks are expensive and not always good. To make your own, see page 212.

Nuts to Soup. Adding ground nuts gives soup instant richness and body. Green Gazpacho (page 204).

Easy Puréeing. Turn all sorts of vegetables into silky purées. Creamy Parsnip Soup with Parsley Pesto (page 218) and Butternut Squash Soup with Apples and Bacon (page 220).

Chopping Canned Tomatoes. Don't pour canned tomatoes on your cutting board to chop them; there's a better way. Canned Tomato Tricks (page 227).

One Method, Infinite Soups. A single formula of browning, boiling, and bubbling is a soup recipe for the rest of your life. Recipe-Free Soups (page 232).

Simmer Down Now. The pros and cons of long and short simmering and why your soup is done when you say it's done. The Time-Texture Continuum (page 215).

Mastering Miso. Learn about one of the world's most wonderful and underused ingredients. Miso Soup with Scallops, Soba, and Spinach (page 234).

Noodling with Soup. Save time (and pots) by cooking the noodles right in the broth. Homemade Chicken Ramen (page 238), Bone-In Chicken Noodle Soup (page 256), Broken Wonton Soup (page 248).

The Mushroom Myth. The "rule" that you can't rinse mushrooms is nonsense; don't let it slow you down: Mushroom and Chicken Stew with Dill and Paprika (page 264).

Caramelizing, Fast. Think it's impossible to caramelize onions quickly? Think again. American Onion Soup (page 258).

Cooling Down Quick. The fridge isn't the coldest appliance in your kitchen, so why use it to chill cold soups? Use the freezer. Melon Gazpacho with Crisp Prosciutto (page 202) and Green Gazpacho (page 204).

SPEED SERVES 4

Melon Gazpacho with Crisp Prosciutto

Tomatoes are a fruit, so it's natural to play with other juicy summertime favorites in this classic cold soup. Prosciutto adds a pleasant saltiness and crisp texture and turns this colorful dish into a light meal. And the trick to quick chilling: ice cubes.

Ingredients

5 tablespoons olive oil, plus more for garnish

4 ounces sliced prosciutto

1 garlic clove

Any large melon or small seedless watermelon (2 pounds)

3 large ripe tomatoes (1½ pounds)

1 bunch fresh basil for garnish

2 tablespoons sherry vinegar, or to taste

Salt and pepper

Ice cubes

Prep | Cook

1. Put 1 tablespoon olive oil in a medium skillet over medium-low heat.

   Chop the prosciutto into small pieces.

2. When the oil is warm, add the prosciutto to the skillet and cook, stirring occasionally, until crisp, 5 to 10 minutes.

   Line a plate with paper towels.

   Peel 1 garlic clove and put it in a food processor or blender. Pulse once or twice to chop.

   Halve the melon, remove any seeds, and scoop the flesh into the food processor or blender.

   Core and quarter the tomatoes.

   Strip ½ cup basil leaves from the stems and chop.

3. When the prosciutto is crisp, transfer it to the paper towels with a slotted spoon.

4. Add the tomatoes to the melon mixture, along with 2 tablespoons sherry vinegar, 4 tablespoons olive oil, and a sprinkle of salt and pepper.

5. Let the machine run if you want a smooth gazpacho or pulse if you want it chunky, adding ice cubes one at a time until you get the consistency you like and scraping down the sides if necessary. Taste and adjust the seasoning and divide among 4 bowls. Garnish with the prosciutto, basil, and a drizzle of olive oil and serve.

VARIATIONS

Cucumber Gazpacho with Crisp Prosciutto
Closer to classic: Instead of the melon, peel and seed 2 medium cucumbers; cut 1 red bell pepper and 1 small red onion into chunks. Tear 2 slices crusty white bread into pieces. Add the vegetables and bread with the tomatoes in Step 4.

Tomato and Peach Gazpacho with Crisp Bacon
Use bacon instead of prosciutto, peaches instead of the melon, and balsamic instead of sherry vinegar.

Gazpacho with Goat Cheese
Works for any of the recipes here: Skip the prosciutto if you like. Crumble 1 cup (about 8 ounces) goat cheese over the top just before serving.

NOTES

IF YOU HAVE MORE TIME
Chill the gazpacho in the freezer for a few minutes or in the fridge for 2 to 6 hours before serving.

SIDES

Bruschetta 909

Warm Flour or Corn Tortillas 907

Fennel Salad 917

SPEED  SERVES 4

Green Gazpacho

This vibrant green gazpacho is way more interesting than its better-known cousin. Tangy with grapes and rich with avocados and nuts, it's a refreshing soup with just the right amount of heft. And though it's best in late summer, you can vary it for winter.

Ingredients

1 garlic clove

1 medium cucumber

3 medium avocados (1 ½ pounds)

1 bunch fresh cilantro

1 pound seedless green grapes

2 slices rustic white bread

4 ounces manchego or feta cheese (optional)

½ cup almonds

2 tablespoons olive oil, plus more for garnish

2 tablespoons sherry vinegar

Salt and pepper

Ice cubes

Prep | Cook

As you work, put everything into a blender:

Peel and chop 1 garlic clove.

Trim the cucumber and peel if necessary; cut it in half lengthwise and scoop out the seeds with a spoon; cut into large chunks.

Halve and pit the avocados; scoop out the flesh.

Pull ½ cup cilantro sprigs from the bunch.

Pluck the grapes from the stems.

1. Turn the machine on, adding a little cold water to get it going, and blend until there is enough room to add more ingredients.

   Tear 2 slices bread into a few pieces and add.

   Shave the manchego into thin ribbons with a vegetable peeler or crumble the feta if you're using cheese (but don't add it yet).

2. Add ½ cup almonds, 2 tablespoons olive oil, 2 tablespoons sherry vinegar, and a sprinkle of salt and pepper to the ingredients in the blender.

3. Pulse the machine to combine the ingredients, then blend, adding ice cubes one at a time (or small amounts of cold water) until the soup is smooth and thin enough to pour. Taste and adjust the seasoning.

4. Divide the soup among 4 bowls. Scatter the cheese over the top, if you're using it, along with a drizzle of olive oil, and serve.

VARIATIONS

Spicy Green Gazpacho with Chile and Lime
Use lime juice instead of the sherry vinegar and skip the cheese. Remove the stem (and seeds if you'd like) from a jalapeño or serrano chile and add it to the blender in Step 1.

Grapefruit Gazpacho
Use mint instead of cilantro. Substitute 3 grapefruits for the grapes; peel and chop them and remove the seeds before adding them to the blender. Sweeten the gazpacho with a little honey if you'd like.

NOTES

IF YOU HAVE MORE TIME
Chill the gazpacho in the freezer for a few minutes or in the fridge for 2 to 6 hours before serving.

SIDES

Bruschetta 909

Jícama and Radish Salad 918

Ripe Plantains with Smoked Paprika 960

SPEED ◔ SERVES 4

Avocado Soup with Crab and Corn

One of the all-time best combinations—avocados, crab, and corn—makes a soup that's creamy, crunchy, rich, briny, and beautifully colored. If you substitute good store-bought chips (see Notes) you don't even have to turn on the stove.

Ingredients

3 medium avocados (1 ½ pounds)

1 lime

3 cups milk

½ teaspoon chili powder, or more to taste

Salt

2 ears fresh corn

Vegetable oil for frying

8 small (4-inch) corn tortillas

2 cups lump crabmeat (about 1 pound)

4 scallions

Hot sauce

Pepper

Prep | Cook

Halve the avocados and the lime.

Pit the avocados and scoop the flesh into a blender.

1. Add 3 cups milk, ½ teaspoon chili powder, and a sprinkle of salt to the blender. Squeeze in the juice of half of the lime; reserve the rest.
2. Purée until smooth, then put the blender in the freezer. If the blender won't fit, transfer the soup to a container that will.

   Husk the corn and cut the kernels off the cobs.
3. Put ½ inch vegetable oil in a large skillet over medium heat.

   Cut the tortillas in half, stack the halves, and cut into thin strips.

   Line a plate with paper towels.
4. When the oil is hot (try a tortilla strip; it will sizzle), add the tortilla strips. Cook, stirring constantly, until they are golden brown and crisp, 1 to 2 minutes. Transfer the strips to the paper towels with a slotted spoon and sprinkle with salt.

   Pick through the crabmeat, discarding any pieces of shell or cartilage.

   Trim and chop the scallions.

5. Put the crab, corn, and scallions in a medium mixing bowl. Squeeze in the juice of the remaining ½ lime, add a dash of hot sauce, sprinkle with salt, and toss to combine.

6. Retrieve the avocado soup from the freezer, taste, and adjust the seasoning. Divide the soup among 4 large bowls. Top each with the crab mixture and tortilla strips, sprinkle with pepper, and serve immediately.

VARIATIONS

Avocado Soup with Crab and Daikon
Substitute 1 tablespoon soy sauce for the chili powder (go easy on the salt). Slice and fry 4 egg roll wrappers instead of the tortillas and substitute 1 small daikon radish, peeled and shredded, for the corn.

NOTES

MAKE YOUR OWN
Chili Powder 758

EVEN FASTER
You can use frozen corn kernels here, although it will taste like cooked, not raw, corn and lack the crunch and sweetness of the fresh stuff in season. A better way to save time is to crumble store-bought tortilla chips over the soup instead of frying your own.

IF YOU HAVE MORE TIME
Halve 1 pint cherry tomatoes and scatter them on top of the crab before serving.

SHUCKING CORN
Don't mess around: Yank down on the husks and tear them off quickly, then rub the cob under running water to rinse and pull the silk free. To strip corn kernels from the cob, hold the cob firmly from the top, with the bottom resting in a stable position. Cut downward with a paring or chef's knife to scrape off kernels; turn the corn and repeat all the way around. (See the illustrations on page 32.)

SIDES

Chopped Salad 912

Jícama and Radish Salad 918

Chile-Cumin Black Beans 937

SPEED SERVES 4

Spicy Black Bean Soup

With canned or precooked beans, you can make an authentic, bold-flavored black bean soup in 15 minutes. If you use canned beans, rinse them thoroughly before adding.

Ingredients

2 tablespoons olive oil

1 large onion

2 garlic cloves

1 chipotle chile (or more) in adobo

1 tablespoon cumin

4 cups cooked or canned black beans (two 15-ounce cans)

4 cups chicken or vegetable stock or water

Salt and pepper

Several sprigs fresh cilantro for garnish

1 lime

Sour cream for garnish

Prep | Cook

1. Put 2 tablespoons olive oil in a large pot over medium heat.
   Trim, peel, and chop the onion.

2. Add the onion to the oil and cook, stirring occasionally until softened, 3 to 5 minutes.
   Peel and mince 2 garlic cloves; add them to the pot and stir.
   Chop 1 (or more) chipotle and add it to the pot with a little of its adobo sauce and 1 tablespoon cumin and stir.
   If you're using canned beans, drain and rinse them.

3. Add the beans, 4 cups stock or water, and a sprinkle of salt and pepper to the pot. Raise the heat to high and bring the soup to a boil, then turn the heat down to medium-low, cover, and simmer until the beans begin to break down, 5 to 10 minutes.
   Chop several sprigs cilantro.
   Halve the lime.

4. When the beans are beginning to break down, run a potato masher or immersion blender through the pot, just enough to mash or purée about half of the beans.

5. Squeeze in the lime juice. Taste and adjust the seasoning, divide among 4 bowls, garnish with the cilantro and a dollop of the sour cream, and serve.

VARIATIONS

Smoky Black Bean Soup
Instead of the chipotle, add 2 teaspoons smoked paprika along with the cumin in Step 2.

White Bean Soup with Rosemary and Lemon
Omit the cumin. Substitute a lemon for the lime. Instead of the chipotle, add 1 tablespoon chopped fresh rosemary leaves with the garlic in Step 2. Use parsley or basil instead of cilantro and a drizzle of olive oil instead of lime.

Minty Fava Bean Soup
Skip the chipotle and cumin. Substitute frozen green fava beans for the black beans, lemon for the lime, and mint for the cilantro. Garnish with crème fraîche or a drizzle of olive oil instead of sour cream.

NOTES

MAKE YOUR OWN

Cooked Beans 496

Chicken Stock 213

Vegetable Stock 212

EVEN FASTER
If you've got precooked beans in the fridge or freezer—black or any kind really—this soup is a little faster and way better. No need to drain them; you can (and should) include some of the cooking liquid; reduce the amount of stock to compensate.

IF YOU HAVE MORE TIME
The longer you let the soup simmer, the more the flavors will develop. Up to an hour is fine; just add more liquid if the soup starts to look dry.

SIDES

Warm Tortillas 907

Cucumber Salad with Hot Sauce and Lime Juice 915

Coleslaw 923

SPEED ◔ SERVES 4

Bacon and Egg Drop Soup

Eggs are naturally fast cooking. Use this technique from the Chinese dish and you magically get gorgeous flowerlike petals in every bite. And it works with nontraditional flavors too.

Ingredients

8 slices bacon

6 cups any stock

Salt and pepper

4 eggs

Several sprigs fresh parsley for garnish

4 ounces Parmesan cheese (1 cup grated)

Prep | Cook

1. Put a large pot over medium heat.

   Chop the bacon into 1-inch pieces.

2. Add the bacon to the pot. Cook, stirring occasionally until crisp, 5 to 10 minutes.

   Line a plate with paper towels.

3. Transfer the bacon to the paper towels with a slotted spoon and pour off all but 1 tablespoon of the fat.

4. Put 6 cups stock in the pot and raise the heat to high. Add a sprinkle of salt (if the stock needs it) and pepper.

   Crack the eggs into a liquid measuring cup (or medium pitcher) and beat them lightly.

   Strip the parsley leaves from several sprigs and chop.

   Grate 1 cup Parmesan cheese.

5. When the stock is bubbling gently, slowly pour in the eggs, stirring constantly, so that they cook softly and appear as silky flowerlike strands; don't let them overheat and curdle. Remove from the heat; taste and adjust the seasoning.

6. Divide the soup among 4 bowls. Sprinkle each with Parmesan and bacon, garnish with the parsley, and serve.

VARIATIONS

Classic Egg Drop Soup
Better than takeout: Go easy on the salt; omit the bacon and parsley and substitute 4 chopped scallions for the cheese. Stir in 2 tablespoons soy sauce and 1 tablespoon sesame oil after the eggs in Step 5 and garnish with the scallions. Add tofu cubes or cooked chicken or pork to make the soup more substantial.

Bacon and Egg Drop Soup with Greens
Skip the parsley. Before adding the eggs in Step 5, stir in 4 cups chopped or baby spinach leaves; let them cook while the stock returns to a gentle bubble, then stir in the eggs and finish the soup.

Toast, Bacon, and Egg Drop Soup
While the bacon cooks in Step 2, toast 4 thick slices of any bread. Put the toast in each bowl before adding the soup and garnishing.

Carbonara Soup
Two or 3 cups leftover plain or lightly sauced pasta is perfect here; add it to the stock after the eggs cook—but before you take the soup off the heat—in Step 5. If you don't have any handy, boil 12 ounces any pasta in salted water until tender but not mushy, 8 to 12 minutes; start the recipe while it cooks. Use pancetta instead of bacon. Drain the pasta and divide it among the bowls before serving and garnishing the soup.

NOTES

MAKE YOUR OWN

Chicken Stock 213

Vegetable Stock 212

TURNING EGGS INTO FLOWER PETALS
To get eggs to this ideal texture, the temperature of the stock needs to remain consistent even as you add the cool eggs. So adjust the heat to maintain a steady but gentle bubble and then add the eggs in a slow, steady stream, using a container with a pour spout. Too fast and they will drop the temperature of the stock and simply thicken the soup without forming strands; too hot and they'll curdle like scrambled eggs. Either way, the soup will still be delicious, just not as beautiful.

SIDES

Bruschetta 909

Warm Buttery Bread 906

Green Salad 911

Tomato Salad 913

Fast Stocks

Here are recipes for five different fast-but-good stocks. The vegetable and chicken stock recipes yield about 12 cups; beef about 14 cups; fish 4 cups; and dashi 8. You can always cook larger quantities and store some for later. Either keep the stock in the refrigerator and use it within a few days or freeze it in convenient-sized containers (like pints or quarts) or in ice cube trays, which lets you use a few tablespoons at a time. Frozen stock will keep for months.

Vegetable Stock

1 Prepare the Vegetables

Slice or chop the following ingredients and put them in a stockpot as they're ready: 4 large carrots, 2 large onions (leave the skin on), 1 large potato, 2 celery stalks, 5 or 6 garlic cloves (leave the skin on), 15 button mushrooms, 2 medium tomatoes, and 15 parsley stems.

2 Simmer

Add some black pepper and 14 cups water. Bring to a boil, then adjust the heat so the mixture bubbles gently but steadily. Cook until the vegetables are tender, 30 to 60 minutes. The longer it goes, the deeper the flavor.

3 Strain

Cool the mixture slightly, then strain it, pressing on the vegetables to extract as much liquid as possible.

Beef Stock

1 Combine the Ingredients

Rinse 3 to 4 pounds meaty beef bones like shin or oxtail under cold water; combine them in a stockpot with 2 medium onions, roughly chopped (leave the skin on), 2 medium carrots, cut into chunks, 2 celery stalks, cut into chunks, 1 bay leaf, 1 teaspoon salt, and 10 peppercorns. Add 16 cups water (or enough to cover by a couple inches).

2 Simmer

Bring almost to a boil, then partially cover and adjust the heat so the mixture sends up a few bubbles at a time. Cook, skimming off the foam that accumulates on top, for 2 to 3 hours.

3 Strain

Cool the mixture slightly, then strain it, pressing on the bones and vegetables to extract as much liquid as possible. Discard the solids and season the stock to taste.

Chicken Stock

1 Prepare the Chicken

Cut a 3- to 4-pound chicken into parts (or buy it precut if you like). Don't forget the back and neck (and feet if you can get 'em.) You can also leave the chicken whole, but it will take a little longer to cook; or you can use specific parts: wings and/or legs are the best common ones.

2 Combine and Simmer

Put the chicken in a stockpot along with 1 halved large onion (leave the skin on), 1 large carrot (cut into chunks), 1 celery stalk (cut into chunks), 1 bay leaf, salt, and pepper. Add 14 cups water and bring to a boil, then lower the heat so the mixture sends up just a few bubbles at a time. Cook, skimming any foam that accumulates on the surface, until the chicken is done, 30 to 60 minutes (depending on how big it is and whether it's cut up).

3 Strain

Cool the mixture slightly, then strain it, pressing on the chicken and vegetables to extract as much liquid as possible. Remove the chicken and save the meat for chicken salad or the like; discard the remaining solids and season the stock to taste.

Fish Stock

1 Combine the Ingredients

In a stockpot, combine 1 medium onion, roughly chopped (leave the skin on), 1 carrot, cut into chunks, 1 celery stalk, cut into chunks, ½ cup white wine, 1 pound bones and/or cleaned head from a white fish, and 1 bay leaf.

2 Simmer

Add 4 cups water and bring nearly to a boil, then adjust the heat so the mixture sends up just a few bubbles at a time. Cook for about 30 minutes.

3 Strain

Cool the mixture slightly, then strain it, pressing on the fish and vegetables to extract as much liquid as possible.

Dashi

1 Simmer Kelp

Combine one 4- to 6-inch piece dried kelp (kombu) and 8 cups water in a medium saucepan over medium heat. Don't let the mixture come to a boil; as soon as it's about to, turn off the heat and remove the kelp (you can slice it up for salads or stir-fries if you like).

2 Add Bonito Flakes

Add ½ to 1 cup dried bonito flakes and stir; let the mixture sit for a few minutes, then strain.

SPEED ◐ SERVES 4

Frozen Vegetable Soup

Minimally processed and flash-frozen right after harvest, frozen vegetables are a real anomaly in the frozen-food aisle (see page 19). They're a true gift to hurried cooks, and this recipe coaxes out every bit of flavor from any vegetable.

Ingredients

¼ cup olive oil, plus more for drizzling

1 large onion

Salt and pepper

2 garlic cloves

8 cups any chopped frozen vegetables

6 cups chicken or vegetable stock or water

Prep | Cook

1. Put ¼ cup olive oil in a large pot over medium-high heat.

   Trim, peel, and chop the onion; add it to the pot, sprinkle with salt and pepper, and stir.

   Peel and mince 2 garlic cloves; add them to the pot and stir.

2. Cook, stirring occasionally until the onion softens, 3 to 5 minutes.

   Organize the packages of vegetables on your counter from the firmest, longest cooking—like squash or shell beans—to the most tender, quickest cooking, like spinach and other greens.

3. When the onion mixture is soft, start adding the vegetables, firmest first, stirring occasionally until they thaw and begin to get tender. (Timing will depend on the vegetable; keep an eye on the pot and test frequently.)

4. Continue adding and stirring, adjusting the heat to prevent burning, until the vegetables in the pot begin to brown in places and become almost as soft as you like.

5. Add 6 cups stock or water, raise the heat to high, and cook, stirring once or twice, until the soup just comes to a boil. Taste and adjust the seasoning, divide among 4 bowls, and serve.

VARIATIONS

Creamy Frozen Vegetable Soup
When the soup is ready, turn off the heat and purée, using an immersion or upright blender. Add 1 cup cream if you'd like. Reheat before serving.

Hearty Frozen Vegetable Soup
More substantial, and won't take more time if you have any of these ingredients handy: Add cooked chicken, beans (page 496), White Rice (page 941), or Buttered Egg Noodles (page 948) just before serving.

6 Ways to Flavor Frozen Vegetable Soup

1. 1 tablespoon chili powder (with the onion and garlic)
2. The zest of 1 lemon or lime (with the onion and garlic)
3. One 28-ounce can whole peeled or diced tomatoes (with the first vegetables; reduce the stock to 4 cups)
4. 1 tablespoon chopped fresh rosemary, sage, thyme, or oregano (with the last vegetables)
5. 1 cup any grated or crumbled cheese (for garnish)
6. ½ cup chopped fresh parsley, basil, cilantro, or dill (for garnish)

NOTES

MAKE YOUR OWN

Chicken Stock 213

Vegetable Stock 212

IF YOU HAVE MORE TIME
If you've got time to prepare fresh vegetables, go for it. The same technique will work perfectly. Trim and chop whatever vegetables you'd like, then organize and cook them as described.

THE TIME-TEXTURE CONTINUUM
You decide how long your soup cooks based on how much of a hurry you're in and how tender (or not) you like your vegetables. Remember that vegetables release starch and break down as they cook, which thickens soups. Sometimes it's worth an extra 10, 20, 30 minutes for a richer texture and deeper flavor.

SIDES

Garlic Bread 906

Green Salad 911

Bruschetta 909

Warm Buttery Bread 906

SPEED ◐ SERVES 4

Provençal Tomato Soup with Fennel

Fennel, olives, rosemary, and orange zest are four ingredients with punch. If you don't have all four of these or you want to make the soup even more substantial, see the list that follows.

Ingredients

3 tablespoons olive oil, plus more for garnish

1 large onion

2 garlic cloves

Salt and pepper

2 medium fennel bulbs

⅔ cup any olives

2 sprigs fresh rosemary

1 orange

1 tablespoon tomato paste

One 28-ounce can diced tomatoes

4 cups vegetable or chicken stock or water

Prep | Cook

1. Put 3 tablespoons olive oil in a large pot over low heat.

   Trim, peel, and chop the onion; add it to the pot.

   Peel and mince 2 garlic cloves; add them to the pot. Sprinkle with salt and pepper.

2. When the onion and garlic start to sizzle, raise the heat to medium and cook, stirring occasionally until they begin to soften and color, 5 to 10 minutes.

   Trim and chop the fennel bulbs, saving a few of the fronds for garnish.

3. Add the fennel to the pot and cook, stirring occasionally until the fennel begins to soften, 3 to 5 minutes.

   Pit ⅔ cup olives if necessary and chop them up a bit.

   Strip the rosemary leaves from 2 sprigs and chop.

   Grate 1 tablespoon zest from the orange; refrigerate the remaining fruit for another use.

4. Add 1 tablespoon tomato paste to the fennel and cook, stirring constantly until it darkens slightly, a minute or 2.

5. Add the olives, rosemary, and zest and cook, stirring until fragrant, less than a minute.

6. Add the tomatoes and their juice and scrape any browned bits off the bottom of the pot. Add 4 cups stock or water and raise the heat to high.

7. When the soup comes to a boil, adjust the heat so it bubbles gently but steadily and cook, stirring once in a while until the tomatoes break down, 5 to 10 minutes.

   Chop the reserved fennel fronds.

8. Taste and adjust the seasoning and divide the soup among 4 bowls. Garnish with the fennel fronds, drizzle with more olive oil, and serve.

VARIATIONS

Provençal Tomato Soup with Fennel and Shrimp
In Step 7, after the tomatoes break down, add 1 pound peeled shrimp to the pot, raise the heat a bit, and cook, stirring constantly until the shrimp turn pink and are cooked through, 2 or 3 minutes; garnish and serve.

Provençal Tomato Soup with Fennel and Fish
One pound of any 1-inch-thick sturdy white fish fillets—like bass, catfish, or halibut—will work. In Step 7, after about 5 minutes of cooking, lay the fish on top of the soup and cover the pot. Cook undisturbed until it flakes easily with a fork, 3 to 5 minutes. Stir the fish into the soup; garnish and serve.

Provençal Tomato Soup with Fennel and Squid
While the soup is cooking in Step 7, rinse 1 pound squid, cut crosswise into rings, and cut the tentacles free. When the soup is ready, add the squid to the pot, raise the heat a bit, and cook, stirring constantly until the rings and tentacles turn white and are just cooked through, 2 or 3 minutes; garnish and serve.

NOTES

MAKE YOUR OWN

Vegetable Stock 212

Chicken Stock 213

IF YOU HAVE MORE TIME
The longer you let this soup simmer, the more the flavors will develop. Any time up to an hour is fine; just add more liquid if the soup starts to look dry.

SIDES

Crisp Roasted Potatoes 965

Boiled Potatoes 954

Warm Buttery Bread 906

Bruschetta 909

Green Salad 911

SPEED ◐ SERVES 4

Creamy Parsnip Soup with Parsley Pesto

Vegetables that will be puréed need to be cooked until very soft. If you cut them into chunks, getting there can take 20 minutes, even longer. But grated, they're ready in a flash.

Ingredients

2 tablespoons butter

1 medium onion

4 or 5 large parsnips (1 ½ pounds)

Salt and pepper

6 cups vegetable or chicken stock or water

1 bunch fresh parsley

1 garlic clove

⅓ cup pine nuts

3 tablespoons olive oil

Prep | Cook

1. Put 2 tablespoons butter in a large pot over medium-low heat.

   Trim, peel, and chop the onion.

2. When the butter starts to foam, add the onion and cook, stirring occasionally until it softens, 10 to 15 minutes.

   Trim and peel the parsnips. If you're using a food processor, cut them into chunks that will fit through the feed tube.

   Grate the parsnips in a food processor with a grating disk or by hand with a box grater.

3. Raise the heat to high. Add the parsnips, a sprinkle of salt and pepper, and 6 cups stock or water. Bring to a boil, then reduce the heat so that it bubbles gently but steadily and cook until the parsnips are tender, 5 to 10 minutes.

   Chop 1 cup parsley.

   Peel and mince 1 garlic clove.

   Roughly chop ⅓ cup pine nuts.

4. Combine the parsley, garlic, pine nuts, 3 tablespoons olive oil, and a sprinkle of salt and pepper in a small mixing bowl. Mash and stir with a fork against the sides of the bowl until the pesto becomes a loose paste.

5. Turn off the heat under the soup and run an immersion blender through the pot or, working in batches, transfer it to an upright blender and carefully purée.

6. Reheat the soup for 1 or 2 minutes if necessary. Taste and adjust the seasoning. Divide the soup among 4 bowls, spoon the pesto over the top, and serve.

VARIATIONS

Creamy Asparagus Soup with Rustic Mint Pesto
Perfect for spring. Use asparagus, cut into 1-inch pieces, instead of the parsnips (they might take half the time to cook) and mint instead of parsley.

Creamy Potato Soup with Rustic Chive Pesto
Substitute potatoes for the parsnips and chives for the parsley. Double the cooking time in Step 3.

Creamy Celery Root Soup with Rustic Cilantro Pesto
Substitute celery root for the parsnips, one 14-ounce can coconut milk for 1 ½ cups of the stock, and cilantro for the parsley. Use 1 inch fresh ginger instead of garlic and cashews in place of the pine nuts. Instead of olive oil, use 2 tablespoons sesame oil and 1 tablespoon vegetable oil.

NOTES

MAKE YOUR OWN

Vegetable Stock 212

Chicken Stock 213

EVEN FASTER
Don't purée. Or if you don't have a blender but want the soup a little smoother, run a potato masher through the pot a few times.

If you have traditional basil pesto already made, bring it to room temperature, skip Step 4, and use it to top the finished soup. (See page 284 for a recipe.)

IF YOU HAVE MORE TIME
Toast the pine nuts in a dry skillet over medium heat, shaking the pan frequently until they're fragrant and lightly browned, 3 or 4 minutes. Pine nuts burn easily, so keep an eye on them.

SIDES

Green Salad 911

Warm Buttery Bread 906

Asparagus Gratin 929

SPEED ◐ SERVES 4

Butternut Squash Soup with Apples and Bacon

This soup has it all: It's sweet, colorful, and creamy and even features the smoky crunch of bacon on top. The most time-consuming thing about preparing squash is peeling and seeding it (see the Notes for the speediest options).

Ingredients

8 slices bacon

1 medium butternut squash (1 ½ pounds)

2 large apples

1 small onion

1 teaspoon allspice

¼ teaspoon cayenne

Salt and pepper

5 cups chicken or vegetable stock or water

1 cup cream

Prep | Cook

1. Put a large pot over medium heat.

   Chop 8 slices bacon into 1-inch pieces.

2. Add the bacon to the pot. Cook, stirring occasionally, until crisp, 5 to 10 minutes.

   Line a plate with paper towels.

   Cut the squash in half crosswise; peel and trim it, and scoop out the seeds. Cut it into chunks that will fit through the feed tube of a food processor.

   Peel, quarter, and core the apples.

   Trim, peel, and quarter the onion.

3. When the bacon is crisp, transfer it to the paper towels with a slotted spoon. Turn the heat to low.

   Shred the vegetables and fruit in a food processor with a grating disk; empty the work bowl into the pot as it fills.

4. Raise the heat to medium-high. Add 1 teaspoon allspice, ¼ teaspoon cayenne, and a sprinkle of salt and pepper. Cook, stirring, until the spices are fragrant, about a minute.

5. Add 5 cups stock or water and 1 cup cream. Bring to a boil, reduce the heat so that it bubbles gently but steadily, and cook until the squash is fully tender, 10 to 15 minutes.

6. Turn off the heat under the soup and run an immersion blender through the pot or, working in batches, transfer it to an upright blender and carefully purée.

7. Reheat the soup for 1 or 2 minutes if necessary. Taste and adjust the seasoning. Divide the soup among 4 bowls, garnish with the bacon, and serve.

VARIATIONS

Sweet Potato Soup with Pears and Bacon
Substitute sweet potatoes for the squash and pears for the apples.

Pumpkin Soup with Apples and Pumpkin Seeds
A lovely Thanksgiving starter: Substitute pumpkin for the squash. In Step 2, instead of the bacon, cook ½ cup hulled pumpkin seeds in 3 tablespoons olive oil until golden and popping, 3 to 5 minutes. Remove them from the pot and remove the pot from the heat until you grate the vegetables and fruit, then proceed with Step 4.

NOTES

MAKE YOUR OWN

Chicken Stock 213

Vegetable Stock 212

EVEN FASTER
Once the squash is soft, leave the texture as is. Or if you don't have a blender and want the soup a little smoother, run a potato masher through the pot a few times.

PEELING BUTTERNUT SQUASH
Butternut and other winter squash have very tough skins. There are two ways to prepare them: Cut the squash in half around the equator, stabilize the flat side on a cutting board, and work downward with a chef's or paring knife to slice the skin from the flesh, turning the piece as you work, then trim off the ends. (See the illustrations on page 29 for more details.) Or if you've got a sharp and sturdy vegetable peeler, remove the skin from the whole squash, working from top to bottom. The top half of the squash should be pure meat; scoop out the seeds from the bottom half and you're done.

SIDES

Warm Buttery Bread 906

Green Salad 911

Fennel Salad 917

SPEED ◐ SERVES 4

Sweet Pea Soup with Crisp Ham

This soup is brighter and faster than its split pea counterpart, and since the ham isn't cooked in the liquid, it provides contrasting textures. It takes a fair amount of fat to get ham crisp, so if your ham is lean, double the amount of olive oil in Step 3.

Ingredients

2 medium leeks

2 tablespoons butter

Several sprigs fresh tarragon

5 cups chicken or vegetable stock or water

1 tablespoon olive oil

8 ounces sliced ham

Two 10-ounce bags frozen peas

1 cup cream

Salt and pepper

Prep | Cook

Trim the leeks; slice the white and light green parts only.

1. Put 2 tablespoons butter in a large pot over medium heat. When it foams, add the leeks and cook, stirring occasionally until they're soft, 3 to 5 minutes. Do not brown.

   Strip the leaves from several sprigs tarragon and chop.

2. When the leeks are soft, add 5 cups stock or water and raise the heat to high.

3. Put 1 tablespoon olive oil in a medium skillet over medium-high heat.

   Cut the ham into thin strips.

4. When the oil is hot, add the ham and cook, stirring occasionally until crisp, 3 to 5 minutes.

   Line a plate with paper towels.

5. When the stock comes to a boil, add the peas and cook, stirring occasionally until tender, 3 to 5 minutes.

6. When the ham is crisp, transfer it to the paper towels.

7. Add the tarragon and 1 cup cream to the pot along with a sprinkle of salt and pepper; turn off the heat. Run an immersion blender through the pot or, working in batches, transfer the soup to an upright blender and carefully purée. Reheat the soup for 1 or 2 minutes if necessary.

8. Taste and adjust the seasoning and divide the soup among 4 bowls. Garnish with the ham and serve.

VARIATIONS

Minty Pea Soup with Crisp Ham
Super fresh tasting. Use ½ cup fresh mint leaves instead of tarragon.

Tangy Pea Soup with Crisp Ham
Use crème fraîche instead of cream.

Ginger Carrot Soup with Crisp Ham
Omit the tarragon. Use frozen carrots instead of the peas (or fresh carrots, peeled and chopped, and double the cooking time). Peel and chop 2 inches fresh ginger. When you cook the ham in Step 4, add the ginger to the pot.

NOTES

MAKE YOUR OWN

Chicken Stock 213

Vegetable Stock 212

IF YOU HAVE MORE TIME
And access to fresh peas in the pod: Start with 4 pounds, shell them, and use them instead of the frozen peas. They might take a little longer to cook, but check them frequently so they don't get too mushy.

SIDES

Crisp Roasted Potatoes 965

Warm Buttery Bread 906

Green Salad 911

SPEED ◐ SERVES 4

Tomato and Bread Soup with White Beans

When a crusty slice of bread breaks up in hot broth, it can turn even garlic-flavored water into soup. Add olive oil and tomatoes and you've got something truly delicious, with a comforting texture. Beans add smoothness, and their starch makes the broth rich.

Ingredients

2 tablespoons olive oil, plus more for drizzling

1 large onion

Salt and pepper

1 large carrot

4 or 5 medium ripe tomatoes (1 ½ pounds)

2 tablespoons tomato paste

4 sprigs fresh thyme or 1 teaspoon dried

4 thick slices any rustic bread

1 garlic clove

2 cups cooked or canned white beans (one 15-ounce can)

3 cups vegetable or beef stock or water

Several sprigs fresh basil for garnish

Prep | Cook

1. Put 2 tablespoons olive oil in a large pot over medium heat.

   Trim, peel, and chop the onion.

2. When the oil is hot, add the onion and a sprinkle of salt and pepper. Cook, stirring occasionally until the onion softens, 3 to 5 minutes.

   Trim, peel, and chop the carrot; add it to the pot and stir.

   Core and chop the tomatoes.

3. Turn the broiler to high; put the rack 4 inches from the heat.

4. When the onion and carrot are soft, add 2 tablespoons tomato paste and cook, stirring until it darkens a bit, 1 or 2 minutes.

5. Add the tomatoes and cook, stirring occasionally until they break apart, 10 to 15 minutes.

   If you're using fresh thyme, strip the leaves from 4 sprigs and chop them.

   Put 4 thick slices bread on a baking sheet and drizzle each with a little olive oil.

6. Broil the bread, turning once, until browned on both sides, 2 to 5 minutes total.

7. Add the fresh thyme (or 1 teaspoon dried) to the pot and stir.

   Peel and halve 1 garlic clove. If you're using canned beans, rinse and drain them.

   When the bread is toasted, rub the tops with the cut side of the garlic; slice or tear the bread into bite-sized pieces and put in the bottom of 4 soup bowls.

8. Add 3 cups stock or water to the pot along with the beans. Adjust the heat so the soup bubbles gently but steadily; cook, stirring occasionally and adding a little liquid if necessary, until it heats through, another 3 minutes.

   Strip the basil leaves from several sprigs and chop them.

9. Taste and adjust the seasoning. Pour the soup over the bread. Garnish with the basil, drizzle with olive oil, and serve.

VARIATIONS

Tomato and Bread Soup with Eggplant

In Step 1, add another tablespoon olive oil to the pot. Cut 1 large or 3 small eggplant into 1-inch chunks. Add them with the onion in Step 2.

Tomato and Bread Soup with Zucchini

Cut 2 medium zucchini into 1-inch chunks. Add them with the tomatoes in Step 5.

Tomato and Bread Soup with Hearty Greens

Roughly chop 1 ½ pounds kale, escarole, or other hearty green. Add them with the tomatoes in Step 5.

NOTES

MAKE YOUR OWN

Cooked Beans 492

Vegetable Stock 212

Beef Stock 212

EVEN FASTER

This soup is lovely with canned tomatoes; figure one 28-ounce can of the whole peeled kind. Break them up as they cook in Step 5.

SIDES

Green Salad 911

Caprese Salad 922

Fennel Salad 917

SPEED ◐ SERVES 4

Pasta e Fagioli

This Italian classic is thick and satisfying with vegetables, beans, and pasta in every bite. You can skip the parsley, but don't skimp on the Parmesan or olive oil: They add key richness.

Ingredients

3 tablespoons olive oil, plus more for drizzling

1 medium onion

2 medium carrots

2 celery stalks

Salt and pepper

2 garlic cloves

2 cups cooked or canned cannellini or pinto beans (one 15-ounce can)

2 sprigs fresh rosemary

One 14-ounce can whole tomatoes

6 cups chicken or vegetable stock or water

1 cup tiny cut pasta (like ditalini or orzo)

1 bunch fresh parsley for garnish

4 ounces Parmesan cheese (1 cup grated)

Prep | Cook

1. Put 3 tablespoons olive oil in a large pot over low heat.
   Trim, peel, and chop the onion; add it to the pot.
   Trim and peel the carrots. Trim the celery. Chop the vegetables, add them to the pot, and stir.

2. Raise the heat to medium-high. When the vegetables start sizzling, sprinkle with salt and pepper and cook, stirring occasionally until they soften and begin to brown, 3 to 5 minutes.
   Peel and chop 2 garlic cloves; add to the pot and stir.
   If you're using canned beans, rinse and drain them.

3. When the vegetables are ready, add 2 sprigs rosemary to the pot. Stir until fragrant, less than 1 minute.

4. Add the tomatoes and their juice, breaking them up with a spoon and scraping any browned bits off the bottom of the pot. Add 6 cups stock or water and raise the heat to high.

5. When the soup comes to a boil, stir in the beans and 1 cup pasta. Return the mixture to a boil; adjust the heat so it bubbles steadily.

6. Start tasting the pasta after 5 minutes; it should be tender but not mushy. If the pot starts to look dry, add water a little at a time.

   Chop ½ cup parsley.

   Grate 1 cup Parmesan cheese.

7. When the pasta is tender, turn off the heat. Fish out the rosemary sprigs and discard. Taste and adjust the seasoning and divide the soup among 4 bowls. Garnish each with the parsley, ¼ cup Parmesan, and a drizzle of olive oil; serve.

VARIATIONS

Greek-Style Pasta e Fagioli
An unusual change. Instead of the rosemary, use several sprigs fresh oregano. Use frozen green favas for the beans and pearl couscous for the pasta; substitute crumbled feta for the Parmesan.

Spanish-Style Pasta e Fagioli
Substitute 2 teaspoons smoked paprika for the rosemary, chickpeas for the beans, and 6 ounces spaghetti for the tiny pasta. Break the noodles into 1-inch pieces before adding them in Step 5.

NOTES

MAKE YOUR OWN

Cooked Beans 496

Chicken Stock 213

Vegetable Stock 212

EVEN FASTER
Use 3 cups already cooked pasta (see page 316) and stir it into the soup right before serving. If you've got lightly sauced leftovers handy, use them; they'll add even more flavor to the soup.

CANNED TOMATO TRICKS
It's easy enough to break canned tomatoes into smaller pieces with a spoon once they're in the pot, but often, if you have 30 seconds to spare before adding the tomatoes, you can roughly chop them right in the can. Just run a paring knife through the tomatoes. Or transfer them to a bowl and squeeze them with your hand until they're broken up a bit. Of course you can always buy canned diced tomatoes.

SIDES

Garlic Bread 906

Green Salad 911

Fennel Salad 917

Bruschetta 909

Sautéed Greens with Garlic 924

SPEED ◐ SERVES 4

Chickpea and Couscous Stew with Moroccan Spices

When you cook pasta or grains in a thick soup, the result is more like a stew. Once you get things going, there's plenty of time to set the table or get a jump on the dishes.

Ingredients

¼ cup olive oil

1 large onion

1 teaspoon cumin

1 teaspoon coriander

1 teaspoon cinnamon

2 large carrots

Salt and pepper

2 cups cooked or canned chickpeas (one 15-ounce can)

2 garlic cloves

1 tablespoon tomato paste

One 28-ounce can whole peeled tomatoes

4 cups vegetable or chicken stock or water

1 lemon

1 bunch fresh mint for garnish

½ cup couscous

Prep | Cook

1. Put ¼ cup olive oil in a large pot over medium heat.
   Trim, peel, and chop the onion.

2. Add 1 teaspoon cumin, 1 teaspoon coriander, and 1 teaspoon cinnamon to the pot; cook, stirring until dark and fragrant, about 1 minute.

3. Add the onion to the pot and cook, stirring occasionally until it begins to soften, 3 to 5 minutes.
   Trim, peel, and chop the carrots; add them to the pot and stir.

4. Raise the heat to medium-high. When the vegetables start sizzling, sprinkle with salt and pepper and cook, stirring occasionally until they soften and begin to brown, 5 to 10 minutes.
   If you're using canned chickpeas, rinse and drain them.
   Peel and chop 2 garlic cloves; add them to the pot and stir.

5. Add 1 tablespoon tomato paste and cook, stirring until it darkens slightly, a minute or 2. Stir in the chickpeas.

6. Add the tomatoes and their juice, breaking them up with a spoon and scraping any browned bits off the bottom of the pot. Add 4 cups stock or water and raise the heat to high.

   Grate the zest of the lemon; refrigerate the fruit for another use. Chop 1 cup mint leaves.

7. When the stew begins to boil, lower the heat so it bubbles gently. Stir in ½ cup couscous; cover and turn off the heat. After 5 minutes, stir in the lemon zest and mint. Taste, adjust the seasoning, divide the soup among 4 bowls, and serve.

VARIATIONS

Chickpea and Couscous Stew with Cauliflower

Add 1 medium head chopped cauliflower to the stew with the tomatoes and stock in Step 6. After reducing the heat in Step 7, cook, stirring occasionally until the cauliflower is almost as tender as you like it, 5 to 10 minutes. Then add the couscous and proceed with the recipe.

NOTES

MAKE YOUR OWN

Cooked Beans 496

Vegetable Stock 212

Chicken Stock 213

"BLOOMING" GROUND SPICES

It's tempting to skip this if you're in a hurry, but it takes no more than a minute and makes the dish taste like it's been simmering for hours. Spices are said to "bloom" when you toast them in a little butter or oil just long enough to activate their fragrant oils. Here, a classic Moroccan spice blend intensifies a simple broth of canned tomatoes and stock and infuses the chickpeas and couscous with long-cooked flavor.

SIDES

Tahini-Lemon Potato Salad 962

Crisp Seasoned Pita 908

Carrot Salad with Raisins 914

Jícama and Radish Salad with Dried Cranberries and Cinnamon 918

Tahini Slaw 923

Cucumber Raita 916

Seafood Chowder

Since seafood brings the briny character of the ocean to the pot, you can get by with little more than a handful of vegetables and water. Use stock and you'll add even more flavor.

Ingredients

5 cups fish or chicken stock or water

2 tablespoons butter

4 sprigs fresh thyme or 1 teaspoon dried

Salt

Pinch of saffron (optional)

2 or 3 medium russet or Yukon Gold potatoes (1 pound)

2 medium leeks

2 medium carrots

2 celery stalks

2 garlic cloves

1 pound thick white fish fillets

2 pounds littleneck or other hard-shell clams or 1 pound mussels

Pepper

1 cup cream or milk

Fresh parsley for garnish

Prep | Cook

1. Put 5 cups stock or water and 2 tablespoons butter in a large pot over medium-high heat. Add 4 sprigs fresh thyme or 1 teaspoon dried, a sprinkle of salt, and a pinch of saffron if you're using it.

   Scrub the potatoes and peel them if you like. Cut them into small chunks and add them to the pot.

   Trim the leeks and slice the white and light green parts only.

   Trim and peel the carrots and trim the celery. Cut them into small chunks and add them to the pot along with the leeks.

   Peel and slice 2 garlic cloves and add to the pot.

2. When the stock comes to a boil, adjust the heat so it bubbles gently but steadily. Cook, stirring occasionally until the potatoes are fork-tender but not yet breaking apart, 10 to 15 minutes.

   Cut the fish fillets into large chunks; scrub the clams or scrub and debeard the mussels (discard any that don't close when you press the shell together).

3. When the potatoes are tender, add the clams or mussels to the chowder and put the pieces of fish on top. Sprinkle with salt and pepper and pour 1 cup cream or milk over all.

4. Adjust the heat so the liquid bubbles gently but steadily. Cover and cook just until the clams or mussels open and the fish is cooked through, 5 to 10 minutes.

Strip the parsley leaves from several sprigs and chop.

5. When the fish and shellfish are cooked, stir the pot gently to combine everything. Taste and adjust the seasoning. Fish out fresh thyme sprigs and discard. Divide among 4 bowls and serve, shells and all, garnished with sprigs of parsley.

VARIATIONS

All-Clam or -Mussel Chowder
Omit the fish and increase the quantity of clams to 4 pounds and mussels to 2 pounds.

Smoked Salmon Chowder
Easy and distinctive. Omit the white fish and clams and use 12 ounces smoked salmon. Garnish with chives instead of parsley.

Manhattan Seafood or Clam Chowder
Substitute one 28-ounce can diced tomatoes with their juice for 1 cup of the stock or water and the cream. If you like, omit the fish and use 3 pounds clams.

Shrimp and Corn Chowder
Summer special. Instead of the carrots and celery, use 2 cups corn kernels (frozen is fine). Substitute 1 ½ pounds peeled shrimp for the fish and clams or mussels.

NOTES

MAKE YOUR OWN

Fish Stock 213

Chicken Stock 213

IF YOU HAVE MORE TIME

Seafood Chowder with Bacon
Most chowders taste better with bacon. Omit the butter. Start by cutting 8 thick slices bacon into 1-inch pieces. Put them in a large pot over medium heat. Cook, stirring occasionally, until nearly cooked, 5 to 10 minutes. Remove the bacon with a slotted spoon and start the soup using the rendered bacon fat with Step 1. Add the bacon back to the pot just before serving.

For a more elegant presentation, fish the clams or mussels out of the pot, remove shells, and return the seafood to the chowder.

SIDES

Rice Pilaf 944

Bulgur with Lemon and Parsley 946

Warm Buttery Bread 906

Green Salad 911

Fennel Salad 917

Soups

1 Heat the fat.

Browning isn't mandatory (see Chop-and-Drop Soups on page 253), but some of the most flavorful soups and stews start with cooking meat in oil or butter. So put a few tablespoons of either in a large pot or deep skillet over medium-high heat.

2 Brown the meat.

Add some meat—ground meat; chopped bacon, ham, or sausage; or chunks of beef, pork, lamb, or poultry. Cook undisturbed, adjusting the heat so it doesn't burn, until it releases easily from the bottom; then stir or turn and cook some more. The less you fuss, the better the browning, plus it gives you time to focus on chopping vegetables.

3 Add seasonings and vegetables.

Remove the meat and add aromatics like onions or garlic. Once they've cooked a bit, add seasonings like spices, herbs, or tomato paste. Stir for a minute, then add the vegetables as you finish chopping them. Cook until they begin to get tender, usually 5 to 10 minutes.

④ Add the liquid.

Add about 6 cups liquid to the pot. This could be stock, water, beer, wine, or canned tomatoes—or a combination. Then stir to scrape up any browned bits from the bottom. You're no longer in danger of burning anything; crank the heat to high so the liquid will come to a boil.

⑤ Build substance.

Return the meat to the pot now. If you have any other ingredients to add that need time to cook, like grains, pasta, or more vegetables, prep and add them to the pot as you work. Once the soup comes to a boil, lower the heat so it bubbles gently but steadily.

⑥ Simmer.

Cook, stirring only once in a while and adding more water or stock as needed to keep everything submerged. Prepare garnishes, then add quick-cooking seafood or any precooked ingredients—leftover vegetables, meat, poultry, noodles, grains, or beans—to heat them through.

⑦ Taste and serve.

When the texture and color look right, taste. Adjust the seasoning, adding salt, pepper, or more of the original flavorings. Finishing touches might include soy, hot sauce, or vinegar; a pat of butter or drizzle of olive oil; citrus zest; or fresh herbs.

SPEED ◑ SERVES 4

Miso Soup with Scallops, Soba, and Spinach

Japanese stock—dashi—is a real change from chicken or vegetable broth, and since the main ingredients are sea greens and fish flakes, it's as simple as steeping tea.

Ingredients

1 large piece dried kelp (kombu), 4 to 6 inches long

Salt

1 bunch spinach (1 pound)

8 ounces sea scallops

½ cup dried bonito flakes

8 ounces soba noodles

4 scallions

⅓ cup any miso

Prep | Cook

1. Put 1 piece dried kelp and 8 cups water in a large pot over medium heat. Bring another large pot of water to boil and salt it.

   Trim off any thick stems from the spinach and chop the leaves. Cut each scallop crosswise into 2 or 3 thin rounds.

2. When the water with the kelp just starts to bubble, turn off the heat, remove the kelp (you can save it for stir-fries if you want), and stir in ½ cup bonito flakes.

3. When the pot of salted water comes to a boil, add 8 ounces soba noodles. Cook, stirring occasionally, until the noodles are barely tender, 3 to 5 minutes.

   Trim and slice the scallions.

4. When the noodles are ready, drain and rinse them under warm water, then return them to the pot. Add the spinach and put the raw scallop slices on top.

5. Strain all but 1 cup of the dashi into the pot with the noodles and cover. Return the pot to high heat. Cook, undisturbed, until it just starts to bubble and the spinach is wilted, 3 to 5 minutes.

   Strain the remaining dashi into a small bowl. Add ⅓ cup miso and whisk until smooth.

6. When the soup is ready, turn off the heat and stir the miso mixture into the pot.

7. Taste and add more salt if necessary. Ladle the soup into 4 bowls and garnish with the scallions.

VARIATIONS

Miso Soup with Shrimp, Soba, and Spinach
Substitute peeled shrimp for the scallops. Chop them into bite-sized pieces or—slightly fancier—slice them in half lengthwise.

Miso Soup with Tofu, Soba, and Bok Choy
Substitute one 12-ounce box silken tofu for the scallops and sliced bok choy for the spinach. When you stir in the miso mixture, break the tofu into big, irregular pieces with a large spoon.

Miso Soup with Chicken, Udon, and Snow Peas
Quite substantial: Use thinly sliced chicken breast instead of the scallops and whole snow peas instead of spinach. Substitute udon for the soba; they will take a minute or 2 longer to become tender in Step 3.

NOTES

MISO
Miso paste isn't in every American refrigerator, but it should be. This fermented soybean paste adds tremendous flavor to soups, sauces, rubs, and marinades. You can find miso at many supermarkets these days, and always at Japanese or other Asian markets. It lasts for about a year in the fridge, so there's no excuse not to keep some handy.

In general, the darker the miso, the more assertive the taste. White and yellow varieties are mild with a touch of sweetness (that's what I usually use for miso soup); red, brown, and black misos all taste a bit stronger, more fermented, and are better for sauces and seasoning; nontraditionalists can use them all interchangeably.

SIDES

Scallion Pancakes 940

Sautéed Sweet Potatoes with Ginger and Soy 964

Edamame with Chili Salt 881

Cucumber Salad with Soy Sauce and Mirin 915

SPEED ◐ SERVES 4

Fast Pho

Pho (pronounced *fuh*) is a classic Vietnamese soup that often contains as many raw ingredients as cooked. While the seductive broth simmers, you prep a few things to stir in near the end or to put on the table for individual sprinkling.

Ingredients

2 tablespoons peanut or sunflower oil

4 garlic cloves

2 inches fresh ginger

1 teaspoon star anise or coriander

1 teaspoon cloves

½ teaspoon cinnamon

⅓ cup fish sauce, or more to taste

1 brick firm tofu (12 to 14 ounces)

Several sprigs fresh cilantro

Several sprigs fresh Thai or regular basil

Several sprigs fresh mint

2 cups bean sprouts

4 scallions

2 fresh hot green chiles

2 limes

2 cups frozen edamame

4 ounces dried rice vermicelli noodles

Salt and pepper

Prep | Cook

1. Put 2 tablespoons peanut or sunflower oil in a large pot over medium-low heat.

   Peel 4 garlic cloves and 2 inches of fresh ginger; mince them together.

2. Add the garlic and ginger to the pot and raise the heat to medium-high. Cook, stirring frequently until soft, about 1 minute.

3. Add 1 teaspoon star anise or coriander, 1 teaspoon cloves, and ½ teaspoon cinnamon and cook, stirring until fragrant, another minute.

4. Add 10 cups water and ⅓ cup fish sauce, raise the heat to high, and bring to a boil. Reduce the heat so the mixture bubbles steadily.

   Cut the brick of tofu into ½- or ¼-inch cubes.

   Trim several sprigs each cilantro, basil, and mint and put the sprigs on a platter (the leaves can be plucked at the table).

   Pick over the bean sprouts to remove any bad bits and put them on the platter.

Trim and chop the scallions; trim, seed, and thinly slice the chiles. Add both to the platter. Cut the limes into wedges and add them to the platter.

5. When the broth is simmering, add 2 cups edamame. Cook for 2 minutes, then add the cubed tofu and 4 ounces rice noodles. Cook, stirring once or twice, until the noodles are almost tender, 2 or 3 minutes.

6. Taste the soup and sprinkle with salt and pepper or add more fish sauce if necessary. Divide among 4 big bowls, passing the platter of garnishes at the table.

VARIATIONS

7 Easy Vegetable Additions
Stir in 4 cups of the following vegetables, thinly sliced, 2 minutes before you add the noodles:

1. Bok choy
2. Napa cabbage
3. Mustard greens
4. Broccoli rabe
5. Carrots
6. Green beans or snow peas
7. Summer squash

5 Easy Meat and Seafood Additions
Stir in 8 ounces of the following meat or seafood, thinly sliced, 2 minutes before you add the noodles:

1. Boneless beef sirloin or rib-eye
2. Boneless pork loin
3. Boneless chicken breast or thighs
4. Shrimp, peeled and butterflied
5. Scallops

NOTES

IF YOU HAVE MORE TIME

Slow Pho with Meat
Add up to 3 pounds meaty beef or pork bones to the pot along with the water. Once the broth comes to a boil, reduce the heat so that it simmers; after 2 or 3 hours, which is ideal, you'll be able to pull the meat from the bones (otherwise you'll have to cut the meat from the bones with a knife). Add the reserved meat along with the noodles in Step 5.

SIDES

Scallion Pancakes 940

Cucumber Salad with Soy Sauce and Mirin 915

Stir-Fried Bok Choy 927

Homemade Chicken Ramen

Packaged ramen can be jazzed up with little more than egg, scallions, and soy sauce. Dump the packet of fake seasoning in the trash and make a quick broth, then add the noodles and some sliced chicken to the same pot.

Ingredients

3 boneless, skinless chicken thighs (about 8 ounces)

1 inch fresh ginger

1 teaspoon sesame oil

¼ teaspoon red chile flakes

3 tablespoons soy sauce

6 cups chicken or vegetable stock

3 garlic cloves

6 scallions

8 ounces ramen or somen noodles or 4 packages ramen soup

1 tablespoon vegetable oil

4 eggs

Prep | Cook

Thinly slice the chicken thighs.

Peel and mince 1 inch fresh ginger.

1. Combine the chicken, ginger, 1 teaspoon sesame oil, ¼ teaspoon red chile flakes, and 1 tablespoon soy sauce in a bowl.
2. Put 6 cups stock and 2 tablespoons soy sauce in a large pot over high heat.

   Peel and thinly slice 3 garlic cloves.

   Trim and chop the scallions, keeping the white and green parts separate.
3. When the stock comes to a boil, add the garlic, the white parts of the scallions, and the chicken along with its marinade. Adjust the heat so the broth bubbles steadily and cook, stirring once or twice, until the chicken is cooked through, 3 to 5 minutes.
4. Put a large skillet over medium-high heat for 1 minute.
5. Add the noodles to the pot (discard the seasoning packets if there are any); break them apart with a fork if necessary and adjust the heat so the broth keeps bubbling gently. Cook, stirring occasionally, until just tender, 3 to 5 minutes.

6. Add 1 tablespoon vegetable oil to the skillet and swirl it to coat the bottom. Crack the eggs into the pan and turn the heat to low.
7. Cover the pan and cook, undisturbed, until the whites are just set and the yolks are still runny, 3 or 4 minutes. Turn off the heat.
8. When the noodles and chicken are done, taste the broth and adjust the seasoning. Divide the soup among 4 bowls, top each with a fried egg and the green parts of the scallions, and serve.

VARIATIONS

6 No-Cook Ramen Toppers

1. Canned mackerel
2. Thinly sliced smoked sausage
3. Tomato wedges
4. Sliced avocado
5. Chopped fresh pineapple
6. Cubed mango

NOTES

MAKE YOUR OWN

Chicken Stock 213

Vegetable Stock 212

EVEN FASTER

Instead of frying the eggs, beat them in a bowl and slowly pour them into the pot at the end of Step 5, stirring the whole time. (See Bacon and Egg Drop Soup, page 210.)

Or you can crack the eggs into a saucer and slide them into the bubbling broth during Step 5. Let them poach until they're as soft or firm as you like, 2 to 4 minutes, then carefully serve 1 in each bowl of soup.

FINDING RAMEN

One of the fastest and most popular meals of all time is ramen—the name for both a curly Japanese-style wheat noodle and the packaged instant soup that includes them. Since the noodles can be hard to find outside their iconic single-serve packages, just buy those and ditch the seasoning. If you can find big, seasoning-free packages, so much the better; ordinary somen noodles work fine in this recipe too.

SIDES

Edamame with Chili Salt 881

Scallion-Miso Bean Sprouts 919

Avocado with Lime and Chili Salt 920

Cucumber Salad with Soy Sauce and Mirin 915

Chicken Tamale Soup

If you like the flavor of corn tortillas and the pleasantly gritty texture of tamales, this is your soup. And you get it all without patting, filling, or wrapping sticky dough. Just assemble similar ingredients in a pot and let it bubble for a few minutes.

Ingredients

8 cups chicken or vegetable stock

1 small onion

1 bunch fresh cilantro

8 boneless, skinless chicken thighs (about 1 ½ pounds)

2 chipotle chiles in adobo, with their sauce to taste

¼ cup masa harina or finely ground cornmeal

Salt and pepper

2 avocados

4 ounces melting cheese, like Oaxaca or Jack (1 cup grated)

1 lime

Prep | Cook

1. Put 8 cups stock in a large pot over high heat.

   Trim, peel, and halve the onion. Chop 1 half for garnish and leave the other half intact.

   Chop 1 cup cilantro; put ½ cup in a blender and reserve the rest.

   Cut the chicken into small chunks or thin slices.

2. Add the onion half to the blender, along with 2 chipotles and some of their sauce, ¼ cup masa harina or finely ground cornmeal, and a sprinkle of salt and pepper.

3. When the stock comes to a boil, turn off the heat and carefully ladle about 2 cups into the blender. Purée until smooth.

4. Add the purée and the chicken to the remaining stock in the pot and adjust the heat so it bubbles gently. Cook, stirring occasionally, until the chicken just cooks through and the soup has thickened slightly, 5 to 10 minutes.

   Halve and pit the avocados, cut the flesh into cubes, and scoop it out of the skin.

   Grate 1 cup cheese.

   Cut the lime into wedges.

5. When the soup is ready, taste and adjust the seasoning and divide among 4 bowls. Garnish with the avocados, cheese, and chopped onion and cilantro. Serve with the lime wedges.

VARIATIONS

Pork Tamale Soup

Substitute 4 thin boneless pork chops for the chicken.

Chicken Tortilla Soup

Omit the salt. Substitute 2 cups broken tortilla chips for the masa. Serve garnished with more chips if you like.

NOTES

MAKE YOUR OWN

Chicken Stock 213

Vegetable Stock 212

IF YOU HAVE MORE TIME

The longer you let the soup simmer—up to an hour or so—the more the flavors will develop. But you don't want to overcook the chicken, so don't add it until about 10 minutes before you're ready to serve.

MASA HARINA

Masa harina is a fine, flourlike meal made from corn that has been processed with lime. It's a staple in Mexico, and in the kitchens of Mexicans-Americans, and since it's the main ingredient in corn tortillas and tamales, everyone else knows the flavor as well. And masa is useful for its ability to quickly add flavor and texture to soups and stews. Like cornmeal, it will clump in liquids, so either make a slurry with a small amount of hot liquid, as in this recipe, or add it slowly, in a steady stream, whisking constantly.

SIDES

Warm Flour or Corn Tortillas 907

Coleslaw 923

Mexican Street Corn 932

Chile-Cumin Black Beans 937

Ripe Plantains 960

SPEED ◐ SERVES 4

Spicy Peanut Soup with Chicken and Collards

Peanuts and collards have a natural affinity. This African-inspired soup demonstrates how delicious these greens can be when cooked quickly.

Ingredients

2 tablespoons vegetable oil

6 boneless, skinless chicken thighs (1 pound)

1 large red onion

2 garlic cloves

1 inch fresh ginger

1 fresh hot green chile (like jalapeño)

1 cup peanut butter

1 tablespoon tomato paste

6 cups chicken or vegetable stock or water

Salt and pepper

1 large or 2 small bunches collard greens (1 pound)

¼ cup roasted peanuts for garnish

Prep | Cook

1. Put 2 tablespoons vegetable oil in a large pot over medium-high heat.

   Cut the chicken into ½-inch chunks.

2. When the oil is hot, add the chicken to pot and cook, undisturbed, until the pieces brown and release easily, 2 or 3 minutes. Then cook, stirring occasionally, until the meat is no longer pink, 2 or 3 more minutes.

   Trim, peel, halve, and slice the onion.

   Peel and mince 2 garlic cloves and 1 inch fresh ginger.

   Trim the chile, remove the seeds if you'd like, and mince it.

3. Add the onion to the pot and cook, stirring occasionally until softened, 2 or 3 minutes.

   Whisk together 1 cup peanut butter and ½ cup water in a small bowl until smooth.

4. Add the garlic, ginger, chile, and 1 tablespoon tomato paste to the pot. Cook, stirring until the mixture darkens and becomes fragrant, 1 or 2 minutes.

5. Add 6 cups stock or water, scraping up any browned bits from the bottom of the pot. Stir in the peanut butter mixture and sprinkle with salt and pepper. Raise the heat to high and bring to a boil.
   Trim the collards; slice the leaves in half along the stem, then crosswise into thin ribbons.

6. When the liquid boils, stir the collards into the pot and lower the heat so the soup bubbles gently. Cover and cook, undisturbed, until the greens soften and the chicken cooks through, 5 to 10 minutes.
   Chop 1/4 cup peanuts (or crush them with the flat side of a knife).

7. Taste and adjust the seasoning. Divide the soup among 4 bowls, garnish with the peanuts, and serve.

VARIATIONS

Spicy Curried Peanut Soup with Chicken and Spinach
Substitute a yellow onion for the red, roughly chopped spinach for the collards, curry powder for the tomato paste, and one 14-ounce can coconut milk for 2 cups of the stock. The spinach will take only 3 to 5 minutes to soften.

Chinese-Style Peanut Soup with Tofu and Bok Choy
I like this a lot. Use 1 bunch scallions instead of the red onion, 2 cups cubed firm tofu in place of the chicken, bok choy instead of collards, and 2 tablespoons soy sauce rather than tomato paste. Add the soy sauce when you add the stock.

NOTES

MAKE YOUR OWN

Chicken Stock 213

Vegetable Stock 212

SIDES

White Rice 941

Quinoa 945

Warm Flour or Corn Tortillas 907

SPEED ◐ SERVES 4

Cabbage Soup with Smoked Sausage

Thanks to the crisp-tender texture of the cabbage, this soup is surprisingly light even though its flavors are hearty and warming. Using whole spices and browning everything creates intense flavor in a short time.

Ingredients

2 tablespoons olive oil

1 pound bratwurst, kielbasa, or other smoked sausage

1 large onion

1 small head Savoy or green cabbage (1 pound)

Salt and pepper

1 tablespoon caraway seeds

6 cups chicken or beef stock

1 cinnamon stick

8 sprigs fresh thyme

Prep | Cook

1. Put 2 tablespoons olive oil in a large pot over medium heat.

   Cut the sausage into bite-sized pieces.

2. When the oil is hot, add the sausage and cook, stirring occasionally, until browned on most sides, 5 to 10 minutes.

   Trim, peel, and halve the onion. Slice each half crosswise ½ inch thick.

   Trim, core, and quarter the cabbage. Cut each quarter crosswise into ½-inch ribbons.

3. Remove the browned sausage from the pot with a slotted spoon. Raise the heat to medium-high and add the onion and cabbage. Sprinkle with salt and pepper and cook, stirring occasionally until they begin to soften, 3 to 5 minutes.

4. Add 1 tablespoon caraway seeds and cook, stirring until fragrant, about 1 minute.

5. Add 6 cups stock, 1 cinnamon stick, and 8 sprigs fresh thyme. Return the sausage to the pot. Bring the mixture to a boil, then adjust the heat so that it bubbles gently but steadily.

6. Cook, stirring once or twice, until the vegetables become tender and the soup thickens, 5 to 10 minutes. Remove the cinnamon stick and thyme if you like. Taste, adjust the seasoning, divide among 4 bowls, and serve.

VARIATIONS

Red Cabbage and Beef Soup
Substitute cumin seeds for the caraway and ground beef for the smoked sausage and add red chile flakes to taste. Use red cabbage and red onion.

Escarole and Italian Sausage Soup
A classic. Omit the caraway and cinnamon. Use fresh hot or sweet Italian sausage and substitute escarole for the cabbage.

Spinach and Chorizo Soup
Use smoked chorizo for the sausage and spinach in place of cabbage; don't add the spinach until the stock bubbles in Step 5 and then cook only until it's just tender, 3 to 5 minutes.

NOTES

MAKE YOUR OWN

Chicken Stock 213

Beef Stock 212

SIDES

Skin-On Mashed Potatoes 961

Quinoa 945

White Rice 941

Buttered Egg Noodles 948

Boiled Potatoes 954

Warm Buttery Bread 906

SPEED ◐ SERVES 4

Sausage, Cannellini, and Kale Soup

Beans and greens are a ubiquitous combination, and they mix and match brilliantly. The combination of cannellini and hearty kale, with the addition of sausage and Parmesan cheese, is one of my all-time favorites.

Ingredients

2 tablespoons olive oil, plus more for garnish

1 pound sweet or hot Italian sausage

3 garlic cloves

1 bunch kale, preferably lacinato (1 pound)

2 cups cooked or canned cannellini beans (one 15-ounce can)

¼ teaspoon red chile flakes, or more to taste

Salt and pepper

6 cups stock or water

1 bay leaf

4 ounces Parmesan cheese (1 cup grated)

Prep | Cook

1. Put 2 tablespoons olive oil in a large pot over medium heat.

   Cut the sausage into small chunks.

2. When the oil is hot, add the sausage and cook, stirring occasionally, until browned on most sides, 5 to 10 minutes.

   Peel and mince 3 garlic cloves.

   Trim and chop the kale.

   If you're using canned cannellini beans, rinse and drain them. Put the beans in a small bowl and mash them with a fork until the pieces are the size of peas.

3. When the sausage is browned, stir in the garlic and ¼ teaspoon red chile flakes (or to taste). Cook, stirring until fragrant, 30 seconds or so.

4. Add the kale, sprinkle with salt and pepper, and cook, stirring until it's coated with oil and just starting to wilt, a minute or 2.

5. Add the beans, 6 cups stock or water, and 1 bay leaf. Bring the mixture to a boil, then adjust the heat so that it bubbles gently but steadily. Cook, stirring occasionally until the broth thickens and the greens are fully tender, 10 to 20 minutes.

   Grate 1 cup Parmesan cheese.

6. Remove and discard the bay leaf. Taste and adjust the seasoning. Divide the soup among 4 bowls, sprinkle each with ¼ cup grated Parmesan, drizzle with olive oil, and serve.

VARIATIONS

Merguez, Chickpea, and Chard Soup
Substitute Merguez or other lamb and/or beef links for the Italian sausage. Substitute chard for the kale and chickpeas for the cannellini beans.

Andouille, Black-Eyed Pea, and Southern Greens Soup
Spicy and smoky. Use andouille sausage. Substitute mustard, collard, or turnip greens for the kale and black-eyed peas for the cannellini beans.

NOTES

MAKE YOUR OWN

Cooked Beans 496

Chicken Stock 213

Vegetable Stock 212

Beef Stock 212

THICKENING WITH BEANS
Even just a little mashing of beans in soup makes the bowlful thick and creamy. The starch released by the beans is water soluble, so it dissolves quickly, creating a viscosity otherwise achieved only by adding fatty foods like butter and cream.

SIDES

Garlic Bread 906

Crisp Roasted Potatoes 965

Bruschetta 909

Green Salad 911

Caprese Salad 922

SPEED ◐ SERVES 4

Broken Wonton Soup

Even with the convenience of packaged wonton skins, no one is going to fill and seal wontons while hurrying to get dinner on the table. But if you deconstruct the whole thing, you can pull together homemade wonton soup in minutes.

Ingredients

8 cups chicken or vegetable stock

4 ounces shiitake mushrooms

2 garlic cloves

½ inch fresh ginger

4 scallions

1 pound ground pork

1 egg

1 tablespoon soy sauce, plus more for serving

2 teaspoons sesame oil, plus more for serving

¼ teaspoon five-spice powder (optional)

Salt

24 wonton skins

Prep | Cook

1. Put 8 cups stock in a large pot over medium heat.

   Twist off the mushroom stems and discard. Thinly slice the caps and add them to the pot.

   Peel and mince 2 garlic cloves and ½ inch fresh ginger.

   Trim and chop the scallions; separate the green and white parts.

2. Combine the ground pork, egg, 1 tablespoon soy sauce, 2 teaspoons sesame oil, ¼ teaspoon five-spice powder if you're using it, the garlic, ginger, white parts of the scallions, and a sprinkle of salt in a medium bowl. Mix gently with a rubber spatula or your hands until just combined.

3. When the stock boils, adjust the heat so it bubbles steadily.

4. Pinch off and shape a walnut-sized piece of the pork mixture; drop it into the stock. Repeat until all the mixture is used. Cook, adjusting the heat so the stock bubbles steadily but not vigorously, until the meatballs firm up a bit, 1 or 2 minutes.

5. Separate 24 wonton skins (refrigerate what remains for another use). Drop them into the pot, stirring carefully after every few to prevent them from sticking together. Cook until the meatballs are cooked through and the wonton skins are just tender, another minute or 2.

6. Taste and adjust the seasoning, adding more soy sauce if necessary. Divide among 4 bowls and serve, garnished with the green parts of the scallions and passing soy sauce and sesame oil at the table.

VARIATIONS

Broken Wonton Soup with Spicy Shrimp
Use peeled shrimp instead of the pork. Pulse it in a food processor with the egg and seasonings from Step 2, adding a bit of chopped fresh green chile, like Thai, and continue with the recipe.

Broken Wonton Soup with Gingered Chicken
Substitute ground chicken for the pork (to grind your own, follow the previous variation) and an additional 2 inches of ginger instead of the garlic.

Broken Ravioli Soup
Omit the ginger, sesame oil, scallions, soy sauce, and five-spice powder. Use cremini instead of shiitake mushrooms and olive instead of sesame oil. Substitute hot or sweet Italian sausage for the ground pork; if you can't find it loose, squeeze it from the casings. When you add the wonton skins to the pot in Step 5, stir in a handful of chopped dried tomatoes if you like. Garnish with grated Parmesan.

Chinese Egg Noodle Soup
Omit the wonton skins. Follow the main recipe or any of the variations, adding 12 ounces dried Chinese egg noodles to the pot with the mushrooms in Step 1, or fresh noodles in Step 5.

NOTES

MAKE YOUR OWN

Chicken Stock 213

Vegetable Stock 212

Five-Spice Powder 759

IF YOU HAVE MORE TIME
Make wontons: You don't have to fold and seal the skins around the filling to get your wontons to hold their shape. Just take the pinch of meat, put it at one pointed end of the wrapper, and roll the skin around it like a cigar. Drop these wontons into the soup in Step 4. Give them 2 to 4 minutes to firm up and cook through.

Make a fried noodle garnish: Cut a few extra wonton skins into thin strips and fry them in 1/4 inch vegetable oil in a skillet over high heat until golden and crisp, just a minute or 2. Drain on paper towels and sprinkle with salt. Use for garnish along with the scallions.

SIDES

White Rice 941

Scallion Pancakes 940

Broiled Radishes with Soy 880

Edamame with Chili Salt 881

SPEED ◐ SERVES 4

Korean-Style Beef Soup with Rice

Sometimes all you need to flavor a soup is to add a seasoned oil just before serving—the reverse of building a soup on a base of cooked aromatics and spices. In this Korean-style soup, the starchy, meaty broth provides the perfect backdrop for the last-minute intensity of a chile-and-sesame–spiked drizzling sauce.

Ingredients

3 tablespoons vegetable oil

1 pound boneless beef chuck

Salt

3 garlic cloves

8 cups beef or chicken stock or water

1 cup long-grain rice

2 tablespoons sesame seeds

1 teaspoon red chile flakes, plus more for serving

4 scallions

6 celery stalks, plus any leaves

1 tablespoon sesame oil, plus more for serving

3 tablespoons soy sauce, plus more for serving

1 tablespoon rice vinegar

Prep | Cook

1. Put 1 tablespoon vegetable oil in a large pot over high heat.
   Cut the beef into ½-inch chunks.
2. When the oil is nearly smoking, add the beef, sprinkle with salt, and cook, stirring once or twice, until it browns in places, 3 to 5 minutes.
   Peel and mince 3 garlic cloves.
3. When the beef is browned, stir in the garlic and cook for 30 seconds. Add 8 cups stock or water, 1 cup rice, and another pinch of salt. Bring to a boil and cook (still boiling) until the rice is just shy of tender, 10 to 15 minutes.
4. Put 2 tablespoons sesame seeds and 1 teaspoon red chile flakes (more or less) in a medium skillet over medium-low heat. Cook, shaking the pan occasionally, until lightly toasted and fragrant, 3 to 5 minutes.
   Trim and chop the scallions, separating the white and green parts.
   Chop the celery stalks and any leaves.

5. When the sesame seeds and red chile flakes are lightly toasted and fragrant, remove the skillet from the heat and stir in 1 tablespoon sesame oil, 2 tablespoons vegetable oil, 3 tablespoons soy sauce, and 1 tablespoon rice vinegar.

6. When the rice is just tender, stir in the celery and celery leaves and the white parts of the scallions. Cook until the rice is fully cooked (it's okay if it's soft) and the celery is crisp-tender, 2 or 3 minutes.

7. Divide the soup among 4 bowls; drizzle with the sesame-chile oil, garnish with the green scallion parts, and serve, passing more soy sauce, sesame oil, and red chile flakes at the table if you like.

VARIATIONS

Beef and Kimchi Soup with Rice
With one little substitution, a huge flavor shift. Use 1 cup kimchi instead of the celery. Chop it before stirring it into the rice.

Korean-Style Pork Soup with Rice
Use boneless pork shoulder instead of beef.

NOTES

MAKE YOUR OWN

Beef Stock 212

Vegetable Stock 212

EVEN FASTER
If you have cooked meat (pages 688 and 744) or vegetables (pages 416 and 954) in the fridge, chop up as many of them as you like and stir into the rice in Step 6. Omit the beef and celery and add the garlic to the rice along with the meat and vegetables.

FROM RICE COMES BROTH
Cooked in soup along with other ingredients, rice releases its starch into the liquid, thickening the broth and making it creamy. But be careful: Rice bulks up considerably, so make sure you have ample liquid or don't use much rice.

SIDES

Tomato Salad with Sesame and Soy 913

Cucumber Salad with Hot Sauce and Lime Juice 915

Stir-Fried Bok Choy 927

Scallion-Miso Bean Sprouts 919

SPEED ◐ SERVES 4

Thai Coconut Soup with Carrots and Beef

This quintessential chop-and-drop soup (see page 253) is inspired by the street food of Bangkok; it's sweet, hot, salty, and delicious.

Ingredients

1 pound boneless beef sirloin or rib-eye steak

4 cups beef or chicken stock or water

2 inches fresh ginger

1 fresh hot green chile (like Thai), or to taste

2 stalks lemongrass (optional)

1 bunch fresh basil (preferably Thai)

2 cups coconut milk (one and a half 15-ounce cans)

5 medium carrots (1 pound)

1 lime

3 tablespoons fish sauce

1 teaspoon sugar

Salt and pepper

Prep | Cook

Put the beef in the freezer.

1. Put 4 cups stock or water in a large pot over high heat and bring to a boil.

   Peel and mince 2 inches fresh ginger; seed the chile and slice it crosswise into thin rounds.

   Trim 2 lemongrass stalks if you're using them, smash them with the flat side of a knife blade, and cut each into 3-inch lengths.

   Strip 1 cup basil leaves from the stems. Save the stems.

   Add the ginger, chiles, lemongrass, and basil stems to the pot.

2. When the liquid comes to a boil, adjust the heat so that it bubbles steadily but not vigorously. Add 2 cups coconut milk; return the mixture to a steady bubble.

   Trim and peel the carrots; slice them crosswise into thin rounds.

   Halve the lime.

   Remove the beef from the freezer and slice it against the grain as thinly as you can.

3. Remove the lemongrass and basil stems from the pot with a slotted spoon and discard.

4. Add the carrots to the pot. Cook, undisturbed, until they're just starting to get tender, 2 or 3 minutes.

5. Add the beef to the pot and cook, stirring once and adjusting the heat so the liquid bubbles steadily, until just cooked through and the carrots are crisp-tender, 2 or 3 minutes.

6. Add 3 tablespoons fish sauce, 1 teaspoon sugar, and a sprinkle of salt and pepper. Squeeze the lime juice into the pot.

7. Stir in the basil leaves, taste and adjust the seasoning, divide the soup among 4 bowls, and serve.

VARIATIONS

Coconut Soup with Carrots and Squid
Use cleaned squid instead of the beef. There's no need to freeze it; just slice it crosswise into rings and separate the tentacles from the body. Add it to the soup during the last minute of cooking; it's ready when it turns white and puffs up a bit.

Coconut Soup with Chicken, Bean Sprouts, and Snow Peas
Use boneless, skinless chicken breast. Freeze and slice as directed for the beef. Substitute 8 ounces each snow peas and bean sprouts for the carrots. Add the sprouts in Step 4, and the peas in Step 5.

NOTES

MAKE YOUR OWN

Beef Stock 212

Chicken Stock 213

CHOP-AND-DROP SOUPS
This is a fantastic way to cook on the fly—and clean out your fridge while you're at it. You get liquid heating in a big pot, then prep and add the ingredients—longest cooking first—while you keep chopping and dropping and the soup simmers.

First the aromatics go in, then the longer-cooking firm vegetables, followed by foods that take less time, like thinly sliced meats, fish, and shellfish and short-cooking greens or sprouts. Just before serving, stir in the top notes: fresh herbs or other seasonings, tomato wedges, soy or fish sauce, maybe a few drops of sesame oil—whatever. Since the soup is bubbling gently, you really don't even need to stir much, and in the end it takes only as long to cook as the sturdiest vegetable in the pot.

SIDES

White Rice 941

Cucumbers with Peanut Vinaigrette 953

Avocado with Hot Sauce and Cilantro 920

SPEED ◐ SERVES 4

Lamb Stew with Green Beans and Tomatoes

The smoky backbone to this tomato-based stew comes from toasted ground cumin, which is balanced by the brightness of lemon zest. If you don't like (or can't find) lamb, use ground beef, pork, or even chicken or turkey instead.

Ingredients

2 tablespoons olive oil, plus more for garnish

1 medium red onion

1 pound ground lamb

Salt and pepper

4 garlic cloves

1 tablespoon cumin

One 28-ounce can diced tomatoes

3 cups chicken or vegetable stock or water

1 ½ pounds green beans

1 lemon

Several sprigs fresh parsley for garnish

Prep | Cook

1. Put 2 tablespoons olive oil in a large pot over medium-high heat.
   Trim, peel, and chop the onion.

2. When the oil is hot, add the lamb and the onion, sprinkle with salt and pepper, and cook, stirring occasionally until the lamb is browned and the onion is golden, 5 to 10 minutes.
   Peel and mince 4 garlic cloves.

3. Add 1 tablespoon cumin to the browned lamb and onion and cook, stirring until fragrant, 30 seconds or so. Add the garlic, cooking and stirring for another 30 seconds.

4. Add the tomatoes and their juice, scraping any browned bits off the bottom of the pot.

5. Add 3 cups stock or water. Bring the stew to a boil, then lower the heat so it bubbles steadily and cook, stirring once in a while until the tomatoes break up and the liquid thickens, 10 to 15 minutes.
   Trim the green beans; chop into 1-inch pieces.

6. When the stew has thickened, stir in the green beans and adjust the heat so that the soup bubbles gently but steadily. Cover and cook undisturbed until the green beans are just tender, 3 to 5 minutes.

   Zest the lemon.

   Strip the parsley leaves from several sprigs and chop.

7. When the green beans are just tender, taste and adjust the seasoning. Divide the stew among 4 bowls. Sprinkle with the lemon zest, drizzle with more olive oil, garnish with the parsley, and serve.

VARIATIONS

Green Bean Stew with Tomatoes, Olives, and Almonds
Substitute 1 cup each pitted black olives and whole almonds for the lamb and cook them with the onion in Step 2.

Curried Chickpea Stew with Tomatoes and Lamb
Use 2 cups cooked or canned chickpeas (one 15-ounce can) instead of the green beans and 2 tablespoons curry powder in place of the cumin.

NOTES

MAKE YOUR OWN

Chicken Stock 213

Vegetable Stock 212

EVEN FASTER
Add the green beans to the pot along with the lamb and onions.

SIDES

Couscous 910

Crisp Seasoned Pita 908

Hummus 939

Cucumber Salad 915

Carrot Salad with Raisins 914

SPEED SERVES 4

Bone-In Chicken Noodle Soup

It doesn't take long for bone-in chicken to turn water into a flavorful broth. Start with whole pieces, don't overcook the meat or fuss with the bones, and you'll have real chicken noodle soup on the table in 30 minutes.

Ingredients

2 tablespoons olive oil

4 bone-in chicken thighs

4 chicken drumsticks

Salt

1 large onion

2 large carrots

3 celery stalks, plus any leaves

4 garlic cloves

5 bay leaves

Pepper

8 ounces egg noodles or any cut pasta

Prep | Cook

1. Put 2 tablespoons oil in a large pot over medium-high heat.

   Pat the chicken dry with a paper towel.

2. Put the chicken in the pot, skin side down, sprinkle with salt, and cook, undisturbed, until browned, 5 or 6 minutes.

   Trim and peel the onion. Trim and peel the carrots. Trim the celery stalks, reserving any leaves.

   Cut the onion, carrots, and celery stalks into ½-inch chunks.

   Peel 4 garlic cloves and smash them with the flat side of a knife.

3. Add the vegetables and garlic to the pot with the chicken. Add 8 cups water, stirring to scrape the chicken and any browned bits from the bottom of the pot. Add 5 bay leaves and a pinch each of salt and pepper.

4. When the broth comes to a boil, adjust the heat so that it bubbles steadily. Cook, undisturbed, until the meat begins to loosen from the bones and is cooked through, 15 to 20 minutes.

   Chop the celery leaves.

5. When the chicken is beginning to fall off the bone, bring the broth to a rolling boil and add 8 ounces egg noodles. Start tasting after 5 minutes; when the noodles are tender but not mushy, turn off the heat.

6. Fish out the bay leaves. Taste and adjust the seasoning, divide the soup among 4 bowls, garnish with the celery leaves, and serve immediately.

VARIATIONS

Herbed Bone-In Chicken Noodle Soup

In Step 2, add 4 sprigs fresh sage or oregano or 2 sprigs rosemary to the pot with the chicken. Remove them when you take out the bay leaves.

Dilly Bone-In Chicken Noodle Soup

Tie 1 bunch fresh dill together with twine. In Step 2, add it to the pot with the chicken. Remove the dill when you take out the bay leaves.

Chinese-Style Bone-In Chicken Noodle Soup

With a few changes, this becomes a completely different soup. In Step 2, add a few pieces of whole or broken star anise, 2 tablespoons soy sauce, and several thinly sliced coins of fresh ginger to the pot with the chicken. Omit the bay leaf. Use fresh or dried Chinese egg noodles (fresh will cook in about 1 minute).

Mexican-Style Bone-In Chicken Noodle Soup

Ditto, really. In Step 2, add 1 or 2 whole fresh or dried chiles to the pot with the chicken, along with a few cilantro sprigs, 1 tablespoon tomato paste, and 1 lime, cut into quarters. When you take out the bay leaves before serving, remove the lime; you can also remove the chiles and herbs if you prefer.

SIDES

Warm Buttery Bread 906

Bruschetta 909

Green Salad 911

SPEED ◔ SERVES 4

American Onion Soup

You can't make real French onion soup for four people in 45 minutes, so why try to fudge it? Introducing American Onion Soup, a faster version that takes its cues from the classic but is distinctly un-French. Beer and cheddar replace cognac and Gruyère. See If You Have More Time for the French original.

Ingredients

4 tablespoons (½ stick) butter

4 large onions

Salt and pepper

½ loaf baguette (a little stale is fine)

8 ounces cheddar cheese (2 cups grated)

1 teaspoon sugar

2 or 3 sprigs fresh thyme or ½ teaspoon dried

½ cup beer or water

5 cups beef or chicken stock

¼ cup cream

Prep | Cook

1. Put 4 tablespoons butter in a large pot over medium heat.

   Trim, peel, halve, and shave the onions in a food processor using the thinnest slicing attachment or slice them as thinly as you can by hand. Add them to the skillet as you go.

2. When you've added all the onions, sprinkle with salt and pepper, cover, and raise the heat to high.

3. Cook, stirring occasionally, until the onions soften, reduce in volume, and start to brown, 10 to 12 minutes. Reduce the heat a little if they start to burn.

4. Heat the broiler as high as it goes and put the rack about 4 inches from the heat.

   Cut 8 slices of bread on the bias. Put them on a baking sheet.

   Grate 2 cups cheddar in the food processor fitted with the grating disk (no need to rinse it out) or by hand with a box grater. Top each slice of bread with a mound of cheese.

5. When the onions are soft, uncover the pot, sprinkle with 1 teaspoon sugar, and cook, stirring occasionally and adding

a splash of liquid if the bottom of the pot starts to burn, until the onions are very soft and golden brown, 10 to 12 minutes.

If you're using fresh thyme, strip the leaves from 2 or 3 sprigs and chop them.

6. When the onions are golden, stir in ½ cup beer or water. Scrape up any brown bits from the bottom and sides of the pot.

7. Add 5 cups stock and the thyme. When the soup comes to a boil, lower the heat so it bubbles steadily and cook, stirring once in a while until the soup thickens a bit and becomes fragrant, 3 to 5 minutes.

8. Broil the bread until the cheese bubbles and browns, 2 or 3 minutes.

9. Stir ¼ cup cream into the soup, taste and adjust the seasoning, and divide the soup among 4 bowls. Top each serving with 2 slices of bread and cheese and serve immediately.

VARIATIONS

Leek Soup with Blue Cheese
Stronger. Use 6 large leeks instead of the onions. Trim away the darkest green parts and slice the leeks crosswise. Be careful not to overcook them; once they start to brown, they'll burn if you don't watch them. Instead of cheddar, use 4 ounces crumbled blue cheese and substitute white wine for the beer.

NOTES

MAKE YOUR OWN

Beef Stock 212

Chicken Stock 213

IF YOU HAVE MORE TIME

Classic French Onion Soup
After uncovering the pot in Step 5, cook the onions over medium-low heat, stirring frequently until they are very dark and jammy, up to an hour; splash with a tablespoon or 2 of cognac, then simmer with the beef stock (no beer, please) for at least another 30 minutes before adding the broiled bread and cheese. Gruyère is traditional.

SPEED ◕ SERVES 4

Shrimp Gumbo

When you cook fat and flour together, you're making a roux, useful in thickening soups and stews. The darker the color, the more complex, less "floury" the flavor. But rushing the process can cause burning. I compromise by cooking the flour just enough to take the rawness off, making a so-called blonde roux, like the one in this New Orleans classic.

Ingredients

4 tablespoons (½ stick) butter

1 medium onion

¼ cup flour

Salt and pepper

1 pound okra

One 28-ounce can diced tomatoes

2 garlic cloves

4 cups vegetable or chicken stock or water

3 sprigs fresh oregano or 1 teaspoon dried

1 pound peeled shrimp

Prep | Cook

1. Put 4 tablespoons butter in a large pot over medium heat.

   Trim, peel, and chop the onion.

2. When the butter starts to sizzle, add the onion and ¼ cup flour, stirring well to combine and break up any lumps.

3. Sprinkle with salt and pepper and cook, stirring occasionally and adjusting the heat to prevent scorching until the mixture turns golden, 4 to 7 minutes.

   Trim the okra and cut it crosswise into ¼-inch slices.

4. If the roux starts to scorch and you're not finished slicing the okra, stir in the tomatoes and their juice, scraping any browned bits off the bottom of the pot.

   Peel and mince 2 garlic cloves and add them to the pot.

5. When the roux and onion turn golden brown, stir in the okra and (if you haven't added them already) the tomatoes and their juice. Scrape any browned bits off the bottom of the pot. Add the 4 cups stock or water and bring to a boil, then lower the heat so the soup bubbles steadily.

6. Cover the pot and cook, stirring occasionally until the okra completely softens and the broth is thickened, 10 to 15 minutes.

If you're using fresh oregano, strip the leaves from 3 sprigs and chop. Chop the shrimp into bite-sized pieces.

7. Add the shrimp and fresh oregano leaves or 1 teaspoon dried to the pot and cook, stirring once or twice until the shrimp turns pink and cooks through, 2 or 3 minutes. Taste and adjust the seasoning and serve.

VARIATIONS

Crab Gumbo
Easier and more luxurious. Use lump crabmeat instead of the shrimp. It will take only a minute or so to heat through.

Chicken Gumbo
Substitute 1 pound boneless, skinless chicken thighs for the shrimp. Cut them into strips and add them after the butter sizzles in Step 2. Let them brown a bit on both sides, then transfer to a plate while you make the roux. Put the seared chicken strips in the pot along with the stock in Step 5.

Sausage Gumbo
Instead of shrimp, use 1 pound andouille or Italian sausage cut into bite-sized bits and add them to the foaming butter in Step 2. Let them brown a little bit on both sides, then transfer to a plate while you make the roux. Add them back with the stock in Step 5.

Tofu Gumbo
Use 1 ½ pounds cubed firm tofu instead of the shrimp. It will take only a minute or so to heat through.

No-Okra Gumbo
Use green beans or zucchini instead of the okra in the main recipe or any of the variations.

NOTES

MAKE YOUR OWN

Vegetable Stock 212

Chicken Stock 213

IF YOU HAVE MORE TIME
Make a fast shrimp stock: Use 1 ½ pounds peel-on shrimp; remove the shells and put them in a medium pot. Add 4 ½ cups water and 2 bay leaves, bring to a boil, then lower the heat so the stock bubbles steadily. Cook, stirring once in a while until fragrant and cloudy, 15 to 20 minutes. Strain and use the shrimp stock as the liquid in Step 5.

For a richer, thicker soup: In Step 2, cook the butter, flour, and onion together until the roux is a deeper, darker brown, 20 to 30 minutes. Skip the okra.

SIDES

White Rice 941

Quinoa 945

Green Salad 911

Succotash 933

SPEED SERVES 4

Curried Chicken and Vegetable Soup with Rice

Bright and spicy. Irresistible.

Ingredients

2 tablespoons vegetable oil

6 boneless, skinless chicken thighs (1 pound)

Salt and pepper

1 medium onion

2 large carrots

2 celery stalks

2 garlic cloves

1 inch fresh ginger

1 fresh hot green chile (like serrano)

2 tablespoons curry powder

1 cinnamon stick

¾ cup white basmati rice

1 bunch fresh cilantro for garnish

Prep | Cook

1. Put 2 tablespoons vegetable oil in a large pot over medium-high heat.

   Cut the chicken into ½-inch chunks.

2. When the oil is hot, add the chicken, sprinkle with salt and pepper, and cook, stirring occasionally, until browned on all sides, 5 to 10 minutes.

   Trim and peel the onion and carrots. Trim the celery.

   Cut everything into ½-inch chunks.

3. When the chicken is browned, add the vegetables to the pot and cook, stirring occasionally and lowering the heat if the vegetables start to burn.

   Peel and mince 2 garlic cloves and 1 inch fresh ginger.

   Trim the chile, seed it if you like, then mince it.

4. Add the garlic, ginger, and chile to the pot, along with 2 tablespoons curry powder and the cinnamon stick. Cook until the spices are fragrant, about 1 minute.

5. Add ¾ cup white basmati rice and raise the heat to high; stir for 30 seconds to toast the rice a bit. Add 8 cups water.

6. When the liquid comes to a boil, adjust the heat so that it simmers and cover the pot. Cook until the rice is tender, 15 to 20 minutes.
   Chop 1/4 cup cilantro.

7. When the rice is tender, fish out the cinnamon stick and discard. Taste and adjust the seasoning, divide among 4 bowls, garnish with the cilantro, and serve.

VARIATIONS

Chicken Soup with Rice and Peas
Use olive oil in place of vegetable. Omit the curry and cinnamon and use chicken stock instead of water for best flavor. Use 1 1/2 cups fresh or frozen peas instead of the celery. Substitute mint leaves for the cilantro and add 1 cup grated Parmesan to the bowls just before serving.

Chicken Soup with Rice and Broccoli
Use olive oil instead of vegetable and substitute 1 1/2 pounds broccoli for the celery and carrots. Skip the curry powder, cinnamon, and cilantro; add 1/2 teaspoon (or more) red chile flakes to the vegetables in Step 3. I like the broccoli to get quite tender and fall apart, but if you like it crisper, wait to add it until the last 5 minutes of cooking in Step 6. Drizzle each bowl with more olive oil just before serving.

NOTES

MAKE YOUR OWN
Curry Powder 758

EVEN FASTER
Put everything but the cilantro—oil, chicken, onion, vegetables, rice, and seasoning—into the pot with the water. Bring to a boil, then lower the heat to a steady bubble, cover the pot, and cook undisturbed until the rice is tender, 15 to 20 minutes.

SIDES

Crunchy Okra 959

Avocado with Hot Sauce and Cilantro 920

Cucumber Raita 916

SPEED SERVES 4

Mushroom and Chicken Stew with Dill and Paprika

This creamy, satisfying stew is based on the Hungarian dish chicken paprikash. The mushrooms add so much flavor that you barely have to sear the chicken. It's delicious served over buttered noodles or rice.

Ingredients

3 tablespoons butter

6 boneless, skinless chicken thighs (about 1 pound)

Salt and pepper

1 ½ pounds button, cremini, or shiitake mushrooms

1 medium onion

2 teaspoons paprika

1 tablespoon all-purpose flour

3 cups chicken or vegetable stock or water

1 bunch fresh dill

½ cup cream, sour cream, or yogurt

Prep | Cook

1. Put 3 tablespoons butter in a large pot over low heat.

   Cut the chicken into bite-sized pieces.

2. When the butter starts to foam, raise the heat to medium-high, add the chicken to the pot, sprinkle with salt and pepper, and cook, stirring occasionally until it is not pink on any side, 5 to 10 minutes.

   Trim and quarter the mushrooms. (If you're using shiitakes, discard the stems.)

   Trim and peel the onion; cut it into small chunks.

3. Transfer the browned chicken to a bowl with a slotted spoon.

4. Add the mushrooms and onion to the pot and cook, stirring occasionally until they soften, 5 to 10 minutes.

5. Add 2 teaspoons paprika and a sprinkle of salt and pepper and cook, stirring until fragrant, less than 1 minute.

6. Add 1 tablespoon flour and cook, stirring occasionally until it toasts it a bit, 3 to 5 minutes.

7. Return the chicken to the pot along with 3 cups stock or water. Cook, stirring occasionally, until the broth is thick and the chicken is fully cooked, 3 to 5 minutes.

   Strip 1/4 cup dill leaves from the stems and chop.

8. Adjust the heat to medium-low, and add the dill and 1/2 cup cream, sour cream, or yogurt. Stir until well combined. Taste and adjust the seasoning and serve right away.

VARIATIONS

Zucchini and Chicken Stew with Paprika and Dill
Substitute zucchini for the mushrooms; cut it in half lengthwise and then into chunks. If you like, let the zucchini cook long enough to break down and thicken the soup, an additional 5 minutes in Step 4.

Cabbage and Chicken Stew with Caraway and Dill
Substitute 1 tablespoon caraway seeds for the paprika. Instead of the mushrooms, shred a small head of red or green cabbage.

NOTES

MAKE YOUR OWN

Chicken Stock 213

Vegetable Stock 212

SIDES

White Rice 941

Quinoa 945

Buttered Egg Noodles 948

Skin-On Mashed Potatoes 961

Boiled Potatoes 954

Warm Buttery Bread 906

SPEED SERVES 4

Lentil Soup, with or Without Ham

Ham obviously adds flavor, but it's optional, and lentils have an earthy taste all their own. Load the pot up with vegetables and you've got a balanced bowl, whichever way you go.

Ingredients

3 tablespoons olive oil, plus more for garnish

8 ounces smoked ham in one piece (optional)

1 large onion

2 large carrots

2 celery stalks

4 garlic cloves

1 ½ cups lentils

2 bay leaves

6 cups chicken or vegetable stock or water, or more as needed

Salt and pepper

Prep | Cook

1. Put 3 tablespoons olive oil in a large pot over medium-low heat.

   If you're using it, cut the ham into cubes.

   Trim and peel the onion.

2. When the oil is hot, add the ham and the onions. Raise the heat to medium-high and cook, stirring occasionally, until the meat and onions brown in places, 3 to 5 minutes.

   Trim and peel the carrots. Trim the celery stalks. Chop both and add them to the pot.

   Peel and mince 4 garlic cloves; add them to the pot.

3. Add 1 ½ cups lentils, 2 bay leaves, and 6 cups stock or water. If you're not using ham, sprinkle with salt and pepper.

4. Bring the soup to a boil, then adjust the heat so that it bubbles gently but steadily. Simmer until the lentils are tender, anywhere from 20 to 40 minutes. If the soup is too thick, stir in more stock or water, ¼ cup at a time.

5. When the soup is ready, fish out the bay leaves and discard, sprinkle with salt and pepper, and divide among 4 bowls. Garnish with a drizzle of olive oil and serve.

VARIATIONS

Lentil Soup with Lemon and Fresh Herbs
When the soup is ready in Step 5, add the zest and juice of 1 lemon and ½ cup chopped fresh dill or parsley or 2 tablespoons chopped fresh tarragon or mint. Stir and serve.

Mustardy Lentil Soup
Lots of flavor with no work: When the soup is ready in Step 5, add 2 tablespoons (or more) coarsely ground mustard. Stir and serve.

Split Pea Soup, with or without Ham
Instead of lentils, use split peas.

NOTES

MAKE YOUR OWN

Chicken Stock 213

Vegetable Stock 212

EVEN FASTER
Put all the ingredients in the pot at the same time. Bring to a boil, then adjust the heat so that it simmers gently but steadily and cook, stirring occasionally until the lentils are tender.

THE FASTEST LEGUMES
Lentils—and split peas for that matter; see the variation—are staples of the fast kitchen (see pages 16 and 485). They're the only legumes that reliably cook in 20 to 40 minutes. And, like all their cousins, they're hearty and satisfying. I usually use common brown or semifancy dark green lentils for this soup, but if you see other kinds and colors, or any small beans like mung beans (which are a lovely green), or pigeon peas for that matter, grab them. This recipe works well with any and all.

SIDES

Warm Buttery Bread 906

Green Salad 911

White Rice 941

Crisp Seasoned Pita 908

Pinzimonio 884

SPEED SERVES 4

Collard Greens Stewed with Smoked Pork

Vegetables take a lot less time to become tender than meat, so when you let them simmer for almost 45 minutes while the ham hocks soften, you're left with a pot of luxurious greens.

Ingredients

2 tablespoons butter

1 large red onion

4 garlic cloves

1 smoked ham hock or 2 smoked pork chops (about 1 pound)

2 bunches collard greens (2 pounds)

Pepper

6 cups chicken or vegetable stock or water

2 bay leaves

Salt

Prep | Cook

1. Put 2 tablespoons butter in a large pot over medium heat.

   Trim, peel, and chop the onion; add it to the pot and stir.

   Peel and mince 4 garlic cloves. Add them to the pot and stir.

2. Add the pork to the pot and cook, stirring occasionally and turning the meat until the onion softens and starts to smell smoky, 3 to 5 minutes.

   Trim the collards. Slice the leaves in half along the stem and cut them crosswise into thick ribbons. Add them to the pot as you work, stirring after each addition.

3. Sprinkle with lots of pepper. Add 6 cups stock or water and 2 bay leaves and raise the heat to high. When the stew comes to a boil, adjust the heat so that it bubbles gently but steadily.

4. Cook, stirring occasionally until the collards become tender, 10 to 15 minutes.

   Fish the pork out of the pot and put it on a cutting board until it's cool enough to handle. (Let the stew keep simmering.)

   Trim and pick the meat and fat from the bone, cutting big chunks of pork into smaller pieces. Put the meat and the bone back into the pot; discard the fat.

5. Cook, stirring once in a while, until the collards are quite tender and the meat is juicy, another 10 to 15 minutes. Remove the bay leaves and discard. Taste and adjust the seasoning, adding salt if necessary, and serve, leaving the bones behind in the pot.

VARIATIONS

Broccoli Rabe Stewed with Tons of Garlic

Yes, you can use less, but trust me: Skip the pork. Use 1/4 cup olive oil instead of the butter. Substitute 20 garlic cloves for the onion; add them to the pot as you peel them in Step 1. Use broccoli rabe instead of collards.

Cauliflower Stewed with Anchovies

Skip the pork and substitute olive oil for the butter. Use cauliflower florets instead of the collards. Add 8 anchovy fillets to the onion in Step 1. Serve with lemon wedges.

NOTES

MAKE YOUR OWN

Chicken Stock 213

Vegetable Stock 212

EVEN FASTER

Skip the smoked pork and increase the butter to 4 tablespoons (1/2 stick). Put everything in the pot at the same time; the vegetables will be ready about 10 minutes earlier.

SEASONING WITH SMOKED PORK

Even a small piece of smoked meat yields loads of flavor in little time, especially if there's a bone involved. What has the potential to take a long time is melting the fat. But this technique—where you yank the meat out partway through cooking, chop it up a bit, and return it to the pot—solves that problem.

Some supermarkets or butchers carry smoked ham hocks or trotters (feet), which add not only smokiness but also a bit of collagen to thicken the broth. If you can't find those, not to worry; a smoked pork chop or even a thick ham steak or a chunk of slab bacon will do the trick too.

SIDES

Warm Flour or Corn Tortillas 907

Creamy Polenta 947

Watermelon, Feta, and Mint Salad 922

Panfried Corn and Onions 933

Ripe Plantains 960

SPEED SERVES 4

Hot and Sour Soup with Bok Choy and Pork

Duplicating the flavor of this restaurant staple isn't the hard part. Preparing all the ingredients is what slows you down. By streamlining the components to a piquant broth, a little meat, and one main vegetable, you'll be spooning this out in no time.

Ingredients

12 ounces pork shoulder

2 garlic cloves

2 inches fresh ginger

1 head bok choy (about 1 ½ pounds)

4 scallions

2 tablespoons vegetable oil

Salt and pepper

Pinch red chile flakes, or more to taste

6 cups chicken or vegetable stock

3 tablespoons rice vinegar, or more to taste

2 tablespoons soy sauce, or more to taste

Prep | Cook

Put the pork in the freezer.

Peel and mince 2 garlic cloves and 2 inches fresh ginger.

Trim the bok choy; cut (or pull) the leaves from the ribs. Slice the stems and cut the leaves into thin ribbons.

Trim and chop the scallions.

1. Put 2 tablespoons vegetable oil in a large pot over low heat.

   Slice the pork thinly against the grain, then stack a few slices and cut them into strips about ½ inch wide.

2. Raise the heat under the pot to high. When the oil is hot but not quite smoking, add the pork, sprinkle with salt and pepper, and cook, undisturbed, until the pieces release from the pan, about 1 minute. Then cook, stirring occasionally until browned, 3 to 5 minutes.

3. Add the garlic, ginger, and a pinch of red chile flakes or to taste. (The soup should not derive its heat from this, so take it easy.) Cook, stirring until fragrant, about 30 seconds.

4. Add the bok choy ribs and cook, stirring occasionally until they begin to soften, 2 or 3 minutes.

5. Add 6 cups stock and bring to a boil.

6. Add the bok choy leaves, stir, and adjust the heat so the liquid bubbles gently but steadily. Cook, stirring once or twice until the bok choy leaves are tender, 3 to 5 minutes.

7. Add 3 tablespoons rice vinegar and 2 tablespoons soy sauce and at least a teaspoon of pepper, then taste and adjust the seasoning, adding more soy sauce and rice vinegar if you like. Divide among 4 bowls and serve, garnished with the scallions.

VARIATIONS

Hot and Sour Soup with Bean Sprouts and Beef
Substitute beef chuck roast for the pork and bean sprouts for the bok choy. Add the sprouts to the pot in Step 6.

Hot and Sour Soup with Napa Cabbage and Chicken
Light and bright tasting. Substitute boneless chicken thighs for the pork and Napa cabbage for the bok choy. There's no need to separate the cabbage ribs from the leaves; just cut the leaves crosswise into ribbons and add them to the pot in Step 6.

Hot and Sour Soup with Asian Greens and Tofu
Instead of the bok choy, use whatever interesting greens you can find: tatsoi, gai lan, pea shoots, or Chinese broccoli. Substitute 1 pound extra-firm tofu for the pork and cut it into ½-inch cubes before cooking in Step 2.

NOTES

MAKE YOUR OWN
Chicken Stock 213

Vegetable Stock 212

THICKENING WITH CORNSTARCH
Most soups don't need thickening; there's nothing wrong with a brothy soup. This one benefits from some body, especially if you are looking for the texture you get in Chinese restaurants. As a rule, to thicken with cornstarch, combine 1 part cornstarch with 2 parts liquid. In this case you can mix 3 tablespoons cornstarch with the rice vinegar, soy sauce, and 1 tablespoon water. Add it to the pot after everything else. Cook at a gentle bubble, stirring, until the soup thickens, which will take just a minute or two.

SIDES

White Rice 941

Sesame Noodles 949

Scallion Pancakes 940

Sesame-Soy Black Beans 937

SPEED SERVES 4

Beef and Butter Bean Chili

Pulse your own meat in a food processor and you'll end up with a less uniform and more pleasing texture and better flavor and quality than any store-bought ground beef.

Ingredients

2 tablespoons olive oil

1 large onion

1 pound boneless beef chuck

Salt and pepper

2 garlic cloves

2 dried hot red chiles (like chile de árbol)

1 teaspoon cumin

1 teaspoon chili powder

1 teaspoon dried oregano

One 28-ounce can whole peeled tomatoes

1 pound frozen butter beans or lima beans

4 cups beef or chicken stock or water

Several sprigs fresh cilantro for garnish

1 lime

Sour cream for garnish

Prep | Cook

1. Put 2 tablespoons olive oil in a large pot over medium heat.

   Trim, peel, and chop the onion.

2. When the oil is hot, add the onion and cook, stirring occasionally until soft and golden, 5 to 10 minutes.

   Cut the beef into chunks and put them in a food processor. Pulse until the meat is coarsely chopped (about the size of peas).

3. Remove the onions from the pot and raise the heat to medium-high. Add the beef, sprinkle with salt and pepper, and cook, stirring frequently until it's browned, 3 to 5 minutes.

   Peel and mince 2 garlic cloves. Trim 2 dried hot red chiles; seed them if you like and mince.

4. Add the garlic and chiles to the pot, along with 1 teaspoon cumin, 1 teaspoon chili powder, and 1 teaspoon dried oregano. Cook, stirring until fragrant, 30 seconds or so.

5. Add the tomatoes and their juice and return the onions to the mixture. Break up the tomatoes with a spoon and scrape any browned bits off the bottom of the pot.

6. Add the beans and 4 cups stock or water. Bring to a boil, then reduce the heat so it bubbles gently. Cover and cook, stirring occasionally until the chili thickens and darkens, 15 to 20 minutes.
   Chop several sprigs cilantro. Cut the lime into wedges.

7. Check the chili. If it's too watery, uncover, raise the heat a bit, and cook, stirring occasionally until it's as thick as you like, just another minute or 2.

8. Taste and adjust the seasoning, divide among 4 bowls, and serve with the lime wedges, garnished with the cilantro and a dollop of sour cream.

VARIATIONS

White Chili
Like chicken-and-bean soup. Substitute boneless, skinless chicken thighs for the beef and use chicken stock or water. Instead of the tomatoes, add 2 cups more liquid.

Lamb and Black Bean Chili
Substitute boneless lamb shoulder for the beef, chicken stock for the beef stock, cinnamon for the oregano, and 4 cups canned or cooked black beans for the butter beans.

NOTES

MAKE YOUR OWN
Chili Powder 758

Beef Stock 212

Chicken Stock 213

EVEN FASTER
Use preground beef instead of grinding your own.

IF YOU HAVE MORE TIME
If you let the chili simmer for another 30 minutes, even deeper flavors will develop, and the beans will break apart and thicken it more.

SIDES

Warm Flour Tortillas 907

White Rice 941

Coleslaw 923

Mexican Street Corn 932

Ripe Plantains with Cinnamon and Cumin 960

Pasta and Noodles

PASTA

Cacio e Pepe (Cheese and Pepper) 278

Mac and Cheese 280

Pasta with Broccoli Rabe and Ricotta 282

Pasta with Pesto and Cherry Tomatoes 284

Pasta with Artichokes, Toasted Bread Crumbs, and Lemon 286

Pasta with Fennel, White Beans, and Stock 288

Spaghetti with Garlicky Fresh Tomato Sauce 290

Pasta with Spicy Eggplant and Tomato Sauce 292

Broiled Ziti 298

Pasta with Greens and Eggs 300

Linguine with Clams 302

Pasta with Tuna and Dried Tomatoes 304

Pasta with Scallops and Potatoes 306

Fideos with Shrimp, Tomatoes, and Peas 308

Pasta with Squid and Tomatoes 310

Three Bs Pasta 312

Pasta with Chicken, Mushrooms, and Wine 314

Spaghetti with Nearly Instant Bolognese 318

Spaghetti and Drop Meatballs with Tomato Sauce 320

Pasta with Squash and Ham, Risotto Style 322

Orzo Risotto with Asparagus and "Poached" Eggs 324

Three-Cheese Lasagna with Fresh Noodles 326

Ricotta Dumplings with Spinach and Brown Butter 328

NOODLES

Cold Peanut Noodles with Whatever You Have 330

Noodles with Snow Peas and Chile Oil 334

Udon with Teriyaki Tofu 336

Noodles, Shrimp, and Sweet Potatoes in Curry Broth 338

Cool Noodles with Chicken and Cilantro-Scallion Pesto 340

Singapore-Style Noodles with Chicken, Peppers, and Basil 342

Stir-Fried Noodles with Beef and Celery 344

Pasta and Noodles

My go-to comfort food, especially when I'm in a hurry, is a bowl of noodles. It may well be yours too: Pasta is satisfying, comforting, and easy. It's also fast.

Its speed, however, is limited by the time it takes to bring a large pot of water to a boil. So cooking pasta is not a process you can easily rush.

This is a good thing. The time it takes for the water to boil gives us the chance to make sauces and side dishes without feeling frantic. Or to say hello to the family without worrying that we haven't even started dinner yet. Consider this scenario: As soon as you get home from work, start the water and walk away. Say hi to your kids and change out of your work clothes. By the time you get back to the kitchen you'll still have plenty of time to whip up a sauce.

You've probably made your fair share of pasta, and there's no shame in relying on a few tried and true recipes to get through the month. But even though noodles may be familiar, they don't have to be routine; I continue to be amazed at the variety of sauces that can be built from a few quick processes and how often I discover new ones.

So here are twists on old favorites, new flavors you can create with common pantry staples, and cunning tricks for making homemade pasta dishes in the simplest possible ways. And if you haven't yet discovered how easy it is to make the noodle dishes of Asia at home, you'll be surprised at the sheer speed with which they come together.

Chapter Highlights

What to Do While the Water Boils You have 19 minutes. Use them wisely: Make a sauce, chop some garnishes, grate some cheese. Possibilities abound. Recipe-Free Pasta (page 316).

More Water, Less Hassle Don't try to cook pasta in a small amount of water. Filling the Pot (page 281).

Salt It Like You Mean It Don't skimp: Salting Pasta Water (page 279).

The Simplest Sauces Sometimes one ingredient is pretty much all you need to make a beautiful sauce. Pasta with Olive Oil and Other Stuff (page 305).

You Say Tomato The tomato primer, including a breakdown of canned tomato varieties. Tomatoes (page 294).

Never Buy Jarred Tomato Sauce Again It's too fast not to make yourself: Tomato Sauce (page 296).

Oil and Anything Why a lot of olive oil, something flavorful, and low heat is a "recipe" for pasta sauces that practically cook themselves. Pasta with Olive Oil and Other Stuff (page 305).

One-Pot Pastas Everything happens in the pot; no colander needed. Orzo Risotto with Asparagus and "Poached" Eggs (page 324); Pasta with Squash and Ham, Risotto Style (page 322); Fideos with Squid, Tomatoes, and Corn (page 309).

Shape Matters Different pasta shapes require different cooking times: For a general rule, see Pasta Cooking Times (page 291).

The Ultimate Shortcut Substitute egg roll wrappers or wonton skins for fresh pasta. Three-Cheese Lasagna with Fresh Noodles (page 326).

Using Fresh Pasta Substitute fresh pasta for dried in any of these recipes. Fresh Pasta Options (page 327).

The Asian Noodle Aisle An introduction to the other (and probably original) pasta: Asian Noodles (page 332).

Noodles Get Company Noodles and vegetables boil together. Noodles with Snow Peas and Chile Oil (page 334); Noodles, Shrimp, and Sweet Potatoes in Curry Broth (page 338).

World's Fastest Noodle Two lightning-quick ways to cook vermicelli rice noodles. Singapore-Style Noodles with Chicken, Peppers, and Basil (page 342); Noodles, Shrimp, and Sweet Potatoes in Curry Broth (page 338).

SPEED ◐ SERVES 4

Cacio e Pepe (Cheese and Pepper)

Among the most fundamental and basic of all Italian pastas. Melting cheese (*cacio*) and fresh pepper (*pepe*) mingle in a simple dish that is much more than the sum of its parts. To be authentic, the cheese should be pecorino (from sheep), and pecorino Romano is widely available; if you can't find that, use (real) Parmesan. And lots of coarsely ground black pepper.

Ingredients

Salt

8 ounces pecorino Romano or Parmesan cheese (2 cups grated)

1 pound pasta, any shape you like

1 tablespoon black pepper, or more to taste

Prep | Cook

1. Bring a stockpot of water to a boil and salt it.

   Grate 2 cups pecorino Romano or Parmesan.

2. When the water boils, add the pasta and stir occasionally. Start tasting after 5 minutes.

3. When the pasta is tender but not mushy, drain it, reserving about 3 cups cooking water. Return the pasta to the pot.

4. Add the cheese, 1 tablespoon pepper, and enough of the cooking water to make it saucy (you may only need a cup or so). Toss, taste and adjust the seasoning, and serve.

VARIATIONS

Buttery Cacio e Pepe

For an even richer version, add 4 tablespoons (½ stick) butter, softened, to the final dish.

Pasta with Blue Cheese and Black Pepper

Tangy and extra creamy. Substitute 1 cup crumbled blue cheese for the pecorino.

Pasta with Ricotta, Pepper, and Nutmeg

Use 1 cup ricotta cheese instead of the pecorino and add about a cup of grated Parmesan and a few gratings of nutmeg (or a couple of pinches of ground nutmeg) along with the black pepper.

Pasta with Mascarpone and Red Pepper

Sweet meets heat. Use 1 cup mascarpone cheese instead of the pecorino and a pinch of red chile flakes instead of the black pepper.

NOTES

SALTING PASTA WATER

A token pinch of salt in a giant pot of water simply isn't enough when you're cooking pasta, because the noodles are seasoned by the cooking water. When you cook pasta, the water should taste noticeably salty, almost like the ocean. If that seems like too much, remember that most of the water is going to be drained off. Be bold and salt your pasta water like you really mean it.

SIDES

Garlic Bread 906

Green Salad 911

Tomato Salad 913

Seared Broccoli or Cauliflower 925

Mac and Cheese

This is simple mac and cheese, not mac with cheese sauce. Instead of making a béchamel, you use the heat of the pasta to melt a load of cheese; a splash of milk makes it saucy. Bread crumbs and a spin under the broiler make the top crisp.

Ingredients

Salt

12 ounces cheddar, Gruyère, or Swiss cheese or a combination (3 cups grated)

4 ounces Parmesan cheese (1 cup grated)

1 pound cut pasta, like elbows, penne, or ziti

½ cup milk

4 tablespoons (½ stick) butter

Pepper

½ cup bread crumbs

Prep | Cook

1. Bring a stockpot of water to a boil and salt it.

   Grate 3 cups cheddar, Gruyère, or Swiss cheese. Grate 1 cup Parmesan.

   Turn the broiler to high; put the rack 4 inches from the heat.

2. When the water boils, add the pasta and stir occasionally. Start tasting after 5 minutes.

3. When the pasta is barely tender, drain it and reserve some cooking water. Return the pasta to the pot.

4. Add the grated cheddar, Gruyère, or Swiss, ½ cup milk, 4 tablespoons butter, and a sprinkle of salt and pepper. Stir until the cheese melts, adding cooking water a tablespoon at a time to thin if necessary. Taste and adjust the seasoning.

5. Transfer the pasta to a 9 × 13-inch baking dish. Sprinkle the Parmesan over the top and sprinkle with ½ cup bread crumbs.

6. Broil until the cheese is bubbly and brown and the bread crumbs crisp, 2 to 5 minutes. Serve.

VARIATIONS

9 Ways to Flavor Mac and Cheese

Stir any of the following, alone or in combination, into the pasta along with the cheese:

1. ½ cup chopped fresh parsley, cilantro, or basil
2. 1 tablespoon chopped fresh rosemary, sage, thyme, or oregano
3. Up to 1 tablespoon Dijon mustard
4. Up to 1 teaspoon nutmeg
5. Dash of hot sauce or Worcestershire
6. Up to 1 cup crumbled cooked bacon or sausage
7. Up to 2 cups chopped tomatoes
8. Up to 2 cups Garlicky Mushrooms (page 956)
9. Up to 2 cups chopped Sautéed Greens with Garlic (page 924)

NOTES

MAKE YOUR OWN

Bread Crumbs 71

IF YOU HAVE MORE TIME

Mac and Cheese Deluxe

If you want to make béchamel—an undeniably luxurious sauce—start by heating 2 ½ cups milk in a small saucepan over medium-low heat. When small bubbles appear around the sides, after about 5 minutes, turn off the heat. In another small saucepan over medium-low heat, melt 3 tablespoons butter. When the butter is foamy, add 3 tablespoons flour and cook, stirring until the mixture browns, about 5 minutes. Start whisking in the milk, about ¼ cup at a time at first, until the mixture is smooth; continue whisking in the milk until the sauce is thick and smooth. Whisk in the cheese until it's melted, sprinkle with salt and pepper, and toss the sauce with the cooked pasta. Top and broil as directed.

FILLING THE POT

There's a limit to how quickly you can throw together a pasta dish—the time it takes a pot of water to boil. It's tempting to save time by skimping on water, but the time saved is soon spent stirring the pasta and pulling it apart when it inevitably clumps together. Do yourself a favor: Fill your pot with ample water—a gallon per pound of pasta is about right—and spend the 20 minutes it takes to boil making something else.

SIDES

Green Salad 911

Tomato Salad 913

Seared Broccoli or Cauliflower 925

Sautéed Greens with Garlic 924

SPEED ◑ SERVES 4 TO 6

Pasta with Broccoli Rabe and Ricotta

Stir a cup of ricotta cheese into hot pasta, add a splash of cooking water, and you've got a rich and creamy sauce that took you 30 seconds to make. Slightly bitter broccoli rabe is the perfect vegetable to cut through the richness of the cheese.

Ingredients

Salt

3 tablespoons olive oil

1 ½ pounds broccoli rabe

Pepper

2 garlic cloves

¼ teaspoon red chile flakes

1 pound cut pasta, like elbows, penne, or ziti

1 cup ricotta cheese

Prep | Cook

1. Bring a stockpot of water to a boil and salt it.
2. Put 3 tablespoons olive oil in a large skillet over low heat.

   Trim and chop the broccoli rabe, separating any thick stems.
3. Raise the heat under the skillet to medium-high. Add any thick stems to the skillet and cook until they begin to soften, 3 or 4 minutes.
4. Add the leaves, a handful at a time if necessary to fit them in, and sprinkle with salt and pepper. Cook until just wilted, 3 or 4 minutes.

   Peel and mince 2 garlic cloves; add them to the skillet along with ¼ teaspoon red chile flakes.
5. When the water boils, add the pasta and stir occasionally. Start tasting after 5 minutes.
6. When the pasta is tender but not mushy, drain it, reserving some cooking water. Return the pasta to the pot.

7. Add the broccoli rabe, 1 cup ricotta, a sprinkle of salt and pepper, and a splash of the cooking water to make it saucy. Toss, taste and adjust the seasoning, and serve.

VARIATIONS

Pasta with Sausage, Broccoli Rabe, and Ricotta
Before adding the broccoli rabe to the skillet, brown 12 ounces crumbled Italian sausage. Remove it from the skillet if needed to make room for the broccoli rabe, then stir it into the pasta in Step 7.

Pasta with Asparagus and Ricotta
With or without the sausage in the first variation. Use asparagus instead of broccoli rabe. After trimming, cut it into 1-inch pieces, separating and cooking any thick stems as described in Steps 2 and 3. The asparagus might take a little longer to cook in Step 4.

Pasta with Spinach, Ricotta, and Lemon
Substitute spinach leaves for the broccoli rabe; it will take a little less time to wilt. Use nutmeg instead of red chile flakes and add the grated zest of a lemon to the sauce as well.

Pasta with Kale, Feta, and Olives
Use kale instead of the broccoli rabe; it will take a little more time to wilt. Substitute 1 cup crumbled feta for the ricotta and add ½ cup chopped pitted kalamata olives to the sauce as well.

SIDES

Green Salad 911

Tomato Salad 913

Garlic Bread 906

Fennel Salad with Olives 917

Celery Salad 917

SPEED ◐ SERVES 4 TO 6

Pasta with Pesto and Cherry Tomatoes

Part pesto, part *salsa cruda*. There's no reason not to combine two standouts in the same dish.

Ingredients

Salt

1 large bunch basil

1 small garlic clove

4 ounces Parmesan cheese (1 cup grated)

2 tablespoons pine nuts

½ cup olive oil

1 pound any pasta

1 pint cherry tomatoes

Prep | Cook

1. Bring a stockpot of water to a boil and salt it.

   Strip about 2 cups basil leaves from the stems. Put in a food processor.

   Peel 1 small garlic clove; add it to the food processor.

   Grate 1 cup Parmesan cheese.

2. Add 2 tablespoons pine nuts, ¼ cup olive oil, and a sprinkle of salt. Process, streaming in another ¼ cup olive oil as you go and stopping to scrape down the sides as necessary until the pesto is smooth.

3. When the water boils, add the pasta and stir occasionally. Start tasting after 3 minutes.

   Halve the cherry tomatoes.

4. When the pasta is tender but not mushy, drain it, reserving some cooking water. Return the pasta to the pot.

5. Add the pesto, tomatoes, about half of the Parmesan, and a splash of the cooking water to make it saucy. Toss, taste and adjust the seasoning, and serve hot, warm, or at room temperature, passing the remaining Parmesan at the table.

VARIATIONS

Pasta with Dill and Lemon Pesto

Substitute dill for the basil, the juice of a lemon for the Parmesan.

Pasta with Buttery Spinach Pesto

Substitute baby spinach leaves for the basil, 1/4 cup chopped walnuts for the pine nuts, and 2 tablespoons softened butter for 2 tablespoons of the olive oil (process in the butter at the end).

NOTES

PLENTY OF PESTOS

Nowadays the word *pesto* has come to describe virtually any herbs, vegetables, or fruit ground with garlic, cheese, and nuts. Cilantro pesto, spinach pesto, broccoli pesto, peach pesto—I've seen it all. Some are better ideas than others, but there's no harm in trying out the foods you like, green or otherwise. Just use the proportions here; double the recipe if you want to skip the tomatoes. The cheese may be stirred into the pesto or omitted entirely. (Cilantro pesto, for example, would not go well with Parmesan.)

STORING PESTO

Unless I have tons of basil growing in my garden or get a huge haul from the farmers' market, I usually just make small batches of pesto and eat them right away. But if you do make a large batch and you want to store it in the freezer for later, two tips will help the pesto keep its bright green color: Don't add Parmesan to the pesto before you store it; wait until after you thaw the frozen pesto to stir in the cheese. Drizzle a layer of olive oil on the top of the pesto before you freeze it. That will help form a seal to keep the air out and prevent the pesto from oxidizing and turning brown.

SIDES

Warm Buttery Bread 906

Green Salad 911

Fennel Salad with Olives 917

SPEED ◑ SERVES 4 TO 6

Pasta with Artichokes, Toasted Bread Crumbs, and Lemon

You can certainly prepare your own artichokes for this dish, but frozen are pretty good. Your prep time is better spent toasting and grinding quality bread. Homemade bread crumbs add an irresistible crunch and flavor to this multitextured dish.

Ingredients

Salt

3 cups frozen artichoke hearts

¼ cup olive oil

4 thick slices any rustic bread (a little stale is fine)

Pepper

2 garlic cloves

1 lemon

2 tablespoons butter

¼ cup white wine

1 pound any pasta

Prep | Cook

1. Bring a stockpot of water to a boil and salt it.
   Take 3 cups artichoke hearts out of the freezer.
2. Put ¼ cup olive oil in a large skillet or large pot over low heat.
   Tear 4 thick slices bread into chunks. Transfer to a food processor and pulse into coarse crumbs.
3. Raise the heat under the skillet to medium-high. Add the bread crumbs to the skillet, sprinkle with salt and pepper, and stir gently to coat in the oil. Cook, stirring frequently and adjusting the heat to prevent burning, until the crumbs are golden and crisp, 3 to 5 minutes.
   Peel and mince 2 garlic cloves.
   Halve the lemon.
4. When the bread crumbs are crisp, transfer them to a bowl, carefully wipe out the skillet, add 2 tablespoons butter, and return the skillet to medium-high heat.
5. When the oil is hot, add the artichokes and cook, stirring occasionally until they're warmed through, 3 to 5 minutes.

6. Add the garlic, sprinkle with salt and pepper, and cook until the garlic is fragrant, about 30 seconds. Add ¼ cup white wine, squeeze in the lemon juice, and scrape any browned bits off the bottom of the skillet.

7. Let the liquid bubble until it reduces by about half, 2 or 3 minutes, then turn the heat as low as it will go.

8. When the water boils, add the pasta and stir occasionally. Start tasting after 5 minutes.

9. When the pasta is tender but not mushy, drain it, reserving some cooking water. Add the pasta to the skillet and return the heat to medium-high. Add a splash of the cooking water to make it saucy, toss, taste, and adjust the seasoning.

10. Divide the pasta among 4 bowls, top with bread crumbs, and serve.

VARIATIONS

Pasta with Fennel, Toasted Bread Crumbs, and Lemon
Substitute 1 large fennel bulb, sliced, for the artichoke hearts. Sauté the fennel in the olive oil until tender and lightly browned, 5 or 6 minutes; proceed with the recipe.

NOTES

EVEN FASTER
Instead of making the bread crumbs described in Step 2, use Bread Crumbs (page 71) you've already made.

FROZEN, JARRED, AND CANNED ARTICHOKES
There is nothing like a fresh artichoke, but unfortunately few vegetables are as time-consuming to prepare. Luckily, their hearts come in some respectable alternative forms, which are quite good in pasta dishes, omelets, dips—pretty much anything. This recipe uses cooked frozen artichoke hearts, which you can thaw ahead of time or toss directly into the hot skillet. They most closely capture the flavor of fresh. Jarred artichoke hearts packed in oil are also fine. They're a bit softer and will break apart into the sauce a little more as you cook them, so add them toward the end of cooking. Avoid water-packed artichokes; they're too . . . well, watery.

SIDES

Garlic Bread 906

Green Salad 911

Tender Vegetables 954

SPEED ◐ SERVES 4 TO 6

Pasta with Fennel, White Beans, and Stock

For an especially hearty and cozy bowl of pasta, try serving it in a shallow bowl with a brothy sauce. The flavorful liquid pools at the bottom of the bowl, wafting savory aromas upward as you eat, and moistens every single bite.

Ingredients

Salt

¼ cup olive oil

2 medium fennel bulbs

2 garlic cloves

2 cups any cooked or canned white beans (one 15-ounce can)

Pepper

1 cup chicken or vegetable stock

1 pound any cut pasta

Prep | Cook

1. Bring a stockpot of water to a boil and salt it.
2. Put ¼ cup olive oil in a large skillet or large pot over medium heat.

   Trim and chop the fennel, saving a few of the fronds for garnish.
3. Add the fennel to the skillet and cook, stirring occasionally until it begins to soften, 3 to 5 minutes.

   Peel and mince 2 garlic cloves.

   If you're using canned beans, rinse and drain them.
4. When the fennel begins to soften, add the garlic, sprinkle with salt and pepper, and cook until the garlic is fragrant, about 30 seconds.
5. Add the white beans and 1 cup stock. Bring the mixture to a simmer, then turn the heat as low as it will go.
6. When the water boils, add the pasta and stir occasionally. Start tasting after 5 minutes.

7. When the pasta is tender but not mushy, drain it, reserving some cooking water. Add the pasta to the skillet and turn the heat to medium-high. Add a splash of the cooking water if you want even more broth. Toss, taste and adjust the seasoning, and serve.

VARIATIONS

Pasta with Sausage, Fennel, White Beans, and Stock
Before adding the fennel, brown 12 ounces crumbled Italian sausage in the skillet.

Pasta with Chorizo, Red Onions, Black Beans, and Stock
Use 2 medium red onions instead of the fennel and black instead of white beans. Before adding them, brown 12 ounces crumbled fresh Mexican chorizo in the skillet.

Pasta with Kale, Lima Beans, and Stock
Substitute 1 pound chopped kale for the fennel and lima beans for the white beans. Cook the kale just until it wilts, 5 or 6 minutes, then proceed with Step 3.

NOTES

MAKE YOUR OWN

Cooked Beans 496

Chicken Stock 213

Vegetable Stock 212

IF YOU HAVE MORE TIME
Whole wheat pasta, which takes only a little longer to cook, is a wonderful option in this dish.

SIDES

Warm Buttery Bread 906

Caprese Salad 922

Broiled Cherry Tomatoes 931

Steamed Tender Vegetables 954

SPEED ◑ SERVES 4 TO 6

Spaghetti with Garlicky Fresh Tomato Sauce

Make this with really good ripe tomatoes and it's astounding. But even made out of season with canned tomatoes it's pretty great. A little saffron goes a long way—to add its distinctive floral flavor—so use just a pinch if you decide to include it.

Ingredients

Salt

2 tablespoons butter

1 tablespoon olive oil

4 garlic cloves

Pinch of saffron (optional)

5 or 6 medium ripe tomatoes (2 pounds)

¼ cup white wine

Pepper

1 pound spaghetti

4 ounces Parmesan cheese (1 cup grated)

Several sprigs fresh parsley for garnish

Prep | Cook

1. Bring a stockpot of water to a boil and salt it.
2. Put 2 tablespoons butter and 1 tablespoon oil in a large skillet or large pot over low heat.

   Peel and thinly slice 4 garlic cloves.
3. Add the garlic to the skillet along with a pinch of saffron if you're using it and raise the heat to medium. Let the garlic and saffron flavor the fat without letting the garlic brown.

   Core and chop the tomatoes; begin adding them to the pan as soon as the garlic is fragrant.
4. Add ¼ cup white wine and a sprinkle of salt and pepper. Bring to a boil, adjust the heat to produce a steady bubble, and cook, stirring occasionally until the tomatoes break down and the sauce thickens, 10 to 15 minutes.
5. When the water boils, add the pasta and stir occasionally. Start tasting after 5 minutes.

   Grate 1 cup Parmesan cheese.

   Strip the parsley leaves from several sprigs and chop.

6. When the pasta is tender but not mushy, drain it, reserving some cooking water. Add the pasta to the skillet and turn the heat to medium-high. Add the Parmesan, parsley, and a splash of the cooking water if you want to make it saucier. Toss, taste and adjust the seasoning, and serve.

VARIATIONS

Spaghetti with Creamy Fresh Tomato–Saffron Sauce
Use cream instead of the wine.

Spaghetti with Chorizo Tomato Sauce
Add 8 ounces chopped smoked Spanish chorizo along with the garlic and saffron in Step 3.

Spaghetti with Clams and Fresh Tomato Sauce
Once the tomato sauce has started to thicken, add 1 ½ pounds littleneck clams to the skillet, cover, and raise the heat to medium-high. Cook until the clams open, 5 to 10 minutes. Toss the pasta with the sauce as directed, skipping the Parmesan if you like.

NOTES

EVEN FASTER
Instead of making the sauce as described in Steps 2 through 4, use 2 cups Tomato Sauce with Lots of Garlic (page 296).

PASTA COOKING TIMES
The cooking time for dried pasta varies wildly depending on the type and, more important, on how old it is and how long it was stored. (And you cannot trust the package timing at all.) The range for dried pasta can be from 3 minutes (for angel hair) to 12 or so minutes; this is why you check it frequently. Smaller and thinner pasta cuts will cook faster than thicker, denser shapes, and whole wheat pasta almost always takes longer to cook than regular pasta.

SIDES

Garlic Bread 906

Green Salad 911

Sautéed Greens with Garlic 924

Seared Broccoli or Cauliflower 925

SPEED ◐ SERVES 4 TO 6

Pasta with Spicy Eggplant and Tomato Sauce

Eggplant is one of my favorite vegetables, in part because it can be meaty and silky at the same time. Browned in olive oil and simmered with tomatoes, it creates a hearty, rich sauce that vies with anything containing meat. For crunch I like to sprinkle this dish with toasted bread crumbs (see If You Have More Time).

Ingredients

Salt

¼ cup olive oil

1 medium onion

1 medium eggplant (about 1 pound)

2 garlic cloves

1 teaspoon red chile flakes

Pepper

One 28-ounce can diced tomatoes

1 pound any pasta

Several sprigs fresh basil

Prep | Cook

1. Bring a stockpot of water to a boil and salt it.
2. Put ¼ cup olive oil in a large skillet or large pot over medium-high heat.

   Trim, peel, and chop the onion.
3. When the oil is hot, add the onion and cook until it begins to soften, 3 to 5 minutes.

   Trim and chop the eggplant into ¼- to ½-inch pieces.

   Peel and mince 2 garlic cloves.
4. When the onion begins to soften, add the eggplant, garlic, 1 teaspoon red chile flakes, and a sprinkle of salt and pepper. Cook, stirring occasionally, until the eggplant is browned all over, 5 to 10 minutes.
5. When the eggplant is browned, add the diced tomatoes with their juice and adjust the heat so the mixture bubbles steadily but not vigorously. Cook, stirring occasionally until the tomatoes start to break down and the eggplant is tender, 5 to 10 minutes.

6. When the water boils, add the pasta and stir occasionally. Start tasting after 5 minutes.

   Strip the basil leaves from several sprigs and chop.

7. When the pasta is tender but not mushy, drain it, reserving some cooking water. Add the pasta to the skillet. Add the basil and a splash of the cooking water if you want to make it saucier. Toss, taste and adjust the seasoning, and serve.

VARIATIONS

Pasta with Eggplant Puttanesca

Along with the diced tomatoes in Step 5, add ½ cup chopped pitted olives, 2 tablespoons capers, and 3 or 4 chopped anchovy fillets.

Pasta with Spicy Curried Cauliflower Tomato Sauce

Substitute 1 small head cauliflower for the eggplant and 1 fresh hot green chile, minced, for the red chile flakes. Add 1 tablespoon minced fresh ginger and 1 teaspoon curry powder along with the garlic and chile in Step 4. Use cilantro instead of basil.

NOTES

EVEN FASTER

Instead of making a tomato sauce as described in Steps 2 through 5, just brown the eggplant in the oil and then add 3 cups Tomato Sauce (page 296).

IF YOU HAVE MORE TIME

Fried Bread Crumbs

Sprinkling some toasted bread crumbs on the pasta before serving is a real crowd-pleaser: Tear 4 thick slices any rustic bread into chunks and pulse them into coarse crumbs in the food processor. Put ¼ cup olive oil in a large skillet over medium heat. When hot, add the bread crumbs and cook, stirring frequently until they are golden and crisp, 3 to 5 minutes.

SIDES

Garlic Bread 906

Green Salad 911

Two-Step Broccoli 926

Asparagus Gratin 929

Tomatoes

Tomatoes range from bright ripe fresh fruit through canned types to the intense flavors of tomato paste and dried tomatoes. All are useful in a fast kitchen, if for slightly different reasons. So if you've always got at least one kind or another on hand, you'll be able to choose from a wide range of dishes, including Fresh Tomato Salsa (page 145), Caprese Salad (page 922), and Tomato Sauce (page 296)—along with all sorts of tomatoey soups and stews.

Tomato Season

The ideal season for growing tomatoes depends on climate—if you're reading this in northern California you're very lucky—but generally tomatoes are in season from summer to early fall. Most supermarket tomatoes are either grown in hothouses or ripened off the vine. Neither is very good, so when it's not tomato season I typically opt for canned, and you should, too.

Types of Tomatoes

There are three main groups of tomatoes: cherry, plum, and slicing. I love cherry tomatoes (and their oblong kin, the so-called grape tomatoes) for both their sweetness and their convenience. You can toss them whole into raw salads, warm them with pastas and grains, sauté them quickly, or broil with olive oil, salt, and pepper. Plum (Roma) tomatoes are the oval-shaped type and famous for being the base of many Italian sauces. They're meaty, perfect for sauces, braises, soups, and stews. Slicing tomatoes are a wide variety of large, spherical tomatoes that you would typically slice into rounds. In season, they are best eaten raw.

Buying and Storing Tomatoes

When buying tomatoes, give them a little squeeze. You want flesh that is soft and yielding to the touch but not mushy. The color should be rich and deep, not light and pale. Store tomatoes at room temperature—never in the fridge.

Canned Tomatoes	What's the Story?
WHOLE PEELED TOMATOES	Many people say that whole peeled canned tomatoes are of a higher quality than diced or crushed, because it's harder to pass off a lackluster tomato if you have to keep it intact. Maybe. In any case, whole peeled tomatoes are generally quite good. They take slightly more time and work than other canned varieties because you either have to chop them up a bit before using or allot some extra time for them to break down while cooking. Typically when I use them in sauces or soups I split the difference, roughly chopping them before adding them, then using a wooden spoon to break them up more as they cook.
DICED TOMATOES	Diced tomatoes occupy the middle ground between whole peeled and crushed. If anything the flesh is slightly firmer than you might get with whole peeled tomatoes, but the difference is negligible, and the time and effort you save with the reduced prep is a help.
CRUSHED TOMATOES	Crushed tomatoes are just that; they have slightly more pulp than what is labeled "Tomato Sauce" (which is actually sweetened and seasoned and to be avoided) or "Tomato Purée" (which is like thick tomato juice). Since the fruit is pulverized, manufacturers can get away with using lower-quality tomatoes than those used for whole canned. Nevertheless, crushed tomatoes can be useful in fast cooking. Unlike whole peeled or diced tomatoes, crushed have the consistency of sauce right out of the can. All they require is a bit of simmering and seasoning and they're ready to eat. If you need to throw together a sauce or soup in a pinch, crushed tomatoes can get you there in just a few minutes.
DRIED TOMATOES	Sun-dried tomatoes have been left in the sun (or in a low oven) to dry, concentrating their sugars and flavors. The tomato flavor is still there, but it's carried to you with an almost candylike sweetness, and a little goes a long way. I don't use dried tomatoes often, but it's nice to have them around for when you want to add a little extra punch to a sauce or a salad. They keep almost indefinitely in the pantry.
TOMATO PASTE	Tomato paste is tomato purée that has been reduced substantially. Look for tomato paste in tubes instead of cans. It lasts for months in the fridge, allowing you to use a teaspoon or tablespoon at a time, unlike the cans, which go bad after a few days. Stir tomato paste into pasta sauces, bean stews, and soups to give a little extra flavor and body.

Tomato Sauce

This is about as useful a sauce as there is, fast and easy enough to make you forget about buying sauce in a jar. Plus, you can spin the basic recipes in any number of directions, some of which follow.

This recipe makes 4 servings. It's easily doubled and will keep in the fridge for several days. To freeze it, let it cool, then pack it in freezer bags or tightly sealed containers and store for up to 6 months. Pack the sauce in smaller quantities to avoid ever having to thaw and refreeze or use more sauce than you want.

Tomato Sauce

1 Sweat the Onions

Put 2 tablespoons olive oil or butter in a large skillet over medium-high heat. When the oil is hot or the butter is melted, add 1 medium onion, chopped. Cook, stirring occasionally until soft, 2 or 3 minutes.

2 Add the Tomatoes

Add one 28-ounce can whole peeled tomatoes (drained and chopped) and a sprinkle of salt and pepper.

3 Simmer the Sauce

Cook, stirring occasionally until the tomatoes break down and thicken the sauce, 10 to 15 minutes. Taste and adjust the seasoning, and serve or cool and store.

VARIATIONS

Fresh Tomato Sauce

Substitute 2 cups chopped ripe fresh tomatoes for the canned. The cooking time will be about the same.

Tomato Sauce with Lots of Garlic

Skip the onion. Crush and peel up to 10 garlic cloves. Cook them in the oil or butter over medium-low heat, turning occasionally until golden brown, about 5 minutes. Raise the heat to medium-high before adding the tomatoes. Fish out the cloves before serving or serve the sauce with them, as you like.

Tomato Sauce with Wine (Red or White)

Right before adding the tomatoes, add 1/4 cup red or white wine and cook until it's mostly evaporated.

Herby Tomato Sauce

At the last minute, stir in ¼ to ½ cup chopped fresh basil, parsley, mint, or dill or 1 to 2 teaspoons chopped fresh rosemary, thyme, sage, or oregano.

Creamy Tomato Sauce

A few minutes before the sauce is done, stir in ¼ cup cream. (For Vodka Sauce, stir in ¼ cup vodka along with the cream.)

Puttanesca

Skip the onion and use olive oil. When the oil is hot, add a few minced garlic cloves, a few anchovies, 2 tablespoons capers, ½ cup pitted black olives, and a pinch of red chile flakes. Break up the anchovies a bit as you stir, then add the tomatoes.

Mirepoix Tomato Sauce

Add about ½ cup each finely chopped carrot and celery and finely chop the onion. Cook until all the vegetables are soft, 8 to 10 minutes, then add the tomatoes.

Tomato Sauce with Mushrooms

Add about 1 cup chopped or sliced mushrooms along with the onion. Cook until soft and lightly browned, then add the tomatoes.

Roasted Red Pepper and Tomato Sauce

Add at least 1 chopped roasted red pepper (page 417) along with the tomatoes.

Dried Tomato Sauce

Reconstitute about ¼ cup dried tomatoes in warm water, chop them, and add them to the skillet a minute before adding the canned tomatoes.

Smooth Tomato Sauce

When the sauce is finished, let it cool a bit, then purée it in the blender until smooth.

Intense Tomato Sauce

Stir about ¼ cup tomato paste into the onion before adding the tomatoes.

Unexpected Ways to Use Tomato Sauce

Once you have tomato sauce on hand, sure, pasta can be ready in a flash. But so can lots of other dishes. (And all of these ideas work well for the simplest tomato sauce or any of the variations.)

For breakfast (yes, breakfast) bring about an inch of sauce to a gentle bubble in a skillet and use it to poach eggs; just crack in a few eggs, cover with a tight-fitting lid, and cook until the whites set and the yolks are as firm as you like. Or use the heated sauce to fill or garnish an omelet.

For lunch or dinner, smear a thin layer of tomato sauce on thickly sliced bread (or flour tortillas or pocketless pita bread), top with grated cheese, and pop in the broiler for instant "pizzas." Or sear meat, fish, or poultry in some olive oil in a large skillet, then add a little sauce—and cut-up vegetables if you like—for a quick stir-fry. If you've got enough sauce to submerge the meat, bring it to a boil, lower to a steady but gentle bubble, cover, and simmer until it's tender for a quick stew.

Side dishes come to life with tomato sauce. Once hot, you can use it to warm or top already cooked vegetables, or as a liquid to poach raw ones until they're crisp-tender. I also like to reheat whole grains with a few spoonfuls of tomato sauce for extra flavor.

SPEED ◑ SERVES 4 TO 6

Broiled Ziti

All the flavors of a classic baked ziti, but more bubbly crust and way less time. Crowd-pleasers don't come much easier than this.

Ingredients

Salt

3 tablespoons olive oil, plus more for greasing the baking sheet

1 medium onion

2 garlic cloves

One 28-ounce can crushed tomatoes

Pepper

1 pound ziti

1 pound mozzarella cheese, preferably fresh

4 ounces Parmesan cheese (1 cup grated)

Prep | Cook

1. Bring a stockpot of water to a boil and salt it.

2. Put 3 tablespoons oil in a large skillet over medium heat.

   Trim, peel, and chop the onion.

   Peel and mince 2 garlic cloves.

3. Add the onion and garlic to the skillet and cook, stirring occasionally until the onion softens, 3 to 5 minutes.

   Grease a rimmed baking sheet with olive oil.

   Turn the broiler to high; put the rack 4 inches from the heat.

4. When the onion is soft, add the tomatoes, stirring them to combine, sprinkle with salt and pepper, and bring to a boil. Lower the heat so the mixture bubbles gently, and cook, stirring occasionally; if the sauce gets too thick, add a splash of pasta-cooking water.

5. When the water boils, add the pasta and stir occasionally. Start tasting after 5 minutes.

   Chop or grate 1 pound mozzarella.

   Grate 1 cup Parmesan.

6. When the pasta is tender but not mushy, drain it and return the pasta to the pot. Add the tomato sauce and half of the mozzarella and stir. Transfer the pasta to the rimmed baking sheet and spread it in an even layer. Top with the remaining mozzarella and the Parmesan.
7. Broil until the cheese is bubbly and brown and the top layer is crisp, 2 to 5 minutes. Let cool for a few minutes before serving.

VARIATIONS

Creamy Broiled Ziti
Add 1 cup ricotta cheese to the pasta along with the tomato sauce in Step 6.

Broiled Ziti with Sausage
Before adding the onion to the skillet, brown 12 ounces crumbled Italian sausage.

Broiled Ziti with Olives and Feta
Add 1 cup chopped pitted kalamata olives along with the tomatoes in Step 4. Substitute feta cheese for half of the mozzarella and omit the Parmesan.

NOTES

EVEN FASTER
Instead of making a sauce as described in Steps 2 through 4, use 3 cups Tomato Sauce (page 296).

SIDES

Garlic Bread 906

Green Salad 911

Sautéed Greens with Garlic 924

Tender Vegetables 954

SPEED ◐ SERVES 4 TO 6

Pasta with Greens and Eggs

With the richness of eggs and Parmesan and the fresh bite of sautéed spinach and garlic, this dish is like a meatless version of pasta carbonara. You can use kale, collards, chard, or broccoli rabe as well; each will take a minute or two longer to cook than the spinach. (For classic carbonara, see the Variations.)

Ingredients

Salt

3 tablespoons olive oil

1 ½ pounds spinach

2 garlic cloves

1 pound any pasta

3 eggs

4 ounces Parmesan cheese (1 cup grated)

Pepper

Prep | Cook

1. Bring a stockpot of water to a boil and salt it.
2. Put 3 tablespoons olive oil in a large skillet over low heat.
   Trim off any thick stems from the spinach.
3. Raise the heat under the skillet to medium-high. Cook the spinach, adding a handful at a time and stirring between batches until the leaves are just wilted, about 5 minutes.
   Peel and mince 2 garlic cloves; add them to the skillet.
4. When the spinach is wilted, turn off the heat.
5. When the water boils, add the pasta and stir occasionally. Start tasting after 5 minutes.
   Crack the eggs into a bowl.
   Grate 1 cup Parmesan cheese and add to the bowl; sprinkle with salt and lots of pepper.
6. When the pasta is tender but not mushy, drain it, reserving some cooking water. Add the pasta to the skillet and pour in the egg mixture. Toss, adding a splash of the cooking water if you want to make it saucier. Taste and adjust the seasoning and serve.

VARIATIONS

Pasta Carbonara

Skip the spinach. Sauté 8 ounces chopped guanciale, pancetta, or bacon in the olive oil until crisp. Drain off some of the fat if you like—or not. Keep the garlic if you like or skip it. If you do use garlic, turn off the heat before adding it to the skillet. Proceed as directed.

Pasta with Cherry Tomatoes and Eggs

Substitute 1 pint cherry tomatoes, halved, for the spinach. Cook them in the olive oil until they begin to break down and release some of their juice, 5 or 6 minutes. Proceed as directed.

Pasta with Mushrooms and Eggs

Use 1 pound mushrooms, sliced, instead of the spinach. Cook them in the olive oil until they are tender and beginning to dry out, 10 to 15 minutes. Proceed as directed.

SIDES

Green Salad 911

Chopped Salad 912

Tomato Salad 913

Garlic Bread 906

Broiled Cherry Tomatoes 931

SPEED ◐ SERVES 4 TO 6

Linguine with Clams

Clams, butter, olive oil, garlic, and parsley are one of the great flavor combinations. If you were truly shooting for speed, you could just skip the pasta and serve this with grilled bread. Tossed with linguine, it's heaven.

Ingredients

Salt

3 pounds littleneck or other small hard-shell clams

2 tablespoons olive oil

2 garlic cloves

1 teaspoon red chile flakes, or to taste

Pepper

1 pound linguine or other long pasta

Several sprigs fresh parsley

2 tablespoons butter

Prep | Cook

1. Bring a stockpot of water to a boil and salt it.

   Scrub the clams.

2. Put 2 tablespoons olive oil in a large skillet or large pot over medium heat.

3. When the oil is hot, add the clams and turn the heat to high. Cook, shaking the skillet occasionally until the first few start to open, about 5 minutes.

   Peel and mince 2 garlic cloves.

4. When a few clams have opened, add the garlic and 1 teaspoon red chile flakes and sprinkle with pepper. Cover the skillet and cook until all the clams open, 3 to 5 minutes. Turn off the heat and leave the clams covered.

5. When the water boils, add the pasta and stir occasionally. Start tasting after 5 minutes.

   Strip the parsley leaves from several sprigs and chop.

6. When the pasta is tender but not mushy, drain it, reserving some cooking water. Add the pasta to the skillet and turn the heat to medium-high. Add 2 tablespoons butter, the parsley, and a splash of the cooking water to make it saucier. Toss, taste and adjust the seasoning, adding more chile flakes, if you like, and serve.

VARIATIONS

Linguine with Mussels
Substitute 1 ½ pounds mussels for the clams; in addition to scrubbing them, you'll want to pull off their fibrous "beards." Mussels will open a few minutes faster than clams.

Linguine with Red Clam Sauce
Just before adding the pasta to the clams in Step 6, stir about 2 cups chopped fresh or canned tomatoes into the skillet.

Linguine with Clams, White Wine, and Cream
Add ¼ cup white wine and ½ cup cream along with the garlic, red chile flakes, and pepper in Step 4.

NOTES

IF YOU HAVE MORE TIME
If you like unimpeded eating, remove the clam meat from the shells after they've opened; discard the shells.

SIDES

Garlic Bread 906

Green Salad 911

Fennel Salad 917

Tomato Salad 913

SPEED ◐ SERVES 4 TO 6

Pasta with Tuna and Dried Tomatoes

Don't let painful memories of childhood tuna noodle casserole sour you on the idea of mixing tuna with pasta. When you use tuna packed in olive oil, especially the kinds imported from the Mediterranean, you'll see the combination is terrific. Both the tuna and dried tomatoes have been prepared ahead of time by someone else, so there's not much work left for you other than cooking the pasta.

Ingredients

Salt

2 tablespoons olive oil

2 garlic cloves

1 cup dried tomatoes

Two 6-ounce jars or cans tuna, packed in olive oil

Pepper

1 pound any pasta

Several sprigs fresh parsley

Prep | Cook

1. Bring a stockpot of water to a boil and salt it.
2. Put 2 tablespoons olive oil in a large skillet or large pot over low heat.

   Peel and thinly slice 2 garlic cloves; add them to the skillet.

   Chop 1 cup dried tomatoes; add them to the skillet.
3. Add the tuna (with its oil) to the skillet, sprinkle with salt and pepper, and stir to break it up a bit. Let everything warm up slowly in the skillet as the pasta cooks.
4. When the water boils, add the pasta and stir occasionally. Start tasting after 5 minutes.

   Strip the parsley leaves from several sprigs and chop.
5. When the pasta is tender but not mushy, drain it, reserving some cooking water. Add the pasta to the skillet. Add the parsley and a splash of the cooking water if you want to make it saucier. Toss, taste and adjust the seasoning, and serve.

VARIATIONS

Pasta with Tuna, Capers, and Lemon
Substitute ½ cup capers and the grated zest of a lemon for the dried tomatoes.

Pasta with Anchovies and Garlic
Intense. Skip the dried tomatoes and increase the olive oil to ¼ cup and the garlic to 4 cloves. Use about a dozen chopped anchovy fillets instead of the tuna.

NOTES

PASTA WITH OLIVE OIL AND OTHER STUFF
Olive oil, warmed in a skillet and seasoned with salt and pepper, is a pasta sauce in itself; in fact it's nearly perfect. But you can also use the time that the water's boiling to slowly warm up a host of other ingredients in that oil to create even more flavorful pasta sauces. The tuna and dried tomato sauce here is one example, but you needn't get fussy. Garlic; anchovies; olives; capers; lemon zest; chopped fresh rosemary, sage, or oregano; red chile flakes or minced fresh chiles; chopped shallots; fresh tomatoes; cured sausage; and prosciutto are all wonderful. Combine any of those things with a big glug of olive oil in a skillet over low heat and by the time you've cooked the pasta you'll have a delicious, olive oil–based sauce ready for tossing.

SIDES

Warm Buttery Bread 906

Green Salad 911

Grape Salad with Mint 913

Carrot Salad with Olives and Rosemary 914

Celery Salad 917

SPEED ◐ SERVES 4 TO 6

Pasta with Scallops and Potatoes

Pasta tossed with a humble mixture of chopped potatoes and onions takes a turn toward the luxurious with the addition of sweet seared scallops nestled in at the end.

Ingredients

Salt

4 tablespoons olive oil, plus more as needed

1 medium onion

2 or 3 medium russet or Yukon Gold potatoes (1 pound)

Pepper

1 pound sea scallops

Several sprigs fresh parsley

1 pound any long pasta

2 tablespoons butter

¼ cup white wine

Prep | Cook

1. Bring a stockpot of water to a boil and salt it.
2. Put 2 tablespoons olive oil in a large skillet or large pot over medium-high heat.

   Trim, peel, and chop the onion; add it to the skillet.

   Chop the potatoes into ¼-inch pieces.
3. Add the potatoes to the skillet, sprinkle with salt and pepper. Cook, stirring frequently and adjusting the heat or adding olive oil so they don't burn, until the potatoes and onions are well browned and tender, 10 to 15 minutes.

   Pat the scallops dry with a paper towel.

   Strip the parsley leaves from several sprigs and chop.
4. When the potatoes and onions are browned and tender, transfer them to a plate and wipe out the skillet (you may need to rinse some stuck potato bits off the bottom).
5. When the water boils, add the pasta and stir occasionally. Start tasting after 5 minutes.
6. Add 2 tablespoons butter and 2 tablespoons olive oil to the skillet and return it to medium heat; when they're hot, add the scallops and sprinkle with salt and pepper.

7. Cook, turning once, until the scallops are nicely browned on both sides, 2 or 3 minutes per side.

8. When the scallops are browned, add ¼ cup white wine and let it bubble mostly away; turn off the heat and transfer the scallops to a plate with a slotted spoon.

9. When the pasta is tender but not mushy, drain it, reserving some cooking water. Add the pasta to the skillet along with the potatoes and onions. Add the parsley and a splash of the cooking water if you want to make it saucier. Toss, taste, and adjust the seasoning. Divide among 4 plates, nestle the scallops back into the pasta, drizzle with a little more olive oil if you like, and serve.

VARIATIONS

Pasta with Shrimp and Potatoes
Substitute shrimp for scallops. Cook until they are lightly browned on the outside and cooked all the way through, 2 or 3 minutes total.

Pasta with Scallops, Potatoes, and Chorizo
Before adding the onion to the skillet in Step 2, brown 12 ounces crumbled fresh Mexican chorizo.

SIDES

Garlic Bread 906

Asparagus Gratin 929

Tomatoes with Fried Bread Crumbs 930

Brussels Sprouts with Bacon 958

SPEED ◐ SERVES 4 TO 6

Fideos with Shrimp, Tomatoes, and Peas

Fideos—short thin noodles, typically used in Spanish cooking—are hard to find at regular supermarkets. Don't kill yourself looking for them; just break up some regular angel hair. Here the noodles are cooked almost risotto style, with shrimp and peas stirred in at the end.

Ingredients

2 tablespoons olive oil

3 garlic cloves

8 ounces angel hair pasta

½ cup white wine

One 28-ounce can diced tomatoes

Salt and pepper

12 ounces peeled shrimp

2 cups frozen peas

Prep | Cook

1. Put 2 tablespoons olive oil in a large skillet over medium heat.
   Peel and mince 3 garlic cloves.
2. Add the garlic to the skillet and raise the heat a bit. Hold the angel hair over the skillet and break it into 1- or 2-inch pieces with your hands. Drop the pieces into the skillet as you go.
3. Toast the pasta, stirring frequently until it is glossy with oil and slightly browned, 3 or 4 minutes.
4. Add ½ cup white wine and cook, stirring until it evaporates, 3 or 4 minutes. Add the tomatoes and their juice and a sprinkle of salt and pepper. Adjust the heat so the mixture bubbles steadily but not vigorously.
5. Cook, stirring occasionally until the pasta is just tender but still has a bit of a bite, 8 to 12 minutes.
   Chop the shrimp.

6. When the pasta is just tender, stir in the shrimp and 2 cups frozen peas. Cook until the peas are warmed through and the shrimp turns pink and cooks through, 2 or 3 minutes. Taste and adjust the seasoning and serve.

VARIATIONS

Fideos with Squid, Tomatoes, and Corn
Substitute 12 ounces sliced squid for the shrimp and 2 cups fresh or frozen corn kernels for the peas. The squid will take only a minute or 2 to cook.

Fideos with Chicken, Tomatoes, and Rosemary
Substitute red wine for white and add a couple sprigs of fresh rosemary along with the tomatoes. About 5 minutes after adding the tomatoes, stir in 12 ounces chopped boneless, skinless chicken thighs instead of the shrimp. By the time the noodles are tender, the chicken should be cooked through. Keep the peas or skip them if you prefer. Remove the rosemary stems before serving.

Fideos with Chorizo, Tomatoes, and White Beans
Add 8 ounces chopped smoked Spanish chorizo along with the garlic in Step 2. Use 2 cups cooked or drained canned white beans instead of the peas.

NOTES

EVEN FASTER
Instead of making the sauce as described in Steps 1 through 4, just toast the pasta and then add 3 cups Tomato Sauce with Wine (page 296), using white wine.

SIDES

Warm Buttery Bread 906

Green Salad 911

Fennel Salad 917

Sautéed Greens with Garlic 924

Crunchy Okra 959

SPEED ◐ SERVES 4 TO 6

Pasta with Squid and Tomatoes

The first time I made this dish I knew it had to be in this book. The simple sauce of garlic, tomatoes, and squid comes together so quickly that you don't have to start cooking it until the pasta is already in the water, and the result is astoundingly delicious.

Ingredients

Salt

3 garlic cloves

2 or 3 medium ripe tomatoes

12 ounces cleaned squid

1 small dried hot red chile

1 pound spaghetti

2 tablespoons olive oil

Pepper

Several sprigs fresh parsley for garnish

Prep | Cook

1. Bring a stockpot of water to a boil and salt it.

   Peel and mince 3 garlic cloves.

   Core and chop the tomatoes.

   Cut the squid bodies into rings and the tentacles (if you have them) in half if they're large.

   Chop the chile.

2. When the water boils, add the pasta and stir occasionally. Start tasting after 5 minutes.

3. Put 2 tablespoons olive oil in a large skillet or large pot over medium-high heat. When it's hot, add the garlic and cook until fragrant, a minute or 2.

4. Add the tomatoes, squid, chile, and a sprinkle of salt and pepper. Raise the heat to high and cook, stirring occasionally until the mixture becomes saucy, 2 or 3 minutes.

   Strip the parsley leaves from several sprigs and chop.

5. When the pasta is tender but not mushy, drain it, reserving some cooking water. Add the pasta to the skillet along with the parsley and a splash of the cooking water if you want to make it saucier. Toss, taste and adjust the seasoning, and serve.

VARIATIONS

Pasta with Shrimp and Tomatoes
Replace the squid with chopped shrimp.

Pasta with Bay Scallops and Tomatoes
Use small whole bay scallops instead of squid.

Pasta with Crab and Tomatoes
Use lump crabmeat instead of the squid. In Step 4, wait to add it until the tomatoes are saucy, then stir it in and let it heat through for a minute or 2 before proceeding.

SIDES

Garlic Bread 906

Green Salad 911

Fennel Salad with Olives 917

Asparagus Gratin 929

SPEED ◑ SERVES 4 TO 6

Three Bs Pasta

Roasted Brussels sprouts are more addictive than potato chips. They are one of the three Bs in this favorite cold-weather recipe, the others being blue cheese and balsamic vinegar.

Ingredients

Salt

1 pound Brussels sprouts

3 tablespoons olive oil

5 boneless, skinless chicken thighs (about 1 pound)

Pepper

½ cup walnuts

4 ounces blue cheese (1 cup crumbled)

1 pound any cut pasta

¼ cup balsamic vinegar

Prep | Cook

1. Bring a stockpot of water to a boil and salt it.

   Trim and halve the Brussels sprouts.

2. Put 3 tablespoons olive oil in a large skillet or large pot over medium-low heat.

   Cut the chicken into ½-inch chunks.

3. Add the chicken to the skillet and sprinkle with salt and pepper. Raise the heat to medium-high and cook, undisturbed, until the pieces brown and release easily, a minute or 2. Then lower the heat to medium and cook, stirring occasionally until the meat is no longer pink, 2 or 3 minutes.

4. When the chicken is no longer pink, transfer it to a plate with a slotted spoon and add the Brussels sprouts to the skillet. Sprinkle with salt and pepper and cook, stirring once or twice, until they are deeply browned and just tender, 5 to 10 minutes.

   Chop ½ cup walnuts.

   Crumble 1 cup blue cheese.

5. When the water boils, add the pasta and stir occasionally. Start tasting after 5 minutes.

6. When the pasta is tender but not mushy, drain it, reserving some cooking water.

7. Return the chicken to the skillet and add 1/4 cup balsamic vinegar. Then add the pasta to the skillet; add the walnuts and the blue cheese, and add a splash of cooking water if you want to make it saucier. Toss, taste and adjust the seasoning, and serve.

VARIATIONS

Pasta with Chicken, Beets, Blue Cheese, and Balsamic
Substitute 1 pound beets, peeled and chopped into 1/4-inch pieces, for the Brussels sprouts, cooking the beets until they are just tender, 10 to 15 minutes.

Pasta with Chicken, Brussels Sprouts, Feta, and Lemon
Substitute feta for the blue cheese and the juice of a lemon for the balsamic.

NOTES

IF YOU HAVE MORE TIME
If you prefer smaller pieces of Brussels sprouts, cut them into quarters or chop them into smaller bits.

SIDES

Warm Buttery Bread 906

Caprese Salad 922

Broiled Cherry Tomatoes 931

Garlicky Mushrooms 956

SPEED ◐ SERVES 4 TO 6

Pasta with Chicken, Mushrooms, and Wine

Use red wine and this dish is hearty for the fall or winter; use white and it becomes lighter for spring or summer. You won't go wrong either way.

Ingredients

Salt

2 tablespoons olive oil

2 tablespoons butter

3 boneless, skinless chicken thighs or 1 boneless, skinless breast (8 ounces)

Pepper

1 ½ pounds button, cremini, or shiitake mushrooms

3 garlic cloves

¾ cup red or white wine

1 pound any cut pasta

Several sprigs fresh parsley

4 ounces Parmesan cheese (1 cup grated)

Prep | Cook

1. Bring a stockpot of water to a boil and salt it.
2. Put 1 tablespoon olive oil and 1 tablespoon butter in a large skillet or large pot over medium-high heat.

   Cut the chicken into ½-inch chunks.
3. Add the chicken to the skillet and sprinkle with salt and pepper. Cook, undisturbed, until the pieces brown and release easily, a minute or 2. Then cook, stirring occasionally until the meat is no longer pink, 2 or 3 minutes.

   Trim and quarter the mushrooms. (If you're using shiitakes, discard the stems.)
4. When the chicken is no longer pink, transfer it to a plate with a slotted spoon.
5. Add 1 tablespoon olive oil and 1 tablespoon butter to the skillet, then the mushrooms. Sprinkle with salt and pepper and cook, stirring occasionally until they soften, 5 to 10 minutes.

   Peel and mince 3 garlic cloves; add them to the mushrooms.

6. When the mushrooms are soft, return the chicken to the skillet, add ¾ cup wine, and scrape any browned bits off the bottom of the skillet. Let the wine bubble away until it reduces by about half; then turn the heat as low as it will go.

7. When the water boils, add the pasta and stir occasionally. Start tasting after 5 minutes.

   Strip the parsley leaves from several sprigs and chop.

   Grate 1 cup Parmesan cheese.

8. When the pasta is tender but not mushy, drain it, reserving some cooking water. Add the pasta to the skillet and turn the heat to medium-high. Add the parsley, Parmesan, and a splash of the cooking water if you want to make it saucier. Toss, taste and adjust the seasoning, and serve.

VARIATIONS

Pasta with Chicken, Leeks, and Wine
Substitute 2 leeks, sliced, for the mushrooms. Cook the leeks until they are soft, 3 to 5 minutes. Omit the garlic if you like and use white wine. Substitute 3 sprigs fresh thyme for the parsley.

Pasta with Chicken, Eggplant, and Balsamic
Use 4 tablespoons olive oil and omit the butter. Substitute 1 medium eggplant, chopped, for the mushrooms. Cook the eggplant until it's tender and browned, 5 to 10 minutes. Use ½ cup red wine and ¼ cup balsamic vinegar.

SIDES

Warm Buttery Bread 906

Green Salad 911

Tomato Salad 913

Carrot Salad with Olives and Rosemary 914

Pasta

1 Bring a large pot of water to boil.

Fill a stockpot or other large pot with a gallon of water for every pound of noodles. Leave a couple inches of headspace so there's room for the pasta. Add several large pinches—at least 2 tablespoons—salt to the pot. Cover and crank up the heat.

2 Make the sauce.

The simplest recipes here call for little more than seasonings and cheese; others are more involved. Make your sauce before you tackle side dishes. If you run out of time and don't get to making something on the side, remember that a bowl of pasta makes a fine dinner.

3 Check the water.

Is it boiling but the sauce isn't ready? Turn it down to a gentle bubble. If the sauce is ready but the water isn't, remove the skillet from the heat.

❹ Cook the pasta.

When the water and the sauce are ready, add the pasta; stir every so often to prevent it from sticking. Start tasting after 5 minutes. Since it will keep softening after draining and saucing, the idea is to anticipate the doneness so it doesn't get too mushy.

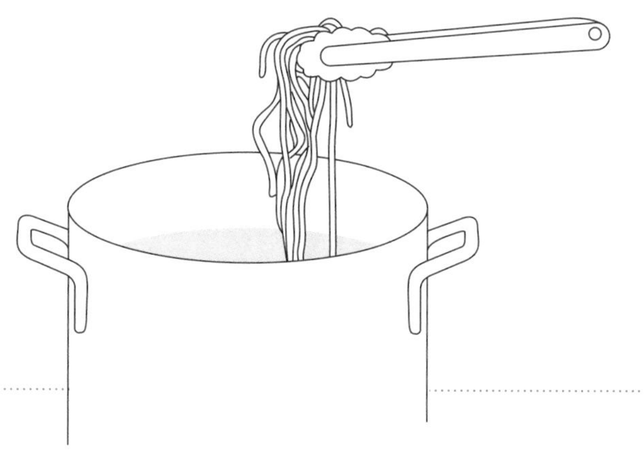

❺ Heat the sauce.

After you first taste the pasta, put the sauce over medium-low heat; you'll need to return to the stove about every minute from now on to check the pasta and stir the sauce. If you turn your attention to other things, set a timer so you don't overcook the pasta.

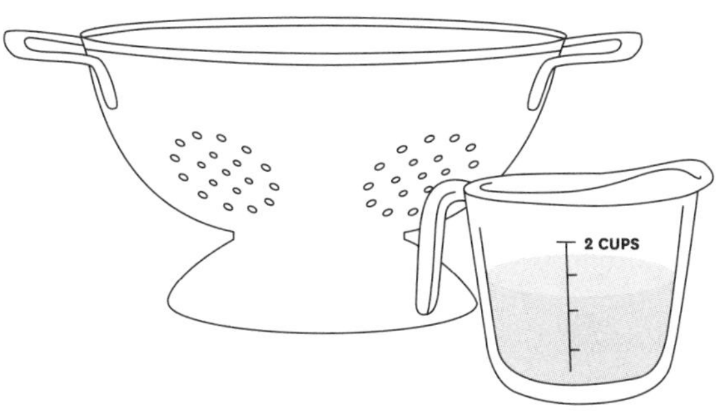

❻ Drain the pasta.

The pasta is ready when there's some resistance when you bite down but it's no longer chalky inside. Remove at least a cup of the cooking water with a ladle or measuring cup, then drain the noodles in a colander. Don't rinse them.

❼ Sauce and toss.

Add the noodles to the skillet (or pour the sauce and pasta back into the large pot and set it over low heat). Stir or toss the pasta with the sauce, adding cooking water if necessary to bring it together. Add cheese, herbs, or other garnishes, and serve right away.

SPEED ◐ SERVES 4 TO 6

Spaghetti with Nearly Instant Bolognese

Traditional Bolognese sauce requires simmering chunks of meat for hours; it's amazing, but not something to make on a weeknight. Enter Instant Bolognese. The flavors still develop into something impressively deep and rich.

Ingredients

Salt

2 tablespoons olive oil

1 pound ground beef, pork, or veal or a combination of all 3

1 small onion

1 carrot

1 celery stalk

2 garlic cloves

Pepper

¼ cup tomato paste

½ cup white or red wine

¼ cup cream

1 pound spaghetti

4 ounces Parmesan cheese (1 cup grated)

Prep | Cook

1. Bring a stockpot of water to a boil and salt it.
2. Put 2 tablespoons olive oil in a large skillet or large pot over medium-high heat.
3. When the oil is hot, add the ground meat and cook, stirring occasionally and breaking it apart with a spoon until it's brown and crisp, 10 to 15 minutes.

   Trim, peel, and finely chop the onion. Trim, peel, and finely chop the carrot. Trim and finely chop the celery stalk. Peel and finely chop 2 garlic cloves. Toss each one as you finish chopping it into the pan with the browning meat.

   Sprinkle with salt and pepper.
4. When the meat is browned, add ¼ cup tomato paste and cook, stirring until it darkens slightly, about a minute. Add ½ cup wine and scrape any browned bits off the bottom of the skillet. Let the wine bubble away until it reduces by about half; stir in ¼ cup cream and turn the heat as low as it will go.

5. When the water boils, add the pasta and stir occasionally. Start tasting after 5 minutes.

   Grate 1 cup Parmesan cheese.

6. When the pasta is tender but not mushy, drain it, reserving some cooking water. Add the pasta to the skillet and turn the heat to medium-high. Add half of the Parmesan and a splash of the cooking water if you want to make it saucier. Toss, taste and adjust the seasoning, and serve with the remaining cheese on top.

VARIATIONS

Tomatoey Spaghetti Bolognese
Add one 14-ounce can diced or crushed tomatoes along with the wine.

More-Veggie-than-Meat Spaghetti Bolognese
Use half as much ground meat and twice as many onions, carrots, and celery. Add more garlic if you'd like.

Spaghetti with Mushroom Bolognese
Use 8 ounces ground meat and add 1 pound finely chopped mushrooms along with it in Step 3. Cook until the meat and mushrooms are nicely browned, 10 to 15 minutes.

NOTES

EVEN FASTER
Instead of chopping the vegetables finely by hand, pulse them in the food processor.

IF YOU HAVE MORE TIME

Slower Bolognese
Still not the classic, but an approximation: Cut 1 pound boneless beef chuck, pork shoulder, or veal shoulder (or a combination) into chunks and pulse them into small pieces (roughly ¼ inch) in the food processor; you can also chop them by hand. Use that in place of the ground meat. Add one 28-ounce can diced tomatoes along with the wine (save the cream for the end). Adjust the heat so the mixture bubbles very gently; simmer, adding a splash of water if the mixture gets too dry, until the meat is very tender, nearly falling apart, 45 minutes to an hour. Stir in the cream before tossing in the pasta.

SIDES

Garlic Bread 906

Green Salad 911

Sautéed Greens with Garlic 924

Seared Broccoli or Cauliflower 925

SPEED ◐ SERVES 4 TO 6

Spaghetti and Drop Meatballs with Tomato Sauce

The most time-consuming part of making meatballs is rolling them. The solution? Don't. Just use two spoons to drop little mounds of the mixture into the hot skillet. (Skipping the rolling also prevents you from overworking the meatballs until they get tough.) Leave them alone to brown beautifully on the bottom while you start building the tomato sauce around them.

Ingredients

Salt

2 tablespoons olive oil

12 ounces ground beef

6 ounces Parmesan cheese (1 ½ cups grated)

1 bunch fresh parsley

¼ cup bread crumbs

1 egg

Pepper

1 large onion

3 garlic cloves

Two 28-ounce cans diced tomatoes

3 bay leaves

1 pound spaghetti

Prep | Cook

1. Bring a stockpot of water to a boil and salt it.
2. Put 2 tablespoons olive oil in a large skillet over medium-high heat.

   Put the ground beef in a medium bowl.

   Grate 1 ½ cups Parmesan cheese and add 1 cup to the bowl.

   Chop ¼ cup parsley leaves and add to the bowl.
3. Add ¼ cup bread crumbs to the bowl, crack in the egg, and sprinkle with salt and pepper. Gently mix together until everything is just combined.
4. When the oil is hot, use 2 spoons to drop rounds of the meatball mixture into the skillet (without touching if you can help it).
5. Once you've used up all the mixture, let the meatballs cook, undisturbed, until they're nicely browned on the bottom, 5 or 6 minutes.

   Trim, peel, and chop the onion; scatter it around the meatballs.

   Peel and mince 3 garlic cloves; scatter them on the onions.

6. When the meatballs are nicely browned on the bottom, add the tomatoes and their juice to the skillet, along with 3 bay leaves and a sprinkle of salt and pepper. Adjust the heat so the mixture bubbles gently, then cover the skillet (by the time the pasta is cooked, the meatballs will be firm).

7. When the water boils, add the pasta and stir occasionally. Start tasting after 5 minutes.

8. When the pasta is tender but not mushy, drain it, reserving some cooking water. Return the pasta to the pot. Discard the bay leaves and spoon about half of the tomato sauce into the pasta pot, leaving the meatballs behind. Toss the pasta, adding a splash of cooking water if you want to make it saucier.

9. Divide the pasta among 4 plates or bowls; top with the meatballs and the remaining sauce, sprinkle the remaining ½ cup Parmesan over the top, and serve.

VARIATIONS

Spaghetti and Pork Drop Meatballs with Tomato Sauce
Use ground pork instead of beef and add 1 tablespoon fennel seeds in addition to the parsley.

Spaghetti and Lamb Drop Meatballs with Tomato Sauce
Substitute ground lamb for the beef and 2 sprigs fresh rosemary for the parsley.

Spaghetti and Drop Chicken Meatballs with Tomato Sauce
Use ground chicken instead of beef and fresh basil instead of parsley.

Spaghetti and Drop Turkey Meatballs with Tomato Sauce
Substitute ground turkey for the beef and 2 sprigs fresh sage for the parsley.

NOTES

MAKE YOUR OWN Bread Crumbs 71

EVEN FASTER
Use Tomato Sauce (page 296) and skip the onion, garlic, and tomato prep. Just add the sauce in Step 6.

SIDES

Garlic Bread 906

Fennel Salad 917

SPEED SERVES 4 TO 6

Pasta with Squash and Ham, Risotto Style

This pasta, cooked in the style of risotto, has *fall* written all over it. With ham, butternut squash, and sage, it would fit nicely on a Thanksgiving table.

Ingredients

2 tablespoons olive oil

2 tablespoons butter

1 large shallot

4 ounces ham

1 small butternut squash (1 ½ to 2 pounds)

1 pound any cut pasta

Salt and pepper

½ cup white wine or water

4 to 5 cups chicken or vegetable stock or water

4 ounces Parmesan cheese (1 cup grated)

2 sprigs fresh sage

Prep | Cook

1. Put 2 tablespoons olive oil and 2 tablespoons butter in a large skillet or large pot over medium heat.

   Trim, peel, and mince the shallot.

   Chop the ham.

2. Add the shallot and ham to the skillet and cook, stirring occasionally until the shallot softens and the ham is lightly browned, 5 or 6 minutes.

   Cut the squash in half crosswise; peel and trim it, and scoop out the seeds. Chop it into ¼-inch pieces (don't worry about making them perfect).

3. When the shallot softens and the ham is lightly browned, add the pasta, sprinkle with salt and pepper, and cook, stirring occasionally until it's glossy, 2 or 3 minutes.

4. Add ½ cup white wine or water, stir, and let it bubble until nearly gone. Add the squash and raise the heat to medium-high.

5. Start adding the stock or water 1 cup at a time; stir after each addition. When the pan is almost dry, add another cup of stock and stir again. Continue this process until the pasta and squash are tender (the pasta should still have a little bite), 15 to 25 minutes.

   Grate 1 cup Parmesan cheese.

   Strip the sage leaves from 2 sprigs and chop.

6. When the pasta and squash are tender, stir in the Parmesan and the sage. Taste and adjust the seasoning and serve.

VARIATIONS

Pasta with Mushrooms and Bacon, Risotto Style
Substitute bacon for the ham; 1 ½ pounds button, cremini, or shiitake mushrooms, quartered, for the squash; and thyme for the sage.

Pasta with Fennel and Sausage, Risotto Style
Use Italian sausage in place of ham, 2 large fennel bulbs, chopped, instead of squash, and parsley instead of sage.

NOTES

MAKE YOUR OWN

Chicken Stock 213

Vegetable Stock 212

EVEN FASTER
Shred the squash in a food processor with a grating disk. This will result in a creamier dish, since the grated squash will get more tender and break apart a bit as it cooks.

SIDES

Warm Buttery Bread 906

Green Salad 911

Fennel Salad 917

SPEED SERVES 4 TO 6

Orzo Risotto with Asparagus and "Poached" Eggs

Cooking orzo in the style of risotto makes it creamy and rich, and it takes little time to coax the starch out of the pasta. A bonus: The bottom develops a delicious crunchy crust. When the dish is just about done, crack a few eggs into the pan and "poach" them right in the skillet.

Ingredients

2 tablespoons butter

1 large shallot

1 pound orzo

Salt and pepper

½ cup white wine or water

4 to 5 cups chicken or vegetable stock or water

1 small bunch asparagus (about 12 ounces)

4 ounces Parmesan cheese (1 cup grated)

4 eggs

Prep | Cook

1. Put 2 tablespoons butter in a large skillet or large pot over medium heat.

   Trim, peel, and mince the shallot.

2. Add the shallot to the butter and cook, stirring occasionally until it softens, 2 or 3 minutes.

3. Add the orzo, sprinkle with salt and pepper, and cook, stirring occasionally until it's glossy, 2 or 3 minutes. Add ½ cup white wine or water, stir, and let it bubble away.

4. Start adding the stock ½ cup at a time; stir after each addition. When the liquid is almost gone, add another ½ cup stock and stir again. Continue this process until the orzo is beginning to get tender but is still a bit too crunchy to eat, about 10 minutes.

   Trim the asparagus and cut it into thin diagonal slices.

   Grate 1 cup Parmesan cheese.

5. When the orzo is beginning to get tender, stir in the asparagus. Continue cooking, adding the stock and stirring as necessary, until the orzo is tender but still has the slightest bit of crunch, 5 to 10 minutes more. At this point the asparagus will be tender.

6. Stir in the Parmesan, taste, and adjust the seasoning. With the back of a spoon, make 4 indentations in the orzo. Crack an egg into each one, turn the heat to medium-low, and cover the skillet.

7. Cook until the eggs are barely set—the yolks should still be runny—7 to 10 minutes. Serve immediately.

VARIATIONS

Lemony Orzo Risotto with Asparagus and "Poached" Eggs
In Step 3, add the grated zest of a lemon along with the orzo and the juice of the lemon along with the wine.

Pasta Risotto with Asparagus and "Poached" Eggs
Instead of orzo, use another small cut pasta like shells, elbows, or orecchiette. The cooking time will be a little longer.

Orzo Risotto with Chard and Ricotta
Substitute 12 ounces chopped chard for the asparagus. Instead of cracking eggs into the pot at the end, just stir in ½ cup ricotta and ½ teaspoon nutmeg along with the Parmesan.

NOTES

MAKE YOUR OWN

Chicken Stock 213

Vegetable Stock 212

EVEN FASTER
If you want to top the orzo with eggs but don't want to cook them in the same skillet, just fry or poach the eggs separately while the orzo finishes cooking. Divide the orzo among 4 plates or bowls and lay the eggs on top.

STEAM-POACHED EGGS
One of my favorite techniques is steaming eggs on top of other ingredients. All you need is a skillet full of something into which you can nestle raw eggs—a mixture that's sturdy enough to cradle and support the eggs but yielding enough to let you make the indentations. The heat of whatever is in the skillet cooks the eggs from the bottom, while the steam that's created when you cover the skillet cooks them from the top.

Besides the orzo here, great mixtures for cooking eggs this way include thick tomato or other vegetables sauces, sautéed greens, puréed vegetables, just-cooked rice or grains, and beans that are starting to break apart. For another example in this book, see Fast Florentine (page 850) in the breakfast chapter.

SIDES

Green Salad 911

Warm Buttery Bread 906

Tomato Salad 913

SPEED SERVES 8

Three-Cheese Lasagna with Fresh Noodles

My trick for lasagna on the fly is treating egg roll wrappers like fresh pasta, which is actually what they are. You don't even need to boil them first; the tomato sauce has enough moisture in it that the wrappers will cook right in the pan. Since lasagna is a dish usually made for a crowd—or with leftovers in mind—I make this in a 9 × 13-inch baking pan.

Ingredients

3 tablespoons olive oil, plus more for greasing the pan

4 garlic cloves

4 ounces Parmesan cheese (1 cup grated)

One 28-ounce can crushed tomatoes

Salt and pepper

1 cup ricotta cheese

1 ½ pounds mozzarella cheese (6 cups grated)

15 egg roll wrappers

Prep | Cook

1. Heat the oven to 450°F. Put 3 tablespoons olive oil in a large skillet over medium-high heat.

   Peel and mince 4 garlic cloves.

   Grate 1 cup Parmesan cheese.

2. When the oil is hot, add the garlic and cook until fragrant, about 30 seconds.

3. Add the tomatoes and a sprinkle of salt and pepper. Bring the sauce to a bubble, then adjust the heat so that it bubbles gently but steadily.

4. Add 1 cup ricotta to the tomato sauce, then add the Parmesan. Stir to incorporate the cheeses; taste and adjust the seasoning. Simmer until you're ready to assemble the lasagna.

   Grate 6 cups mozzarella.

5. Grease a 9 × 13-inch baking pan with a little olive oil. Put down a layer of the egg roll wrappers, using a knife or kitchen scissors to cut them as necessary so they cover the pan but don't overlap

too much (you'll want to do that for each layer). You'll use 3 wrappers per layer, for a total of 5 layers of noodles.

6. Spread a thin layer of the tomato sauce on top of the wrappers, followed by a heaping cup of mozzarella. Make 4 more layers like this, being sure that the final layer is topped with mozzarella.

7. Bake the lasagna (with a rimmed baking sheet underneath in case it drips) until it's bubbly and brown, about 15 minutes. If you want some additional browning on top, put the dish under the broiler at the end. Let it rest for 5 to 10 minutes before cutting and serving.

VARIATIONS

7 Additions to Three-Cheese Lasagna

Layer any of the following along with the cheese and tomato sauce:

1. Sautéed Greens with Garlic (page 924)
2. Garlicky Mushrooms (page 956)
3. Creamed Spinach (page 936)
4. Roasted Squash (page 416)
5. Roasted Red (or Other Large) Peppers (page 417)
6. Olives, capers, or dried tomatoes
7. Cooked crumbled bacon, sausage, or prosciutto

NOTES

EVEN FASTER

Instead of making the sauce as described in Steps 1 through 3, use 3 cups Tomato Sauce (page 296).

EGG ROLL WRAPPERS AND WONTON SKINS

These are nothing more than fresh pasta, which makes them good stand-ins for ravioli wrappers and lasagna. You can also use them as noodles for soup or like fresh pasta handkerchiefs, boiled until tender and tossed with tomato sauce and cheese.

FRESH PASTA OPTIONS

Good fresh pasta is a special treat, and as an added bonus, it cooks in a flash—just a couple of minutes. All the recipes in this chapter also work for fresh pasta; just start checking it after a minute.

SIDES

Garlic Bread 906

Green Salad 911

Cucumber Salad 915

Tender Vegetables 954

SPEED SERVES 4

Ricotta Dumplings with Spinach and Brown Butter

There is no homemade pasta faster to whip up than ricotta dumplings. The only part that requires patience is cooking them in batches so you don't overload the pot. It's worth the short wait, though; these are downright luxurious.

Ingredients

Salt

6 ounces Parmesan cheese (1 ½ cups grated)

2 eggs

2 cups ricotta cheese

Pepper

¾ to 1 cup flour

6 tablespoons (¾ stick) butter

1 bunch spinach (1 pound)

Prep | Cook

1. Bring a stockpot of water to a boil and salt it.
   Grate 1 ½ cups Parmesan.
2. Crack the eggs into a large bowl and beat them. Add 2 cups ricotta, a sprinkle of salt and pepper, and 1 ¼ cups of the Parmesan. Add about ¾ cup of the flour and stir, adding more flour as needed to form a very sticky dough.
3. Put 6 tablespoons butter in a large skillet over medium heat. Cook until the butter just turns light brown. Turn off the heat.
   Trim off any thick stems from the spinach.
4. When the water is very hot, but not yet boiling, add the spinach and cook just until it's wilted, 2 or 3 minutes. Remove the leaves from the pot, rinse them under cold water, squeeze them dry, and chop them.
5. When the water boils, reduce the heat so it bubbles steadily. Pinch off a piece of the dough and boil it to make sure it will hold its shape. If not, stir a bit more flour into the dough until it does.

6. Start dropping rounded tablespoons of the dough into the boiling water (you'll likely want to cook these in 2 batches to avoid overcrowding the pot).

7. The dumplings will sink at first, then rise to the surface. A minute or 2 after they rise to the surface, scoop them out with a slotted spoon and transfer them to a platter. Repeat with the second batch.

8. Add the spinach to the skillet with the brown butter and sprinkle with salt and pepper. Turn the heat to medium and toss to warm the spinach through, adding a splash of cooking liquid if you want to make it saucier.

9. Spoon the butter and spinach over the dumplings, sprinkle the remaining 1/4 cup Parmesan over the top, and serve.

VARIATIONS

Ricotta Dumplings with Spinach and Sage Brown Butter
Once the butter turns light brown, add about 10 sage leaves, let them sizzle for a minute, then turn off the heat and proceed.

NOTES

EVEN FASTER
Instead of blanching the spinach in the boiling water in Step 4, chop the raw spinach leaves and add them to the butter once it turns light brown. Cook just until the spinach wilts, then turn off the heat and proceed.

SIDES

Tomato Salad 913

Fennel Salad 917

Broiled Cherry Tomatoes 931

SPEED ◐ SERVES 4

Cold Peanut Noodles with Whatever You Have

The "whatever you have" part of this recipe could be any number of ingredients hanging around in your fridge—cooked meat, chicken, shrimp, or vegetables, cubes of tofu, or any veggies that you'd eat raw. As long as what you use goes well with peanut butter, these noodles will be a perfect backdrop.

Ingredients

Salt

Stir-In Ingredients: 8 ounces to 1 pound cooked meat, fish, or tofu or any cooked or raw vegetables

½ cup peanut butter

1 tablespoon sesame oil

1 tablespoon honey

3 tablespoons soy sauce

1 tablespoon rice vinegar

Dash of chile oil or hot sauce

Pepper

½ inch fresh ginger

12 ounces udon or soba noodles

3 scallions

Prep | Cook

1. Bring a stockpot of water to a boil and salt it.

   Gather your stir-in ingredients from the fridge and chop or slice as needed.

2. Combine ½ cup peanut butter, 1 tablespoon sesame oil, 1 tablespoon honey, 3 tablespoons soy sauce, 1 tablespoon rice vinegar, a dash of chile oil or hot sauce, and a sprinkle of pepper in a large bowl.

   Peel and mince ½ inch fresh ginger; add it to the bowl.

3. Whisk, thinning the sauce with hot water until it has the consistency of heavy cream. Taste and adjust the seasoning.

4. When the water boils, add the noodles and stir occasionally. Start tasting after 3 minutes.

   Trim and chop the scallions.

5. When the noodles are tender but not mushy, drain them, rinse them under cold water until completely cool, then drain again.

6. Add the noodles to the bowl with the sauce, along with whatever you're stirring in and the scallions. Toss, taste and adjust the seasoning, and serve.

VARIATIONS

Cold Sesame Noodles with Whatever You Have
Use tahini instead of the peanut butter.

Cold Cashew Noodles with Whatever You Have
Use cashew butter—your own (see page 139) or store-bought—instead of the peanut butter.

NOTES

ASIAN NOODLE DISHES WITH PASTA
Of course, the tastiest Asian noodle dishes are made with noodles like udon or soba, but there's certainly nothing about the taste of pasta that excludes it from being used with Asian ingredients. So, if you're craving soy, sesame, coconut, or ginger but don't have any Asian noodles, just use whatever you have on hand. Linguine is often a good option, as is any type of egg noodle.

SIDES

Ginger-Orange Bean Sprouts 919

Cucumber Salad with Soy Sauce and Mirin 915

Avocado with Lemon and Salt 920

Asian Noodles

I've been cooking noodles for a long time, but I still get excited at Asian markets—or in the ever-improving Asian food aisles in supermarkets—when I see just how wide the variety is. You could cook Asian noodles for a week or longer and not use the same one twice. Some are similar in taste and cooking technique to Italian pasta; others are strikingly different. It doesn't really matter which types of Asian noodles you choose to stock in your pantry, but here is a rundown of those you're likely to encounter, including both the ones that I call for here and others that make good substitutes.

Noodle	Description
CHINESE EGG NOODLES	These are the noodles used in lo mein and many other Chinese noodle dishes, and, like fresh Italian pasta, they're made with wheat flour and eggs and come both fresh and dried. They are long, thin, and golden in color; the width of the noodle can vary. The fresh variety cooks in about 3 minutes, the dried in roughly 5. If you're boiling these before stir-frying (as in Stir-Fried Noodles with Beef and Celery, page 344), you'll want to undercook them slightly to account for the extra time in the skillet.
RAMEN AND SAIMIN	Otherwise knows as the crinkly bricks of noodles that come in the instant ramen packages—although you can also find them fresh if you go out of your way. Fun fact: The ones in the instant ramen packages are usually deep fried to remove moisture before they are dried and packaged. Follow the package directions for cooking or soaking time.

Noodle	Description
UDON NOODLES	Japanese wheat noodles, which can be round, square, or flat and come in a wide range of thicknesses and lengths. Udon noodles have a wonderful chew if you don't overcook them; they're often served in soups, but you can also stir-fry them or serve them cold. They come both fresh and dried. Cook the same way you would both fresh and dried pasta.
SOBA NOODLES	Japanese noodles made from a combination of buckwheat and wheat flour. The buckwheat gives them a uniquely nutty flavor and a grayish brown color—they're actually quite beautiful. They're long, thin, and flat, and—although you can find them fresh—almost always dried. Because of the buckwheat flour, they take a little longer to cook than other dried noodles, 5 to 7 minutes. You can find soba noodles that are pure buckwheat (and thus gluten-free). If you use those, cook them carefully according to the directions; they are more fragile than the type that contains wheat.
RICE NOODLES	The thicker versions are called *rice sticks*, while the wispy thin ones are called *rice vermicelli*. Typically used in Southeast Asian cooking, they're made with rice flour and are dried, white, and slightly translucent. They are a revelation for fast cooks because you only need to soak them in hot or boiling water until softened before eating—it could take anywhere from 5 to 30 minutes, depending on the thickness. (To speed things up even more, you can boil them as you would Italian pasta until tender, which takes only a few minutes.) If you're adding them to soup (as in Noodles, Shrimp, and Sweet Potatoes in Curry Broth, page 338), you don't need to presoak them. These are a favorite with gluten-free cooks.
GLASS NOODLES	Also know as *bean threads*, *cellophane noodles*, *mung bean noodles*, and *spring rain noodles*, these are long, thin, translucent noodles made from mung bean starch. Like rice noodles, you only need to soak them in hot or boiling water until tender —somewhere between 5 and 15 minutes— but you can also boil them. And like rice noodles, they do not contain wheat. They tend to be quite long, so use kitchen scissors to cut them into smaller pieces once they're cooked.

SPEED ◐ SERVES 4

Noodles with Snow Peas and Chile Oil

Warning: Don't cook this recipe unless you're prepared never to buy an overpriced bottle of chile oil in the store again. Great chile oil is stunningly easy to make at home—it's not much more than chiles simmered in oil. Dried chiles give you more of a toasted flavor, while fresh chiles produce a brighter-tasting oil. Either version plays very well here.

Ingredients

Salt

¼ cup vegetable oil

5 dried red chiles or 3 fresh hot chiles (like Thai or serrano)

4 garlic cloves

1 inch fresh ginger

12 ounces soba or udon noodles

12 ounces snow peas

Sesame seeds for garnish

Prep | Cook

1. Bring a stockpot of water to a boil and salt it.
2. Put ¼ cup vegetable oil in a small saucepan over low heat.
   If you're using dried chiles, leave them whole; if you're using fresh, slice them thinly. Add them to the saucepan.
   Crush 4 garlic cloves and slice 1 inch fresh ginger (don't bother to peel either). Add them to the saucepan.
3. Adjust the heat so that the oil bubbles ever so slightly, turning it down if anything starts to smell too toasted; let the flavors infuse the oil while you cook the noodles and snow peas.
4. When the water boils, add the noodles and stir occasionally. Start tasting after 3 minutes.
5. When the noodles are almost tender, add the snow peas to the pot. Continue cooking until the noodles are tender but not mushy and the snow peas are softened but still crisp.
6. Drain the noodles and snow peas, rinse them under cold water until they're room temperature, then drain again.

7. Return the noodles and snow peas to the pot. Pour the oil into the pot through a strainer (discarding the solids). Toss, taste and adjust the seasoning, and divide among 4 bowls. Garnish with the sesame seeds and serve.

VARIATIONS

Noodles with Spinach and Chile Oil

Substitute 1 pound chopped spinach for the snow peas.

Noodles with Crisp Pork, Chile Oil, and Snow Peas

Start by cooking 12 ounces ground pork in a medium skillet until browned, 6 to 8 minutes. Then build the chile oil right in that skillet, leaving the pork and any rendered fat to flavor the oil. Since you won't be straining the oil before tossing it with the noodles, mince the chiles and peel and mince the garlic and ginger before adding them.

Noodles with Tofu, Chile Oil, and Edamame

Put a tablespoon of oil in a medium skillet. Add 12 ounces crumbled extra-firm tofu and cook until browned, 5 to 10 minutes. Then build the chile oil right in that skillet, leaving the tofu in the skillet to soak up the oil. Since you won't be straining the oil before tossing it with the noodles, mince the chiles and peel and mince the garlic and ginger before adding them. Substitute 3 cups frozen edamame for the snow peas. Add them to the pot with the noodles to take the chill off.

NOTES

MAKING CHILE OIL

Once you realize how delicious and easy homemade chile oil is, you'll want to have some on hand at all times. It's as useful a condiment as soy sauce or sesame oil, and I use it in all the same ways: drizzling it on noodles and rice, simply cooked vegetables, shrimp, and tofu and stirring it into all sorts of Asian-style sauces (like peanut sauce) to give them a kick. Even though it's made with neutral oil, you want to make sure not to use chile oil to stir-fry other ingredients, since the bits of aromatics that have infused it will burn over high heat. I recommend making chile oil in batches that you feel confident using up in a week or 2 (I usually shoot for about ½ cup). You can store it comfortably in a jar in the fridge for about that long, but after that it may begin to go bad. Luckily, whipping up a new batch every few weeks could hardly be easier.

SIDES

Soy Slaw 923

Scallion-Miso Bean Sprouts 919

Stir-Fried Bok Choy 927

SPEED ◑ SERVES 4

Udon with Teriyaki Tofu

Teriyaki is a consummate crowd-pleaser and a snap to make from scratch. And tofu loves the teriyaki treatment. It soaks up the sauce's flavor like a sponge and emerges with a wonderful syrupy coating that's got the perfect balance of sweet and savory flavors.

Ingredients

Salt

2 tablespoons vegetable oil

1 brick firm tofu (12 to 14 ounces)

2 garlic cloves

1 inch fresh ginger

½ cup soy sauce

½ cup mirin or ¼ cup honey mixed with ¼ cup water

12 ounces udon noodles

4 scallions

Prep | Cook

1. Bring a stockpot of water to a boil and salt it.
2. Put 2 tablespoons vegetable oil in a large skillet or large pot over medium-high heat.

   Pat the tofu dry and cut it into ½-inch cubes.
3. When the oil is hot, add the tofu to the skillet and cook, stirring or shaking the pan occasionally until the tofu is lightly browned, 5 or 6 minutes.

   Peel 2 garlic cloves and 1 inch fresh ginger; mince them together.
4. When the tofu is lightly browned, carefully add ½ cup soy sauce, ½ cup mirin (or ¼ cup honey mixed with ¼ cup water), and the garlic and ginger to the skillet. Bring the mixture to a boil, then adjust the heat so that it bubbles gently.
5. When the water boils, add the noodles and stir occasionally. Start tasting after 3 minutes.

   Trim and chop the scallions.

6. When the noodles are tender but not mushy, drain them and add them to the skillet. Toss to coat with the sauce, being careful not to break up the tofu too much if you can help it. Garnish with the scallions and serve.

VARIATIONS

Udon with Teriyaki Beef
Substitute 12 ounces boneless beef sirloin or rib-eye, thinly sliced, for the tofu. Sauté it in the skillet until it just loses its red color, then build in the teriyaki sauce as directed.

Udon with Teriyaki Chicken
Substitute 12 ounces boneless, skinless chicken thighs or breasts, thinly sliced, for the tofu. Sauté it in the skillet until it just loses its pink color, then build in the teriyaki sauce as directed.

Udon with Teriyaki Pork
Use 12 ounces thinly sliced pork shoulder instead of the tofu. Sauté it in the skillet until it just loses its pink color, then build in the teriyaki sauce as directed.

NOTES

SOY SAUCE
Soy sauce, which has been around for thousands of years, is made by fermenting soybeans, and usually wheat, with salt and bacteria. The vast majority of real soy sauces (as opposed to salt, water, and food coloring; such "soy" sauces are to be avoided) are Japanese, and mostly "dark"; "light" soy sauce is somewhat saltier. ("Low sodium" soy sauce has almost half of its salt removed after brewing and should not be confused with "light.") Tamari is a special variety with a stronger flavor, usually made from 100 percent soy. (If you're incredibly sensitive to gluten, this is the stuff you want.) Chinese soy sauces (less common) can also either be "light" (salty and thin) or "dark" (sweet and viscous). Anything but the viscous kinds will do just fine in these recipes.

SIDES

Green Salad with Sesame-Soy Dressing 911

Soy Slaw 923

Ginger-Orange Bean Sprouts 919

Stir-Fried Bok Choy 927

Scallion-Miso Bean Sprouts 919

Simmered Squash 955

SPEED ◐ SERVES 4

Noodles, Shrimp, and Sweet Potatoes in Curry Broth

This homey Malaysian one-pot meal is somewhere between a regular noodle dish and a soup. You start by building a fragrant broth with aromatics and spices; thin slices of sweet potato and rice noodles thicken the broth with their starch, while lime at the end brightens it up.

Ingredients

One 15-ounce can coconut milk

1 tablespoon curry powder

4 whole star anise

2 bay leaves

Salt

2 garlic cloves

1 inch fresh ginger

1 fresh hot green chile (like serrano)

1 pound sweet potatoes

1 lime

Several sprigs fresh cilantro

4 ounces dried rice vermicelli noodles

3 tablespoons fish sauce

12 ounces peeled shrimp

Prep | Cook

1. Put 4 cups water in a large skillet or large pot over high heat. Add the coconut milk, 1 tablespoon curry powder, 4 whole star anise, 2 bay leaves, and a generous pinch of salt.

   Peel 2 garlic cloves and 1 inch fresh ginger. Trim the chile and seed it if you'd like to reduce the heat. Mince them all together and add them to the pot.

   Peel the sweet potatoes, halve them lengthwise, and cut them into half-moons ⅛ to ¼ inch thick. Add them to the pot.

2. Bring the mixture to a boil, reduce the heat slightly to let the mixture simmer, and cook until the sweet potatoes are just about tender, 6 to 8 minutes.

   Halve the lime.

   Chop several sprigs cilantro.

3. When the sweet potatoes are tender, add the rice noodles and stir. Squeeze in the lime juice, add 3 tablespoons fish sauce, and stir in the shrimp. Cook until the shrimp turns pink and cooks through, 2 or 3 minutes.

4. Fish out the star anise and bay leaves. Taste and adjust the seasoning, divide among 4 bowls, garnish with the cilantro, and serve immediately.

VARIATIONS

Noodles, Chicken, and Sweet Potatoes in Curry Broth
Substitute 12 ounces boneless, skinless chicken thighs for the shrimp. Chop the chicken into ½-inch pieces and add to the pot along with the noodles in Step 3.

Noodles, Shrimp, and Sweet Potatoes in Lemongrass Broth
Omit the bay leaves. Substitute two 3-inch pieces lemongrass for the curry powder and 2 or 3 fresh basil stems for the star anise. Remove the lemongrass and basil stems before serving. Garnish with basil leaves.

NOTES

MAKE YOUR OWN
Curry Powder 758

EVEN FASTER
If you have a mandoline, use it to slice the potatoes very thinly. Not only does it make for faster slicing, but they'll take just a couple of minutes to become tender.

ONE-POT NOODLES
There's no rule saying you have to cook noodles in water by themselves. Cooking them with other ingredients lets the noodles absorb the flavor of the sauce or broth as they cook and, more important, I think, allows the starch that's released by the noodles to thicken the cooking liquid. The result is a wonderfully fortified sauce or broth that makes for a very comforting one-dish meal.

SIDES

Avocado with Lime and Chili Salt 920

Edamame Succotash 933

Sesame-Soy Black Beans 937

Tender Vegetables 954

Cool Noodles with Chicken and Cilantro-Scallion Pesto

We're long past the time when *pesto* meant only basil. Alternative versions abound, and many are wonderful. This loose interpretation uses cilantro, ginger, and quickly blanched scallions. Tossing the pesto with the noodles a bit before serving allows the flavors to develop and is a good use of the time it takes to cook the chicken.

Ingredients

Salt

½ inch fresh ginger

1 bunch fresh cilantro

1 bunch scallions

⅓ cup plus 2 tablespoons vegetable oil

1 tablespoon sesame oil

Pepper

12 ounces udon or fresh Chinese egg noodles

4 chicken cutlets (about 12 ounces)

Prep | Cook

1. Bring a stockpot of water to a boil and salt it. Also bring a small saucepan of water to a boil.
2. Prepare a grill or turn the broiler to high; put the rack 4 inches from the heat.

   Peel and roughly chop ½ inch fresh ginger; put it in a food processor.

   Cut off about 1 cup cilantro. Add it to the food processor.

   Trim and roughly chop the scallions.
3. When the saucepan of water boils, add the scallions and cook for 1 minute. Drain and rinse under cold water until cool; add them to the food processor.
4. Add ⅓ cup vegetable oil and 1 tablespoon sesame oil to the food processor along with a sprinkle of salt and pepper. Process, scraping down the sides and thinning the mixture with a splash of water if necessary, until it becomes a thick, smooth sauce. Transfer half of the sauce to a large bowl.

5. When the stockpot of water boils, add the noodles and stir occasionally. Start tasting after 3 minutes.
   Drizzle the chicken with 2 tablespoons vegetable oil and sprinkle with salt and pepper.

6. When the noodles are tender but not mushy, drain them, rinse them under cold water until completely cool, then drain again. Add the noodles to the bowl with the sauce and toss.

7. When the grill or broiler is hot, cook the chicken, turning once, until lightly browned on both sides and just cooked through, 2 to 5 minutes per side.

8. While the chicken cooks, divide the noodles among 4 bowls.

9. When the chicken is cooked through, transfer it to a cutting board and slice it. Lay the chicken on top of the noodles, top with the remaining sauce, and serve.

VARIATIONS

Cool Noodles with Beef and Spicy Cilantro-Scallion Pesto
Add 1 fresh hot green chile, chopped, to the food processor along with the ginger. Substitute 12 ounces skirt or flank steak for the chicken. Grill or broil it until a bit pinker inside than you like it, 2 to 5 minutes per side. Let it rest for 5 minutes before slicing.

Cool Noodles with Chicken and Peanut-Cilantro-Scallion Pesto
Along with the cilantro, add ¼ cup peanut butter to the food processor. Since it's thick, you'll likely need a little extra water to thin out the pesto.

SIDES

Soy Slaw 923

Ginger-Orange Bean Sprouts 919

Sautéed Sweet Potatoes with Ginger and Soy 964

SPEED ◐ SERVES 4

Singapore-Style Noodles with Chicken, Peppers, and Basil

Since rice vermicelli noodles cook so quickly, there's time for an initial soak to get them almost tender and a final stir-fry to finish them off and coat them with sauce. Inspired by curried noodles from Singapore, this dish is bursting with vibrant flavors.

Ingredients

Salt

6 boneless, skinless chicken thighs (1 pound)

2 garlic cloves

1 inch fresh ginger

2 red bell peppers

4 ounces dried rice vermicelli noodles

2 tablespoons vegetable oil

1 tablespoon curry powder

1 teaspoon sugar

1 tablespoon soy sauce, or more to taste

1 tablespoon fish sauce, or more to taste

1 bunch fresh basil

Prep | Cook

1. Bring a medium saucepan of water to a boil and salt it.
   Cut the chicken into ½-inch chunks.
   Peel 2 garlic cloves and 1 inch fresh ginger; mince them together.
   Core, seed, and slice the bell peppers.
2. When the water comes to a boil, add the noodles, stir once or twice, turn off the heat, and let them steep until they're not quite fully tender, 3 to 5 minutes.
3. Put 2 tablespoons vegetable oil in a large skillet over medium-high heat.
4. When the oil is hot, add the garlic and ginger to the skillet and sauté until fragrant, 1 or 2 minutes. Add the chicken and cook, undisturbed, until the pieces brown and release easily, 2 or 3 minutes. Then cook, stirring occasionally until the meat is no longer pink, 2 or 3 minutes.
5. When the noodles are done, drain well, reserving some of the soaking liquid and shaking off as much excess water as you can.

6. Stir 1 tablespoon curry powder and 1 teaspoon sugar into the skillet. Cook until the curry powder is fragrant, about a minute.

7. Add 1 tablespoon soy sauce, 1 tablespoon fish sauce, and the red peppers and stir to combine.

   Strip about ½ cup basil leaves from the stems.

8. When the peppers begin to soften and the chicken is cooked through, add the noodles and a splash of the reserved soaking liquid. Cook, tossing with tongs, until the noodles are tender and most of the liquid evaporates.

9. Taste and adjust the seasoning, adding more fish sauce or soy sauce if desired. Stir in the basil and serve.

VARIATIONS

Singapore-Style Noodles with Pork, Peppers, and Cilantro
Substitute 1 pound boneless pork shoulder, thinly sliced, for the chicken and cilantro for the basil.

Singapore-Style Noodles with Beef, Onions, and Mint
Use 1 pound boneless beef sirloin or rib-eye, thinly sliced, instead of chicken, 1 large red onion instead of bell peppers, and mint in place of basil.

NOTES

MAKE YOUR OWN
Curry Powder 758

IF YOU HAVE MORE TIME
If you prefer a thicker noodle, use rice sticks or wide rice noodles instead of rice vermicelli. Cook them in a stockpot of boiling water until almost tender (start tasting after 3 minutes). Proceed as directed.

SIDES

Cucumber Salad with Soy Sauce and Mirin 915

Avocado with Lemon and Salt 920

Tomato Salad 913

SPEED ◐ SERVES 4

Stir-Fried Noodles with Beef and Celery

Conventional wisdom for cooking stir-fries says you should prep all of your ingredients first, because once you start cooking, it all goes lightning-quick. That's true if you're using a lot of different ingredients (and have a super-powerful stove), but if you narrow them down to a key few—as in this lo-mein-style dish—you can prep as you go without having to sweat it.

Ingredients

Salt

2 tablespoons vegetable oil

12 ounces boneless beef sirloin or rib-eye

1 medium onion

3 celery stalks, with any leaves

1 lemon

2 tablespoons soy sauce

12 ounces fresh or dried Chinese egg noodles

Prep | Cook

1. Bring a stockpot of water to a boil and salt it.
2. Put 2 tablespoons vegetable oil in a large skillet or large pot over medium-high heat.

   Slice the beef as thinly as you can.
3. When the oil is very hot, add the beef and sprinkle with salt. Cook, stirring once or twice, until it loses its pink color, 3 or 4 minutes.

   Trim, peel, halve, and slice the onion.

   Trim and slice the celery; chop and save the leaves for garnish.
4. When the beef loses its pink color, remove it from the skillet. Add the onion and celery and sprinkle with salt. Cook, stirring occasionally until the onion begins to brown and the celery is just tender (but still has some crunch), 3 to 5 minutes.

   Halve the lemon.

5. When the vegetables are done, return the beef to the skillet. Squeeze in the lemon juice and add 2 tablespoons soy sauce. Cook for 30 seconds to a minute, then turn off the heat.

6. When the water boils, add the noodles and stir occasionally. Start tasting after 3 minutes.

7. When the noodles are tender but not mushy, drain them, reserving some of the cooking water. Add the noodles to the skillet along with a small splash of cooking water and turn the heat to medium-high.

8. Add the celery leaves and cook, tossing with tongs, until the noodles are coated with sauce. Taste and adjust the seasoning and serve immediately.

VARIATIONS

Stir-Fried Noodles with Beef and Bean Sprouts
Substitute 8 ounces bean sprouts for the celery. To keep them nice and crunchy, instead of cooking them along with the onion, add them to the skillet when you return the beef in Step 5.

Stir-Fried Noodles with Tofu and Celery
Use a brick of firm tofu (12 to 14 ounces) instead of the beef. Cut the tofu into ½-inch cubes and cook it in the skillet until it's lightly browned, 5 or 6 minutes. Remove it from the skillet and proceed as directed.

SIDES

Green Salad with Sesame-Soy Dressing 911

Soy Slaw 923

Steamed Tender Vegetables 954

Rice and Grains

RICE

Rice, Beans, and Broccoli 350

Rice with Cabbage, Scrambled Eggs, and Scallions 356

Creamy Chinese Rice with Clams 358

Fast Jook with Chicken and Snow Peas 360

Hoppin' John with Collards 362

Chipotle Rice and Corn with Seared Beef 366

Rice Bowl with Sausage 368

Three-Stir Mushroom Risotto 370

Curried Lentils and Rice with Fried Onions 372

Fast Thai Sticky Rice with Meaty Vegetable Sauce 374

Rice and Smoked Salmon Cakes with Cucumber Salsa 376

Shrimp and Tomato Paella 378

Jambalaya des Herbes with Shrimp 380

Rice and Wings 382

GRAINS

Quinoa Pilaf with Chickpeas and Dried Fruit 384

Smoky Bulgur with Eggplant, Dried Tomatoes, and Feta 386

Quinoa Puttanesca with Fresh Mozzarella 388

Couscous Gratin with Leeks and Gruyère 390

Masa and Rajas 392

Farro with White Beans and Tuna 394

Warm Tabbouleh with Mussels 396

Shrimp over Grits 398

Couscous Helper 400

Polenta with Sausage and Mushrooms 402

Pozole and Pork Chops 404

Couscous Paella with Chicken and Zucchini 406

Skillet Shepherd's Pie with Quinoa Crust 408

Rice and Grains

Rice and other grains are the human race's main source of calories; they have been staples since the beginning of agriculture. But I'm guessing none of that crosses your mind when you're staring into your pantry, looking for something to get on the table quickly.

If it did, you might consider the tremendous variety of grain dishes, many substantial and many quite quick. A pot of rice—which could be the most loved food on the planet—takes maybe 15 unattended minutes to cook and can be taken in infinite directions; bulgur or couscous takes even less time.

Some rices and grains take too long to cook to fall within the scope of this book, so I call for only varieties that you can cook in 45 minutes or less. That said, there's certainly no need to walk down the dark path toward products like "instant rice" or other overly processed convenience foods.

A word on washing: I wash all my grains, organic or not, in several changes of water before cooking them. You never know what kind of residue may be on them, and washing does help.

Take a look at the impressive variety of stir-ins, season-withs, and scatter-on-tops that transform plain grains into satisfying and often stunning main dishes.

Chapter Highlights

Rice and Grains 101 Notes on the different kinds of rices and grains that you might want to incorporate into your rotation. Rice and Grains (page 352).

Brown Rice for White Want to use brown rice? Here's how. Substituting Brown Rice for White (page 351).

Cooking Grains A master recipe for cooking all different kinds of grains. Rice and Other Grains, Fast and Slow (page 354).

Pilaf Aplenty Pilaf—a grain dish in which aromatic ingredients are simmered along with the grain—is one of the most useful dishes in the world. Recipe-Free Pilaf (page 364).

Almost Fried Rice Classic flavors, fast. Rice with Cabbage, Scrambled Eggs, and Scallions (page 356).

Lazy Man's Risotto You might think risotto requires constant stirring and unwavering attention; it doesn't. Three-Stir Mushroom Risotto (page 370).

Paella, Easier than You Might Think Paella is not a huge production, but a simple (and relatively fast) baked rice dish. Shrimp and Tomato Paella (page 378); Couscous Paella with Chicken and Zucchini (page 406).

Overcooking Rice It's not something you want to do all the time, but sometimes overcooking rice—until the kernels burst and release starch—has its advantages. Fast Thai Sticky Rice with Meaty Vegetable Sauce (page 374), Rice and Smoked Salmon Cakes with Cucumber Salsa (page 376), Fast Jook with Chicken and Snow Peas (page 360), Creamy Chinese Rice with Clams (page 358).

A Sticky Shortcut A shortcut that gets you firm, chewy sticky rice in no time. Fast Thai Sticky Rice with Meaty Vegetable Sauce (page 374).

Rice Cakes The fastest way to turn rice into cakes. Rice Cakes (page 377).

Grain Casseroles Though we may not think of them as such, grains are perfect for casseroles. Quinoa Puttanesca with Fresh Mozzarella (page 388), Couscous Gratin with Leeks and Gruyère (page 390), Skillet Shepherd's Pie with Quinoa Crust (page 408).

Crunchy Grains Aren't Just for Cereal Crisp grains add wonderful texture to all sorts of dishes. Crisp Grains (page 409).

Deconstructed Tamales Tamale flavor without much of the work. Masa and Rajas (page 392).

SPEED ◐ SERVES 4

Rice, Beans, and Broccoli

An incredibly hearty one-pot meal. Here I use white beans, which begin to break down and get creamy as the rice cooks. If you want your beans more intact, cook the rice first, then toss the beans in at the end, just long enough to warm them.

Ingredients

2 cups any cooked or canned white beans (one 15-ounce can)

1 ½ cups long-grain white rice

Salt

Water or stock (2 ½ to 3 cups)

2 garlic cloves

1 medium head broccoli (1 to 1 ½ pounds)

2 ounces Parmesan cheese (½ cup grated)

1 large bunch fresh basil (2 cups leaves)

2 tablespoons olive oil or butter

Pepper

Prep | Cook

If you're using canned beans, rinse and drain them.

1. Put the beans and 1 ½ cups rice in a large pot or deep skillet; add a big pinch of salt and water or stock to cover by about an inch. Bring to a boil.

   Peel and thinly slice 2 garlic cloves; add them to the pot.

2. When the liquid boils, adjust the heat so it bubbles steadily but not vigorously; cover. Cook, undisturbed, until the rice is beginning to get tender but is still too hard to eat, 5 to 7 minutes.

   Trim the broccoli and separate into florets; slice any thick stems.

   Grate ½ cup Parmesan.

   Strip about 2 cups basil leaves from the stems. Roughly shred the leaves with your hands.

3. When the rice is beginning to get tender, stir in the broccoli, adding more liquid if necessary. Cover the pot and cook, undisturbed, until the rice and broccoli are tender, 5 to 7 minutes more. Tip the pot; if any liquid remains, cover and keep cooking until the rice is dry, checking every minute or 2.

4. Stir in 2 tablespoons olive oil or butter, the Parmesan, basil, and some pepper. Taste and adjust the seasoning and serve.

VARIATIONS

Curried Rice, Beans, and Hearty Greens
Use chickpeas instead of white beans. Substitute one 15-ounce can coconut milk for 1 ½ cups of the water. Add 1 inch fresh ginger, minced, 1 fresh hot green chile, minced, and 1 tablespoon curry powder to the pot along with the garlic. Substitute 1 bunch kale or collards, chopped, for the broccoli.

Rice, Beans, and Broccoli with Bacon or Prosciutto
Before you add the rice and beans to the saucepan, cook 4 ounces chopped bacon or prosciutto in a little olive oil until crisp. You can either leave it in to cook with the rice and beans or, to keep it crisp, remove it, then add it back right before serving.

NOTES

MAKE YOUR OWN

Cooked Beans 496

Chicken Stock 213

Vegetable Stock 212

Beef Stock 212

IF YOU HAVE MORE TIME
Peel off the broccoli stem's tough skin before chopping.

SUBSTITUTING BROWN RICE FOR WHITE
Since brown rice takes a long time to cook, I don't call for it in the main recipes in this book, but you can easily substitute it: Bring a pot of salted water to a boil, then stir in the same quantity of brown rice as is called for in the recipe. Adjust the heat so the water bubbles steadily but not too vigorously. Cook, undisturbed, for 10 to 15 minutes, then drain it. Now it's ready to use in any recipe that calls for white rice; you can parcook the rice up to an hour before you use it. And once it's finished cooking, you can refrigerate it for a few days. Microwave it to reheat, adding a little water if it seems dry.

SIDES

Warm Buttery Bread 906

Cucumber Salad 915

Broiled Cherry Tomatoes 931

Carrot Salad with Olives and Rosemary 914

Rice and Grains

There are thousands of varieties of rice and grains. This chart describes the handful that can be cooked quickly—the ones you'll use in this chapter—as well as a few more that are useful to know about. For a master recipe and cooking times for everything here, see page 355.

Rice or Grain	Description
SOUTHERN LONG-GRAIN RICE	The most common long-grain rice in the world, grown widely in the United States. Any rice at the supermarket simply labeled *long-grain* is likely to be this.
BASMATI RICE	Originally from India, basmati has a supremely nutty aroma and fantastic flavor, and the grains separate from each other beautifully when cooked. The various American aromatic varieties, like Texmati, Kasmati, Calmati, and Jasmati, are not as flavorful as the original but are still pretty good.
JASMINE RICE	Usually associated with Thailand, this has a milder flavor than basmati, a slightly stickier texture, and a distinctive aroma.
LONG-GRAIN STICKY RICES	Southeast Asian, mostly, where the grains are formed into balls or squares and eaten like bread; they're aromatic, sweet, and uniquely textured. Look for variety names like *Thai*, *sticky jasmine*, *glutinous*, and *sweet*. (You'll also find short-grain sticky rices, which are plump and slightly sweet and often used in desserts.)
COMMON SHORT- AND MEDIUM-GRAIN RICES	Most commonly found in Southeast Asia and Japan (where they are used for sushi), these are glossy, sticky, and firm, with a neutral flavor. I like to keep both white and brown versions on hand; both are a good substitute for more expensive varieties like Arborio and Valencia.
RISOTTO RICES	Arborio is the most common, but other versions include Carnaroli and Vialone Nano. Their starchy outer layers absorb liquid and give risotto its creamy texture, while their centers remain firm and al dente, as long they're not overcooked.

Rice or Grain	Description
COUSCOUS	Not a grain but rather tiny bits of pasta, couscous comes in white (which takes 5 to 10 minutes to cook) and whole wheat (10 to 15). There's also pearl or Israeli couscous, which are larger, toasted pieces that have more chew. Most cooks treat couscous more like a grain than a pasta, which is why it's included here.
BULGUR	Wheat kernels that are steamed, hulled, dried, and ground to fine, medium, and coarse, sometimes identified by numbers: #1 for fine and #3 or #4 for the coarsest. It takes 10 to 20 minutes to become tender, depending on the grind, and has a nutty, mild flavor and a dry, fluffy texture.
ROLLED OATS	Oats flattened with giant rollers into the flakes we all know. Avoid the quick-cooking and instant varieties. Oats almost always get a breakfast or sweet treatment, though some adventurous cooks use them in savory dishes.
QUINOA	Shaped like disks and about the size of pinheads, quinoa has a distinctly grassy and nutty flavor and an almost crunchy texture when cooked (it takes about 20 minutes). The most common variety is light tan in color, but you can also find it in red and black.
PEARLED BARLEY	This is the kind of barley that's sold everywhere, as opposed to hulled barley, which takes much longer to cook. Pearled barley has been hulled, steamed, and polished. It cooks in about 20 minutes and has a creamy yet chewy texture.
CORNMEAL	Most commonly yellow or white (but sometimes blue or red), cornmeal is dried corn kernels that are ground to varying degrees. The fine grind is best for baking, while the medium grind is best for polenta. It cooks in 20 to 30 minutes. Grits and pozole are made from hominy, corn kernels that have been dried and processed with lime or lye.
CRACKED WHEAT	Often confused with bulgur, but instead of being steamed, it's completely raw, which means it takes a little longer to cook—20 to 30 minutes. It has the same nutty flavor as bulgur but is chewier and heartier.
MILLET	Purported to be one of the first grains used by humans, millet has a mildly nutty, almost cornlike flavor. It's fluffy when cooked and takes 20 to 30 minutes.
FARRO	A chewy ancient wheat-related grain that has a nutty, wheaty flavor. Makes a wonderful whole grain substitute in risotto; takes 20 to 30 minutes to cook.

Rice and Other Grains, Fast and Slow

The happy truth about grains is that you can cook almost every kind perfectly using the simple method here. (The most notable exceptions are bulgur and couscous, which get their own recipes—see pages 125 and 910—and wild rice, which takes quite a while to cook.)

The only significant variable is the timing: Some grains—like couscous—will take as little as 10 minutes, while others, like wheat berries, could take more than an hour. Cooking times are never quite exact, so taste the grains every now and then and trust your judgment; they should be tender enough to eat but still have a little bite. This recipe makes 3 or 4 cups, but if you're cooking a big batch—which I recommend—see the final step for tips on storing. And see the list that follows for a few ideas for flavoring grains once they are cooked.

My method for cooking rice has become more casual over the years. I no longer bother to measure the liquid and the grains (usually a ratio of 2:1, liquid to grains). Instead, I rinse the grains, put them in the pot, cover them by about an inch of liquid, and boil them, adding more liquid if the grains start drying out before they finish. The results are just as good. You can use the more traditional "boil, cover, simmer, let rest" method if you prefer. You can also boil the grains in abundant water as you would pasta and drain them in a strainer.

Easy Cooked Grains

1 Wash the Grains

Put 1 cup of grains in a large bowl and rinse them in several changes of water. Drain them.

2 Combine Grains and Water

Put the washed grains and a large pinch of salt in a small to medium saucepan. Add water to cover by about an inch. Bring to a boil, then adjust the heat so the mixture bubbles gently.

3 Cook Until Tender

Cook, stirring occasionally until the grain is tender, anywhere from 7 or 8 minutes to over an hour, depending on the type of grain. Like pasta, the grain should retain a little bite when it's done. Whole grains will always have a certain amount of chew to them, but milled or cut grains will become mushy if you cook them for too long, so taste frequently. Ideally, by the time the grain is tender all of the liquid will have been absorbed. If at any point the pot gets too dry before the grain is tender, add more water. If any water remains when the grain is tender, drain it.

4 Serve or Store

If you're serving the grain right away, toss it with olive oil or butter to taste, with any of the ingredients from the following list or really anything that you feel like. Or cover (toss with a little oil first if you want to prevent sticking) and store in the refrigerator for up to 4 or 5 days or the freezer for up to a few months. Reheat with a little water or oil.

Cooking Times for Rice and Other Grains

Long-Grain Rice: 10 to 15 minutes
Basmati Rice: 15 to 20 minutes
Jasmine Rice: 15 to 20 minutes
Long-Grain Sticky Rice: 20 to 25 minutes
Short- and Medium-Grain Rice: 25 to 30 minutes
Risotto Rice: 20 to 30 minutes
Couscous: 5 to 10 minutes
Bulgur: 10 to 25 minutes
Rolled Oats: 10 to 15 minutes
Quinoa: 15 to 20 minutes
Pearled Barley: 20 minutes
Cornmeal: 20 to 30 minutes
Cracked Wheat: 20 to 30 minutes
Millet: 20 to 30 minutes
Farro: 20 to 30 minutes

VARIATIONS

11 Ways to Flavor Cooked Grains

Toss any of the following, alone or in combination, with the cooked grains along with olive oil or butter:

1. 1 tablespoon chopped fresh herbs
2. A few spoonfuls of simple vinaigrette (page 70)
3. Lots of pepper
4. ½ cup grated or crumbled cheese
5. 1 to 2 cups cooked beans, peas, or lentils
6. 1 to 1 ½ cups dried fruit
7. ½ cup chopped scallions
8. ½ cup tomato sauce or salsa
9. ½ to 1 teaspoon ground spices
10. ½ cup crumbled cooked bacon
11. ½ cup chopped nuts or dried fruit

SPEED ◐ SERVES 4

Rice with Cabbage, Scrambled Eggs, and Scallions

Tender, slightly crisp stir-fried cabbage, scrambled eggs, and crunchy sharp scallions are a stellar combination, and freshly made rice gives this dish a fluffy quality that's different from standard fried rice; I like it a lot.

Ingredients

3 tablespoons vegetable oil, plus more if needed

1 tablespoon sesame seeds

1 ½ cups long-grain white rice

Salt

1 small head Napa or Savoy cabbage (1 pound)

4 eggs

4 scallions

Soy sauce for serving

Prep | Cook

1. Put 1 tablespoon vegetable oil in a medium saucepan over medium heat.
2. When the oil is hot, add 1 tablespoon sesame seeds, 1 ½ cups rice, and a sprinkle of salt. Cook, stirring frequently until the rice is glossy and starting to color slightly, 3 to 5 minutes.
3. Add 3 cups of water. Bring to a boil, then adjust the heat so the mixture bubbles steadily but not vigorously. Cover and cook, undisturbed, until small craters appear on the surface, 10 to 15 minutes.
4. Put 2 tablespoons vegetable oil in a large skillet over low heat.

   Trim, core, and quarter the cabbage. Cut each quarter crosswise into thin ribbons.
5. Turn the heat up to medium-high. Add the cabbage to the skillet and sprinkle with salt. Cook, stirring occasionally until the cabbage is lightly browned and wilted (it should still have a little crunch), 6 to 8 minutes.

   Crack the eggs into a bowl, sprinkle with salt, and beat them.

   Trim and chop the scallions.

6. Move the cabbage to one side of the skillet and add a drizzle of oil to the empty space if it looks dry. Add the eggs and cook, stirring constantly until they're scrambled and set, a minute or 2.

7. Toss the eggs and cabbage together in the skillet and turn off the heat.

8. When small craters appear on the surface of the rice, tip the pot to see if any liquid remains. If so, cover and keep cooking until the rice is dry, checking every minute or 2.

9. Add the cooked rice to the skillet with the cabbage and eggs. Add the scallions and stir to combine. Taste and adjust the seasoning and serve, passing soy sauce at the table.

VARIATIONS

Rice with Bok Choy, Scrambled Eggs, and Scallions
Substitute bok choy, stems and leaves sliced crosswise, for the cabbage. If you want the stems to be nice and crunchy, add them at the same time as the leaves. Otherwise, add them by themselves first and cook for 2 or 3 minutes before adding the leaves.

Rice with Tomatoes, Scrambled Eggs, and Basil
Use olive oil instead of vegetable and skip the sesame seeds. Substitute 1 ½ pounds ripe fresh tomatoes, chopped, for the cabbage. Cook the tomatoes just until they start to release some of their juice but not so much that they turn into sauce, 3 or 4 minutes. Then add the eggs and proceed as directed, substituting ½ cup torn fresh basil for the scallions. Pass Parmesan cheese instead of soy sauce.

NOTES

EVEN FASTER
More Like Fried Rice
If you have 3 to 4 cups leftover refrigerated rice on hand, use that and start at Step 4. Toast the sesame seeds in a dry pan and add them with the rice in Step 9.

SIDES

Tomato Salad with Sesame and Soy 913

Daikon Salad with Fish Sauce and Peanuts 918

SPEED ◐ SERVES 4

Creamy Chinese Rice with Clams

Soft and creamy rice is the perfect plain foil for this quick and intensely flavored stir-fry of clams, chile, and fermented Chinese black beans (more on those in the Notes).

Ingredients

1 ½ cups short-grain white rice

Salt

¼ cup fermented black beans

½ cup rice wine

3 pounds littleneck or other hard-shell clams

2 tablespoons vegetable oil

2 garlic cloves

1 fresh hot green chile (like serrano)

4 scallions

Sesame oil for serving

Prep | Cook

1. Put 1 ½ cups rice in a medium saucepan; add a big pinch of salt and water to cover by about 1 ½ inches. Bring to a boil.

   Put ¼ cup fermented black beans in a small dish with ½ cup rice wine.

2. When the water boils, adjust the heat so the mixture bubbles steadily but not vigorously. Cover and cook, stirring occasionally until the rice is soft and slightly creamy and most of the liquid is absorbed, 15 to 20 minutes.

   Scrub the clams.

3. Put 2 tablespoons vegetable oil in a large skillet over low heat.

   Peel 2 garlic cloves and trim the chile. Mince them together.

4. Turn the heat up to medium-high and add the garlic and chile to the skillet. Cook, stirring until fragrant, 30 seconds to a minute.

5. Add the clams and ¼ cup water and cover the skillet. Cook until the clams open, 5 to 10 minutes.

   Trim and chop the scallions.

6. When the clams open, uncover the skillet and stir in the fermented black bean mixture. Cook, stirring to toss the clams in the sauce. Turn off the heat.

7. When the rice is soft and slightly creamy, divide it among 4 plates or shallow bowls. Top with the clams, garnish with the scallions, and serve, passing sesame oil for drizzling at the table.

VARIATIONS

Creamy Rice with Chipotle Clams

Substitute 1 (or more) chipotle in adobo for the fermented black beans. No need to soak; just chop it and stir it (with some of the adobo sauce) into the skillet in Step 6. Skip the sesame oil.

NOTES

EVEN FASTER

Cook the rice normally: Cover with 1 inch of water, add the salt, bring to a boil, then adjust the heat so the mixture bubbles steadily but not vigorously. Cook, undisturbed, until small craters appear on the surface of the rice, 10 to 15 minutes.

FERMENTED BLACK BEANS

Fermented black beans, made from black soybeans, are earthy and salty. Even in small quantities, they add huge flavor to stir-fries and require only a quick soak in liquid (something flavorful like rice wine or sherry is traditional) before they're ready to go. You can find them at any Chinese market and even many supermarkets.

SIDES

Tomato Salad with Sesame and Soy 913

Soy Slaw 923

Carrot Salad with Soy Sauce and Scallions 914

Stir-Fried Bok Choy 927

SPEED ◐ SERVES 4

Fast Jook with Chicken and Snow Peas

Jook is a traditional Chinese porridge made by simmering rice for hours until it breaks apart into a mass of silky starch. Since we don't have hours here, I've expedited the process, cooking the rice in stock over high heat until thick and creamy. While that happens you stir-fry some chicken and snow peas to top the rice at the end.

Ingredients

1 ½ cups short-grain white rice

4 cups chicken or vegetable stock or water

Salt

1 pound boneless, skinless chicken thighs

2 tablespoons vegetable oil

2 garlic cloves

1 inch fresh ginger

12 ounces snow peas

Pepper

3 scallions

Soy sauce for serving

Prep | Cook

1. Put 1 ½ cups rice, 4 cups stock or water, and a pinch of salt in a medium saucepan. Bring to a boil.

   Cut the chicken into ½-inch chunks.

2. When the water boils, adjust the heat so the mixture bubbles steadily but not vigorously. Cook, stirring occasionally and adding more liquid if necessary until the rice is very soft and its starch has thickened the liquid to the consistency of porridge, about 15 minutes.

3. Put 2 tablespoons vegetable oil in a large skillet over medium-high heat.

4. When the oil is hot, add the chicken to the skillet and cook, undisturbed, until the pieces brown and release easily, 3 or 4 minutes. Then cook, stirring occasionally until the meat is no longer pink, 2 or 3 more minutes.

   Peel 2 garlic cloves and 1 inch fresh ginger; mince them together.

5. When the chicken is no longer pink, stir in the garlic and ginger and cook until fragrant, about a minute.

6. Stir in the snow peas, sprinkle with salt and pepper, and cook, stirring occasionally until they soften slightly (they should still be mostly crunchy), 3 or 4 minutes. Turn off the heat.
   Trim and chop the scallions.

7. When the rice reaches the consistency of porridge, divide it among 4 bowls. (If you feel the rice is too thick, stir in some water to thin it out.) Top with the chicken and snow peas, garnish with the scallions, and serve, passing soy sauce at the table.

VARIATIONS

Fast Jook with Beef and Bean Sprouts
Use beef stock to cook the rice. Swap beef sirloin, thinly sliced, for the chicken, and 8 ounces bean sprouts for the snow peas. As soon as you stir in the bean sprouts, turn off the heat.

Brown Rice Jook with Chicken and Snow Peas
Substitute short-grain brown rice for white. It will take an extra 20 minutes or so to reach the desired consistency.

NOTES

MAKE YOUR OWN

Chicken Stock 213

Vegetable Stock 212

IF YOU HAVE MORE TIME
For extra-creamy jook, once the liquid boils, adjust the heat so that it bubbles very gently. Cook, stirring occasionally and adding more liquid if necessary until the rice almost completely breaks apart, at least an hour.

SIDES

Soy Slaw 923

Tomato Salad with Sesame and Soy 913

Cucumber Salad with Soy Sauce and Mirin 915

SPEED ◐ SERVES 4

Hoppin' John with Collards

The best American rice and beans dish, boosted by the addition of collards, which are not traditional but are hearty and delicious.

Ingredients

4 ounces bacon (preferably slab)

1 medium onion

3 garlic cloves

2 sprigs fresh thyme

1 small bunch collard greens (8 ounces)

4 cups cooked or canned black-eyed peas (two 15-ounce cans)

Red chile flakes to taste

Salt and pepper

1 ½ cups long-grain white rice

Prep | Cook

1. Put 3 ½ cups water in a large pot; bring to a boil.

   Chop the bacon into pieces; add it to the pot.

   Trim, peel, and chop the onion; peel and mince 3 garlic cloves. Add them to the pot.

   Strip the leaves from 2 sprigs fresh thyme and add to the pot.

   Trim the collards; slice the leaves in half along the stem, then crosswise into thin ribbons; add them to the pot.

   If you're using canned black-eyed peas, rinse and drain them; add the beans to the pot.

2. When the mixture boils, season with red chile flakes, salt, and pepper to taste. Stir in 1 ½ cups rice and adjust the heat so the mixture bubbles steadily but not vigorously. Cover and cook until the rice is tender and the liquid is absorbed, 15 to 20 minutes. Taste and adjust the seasoning and serve.

VARIATIONS

Hoppin' John, Portuguese Style
Substitute linguiça or smoked Spanish chorizo for the bacon, kale for the collard greens, and chickpeas for the black-eyed peas.

Hoppin' John with Green Beans and Ham
Instead of the bacon, use 4 ounces chopped ham. Substitute 1 pound green beans for the collards, sliced into 1-inch pieces. If you want them crisp-tender, wait to add them to the pot until the rice has cooked for 10 minutes. Then put them on top and return the lid. Fluff with a fork just before serving.

NOTES

MAKE YOUR OWN
Cooked Beans 496

EVEN FASTER
Cook the rice in a separate pot. Instead of simmering the bacon, collards, and black-eyed peas, start by rendering some of the bacon fat in the pan, then add the remaining ingredients as you finish prepping them. Cook until the onions are soft and the collards are wilted, then stir the mixture into the cooked rice at the end.

SIDES

Warm Flour Tortillas 907

Coleslaw 923

No-Mayo Slaw 923

Succotash 933

Pilaf

❶ Pick a grain.

If you're using rice, you'll want a long-grain variety; basmati is ideal. Bulgur, quinoa, farro, millet, and cracked wheat all make excellent pilafs too. The cooking time for these alternatives will vary so check them for tenderness occasionally as they cook.

❷ Sauté something flavorful.

Put 2 or more tablespoons butter or oil in a large, deep skillet with a lid over medium-high heat. Add chopped aromatic vegetables, mushrooms, and/or raw ground or chopped meat. Cook until the vegetables have slightly softened and the meat is browned.

❸ Toast the grain.

Add 1 ½ cups rice or other grains and lower the heat to medium. Cook, stirring frequently until the grains are glossy, coated with the butter or oil, and barely beginning to brown, about 5 minutes. At this point, add any spices, chopped nuts, or dried fruit.

④ Add liquid.

Add 2 ½ cups stock or water, bring to a boil, then turn the heat down so it bubbles gently. At any point during cooking you can add other ingredients—chopped vegetables or greens, cooked meat, fish, or shellfish—timed so that they're ready when the grain becomes tender.

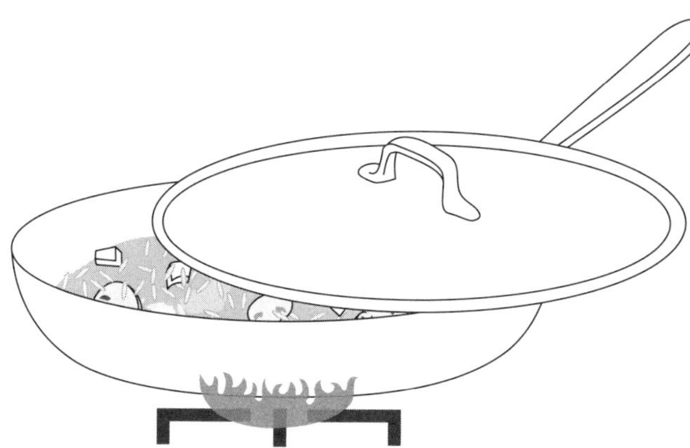

⑤ Let the magic happen.

Cover and cook until the liquid is absorbed, 15 to 30 minutes, depending on the grain, and holes form on top. If the rice sticks before getting tender, add a little more water and adjust the heat. When it's ready turn the heat off; you can let pilaf sit for up to 10 minutes before serving.

⑥ Garnish, fluff, and serve.

Stir in any last-minute additions like chopped fresh herbs, citrus zest, soy sauce, or more butter or oil. Toss gently with a fork to fluff the grains, taste and adjust the seasoning, and serve.

SPEED ◐ SERVES 4

Chipotle Rice and Corn with Seared Beef

Rice simmered with smoky, spicy chipotles in adobo and finished with fresh corn and scallions turns into a southwestern pilaf. The seared chili-rubbed steak served on top would be good on anything but is especially welcome here.

Ingredients

3 tablespoons vegetable oil

2 garlic cloves

1 chipotle chile (or more) in adobo

1 ½ cups long-grain white rice

Salt and pepper

1 ½ pounds skirt or flank steak

1 teaspoon chili powder

2 ears fresh corn

3 scallions

Prep | Cook

1. Put 2 tablespoons vegetable oil in a medium saucepan over medium-high heat.

   Peel and mince 2 garlic cloves.

   Chop 1 (or more) chipotle.

2. Add the garlic and chipotle (with some of its adobo sauce) to the pan. Cook, stirring until the garlic is fragrant, about a minute.

3. Add 1 ½ cups rice, sprinkle with salt and pepper, and cook, stirring occasionally until coated with the chipotle mixture and lightly toasted, 1 to 2 minutes.

4. Add water to cover by about an inch. Bring to a boil, then adjust the heat so the mixture bubbles steadily but not vigorously. Cover and cook, undisturbed, until small craters appear on the surface, 10 to 15 minutes.

5. Put a large skillet over high heat. Pat the steak dry with a paper towel and rub with 1 teaspoon chili powder and a sprinkle of salt and pepper. Cut the steak in half if needed to fit in the skillet. When the skillet is very hot, add 1 tablespoon vegetable oil and swirl it around.

6. Add the steak and cook, turning once, until browned on both sides but still a bit pinker inside than you like it, 3 to 5 minutes per side.
   Husk the corn and cut the kernels off the cob.
   Trim and chop the scallions.

7. When the steak is done, transfer it to a cutting board. Carefully add 1/4 cup water to the skillet and turn off the heat (it will release the drippings and make a little sauce).

8. When small craters appear on the surface of the rice, tip the pot to see if any liquid remains. If so, cover and keep cooking until the rice is dry, checking every minute or 2.

9. Add the corn and scallions to the rice, fluff with a fork, taste, and adjust the seasoning. Divide the rice among 4 plates.

10. Thinly slice the steak against the grain and lay it on top of the rice. Spoon the pan sauce over the top of the steak and serve.

VARIATIONS

Chipotle Rice with Corn and Pinto Beans
Skip the steak and stir in 2 cups cooked pinto or other beans after you've toasted the rice in Step 3. If you prefer the beans to remain intact, stir them in along with the corn.

Tomato Rice with Corn and Seared Shrimp
Substitute 2 tablespoons tomato paste for the chipotle and 1 pound peeled shrimp for the steak. Sauté the shrimp over medium-high heat, stirring occasionally until they turn pink and cook through, 2 or 3 minutes.

Miso Rice with Snow Peas and Seared Chicken
Substitute 2 tablespoons miso paste for the chipotle and stir in 1 teaspoon rice vinegar as the rice cooks. Use 1 pound chicken cutlets instead of steak. Sprinkle with salt and pepper and sear for 2 or 3 minutes per side. Substitute 1 cup sliced snow peas for the corn. Skip the pan sauce after cooking the chicken. Instead, once the dish is plated, just drizzle on a little soy sauce.

SIDES

Avocado with Lime and Chili Salt 920

Warm Flour Tortillas 907

Jícama and Radish Salad 918

SPEED ◐ SERVES 4

Rice Bowl with Sausage

In the Japanese tradition of *chirashi*, bowls of sushi rice have all sorts of ingredient combinations scattered on top. This one is not at all Japanese, although the flavors can go in any direction you like; see the variations.

Ingredients

1 ½ cups short-grain white rice

Salt

2 tablespoons olive oil, plus more for drizzling

1 pound hot or sweet Italian sausage links

2 large fennel bulbs

Pepper

4 ounces Parmesan cheese (1 cup shaved)

Several sprigs fresh basil for garnish

Prep | Cook

1. Put 1 ½ cups rice in a medium saucepan; add a big pinch of salt and water to cover by about an inch. Bring to a boil.
2. Put 2 tablespoons olive oil in a large skillet over medium heat.
   Cut the sausages into slices; add them to the skillet.
   Trim and slice the fennel; add it to the skillet.
3. Sprinkle the sausage and fennel with salt and pepper and cook, stirring occasionally until the sausage is browned and the fennel is golden, 10 to 15 minutes.
4. When the water boils, adjust the heat so the mixture bubbles steadily but not vigorously. Cover and cook, undisturbed, until small craters appear on the surface, 10 to 15 minutes.
   Shave 1 cup Parmesan cheese with a vegetable peeler.
   Strip the basil leaves from several sprigs and chop.
5. When small craters appear on the surface of the rice, tip the pot to see if any liquid remains. If so, cover and keep cooking until the rice is dry, checking every minute or 2.

6. Divide the rice among 4 bowls, and spoon the sausage and fennel over the top. Garnish with the Parmesan and basil, and a drizzle of olive oil if you like, and serve.

VARIATIONS

Rice Bowl with Chorizo and Pineapple
Substitute fresh Mexican chorizo for the Italian sausage and 2 medium red onions for the fennel. When the chorizo and onions are a few minutes shy of being done, stir in 1 cup chopped pineapple. Use queso fresco instead of Parmesan and cilantro instead of basil.

Rice Bowl with Andouille
Use andouille or another spicy sausage instead of Italian sausage and 2 small red bell peppers and 1 cup corn kernels instead of fennel. Skip the cheese and garnish with scallions instead of basil.

SIDES

Tomato Salad 913

Green Salad 911

No-Mayo Slaw 923

Sautéed Greens with Garlic 924

SPEED  SERVES 4

Three-Stir Mushroom Risotto

While risotto does need to be stirred, it does not demand laborious babysitting. Add the stock in three larger additions—as opposed to many smaller ones—and stir the rice three times; the effort is minimal. For even better results, warm your plates in the oven while the risotto cooks. The rice will stay loose and creamy (as it should), as opposed to firming up as you eat.

Ingredients

½ cup dried porcini mushrooms

1 cup hot water

4 tablespoons (½ stick) butter

1 medium onion

1 ½ cups Arborio or other short- or medium-grain white rice

Salt and pepper

½ cup dry white wine or water

3 ½ cups stock or water

8 ounces button, cremini, or shiitake mushrooms

4 ounces Parmesan cheese (1 cup grated)

Prep | Cook

Put ½ cup dried mushrooms in a bowl with 1 cup hot water to cover and leave them to soak.

1. Put 2 tablespoons butter in a large skillet or large pot over medium heat.

   Trim, peel, and chop the onion.

2. When the butter is melted, add the onion and cook, stirring occasionally until it softens, 3 to 5 minutes.

3. Add 1 ½ cups rice and cook, stirring occasionally until it is glossy and coated with butter, 2 to 3 minutes.

4. Sprinkle with salt and pepper and add ½ cup dry white wine or water. Stir and let the liquid bubble until nearly evaporated.

   Remove the mushrooms from the soaking water, chop, and add them to the rice.

5. Add ½ cup stock or water and the mushroom soaking liquid, being careful to leave behind any sediment in the bowl. Let the rice cook, undisturbed, until the liquid is almost completely evaporated, 5 to 8 minutes.

6. Put 2 tablespoons butter in a medium skillet over high heat.

   Trim and chop the fresh mushrooms.

7. Add the fresh mushrooms to the skillet and cook, stirring occasionally until they soften and brown, 8 to 10 minutes. Remove the skillet from the heat.

   Grate 1 cup Parmesan.

8. When the stock is almost completely evaporated, add another 1 ½ cups stock and stir vigorously. Again, let the rice cook undisturbed until the liquid is almost completely evaporated, 5 to 8 minutes. Add the final 1 ½ cups stock and stir vigorously.

9. As the final addition of stock is absorbed, taste the rice; it should be tender but still have a bit of crunch. Continue cooking until the liquid is almost completely evaporated. Add the cooked fresh mushrooms and stir.

10. Add the Parmesan and stir vigorously one more time. Taste and adjust the seasoning and serve immediately.

VARIATIONS

Three-Stir Sausage Risotto
Skip the dried and fresh mushrooms. While the rice is cooking, sauté 8 ounces chopped or crumbled Italian sausage in olive oil until browned and slightly crisp. Stir it into the rice in the final step.

Three-Stir Smoky Shrimp Risotto
Skip the dried and fresh mushrooms. Add 2 teaspoons smoked paprika to the rice as it toasts in Step 3. As the final addition of stock bubbles away, stir in 8 ounces peeled shrimp, chopped. In the time it takes to finish the risotto, the shrimp will cook through.

NOTES

MAKE YOUR OWN
Chicken Stock 213

Vegetable Stock 212

Beef Stock 212

SIDES

Green Salad 911

Tomato Salad 913

Broiled Cherry Tomatoes 931

SPEED ◔ SERVES 4

Curried Lentils and Rice with Fried Onions

Lentils are the fastest legume to cook from scratch, but they still take a little while. So, rather than building flavor in the pot before adding the lentils, start them right away and add flavor as they cook. Here a classic Indian *tarka*—spices toasted in butter—is key.

Ingredients

1 cup dried brown lentils

1 bay leaf

5 cups chicken or vegetable stock or water, plus more if needed

4 tablespoons (½ stick) butter

1 inch fresh ginger

2 tablespoons cumin seeds

1 teaspoon coriander

1 teaspoon turmeric

3 tablespoons olive oil

2 medium onions

1 ½ cups white basmati rice

Salt and pepper

Several sprigs fresh cilantro for garnish

Prep | Cook

1. Put 1 cup brown lentils, a bay leaf, and 5 cups stock or water in a large pot. Bring to a boil.
2. Put 4 tablespoons butter in a large skillet over medium heat.
   Peel and mince 1 inch fresh ginger.
3. When the butter is melted, add the ginger, 2 tablespoons cumin seeds, 1 teaspoon coriander, and 1 teaspoon turmeric. Cook, stirring until the ginger and spices are fragrant, a minute or 2. Add the mixture to the lentils.
4. When the liquid boils, adjust the heat so the mixture bubbles gently but steadily, partially cover, and cook for 20 minutes.
5. Put 3 tablespoons olive oil in the skillet (no need to clean it) over medium-high heat.
   Trim, peel, halve, and slice the onions.
6. Add the onions to the skillet and cook, stirring occasionally and adjusting the heat if they start to burn, until they are deeply browned and slightly crisp, 10 to 15 minutes.

7. After the lentils have simmered for 20 minutes (they shouldn't be tender yet, and there should still be about 3 cups liquid in the pot), stir in 1 ½ cups rice and a sprinkle of salt and pepper. Cover and cook until the lentils and rice are tender, 10 to 15 minutes, adding a splash of stock or water of the pot gets too dry along the way.
   Chop several sprigs cilantro.

8. When the onions are dark brown and slightly crisp, sprinkle them with salt and turn off the heat.

9. When the lentils and rice are tender, remove the bay leaf, stir in the onions, taste and adjust the seasoning, and serve, garnished with the cilantro.

VARIATIONS

Smoky Lentils and Rice with Fried Onions
Use ¼ cup olive oil instead of the butter. Substitute 3 garlic cloves for the ginger, 1 tablespoon smoked paprika for the cumin seeds, and 1 teaspoon ground cumin for the coriander. Skip the turmeric. Garnish with parsley instead of cilantro.

Curried Lentils and Rice with Fried Onions and Tomatoes
Stir in a cup or 2 of chopped fresh tomatoes when you add the cooked onions in Step 9. For extra brightness, squeeze in the juice of a lime.

NOTES

MAKE YOUR OWN

Chicken Stock 213

Vegetable Stock 212

SIDES

Cucumber Raita 916

Tomato Salad with Olive Oil and Yogurt 913

Fennel Salad with Olives 917

SPEED SERVES 4 TO 6

Fast Thai Sticky Rice with Meaty Vegetable Sauce

Thai sticky rice traditionally takes a while, but in this method you boil the rice and then freeze it. The result is a wonderful canvas for a Thai meat and vegetable sauce.

Ingredients

1 ½ cups short-grain white sushi rice or glutinous rice

Salt

1 large carrot

1 celery stalk

1 small onion

2 tablespoons vegetable oil

1 pound ground pork

Pepper

1 fresh hot green chile (like serrano)

2 garlic cloves

1 inch fresh ginger

2 cups coconut milk

2 teaspoons fish sauce

Several sprigs fresh Thai basil or regular basil for garnish

1 lime

Prep | Cook

1. Put 1 ½ cups rice in a medium saucepan; add a big pinch of salt and 5 cups water. Bring to a boil.

   Trim, peel, and chop the carrot.

   Trim and chop the celery.

   Trim, peel, and chop the onion.

2. When the water boils, continue to cook over high heat, stirring frequently and adding more water if the pot gets too dry, until the rice is soft and the starch has released into the water to form a thick, risottolike mixture, 8 to 10 minutes.

   Line a large plate or a rimmed baking sheet with plastic wrap.

3. Put 2 tablespoons vegetable oil in a large skillet over medium-high heat.

4. When the oil is hot, add the ground pork, carrot, celery, onion, and a sprinkle of salt and pepper. Cook, stirring occasionally until the pork is browned and the vegetables are soft, 5 to 10 minutes.

5. When the rice is done, pour it out onto the prepared plate and spread it with the back of a spoon into an even ½-inch-thick layer. Put the plate in the freezer until the rice is firm enough to cut, 10 to 15 minutes.

   Trim the chile. Peel 2 garlic cloves and 1 inch fresh ginger. Mince them all together and stir them into the skillet.

6. When the pork is browned and the vegetables are tender, stir in 2 cups coconut milk and 2 teaspoons fish sauce. Bring to a boil and let the liquid bubble away until it reduces into a thick sauce. Taste and adjust the seasoning and turn off the heat.

   Strip the basil leaves from several sprigs and chop.

   Cut the lime into wedges.

7. When the rice is firm, cut it into 4 or 6 equal pieces. Use the plastic wrap to lift out each piece and divide the pieces among 4 or 6 plates or shallow bowls. Spoon the sauce over the top. Garnish with the basil and lime and serve.

VARIATIONS

Fast Thai Sticky Rice with Pork and Mustard Greens

Substitute 1 bunch mustard greens, chopped, for the carrot and celery.

NOTES

EVEN FASTER

Don't bother freezing the rice. As soon as it's tender, spoon it out onto 4 plates or shallow bowls. It will firm up a bit as it sits there. Then just top with the sauce when it's ready.

SIDES

Green Salad with Sesame-Soy Dressing 911

Ginger-Orange Bean Sprouts 919

Stir-Fried Bok Choy 927

SPEED  SERVES 4

Rice and Smoked Salmon Cakes with Cucumber Salsa

The key to this dish is overcooking the rice so it releases its starch. That, along with an egg and a quick chill in the freezer, lets you form the rice into cakes that will hold together enough to panfry until golden and crisp.

Ingredients

1 ½ cups short-grain white rice

Salt

1 large cucumber

1 small red onion

1 bunch fresh dill

1 lemon

4 tablespoons olive oil, plus more as needed

Pepper

6 ounces smoked salmon

2 eggs

Prep | Cook

1. Put 1 ½ cups rice in a medium saucepan; add a big pinch of salt and 5 cups of water to cover by about 2 inches. Bring to a boil.

2. When the water boils, continue to cook over high heat, stirring frequently and adding more water if the pot gets too dry, until the rice is soft and the starch has released into the water to form a thick, risotto-like mixture, 15 to 20 minutes.

   Peel the cucumber if necessary; cut it in half lengthwise and scoop out the seeds with a spoon. Finely chop and put in a medium bowl.

   Trim, peel, and chop the onion; add it to the bowl.

   Strip ¼ cup dill leaves from the stems and chop; add them to the bowl.

   Halve the lemon; squeeze the juice into the bowl.

3. Add 2 tablespoons olive oil and a sprinkle of salt and pepper to the bowl; stir to combine, taste, and adjust the seasoning.

4. When the rice is done, pour it into a shallow baking dish, spread it in a thin layer, and put it in the freezer for 5 minutes to cool.

   Chop the smoked salmon.

5. Remove the rice from the freezer; crack in the eggs and add the smoked salmon and a sprinkle of pepper. Mix gently.
6. Put 2 tablespoons olive oil in a large skillet over medium-high heat.
7. Form the rice mixture into 12 small patties and add them to the skillet as you go. (Cook in 2 batches, 6 at a time.) Cook, turning once, until they're browned and crisp on both sides, 3 to 5 minutes per side. Add a little more oil as needed and cook the remaining 6 patties. Serve with the salsa.

VARIATIONS

Rice and Smoked Trout Cakes with Cucumber Salad
Substitute smoked trout for smoked salmon.

Rice and Chorizo Cakes with Tomato Salsa
Substitute 4 ounces fresh Mexican chorizo for the smoked salmon (take the meat out of the casings). For the salsa, use 2 medium tomatoes instead of cucumber, cilantro in place of dill, and 2 limes instead of lemon.

NOTES

IF YOU HAVE MORE TIME
Let the rice mixture chill in the refrigerator until firm, about an hour.

RICE CAKES
As you can see in this recipe and the one before it, a quick way to make firm patties out of rice is to use starchy rice (short-grain rice or a glutinous long-grain variety is best), cook it high and fast so that the starch seeps out, then rapidly cool the rice down in the freezer so it becomes firm. While the individual grains of rice will be overcooked, the process of binding the rice with its own starch leaves you with cakes that have a wonderful chew.

SIDES

Tomato Salad 913

Broiled Cherry Tomatoes 931

Creamed Spinach 936

SPEED SERVES 4

Shrimp and Tomato Paella

Paella need not be a huge ordeal; if it were called baked rice and shrimp in a skillet, you'd think it was a piece of cake—which it is.

Ingredients

3 ½ cups shrimp or vegetable stock or water, plus more if needed

Pinch of saffron

3 tablespoons olive oil

1 medium onion

Salt and pepper

1 pound peeled shrimp

3 large ripe tomatoes (1 ½ pounds)

2 cups short- or medium-grain white rice, preferably paella or Arborio rice

Several sprigs fresh parsley for garnish

Prep | Cook

1. Heat the oven to 450°F. Put 3 ½ cups stock or water and a pinch of saffron in a small saucepan over medium heat.
2. Put 3 tablespoons olive oil in a large ovenproof skillet over medium-high heat.

   Trim, peel, and chop the onion.
3. Add the onion to the skillet, sprinkle with salt and pepper, and cook, stirring occasionally until it softens, 3 to 5 minutes.

   Cut the shrimp into ½-inch chunks.

   Core the tomatoes and cut them into wedges.
4. When the onion is soft, stir in 2 cups rice and cook, stirring occasionally, until it's glossy, a minute or 2. Add the warmed stock and stir in the shrimp.
5. Lay the tomato wedges on top of the rice and put the skillet in the oven. Cook, undisturbed, for 15 minutes.
6. After 15 minutes, check to see if the rice is dry and just tender. If not, return the skillet to the oven for another 5 minutes. If the rice looks too dry but still not quite done, add a small splash of stock or water.

7. When the rice is ready, turn off the heat and let the pan sit in the oven for 5 minutes.

   Chop several sprigs parsley.

8. Remove the skillet from the oven, sprinkle with the parsley, and serve hot or warm.

VARIATIONS

Squid and Tomato Paella
Substitute 1 pound cleaned squid for the shrimp. Cut the bodies into thin rings and the tentacles (if there are any) in half vertically into small pieces. Add them to the stock and saffron at the very beginning.

Chorizo and Tomato Paella
Substitute 8 ounces sliced smoked Spanish chorizo for the shrimp. Add the chorizo to the skillet along with the onion in Step 3.

NOTES

MAKE YOUR OWN

Shrimp Stock 261

Vegetable Stock 212

IF YOU HAVE MORE TIME
To develop more of a crust on the bottom of the rice (soccarat, the hallmark of great paella), after removing the skillet from the oven, put it on a burner over high heat and cook, undisturbed, for 2 or 3 minutes. Do not burn.

PAELLA RICE
Arborio or other short- or medium-grain rice will work just fine in paella, but there are rices that are particularly well suited to the job. These are medium-grain varieties that get creamy, like Arborio, but the grains remain more separate. The different types that you might come across, generically called *Spanish paella rice*, are Valencia, Bomba, Bahia, and Granza.

SIDES

Green Salad 911

Chopped Salad 912

Warm Buttery Bread 906

Sautéed Greens with Garlic 924

Crunchy Okra 959

SPEED SERVES 4 TO 6

Jambalaya des Herbes with Shrimp

To accommodate Catholics who were abstaining from meat during Lent, a vegetarian version of gumbo with lots of greens—gumbo z'herbes—was often served in New Orleans. This recipe takes the same approach with another bayou classic, jambalaya.

Ingredients

3 tablespoons olive oil

1 large onion

2 celery stalks

2 green bell peppers

3 garlic cloves

Salt and pepper

1 ½ cups long-grain white rice

2 large ripe tomatoes (1 pound)

1 teaspoon paprika

½ teaspoon cayenne

1 teaspoon dried thyme

3 bay leaves

1 bunch fresh parsley

1 pound peeled shrimp

Hot sauce for serving (optional)

Prep | Cook

1. Put 3 tablespoons olive oil in a large skillet over medium-high heat.

   Trim, peel, and chop the onion; add it to the skillet.

   Trim and chop the celery; add it to the skillet.

   Trim, core, seed, and chop the peppers; add them to the skillet.

   Peel and mince 3 garlic cloves; add them to the skillet.

2. Sprinkle the vegetables with salt and pepper and cook, stirring occasionally until they soften, 5 to 10 minutes.

3. Put 1 ½ cups rice in a large pot; add a big pinch of salt and water to cover by about ½ inch (2 ½ cups water). Bring to a boil.

   Core and chop the tomatoes.

4. When the water boils, adjust the heat so the mixture bubbles steadily but not vigorously; cover.

5. When the vegetables are soft, stir in 1 teaspoon paprika, ½ teaspoon cayenne, and 1 teaspoon dried thyme. Cook, stirring, for a minute.

6. Add the vegetable mixture, tomatoes, and 3 bay leaves to the rice; stir and cover. Cook, checking occasionally until the rice is just tender, 10 to 15 minutes. If the rice begins to get tender and

there is too much liquid in the pot, remove the cover and continue cooking to let some of the liquid evaporate.

Chop 1 cup parsley.

7. When the rice is just tender, fish out the bay leaves, add the shrimp and parsley, and toss with a fork. Cover and cook until the shrimp turn pink and cook through, 2 or 3 minutes.

8. Taste and adjust the seasoning. Serve, passing a bottle of hot sauce at the table if you like.

VARIATIONS

Jambalaya des Herbes with Fish
Substitute 1 pound thin white fish fillets, cut into chunks, for the shrimp. They take just a few minutes longer to cook than the shrimp, so add them just before the rice is tender.

Jambalaya with Lots of Herbes
Use 10 ounces baby spinach instead of the shrimp. Stir the leaves into the pot in Step 7, cover, and cook until the spinach is just wilted, 2 or 3 minutes. The raw spinach will take up a lot of room before it wilts, so consider that when choosing a pot.

Jambalaya with Collards
Substitute 1 pound collard greens, sliced into ribbons, for the shrimp. Stir them into the pot along with the vegetables in Step 6.

NOTES

EVEN FASTER
Bring the rice to a boil at the very beginning. By the time you're ready to add the softened vegetables, the rice will be pretty close to tender, so you'll essentially just be stirring everything into the cooked rice at the end. The rice picks up a little less flavor when it isn't cooked with the vegetables, but this is a fine compromise and certainly a time-saver.

SIDES

Green Salad 911

Warm Flour Tortillas 907

Crunchy Okra 959

Coleslaw 923

SPEED ◕ SERVES 4

Rice and Wings

The one-pot magic of *arroz con pollo* meets the flavors and fixings of the chicken and rice that you get at Middle Eastern street carts in New York City.

Ingredients

3 tablespoons olive oil

2 tablespoons butter

1 ½ pounds chicken wings

Salt and pepper

2 medium ripe tomatoes

1 small head iceberg lettuce (you'll need only half)

2 teaspoons turmeric

1 teaspoon cumin

1 ½ cups long-grain white rice

3 cups chicken stock or water

One 8-inch pita

1 garlic clove

¼ cup mayonnaise

¼ cup Greek yogurt

Prep | Cook

1. Put 2 tablespoons olive oil and 2 tablespoons butter in a large skillet or large pot over medium-high heat.
2. When the fat is hot, add the chicken wings and sprinkle with salt and pepper. Cook, turning as necessary until browned on both sides, 5 to 10 minutes.
   Core and chop the tomatoes; put them in a medium bowl.
   Cut the head of lettuce in half; chop 1 half and add it to the bowl. Refrigerate the other half for another use.
3. When the wings are browned, stir in 2 teaspoons turmeric and 1 teaspoon cumin. Cook, stirring until the spices are fragrant, about a minute. Add 1 ½ cups rice and cook, stirring occasionally until glossy and coated with the spices, 2 or 3 minutes.
4. Add 3 cups chicken stock or water and bring to a boil.
   Chop the pita into 1-inch pieces.
5. When the mixture boils, adjust the heat so the mixture bubbles steadily but not vigorously. Cover and cook until the rice is tender and the liquid is absorbed, 10 to 20 minutes.
6. Put 1 tablespoon olive oil in a medium skillet over medium heat. When it's hot, add the pita and a sprinkle of salt and pepper.

Cook, stirring occasionally until the pita is golden and crisp, 4 or 5 minutes.

Peel and mince the garlic clove; put it in a small bowl.

Add 1/4 cup mayonnaise and 1/4 cup yogurt to the bowl; stir in enough water to make the sauce pourable. Season with salt and pepper.

7. When the pita is golden and crisp, turn off the heat.

8. When the rice is tender and the liquid absorbed, divide the rice and wings among 4 plates. Top with the chopped tomatoes, lettuce, and toasted pita. Drizzle the white sauce over the top and serve.

VARIATIONS

Rice and Thighs
For a meatier dish, substitute boneless, skinless chicken thighs.

Rice and Wings with Mexican Flavors
Substitute chili powder for the turmeric, 2 corn tortillas for the pita, and sour cream for the yogurt. In addition to the tomatoes and lettuce, garnish with chopped cilantro, lime wedges, and hot sauce if you like.

NOTES

MAKE YOUR OWN

Chicken Stock 213

Mayonnaise 144

SIDES

Hummus 939

Tahini-Creamed Spinach 936

Crunchy Okra 959

SPEED ◑ SERVES 4

Quinoa Pilaf with Chickpeas and Dried Fruit

You won't find a pilaf with better textures than this one. Toasted and simmered nuts retain their crunch, dried fruit becomes creamy, chickpeas are meaty yet soft, and quinoa adds its unique pop. With parsley, mint, and lemon zest stirred in at the end, this dish isn't shy in the flavor department either.

Ingredients

2 tablespoons olive oil

1 cup walnuts, almonds, pecans, pistachios, or a combination

2 cups cooked or canned chickpeas (one 15-ounce can)

1 ½ cups quinoa

Salt and pepper

1 cup dried cranberries, cherries, apricots, or raisins

1 bunch fresh parsley

1 bunch fresh mint

1 lemon

Prep | Cook

1. Put 2 tablespoons olive oil in a medium saucepan over medium heat.

   Chop 1 cup nuts.

2. Add the nuts to the skillet and cook, shaking the pan occasionally until lightly browned and fragrant, 2 or 3 minutes.

   If you're using canned beans, rinse and drain them.

3. Stir 1 ½ cups quinoa into the lightly browned nuts and add a sprinkle of salt and pepper. Cook, stirring occasionally until the quinoa is glossy and coated with oil, 2 or 3 minutes.

   Measure 1 cup dried fruit, chopping up larger items like apricots.

4. When the quinoa is glossy, stir in the chickpeas and dried fruit and add 4 cups water. Bring to a boil, then adjust the heat so the liquid bubbles gently. Cover and cook, undisturbed, until small craters appear on the surface, 15 to 20 minutes.

   Chop ½ cup parsley and ¼ cup mint leaves.

5. When small craters appear on the surface of the quinoa, tip the pot to see if any liquid remains. If so, cover and keep cooking until the quinoa is dry, checking every minute or 2.

6. Stir in the parsley and mint and grate in the zest of a lemon. Taste and adjust the seasoning and serve.

VARIATIONS

7 Dried Fruit and Nut Combos for Pilaf

1. Dried apples and walnuts
2. Dried peaches and pecans
3. Dried cherries and pistachios
4. Dried tomatoes and pine nuts
5. Dried cranberries and almonds
6. Dried dates and walnuts
7. Dried currants and cashews

NOTES

MAKE YOUR OWN

Cooked Beans 496

EVEN FASTER

Instead of toasting the nuts at the beginning, just chop them and add them (raw) along with the herbs and lemon zest in Step 6.

STOCK FOR WATER

Any pilaf can benefit from being cooked in stock instead of water, so if you have some on hand, by all means use it in the same quantities as water. Chicken, vegetable, and beef stock are the most useful options, but if the ingredients lend themselves to fish or shrimp stock, you can use those as well.

SIDES

Fennel Salad with Olives 917

Carrots with Curry Vinaigrette 953

Simmered Squash 955

SPEED ◐ SERVES 4

Smoky Bulgur with Eggplant, Dried Tomatoes, and Feta

Finely ground bulgur steeps in a broth of browned eggplant and onions, dried tomatoes, smoked paprika, and cumin, and a spectacular pilaf results. This is also stellar left over, cold or at room temperature.

Ingredients

¼ cup olive oil

1 medium eggplant (about 1 pound)

1 medium red onion

1 cup dried tomatoes

Salt and pepper

2 garlic cloves

1 teaspoon smoked paprika

1 teaspoon cumin

1 cup finely ground bulgur

1 bunch fresh parsley

4 ounces feta cheese (1 cup crumbled)

1 lemon

Prep | Cook

1. Bring 2 cups water to a boil.
2. Put ¼ cup oil in a large skillet over medium-high heat.

   Trim and chop the eggplant into ½-inch pieces; put it in the skillet.

   Trim, peel, and chop the onion; add it to the skillet.

   Chop 1 cup dried tomatoes; add them to the skillet.
3. Sprinkle with salt and pepper and cook, stirring occasionally until the vegetables are browned and soft, 10 to 12 minutes.
4. When the water comes to a boil, turn the heat to low.

   Peel and mince 2 garlic cloves.
5. When the vegetables are browned and soft, stir in the garlic, 1 teaspoon smoked paprika, and 1 teaspoon cumin. Cook, stirring until fragrant, a minute.

6. Stir 1 cup bulgur and the boiled water into the skillet; cover and turn off the heat. Let steep until the bulgur is tender, 10 to 15 minutes.

   Chop ½ cup parsley.

   Crumble 1 cup feta cheese.

   Halve the lemon.

7. When the bulgur is tender, add the parsley, feta, and squeeze in the lemon juice; fluff with a fork. Taste and adjust the seasoning and serve.

VARIATIONS

Smoky Bulgur with Eggplant, Dates, and Feta
Substitute 1 cup chopped dates for the dried tomatoes.

Lemony Bulgur with Zucchini, Olives, and Ricotta Salata
Gets nice and creamy as the zucchini breaks down. Substitute 1 pound zucchini for the eggplant and ½ cup chopped olives for the dried tomatoes. Substitute the zest and juice of a lemon for the smoked paprika and cumin and ricotta salata for the feta.

Smoky Bulgur with Eggplant, Roasted Red Peppers, and Manchego
Substitute 1 cup chopped roasted red peppers (page 417) for the dried tomatoes. Use 2 teaspoons smoked paprika and no cumin and substitute grated manchego cheese for the feta.

NOTES

EVEN FASTER
As soon as the water boils, stir in the bulgur, turn off the heat, cover, and cook it by itself. Continue sautéing the vegetables until they are very tender and well browned, then stir the cooked bulgur into the vegetables at the end.

SIDES

Crisp Seasoned Pita 908

Cucumber Salad 915

Sautéed Greens with Garlic 924

Garlicky Fresh and Dried Mushrooms 956

SPEED ◐ SERVES 4

Quinoa Puttanesca with Fresh Mozzarella

Noodle casseroles—think mac and cheese—are beloved, while grain casseroles (can you even name any?) not so much. There's no reason this should be the case.

Ingredients

Salt

2 tablespoons olive oil

2 garlic cloves

3 or 4 anchovy fillets

½ cup black olives

2 tablespoons capers

½ teaspoon red chile flakes

One 28-ounce can diced tomatoes

Pepper

1 ½ cups quinoa

4 ounces Parmesan cheese (1 cup grated)

8 ounces fresh mozzarella cheese

Several sprigs fresh basil for garnish

Prep | Cook

1. Bring a medium saucepan of water to a boil and salt it.
2. Put 2 tablespoons oil in a large ovenproof skillet over medium heat.

   Peel 2 garlic cloves; mince them together with 3 or 4 anchovies.

   Pit ½ cup olives if necessary and chop them up a bit.
3. Add the garlic, anchovies, and olives to the skillet along with 2 tablespoons capers and ½ teaspoon red chile flakes. Turn the heat to medium-high and cook, stirring, for a minute.
4. Add the tomatoes with their juice and a sprinkle of salt and pepper. Cook, stirring occasionally until the tomatoes break down and thicken the sauce, 10 to 15 minutes.
5. When the water boils, add 1 ½ cups quinoa, adjust the heat so it bubbles steadily, and stir occasionally. Start tasting after 7 minutes.

   Turn the broiler to high; put the rack 4 inches from the heat.

   Grate 1 cup Parmesan.

   Thinly slice 8 ounces fresh mozzarella.

   Strip the basil leaves from several sprigs and chop.

6. When the quinoa is tender, drain it, reserving some cooking water. Add the quinoa to the skillet along with the Parmesan and a splash of the cooking water if you want to make it saucier. Taste and adjust the seasoning.

7. Lay the sliced mozzarella on top and broil until the cheese is bubbly and brown, 2 or 3 minutes. Let the dish cool for a few minutes, then garnish with the basil and serve.

VARIATIONS

Quinoa Puttanesca with Ricotta

Instead of the mozzarella, use 2 cups ricotta. You can season it with ⅛ teaspoon nutmeg if you'd like. In Step 7, drop tablespoons of the cheese on top of the quinoa, spread it around a little with the back of the spoon, and broil as directed.

NOTES

EVEN FASTER

Use crushed tomatoes instead of diced; the sauce will be ready 5 to 10 minutes after you add the tomatoes.

Instead of making the tomato sauce in Steps 2 to 4, use Puttanesca Sauce, page 299.

SIDES

Green Salad 911

Sautéed Greens with Garlic 924

Seared Broccoli or Cauliflower 925

SPEED ◐ SERVES 4

Couscous Gratin with Leeks and Gruyère

Adding cooked couscous to the classic leeks au gratin is a fast and easy way to turn a side dish into a hearty meal. Treat this as the model for grain-bolstered vegetable gratins—see the variations for a few other ideas.

Ingredients

2 cups couscous

Salt

4 medium leeks

3 tablespoons butter

Pepper

8 ounces Gruyère cheese (2 cups grated)

Prep | Cook

1. Put 2 cups couscous in a medium saucepan; add 3 cups water and a big pinch of salt. Bring to a boil.

   Trim the leeks and slice the white and light green parts only.

2. As soon as the water boils, cover and remove from the heat.

3. Put 3 tablespoons butter in a large ovenproof skillet over medium heat. When it foams, add the leeks, sprinkle with salt and pepper, and cook, stirring occasionally until they're soft, 6 to 8 minutes. Do not brown.

   Turn the broiler to high; put the rack 4 inches from the heat.

   Grate 2 cups Gruyère.

4. When the leeks are soft, turn off the heat and spread them evenly in the bottom of the skillet.

5. Fluff the couscous with a fork and layer it on top of the leeks. Sprinkle the cheese on top and broil until bubbly and brown, 2 or 3 minutes. Let the dish cool for a minute before serving.

VARIATIONS

Quinoa Gratin with Leeks and Gruyère

Use cooked quinoa (or any other cooked grain) in place of couscous. Add it in Step 5.

Couscous Gratin with Onions and Broccoli and Cheddar

Substitute 1 large head broccoli, chopped, for the leeks. In Step 3, cook until the broccoli is just tender, 5 to 10 minutes, and proceed as directed. Use cheddar cheese instead of Gruyère if you like.

Couscous Gratin with Mushrooms and Parmesan

Substitute 1 ½ pounds chopped button, cremini, or shiitake mushrooms for the leeks. In Step 3, cook until the mushrooms are tender and starting to dry out, 10 to 15 minutes, and proceed as directed, using Parmesan cheese instead of Gruyère.

Couscous Gratin with Poblanos and Jack

Nice and spicy. Use olive oil instead of butter. Substitute 1 ½ pounds sliced poblano peppers for the leeks. Cook over medium-high heat until the peppers are tender and lightly browned, 5 to 10 minutes, and proceed as directed. Use Jack cheese instead of Gruyère if you like.

SIDES

Green Salad 911

Refried White Beans with Rosemary 938

Bruschetta 909

SPEED ◑ SERVES 4

Masa and Rajas

Tamale flavors without fuss: Make a masa dough and cook it as one big cake in a covered skillet; this way it gets golden and crisp on the bottom but remains puffy and tender on top. Finish with a stir-fry of poblanos (*rajas* means "slices" and refers to the small pieces of poblano), onions, and a touch of cream.

Ingredients

1 ½ cups masa harina

¾ teaspoon baking powder

Salt and pepper

5 tablespoons vegetable oil

1 large onion

4 poblano peppers

2 garlic cloves

¼ cup cream

Prep | Cook

1. Combine 1 ½ cups masa harina, ¾ teaspoon baking powder, a sprinkle of salt and pepper, and 1 tablespoon vegetable oil in a medium bowl. Stir to combine into a coarse meal, then add 1 ½ cups warm water and stir to make a thick batter.
   Trim, peel, and chop the onion.
   Trim, core, seed, and slice the poblanos.

2. Put 2 tablespoons vegetable oil in a large skillet over medium-high heat.
   Peel and mince 2 garlic cloves.

3. When the oil is hot, add the onion, peppers, and garlic and sprinkle with salt and pepper. Cook, stirring occasionally until the vegetables are soft, 8 to 12 minutes.

4. Put 2 tablespoons vegetable oil in another large skillet over medium-high heat. When it's hot, add the masa batter, spreading it into an even layer (about ½ inch thick) with a rubber spatula or carefully pressing it with the palm of your hand.

5. Cover the skillet and cook, adjusting the heat so the bottom doesn't burn, until the cake is crisp on the bottom and slightly puffed up and firm on the top, 5 to 10 minutes.

6. When the cake is done, cut it into 4 wedges and put them on plates.

7. When the vegetables are soft, stir in ¼ cup cream and cook until it reduces slightly, a minute or 2. Taste and adjust the seasoning, spoon the mixture over the top of the masa cakes, and serve.

VARIATIONS

Masa and Rajas with Chicken
Before adding the vegetables, slice 3 boneless, skinless chicken thighs and cook them in the skillet, undisturbed, until they brown and release easily, 2 or 3 minutes. Then cook, stirring occasionally until the meat is no longer pink, 2 or 3 more minutes. Remove the chicken from the skillet while you cook the vegetables, than stir it back in along with the cream in Step 7.

Masa and Rajas with Chorizo
Before adding the vegetables, cook 8 ounces fresh Mexican-style chorizo until lightly browned. Add the vegetables to the skillet and proceed as directed.

SIDES

Carrot Salad with Cilantro and Lime 914

Fresh Tomato Salsa 145

Chile-Cumin Black Beans 937

SPEED ◐ SERVES 4

Farro with White Beans and Tuna

Farro, an ancient grain that's become popular again, has a distinctively nutty flavor and chewy texture. It's a fabulous base for salads, tossed with olive oil, lemon, and whatever else you've got—here it's tuna and white beans. You can cook farro as you would most other grains, but it's faster to boil it like pasta.

Ingredients

Salt

¼ cup olive oil

1 lemon

1 small red onion

4 cups any cooked or canned white beans (two 15-ounce cans)

One 6-ounce jar or can tuna, packed in olive oil

¼ cup capers

1 ½ cups farro

1 bunch fresh parsley

Pepper

Prep | Cook

1. Bring a medium pot of water to a boil and salt it.

   Put ¼ cup olive oil in a large bowl.

   Halve the lemon; squeeze the juice into the bowl.

   Trim, peel, halve, and slice the onion; add it to the bowl.

   If you're using canned beans, rinse and drain them. Add the beans to the bowl.

2. Add the tuna (with its oil) to the bowl along with ¼ cup capers (with or without any brine).

3. When the water boils, add the farro and stir occasionally. Start tasting after 10 minutes.

   Chop ½ cup parsley and add it to the bowl.

4. When the farro is tender, drain it. Add it to the bowl, sprinkle with salt and pepper, and toss. Taste and adjust the seasoning and serve.

VARIATIONS

Farro with White Beans, Tomatoes, and Fennel
Skip the tuna. Substitute 1 large fennel bulb for the red onion and add 2 medium ripe tomatoes, chopped.

Farro and White Beans, Greek Style
Skip the tuna. Add 2 medium ripe tomatoes, chopped; 1 cucumber, chopped; ½ cup kalamata olives; and 1 cup crumbled or chopped feta cheese.

Farro with White Beans, Arugula, and Parmesan
Instead of the tuna use 3 ounces grated Parmesan cheese (¾ cup). Skip the capers and substitute 1 large bunch arugula for the parsley.

NOTES

MAKE YOUR OWN

Cooked Beans 496

SUSTAINABLE CANNED TUNA
When we think about "sustainable seafood," we usually focus on the seafood counter. But sustainability applies as much to canned fish as to fresh. The tuna industry has relied notoriously on unsustainable methods to keep the price of canned tuna low. For instance, the most common devices used to catch skipjack (aka "chunk light") tuna (like Fish Aggregating Devices, or FADs) result in huge amounts of "bycatch," the capturing of species that aren't intended to be caught. In the case of albacore (aka "solid white") tuna, fishing vessels generally rely on conventional longline operations that kill thousands of sharks, turtles, seabirds, and other animals.

If you do a little poking around in the grocery store you might come across canned tuna that is caught in a more responsible way. When buying "light" tuna, look for what's called "pole-and-line skipjack" or "FAD-free seined skipjack." When buying "white" tuna, look for "pole-and-line albacore," or any indicator of a company that is using better and more progressive longline practices (like, as of this writing, Safeway's "Responsibly Caught" albacore). It's also important to note that the "Dolphin Safe" logo is not an indication of these practices and does not guarantee that the tuna in question has been captured in a sustainable manner.

SIDES

Green Salad 911

Chopped Salad 912

Tomato Salad 913

SPEED ◐ SERVES 4

Warm Tabbouleh with Mussels

Like no tabbouleh you've had before. Instead of steeping in plain water, the bulgur soaks in briny mussel-cooking liquid. The result is a meal studded with gems of mussel meat and infused with the flavor of the sea.

Ingredients

2 pounds mussels

3 large ripe tomatoes (1 ½ pounds)

4 scallions

1 bunch fresh parsley

1 bunch fresh mint

1 cup finely ground bulgur

1 lemon

⅓ cup olive oil

Salt and pepper

Prep | Cook

1. Bring 2 ½ cups water to a boil in a large pot with a lid.

   Rinse and debeard the mussels; discard any that don't close when you press the shell together.

2. When the water boils, add the mussels and cover the pot. Cook, undisturbed, until the shells open, 5 to 10 minutes.

   Core and chop the tomatoes; put them in a large serving bowl.

   Trim and chop the scallions; add them to the bowl.

   Chop about ¾ cup parsley and ¼ cup mint leaves; add them to the bowl.

3. Remove the mussels from the pot with a slotted spoon, leaving the liquid behind. If the mussels have released a lot of sediment, strain the liquid through a cheesecloth-lined strainer and return the clear liquid to the pot.

4. Stir 1 cup bulgur into the pot, cover, and turn off the heat. It will take 10 to 15 minutes to become tender.

   Remove the mussel meat from the shells and add it to the bowl.

   Halve the lemon; squeeze the juice into the bowl.

5. Add ⅓ cup olive oil and a sprinkle of salt and pepper to the bowl; toss until combined.

6. When the bulgur is tender, drain it in a strainer, pressing out any excess liquid with a spoon, and add it to the bowl.

7. Toss the contents of the bowl, taste and adjust the seasoning, and serve.

VARIATIONS

Warm Tabbouleh with Tuna
Skip the mussels and just steep the bulgur in 2 ½ cups boiling water. Add one 6-ounce can oil-packed tuna to the bowl along with the tomatoes.

Warm Tabbouleh with Clams
Substitute about 4 pounds littleneck or other hard-shell clams for the mussels. They generally take a few more minutes to steam open than mussels.

NOTES

EVEN FASTER
Put the herbs in the food processor and pulse until finely chopped. Then add the tomatoes and scallions and pulse until coarsely chopped.

SAVING SHELLFISH LIQUID
Most of the time that you steam mussels and clams you'll serve the steaming liquid right along with them, but if there are ever occasions when you don't have any plans for the liquid, make sure to save it. The seawater remaining in mussels and clams releases into the pot as you cook the mollusks. When mixed with plain water, white wine, or aromatics, the briny water creates an irresistible broth that can be used for cooking grains, as it is here, or bolstering all sort of dishes that already contain seafood, from soups and braises to pastas and stir-fries. Any extra shellfish liquid that you might have will keep in the fridge for a few days—just long enough to figure out what to do with it.

SIDES

Crisp Seasoned Pita 908

Sautéed Greens with Garlic 924

Seared Broccoli or Cauliflower 925

SPEED ◐ SERVES 4

Shrimp over Grits

This sublime southern classic is easy to make: Simmer a pot of grits while a pan of smoked sausage or ham, vegetables, and shrimp sizzles alongside. The vegetables need to cook long enough get soft and luscious, but other than that it all goes quickly.

Ingredients

1 ¼ cups milk

Salt

2 tablespoons butter

4 ounces andouille sausage or tasso ham

1 cup grits, preferably stone-ground

1 medium onion

2 celery stalks, with any leaves

1 green bell pepper

2 garlic cloves

Pepper

2 large ripe tomatoes (1 pound)

1 pound peeled shrimp

Prep | Cook

1. Put 1 ¼ cups milk, 1 ¼ cups water, and a pinch of salt in a small saucepan over medium-high heat.

2. Put 2 tablespoons butter in a medium skillet over medium heat.

   Chop 4 ounces andouille or tasso; put it in the skillet.

3. When the liquid comes to a boil, turn the heat to low and slowly whisk in 1 cup grits, trying to eliminate any lumps.

4. Cover and cook, stirring occasionally and adding more liquid if the grits become too thick, until the liquid is absorbed and the grits are creamy, 10 to 15 minutes. Stir the meat as necessary.

   Trim, peel, and chop the onion; add it to the skillet.

   Trim and chop the celery (saving any leaves for garnish). Add it to the skillet.

   Trim, core, seed, and chop the pepper; add it to the skillet.

   Peel and mince 2 garlic cloves; add them to the skillet.

5. Sprinkle the meat and vegetables with salt and pepper and cook, stirring occasionally until they soften, 5 to 10 minutes.

   Core and chop the tomatoes.

6. When the vegetables are soft, stir in the tomatoes and cook, stirring once or twice until they begin to release their juice, 3 or 4 minutes.

7. Stir in the shrimp, sprinkle with salt and pepper, and cook, stirring occasionally until they turn pink and cook through, 2 or 3 minutes.

8. Divide the grits among 4 bowls. Spoon the shrimp mixture over the top, garnish with the celery leaves, and serve.

VARIATIONS

Creamy Shrimp over Grits
Stir 1/4 cup cream into the vegetable mixture right before adding the shrimp.

Shrimp over Polenta
A couple switches and the dish veers toward Italy. Use sweet or hot Italian sausage or prosciutto instead of the andouille and medium-grind cornmeal instead of the grits.

NOTES

IF YOU HAVE MORE TIME

Shrimp over Shrimpy Grits
Buy shrimp with the shells on and take them off yourself. Add the shrimp shells to the milk and water mixture as you bring it to a boil, then use a slotted spoon to fish them out before stirring in the grits. What you're basically doing is making a shrimp stock that will flavor the grits as they cook.

SIDES

Green Salad 911

Chopped Salad 912

Mexican Street Corn 932

SPEED ◐ SERVES 4

Couscous Helper

Hamburger Helper (with real ingredients) goes to Morocco, in a road trip to remember.

Ingredients

4 tablespoons olive oil

1 large red onion

12 ounces ground beef

Salt and pepper

3 garlic cloves

2 oranges

2 teaspoons cumin

½ teaspoon cinnamon

1 cup couscous

Several sprigs fresh parsley for garnish

Prep | Cook

1. Put 2 tablespoons olive oil in a large skillet over medium-high heat.

   Trim, peel, and chop the onion.

2. When the oil is hot, add the beef and the onion, sprinkle with salt and pepper, and cook, stirring occasionally until the beef is browned and the onions are golden, 5 to 10 minutes.

   Peel and mince 3 garlic cloves.

   Half the oranges and squeeze them to get ½ cup juice; refrigerate any remaining fruit.

3. When the beef is browned and the onions are golden, stir in the garlic, 2 teaspoons cumin, ½ teaspoon cinnamon, and 1 cup couscous.

4. Cook, stirring until the spices are fragrant and the couscous is lightly toasted, a minute or 2.

5. Add the orange juice and 1 cup water, bring to a boil, then cover and turn off the heat. Let it steep until the couscous is tender and the liquid is absorbed, about 5 minutes.

   Strip the parsley leaves from several sprigs and chop.

6. When the couscous is ready, add the parsley and 2 tablespoons olive oil and fluff with a fork. Taste and adjust the seasoning and serve immediately.

VARIATIONS

Couscous Helper, Chinese Style
Substitute vegetable oil for the olive oil, ground pork for the beef, and yellow onion for red. Instead of the cumin and cinnamon, use 2 teaspoons five-spice powder. For the liquid, use 1 ½ cups chicken stock or water with a dash of soy sauce mixed in. Garnish with scallions and some sesame oil instead of the parsley and olive oil.

Couscous Helper, Italian Style
Substitute ground chicken or turkey for the beef, 1 tablespoon fennel seeds for the cumin, and ½ teaspoon red chile flakes for the cinnamon. For the liquid, use 1 ¼ cups chicken stock or water and ¼ cup white wine. Garnish with basil instead of parsley and a little grated Parmesan if you like.

Vegetarian Couscous Helper
Instead of the beef use 3 cups drained cooked or canned chickpeas (if canned rinse them first). In Step 2, wait to add the chickpeas until the onions are almost ready. Then stir them into the pan with a fork or potato masher, breaking them up as they warm before proceeding.

SIDES

Crisp Seasoned Pita 908

Hummus 939

Tahini Creamed Spinach 936

Watermelon, Feta, and Mint Salad 922

SPEED ◐ SERVES 4

Polenta with Sausage and Mushrooms

There's not much that's cozier than a dish of creamy Parmesan polenta topped with a meaty sauté of Italian sausage and mushrooms. All you need is a glass of wine and a cool day.

Ingredients

½ cup milk, plus more if needed

Salt

4 tablespoons olive oil, plus more if needed

1 pound sweet or hot Italian sausage

1 cup cornmeal

1 medium red onion

1 ½ pounds button, cremini, or shiitake mushrooms

Pepper

Several sprigs fresh parsley for garnish

4 ounces Parmesan cheese (1 cup grated)

Prep | Cook

1. Put ½ cup milk, 2 cups water, and a big pinch of salt in a medium saucepan and bring to a boil.

2. Put 2 tablespoons olive oil in a large skillet over medium-high heat.

   Chop the sausage or remove the meat from the casings and break it up.

3. Add the sausage to the skillet and cook, stirring occasionally until it starts to brown, 3 or 4 minutes.

4. When the liquid comes to a boil, add 1 cup cornmeal in a steady stream, whisking constantly to prevent lumps. Adjust the heat so that it simmers and cook, whisking frequently until the mixture is creamy and the grains are soft, 10 to 15 minutes. If the mixture becomes too thick, whisk in more water or milk.

   Peel, trim, and chop the onion; add it to the skillet.

   Trim and slice the mushrooms. (If you're using shiitakes, discard the stems.) Add them to the skillet as you work.

5. Sprinkle the mushrooms with salt and pepper and cook, stirring occasionally and adding more olive oil if the skillet gets too dry, until the sausage is nicely browned and the mushrooms are tender, 8 to 12 minutes.

   Strip the parsley leaves from several sprigs and chop.

   Grate 1 cup Parmesan cheese.

6. When the polenta is done, stir in the Parmesan, 2 tablespoons olive oil, and lots of pepper. Taste and adjust the seasoning and divide among 4 bowls.

7. Top with the sausage and mushroom mixture, garnish with the parsley, and serve.

VARIATIONS

Polenta with Chicken and Asparagus

Substitute boneless, skinless chicken thighs, cut into ½-inch chunks, for the sausage, and 1 pound asparagus, cut into 1-inch pieces, for the mushrooms. Cook the chicken until it loses its pink color, then add the asparagus and continue cooking until the asparagus is just tender and the chicken is cooked through, 5 or 6 minutes. Garnish with tarragon instead of parsley.

Polenta with Sausage and Fennel

Substitute 2 medium fennel bulbs, thinly sliced, for the mushrooms.

SIDES

Green Salad 911

Caprese Salad 922

Tomato Salad 913

Bruschetta 909

SPEED ◐ SERVES 4

Pozole and Pork Chops

Pozole—also known as *hominy*—is corn that has been processed with lime (or lye; in any case, calcium hydroxide) to remove the outer germ and bran. It is an intoxicatingly corny ingredient, but in its dried form it can take up to 4 hours to cook. Luckily, it also comes canned and ready to go, which makes this Mexican-inspired dish a weeknight treat.

Ingredients

2 tablespoons olive oil

4 bone-in pork chops (about 2 pounds)

Salt and pepper

1 medium red onion

3 garlic cloves

1 small head green cabbage (1 pound)

1 tablespoon chili powder

One 15-ounce can hominy (2 cups)

1 cup chicken or vegetable stock or water

4 radishes

Several sprigs fresh cilantro for garnish

Sour cream for garnish

Prep | Cook

1. Put 2 tablespoons olive oil in a large skillet or large pot over medium-high heat.
2. When the oil is hot, add the pork chops and sprinkle with salt and pepper. Cook, turning once, until browned on both sides, 3 to 5 minutes per side.

   Trim, peel, and chop the onion.

   Peel and mince 3 garlic cloves.
3. When the pork chops are browned on both sides, remove them from the skillet and add the onion and garlic. Cook, stirring occasionally until the onion starts to soften, 2 or 3 minutes.

   Trim, core, and quarter the cabbage. Cut each quarter crosswise into wide ribbons.
4. When the onion starts to soften, stir in 1 tablespoon chili powder and cook, stirring once or twice, until fragrant, a minute or 2.

   Drain and rinse the hominy.
5. When the chili powder is fragrant, add the cabbage and hominy to the pot, along with a sprinkle of salt and pepper and 1 cup stock or water.

6. Nestle the pork chops back into the skillet and adjust the heat so the mixture bubbles steadily but not vigorously. Cover and cook until the cabbage and pork chops are tender, 5 to 10 minutes.

   Trim and thinly slice 4 radishes.

   Chop several sprigs cilantro.

7. When the cabbage and pork chops are tender, divide the mixture among 4 plates or shallow bowls, spooning a little extra liquid over the top.

8. Garnish with the radishes, cilantro, and a dollop of sour cream and serve immediately.

VARIATIONS

Pozole and Chicken Thighs
Substitute 4 to 6 bone-in chicken thighs for the pork chops. Brown them on both sides just as you would the pork and proceed as directed.

NOTES

MAKE YOUR OWN
Chili Powder 758

Chicken Stock 213

Vegetable Stock 212

SIDES

Avocado with Lime and Chili Salt 920

Corn Bread Skillet Stuffing 952

White Rice 941

SPEED ◐ SERVES 4

Couscous Paella with Chicken and Zucchini

The technique of letting couscous cook and crisp slightly in a hot oven—accompanied by bone-in chicken and vegetables—is derived from paella. Call it whatever; it's quite tasty.

Ingredients

2 tablespoons olive oil

4 chicken thighs

Salt and pepper

2 medium zucchini

3 garlic cloves

1 ½ cups chicken stock or water

1 cup couscous

Prep | Cook

1. Heat the oven to 450°F. Put 2 tablespoons olive oil in a large ovenproof skillet over medium-high heat.

   Pat the chicken dry with a paper towel.

2. Put the chicken in the skillet, skin side down, sprinkle with salt and pepper, and cook, undisturbed, until browned, 4 or 5 minutes.

   Trim the zucchini; cut them into ¼-inch coins.

   Peel and mince 3 garlic cloves.

3. When the skin side of the chicken is browned, turn it over and add the zucchini, garlic, and 1 ½ cups chicken stock or water.

4. Adjust the heat so the mixture bubbles steadily but not vigorously. Cover and cook until the chicken cooks through and the zucchini is tender, 6 to 8 minutes.

5. Remove the chicken thighs and bring the mixture to a boil. Stir in 1 cup couscous and a sprinkle of salt and pepper, nestle the chicken back in, and put the skillet (uncovered) in the oven.

6. Cook until the couscous is tender, the liquid has evaporated, and the top of the couscous and chicken is starting to crisp, 10 to 12 minutes. Serve hot or warm.

VARIATIONS

Couscous Paella with Chicken and Fennel
Substitute 2 large fennel bulbs, sliced, for the zucchini. They won't quite break apart like the zucchini, but they will get tender and add a ton of flavor.

Warm-Spiced Couscous Paella with Chicken and Zucchini
Add 1 cinnamon stick, 4 allspice berries, 1 teaspoon ground cumin, and 1 teaspoon ground coriander right before adding the zucchini and stock in Step 3.

NOTES

MAKE YOUR OWN
Chicken Stock 213

EVEN FASTER
Use boneless, skinless chicken thighs and cut the zucchini into thinner coins. Once the chicken is browned and you add the zucchini and stock, you'll need only a few minutes for the chicken to cook through and the zucchini to become tender.

SIDES

Green Salad 911

Crisp Seasoned Pita 908

Warm Buttery Bread 906

SPEED SERVES 4

Skillet Shepherd's Pie with Quinoa Crust

In this twist on shepherd's pie, nutty, crisped quinoa replaces the mashed potatoes. You still get that beautiful browning on top, but the quinoa brings more texture to the party.

Ingredients

1 ½ cups quinoa

Salt and pepper

4 tablespoons olive oil

2 carrots

1 medium onion

2 garlic cloves

1 pound ground lamb

1 tablespoon tomato paste

2 teaspoons fennel seeds

1 cup beef or chicken stock or water

1 cup frozen peas

Several sprigs fresh parsley for garnish

Prep | Cook

1. Put 1 ½ cups quinoa in a medium saucepan; add a big pinch of salt, a sprinkle of pepper, and water to cover by about an inch. Bring to a boil.
2. Put 2 tablespoons olive oil in a large ovenproof skillet over low heat.
   Trim, peel, and chop the carrots. Add them to the skillet.
   Trim, peel, and chop the onion. Add it to the skillet.
   Peel and mince 2 garlic cloves. Add them to the skillet.
3. When the water boils, adjust the heat so it bubbles gently. Cover and cook, undisturbed, until small craters appear on the quinoa's surface, 15 to 20 minutes.
4. Add the lamb to the skillet, sprinkle with salt and pepper, and raise the heat to medium-high. Cook, stirring to break up the meat until the lamb is browned and the onions are golden, 5 to 10 minutes.
5. When the lamb is browned and the onions are golden, stir in 1 tablespoon tomato paste and 2 teaspoon fennel seeds; cook for a minute.

6. Add 1 cup stock or water, 1 cup frozen peas, and some salt and pepper. Bring to a boil and let the liquid bubble until it reduces to a thin gravy. Turn off the heat. Taste and adjust the seasoning.

7. Turn the broiler to high; put the rack 4 inches from the heat.

8. When small craters appear on the surface of the quinoa, tip the pot to see if any liquid remains. If so, cover and keep cooking until the quinoa is dry, checking every minute or 2.

   Strip the parsley leaves from several sprigs and chop.

9. Stir 2 tablespoons olive oil into the quinoa. Spread the quinoa on top of the lamb mixture, pressing it down into a flat layer, and put the skillet in the broiler. Cook until the crust is browned, 2 or 3 minutes. Remove from the broiler and let it sit for a few minutes before serving, garnished with the parsley.

VARIATIONS

Bolognese-Style Skillet Shepherd's Pie with Quinoa Crust
Substitute 8 ounces ground beef and 8 ounces ground pork for the lamb. Up the tomato paste to 2 tablespoons, use 1/4 cup cream instead of the fennel seeds, and replace 1/2 cup of the stock or water with white wine. Skip the peas if you like.

NOTES

MAKE YOUR OWN

Beef Stock 212

Chicken Stock 213

CRISP GRAINS
We don't usually think of broiling grains, but they're particularly well suited to being crisped under high heat; think of them as an alternative to bread crumbs. You can sprinkle them on top of dishes and run them under the broiler for a little added crunch, or you can create an even layer for a uniform crust. Any cooked grain can achieve this effect. It helps to toss them in olive oil first or drizzle some on top; the fat facilitates the browning.

SIDES

Tender Vegetables 954

Green Salad 911

Vegetables

Bubbling Caprese 414

Sweet Pepper Queso Fundido 418

Eggplant Steaks with Fresh Tomato–Garlic Sauce 420

Glazed Brussels Sprouts with Vietnamese Flavors 422

Unstuffed Cabbage 424

Potato Rösti with Fresh Apple Sauce 426

Squash au Gratin with Toasted Nuts 430

Cauliflower "Polenta" with Mushrooms 432

Stuffed Poblanos with Black Beans and Cheese 434

Sweet Potato Flautas 436

Potato and Spinach Saag 438

Zucchini Fattoush 440

Scrambled Broccoli with Parmesan and Lemon 442

Bok Choy Pancake with Soy Dipping Sauce 444

Fried Fennel and Arugula 446

Celery Root Tempura with or Without Shrimp 448

Quick-Stewed Green Beans with Bacon 450

Braised Cabbage, Sauerkraut, and Ham 452

Pan-Seared Corn and Pork 454

Roasted Spaghetti Squash with Brown Butter and Walnuts 458

Spanish Tortilla 460

Vegetable Flatbread with Kale and White Bean Stew 462

Cherry Tomato Cobbler 464

Tortilla Lasagna 466

Skillet Spanakopita 468

Cauliflower Tikka with Boiled Eggs 470

Vegetables

Cooking vegetables is among the most important skills you'll ever learn, up there with driving a car. If we all had to pass a vegetable cooking test when we were sixteen, our general health would be much improved. Since vegetables should be the largest component of our diet, we should be just as good at cooking them—and using them creatively—as we are at cooking ingredients like meat or pasta.

Many cookbooks feature vegetable recipes only as side dishes (you'll find those in the Sides chapter on page 902), but here we move vegetables to the center of the plate, spanning a variety of cooking methods and expanding the way we think about incorporating them in daily cooking. Many include small amounts of eggs, nuts, or bacon, which boost flavor and add protein; these can easily be made vegetarian. Some are made better with bread or rice on the side; many others are satisfying alone.

Vegetables do require more prep work than other ingredients—the illustrations starting on page 28 offer helpful tips—so only a few of these recipes take 15 minutes or less. But the cooking moves along quickly. This chapter constitutes a repertoire of delicious, healthy, and filling dishes that should be the cornerstone of our diets.

Chapter Highlights

Braising and Glazing One of the best methods for cooking vegetables. Braising and Glazing (page 423).

Potato, the Pancake One big pancake is a fine main dish. Potato Rösti with Fresh Apple Sauce (page 426).

Take It Apart Classic, labor-intensive recipes reworked for speed and ease. Unstuffed Cabbage (page 424), Skillet Spanakopita (page 468).

Pepper Primer All about fresh or dried chile peppers; see page 456.

Vegetable Polenta A vegetable base for your vegetables. Cauliflower "Polenta" with Mushrooms (page 432).

Roast 'Em Roast vegetables in large batches to have on hand at all times. Roasted Vegetables (page 416).

The Incredible Egg Eggs and veggies are a magical and easy combination. Eggs to the Rescue (page 443).

Lasagna, Hold the Noodles Faster with tortillas. Tortilla Lasagna (page 466).

Crust Gone Wild Three recipes with unconventional crusts. Squash au Gratin with Toasted Nuts (page 430), Skillet Spanakopita (page 468), Cherry Tomato Cobbler (page 464).

Batter Up The key to fast and easy flatbreads from scratch. Vegetable Flatbread with Kale and White Bean Stew (page 462).

A Cheesy Refuge for Vegetables Give your vegetables a home in lasagnas or gratins. Impromptu Lasagnas and Gratins (page 467).

Eat on Your Feet The rare occasions when eating standing up, crowded around the stove is the thing to do. Eating Around the Stove (page 449).

SPEED SERVES 4

Bubbling Caprese

The hard-to-beat trio of tomatoes, mozzarella, and basil, made all hot and bubbly in the broiler. The quantities here are flexible; tinker according to taste and what you have on hand. You could add some chicken or eggplant underneath for a full-on Parmigiana (see page 618), but my favorite way to eat this dish is simply with a crusty hunk of bread.

Ingredients

5 or 6 medium ripe tomatoes (2 pounds)

Olive oil for drizzling

12 ounces fresh mozzarella cheese

Salt and pepper

1 bunch fresh basil

2 tablespoons balsamic vinegar

Prep | Cook

1. Turn the broiler to high; put the rack 4 inches from the heat.

   Core the tomatoes; slice crosswise into rounds about ½ inch thick; put them on a rimmed baking sheet. Drizzle with some olive oil.

   Slice the mozzarella about the same thickness.

2. Sprinkle the tomatoes with salt and pepper and lay the mozzarella on top of the tomatoes. (You may have to cut some of the cheese slices in half.) Drizzle with a little more olive oil and broil until the cheese is bubbly and browned, about 5 minutes.

   Strip about ½ cup basil leaves from the stems.

3. When the cheese is browned, remove from the broiler and drizzle with 2 tablespoons balsamic vinegar. Tear the basil leaves over the top and serve.

VARIATIONS

6 Other Cheese, Herb, and Drizzle Combinations

1. Blue cheese, tarragon, and balsamic vinegar
2. Cheddar, scallions, and hot sauce
3. Manchego cheese, parsley, and sherry vinegar
4. Feta cheese, mint, and lemon juice
5. Oaxaca cheese, cilantro, and lime juice
6. Gruyère cheese, thyme, and red wine vinegar

NOTES

IF YOU HAVE MORE TIME
If you'd like the tomatoes to get a little browned as well, broil them on their own for 5 to 8 minutes before topping with the cheese.

SIDES

Warm Buttery Bread 906

Garlic Bread 906

Bruschetta 909

Green Salad 911

Pasta, Plain and Simple 948

Roasted Vegetables

When vegetables roast, their flavors concentrate; they brown outside and soften inside. If you have roasted vegetables on hand in your refrigerator, when you need a shortcut for dinner, inspiration for lunch, or just something healthy to snack on, your everyday cooking will be much easier and more enjoyable.

You can roast vegetables in small quantities if you like, but since the same method works for all different vegetables and you've already got the oven cranking, you might as well make the biggest batch you can. Spread the vegetables you want to roast between two or more rimmed baking sheets or roasting pans. Make sure not to crowd them or they won't brown. Arrange the vegetables in groups on the baking sheets, keeping like with like so you can easily remove those that cook quickest and give more time to bigger, slower ones.

Here are the vegetables that are best for roasting, roughly in order from quickest cooking to slowest: asparagus, summer squash and zucchini, leeks, fennel, mushrooms, shallots, onions, eggplant (use a little extra oil or butter), broccoli, cauliflower, radishes, Brussels sprouts, carrots, parsnips, potatoes, sweet potatoes, turnips, rutabaga, celery root, winter squash. Leave small or narrow things whole (asparagus, shallots, thin carrots), break broccoli and cauliflower into florets, and cut other vegetables into thick slices or chunks.

The Roasted Peppers recipe here will work for any bell pepper, poblanos, or other large long or round peppers.

Roasted Vegetables

1 Prepare the Vegetables

Heat the oven to 425°F. Drizzle some olive oil or melted butter on the bottom of your baking sheets or roasting pans. Prepare the vegetables and spread them evenly, leaving enough space between them for them to brown properly. Drizzle with a little more olive oil or butter and sprinkle with salt and pepper; toss or stir to coat.

2 Roast

Roast the vegetables, stirring gently and/or turning once or twice, until they are tender and beginning to brown. The fastest vegetables can take as little as 15 minutes and the slower ones around an hour. If they are browning too quickly, lower the temperature to 400°F and stir more frequently. Sample the vegetables occasionally to check for tenderness, removing them from the oven as they finish cooking. Taste and adjust the seasoning.

3 Store

If you are not using the vegetables right away, let them cool, then store them in airtight containers in the refrigerator for up to a week.

VARIATIONS

8 Ways to Flavor Roasted Vegetables

Toss any of the following with the vegetables:

1. Chopped fresh herbs
2. Citrus juice or grated zest
3. Toasted Bread Crumbs or Croutons (page 71)
4. Chopped nuts
5. Any flavorful oil, like olive, sesame, or nut oils
6. Vinaigrette
7. Spices or spice blends (page 758)
8. Butter (simple and classic)

Roasted Peppers

1 Pick Your Heat Source

Heat the oven to 450°F, turn the broiler to high and put the rack 4 inches from the heat, heat a charcoal or gas grill to moderately high heat and put the rack 4 inches from the heat, or turn on a few gas burners on your stove.

2 Blacken the Peppers

Roast, broil, grill, or cook the peppers right in the gas flame, turning as necessary until they're dark brown or black all over and they collapse in on themselves. Roasting can take up to an hour, broiling and grilling about 15 minutes, and cooking in the gas flame about 10.

3 Peel the Peppers

Wrap the cooked peppers in foil or put them in a bowl and cover it tightly with plastic wrap; the steam will help the skins peel off easily. When they are cool enough to handle, remove the skins, seeds, and stems—doing this under running water is easiest. It's okay if they fall apart a bit. Now they're ready to serve or store in the fridge for a few days or the freezer for a few months.

SPEED SERVES 4

Sweet Pepper Queso Fundido

Queso fundido is Mexico's answer to fondue. It's usually served as a snack, often with a token scattering of poblanos, mushrooms, or chorizo, but bulked up with vegetables and served with warm tortillas or tortilla chips, it makes a great dinner.

Ingredients

3 tablespoons olive oil

4 large bell peppers of the same color

2 garlic cloves

Salt and pepper

12 ounces Jack, Oaxaca, or mozzarella cheese (3 cups grated)

Several sprigs fresh cilantro for garnish

Prep | Cook

1. Turn the broiler to high; put the rack 4 inches from the heat.
2. Put 3 tablespoons olive oil in a medium ovenproof skillet over medium-high heat.

   Trim, core, seed, and slice the peppers.

   Peel and mince 2 garlic cloves.
3. Add the bell peppers and garlic to the skillet, sprinkle with salt and pepper, and cook, stirring occasionally until the peppers soften, 5 to 10 minutes.

   Grate 3 cups cheese.

   Chop several sprigs cilantro.
4. When the peppers are soft, turn off the heat, add the cheese to the skillet, and toss so the peppers are well distributed throughout.
5. Broil until the cheese is bubbly and brown, 2 or 3 minutes. Garnish with the cilantro and serve.

VARIATIONS

5 Other Vegetables to Use Instead of Bell Peppers

1. Poblano peppers
2. Mushrooms (1 pound)
3. Spinach (8 ounces; sauté until it wilts and its water evaporates)
4. Tomatoes (don't sauté first)
5. Red onions (just 1)

SIDES

Warm Flour or Corn Tortillas 907

White Rice 941

Avocado with Hot Sauce and Cilantro 920

Jícama and Radish Salad 918

SPEED ◐ SERVES 4

Eggplant Steaks with Fresh Tomato-Garlic Sauce

Grilling or broiling the eggplant gives this dish a delicious smokiness, and this quick, garlicky sauce is hard to beat. Feel free to use chopped canned tomatoes if fresh ones aren't in season.

Ingredients

6 tablespoons olive oil, plus more as needed

4 medium ripe tomatoes

4 garlic cloves

Salt and pepper

1 large or 2 medium eggplant (about 2 pounds)

1 bunch fresh basil

4 ounces Parmesan cheese (1 cup grated)

Prep | Cook

1. Prepare a grill or turn the broiler to high; put the rack 4 inches from the heat.
2. Put 2 tablespoons olive oil in a medium skillet over medium heat.
   Core and chop the tomatoes; add them to the skillet as you go.
   Peel and mince 4 garlic cloves; add them to the skillet.
3. Sprinkle the tomatoes with salt and pepper and cook, stirring occasionally until they begin to break down, 8 to 10 minutes.
   Trim and slice the eggplant into ½-inch-thick rounds.
   Rub the eggplant with 4 tablespoons olive oil; sprinkle with salt and pepper.
4. Grill or broil the eggplant, turning once or twice and brushing with more oil if it looks dry, until tender and browned on both sides, about 10 minutes total.
   Strip ½ cup basil leaves from the stems.
   Grate 1 cup Parmesan.

5. When the tomatoes start to break down, turn off the heat; taste and adjust the seasoning.
6. When the eggplant is tender and browned on both sides, put the slices on a platter and spoon the tomato sauce over them. Sprinkle the Parmesan over the top, tear the basil leaves and scatter them all around, and serve.

VARIATIONS

Eggplant Steaks with Tomatillo Sauce
Substitute 2 cups chopped husked tomatillos for the tomatoes and add a seeded and chopped poblano pepper. Garnish with crumbled queso fresco instead of the Parmesan and 1/4 cup chopped cilantro instead of the basil.

Eggplant Steaks with Fresh Tomato-Olive Sauce
Add 1/2 cup or more pitted black olives along with the tomatoes.

NOTES

EVEN FASTER
Instead of making the sauce as described in Steps 2 and 3, use 1 or 2 cups Tomato Sauce (page 296).

Serve the eggplant with a raw tomato "sauce": Combine chopped tomatoes with a little minced garlic, olive oil, chopped basil, salt, and pepper.

SIDES

Pasta, Plain and Simple 948

Bruschetta 909

Garlic Bread 906

Green Salad 911

SPEED ◐ SERVES 4

Glazed Brussels Sprouts with Vietnamese Flavors

A Vietnamese-style glaze breathes sweet and spicy life into Brussels sprouts; add more chiles if you want to kick up the heat. Serve with some white rice or noodles and this becomes a meal.

Ingredients

2 tablespoons vegetable oil

2 pounds Brussels sprouts

Salt and pepper

1 garlic clove

1 fresh hot chile (like Thai or jalapeño)

2 limes

2 tablespoons fish sauce

2 teaspoons sugar

Several sprigs fresh cilantro for garnish

Prep | Cook

1. Put 2 tablespoons vegetable oil in a large skillet with a lid over low heat.

   Trim the Brussels sprouts.

2. Add the Brussels sprouts to the skillet along with a sprinkle of salt and pepper and ⅓ cup water. Raise the heat to medium-high.

3. Cover and cook, checking once or twice and adding small amounts of water if the pan looks dry, until the Brussels sprouts are a little shy of tender, 6 to 10 minutes, depending on their size.

   Peel 1 garlic clove. Trim the chile. Mince them together and put them in a small bowl.

   Halve the limes; squeeze the juice into the bowl.

   Add 2 tablespoons fish sauce, 2 teaspoons sugar, and ⅓ cup water to the bowl and stir to combine.

4. When the Brussels sprouts are a little shy of tender, remove the cover, add the lime and fish sauce mixture, and raise the heat to high. Cook, stirring just a few times to coat the Brussels sprouts, until the liquid reduces to a thick glaze and the Brussels sprouts become brown and crisp in places, 4 to 6 minutes.

   Chop several sprigs cilantro.

5. Taste and adjust the seasoning. Sprinkle with the cilantro and serve hot or warm.

NOTES

HEARTIER BRAISED VEGETABLES

Add any of the following to the Brussels sprouts during the final few minutes of cooking:

1. Chopped peanuts, cashews, or almonds
2. Tofu cubes
3. Cooked chicken or meat
4. Raw shrimp, scallops, or squid
5. Cooked rice, noodles, or grains

BRAISING AND GLAZING

This has become one of my favorite ways to cook firmer vegetables that take some time to become tender, like Brussels sprouts, winter squash, parsnips, or other roots like beets and carrots. The braising part consists of nothing more than simmering the vegetables with a little water and oil or butter in a covered skillet until they are nearly tender—the steam from the liquid helps get this done fairly quickly. Then you uncover the pot, turn the heat to high, and let the liquid bubble away until the skillet is dry and the near-tender vegetables become glazed with fat. (You can let them brown a bit too.) By that time the vegetables will be tender and ready to go.

SIDES

White Rice 941

Fire and Ice Noodles 950

Scallion Pancakes 940

SPEED ◐ SERVES 4

Unstuffed Cabbage

The most onerous part about making stuffed cabbage is actually stuffing and rolling the cabbage, which requires blanching the leaves to make them pliable. When you use the cabbage leaves as a base instead of a wrapper, all that work becomes unnecessary.

Ingredients

1 large head Savoy or green cabbage

2 garlic cloves

1 cup couscous

1 tablespoon olive oil, plus more for drizzling

1 cup canned diced tomatoes with juice

2 teaspoons smoked paprika

Salt and pepper

1 cup vegetable or chicken stock or water

1 bunch fresh parsley

Prep | Cook

Core the cabbage; peel away 8 to 12 large outer leaves. Refrigerate the remaining cabbage for another use. If your cabbage leaves have thick stems, cut out the spines.

1. Line the bottom of a large skillet with the cabbage leaves.

   Peel and mince 2 garlic cloves; put them in a medium bowl.

2. Add 1 cup couscous, 1 tablespoon olive oil, 1 cup canned diced tomatoes, 2 teaspoons smoked paprika, and a sprinkle of salt and pepper to the bowl. Stir to combine.

3. Spread the couscous mixture over the top of the cabbage; add 1 cup stock or water and bring to a boil.

4. Reduce the heat to a simmer, cover, and cook until the cabbage and couscous are tender and most of the liquid is absorbed, 5 to 10 minutes.

   Chop about ¼ cup parsley.

5. When the cabbage and couscous are tender, taste and adjust the seasoning. Drizzle with a little more olive oil, garnish with the parsley, and serve.

VARIATIONS

Unstuffed Cabbage with Ground Meat
Brown 8 to 12 ounces ground beef, lamb, pork, chicken, turkey, or sausage and 1 small onion, chopped, in the skillet, then transfer to a large bowl and line the skillet with the cabbage leaves. Make the couscous mixture in the bowl with the browned meat, then layer on top of the cabbage and proceed as directed.

NOTES

MAKE YOUR OWN

Vegetable Stock 212

Chicken Stock 213

SAVOY CABBAGE
This versatile, long-storing vegetable is worth grabbing whenever you see it. Like green and red cabbages, Savoy comes in a tightly packed head, only the leaves are curly and less firm, and the flavor is a little milder. So it's perfect for salads and slaws and has a supple texture when cooked.

SMOKED PAPRIKA
I don't really do favorites, but this is as close as it gets. Even if you haven't heard of smoked paprika—or pimentón—you've almost certainly eaten some in chorizo, where its sweet-smoky flavor is dominant. Thankfully even supermarkets carry it now, so you can incorporate its pleasantly haunting taste into all sorts of dishes. Like all paprika, it's made from dried chiles, but in this case, they're smoked first. Pimentón may be either hot or picante (which is not that hot) or sweet or dulce (which is not sweet but mild). It adds as much smokiness as bacon and a stunning brick-red color to any dish it touches, Spanish or not.

SIDES

Steamed Tender Vegetables 954

Hummus 939

Carrot Salad with Olives and Rosemary 914

Cucumber Raita with Cinnamon and Mint 916

Skin-On Mashed Potatoes 961

SPEED ◐ SERVES 4

Potato Rösti with Fresh Apple Sauce

Potato pancakes with apple sauce is a classic of eastern European cooking, but it's a lot easier to cook one giant pancake than many little ones. That's just what they do in Switzerland, where rösti are beloved. Call it whatever you want, a crisp potato cake with apple sauce and a dollop of sour cream is good eating.

Ingredients

4 to 6 medium russet or Yukon Gold potatoes (2 pounds)

Salt and pepper

3 tablespoons olive oil, plus more as needed

4 tablespoons (½ stick) butter

3 medium apples (about 1 pound)

½ teaspoon cinnamon

Sour cream for garnish (optional)

Prep | Cook

Peel the potatoes if you like. Shred them in a food processor with a grating disk or by hand with a box grater.

Drain the potatoes well in a colander or strainer, patting them dry with a paper towel and squeezing out the moisture. Sprinkle with salt and pepper and toss.

1. Put 3 tablespoons olive oil in a large nonstick skillet over medium-high heat.
2. Put the potatoes in the skillet and press them down with a spatula. Cook, shaking the pan occasionally until the bottom of the cake is crisp, 6 to 8 minutes.
3. Put 4 tablespoons butter in a large pot over medium heat.
   Core the apples and cut them into thin slices.
4. When the butter has melted, add the apples, ½ teaspoon cinnamon, a sprinkle of salt, and ⅓ cup water. Cook, stirring occasionally and adding more water if the mixture gets too dry, until the apples break down slightly into a sauce, 10 to 15 minutes.

5. When the first side of the rösti is browned, slide it onto a plate, top that plate with another plate, and flip. Add a little more oil to the skillet and slide the potatoes back in. Continue to cook, adjusting the heat if necessary, until the second side is browned, 5 to 10 minutes.

6. Cut the rösti into slices, top with warm apple sauce and a dollop of sour cream if you like, and serve.

VARIATIONS

Beet Rösti with Fresh Pear Sauce
Use peeled beets instead of the potatoes and pears in place of the apples. Skip the cinnamon and garnish with crumbled blue cheese instead of sour cream.

Sweet Potato Rösti with Orange Sauce
Like warm marmalade, only better. Use sweet potatoes. Instead of the apples use 3 oranges. Grate the zest from 1 of them, then peel them all. Chop into chunks and add the pulp and the zest to the pot in Step 4. (Wait to see if you need to add water; you might not.)

SIDES

Green Salad 911

Brussels Sprouts with Sausage 958

Tahini Slaw 923

Casseroles

1 Sauté aromatics.

Heat the oven to 375°F. Cook aromatics like onions, leeks, shallots, garlic, ginger, or chiles in a few tablespoons oil or butter over medium heat until softened and fragrant. A large ovenproof skillet is best, so you can build the casserole right in the pan.

2 Vary the flavors.

Stir spices or other seasonings into the aromatics to give the casserole its characteristic flavor. Chipotle chiles in adobo lend a smoky heat; Dijon mustard and thyme or tarragon lend a French flair; for Italian flavors, try rosemary and lemon zest; for Chinese, five-spice powder and soy sauce do the trick; and for Indian flavors, add curry powder or garam masala.

3 Build in the main ingredients.

Casseroles are the perfect place for leftovers like cooked vegetables, grains, pasta, beans, or meat. You can also stir in frozen or quick-cooking raw vegetables or greens (sauté those until just short of tender before proceeding).

4 Add liquid if you want.

For saucy casseroles, add cream, tomato sauce, salsa, pesto, or even beaten eggs (to make something akin to a frittata). You want the main ingredients moistened, but not swimming. (If the vegetables or grains are raw or underdone, add extra liquid and cover the pan with foil for the first half of baking.)

5 Top.

The best part is the cheesy, crunchy topping. Any decent melting cheese will work; bread crumbs are classic for crunch, but chopped nuts or crushed potato chips, tortillas chips, or pretzels could all get the job done. Sprinkle everything in an even layer.

6 Bake.

Bake until the cheese is bubbly and the top is brown, 15 to 30 minutes, depending on how much you have in the pan. For extra browning, run the casserole under the broiler for a minute or 2. Let it rest for a few minutes before serving.

SPEED ◑ SERVES 4

Squash au Gratin with Toasted Nuts

A luxurious treat. The cream is infused with sage, and the shredded squash becomes velvety. The top offers a crunchy contrast in the form of chopped nuts and grated Parmesan. This could be the star at your next Thanksgiving.

Ingredients

1 large butternut or other winter squash (2 to 2 ½ pounds)

3 sprigs fresh sage

2 tablespoons olive oil

Salt and pepper

1 cup cream

1 cup hazelnuts, pecans, or pistachios

4 ounces Parmesan (1 cup grated)

Prep | Cook

1. Heat the oven to 450°F.

   Cut the squash in half crosswise, trim and peel it, scoop out and discard the seeds, and cut it into chunks. Shred the squash in a food processor with a grating disk (by far the easier method) or by hand with a box grater.

   Strip the sage leaves from 3 sprigs and chop them.

2. Put the squash in a 9 × 13-inch baking dish. Add the sage, 2 tablespoons olive oil, and a sprinkle of salt and pepper; toss and spread in an even layer. Pour 1 cup cream over the top.

3. Cover the baking dish with aluminum foil and bake until the squash is tender and the cream is bubbly and thick, 15 to 20 minutes.

   Chop 1 cup nuts.

   Grate 1 cup Parmesan.

4. When the squash is tender, uncover the dish, sprinkle the Parmesan over the top, and sprinkle with the nuts. Return to the oven and bake, uncovered, until the top is lightly browned, about 5 minutes more.

5. Let cool for a minute or 2 before serving.

VARIATIONS

Beet Gratin with Toasted Nuts
Substitute beets for the squash, tarragon for the sage, and add a few dollops of goat cheese along with the cream. Use pistachios and skip the Parmesan.

Celery Root Gratin with Toasted Nuts
Replace the squash with celery root and the sage with dill. Use hazelnuts and substitute Gruyère for the Parmesan.

NOTES

EVEN FASTER
Sauté the squash and sage in a large ovenproof skillet with olive oil until slightly softened, then stir in ½ cup cream and simmer until the squash is tender, about 5 minutes. Sprinkle with the cheese and nuts and broil until browned and bubbling.

SIDES

Rice Pilaf 944

Quinoa 945

Warm Buttery Bread 906

Green Salad 911

Refried White Beans with Rosemary 938

SPEED ◐ SERVES 4

Cauliflower "Polenta" with Mushrooms

Polenta is a great comfort food of Italy and a wonderful venue for all kinds of toppings from meat stews to vegetable ragouts. With the right seasonings puréed cauliflower impersonates it brilliantly, increasing your vegetable intake without decreasing your pleasure.

Ingredients

4 tablespoons olive oil

1 cup chicken or vegetable stock, water, or white wine

12 ounces button, cremini, or shiitake mushrooms

1 large head cauliflower

Salt and pepper

1 large shallot

3 tablespoons butter

2 tablespoons sour cream

2 sprigs fresh rosemary

4 ounces Parmesan or pecorino cheese (1 cup grated)

Prep | Cook

1. Put 2 tablespoons olive oil in a large skillet or large pot over medium-low heat.
2. Put 1 cup stock, water, or wine in a saucepan over high heat.

   Trim and slice the mushrooms. (If you're using shiitakes, discard the stems.) Add them to the skillet as you work.

   Trim the cauliflower and cut into small florets.
3. Sprinkle the mushrooms with salt and pepper and raise the heat to medium. Cook, stirring occasionally until tender and lightly browned, about 10 minutes.
4. Add the cauliflower to the saucepan, lower the heat to medium, and cook until quite tender, at least 10 minutes.

   Trim, peel, and chop the shallot.
5. When the mushrooms are tender and lightly browned, add 2 tablespoons olive oil and the shallot. Cook, stirring, for a minute, then remove from the heat.
6. Transfer the florets from the cooking liquid to the food processor. Process them in batches, adding 2 tablespoons

cooking liquid to each, until they are as smooth as polenta. Transfer each batch to a large bowl. Stir 2 tablespoons butter and 2 tablespoons sour cream into the finished purée.

Strip the leaves from 2 sprigs rosemary and chop finely.

Grate 1 cup Parmesan.

7. Add the rosemary, 1 tablespoon butter, and the Parmesan to the bowl and stir to combine.

8. Spoon the cauliflower "polenta" into bowls, top with the mushrooms, and serve.

VARIATIONS

Mashed Potatoes with Mushrooms
Substitute peeled potatoes for the cauliflower. Mash by hand. They may need 10 minutes more cooking time.

Red Cauliflower "Polenta" with Mushrooms
Use red wine for half of the liquid.

NOTES

MAKE YOUR OWN

Chicken Stock 213

Vegetable Stock 212

STRIPPING ROSEMARY
Stripping rosemary leaves from their stems is one of the more satisfying bits of kitchen prep (see the illustration on page 29). Hold the sprig from the top with the leaves pointed up (like an open flower), pinch the top of the sprig with the thumb, forefinger, and middle finger on your other hand, and pull all the way down. The leaves will strip right off as you slide your fingers down toward the bottom. Now they're ready to chop.

SIDES

Asparagus Gratin 929

Green Salad 911

Broiled Cherry Tomatoes 931

SPEED ◑ SERVES 4

Stuffed Poblanos with Black Beans and Cheese

Stuffed poblano recipes usually have you wrangling with fragile roasted peppers, struggling to keep them intact. That's too much work. If you treat poblanos like normal bell peppers—that is, stuff them raw—the process is utterly manageable.

Ingredients

8 poblano peppers

1 cup cooked or canned black beans

1 small red onion

1 bunch fresh cilantro

4 ounces manchego or Jack cheese (1 cup grated)

Salt and pepper

2 tablespoons olive oil

2 limes

Prep | Cook

1. Turn the broiler to high; put the rack 6 inches from the heat.

   Cut a slit down the length of each poblano and carefully pry each one open just wide enough to remove the seeds (and later to stuff them).

   If you're using canned beans, rinse and drain them; put the beans in a bowl.

   Trim, peel, and chop the onion; add it to the bowl.

   Chop ⅓ cup cilantro and add it to the bowl.

   Grate 1 cup cheese and add to the bowl.

2. Sprinkle the mixture with salt and pepper and stir to combine.

3. Using your fingers, gently stuff the poblanos with the bean mixture. When all the peppers are stuffed, put them on a rimmed baking sheet, rub with 2 tablespoons olive oil, and sprinkle with salt and pepper.

4. Broil, turning occasionally to avoid burning until the peppers are soft and lightly charred on all sides and the cheese is melted, 10 to 15 minutes.

   Cut the limes into wedges.

5. When the peppers are done, put them on plates or a platter and serve with the lime wedges.

VARIATIONS

Stuffed Poblanos with Corn and Cheese
Substitute fresh or frozen corn kernels for the black beans (or do half and half).

Stuffed Poblanos with White Beans and Mozzarella
Substitute white beans for black, parsley for the cilantro, mozzarella for the manchego, and lemons for the limes.

NOTES

MAKE YOUR OWN

Cooked Beans 496

IF YOU HAVE MORE TIME
If you want to roast, peel, and seed the peppers first, see page 417 for instructions. Once the peppers are ready to go, carefully stuff them, put them on a baking sheet, and bake them at 375°F until the cheese is hot and melted, about 20 minutes.

SIDES

Warm Flour or Corn Tortillas 907

Jícama and Radish Salad 918

Avocado with Lime and Chili Salt 920

White Rice 941

SPEED ◑ SERVES 4

Sweet Potato Flautas

Flautas—stuffed and rolled tortillas—are typically fried, which is a bit of work. You can get some of the same shattering crunch by brushing them with oil and broiling them, the crisp tortillas giving way to tender sweet potatoes inside. These are perfect for a casual party.

Ingredients

3 tablespoons olive oil, plus more as needed

2 pounds sweet potatoes

Salt and pepper

6 scallions

1 fresh hot green chile (like serrano)

Twelve 8-inch flour tortillas

Sour cream for garnish

Salsa for garnish

Prep | Cook

1. Turn the broiler to high; put the rack 4 inches from the heat.
2. Put 3 tablespoons olive oil in a large skillet over low heat.

   Peel the sweet potatoes; shred them in a food processor with a grating disk or by hand with a box grater.
3. Put the sweet potatoes in the skillet with ½ cup water, sprinkle with salt and pepper, and raise the heat to medium-high.
4. Cook, stirring occasionally until they begin to soften and lighten in color, 8 to 10 minutes. Add a tablespoon or 2 more oil if they start to stick to the skillet.

   Trim and chop the scallions.

   Trim and mince the chile.
5. When the sweet potatoes begin to lighten in color, add the scallions and chile. Cook, stirring frequently until the potatoes are tender but not mushy, 2 or 3 minutes.
6. Spoon about ¼ cup of the mixture onto each of 12 tortillas. Roll them up tightly, leaving the ends open, and brush the outsides with some olive oil.

7. Put the flautas on a rimmed baking sheet, seam side down so they stay closed. Broil until the tops are brown and crisp, 2 to 3 minutes. Turn and brown the other side, about 2 minutes. Watch them so the tortillas don't burn. Serve with sour cream and salsa on top or alongside.

VARIATIONS

Potato and Chorizo Flautas
Substitute russet or Yukon Gold potatoes for the sweet potatoes. Before adding the potatoes to the skillet, sauté 8 ounces fresh Mexican chorizo until brown.

NOTES

MAKE YOUR OWN
Fresh Tomato Salsa 145

IF YOU HAVE MORE TIME
Soak 8 toothpicks in water for 15 minutes and use them to fasten the flautas shut. Broil, turning once, until both sides are brown and crisp.

Fasten the flautas shut with toothpicks (as described above) and fry them in about ½ inch of vegetable oil over medium-high heat (350°F; a pinch of flour will sizzle but not burn) until golden and crisp, about 2 minutes.

SIDES

White Rice 941

Chile-Cumin Black Beans 937

Jícama and Radish Salad 918

Avocado with Lime and Chili Salt 920

SPEED ◑ SERVES 4

Potato and Spinach Saag

Saag, an Indian stew of spinach and aromatics, is even more luxurious when bolstered with cream. The potatoes lend some of their starch to the sauce, which thickens it even further. You'll want rice or bread to sop it up.

Ingredients

Salt

1 ½ pounds russet or Yukon Gold potatoes

1 ½ pounds spinach

2 tablespoons vegetable oil

1 inch fresh ginger

2 garlic cloves

1 fresh hot green chile (like serrano)

1 tablespoon garam masala or curry powder

Pepper

1 ¼ cups cream

Prep | Cook

1. Put a stockpot of water over high heat and salt it.

   Peel the potatoes and cut them into ½-inch cubes, adding them to the pot as you finish.

2. Cover the pot, bring to a boil, and cook until the potatoes are tender, 5 to 15 minutes.

   Trim and finely chop the spinach; discard any thick stems.

3. Put 2 tablespoons vegetable oil in a large skillet with a lid over medium-high heat.

   Peel 1 inch ginger and 2 garlic cloves; trim the chile. Mince them all together.

4. Add the ginger, garlic, and chile, 1 tablespoon garam masala or curry powder, and a sprinkle of salt to the skillet. Cook, stirring until fragrant, about a minute.

5. Add the spinach to the skillet, a handful at a time if necessary to fit it in, and sprinkle with salt and pepper. Cook, stirring until just wilted, 5 to 8 minutes.

6. When the potatoes are fully tender but not mushy, drain them in a colander or strainer.

7. When the spinach is wilted, add the potatoes to the skillet along with 1 ¼ cups cream. Stir to combine and heat through, taste and adjust the seasoning, and serve.

VARIATIONS

Mushroom and Spinach Saag
Substitute 1 pound mushrooms, sliced or quartered, for the potatoes. Instead of boiling them, sauté them for 5 or 10 minutes in the oil at the beginning of Step 3 before you add the aromatics.

Tofu and Spinach Saag
Use 2 bricks firm or extra-firm tofu instead of the potatoes. Add directly to the sauce in Step 7 and cook until the tofu warms through and the sauce thickens.

NOTES

MAKE YOUR OWN
Curry Powder 758

EVEN FASTER
Cut the potatoes into smaller cubes, or thinly slice them so they take less time to cook.

CREAMY GREEN SAUCES
Stirring a creamy liquid into sautéed greens can turn them into a fantastic sauce. Cream is most commonly used for this (like creamed spinach), but coconut milk, yogurt, tahini thinned with a little water, or puréed silken tofu (or any combination of these) will all provide that thick, rich base into which the greens can just melt away. The rule of thumb for measuring is 1 ½ pounds of greens to 1 to 2 cups creamy base. Once the greens are wilted and the creamy component is added, the sauce is ready to serve, but simmering the mixture for a bit not only allows all the flavors to come together but also gives you the opportunity to cook something else—like potatoes or chopped chicken—directly in the sauce. Note that very delicate greens like arugula and spinach will meld into a sauce almost instantly. Collards and other thick ones will take more time to cook or retain some crunch if you pull them off the heat early. If you can chop them very finely before you work with them, they'll break down faster, and it's also helpful to add up to a cup of water, ¼ cup at a time, to the creamy base as the thick greens cook.

SIDES

Cucumber Raita 916

White Rice 941

Carrots with Curry Vinaigrette 953

SPEED ◐ SERVES 4

Zucchini Fattoush

Fattoush is usually a cold salad composed of raw tomatoes and toasted bread. Adding other vegetables to the mix—zucchini here—and serving it warm makes the dish feel heartier and adds only a few minutes to the prep time.

Ingredients

Two 8-inch pitas

4 tablespoons olive oil

2 large zucchini

Salt and pepper

2 garlic cloves

3 or 4 medium ripe tomatoes

½ cup olives

1 bunch fresh parsley

1 lemon

Prep | Cook

1. Heat the oven to 350°F. Put the pitas on a baking sheet, brush with 1 tablespoon olive oil, and put in the oven (it's okay that it isn't heated yet). Bake, turning once, until crisp, about 15 minutes.

2. Put 3 tablespoons olive oil in a large skillet over medium-high heat.

   Trim and chop the zucchini.

3. Add the zucchini to the skillet, sprinkle with salt and pepper, and cook, stirring occasionally until tender, 5 or 6 minutes.

   Peel and mince 2 garlic cloves.

   Core and chop the tomatoes.

   Pit ½ cup olives if necessary.

4. When the zucchini is tender, add the garlic, tomatoes, and olives. Cook, stirring occasionally until the tomatoes are warmed and slightly softened but the mixture isn't yet saucy, 2 or 3 minutes.

   Chop ½ cup parsley.

   Halve the lemon.

5. When the tomatoes are warmed and slightly softened, turn off the heat. When the pita is crisp, crumble it into the skillet, add the parsley, and squeeze in the lemon juice. Toss to combine, taste and adjust the seasoning, and serve.

VARIATIONS

Warm Pita Fattoush with Feta
Toss in some cubes of feta cheese right before serving.

Warm Pita Fattoush with Shrimp
Add 8 to 12 ounces chopped shrimp along with the tomatoes and olives in Step 4. By the time the tomatoes are warmed and softened, the shrimp will be cooked through.

NOTES

EVEN FASTER
Grill or broil the pita instead of baking it. You'll have to keep a closer eye on it, but it will take less time to crisp up.

SIDES

Refried White Beans with Rosemary 938

Tahini Slaw 923

Rice Pilaf 944

Bulgur with Lemon and Parsley 946

Couscous 910

Hummus 939

SPEED ◑ SERVES 4

Scrambled Broccoli with Parmesan and Lemon

Somewhere between scrambled eggs and a broccoli frittata, this dish pairs the hearty richness of eggs and Parmesan with the bright punch of lemon juice. If you're not enthralled by broccoli, there are plenty of other vegetables that you can treat the same way; see the list that follows. And any will work with the completely different taste of the variations.

Ingredients

2 tablespoons olive oil, plus more if needed

1 large head broccoli (1 ½ to 2 pounds)

8 eggs

1 lemon

4 ounces Parmesan cheese (1 cup grated), plus a little more for garnish

Salt and pepper

Prep | Cook

1. Put 2 tablespoons olive oil in a large skillet over medium-high heat.

   Break or chop the broccoli into small florets.

2. Add the broccoli to the skillet along with ⅓ cup water. Partially cover and cook until the broccoli is just tender and the skillet is dry, 5 or 6 minutes.

   Crack the eggs into a medium bowl.

   Grate the lemon zest into the bowl, then halve the lemon.

   Grate 1 cup Parmesan and add to the bowl.

3. Sprinkle the eggs with salt and lots of pepper and beat.

4. When the broccoli is just tender and the pan is dry (there should still be some oil left; if not, add some), turn the heat to low and pour in the egg mixture.

5. Cook, uncovered, stirring occasionally until the eggs are just set, just a few minutes. Grate a little more Parmesan over the top and squeeze the lemon juice over the top to taste. Taste and adjust the seasoning and serve.

VARIATIONS

Scrambled Broccoli with Soy Sauce and Lime
Substitute 1 tablespoon vegetable oil and 1 tablespoon sesame oil for the olive oil, 2 limes for the lemon, and 2 tablespoons soy sauce for the Parmesan.

8 Other Vegetables to Cook Like This with Eggs

1. Asparagus
2. Green beans
3. Cauliflower
4. Greens
5. Mushrooms
6. Bell peppers
7. Summer squash or zucchini
8. Eggplant

NOTES

EVEN FASTER
Chop the broccoli into small pieces, but keep an eye on them, because they will become tender fairly quickly.

EGGS TO THE RESCUE
If you ever have vegetables in the fridge and feel totally uninspired, turn to eggs. They cook almost instantly and can turn sautéed vegetables—which might otherwise feel like a side dish—into something far more substantial. Whether you scramble them (page 844), broil them (page 848), make an omelet (page 834), or turn them into a frittata (page 494), eggs offer a fast and foolproof canvas for all sorts of vegetables that you might have lying around.

SIDES

Warm Buttery Bread 906

Garlic Bread 906

Bruschetta 909

White Rice 941

SPEED ◐ SERVES 4

Bok Choy Pancake with Soy Dipping Sauce

Think of a thicker scallion pancake with lots of stir-fried bok choy coursing through it instead of scallions and you've got the idea.

Ingredients

3 tablespoons vegetable oil, plus more if needed

1 large head bok choy (1 ½ pounds)

Salt and pepper

1 egg

¾ cup flour, plus more if needed

3 tablespoons soy sauce

½ teaspoon sesame oil

1 tablespoon mirin or 1 ½ teaspoons water and 1 ½ teaspoons honey

Prep | Cook

1. Put 3 tablespoons vegetable oil in a large skillet (preferably nonstick) over medium heat.

   Trim the bok choy; cut or pull off the leaves and thinly slice the stems.

2. Add the stems to the skillet and raise the heat to medium-high. Cook, stirring occasionally until they start to soften, 3 to 5 minutes.

   Cut the bok choy leaves into thin ribbons.

3. Add the leaves, a little salt, and some pepper to the skillet. Cook, stirring occasionally until the leaves wilt and the stems are nearly tender but still have some crunch, 3 or 4 minutes.

4. Meanwhile, in a large bowl combine the egg, ¾ cup flour, 1 tablespoon soy sauce, ½ teaspoon sesame oil, and ½ cup water. Whisk until smooth. It should have the consistency of thin pancake batter; if it doesn't, add more water or flour as necessary.

5. When the bok choy is done, stir it into the batter. Put a thin film of vegetable oil in the skillet if necessary.

6. When the oil is hot, pour the batter into the skillet and spread it into an even layer with a spatula. Cook, undisturbed, until the edges crisp and the batter sets, 4 to 6 minutes; adjust the heat so the pancake sizzles but doesn't burn.

   In a small bowl, whisk together 2 tablespoons soy sauce and 1 tablespoon mirin (or 1 ½ teaspoons honey mixed with 1 ½ teaspoons water).

7. Flip the pancake with a broad spatula and cook until the second side is crisp and the pancake is cooked all the way through (use a paring knife to cut into it and peek), another 4 to 6 minutes.

8. Transfer the pancake to a cutting board. Cut it into wedges and serve with the dipping sauce.

VARIATIONS

Broccoli Rabe Pancake with Ricotta Dipping Sauce
Substitute olive oil for the vegetable oil and broccoli rabe for the bok choy. Instead of adding soy sauce and sesame oil to the batter, add 1 tablespoon olive oil, 1 garlic clove, minced, and some red chile flakes. For the dipping sauce, thin some ricotta cheese with olive oil and season with lemon zest, salt, and pepper.

SIDES

Tomato Salad with Sesame and Soy 913

Cucumber Salad with Soy Sauce and Mirin 915

SPEED ◐ SERVES 4

Fried Fennel and Arugula

If anything can be deep-fried, dipped in mayonnaise, and still manage to feel light, it's fennel. Even if you slice it thinly, it stays crunchy and turns slightly sweet. Meanwhile, the lemon in the mayonnaise keeps every bite tart and bright.

Ingredients

Vegetable oil for frying

1 large fennel bulb

1 bunch fresh parsley

2 cups all-purpose flour

1 teaspoon baking powder

Salt and pepper

1 egg

¾ cup beer or sparkling water

1 lemon

⅓ cup mayonnaise

⅓ cup olive oil

1 pound arugula

2 large tomatoes

1 small red onion

2 ounces Parmesan cheese (½ cup grated)

Prep | Cook

1. Heat the oven to 200°F. Put an inch of vegetable oil in a large deep skillet over medium heat (the oil should reach 350°F).

   Trim the fennel and thinly slice crosswise to get a pile of crescent-shaped pieces (pull apart any that are stuck together). Discard any hard center pieces.

   Chop ½ cup parsley.

2. Mix 1 cup flour and 1 teaspoon baking powder in a large bowl and sprinkle with salt and pepper. Add the egg and ¾ cup beer or sparkling water and whisk until just combined; it should be the consistency of pancake batter. Stir in the parsley.

   Put 1 cup flour on a shallow plate. Line another plate with paper towels.

3. When a pinch of flour sizzles in the oil but doesn't burn (around 350°F), dredge the fennel pieces lightly in the flour, dip into the batter, and add to the oil, a few pieces at a time, until the pot is full but not overcrowded.

4. Cook in batches, adjusting the heat to maintain the temperature of the oil and turning the fries once, until they are nicely browned all over, 4 to 6 minutes per batch.

5. Drain the fries on paper towels, sprinkle with a little salt, and keep them warm in the oven while you cook the rest.

   Grate the lemon zest into a small bowl. Halve the lemon and add the juice to the bowl.

6. Add ⅓ cup mayonnaise, ⅓ cup olive oil, and a sprinkle of salt and pepper to the bowl; stir to combine.

   Trim the arugula; add it to a large serving bowl.

   Core the tomatoes and cut them into wedges; add them to the serving bowl.

   Peel and thinly slice the onion; add it to the serving bowl.

   Grate ½ cup Parmesan.

7. When you've cooked all of the fries, add them to the arugula and tomato salad, sprinkle with the Parmesan, and serve with the lemon-mayonnaise dressing.

VARIATIONS

Parmesan Fennel Fries
Omit the arugula, tomato, and onion. Add the Parmesan directly to the batter in Step 2. Omit the olive oil to make a lemon-mayonnaise dipping sauce.

Arugula and Jícama Fry Salad with Creamy Lime Sauce
Substitute jícama matchsticks for the fennel, cilantro for the parsley, cotija cheese or finely crumbled queso fresco for the Parmesan, and lime for the lemon.

NOTES

MAKE YOUR OWN
Mayonnaise 144

SIDES

Panfried Corn and Onions 933

Peas with Prosciutto and Mint 934

Simmered Squash 955

SPEED ◑ SERVES 4

Celery Root Tempura with or Without Shrimp

Root vegetables make great tempura. Sweet potato is a common choice, but celery root is even better. (Of course you can do mixed vegetables too.) If you like shrimp, throw in some of those. These are delicious dipped in wasabi-spiked soy sauce or mayonnaise with soy sauce in it.

Ingredients

Vegetable oil for deep frying

Ice cubes

3 eggs

2 ½ cups flour

2 pounds celery root

6 or 8 large peeled shrimp (optional)

Soy sauce for serving

Wasabi for serving

Prep | Cook

1. Put at least 2 inches of oil in a large deep skillet over medium heat (you want the oil to get to 350°F).
2. Combine 2 cups cold water and a cup or 2 of ice in a large bowl and let it sit for a minute.

   Separate 3 eggs; put the yolks in another large bowl and discard the whites or save for another use.
3. Measure out 2 cups of the ice water (without the ice) and add it to the yolks along with 1 ½ cups flour. Beat the mixture lightly; the batter should be lumpy and very thin.

   Trim and peel the celery root; cut it into thin disks or batons (not so big that you can't eat a piece in a few bites).

   If you're using shrimp, slice them in half lengthwise.

   Put 1 cup flour in a shallow bowl for dredging.

   Line a plate with paper towels.
4. When a pinch of flour sizzles in the oil but doesn't burn (around 350°F), begin dipping pieces of celery root and shrimp in the

flour, then in the batter. Fry in batches, adjusting the heat to maintain the temperature and turning once if necessary, until each piece is golden, 3 to 5 minutes.

Mix together some soy sauce and wasabi to taste.

5. Drain the pieces on paper towels as they finish and serve immediately with the soy and wasabi for dipping. Continue frying and eating as you go until there's nothing left.

VARIATIONS

7 Other Root Vegetables for Tempura

1. Sweet potato
2. Rutabaga
3. Daikon
4. Turnip
5. Kohlrabi
6. Butternut or any winter squash
7. Beets

NOTES

EATING AROUND THE STOVE

Eating dinner standing up in the kitchen is not something I usually recommend, but some dishes are not only fun but optimal when consumed while gathered around the stove, and tempura is one of them. So are other delicate, fried dishes that don't do too well just sitting around on a counter or in a low oven. The sooner you eat it, the better it will taste, so instead of seeing the timing as stressful, embrace the opportunity to do something different. Besides, there's nothing quite like nibbling on something crispy and fried while you're watching the next batch bubble away in the oil.

SIDES

White Rice 941

Edamame Succotash 933

Peas with Ginger 934

Stir-Fried Bok Choy 927

SPEED ◐ SERVES 4

Quick-Stewed Green Beans with Bacon

As wonderful as barely cooked, perfectly crisp-tender green beans are, sometimes you want them soul food style: soft and stewed. Bacon and beer send this over the top.

Ingredients

2 tablespoons olive oil

4 slices bacon

1 large onion

2 garlic cloves

2 pounds green beans

One 28-ounce can diced tomatoes

1 cup beer

Salt and pepper

4 scallions

Prep | Cook

1. Put 2 tablespoon olive oil in a large skillet or large pot over medium heat.

   Chop the bacon and add it to the skillet.

   Trim, peel, and chop the onion; add it to the skillet.

   Peel and mince 2 garlic cloves; add them to the skillet.

2. Cook, stirring occasionally until the bacon is crisp and the onion is golden and soft, 5 to 10 minutes.

   Trim the green beans.

3. Add the green beans to the cooked bacon and onion, along with the tomatoes with their juice, 1 cup beer, and a sprinkle of salt and pepper.

4. Turn the heat to high and let the mixture bubble vigorously, adding a splash of water if the pan gets too dry, until the tomatoes break down into a thick sauce and the green beans are very tender, 10 to 15 minutes.

   Trim and chop the scallions.

5. When the beans are ready, taste and adjust the seasoning. Garnish with the scallions and serve.

VARIATIONS

Quick-Stewed Green Beans with Sausage or Ham
Substitute chopped or sliced sausage or chopped smoked ham for the bacon.

Quick-Stewed Green Beans with Shrimp
You can omit the bacon if you like, but you can also keep it in. When the green beans are just about as tender as you want them to be, stir in 12 ounces peeled shrimp. Make sure they are coated in the sauce and simmer until they are just cooked through, 3 or 4 minutes.

Quick-Stewed Green Beans with Chicken
Add 12 ounces boneless, skinless chicken thighs, cut into large chunks, along with the bacon. Let them brown a bit with the bacon and onions, then keep it in the skillet for the entire cooking process.

NOTES

COOKING WITH BEER
Wine is called for as an ingredient much more often than beer, but cooking with beer makes just as much sense. For starters, beer is a logical option when you need a flavorful cooking liquid: It has a better flavor than store-bought stocks, and it's not unlikely that you'll have some in your fridge. And, like wine, if you don't finish a beer you can drink it or pop it into the fridge and cook with it over the next few days. (Flat beer is fair game for cooking.) Whole books cover the intricacies of beer flavors. For now, just know that lagers and wheat beers will produce a lighter, fruitier dish; porters will add richness; and stouts will impart deep, caramelized flavors.

SIDES

White Rice 941

Warm Flour Tortillas 907

Warm Buttery Bread 906

SPEED ◐ SERVES 4

Braised Cabbage, Sauerkraut, and Ham

Sauerkraut is a valuable staple of the fast pantry, and it's about as natural and healthy as a store-bought food can be. You can serve it straight from the jar, but when you treat it like an ingredient and braise it with seasonings like ham, dill, and beer, everything tastes as if you've been cooking for hours. The fresh cabbage increases the mileage you get out of the kraut, and the crunch is a wonderful counterpart.

Ingredients

2 tablespoons vegetable oil

8 ounces smoked ham steak

1 large onion

1 pound sauerkraut

1 head Savoy cabbage (about 1 ½ pounds)

1 bunch fresh dill

2 bay leaves

Salt and pepper

2 cups water or beer

Mustard for serving (optional)

Prep | Cook

1. Put 2 tablespoons vegetable oil in a large skillet or large pot over medium-high heat.

   Cut the ham into ½-inch cubes.

2. Add the ham to the skillet and cook, stirring occasionally until it's nicely browned all over, 5 to 10 minutes.

   Trim, peel, halve, and slice the onion.

   Rinse and drain the sauerkraut.

3. Add the onion to the browned ham and cook, stirring occasionally until it softens, 3 to 5 minutes.

   Core and shred the cabbage.

   Strip ⅓ cup dill leaves from the stems and chop.

4. When the onion softens, add the sauerkraut, cabbage, and dill, along with 2 bay leaves, a sprinkle of salt and pepper, and 2 cups water or beer. Bring the mixture to a boil, then adjust the heat so that it bubbles steadily.

5. Cook, stirring occasionally and adding more liquid if the mixture gets too dry, until the cabbage is tender and most of the liquid is gone, 8 to 12 minutes.

6. Remove the bay leaves from the pot, taste and adjust the seasoning, and serve with mustard on the side if you like.

VARIATIONS

Braised Cabbage, Kimchi, and Bacon
Substitute slab bacon for the ham (drain the fat after cooking), kimchi for the sauerkraut, and Napa cabbage for Savoy. Omit the dill and mustard.

NOTES

EVEN FASTER
If you've got a lot of sauerkraut to burn through, feel free to double the amount and skip the fresh cabbage. Once you add it to the pan you'll only need to simmer it with a splash of liquid until it heats through.

SIDES

Warm Buttery Bread 906

Skin-On Mashed Potatoes 961

Quinoa 945

German-Style Potato Salad 962

SPEED ◐ SERVES 4

Pan-Seared Corn and Pork

Skillet-charred corn kernels are fantastic. Combine them with crisp bits of pork shoulder and a bit of tropical flavor and you have a meal.

Ingredients

2 tablespoons olive oil

1 pound boneless pork shoulder

Salt and pepper

8 ears fresh corn

1 fresh hot green chile (like serrano)

1 lime

1 bunch fresh cilantro

Prep | Cook

1. Put 2 tablespoons olive oil in a large skillet (preferably cast iron) over low heat.

   Chop the pork shoulder into small bits (about 1/4 inch, but no need to be exact).

2. Add the pork to the skillet, sprinkle with salt and pepper, and raise the heat to medium-high. Cook, stirring once or twice until the pork is browned and crisp on at least a few sides, 5 to 10 minutes.

   Husk the corn and strip the kernels off the cobs.

   Trim and mince the chile.

3. When the pork is browned and crisp, transfer it to a bowl with a slotted spoon. Add the corn and chile to the skillet and sprinkle with salt and pepper.

4. Cook, shaking the pan occasionally and keeping the corn in as much of a single layer as possible, until the kernels are well browned on at least one side, 5 to 10 minutes.

   Halve the lime.

   Chop 1/4 cup cilantro.

5. When the corn is ready, stir the pork back into the skillet and cook until it warms through, a few minutes more. Squeeze the lime juice over the top, garnish with the cilantro, and serve.

VARIATIONS

Pan-Seared Corn and Poblanos
Instead of the pork, sauté 4 sliced poblanos until tender and lightly browned. Then stir them back into the corn in Step 5.

Pan-Seared Corn and Steak
Substitute 1 pound skirt or flank steak, cut into small cubes, for the pork. Sear the steak until browned and crisp on at least a few sides.

Pan-Seared Corn and Shrimp
Start the corn and chile in the skillet first. When they're browned in places, stir in 1 pound chopped peeled shrimp, sprinkle with a little more salt and pepper, and cook, stirring occasionally until the shrimp is just cooked through, 3 or 4 minutes.

NOTES

EVEN FASTER
Use frozen corn (about 3 cups). Since the kernels usually have some moisture clinging to the outside, they won't brown quite as well as fresh corn kernels, so pat them dry as best you can before adding them to the skillet.

SIDES

Warm Flour or Corn Tortillas 907

Jícama and Radish Salad 918

White Rice 941

Fajita Peppers and Onions 928

Peppers

Here is a list of some of the peppers you'll be turning to often, starting with fresh hot chiles and moving to dried chiles and then sweet peppers. Smaller peppers tend to be hotter than larger ones, while mature peppers (red and orange) are hotter than green ones. The seeds and white veins inside the pepper are the hottest part, so you can control the heat to a certain extent by including those or leaving them out.

Chiles can actually burn you, so wash your hands well after you work with them and try to avoid touching your eyes or other sensitive areas. If you want to quench the heat of a hot chile that you've just eaten, milk, bread, crackers, or bananas will do a much better job than thin liquids, which just slosh the heat all around your mouth.

Peppers	Description	Heat
HABANERO AND SCOTCH BONNET	Not technically the same, but you can use them interchangeably. They are walnut size, ranging in color from neon green to red, yellow, and orange. Both are incredibly hot but also slightly fruity.	Very hot
THAI	Also known as *Thai bird*. Pinky size or smaller; green when young, red when mature.	Very hot
SERRANO	Finger size or smaller, thin skinned; green when young (most common), red when mature.	Hot
JALAPEÑO	Usually sold when green but sometimes red; the flavor is slightly herbaceous.	Hot to medium
FRESNO	Like jalapeños, but with thinner flesh, usually sold when red (mature) but sometimes green.	Hot to medium

Peppers	Description	Heat
POBLANO	Like a smaller, flatter bell pepper, but with a mild heat; usually dark green but sometimes red.	Medium to mild
ANAHEIM	Long, wide, and somewhat flat; green and red.	Medium to mild
CHIPOTLE	Smoked jalapeños; the flavor is incomparable. You'll find them either canned with adobo (seasoned vinegar sauce) or dried.	Very hot to hot
CHILE DE ÁRBOL	Unlike many dried chiles, these retain a bright reddish brown to almost orange color; narrow and a couple inches long; nice heat and depth of flavor.	Very hot to hot
DRIED THAI	Dried Thai chiles (see above); small, narrow, and brownish red.	Hot
RED CHILE FLAKES	The familiar combination of dried seeds and bits from a variety of peppers, always red/yellow in color. Great for adding plain old heat.	Hot to medium
GUAJILLO	Dark reddish brown with shiny, thick skin; flat and about an inch wide and a few inches long.	Medium
ANCHO	Dried poblanos. Almost purple or black; compact, squarish; medium size. The classic in mild chili powder and an excellent mild dried chile.	Medium to mild
PASILLA	Almost black, very wrinkled, long, and narrow.	Hot to mild
BELL PEPPERS	The ubiquitous red, orange, yellow, and green peppers with crisp flesh that has a grassy, sweet flavor. Immature (green) ones are slightly bitter.	None or almost none
SHISHITO	Finger sized and pale green, they are wonderful fried or grilled whole and served with salt.	Mostly mild, but one out of every ten or so is hot

SPEED ◔ SERVES 4

Roasted Spaghetti Squash with Brown Butter and Walnuts

Silky strands of squash soaking up nutty, earthy brown butter taste like fall. It takes a little time for the squash to become tender, but once you get it roasting you can walk away until it's time to make the brown butter, which is best done at the last minute.

Ingredients

2 medium spaghetti squash

Olive oil

Salt and pepper

½ cup walnuts

2 sprigs fresh sage

4 tablespoons (½ stick) butter

Prep | Cook

1. Heat the oven to 500°F.

   Halve the squash lengthwise and scrape out the seeds.

2. Put the squash on a rimmed baking sheet, drizzle with olive oil, and sprinkle with salt and pepper. Turn them cut side down.

3. Put the squash in the oven—it doesn't have to be fully heated. Roast until the squash are tender and a knife easily pierces the skin, 30 to 40 minutes.

   Chop ½ cup walnuts.

   Strip the leaves from 2 sprigs sage and chop.

4. After the squash has cooked for 25 minutes or so, put 4 tablespoons butter in a small saucepan over medium heat. Cook, swirling occasionally until the foam subsides and the butter turns nut brown, 3 to 5 minutes. Stir in the walnuts, sage, and a sprinkle of salt and pepper. Turn off the heat.

5. When the squash are tender, carefully use a fork to scrape and loosen the strands of squash, keeping them inside the skin.

6. Put each squash half on a plate, sprinkle with salt and pepper, spoon the butter mixture over the top, and serve.

VARIATIONS

Roasted Spaghetti Squash with Rosemary-Garlic Oil and Walnuts
Instead of the butter, put ⅓ cup olive oil, some chopped fresh rosemary, and sliced garlic in a saucepan over medium-low heat. Let the oil bubble gently and infuse with the flavor of the rosemary and garlic, 5 to 10 minutes.

Roasted Spaghetti Squash with Hazelnuts and Gorgonzola
Skip the butter and chop ¾ cup hazelnuts instead of the walnuts. When the squash is tender, remove it from the oven, turn the broiler to high, and move the rack 6 inches from the heat. After loosening the squash strands in Step 5, sprinkle first with the sage, then with the nuts. Crumble 4 ounces (1 cup) Gorgonzola over all and broil until bubbly and fragrant.

SIDES

Warm Buttery Bread 906

Green Salad 911

Quinoa 945

SPEED ◔ SERVES 4

Spanish Tortilla

One of the world's great vegetarian dishes, Spanish tortilla takes the humblest of ingredients—potatoes, onion, and eggs—and turns them into a meal fit for any time of day. Don't skimp on the olive oil; it's the key to success. See the list of ingredient additions that follows for ways to spike tortilla with a little more flavor.

Ingredients

1 cup olive oil

1 medium onion

1 ½ pounds Yukon Gold potatoes

Salt and pepper

8 eggs

Prep | Cook

1. Put 1 cup olive oil in a large skillet (preferably nonstick) over medium heat.

   Trim, peel, halve, and slice the onion.

   Thinly slice the potatoes.

2. Add the onion and potatoes to the skillet and sprinkle with salt and pepper. Adjust the heat so the oil bubbles gently and cook, turning the potatoes every few minutes until you can easily pierce them with the tip of a knife (don't let the potatoes brown), about 20 minutes.

   Crack the eggs into a large bowl, sprinkle with salt and pepper, and beat.

3. When the potatoes are tender, drain them and the onion in a colander, reserving the cooking oil. Wipe out the skillet, return it to medium heat, and add 2 tablespoons of the reserved oil.

4. Add the potatoes and onion to the eggs, then pour the mixture into the skillet. Cook just until the edges are firm, a minute or 2, then reduce the heat to medium-low and cook, undisturbed, for 5 minutes.

5. Run a rubber spatula around the edges to make sure the tortilla will slide out of the skillet, then gently slide it onto a plate. Add another tablespoon of the reserved oil to the skillet.

6. Cover the tortilla with another plate and, holding the plates tightly together, invert the tortilla. Slide it back into the skillet and cook until it's just set all the way through, 3 to 5 minutes.

7. Slide the tortilla onto a plate or cutting board and serve warm or at room temperature.

VARIATIONS

8 Additions to Spanish Tortilla

Stir any of the following into the beaten eggs in Step 4:

1. ½ cup chopped pitted olives
2. ¼ cup capers
3. 1 tablespoon minced garlic or fresh chiles
4. 2 teaspoons smoked paprika
5. Up to 1 cup grated manchego cheese
6. ½ cup chopped smoked Spanish chorizo or Serrano ham
7. ½ cup chopped roasted red peppers (page 417)
8. A few chopped anchovy fillets

NOTES

EVEN FASTER

If you have a mandoline, use that to slice the potatoes very thinly. Not only will the slicing go more quickly, but the potatoes will cook a lot faster as well; start checking after 5 minutes.

SIDES

Green Salad 911

Warm Buttery Toast 906

Tomato Salad 913

Sautéed Greens with Garlic 924

SPEED SERVES 4

Vegetable Flatbread with Kale and White Bean Stew

Try chickpea flour (excellent stuff) and you'll get a variation of the Provençal favorite, *socca*. Use the baking time to make a quick kale and white bean stew, perfect for serving with or spooning over the bread.

Ingredients

8 tablespoons olive oil

4 ounces button or cremini mushrooms

1 small onion

Salt and pepper

1 cup flour (all-purpose, whole wheat, or chickpea), plus more as needed

2 or 3 sprigs fresh rosemary

1 pound kale

2 garlic cloves

2 cups cooked or canned white beans (one 15-ounce can)

½ cup chicken or vegetable stock or water

2 ounces Parmesan cheese (½ cup grated)

Prep | Cook

1. Heat the oven to 450°F. Put 2 tablespoons olive oil in a large ovenproof skillet over medium heat.
   Trim and thinly slice the mushrooms; trim, peel, halve, and thinly slice the onion.
2. Add the vegetables to the skillet, sprinkle with salt and pepper, and cook, stirring occasionally until soft, 5 to 10 minutes.
3. Put 1 cup flour in a medium bowl; sprinkle with salt and pepper, then slowly add 1 ½ cups warm water, whisking to eliminate lumps. The batter should be the consistency of thin pancake batter. Cover with a towel and let sit while the oven heats.
   Strip the rosemary leaves from 2 or 3 sprigs and chop; add them to the batter.
4. When the vegetables are soft, add them to the batter. Put 4 tablespoons olive oil in the skillet and let it heat up.
5. Pour in the batter and swirl it around to make sure the vegetables are spread out evenly. Bake until the flatbread is browned and crisp around the edges (it will release easily

from the pan when it's done and a toothpick inserted will come out clean), about 30 minutes.

6. Put 2 tablespoons olive oil in a medium skillet over medium heat.

   Trim and chop the kale. Discard any very thick stems.

7. Add the kale to the skillet, sprinkle with salt and pepper, and cook until the leaves are just wilted, 4 or 5 minutes.

   Peel and mince 2 garlic cloves.

   If you're using canned beans, rinse and drain them.

8. When the kale is just wilted, add the garlic and cook, stirring until fragrant, about a minute. Add the beans and ½ cup stock or water. Adjust the heat so the mixture simmers very gently; cover and cook, adding more liquid if the pan gets too dry, until the flatbread is done.

9. When the flatbread is browned and crisp and a toothpick comes out clean, transfer it to a cutting board and let it rest for a few minutes. Taste the kale and white bean stew and adjust the seasoning; divide it among shallow bowls. Grate ½ cup Parmesan over the top.

10. Cut the bread into wedges and serve alongside the stew.

VARIATIONS

"Pizza" with Kale and White Bean Stew

When the bread is done, top as you would a pizza—smear a thin layer of tomato sauce (like the one on page 296) on first if you like, then add a sprinkling of cheese and any other toppings you like. Broil until the cheese is bubbly and browned.

NOTES

MAKE YOUR OWN

Cooked Beans 496

Chicken Stock 213

Vegetable Stock 212

SIDES

Green Salad 911

Tomato Salad 913

Caprese Salad 922

Fennel Salad 917

Sautéed Greens with Garlic 924

SPEED ◔ SERVES 4

Cherry Tomato Cobbler

This is a classic cobbler turned savory with tomatoes, onions, and garlic. You don't get to put whipped cream on it, but you do get to shower the crisp biscuit top with Parmesan cheese.

Ingredients

Olive oil

2 tablespoons cold butter, plus some for greasing the pan

1 egg

¾ cup flour, plus more if needed

¾ cup finely ground cornmeal

¾ teaspoon baking powder

¼ teaspoon baking soda

Salt

½ cup buttermilk, plus more if needed

2 pints cherry tomatoes

2 garlic cloves

1 medium red onion

Pepper

Several sprigs fresh basil for garnish

2 ounces Parmesan cheese (½ cup grated)

Prep | Cook

1. Heat the oven to 425°F.

   Grease a medium ovenproof skillet (preferably not cast iron) with olive oil or butter.

   Cut 2 tablespoons cold butter into cubes.

   Crack the egg into a small bowl and beat it.

2. Put ¾ cup flour, ¾ cup cornmeal, ¾ teaspoon baking powder, ¼ teaspoon baking soda, and a sprinkle of salt in a food processor. Add the cubed butter and pulse until the mixture looks like coarse bread crumbs.

3. Add the beaten egg and ½ cup buttermilk and pulse a few more times until the mixture comes together in a thick, sticky batter. (If the mixture seems too wet, add more flour; if too dry, add more buttermilk.)

   Halve the cherry tomatoes and put them in a medium bowl.

   Peel and thinly slice 2 garlic cloves; add them to the bowl.

   Trim, peel, halve, and slice the red onion; add it to the bowl.

4. Drizzle the tomato mixture with some olive oil, sprinkle with salt and pepper, and toss.

5. Put the tomato mixture in the skillet; spoon dollops of the biscuit batter across the top.

6. Bake until the biscuits are golden and cooked through and the tomatoes and onions are softened, 20 to 25 minutes.

   Strip the basil leaves from several sprigs.

   Grate ½ cup Parmesan.

7. When the cobbler is done, sprinkle the Parmesan on top and tear the basil leaves over all. Drizzle with a little olive oil if you like. Serve hot, warm, or at room temperature.

VARIATIONS

Tomato Cobbler with Olives and Fennel
Substitute 1 cup pitted olives for half of the tomatoes (no need to halve them) and fennel for the red onion.

Tomato and Corn Cobbler
Especially great in summer. Fold 1 cup fresh corn kernels into the biscuit batter by hand at the end of Step 3.

NOTES

EVEN FASTER
Put the biscuit batter on a greased rimmed baking sheet and press until it's ½ inch thick. Bake until golden and cooked through, 8 to 12 minutes. Sauté the tomato, garlic, and onion mixture in a little olive oil in a large skillet until the tomatoes just start to break down. When the biscuit is done, spread the tomato mixture over the top.

SIDES

Green Salad 911

Chopped Salad 912

Fennel Salad 917

Pinzimonio 884

Refried White Beans with Rosemary 938

SPEED SERVES 4

Tortilla Lasagna

In the Pasta and Noodles chapter, egg roll wrappers stand in for lasagna noodles; here flour tortillas do the job. The tortillas on the bottom soak up the juices from the vegetables, while the ones on top become wonderfully crisp.

Ingredients

3 tablespoons vegetable oil, plus more for greasing the skillet

1 onion

3 poblano peppers

12 ounces button, cremini, or shiitake mushrooms

Salt and pepper

3 or 4 medium ripe tomatoes

2 teaspoons chili powder

1 teaspoon cumin

8 ounces Jack or cheddar cheese (2 cups grated)

Eight to ten 6-inch flour tortillas

1 bunch fresh cilantro

6 radishes

Prep | Cook

1. Heat the oven to 425°F. Put 3 tablespoons vegetable oil in a large ovenproof skillet over medium-high heat.

   Trim, peel, and chop the onion; add it to the skillet.

   Core, seed, and chop the poblanos; add them to the skillet.

   Trim and slice the mushrooms. (If you're using shiitakes, discard the stems.) Add them to the skillet.

2. Sprinkle the vegetables with salt and pepper and cook, stirring occasionally until they're soft, 8 to 12 minutes.

   Core and chop the tomatoes.

3. When the vegetables are soft, add 2 teaspoons chili powder and 1 teaspoon cumin and cook, stirring until fragrant, about a minute. Add the tomatoes and cook, stirring occasionally until they begin to break down, 3 to 5 minutes.

   Grate 2 cups Jack cheese.

4. When the tomatoes begin to break down, transfer the vegetable mixture to a bowl and wipe out the skillet. Grease the skillet with a little vegetable oil, then layer about half of the tortillas in the bottom of the skillet and curling up along the sides.

5. Top with the vegetable mixture and about half of the cheese, then layer the remaining tortillas on top, sprinkle with the rest of the cheese, and drizzle with a little more oil.

6. Cover and bake until the cheese is melted and the vegetables are bubbly, 20 minutes. Then remove the cover and continue baking until the top is crisp, about 5 minutes more.

   Chop ¼ cup cilantro.

   Chop the radishes.

7. When the top of the lasagna is crisp, remove the skillet from the oven, garnish with the cilantro and radishes, and let it cool for a few minutes before cutting into wedges and serving.

VARIATIONS

Green Tortilla Lasagna
Use spinach tortillas if you can find them and substitute 1 bunch spinach, chopped, for the mushrooms and 6 to 8 tomatillos for the tomatoes. Garnish with chopped avocado instead of or in addition to the radishes.

NOTES

MAKE YOUR OWN
Chili Powder 758

EVEN FASTER
After layering the lasagna in the skillet, just run it under the broiler until the top is bubbly and brown.

IMPROMPTU LASAGNAS AND GRATINS
If you ever find yourself staring into a refrigerator dotted with random vegetables that aren't pulling you in one direction or another, you can always fall back on the lasagna treatment. Sauté a collection of vegetables until they are all more or less tender, then layer them in an ovenproof skillet or baking dish with cheese and some stand-in for lasagna noodles, be it tortillas, sliced bread, or cooked noodles or grains. Then bake or broil until bubbly and hot. It gives those random vegetables an immediately recognizable and delicious context and is a great way to use up what's in your fridge.

SIDES

Mexican Street Corn 932

Chile-Cumin Black Beans 937

Jícama and Radish Salad 918

SPEED  SERVES 4

Skillet Spanakopita

Buttering individual sheets of phyllo dough is not fast. This skillet spanakopita preserves all the flavors and textures of the classic dish but eliminates much of the busywork.

Ingredients

10 to 12 sheets phyllo dough

3 tablespoons olive oil

4 scallions

Two 10-ounce bags spinach

Salt and pepper

2 eggs

6 ounces feta cheese (1 ½ cups crumbled)

1 teaspoon dried dill

¼ teaspoon nutmeg

4 tablespoons (½ stick) butter

Prep | Cook

Remove 10 to 12 sheets of phyllo (typically one plastic-wrapped roll) from the freezer.

1. Heat the oven to 350°F. Put 3 tablespoons olive oil in a medium ovenproof skillet over low heat.

   Trim and chop the scallions and the spinach.

2. Raise the heat to medium-high and add the scallions and spinach, a handful at a time; sprinkle with salt and pepper. Cook, stirring frequently until the spinach leaves are just wilted, 2 or 3 minutes after the last addition.

   Crack the eggs into a medium bowl and beat them.

   Crumble 1 ½ cups feta and add to the bowl. Add 1 teaspoon dill and ¼ teaspoon nutmeg.

   Melt 4 tablespoons butter in the microwave or in a small pot over medium-low heat.

   On a dry surface, cut the phyllo into thin shreds.

3. When the spinach is wilted, stir in the egg and feta mixture and sprinkle the shredded phyllo dough over the top. Drizzle the melted butter over the phyllo.

4. Bake until the phyllo is crisp, about 30 minutes. Cut the pie into wedges and serve hot, warm, or at room temperature.

VARIATIONS

Deconstructed Spinach, Tomato, and Ricotta Pie

Replace the feta with ricotta and add some grated lemon zest and red chile flakes to the mixture along with the nutmeg. Stir in ½ cup chopped tomato or ¼ cup chopped dried tomatoes when you add the egg and cheese mixture to the spinach in Step 3.

NOTES

IF YOU HAVE MORE TIME

Classic Spanakopita

Start with a 1-pound package phyllo. Brush the bottom of a 9 × 13-inch baking dish with butter. Lay 6 phyllo sheets in the pan (they should hang over the side), brushing each one with melted butter as you go. Spread half of the spinach and feta mixture over the phyllo, then top with another 4 or 5 sheets, again brushing each one with butter. Top with the remaining spinach mixture and fold in the edges to close the pie. Add some of (or all of) the remaining phyllo to close any open spaces if necessary and brush the top with butter. Score the pie into squares or triangles and bake until golden brown.

SIDES

Bulgur with Lemon and Parsley 946

Rice Pilaf 944

Chopped Salad 912

Tomato Salad with Olive Oil and Yogurt 913

SPEED ◕ SERVES 4

Cauliflower Tikka with Boiled Eggs

Tossed with a yogurt-curry marinade and roasted in a hot oven, cauliflower florets become tender and beautifully charred in places. A boiled egg is a rich and welcome addition.

Ingredients

¾ cup yogurt

2 tablespoons vegetable oil

1 tablespoon curry powder or garam masala

Salt and pepper

1 large head cauliflower (about 2 pounds)

4 eggs

Several sprigs fresh parsley for garnish

Prep | Cook

1. Heat the oven to 450°F.
2. Combine ¾ cup yogurt, 2 tablespoons vegetable oil, 1 tablespoon curry powder or garam masala, and a sprinkle of salt and pepper in a large bowl.

   Break or chop the cauliflower into small florets.
3. Add the cauliflower to the bowl and toss to coat in the yogurt mixture. Spread the cauliflower out on a rimmed baking sheet.
4. When the oven is hot, roast the cauliflower, turning occasionally until it's tender and charred in a few places, 15 to 20 minutes.
5. While the cauliflower roasts, fill a medium saucepan about two-thirds full of water and bring it to a boil.
6. When the water boils, use a spoon to lower the eggs into the gently boiling water. Adjust the heat so the water barely simmers, then cook until as runny or firm as you like (6 minutes for soft-boiled, 10 minutes for hard).

   Chop several sprigs parsley.

7. When the eggs are cooked to your liking, put the pot under cold running water for 30 to 60 seconds. If the eggs are firm, peel away the shells; if they are still runny, wait until the cauliflower is on the plates, then scoop them out of the shells onto the cauliflower.
8. When the cauliflower is tender and charred in spots, divide it among 4 plates. Top each one with an egg, sprinkle the eggs with a little salt and pepper, garnish with the parsley, and serve.

VARIATIONS

BBQ Cauliflower with Boiled Eggs
Substitute ketchup for the yogurt, 2 teaspoons chili powder and 1 teaspoon cumin for the curry powder, and 1 tablespoon Worcestershire sauce for 1 tablespoon of the vegetable oil. Garnish with chopped scallion instead of the parsley.

Chipotle Cauliflower with Boiled Eggs
Substitute mayonnaise for the yogurt and 2 chopped chipotles with some of their adobo for the curry powder. Garnish with cilantro instead of parsley.

NOTES

MAKE YOUR OWN
Curry Powder 758

EVEN FASTER
Chop the cauliflower into smaller pieces and broil them 6 inches away from the heat. Keep an eye on them, because they will start to char pretty quickly,

SIDES

White Rice 941

Crisp Seasoned Pita 908

Cucumber Raita 916

Beans and Tofu

BEANS

Beans on Toast 476

Hot and Sour Black Beans with Bok Choy 478

White Beans with Sausage, Greens, and Garlic 480

Stewed White Beans and Tomatoes with Parmesan Toast 482

Stir-Fried Curried Chickpeas with Potatoes and Carrots 486

Lemony Limas with Broccoli 488

Red Beans and Cabbage in Buttery Tomato Sauce 490

Lima Bean and Cabbage Gratin with Rye Crumbs 492

White Bean and Spinach Frittata 494

Beer-Braised Black Beans with Chicken and Corn 498

White Beans with Pork and Cabbage, Kimchi Style 500

White Bean and Ham Gratin 502

Fast Feijoada 504

Lentil and Mushroom Stew 506

Red Lentils with Toasted Cauliflower 508

Tomato-Braised Lentils and Potatoes 510

Braised Lentils with Salmon 512

BBQ Lima Beans with Collards 514

TOFU

Stir-Fried Tofu and Green Beans 516

Deep-Fried Tofu with Peanut Sauce and Scallions 520

Manchurian Tofu and Cauliflower 522

Eggs Sukiyaki 524

Smoky Tofu and Black Bean Chili 526

Roasted Tofu with Sesame Drizzle 528

Braised Tofu with Tomatoes and Broccoli 530

Beans and Tofu

More of us have come to appreciate beans, and with good reason; not only are they a low-fat, low-calorie source of quality protein and fiber, but they're versatile, they almost never go bad, they're easy on the environment, and they're cheap.

Tofu is a tougher sell for some people, mostly because they think of it as a meat replacement. They shouldn't. Tofu, essentially the simplest form of soy "cheese," is densely packed with protein, ready to eat right out of the package, and delicious once you know what to do with it. Which is minimal and which you'll learn here.

Beans offer a bit of a conundrum for the fast cook. They come in two major categories: dried, which take a long time to cook from scratch but are undeniably superior, and canned, which are as fast and convenient as it gets but not quite as good. This chapter lets you have it both ways; all of the bean recipes (barring those for lentils, which you can cook from scratch quickly) call for cooked or canned beans. If you want to use canned, go for it; if you want to cook beans from scratch to have on hand for any of these recipes, you'll find instructions on page 496.

Either way, the more you integrate beans and tofu into your cooking repertoire, the better off you'll be.

Chapter Highlights

Beans 101 What to know about beans before you start cooking. Beans (page 484).

Beans from Scratch Strategies for using homemade beans every time. Beans, Soaked and Unsoaked (page 496).

Lentil Lexicon Lentils cook from scratch in less than 45 minutes. Here are the three most popular varieties. Lentils (page 485).

Cooking Dal The greatest family of lentil dishes on the planet. Red Lentils with Toasted Cauliflower (page 508).

Tofu 101 An intro to the world of tofu. Tofu (page 518).

Boozy Beans Beer makes a superb cooking liquid, for beans, tofu, and beyond. Cooking with Beer (page 451).

Braising in Beans Beans as a medium for other foods. Braising with Beans (page 511).

Bean Gratins Run 'em under the broiler. Lima Bean and Cabbage Gratin with Rye Crumbs (page 492), White Bean and Ham Gratin (page 502).

Fast Takes on Slow Beans Two dishes that typically take hours, significantly sped up. BBQ Lima Beans with Collards (page 514), Fast Feijoada (page 504).

Thinking Outside the Can Really, there are few rules about which beans should go with which flavor profiles. White Beans with Pork and Cabbage, Kimchi Style (page 500), Hot and Sour Black Beans with Bok Choy (page 478).

Global Tofu Just because tofu comes from Asia doesn't mean we should use it only in Asian dishes. Braised Tofu with Tomatoes and Broccoli (page 530).

The Sticking Point for Tofu Why stir-frying tofu in a nonstick pan makes so much sense. Tofu and Nonstick Cookware (page 519).

SPEED SERVES 4

Beans on Toast

As a snack or for breakfast or lunch, beans on toast is hearty and comforting. With a simple salad on the side, it's suitable for dinner.

Ingredients

8 thick slices any good bread

1 tablespoon olive oil

1 garlic clove

4 cups cooked or canned navy or other white beans (two 15-ounce cans)

1 teaspoon sugar

1 tablespoon Worcestershire sauce

2 teaspoons Dijon mustard

Salt and pepper

Several sprigs chopped fresh parsley for garnish

Prep | Cook

1. Toast 8 slices bread.
2. Put 1 tablespoon olive oil in a medium saucepan over medium-low heat.

   Peel and mince 1 garlic clove.
3. Add the garlic to the pan and cook until fragrant, a minute or 2.

   If you're using canned beans, rinse and drain them.
4. When the garlic is fragrant, add the beans to the pan along with 1 teaspoon sugar, 1 tablespoon Worcestershire, 2 teaspoons Dijon, and a sprinkle of salt and pepper.
5. Raise the heat to medium and cook, stirring occasionally until the beans are warmed through and the mixture is slightly saucy, 3 to 5 minutes.

   Strip the leaves from several sprigs parsley and chop.
6. When the beans are warmed through, taste and adjust the seasoning. Spoon them onto the toast, sprinkle with the parsley, and serve.

VARIATIONS

White Beans on Toast with Parmesan and Sage
Use cannellini or other large white beans. Swap ¼ teaspoon red chile flakes for the sugar, ¼ cup grated Parmesan for the Worcestershire, and 2 teaspoons chopped fresh sage for the Dijon. Skip the parsley.

Smoky Pinto Beans on Toast
Use pinto beans. Swap 1 teaspoon cumin for the sugar, 1 teaspoon chili powder for the Worcestershire, and ½ teaspoon smoked paprika for the Dijon. Add the spices along with the garlic. Garnish with cilantro instead of parsley.

Lima Beans on Toast with Lemon and Rosemary
Use lima beans. Use the grated zest of a lemon in place of sugar and Worcestershire and 2 teaspoons chopped fresh rosemary instead of Dijon.

Edamame on Toast with Sesame Oil and Scallions
Use frozen edamame. Substitute vegetable oil for the olive oil, 1 teaspoon soy sauce for the sugar, and 2 teaspoons sesame oil for the Worcestershire. Skip the Dijon. Garnish with scallions and sesame seeds instead of parsley.

Curried Chickpeas on Toast
Use chickpeas. Replace the olive oil with butter, the sugar with 1 tablespoon curry powder, and the Worcestershire and Dijon with 1 teaspoon cumin seeds. Add the spices along with the garlic. Garnish with cilantro instead of parsley.

NOTES

MAKE YOUR OWN

Cooked Beans 496

IF YOU HAVE MORE TIME
If you prefer, cook the beans, adding a little stock or water and mashing them up as you go, until they are very soft and creamy, 20 to 30 minutes.

SIDES

Green Salad 911

Chopped Salad 912

Tomato Salad 913

SPEED SERVES 4

Hot and Sour Black Beans with Bok Choy

Black beans take on classic Chinese flavors well. (If you come across black soybeans, snap 'em up, but ordinary black turtle beans are just fine.) Here a quick marinade makes them salty, sweet, sour, and hot all at once. A toss with stir-fried bok choy is all it takes to make a meal.

Ingredients

4 cups cooked or canned black beans (two 15-ounce cans)

2 tablespoons soy sauce

1 tablespoon sesame oil

2 tablespoons rice vinegar

1 teaspoon sugar

½ teaspoon red chile flakes, or more to taste

Pepper

3 tablespoons vegetable oil

1 large head bok choy (1 ½ pounds)

2 garlic cloves

Salt

Prep | Cook

If you're using canned beans, rinse and drain them; put the beans in a medium bowl.

1. Add 2 tablespoons soy sauce, 1 tablespoon sesame oil, 2 tablespoons rice vinegar, 1 teaspoon sugar, ½ teaspoon red chile flakes, and a good amount of pepper to the beans. Toss to coat and let sit.

2. Put 3 tablespoons vegetable oil in a large skillet over medium heat.

   Trim the bok choy; cut or pull the leaves from the stems. Thinly slice the stems.

3. Add the stems to the skillet and raise the heat to medium-high. Cook, stirring occasionally until they start to soften, 3 to 5 minutes.

   Cut the leaves into wide ribbons.

   Peel and mince 2 garlic cloves.

4. Add the leaves, garlic, a little salt, and some pepper to the skillet. Cook, stirring occasionally until the leaves wilt and the stems are nearly tender but still have some crunch, 3 or 4 minutes.

5. Stir in the black beans and all of the marinade and cook, stirring to combine, just until the beans are warmed through, 3 or 4 minutes. Taste and adjust the seasoning and serve.

VARIATIONS

Lemony Chickpeas with Kale
Swap chickpeas for the black beans, a sprinkle of salt for the soy sauce, 1 tablespoon olive oil for the sesame oil, and lemon juice for the rice vinegar. Skip the sugar. Use kale instead of bok choy; since the stems are smaller, you need to cook them on their own for only 2 or 3 minutes before adding the leaves.

Hot and Sour Chicken with Bok Choy
Perfect when you have leftover roast chicken. Instead of the beans, use 1 pound plainly cooked white or dark meat chicken. Remove the bones if necessary and shred or chop it into bite-sized pieces, then add it to the marinade in Step 1.

Hot and Sour Beef with Asparagus
You can use any plainly cooked cut: roast beef, grilled steak, or even crumbled ground meat. Remove the bones if necessary and shred or chop it into bite-sized pieces, then add it to the marinade in Step 1. Instead of the bok choy, use 1 ½ pounds asparagus. Cut into 1-inch pieces, keeping any thick stems separate. Give a head start as described for the bok choy stems in Step 3, then proceed with the recipe to cook the tips and add the marinated meat.

NOTES

MAKE YOUR OWN
Cooked Beans 496

SIDES

White Rice 941

Sesame Noodles 949

Scallion Pancakes 940

SPEED ◐ SERVES 4

White Beans with Sausage, Greens, and Garlic

White beans, greens, and Italian sausage make one of the holy trinities of the kitchen. Cook this quickly if you want the beans to remain intact or long and slow if you've got the time and want the beans to fall apart a bit. See the Notes on the opposite page.

Ingredients

2 tablespoons olive oil

12 ounces sweet or hot Italian sausage

1 ½ pounds spinach, kale, collards, escarole, chard, or broccoli rabe

2 garlic cloves

4 cups cooked or canned white beans (two 15-ounce cans)

½ cup chicken stock or water

4 ounces Parmesan cheese (1 cup grated)

Salt and pepper

Prep | Cook

1. Put 2 tablespoons olive oil in a large skillet or large pot over medium-high heat.

   Cut the sausage into slices.

2. Add the sausage to the skillet and cook, stirring occasionally until lightly browned, 5 or 6 minutes.

   Trim and chop the greens, keeping any thick stems separate (discard thick spinach stems).

3. When the sausage is lightly browned, add any chopped stems to the skillet and cook until they begin to soften, 3 or 4 minutes.

   Peel and mince 2 garlic cloves.

   If you're using canned beans, rinse and drain them.

4. When the stems begin to soften, add the leaves, a handful at a time if necessary to fit them in, along with the garlic, beans, and ½ cup chicken stock or water.

5. Cook, stirring occasionally until the beans are warmed through and the greens are just wilted—3 or 4 minutes for spinach; 4 or 5 minutes for escarole, chard, and broccoli rabe; 5 or 6 minutes for kale and collards.

   Grate 1 cup Parmesan.

6. Add the Parmesan to the skillet and stir. Season with salt and pepper. Taste and adjust the seasoning and serve.

VARIATIONS

White Beans with Bacon, Greens, and Garlic
Substitute chopped bacon for the sausage. Cook until crisp and drain the excess fat before adding the stems.

Black Beans with Chorizo, Greens, and Garlic
Substitute fresh Mexican-style chorizo for the Italian sausage and black beans for white. Omit the Parmesan.

Kidney Beans with Ham, Greens, and Garlic
Substitute chopped smoked ham for the Italian sausage and kidney beans for the white beans. Omit the Parmesan and add a dash of hot sauce instead if you like.

NOTES

MAKE YOUR OWN

Cooked Beans 496

Chicken Stock 213

IF YOU HAVE MORE TIME
If you want a soft stewy mixture, let the beans and greens bubble gently, adding more stock or water if the pan gets too dry, until the greens are very tender and the beans begin to break apart, up to 45 minutes.

SIDES

Garlic Bread 906

Bruschetta 909

Caprese Salad 922

SPEED ◑ SERVES 4

Stewed White Beans and Tomatoes with Parmesan Toast

A warm, cozy pot of stewed beans and tomatoes cries out for something crusty and crunchy to dip into it. Thick slices of Parmesan-topped toast is the ultimate accompaniment.

Ingredients

3 tablespoons olive oil, plus more for drizzling

1 medium onion

3 garlic cloves

3 or 4 medium ripe tomatoes

Salt and pepper

4 cups cooked or canned white beans

4 thick slices any rustic bread

½ cup white wine

2 cups chicken or vegetable stock or water, plus more if needed

4 ounces Parmesan cheese (1 cup grated)

Several sprigs fresh basil

Prep | Cook

1. Put 3 tablespoons olive oil in a large skillet or large pot over medium-high heat.

   Trim, peel, and chop the onion.

   Peel and mince 3 garlic cloves.

2. Add the onion and garlic to the skillet and cook, stirring occasionally until the onion softens, 3 to 5 minutes.

   Core and chop the tomatoes.

3. When the onion softens, add the tomatoes and sprinkle with salt and pepper. Cook, stirring occasionally until the tomatoes begin to soften, about 5 minutes.

4. Turn the broiler to high; put the rack 4 inches from the heat.

   If you're using canned beans, rinse and drain them.

   Put 4 slices bread on a rimmed baking sheet.

5. When the tomatoes begin to soften, add ½ cup white wine and let it bubble until evaporated. Add 2 cups stock or water, the beans, and a sprinkle of salt and pepper. Bring the mixture to a boil, then adjust the heat so it bubbles gently but steadily.

6. Cook, stirring occasionally and adding more liquid if the mixture gets too dry, until the tomatoes break down and the beans soften, 10 to 15 minutes.

   Grate 1 cup Parmesan.

   Strip the basil leaves from several sprigs and chop.

7. Drizzle both sides of the bread with a little olive oil. Broil until the tops are golden, a minute or 2. Remove, flip the bread, and sprinkle the untoasted sides with the Parmesan. Broil until the cheese is bubbly and brown, another minute or 2.

8. When the tomatoes are ready, taste and adjust the seasoning. Divide among 4 bowls, scatter the basil over the top, drizzle with olive oil, and serve with the Parmesan toast for dipping.

VARIATIONS

Stewed White Beans and Kale with Parmesan Toast

Substitute 1 pound chopped kale (preferably lacinato) for the tomatoes. After adding it to the skillet in Step 3, cook until it wilts down a bit, 5 to 10 minutes, then proceed with the recipe.

Stewed Pinto Beans and Tomatoes with Cheesy Tortillas

Substitute vegetable oil for olive oil, pinto beans for the white beans, and beer for the white wine. Instead of bread, use four 6-inch flour or corn tortillas and top them with cheddar or Jack instead of Parmesan. Garnish with cilantro instead of basil.

NOTES

MAKE YOUR OWN

Cooked Beans 496

Chicken Stock 213

Vegetable Stock 212

EVEN FASTER

After the onion softens, add the wine and let it bubble until evaporated, then add the tomatoes, beans, and stock. Simmer together just until you've made the Parmesan toast.

SIDES

Green Salad 911

Sautéed Greens with Garlic 924

Brussels Sprouts with Sausage 958

Beans

Beans are convenient and delicious, the perfect food to keep on hand to toss into salads and stir-fries, stews and gratins, and many other dishes. Here's all you need to know to become a bean lover.

Dried vs. Canned

Other than those made with lentils, none of the recipes in this chapter calls for cooking dried beans from scratch. That's because without a pressure cooker you can't cook a dried bean in less than 45 minutes, which is the upper time limit for recipes in this book. (If you have a pressure cooker, you can use it to cook beans from scratch in less than half an hour.) For speed, I use dried beans cooked ahead of time or canned beans. Canned beans are incredibly useful, and it's worth keeping them stocked in your pantry, but like anything else that isn't home-cooked, there are some disadvantages:

- You can't control their texture: The texture of canned beans is what it is, and it tends to be on the soft side.
- The flavor of canned beans is never as deep as that of home-cooked.
- The liquid from beans you cook yourself is usually delicious and usable; the viscous liquid that comes in the can is something you want to rinse off.
- Only the most common bean varieties are canned.
- Canned beans are more expensive.

Freezing Beans

Since frozen beans keep perfectly, the best way to avoid canned beans is to cook large batches of beans (see Beans, Soaked and Unsoaked, page 496) and freeze whatever you don't use in the next day or two. (You can refrigerate cooked beans for up to 5 days.) To freeze cooked beans, let them cool in their liquid, then put them, liquid and all, in zipper bags or plastic containers with tight-fitting lids. You can freeze them like this for up to 6 months. To thaw frozen beans, either leave them in the refrigerator for about a day, defrost them in the microwave, or put the frozen block in a covered pan with a little water over medium-low heat. (Don't stir too much or the beans will break apart.)

Storing Dried Beans

Dried beans don't go bad, but they do get old and stale, and older beans take longer to soften. While you have no way of knowing when beans were dried, broken or discolored beans and beans with imperfect skins are clues that they might not be the freshest. Try to use all the beans you've accumulated throughout the year over the summer, then buy new ones in the fall. That ensures that you're not keeping beans in the pantry for more than a year and gives you a chance of getting beans from the latest crop.

Lentils

Dried lentils are essential ingredients in the fast kitchen—they cook from scratch in as little as 15 minutes. These are the varieties you're likely to cook with the most.

Type of Lentil	Description
BROWN LENTILS	The most ubiquitous variety of lentil, ranging from khaki colored to dark brown and black, with a mild, earthy flavor. They cook in 20 to 30 minutes and tend to hold their shape during cooking.
RED LENTILS	They should really be called *orange lentils* because few are actually red. They are usually peeled and split, which means they cook very quickly, in about 15 minutes. Even if you don't overcook them, they get very soft and fall apart when tender, so they're an excellent choice for dals, soups, or any dish you want to thicken a bit as the lentils break apart. There are yellow lentils as well, which you can use in place of red; split peas are acceptable substitutes.
GREEN LENTILS	Green lentils range from dark green to greenish brown and have a very deep, full flavor. They take the longest to cook of all the lentils (could be 45 minutes) and hold their shape perfectly, which makes them ideal for lentil salads. The best variety are French green lentils, called *Puy* or *lentilles du Puy*.

Store-Bought Frozen Beans

Some stores sell frozen cooked beans, and that's another excellent option. The beans you see most often frozen are lima beans, butter beans, black-eyed peas, and edamame; white, black, red, and pink beans are sometimes frozen as well. Thaw them in the microwave before incorporating them into the dish or just let the heat of whatever you're cooking warm the beans right in the pan. You can use frozen lima beans and frozen shelled edamame interchangeably.

SPEED ◑ SERVES 4

Stir-Fried Curried Chickpeas with Potatoes and Carrots

Crisp spiced chickpeas are one of the great snack foods of all time, too good to confine to nibbling. Here they're added to a grated-root-vegetable stir-fry, which benefits greatly from the extra crunch and seasoning.

Ingredients

4 tablespoons vegetable oil

4 cups cooked or canned chickpeas (two 15-ounce cans)

1 ½ pounds russet or Yukon Gold potatoes

1 pound carrots

2 garlic cloves

1 inch fresh ginger

1 tablespoon curry powder

Salt and pepper

1 bunch fresh cilantro

¼ cup coconut milk

Prep | Cook

1. Put 2 tablespoons vegetable oil in a large skillet over medium-high heat.

   If you're using canned chickpeas, rinse and drain them.

2. Add the chickpeas to the skillet and cook, stirring or shaking the pan occasionally until they are golden and crisp, 10 to 15 minutes.

   Scrub the potatoes; trim and peel the carrots. Shred both in a food processor with a grating disk or by hand.

   Peel 2 garlic cloves and 1 inch fresh ginger; mince them together.

3. When the chickpeas are golden and crisp, add 1 tablespoon curry powder and a sprinkle of salt and pepper. Cook, stirring until the curry powder is fragrant, a minute or 2. Transfer the chickpeas to a plate.

4. Add 2 tablespoons vegetable oil to the skillet along with the garlic and ginger. Cook, stirring until they're fragrant, 30 seconds to a minute.

5. Add the potatoes and carrots, stirring them around to coat in whatever curry powder was left behind. Cook, stirring occasionally until the vegetables are tender and lightly browned, 8 to 12 minutes. Chop ½ cup cilantro.

6. When the vegetables are tender and lightly browned, sprinkle with salt and pepper. Stir in ¼ cup coconut milk, scraping any browned bits off the bottom of the skillet.

7. Stir in the cilantro and the chickpeas, taste and adjust the seasoning, and serve.

VARIATIONS

Spicy Stir-Fried Chickpeas with Sweet Potatoes
Swap 2 ½ pounds sweet potatoes for the potatoes and carrots, 1 minced fresh hot green chile for the ginger, and 2 teaspoons chili powder and ½ teaspoon cayenne for the curry powder. Omit the coconut milk.

Stir-Fried Curried Chickpeas with Chicken and Carrots
Skip the potatoes. Before adding the garlic and ginger in Step 4, cook 12 ounces chopped boneless, skinless chicken thighs until they lose their pink color and are cooked through, 5 or 6 minutes. Add them to the chickpeas and stir both of them back into the skillet in Step 7.

NOTES

MAKE YOUR OWN
Cooked Beans 496

Curry Powder 758

EVEN FASTER
Cook the garlic, ginger, and vegetables in another skillet while the chickpeas are crisping.

SIDES

White Rice 941

Cucumber Raita 916

Crisp Seasoned Pita 908

SPEED  SERVES 4

Lemony Limas with Broccoli

These are not the soggy, gray canned limas of myth. Frozen limas are bright, convenient, and delicious and even more so with a squeeze of lemon and a savory broccoli stew. Add a sprinkle of grated Parmesan or crumbled feta cheese if you like.

Ingredients

2 tablespoons butter

2 large shallots

1 medium head broccoli (1 to 1 ½ pounds)

½ cup white wine

4 cups frozen lima beans

1 cup chicken or vegetable stock or water

Salt and pepper

1 lemon

Several sprigs fresh parsley

Prep | Cook

1. Put 2 tablespoons butter in a large skillet or large pot over medium heat.

   Trim, peel, and chop 2 shallots.

2. Add the shallots to the skillet and cook, stirring occasionally until they soften, 2 or 3 minutes.

   Trim and break or chop the broccoli into small florets.

3. When the shallots soften, add ½ cup white wine and let it bubble until mostly evaporated. Add the broccoli, 4 cups lima beans, and 1 cup stock or water and sprinkle with salt and pepper.

4. Turn the heat to high, bring to a boil, then bring the heat back to medium. Cover and cook, stirring occasionally until the broccoli is just tender, 5 to 10 minutes.

   Grate the zest from the lemon, then cut it in half.

   Strip the leaves from several sprigs parsley and chop.

5. When the broccoli is just tender, squeeze in the lemon juice and stir in the zest and the parsley. Taste and adjust the seasoning and serve hot or at room temperature.

VARIATIONS

Soy-Lemon Edamame and Asparagus

Substitute 1 large bunch asparagus, cut into 2-inch pieces, for the broccoli, frozen edamame for the lima beans, and ¼ cup soy sauce for the white wine. The asparagus will take less time to become tender than the broccoli, so keep an eye on it. Use cilantro or scallions instead of the parsley.

Limy Limas and Poblanos

Substitute a small red onion for the shallots, 3 or 4 poblano peppers, cut into strips, for the broccoli, and beer for the wine. The poblanos will take less time to become tender than the broccoli, but it's okay if they get soft. Swap a lime or 2 for the lemon and cilantro for the parsley. If you have any queso fresco, crumble some on at the end.

Lemony Limas with Spinach and Eggs

Substitute 1 pound spinach for the broccoli. In Step 4, cook, stirring occasionally, until the leaves just start to wilt. Then adjust the heat so the liquid bubbles gently; make 4 indentations in the vegetable mixture and crack an egg into each. Cover and cook until the vegetables are hot and the eggs set to your liking, 3 to 10 minutes.

NOTES

MAKE YOUR OWN

Chicken Stock 213

Vegetable Stock 212

SIDES

Grape Salad with Mint 913

Caprese Salad 922

Quick Brown Rice 941

SPEED ◐ SERVES 4

Red Beans and Cabbage in Buttery Tomato Sauce

Here you get the soft, silky texture of braised cabbage, beans, and tomatoes, the richness of butter, and the sharp bite of ginger. This has the feeling of a long-cooked dish but takes only as long as the tomatoes need to break down and the cabbage needs to become tender.

Ingredients

4 tablespoons (½ stick) butter

2 inches fresh ginger

One 28-ounce can diced tomatoes

1 small head Savoy or green cabbage (1 pound)

4 cups cooked or canned red beans (two 15-ounce cans)

½ cup chicken or vegetable stock or water, plus more if needed

Salt and pepper

Prep | Cook

1. Put 2 tablespoons butter in a large pot over medium heat.
   Peel and mince 2 inches fresh ginger.
2. Add the ginger to the skillet and cook, stirring occasionally until fragrant, a minute or 2.
3. Add the tomatoes and turn the heat to medium-high.
   Trim, core, quarter, and chop the cabbage; add it to the pot as you go.
   If you're using canned beans, rinse and drain them; add the beans to the pot.
4. Add ½ cup stock or water, sprinkle the whole mixture with salt and pepper, and stir to combine.
5. Reduce the heat to medium and cook, stirring occasionally and adding more liquid if the mixture gets too dry, until the tomatoes break down, the cabbage becomes tender, and the beans get creamy, 10 to 15 minutes.
6. Stir in 2 tablespoons butter, taste and adjust the seasoning, and serve immediately.

VARIATIONS

Pintos and Peppers in Buttery Tomato Sauce
Substitute 2 garlic cloves and 1 fresh hot green chile, both minced, for the ginger, 4 sliced bell peppers for the cabbage, and pinto beans for the red beans.

Red Beans and Okra in Buttery Tomato Sauce
Swap 1 pound okra, cut into thin rounds, for the cabbage. If you don't like the slimy texture of okra, you can add a little more liquid to the pot and simmer the mixture, partially covered, until the okra more or less melts into the sauce, about an hour.

Red Beans and Cabbage in Coconutty Tomato Sauce
Use coconut milk instead of stock or water. Omit the 2 tablespoons butter at the end.

NOTES

MAKE YOUR OWN

Cooked Beans 496

Chicken Stock 213

Vegetable Stock 212

SIDES

White Rice 941

Warm Buttery Bread 906

Celery Salad 917

SPEED ◐ SERVES 4

Lima Bean and Cabbage Gratin with Rye Crumbs

A lighter and even vegetarian ode to the Reuben sandwich. While lima beans are certainly not corned beef, they do offer satisfying heft, and you can eat this dish often, without guilt. (If you don't mind guilt, see the Notes.)

Ingredients

4 tablespoons (½ stick) butter

1 small head red cabbage (1 pound)

¼ cup red wine vinegar

Salt and pepper

2 slices rye bread (a little stale is fine)

4 ounces Gruyère cheese (1 cup grated)

4 cups frozen lima beans

1 tablespoon Dijon mustard

Prep | Cook

1. Turn the broiler to high; put the rack 6 inches from the heat. Put 4 tablespoons butter in a large ovenproof skillet over low heat.

   Trim, core, quarter, and chop the cabbage.

2. Turn the heat under the skillet to medium-high and add the cabbage to the skillet along with ¼ cup red wine vinegar and a sprinkle of salt and pepper. Cook, stirring occasionally until the cabbage is softened, 8 to 10 minutes.

   Tear 2 slices rye bread into pieces, transfer to a food processor, and pulse into coarse crumbs.

   Grate 1 cup Gruyère.

3. When the cabbage softens, stir in 4 cups lima beans and 1 tablespoon Dijon. Cook, stirring occasionally until the lima beans are warmed through, 2 or 3 minutes. Taste and adjust the seasoning.

4. Spread the mixture out evenly in the skillet, sprinkle it with the Gruyère, and scatter the bread crumbs over the top.

5. Broil until the cheese is bubbly and brown and the bread crumbs are crisp. Let it cool for a minute or 2, then serve.

VARIATIONS

Black Bean and Cabbage Gratin with Tortilla Crumbs and Jack

Substitute olive oil for the butter, green cabbage for red, and the juice of 2 limes for the red wine vinegar. Instead of pulsing rye bread in the food processor, roughly crumble tortilla chips with your hands (enough to make ½ to ¾ cup). Swap Jack cheese for the Gruyère, rinsed and drained black beans for the lima beans, and 1 or 2 chopped chipotles in adobo for the Dijon. Garnish with chopped fresh cilantro or scallions.

NOTES

EVEN FASTER

Instead of making the rye crumbs as described in Step 2, use Bread Crumbs (page 71) you've already made.

IF YOU HAVE MORE TIME

Corned Beef Cabbage Gratin with Lima Beans

Before adding the cabbage to the skillet, sauté about 1 cup chopped corned beef or pastrami until the edges start to get crisp, 5 to 10 minutes. Remove it with a slotted spoon, then add the cabbage and proceed. Either stir the meat back in along with the beans and Dijon in Step 3 or, for extra crunch, sprinkle it on top along with the bread crumbs. Or do a little of each.

SIDES

Warm Buttery Bread 906

Broiled Cherry Tomatoes 931

Garlicky Mushrooms 956

Quinoa 945

SPEED ◐ SERVES 4

White Bean and Spinach Frittata

Frittata is as versatile a dish as there is: You put nearly anything in it—including leftovers—and it's appropriate to eat at any time of day. Beans are an uncommon addition but contribute wonderful heartiness and a nice contrast to the spinach.

Ingredients

2 tablespoons olive oil

1 small onion

1 pound spinach

Salt and pepper

6 eggs

4 ounces Parmesan cheese (1 cup grated)

2 cups cooked or canned white beans (one 15-ounce can)

Several sprigs fresh basil

Prep | Cook

1. Put 2 tablespoons olive oil in a large ovenproof skillet over medium heat.

   Trim, peel, and chop the onion.

2. Add the onion to the skillet and cook, stirring occasionally until it's softened, 3 to 5 minutes.

   Trim and chop the spinach, discarding any thick stems.

3. Raise the heat to medium-high. Add the spinach to the softened onion, a handful at a time, and sprinkle with salt and pepper. Stir and cook until the spinach is just wilted and the liquid has evaporated, 5 to 10 minutes.

   Crack the eggs into a medium bowl.

   Grate 1 cup Parmesan and add it; sprinkle with salt and pepper and beat the mixture.

   If you're using canned beans, rinse and drain them.

   Strip the basil leaves from several sprigs and chop.

4. When the spinach is wilted and the liquid has evaporated, add the beans, basil, and a sprinkle of salt and pepper. Stir to combine and turn the heat to low.

5. Pour the eggs into the skillet, tilting it or using a spoon to distribute them evenly. Cook until the eggs are barely set, 5 to 10 minutes.

6. Turn the broiler to high; put the rack 4 inches from the heat.

7. When the eggs are barely set, transfer the skillet to the broiler and cook just until the top turns golden, a minute or 2.

8. Cut the frittata into wedges and serve, hot, warm, or at room temperature.

VARIATIONS

Pinto Bean and Poblano Frittata
Substitute red onion for yellow and 4 poblano peppers, chopped, for the spinach. Cook the onions and poblanos together until both are soft. Use grated Oaxaca cheese (or any melting cheese—Jack would work well) instead of the Parmesan, pinto beans instead of the white beans, and cilantro instead of the basil.

Pea and Arugula Frittata
Shouts of spring. Substitute arugula for the spinach and fresh or frozen peas for the white beans. Sauté the arugula leaves until they are barely wilted, a couple of minutes. Parmesan is perfect here, but you can beat 4 ounces soft goat cheese into the eggs instead. Use mint or chives instead of the basil.

NOTES

MAKE YOUR OWN

Cooked Beans 496

SIDES

Green Salad 911

Tomato Salad 913

Fennel Salad with Olives 917

Beans, Soaked and Unsoaked

The value of soaking beans is arguable, but most experienced cooks now consider it optional. The benefit of soaking is that you don't have to check on the beans as often while they're cooking or add as much water; the downside, of course, is that you have to think a little farther ahead. Cooking time, ultimately, is not much different. Here, then, are two methods for cooking beans, which take the same amount of time and result in the same taste and texture. No matter which method you choose, see the lists that follow for ideas about flavoring the beans either during or after cooking.

No-Soak Beans

1 Wash and Pick Over

Rinse beans, lentils, or split peas (a pound is a nice amount, since they're packaged that way) and discard any broken bits or discolored beans.

2 Combine Beans and Water

Put them in a large pot and cover with cold water by 2 or 3 inches. Bring to a boil, then reduce the heat so the liquid bubbles gently.

3 Simmer Until Tender

Partially cover the pot and cook, stirring only once in a while and adding water if the liquid gets low before the beans are done; check for doneness every 15 minutes or so. When the beans start to get tender, sprinkle with salt and pepper and continue cooking until the beans are done the way you like them, a total of 20 to 45 minutes for lentils and up to an hour or more for other beans. Pour off any extra water if the beans are done before the water has evaporated. Taste and adjust the seasoning and use immediately or store (see page 484 for storing instructions).

Quick-Soaked Beans

Use this method for any beans except for lentils and split peas or split beans.

1 Boil—Then Soak—the Beans

Put the beans in a large pot and cover with cold water by 2 or 3 inches. Bring to a boil and let it boil for about 2 minutes. Cover the pot, turn off the heat, and let the beans soak for 2 hours.

2 Start Cooking

After 2 hours, taste a bean. If it's tender (it won't yet be fully done), sprinkle with salt and pepper and make sure the beans are covered with about an inch of water. If the beans are still hard, don't add any salt; cover with about 2 inches of water. Bring to a boil, then adjust the heat so the liquid bubbles gently. Partially cover the pot and cook, stirring only once in a while and adding water if the pot gets too dry.

3 Simmer Until Tender

Check for doneness every 15 minutes or so. If you haven't added salt and pepper yet, add them when the beans start to get tender. Continue cooking until the beans are done the way you like them. Taste and adjust the seasoning and use immediately or store (see page 484 for storing instructions).

VARIATIONS

5 Ways to Flavor Beans as They Cook

Add any of the following ingredients to the pot, alone or in combination, when you start cooking the beans:

1. **Herbs or spices:** A bay leaf, a couple of cloves, some peppercorns, thyme sprigs, parsley leaves and/or stems, chili powder (page 758), or other herbs and spices
2. **Aromatics:** An unpeeled onion, a carrot, a celery stalk, and/or 3 or 4 cloves of garlic
3. **Stock:** Chicken, beef, or vegetable stock (page 212) in place of all or part of the water
4. **Other beverages:** A cup or so of beer or wine or, if you feel like experimenting, coffee, tea, or juice
5. **Smoked meat:** Ham hock, pork chop, beef bone, bacon, or sausage, fished out after cooking, the meat chopped and stirred back into the beans

8 Ways to Flavor Cooked Beans

Add any of the following ingredients to cooked beans (the quantities are for 4 servings of beans):

1. 2 tablespoons butter, olive oil, or sesame oil
2. ½ cup chopped fresh parsley, cilantro, mint, or any basil leaves
3. 2 tablespoons chopped fresh rosemary, tarragon, oregano, thyme, or sage leaves
4. Up to ½ cup any vinaigrette (page 70)
5. A tablespoon or so of curry powder or chili powder (page 758)
6. Soy, Worcestershire, or Tabasco sauce to taste
7. 1 or 2 tablespoons miso thinned with hot bean-cooking liquid and warmed gently with the beans
8. Chopped onion or other aromatic vegetables added during reheating

SPEED ◐ SERVES 4

Beer-Braised Black Beans with Chicken and Corn

Toasting tomato paste, garlic, and spices along with the chicken and onions sets the stage for the addition of beer, which pulls all those deep flavors together into a saucy glaze.

Ingredients

2 tablespoons olive oil

6 boneless, skinless chicken thighs (about 1 pound)

1 onion

2 garlic cloves

4 cups cooked or canned black beans (two 15-ounce cans)

1 tablespoon tomato paste

1 teaspoon chili powder

1 teaspoon cumin

1 cup beer

3 cups frozen corn

Salt and pepper

1 bunch fresh cilantro

4 ounces queso fresco (1 cup crumbled)

Prep | Cook

1. Put 2 tablespoons olive oil in a large skillet over medium-high heat.

   Cut the chicken into ½-inch chunks.

2. When the oil is hot, add the chicken to the skillet and cook, undisturbed, until the pieces brown and release easily, 2 or 3 minutes. Then cook, stirring occasionally until the meat is no longer pink, 2 or 3 minutes longer.

   Trim, peel, and chop the onion.

   Peel and mince 2 garlic cloves.

3. Add the onion to the skillet and cook, stirring occasionally until it softens, 2 or 3 minutes.

   If you're using canned beans, rinse and drain them.

4. Add the garlic, 1 tablespoon tomato paste, 1 teaspoon chili powder, and 1 teaspoon cumin to the skillet. Cook, stirring until the mixture darkens and becomes fragrant, 1 or 2 minutes.

5. Add 1 cup beer, stirring to scrape up any browned bits. Add the beans, 3 cups corn, and a sprinkle of salt and pepper.

6. Adjust the heat so the mixture simmers gently but steadily and cook until the liquid reduces to a glaze, 3 or 4 minutes.

   Chop ½ cup cilantro.

7. When the liquid has reduced to a glaze, taste and adjust the seasoning. Stir in the cilantro and divide among 4 bowls. Sprinkle with the queso fresco and serve.

VARIATIONS

Beer-Braised Black Beans and Corn with Chorizo
Cook 4 to 8 ounces smoked Spanish chorizo, cut into cubes or small pieces, over medium heat until crisp. Scoop out the chorizo with a slotted spoon and use the fat to cook the onion. Proceed with the recipe, stirring in the cooked chorizo at the last minute.

Beer-Braised Pinto Beans with Chiles and Sour Cream
Use pinto beans instead of black beans. Cook 2 chopped poblano chiles with the onion (add some seeded chopped jalapeños as well if you want more heat). Add the juice of a lime along with the beer and top each serving with a dollop of sour cream.

Wine-Braised White Beans with Cherry Tomatoes and Parmesan
Substitute white beans for the black beans, white wine for the beer, cherry tomatoes for the corn, and basil for the cilantro. Skip the chili powder and cumin. Garnish with freshly grated Parmesan and lots of olive oil.

NOTES

MAKE YOUR OWN

Cooked Beans 496

Chili Powder 758

EVEN FASTER
Instead of cooking chicken as described in Step 2, cut 1 cup Whole Roast Chicken (page 688) into chunks and add in Step 5.

IF YOU HAVE MORE TIME
Cut fresh corn kernels off the cob instead of using frozen.

SIDES

Coleslaw 923

White Rice 941

Warm Tortillas 907

Jícama and Radish Salad 918

SPEED ◐ SERVES 4

White Beans with Pork and Cabbage, Kimchi Style

An impromptu skillet kimchi is bolstered by stir-fried pork and white beans and spreads its salty-sweet-spicy flavors all across the dish. The Korean red pepper paste gochujang is available at many Asian markets, but if you can't find it, red chile flakes, or even a few shakes of Sriracha to taste, will add the heat you're looking for.

Ingredients

2 tablespoons vegetable oil

8 ounces boneless pork shoulder

4 garlic cloves

1 inch fresh ginger

Salt and peper

1 small head Savoy or Napa cabbage (1 ½ pounds)

3 tablespoons gochujang or 1 tablespoon red chile flakes

3 tablespoons soy sauce

2 tablespoons sugar

2 cups cooked or canned white beans (one 15-ounce can)

4 scallions

Prep | Cook

1. Put 2 tablespoons vegetable oil in a large skillet or large pot over low heat.

   Cut the pork into thin slices or strips.

   Peel 4 garlic cloves and 1 inch ginger; mince them together.

2. Raise the heat under the skillet to high. When the oil is hot but not quite smoking, add the pork and sprinkle with salt and pepper. Cook undisturbed until the pieces release from the pan, about 1 minute. Then cook, stirring occasionally until browned, 3 to 5 minutes.

   Trim, core, quarter, and roughly chop the cabbage.

3. When the pork is browned, add the garlic and ginger and cook, stirring until fragrant, 30 seconds to a minute. Add the cabbage to the skillet, a handful at a time if necessary to fit it in. Reduce the heat to medium.

4. Once all the cabbage is added, stir in 3 tablespoons gochujang or 1 tablespoon red chile flakes, 3 tablespoons soy sauce, and 2 tablespoons sugar. Cook, tossing occasionally until the cabbage is softened and coated in the sauce, 5 or 6 minutes.

   If you're using canned beans, rinse and drain them.

   Trim and chop the scallions.

5. When the cabbage is softened, stir in the beans and cook just until warmed through, 2 or 3 minutes. Taste and adjust the seasoning, garnish with the scallions, and serve.

VARIATIONS

Edamame with Pork, Cabbage, and Miso
Substitute miso for the gochujang and frozen edamame for the white beans.

Edamame with Chicken and Cabbage
Use boneless chicken thighs instead of the pork in the main recipe (or the first variation).

NOTES

MAKE YOUR OWN
Cooked Beans 496

EVEN FASTER
Omit the garlic and ginger. Instead of using the cabbage and the sauce ingredients, just stir in 2 cups store-bought kimchi in Step 5.

IF YOU HAVE MORE TIME
If you prefer a softer cabbage, cook it longer in Step 4 until it loses most of its crunch.

SIDES

White Rice 941

Sesame Noodles 949

Scallion Pancakes 940

Cucumber Salad 915

SPEED ◐ SERVES 4

White Bean and Ham Gratin

A hurry-up cassoulet: Combine beans with meat, top with crispy bread crumbs, and eat. Pork and white beans are the classic combination, but the variations are also terrific.

Ingredients

¼ cup olive oil, plus more for drizzling

1 medium red onion

2 garlic cloves

8 ounces smoked ham

4 cups cooked or canned white beans (two 15-ounce cans)

1 lemon

¼ cup white wine or water

Salt and pepper

½ cup bread crumbs

Several sprigs fresh basil for garnish

Prep | Cook

1. Turn the broiler to high; put the rack 6 inches from the heat. Put ¼ cup olive oil in a large ovenproof skillet over medium-high heat.

   Trim, peel, halve, and slice the onion.

   Peel and mince 2 garlic cloves.

2. Add the onion and garlic to the skillet and cook, stirring occasionally until the onion softens, 3 to 5 minutes.

   Chop the ham.

   If you're using canned beans, rinse and drain them.

   Grate the zest from the lemon; refrigerate the fruit for another use.

3. When the onion softens, stir in the ham, beans, lemon zest, ¼ cup white wine or water, and a sprinkle of salt and pepper.

4. Spread the mixture out evenly in the skillet, scatter the bread crumbs over the top, and drizzle with a little more olive oil.

5. Broil until the beans are hot and bubbly and the bread crumbs are crisp, 3 to 5 minutes.

   Strip the basil leaves from several sprigs and chop.

6. When the beans are bubbly and the bread crumbs are crisp, garnish with the basil, let cool for a minute or 2, and serve.

VARIATIONS

White Bean and Smoked Fish Gratin
Substitute 8 ounces smoked salmon or trout for the ham. Garnish with dill instead of the basil.

Chickpea and Chorizo Gratin
Swap 8 ounces smoked Spanish chorizo for the ham and chickpeas for the white beans. Stir ½ teaspoon smoked paprika into the bread crumbs before sprinkling them over the top. Garnish with parsley instead of the basil.

NOTES

MAKE YOUR OWN

Cooked Beans 496

Bread Crumbs 71

COOKING WITH HAM
Most recipes in this book (and others) use ham that's cut into chunks. If you can't find thick-cut smoked ham steaks or smoked pork chops (those will work too), just ask for 1 extra-thick slice (between ¼ and ½ inch) of ham at the deli counter. When you want really crisp ham—great to sprinkle on soups and salads—start with thin slices, slice them into wispy shreds, and sauté in oil, stirring frequently, until they become crunchy. This process (I call it frizzling), works fine for regular deli ham, but is even tastier with dry varieties like prosciutto and Serrano.

SIDES

Green Salad 911

Chopped Salad 912

Sautéed Greens with Garlic 924

Simmered Squash 955

SPEED ◐ SERVES 4

Fast Feijoada

Feijoada (pronounced *fay-JWA-da*) is the cassoulet of Brazil, a one-pot dish of dried beans and cured meats that inspires rhapsodies, arguments, memories, and other passions. This version uses canned beans (or your own precooked beans) to cut way back on the cook time. It may not inspire you to write a poem, but it's super-tasty.

Ingredients

2 tablespoons vegetable oil

1 large onion

3 garlic cloves

8 ounces linguiça or kielbasa

8 ounces bacon (preferably slab)

8 ounces smoked pork chops or ham steak

6 cups cooked or canned black beans (three 15-ounce cans)

2 dried hot red chiles (like chile de árbol), or more to taste

1 cup chicken stock or water

Salt

Prep | Cook

1. Put 2 tablespoons vegetable oil in a large skillet or large pot over medium-high heat.

   Trim, peel, and chop the onion.

   Peel and mince 3 garlic cloves.

2. Add the onion and garlic to the skillet and cook, stirring occasionally until the onion softens, 3 to 5 minutes.

   Cut all the meat into chunks.

3. When the onion softens, add the meat and cook, stirring occasionally until it browns and crisps, 8 to 12 minutes.

   If you're using canned beans, rinse and drain them.

   Trim the dried chiles; seed them if you like and mince.

4. When the meat is brown, stir in the beans, chiles, and 1 cup stock or water. Bring to a boil, then adjust the heat so the mixture bubbles steadily but not vigorously.

5. Cook, stirring occasionally until the liquid mostly disappears, 5 to 10 minutes. Stir in salt to taste and serve.

VARIATIONS

Fast Cassoulet

This dish usually takes days, so doing it in 30 minutes is obviously cheating, but it still satisfies. Use an ovenproof skillet or large pot. Substitute boneless, skinless duck breast for the linguiça. Cut it into cubes and brown it along with the rest of the meat. Substitute cannellini beans for black beans and 2 teaspoons fresh thyme for the chiles. Once you've simmered the beans and meat, sprinkle Bread Crumbs (page 71) over the top and broil until bubbly and browned.

NOTES

MAKE YOUR OWN

Cooked Beans 496

Chicken Stock 213

IF YOU HAVE MORE TIME

Start with dried beans. After the meat is browned, add about 3 cups dried black beans, the chiles, and enough stock or water to cover by about an inch. Bring to a boil, then adjust the heat so the mixture simmers gently but steadily. Cook, adding more liquid if the mixture gets too dry, until the beans are tender and the liquid is mostly absorbed, up to 1 ½ hours.

SIDES

White Rice 941

Crisp Seasoned Pita 908

Green Salad 911

Ripe Plantains 960

SPEED SERVES 4

Lentil and Mushroom Stew

The addition of dried and fresh mushrooms to earthy lentils gives this stew an irresistible depth of flavor. Add some grated Parmesan at the end to make it even better.

Ingredients

1/4 cup any dried mushrooms

2 medium leeks

1 1/2 pounds button, cremini, or shiitake mushrooms

2 tablespoons olive oil, plus more for garnish

1 1/2 cups lentils

4 cups stock or water

3 sprigs fresh thyme

Salt and pepper

2 ounces Parmesan cheese (1/2 cup grated; optional)

Prep | Cook

1. Put 1/4 cup dried mushrooms in a small bowl with hot water to cover.

   Trim the leeks and slice the white and light green parts only.

   Trim and quarter the fresh mushrooms. (If you're using shiitakes, discard the stems.)

2. Put 2 tablespoons olive oil in a large pot over medium-high heat. Add the leeks and fresh mushrooms to the pot and cook, stirring occasionally until they soften, 5 to 10 minutes.

3. Add 1 1/2 cups lentils, 4 cups stock or water, and 3 sprigs thyme.

4. Remove the dried mushrooms from their soaking liquid, chop, and add them to the pot. Pour in the soaking liquid as well, being careful to leave any sediment behind.

5. Bring to a boil, then adjust the heat so the liquid bubbles gently but steadily. Simmer, adding more liquid if the mixture gets too dry, until the lentils are tender, anywhere from 20 to 40 minutes.

   Grate 1/2 cup Parmesan if you're using it.

6. When the lentils are tender, sprinkle with salt and pepper. Fish out the thyme sprigs and divide among 4 bowls. Sprinkle the Parmesan over the top if you like; drizzle with a little more olive oil and serve.

VARIATIONS

Creamy Lentil and Mushroom Stew
Particularly luxurious. Stir in ½ cup cream during the last few minutes of cooking. Skip the Parmesan.

Lentil and Chile Stew
Swap 3 dried hot red chiles for the dried mushrooms, 1 medium onion for the leeks, and 4 poblano peppers, chopped, for the mushrooms. Use fresh oregano instead of the thyme and garnish with a little sour cream and cilantro if you like instead of the Parmesan.

Beefy Lentil Stew with Dried Mushrooms
Keep the dried mushrooms, but instead of the fresh mushrooms use 1 pound chuck steak, cut into ½-inch pieces. In Step 2, cook the meat by itself in the hot olive oil, stirring occasionally, until browned in places, 3 to 5 minutes. Then add the leeks and cook until they soften, another 5 minutes or so. Then proceed with the recipe.

NOTES

MAKE YOUR OWN

Chicken Stock 213

Beef Stock 212

Vegetable Stock 212

EVEN FASTER
Since the lentils don't start cooking until a little way into the recipe, choosing a quicker-cooking lentil like red (see page 485) will guarantee that you finish this in less than 45 minutes.

SIDES

Warm Buttery Bread 906

Carrot Salad with Raisins 914

Sautéed Greens with Garlic 924

SPEED ◔ SERVES 4

Red Lentils with Toasted Cauliflower

There is no better use for lentils than dal, the stewed, spiced lentil dishes ubiquitous in India. The idea is to cook them long enough so they begin to break apart and become creamy. Toasted cauliflower adds another layer of texture.

Ingredients

5 tablespoons vegetable oil

1 small onion

1 garlic clove

1 inch fresh ginger

1 tablespoon curry powder

3 cups coconut milk (two 15-ounce cans)

1 ½ cups red lentils

1 large head cauliflower (about 2 ½ pounds)

Salt and pepper

4 scallions

Prep | Cook

1. Put 2 tablespoons vegetable oil in a medium saucepan over medium-high heat.

   Trim, peel, and chop the onion.

2. Add the onion to the pan and cook, stirring occasionally until it softens, 3 to 5 minutes.

   Peel the garlic clove and 1 inch ginger; mince them together.

3. When the onion softens, add the garlic and ginger and 1 tablespoon curry powder. Cook, stirring until they're fragrant, a minute or 2.

4. Add 3 cups coconut milk, 1 ½ cups water, and 1 ½ cups red lentils. Bring to a boil, then adjust the heat so the mixture bubbles gently but steadily. Partially cover and cook, adding more water if the mixture gets too dry, until the lentils are tender and begin to break down and become saucy, 25 to 30 minutes.

5. Turn the broiler to high; put the rack 6 inches from the heat.
   Trim and chop the cauliflower into small pieces (roughly ½ inch, but you don't need to be exact).

6. Put the cauliflower on a rimmed baking sheet, toss with 3 tablespoons oil and a sprinkle of salt and pepper, and spread it out in an even layer.

7. Broil, undisturbed, until the cauliflower is tender and nicely browned and crisp on top, 15 to 20 minutes.
   Trim and chop the scallions.

8. When the lentils are tender and beginning to break down, stir them vigorously with a spoon for a minute. Sprinkle them with salt and pepper and divide them among 4 bowls. Spoon the cauliflower on top of the lentils, garnish with the scallions, and serve immediately.

VARIATIONS

Yellow Lentils with Charred Broccoli
Broccoli gives this dish an entirely different flavor. Substitute yellow lentils for red and cook them the same way. Use broccoli, chopped into roughly ½-inch pieces, instead of the cauliflower. It takes a bit less time to become tender, but make sure to brown and crisp it well, stirring and tossing as necessary until the outside has a bit of a crunch.

NOTES

MAKE YOUR OWN
Curry Powder 758

SIDES

White Rice 941

Cucumber Raita 916

Tender Steamed Vegetables 954

SPEED SERVES 4

Tomato-Braised Lentils and Potatoes

Tomato juice mixed with water adds a welcome acidity to this dish of lentils and potatoes, a hearty creation that falls somewhere between soup and stew.

Ingredients

2 tablespoons olive oil

1 medium onion

2 garlic cloves

½ teaspoon red chile flakes

One 28-ounce can whole tomatoes

5 cups water or a combination of water and chicken stock

1 ½ cups lentils

Salt and pepper

2 or 3 medium russet or Yukon Gold potatoes (1 pound)

2 sprigs fresh oregano

Prep | Cook

1. Put 2 tablespoons olive oil in a large pot over medium-high heat.

   Trim, peel, and chop the onion.

   Peel and mince 2 garlic cloves.

2. Add the onion, garlic, and ½ teaspoon red chile flakes to the pot and cook, stirring occasionally until the onion softens, 3 to 5 minutes.

3. Add the tomatoes with their juice, 5 cups water or a combination of water and stock, and 1 ½ cups lentils. Sprinkle with salt and pepper. Bring to a boil, then adjust the heat so it bubbles gently but steadily. Simmer, adding more liquid if the mixture gets too dry, until the lentils are tender, anywhere from 20 to 40 minutes.

   Scrub the potatoes and peel them if you like; cut them into ½-inch cubes.

4. Add the potatoes to the pot; by the time the lentils are cooked, the potatoes will be tender.

   Strip the oregano leaves from 2 sprigs and chop.

5. When the lentils and potatoes are tender, stir in the oregano, sprinkle with salt and pepper, and serve.

VARIATIONS

Tomato-and-Soy-Braised Lentils and Potatoes
For the liquid, use 2 cups tomato juice, 1 3/4 cups water, 1/4 cup soy sauce, and 2 tablespoons sesame oil. Instead of stirring in oregano, garnish with cilantro.

Tomato-and-Dijon-Braised Lentils and Potatoes
Add 2 tablespoons Dijon mustard to the cooking liquid and use 2 tablespoons chopped fresh tarragon instead of the oregano.

NOTES

MAKE YOUR OWN

Chicken Stock 213

EVEN FASTER
If you use a quicker-cooking variety of lentil (see page 485) and chop the potatoes into small pieces, they'll both become tender faster.

IF YOU HAVE MORE TIME
For a little crunch, cook the lentils and potatoes, then transfer everything to an ovenproof dish, scatter some Bread Crumbs (page 71) over the top, and drizzle with olive oil. Bake in a 400°F oven until the bread crumbs are brown and crisp.

BRAISING WITH BEANS
Ingredients that need to be braised for a longer amount of time can always be added to a pot of beans at the beginning: think ham, beef, or root vegetables. But the point at which beans and lentils are close to fully cooked but haven't yet absorbed all of their cooking liquid is a perfect moment to add in something that needs only a quick simmer to cook. Shrimp, scallops, or thin fish fillets can go in raw since they don't take much time to cook, and certainly tofu or fairly tender vegetables and greens are fair game; partly cooked fish fillets or cuts of meat and poultry work too. Cover the pot so whatever you've added will warm from both below and the steam above, cooking quickly and evenly.

SIDES

Garlicky Mushrooms 956

Crunchy Okra 959

Brussels Sprouts with Sausage 958

Creamy Polenta 947

Braised Lentils with Salmon

Lentils and salmon are great partners, an old-style surf and turf. This wine-based lentil stew with sautéed salmon on top is bistro cooking at its best.

Ingredients

2 medium leeks

2 tablespoons butter

1 cup white wine

6 cups chicken or vegetable stock or water

1 ½ cups lentils

1 small shallot

4 sprigs fresh tarragon

2 tablespoons tomato paste

1 tablespoon sherry vinegar

5 tablespoons olive oil

Handful of fresh chives for garnish (about 1 cup chopped)

Salt and pepper

1 ½ pounds skin-on salmon fillet

Prep | Cook

Trim the leeks and slice the white and light green parts only.

1. Put 2 tablespoons butter in a medium saucepan over medium heat. When it foams, add the leeks and cook, stirring occasionally until they're soft, 3 to 5 minutes. Do not brown.

2. Add 1 cup white wine to the softened leeks and let it bubble until evaporated. Add 6 cups stock or water and 1 ½ cups lentils. Bring to a boil, then adjust the heat so it bubbles gently but steadily.

3. Simmer, adding more liquid if the mixture gets too dry, until the lentils are just tender and the liquid is absorbed, anywhere from 15 to 35 minutes.

   Peel and mince the shallot. Strip the tarragon leaves from 4 sprigs and mince. (You should have about 2 tablespoons.)

4. Stir together 2 tablespoons tomato paste, 1 tablespoon sherry vinegar, the minced shallot and tarragon, and 4 tablespoons olive oil.

   Chop the chives.

5. When the lentils are just tender and the liquid is absorbed, season with salt and pepper and stir in the dressing; whisk to combine. Turn off the heat and let marinate while you cook the salmon.

6. Put a large skillet over medium-high heat. Rub the salmon with 1 tablespoon olive oil and sprinkle with salt and pepper.
7. When the pan is smoking hot, add the salmon skin side down and cook until the skin is browned and crisp, 3 to 5 minutes. Flip the salmon, cook until the outside is crisp and the interior medium-rare, another minute or 2, then remove from heat.
8. Divide the salmon into 4 portions and serve them over the lentils.

VARIATIONS

Braised Lentils with Pork Chops
Substitute bone-in or boneless pork chops for the salmon. Sear them on both sides until a crust forms, then add ½ cup white wine and lower the heat to medium; after the wine evaporates, add ½ cup water and turn the heat to low. Cover and cook for 10 to 15 minutes.

Braised Lentils with Chicken
Substitute bone-in chicken thighs for the salmon. Sear them skin side down until the skin is brown and crisp, then flip them over and cook for the same amount of time on the other side, about 15 minutes total.

NOTES

MAKE YOUR OWN
Chicken Stock 213

Vegetable Stock 212

EVEN FASTER
Instead of searing the salmon, you can skin it, cut it into cubes, and stir the pieces into the lentils a few minutes before the lentils are done cooking.

SIDES

White Rice 941

Cucumber Salad 915

Tender Vegetables 954

Crisp Roasted Potatoes 965

SPEED SERVES 4

BBQ Lima Beans with Collards

Limas are so meaty that it makes sense to give them the classic BBQ treatment. Adding greens turns a side dish into a satisfying meal.

Ingredients

4 tablespoons olive oil

1 medium onion

2 garlic cloves

1 cup ketchup

¼ cup cider vinegar

2 tablespoons molasses

1 tablespoon Dijon mustard

Salt and pepper

2 ½ cups frozen or fresh lima beans

8 ounces bacon (preferably slab)

1 large or 2 small bunches collard greens (1 pound)

Prep | Cook

1. Heat the oven to 450°F. Put 2 tablespoons olive oil in a large ovenproof skillet or large pot over medium-high heat.

   Trim, peel, and chop the onion.

   Peel and mince 2 garlic cloves.

2. Add the onion and garlic to the skillet and cook, stirring occasionally until the onion softens, 3 to 5 minutes.

3. Add 1 cup ketchup, ¼ cup cider vinegar, 2 tablespoons molasses, 1 tablespoon Dijon, 1 tablespoon water, ½ teaspoon salt, and ½ teaspoon pepper. Cook until the mixture bubbles, then add 2 ½ cups lima beans and turn the heat to low.

4. Put 2 tablespoons oil in a large skillet over medium heat.

   Chop the bacon into small pieces.

5. Add the bacon to the skillet and cook, stirring occasionally until crisp, 5 to 10 minutes.

   Trim the collards; slice the leaves in half lengthwise along the stem, then crosswise into thin ribbons.

6. When the bacon is crisp, add the collards and cook, stirring occasionally until they wilt, 3 to 5 minutes.

7. Add the collards and bacon to the beans and stir to combine. Taste and adjust the seasoning, then put the pot in the oven.
8. Bake, uncovered, just until the top gets a little brown and crisp, 10 to 15 minutes. Serve hot or warm.

VARIATIONS

Spicy Kidney Beans with Chorizo and Kale
Swap kidney beans for the lima beans, fresh Mexican chorizo for the bacon, and kale for the collard greens. For a little extra spice, add 1 chopped chipotle in adobo or some cayenne to the barbecue sauce.

Creamy White Beans with Prosciutto and Escarole
Substitute white beans for the lima beans, prosciutto for the bacon (it will crisp in 3 to 5 minutes), and escarole for the collard greens. Instead of the barbecue sauce mixture, add about 1 cup of the white beans, ¼ cup olive oil, ½ cup water, and the juice of a lemon in Step 3. Mash it together until the mixture becomes creamy, then stir in the rest of the beans and proceed.

NOTES

EVEN FASTER
Instead of mixing the barbecue sauce ingredients as described in Step 3, use the Barbecue Sauce on page 145.

Skip the baking; just serve after combing the collards with the lima beans.

IF YOU HAVE MORE TIME
To develop an even crispier crust on top, bake the dish for up to 30 minutes.

SIDES

Warm Flour Tortillas 907

Coleslaw 923

Mexican Street Corn 932

SPEED SERVES 4

Stir-Fried Tofu and Green Beans

A stir-fry in two parts: Get the tofu started right away, then turn your attention to the green beans and sauce. Since the tofu will be partly soft when you're tossing everything in the sauce at the end, do it as gently as you can so it doesn't crumble too much.

Ingredients

3 tablespoons vegetable oil

2 bricks firm tofu (12 to 14 ounces each)

Salt and pepper

1 pound green beans

1 garlic clove

1 fresh hot green chile (like serrano)

3 tablespoons soy sauce

2 tablespoons honey

2 teaspoons sesame oil

Sesame seeds for garnish

Prep | Cook

1. Put 3 tablespoons vegetable oil in a large skillet (preferably nonstick) over medium-high heat.

   Cut the tofu into slices or cubes.

2. Add the tofu to the skillet, sprinkle with salt and pepper, and cook, stirring and turning occasionally until it's golden and crisp on at least a few sides, 5 to 10 minutes total.

   Trim the green beans.

   Peel 1 garlic clove; trim the chile. Mince them together and put them in a small bowl.

3. When the tofu is golden and crisp on at least a few sides, remove it from the pan.

4. Add the green beans, sprinkle with salt and pepper, and cook, stirring occasionally until they brown lightly, 3 to 5 minutes.

   Add 3 tablespoons soy sauce, 2 tablespoons honey, and 2 teaspoons sesame oil to the bowl with the garlic and chile. Whisk to combine.

5. When the green beans are lightly browned, return the tofu to the skillet and add the sauce. Toss gently to coat everything. Taste and adjust the seasoning.

6. Sprinkle with sesame seeds and serve.

VARIATIONS

Gingery Stir-Fried Tofu and Green Beans
Add 1 inch minced fresh ginger to the sauce.

Stir-Fried Tofu and Snow Peas
Swap snow peas for green beans. Reduce the amount of honey to 1 tablespoon and increase the sesame oil to 1 tablespoon.

Stir-Fried Tofu and Carrots with Soy and Mustard
Use 4 or 5 carrots, thinly sliced on the bias, instead of green beans. After removing the tofu, stir-fry them until they're lightly browned and just tender, 6 to 8 minutes. Add 2 teaspoons Dijon mustard to the sauce. Garnish with cilantro.

NOTES

IF YOU HAVE MORE TIME
To get the tofu firmer and crisper, let it get golden and crisp all over. This could take up to 15 minutes, depending on the size of your skillet.

SIDES

Tomato Salad with Sesame and Soy 913

White Rice 941

Sesame Noodles 949

Tofu

Tofu, aka *bean curd*, is as versatile as it gets. Think of it as a unique ingredient and you'll be won over, if you haven't been already. All tofu is made in pretty much the same way—it's coagulated soy milk, just as cheese is coagulated cow's milk—and it comes in a few main varieties:

Type of Tofu	Description
"REGULAR" TOFU	Also known as *brick* or *Chinese tofu*, this is the block that you most often see in sealed plastic tubs filled with water. It has a dense and crumbly texture and comes in four levels of firmness: soft, medium, firm, and extra-firm. Firm and extra-firm—what I call for most of the time in this book—hold their shape during cooking, which means they are suitable for stir-frying, grilling, broiling, baking, or braising. Unless you cook them in liquid, soft and medium tofu break apart during cooking, so they are best served raw or used as thickeners in places that you might otherwise use yogurt or milk, like smoothies.
SILKEN TOFU	Also known as *Japanese tofu*, it's also brick shaped and sold in soft, firm, and extra-firm varieties; all of these are soft and creamy, with a jiggly texture almost like custard. Like soft or medium "regular" tofu, silken tofu is an ideal thickener or replacement for eggs or dairy. The firm and extra-firm versions can be cut into cubes and added to broths and soup, stir-fried or deep-fried if you're careful, or crumbled into anything you like.
PRESSED TOFU	While pressed tofu has popped up in some supermarkets, it's mostly available at Asian markets. Regular tofu is subjected to high pressure until it becomes dense and chewy. (If you're looking for tofu that comes closest to the texture of meat, this is it.) Pressed tofu ranges in color from beige to dark brown and comes plain, seasoned, and sometimes "smoked" or even fried. Slice and stir-fry pressed tofu—it will not fall apart—or marinate and grill or broil it, use it raw in salads, or toss it into soups for texture. It's also good as a snack.

Storing Tofu

Once opened, tofu can be stored in the refrigerator for a few days; put it in a container, cover it with fresh water, and change the water daily. (If it starts to smell sour, you can shave the ends off the rectangle; the interior is probably still good. Again, it's just like cheese.) To freeze tofu, drain it and pat it dry, then wrap it in plastic or put it in a container; use within 3 months. The benefit of freezing tofu is that it completely changes its texture, so that it's darker, firmer, chewier, and meatier. If you find you like it more after freezing, just keep some in the freezer and take it out so it defrosts before you cook with it.

Pressing Tofu

Just the way that packaged pressed tofu has much of the water squeezed out of it to give it a firmer texture, regular tofu can be subjected to the same process to make it drier and firmer. You won't achieve nearly the same consistency as commercially pressed tofu, but it does make a difference. Cut the brick of tofu (firm or extra-firm is best) in half through its equator. Put the halves on a clean kitchen towel and cover them with another towel (or use several layers of paper towel above and below). Put something heavy on top so the tofu bulges at the sides slightly but doesn't get crushed or cracked. Wait, changing the towels if they become saturated, for 20 to 30 minutes, or longer if you have time. The longer you press it, the more liquid it will release and the drier and easier to handle the tofu will be, but even the few minutes that it takes to get your other ingredients ready will make a difference.

Tofu and Nonstick Cookware

Tofu will stick to the bottom of most regular skillets, even well-seasoned ones, so if you have a large nonstick skillet, now's the time to use it. If you must use a regular skillet, try to get as much moisture as you can out of the tofu before you start (see above) and make sure the skillet and oil are very hot when you put the tofu in the pan. Then wait until the pieces release to start turning or stirring.

SPEED ◐ SERVES 4

Deep-Fried Tofu with Peanut Sauce and Scallions

If you think you don't like tofu, try deep-frying it until golden and serving with this peanut sauce—then we'll talk. Serve it with rice, noodles, or vegetables on the side.

Ingredients

Vegetable oil for frying

2 bricks firm tofu (12 to 14 ounces each)

1 garlic clove

½ inch fresh ginger

¼ cup peanut butter

1 tablespoon soy sauce

1 tablespoon rice vinegar

2 teaspoons sesame oil

Salt

3 scallions

Prep | Cook

1. Put at least 2 inches of vegetable oil in a deep heavy skillet or saucepan over medium heat (you want the temperature to reach 350°F).

   Cut each brick of tofu in half across its equator, then cut each of those halves into 2 triangles; pat them dry with a paper towel. You'll end up with 4 pieces for each brick.

   Peel 1 garlic clove and ½ inch ginger; mince them together and put them in a small bowl.

2. Add ¼ cup peanut butter, 1 tablespoon soy sauce, 1 tablespoon rice vinegar, and 2 teaspoons sesame oil to the bowl. Stir to combine, adding enough hot water to turn it into a sauce.

3. When the oil reaches 350°F, fry the tofu in batches, turning occasionally until golden brown and puffed up, 2 to 4 minutes.

4. As each batch is finished, remove the pieces with a slotted spoon to drain on paper towels; sprinkle with salt.

   Trim and chop the scallions.

5. When all the tofu is fried, pile it on a platter, scatter the scallions over the top, and serve the peanut sauce on the side for dipping.

VARIATIONS

Deep-Fried Tofu with Pistachio Sauce and Cilantro

Use ½ cup pistachios for the peanut butter. Substitute 2 tablespoons lime juice for the soy sauce and rice vinegar, ¼ cup coconut milk for the sesame oil, and a few cilantro sprigs for the scallions. While the oil is heating, put the sauce ingredients in a blender and purée.

5 More Dipping Sauces for Fried Tofu

Just like Roasted Tofu (page 528), fried tofu is a blank canvas for all sorts of dipping sauces:

1. Tomato Sauce (page 296)
2. Fresh Tomato Salsa (page 145)
3. Vinaigrette (page 70)
4. Barbecue Sauce (page 145)
5. Mayonnaise (page 144)

SIDES

White Rice 941

Sesame Noodles 949

Stir-Fried Bok Choy 927

SPEED ◑ SERVES 4

Manchurian Tofu and Cauliflower

This Chinese-Indian dish is a riff on a recipe from my friend (and phenomenal Indian chef) Suvir Saran. The ketchup-based sauce is addictive.

Ingredients

5 tablespoons vegetable oil

2 bricks firm tofu (12 to 14 ounces each)

Salt and pepper

1 small head cauliflower

2 garlic cloves

1 cup ketchup

½ teaspoon cayenne

Prep | Cook

1. Put 3 tablespoons vegetable oil in a large skillet (preferably nonstick) over medium-high heat.

   Cut the tofu into slices or cubes.

2. Add the tofu to the skillet, sprinkle with salt and pepper, and cook, stirring and turning occasionally until it's golden and crisp on at least a few sides, 5 to 10 minutes total.

   Trim and break or chop the cauliflower into small florets.

3. When the tofu is golden and crisp on at least a few sides, remove it from the pan.

4. Add 2 tablespoons oil and the cauliflower to the skillet, sprinkle with salt and pepper, and raise the heat to high. Cook undisturbed until the florets brown, 3 to 5 minutes.

   Peel and mince 2 garlic cloves.

5. When the florets are brown on the bottom, turn and sear on the other side, another 2 or 3 minutes.

6. Add the garlic to the skillet along with 1 cup ketchup and ½ teaspoon cayenne. Cook, stirring until the ketchup starts to bubble and caramelize around the edges of the skillet.

7. Return the tofu to the skillet and toss to coat with the sauce; add a splash of water if the mixture needs to be a bit saucier.

8. Turn the heat to medium, cover, and cook until the tofu is warmed back through and the cauliflower is tender, 2 or 3 minutes. Serve.

VARIATIONS

BBQ Tofu and Cauliflower

Substitute 1 teaspoon paprika for the cayenne and add 1 teaspoon yellow mustard, 1 tablespoon molasses, and 1 tablespoon cider vinegar along with the ketchup.

Chipotle-Orange Tofu and Cauliflower

Along with the ketchup in Step 6, add 1 chopped chipotle in adobo (or more to taste) and the juice of an orange. The orange juice will make the mixture saucier, so you won't need to add much extra water (if any).

SIDES

White Rice 941

Quick Brown Rice 941

Stir-Fried Bok Choy 927

Peas with Ginger 934

SPEED ◐ SERVES 4

Eggs Sukiyaki

Sukiyaki is a category of slow-simmered soups and stews from Japan, where the meat may be cooked in the broth right at the table. The dish often contains eggs, which here are poached in a thick, flavorful broth of stewed onions, ginger, and soy.

Ingredients

2 tablespoons sesame oil

2 inches fresh ginger

2 onions

1 pound shiitake mushrooms

¼ cup soy sauce

1 tablespoon brown sugar

8 ounces firm tofu

1 pound spinach

1 cup dashi or water

8 eggs

4 scallions

Prep | Cook

1. Put 2 tablespoons sesame oil in a large skillet over medium-low heat.

   Peel and mince 2 inches ginger; add it to the skillet.

   Trim, peel, halve, and slice the onions.

2. Add the onions to the skillet and raise the heat to medium. Cook, stirring occasionally until they are very tender, 5 to 8 minutes.

   Trim and slice the mushrooms, discarding the stems.

3. When the onions are tender, add the mushrooms. Stir and cook for 1 minute, then add ¼ cup soy sauce and 1 tablespoon brown sugar; stir to combine. Cook until the mushrooms are soft, 5 to 10 minutes.

   Cut the tofu into ½-inch cubes. Trim the spinach, discarding any thick stems.

4. Add the tofu and spinach to the skillet; stir and cook until tender, 5 minutes.

5. Add 1 cup dashi or water, or just enough to almost cover the vegetables, and cook for another minute. Taste and adjust the seasoning.

6. Crack the eggs over the broth, turn the heat to medium, and cover the skillet. Cook until the eggs are barely set (the yolks should still be runny), 5 to 10 minutes.

   Trim and chop the scallions.

7. When the eggs are barely set, sprinkle with the scallions and serve immediately.

VARIATIONS

Eggs Poached in Fennel
Omit the tofu. Substitute olive oil for the sesame oil; 3 garlic cloves for the ginger; 3 fennel bulbs, sliced, for the onions, mushrooms, and spinach; white wine for the soy sauce; and ½ teaspoon red chile flakes for the brown sugar. Garnish with parsley instead of the scallions and sprinkle on some Parmesan if you like.

Eggs Poached in Poblanos and Cream
Skip the tofu. Substitute olive oil for the sesame oil, 3 garlic cloves for the ginger, 4 large poblanos for the onions and mushrooms, cream for the soy sauce, and ½ teaspoon cumin for the brown sugar. Garnish with cilantro instead of or in addition to the scallions.

NOTES

MAKE YOUR OWN
Dashi 213

EVEN FASTER
To soften the vegetables faster, cook them over medium-high heat. If at any point the pan gets too dry, add a splash of water, scrape any browned bits off the bottom, and continue cooking.

SIDES

Soy Slaw 923

White Rice 941

Sesame Noodles 949

SPEED  SERVES 4

Smoky Tofu and Black Bean Chili

A superior vegetarian chili. Browning crumbled tofu instead of beef sounds sacrilegious, but this chili is brimming with enough earthy, spicy flavors that you won't miss the meat.

Ingredients

3 tablespoons vegetable oil

1 brick firm tofu (12 to 14 ounces)

1 medium onion

2 garlic cloves

2 canned chipotles in adobo

4 cups cooked or canned black beans (two 15-ounce cans)

1 tablespoon chili powder

1 tablespoon cumin

Salt

One 28-ounce can diced tomatoes

2 cups beer, water, or a combination

4 ounces cheddar cheese (1 cup grated)

3 scallions

Sour cream for garnish

Prep | Cook

1. Put 3 tablespoons vegetable oil in a large pot over medium-high heat.
2. When the oil is hot, crumble the tofu into the pot. Cook, stirring and scraping occasionally until the tofu bits are lightly browned, 5 or 6 minutes.

   Trim, peel, and chop the onion.

   Peel and mince 2 garlic cloves.
3. When the tofu is lightly browned, add the onion and garlic; cook until the onion softens, 3 to 5 minutes.

   Finely chop 2 chipotles in adobo.

   If you're using canned beans, rinse and drain them.
4. When the onion is softened, stir in the chipotles with some of their adobo if you like, 1 tablespoon chili powder, 1 tablespoon cumin, and a sprinkle of salt. Cook, stirring until the spices are fragrant, a minute or 2.
5. Stir in the beans, the tomatoes and their juice, and 2 cups beer, water, or a combination. Bring to a boil, then adjust the heat so the mixture bubbles steadily but not vigorously.

6. Partially cover and cook, stirring occasionally and adding more liquid if the mixture gets too dry, until the tomatoes and beans start to break down and the chili thickens, 15 to 20 minutes.

   Grate 1 cup cheddar cheese.

   Trim and chop the scallions.

7. When the chili thickens, taste and adjust the seasoning and divide it among 4 bowls. Top with some cheddar and a dollop of sour cream, sprinkle with the scallions, and serve.

VARIATIONS

Spicy Tofu and White Bean Chili
Substitute olive oil for the vegetable oil, 1 tablespoon tomato paste for the chipotles, 1 teaspoon dried oregano for the chili powder, and 1 teaspoon red chile flakes for the cumin. For the liquid, use 1 ½ cups water or stock and ½ cup red wine. Use Parmesan instead of cheddar, basil in place of scallions, and a drizzle of olive oil instead of a dollop of sour cream.

Smoky Tofu and Black-Eyed Pea Chili with Collards
Use 2 cups black-eyed peas in place of the black beans and add 1 pound collard greens, sliced into thin ribbons, in Step 5.

NOTES

MAKE YOUR OWN

Cooked Beans 496

Chili Powder 758

IF YOU HAVE MORE TIME
The longer you simmer the chili, the more the beans will break down and become creamy, and the more the flavors will develop—even up to a couple of hours.

SIDES

Avocado with Lemon and Salt 920

Warm Tortillas 907

White Rice 941

SPEED SERVES 4

Roasted Tofu with Sesame Drizzle

Roasting whole bricks is a fantastic way to prepare tofu. The outsides become golden and slightly chewy, while the insides remain wonderfully creamy. It takes some time for this to happen, but the upside is that it's absolutely effortless.

Ingredients

2 bricks firm tofu (12 to 14 ounces each)

3 scallions

Sesame oil for drizzling

Soy sauce for drizzling

Sesame seeds for garnish

Prep | Cook

1. Heat the oven to 425°F.

   Pat the tofu dry and put it in a large ovenproof skillet (the bricks shouldn't be touching).

2. When the oven is hot, roast the tofu, turning once halfway through, until the outsides are golden and crisp, 30 to 35 minutes total.

   Trim and chop the scallions.

3. When the tofu is crisp, transfer it to a cutting board and slice it between ¼ and ½ inch thick.

4. Put the tofu on a platter or plates, drizzle with sesame oil and soy sauce, garnish with scallions and sesame seeds, and serve.

VARIATIONS

5 More Things to Put on Roasted Tofu

1. Tomato Sauce (page 296)
2. Fresh Tomato Salsa (page 145)
3. Vinaigrette (page 70)
4. Barbecue Sauce (page 145)
5. Spice Blends (page 758) (rub them on the outside before roasting)

5 Ways to Use Roasted Tofu, with or Without a Drizzle or Sauce

First slice the whole bricks after roasting as described in the main recipe or cut them into cubes.

1. Fill and dress sandwiches.
2. Toss into green or vegetable salads.
3. Stir into soups at any point during cooking.
4. Add to noodle or rice dishes just before serving.
5. Add to stir-fries during the last minute or 2 of cooking.

NOTES

EVEN FASTER

Seared Tofu

Start by putting 2 tablespoons vegetable oil in the skillet and put the skillet in the oven while it heats. When the oven is hot, carefully add the tofu to the skillet; the hot oil will start browning the bottom of the bricks as they roast and cut the cooking time by 10 minutes.

SIDES

Green Salad with Sesame-Soy Dressing 911

White Rice 941

Stir-Fried Bok Choy 927

Braised Tofu with Tomatoes and Broccoli

Something wonderful happens when you cook tofu and tomatoes together; they each soften and begin to break down, and the tofu takes on the acidity of the tomatoes as they cook. The broccoli provides contrast if you leave it crisp-tender. Or try cooking it until completely soft and watch it meld with the tofu and tomatoes.

Ingredients

3 tablespoons olive oil

2 bricks firm tofu (12 to 14 ounces each)

Salt and pepper

1 medium onion

3 garlic cloves

1 small head broccoli (about 1 pound)

One 14-ounce can diced tomatoes

2 bay leaves

Several sprigs fresh basil for garnish

4 ounces Parmesan cheese (1 cup grated; optional)

Prep | Cook

1. Put 3 tablespoons olive oil in a large skillet (preferably nonstick) over medium-high heat.

   Cut the tofu into cubes.

2. Add the tofu to the skillet, sprinkle with salt and pepper, and cook, stirring and turning once in a while until it's golden and crisp on at least a few sides, 5 to 10 minutes total.

   Trim, peel, and chop the onion.

   Peel and mince 3 garlic cloves.

3. When the tofu is golden and crisp on at least a few sides, add the onion and garlic and cook, stirring occasionally until the onion softens, 3 to 5 minutes.

   Trim and break or chop the broccoli into small florets.

4. When the onion softens, stir in the tomatoes with their juice, the broccoli, 2 bay leaves, and a sprinkle of salt and pepper.

5. Bring to a boil, then adjust the heat so the mixture bubbles gently. Cover and cook, adding a splash of water if the mixture gets too dry, until the broccoli is as tender as you like, anywhere from 10 to 20 minutes.

   Strip the basil leaves from several sprigs and chop.

   Grate 1 cup Parmesan if you're using it.

6. When the broccoli is done, remove the bay leaves. Add the Parmesan to the skillet if you like, taste, and adjust the seasoning.

7. Divide among 4 bowls, garnish with the basil, and serve.

VARIATIONS

Curried Tofu with Tomatoes and Peas

Use vegetable oil instead of olive oil. Substitute 1 inch fresh ginger, minced, for the garlic and add 1 tablespoon curry powder when you add the onion and ginger in Step 3. Let the tomatoes simmer with the tofu for about 10 minutes, then add 3 cups frozen peas instead of the broccoli and cook just until they're warmed through. Use 1/4 cup yogurt or cream instead of Parmesan, and garnish with cilantro instead of basil.

Moroccan-Spiced Tofu with Tomatoes and Cauliflower

Add 1 teaspoon cumin, 1 teaspoon coriander, and 1/2 teaspoon cinnamon when you add the onion and garlic in Step 3. Substitute cauliflower for broccoli and garnish with parsley and mint instead of basil.

NOTES

EVEN FASTER

Instead of making a tomato sauce as described in Steps 2–4, use about 1 1/2 cups Tomato Sauce (page 296). Skip browning the tofu. Start by softening the onion and garlic, then add the tofu, tomatoes, broccoli, and bay leaves and proceed from Step 5.

SIDES

White Rice 941

Pasta, Plain and Simple 948

Creamy Polenta 947

Garlic Bread 906

Seafood

Salmon and Asparagus with Toasted Bread Crumbs 536

Salmon with Fresh Salsa 538

Pan-Seared Tuna with Ginger-Scallion Snow Peas 540

Tuna Poke with Daikon and Peanuts 544

Smoky Shrimp Scampi 546

Buffalo Shrimp 548

Black Pepper Scallops and Broccoli 550

Steamed Clams with Chorizo and Cherry Tomatoes 552

Salmon with Gingery Greens 554

Roasted Salmon with Potato Crust 558

Sole (or Other Thin Fillets) with Glazed Carrots 560

Swordfish (or Other Fish Steaks) with Picante Verde 562

Striped Bass (or Other Thick Fillets) and Zucchini Ribbons 564

Cod (or Other Thick Fillets) and Chickpea Stew 566

Caramel-Cooked Cod (or Other Thick Fillets) 568

Olive Oil–Poached Halibut (or Other Thick Fillets) with Endive 570

Blackened Catfish (or Other Thick Fillets) with Green Beans 572

Miso-Glazed Catfish (or Other Thick Fillets) and Mushrooms 574

Fish Kebabs over Bulgur Pilaf 576

Malaysian-Style BBQ Fish with Cool Cucumbers 578

Poached Fish in Creamy Tomato Broth 580

Panfried Trout with Bacon and Leeks 582

Mediterranean Mackerel with Mint 584

Stir-Fried Shrimp with Tomato, Eggs, and Scallions 588

Shrimp and Cauliflower with Rustic Romesco 590

Seared Scallops in Tomato Sauce with Basil and Chiles 592

Fish and Chips with Tartar Sauce 594

Roasted Trout (or Other Whole Fish) with Fennel and Orange 596

Shrimp Simmered in Dal 598

Baked Potato and Crab Cakes 600

Scallop and Corn Pan Broil 602

Mussel and Vegetable Pan Roast with Saffron Aïoli 604

Seafood

The benefits of fish are impressive. It comes in such a wide variety of flavors and textures that you could cook it every day without getting bored. It's the healthiest animal product you can eat. It rewards the simplest preparation. And it's ridiculously fast to cook—usually between 0 and 10 minutes.

But: Buying fish can be difficult. The global fish market is complicated; there is a dizzying variety of fish available to us at the supermarket, composed of species that can be either wild or farmed, caught responsibly or recklessly, shipped from in state or around the world, frozen and thawed (or not), fresh (or not). I've been writing about fish for more than 30 years, and in this chapter I've tried to summarize ways to avoid—or at least reduce—fish counter paralysis.

Cooking Seafood on page 586 contains links to websites that can keep you up to date with the ever-shifting list of which seafood is sustainable and which isn't, along with general groupings of fish that can be cooked in similar ways, so when you're in the store looking for fish they don't have, you can substitute something else without having to change the recipe.

The good news is that once you've got good seafood in your fridge a great meal is minutes away, and this chapter provides a number of fast and delicious ways to get from raw to cooked, including grilling, roasting, steaming, searing, and much more.

Chapter Highlights

Five Categories of Fish Within any of these groups, most fish can be substituted for one another. Seafood (page 534).

Buying Fish Two invaluable resources for learning which seafood you should be buying and which you should avoid. Sustainable Seafood (page 587).

Yes, You Can Make Sushi Some clarity on selecting fish for eating raw. Making the Sushi Grade (page 541).

Shrimp = Squid = Scallops Use shrimp, squid, and scallops interchangeably and watch your seafood repertoire grow exponentially. Shrimp, Squid, and Scallop Doneness (page 551).

And: Mussels = Clams What you need to know about switching between mussels and clams. (Not much.) Swapping Mussels for Clams (page 553).

Fast Oil Poaching A new way to oil-poach fish using less oil and a little steam. Oil Poaching Meets Steaming (page 571).

Blackening A fast way to create big flavor. Blackened Anything (page 573).

Fish for Roasting Thick fish steaks and fillets lend themselves brilliantly to roasting. Fish Roasts (page 575).

Two Skewers Are Better Than One Use two skewers for every kebab and gain confidence at the grill. Two Skewers, One Kebab (page 577).

Steaming Fish with Vegetables The best combo there is: fish and veg. Steamed Fish (page 556).

In Praise of "Oily Fish" Dark-fleshed, fatty fish make for some of the best eating. Oily Fish (page 585).

Whole Fish, No Problem It sure beats carving a turkey. Serving Whole Fish (page 597).

Prepping in Vein I never take the veins out of my shrimp, but here's how. Deveining Shrimp (page 599).

SPEED SERVES 4

Salmon and Asparagus with Toasted Bread Crumbs

Salmon takes 10 minutes to broil, and the same goes for thin asparagus. A large rimmed baking sheet accommodates both, which saves time and keeps skillet juggling to a minimum.

Ingredients

5 tablespoons butter

1 large bunch thin asparagus (1 pound)

4 thick salmon steaks or fillets (1 ½ pounds)

Salt and pepper

2 tablespoons vegetable oil

1 cup bread crumbs

1 lemon

Prep | Cook

1. Turn the broiler to high; put the rack 4 inches from the heat.

   Melt 5 tablespoons butter in the microwave or in a small pot over medium-low heat.

   Trim the asparagus.

2. Put the salmon and asparagus on a rimmed baking sheet, drizzle with the butter, and sprinkle with salt and pepper. If using skin-on fillets, place the skin side up.

3. Broil, turning the salmon and asparagus about halfway through the cooking, until the salmon is cooked as you like (no more than 10 minutes for medium to medium-well, and less if you like your salmon closer to medium-rare) and the asparagus is tender and browned.

4. Put 2 tablespoons vegetable oil in a medium skillet over medium-high heat. When it's hot, add 1 cup bread crumbs, sprinkle with salt and pepper, and stir gently to coat with the oil. Cook, stirring frequently and adjusting the heat to avoid burning, until the crumbs are golden and crisp, 3 to 5 minutes.

   Cut the lemon into wedges.

5. When the salmon and asparagus are done, divide among 4 plates. Then sprinkle the bread crumbs over the top, and serve with the lemon wedges.

VARIATIONS

Scallops with Asparagus and Toasted Bread Crumbs
Substitute scallops for the salmon; give the asparagus a few minutes' head start before adding the scallops to the baking sheet, because they need only a few minutes. (Don't overcook!)

Any Fish Fillets or Steaks and Cherry Tomatoes with Toasted Bread Crumbs
Substitute halibut, tuna, snapper, swordfish, cod, striped bass, catfish, or other thick fish fillets or steaks for the salmon and cherry tomatoes for the asparagus. Cooking time will depend on the thickness of the fish.

Any Fish Fillets or Steaks and Zucchini with Toasted Bread Crumbs
Substitute halibut, tuna, snapper, swordfish, cod, striped bass, catfish, or other thick fish fillets or steaks for the salmon and zucchini, cut lengthwise into planks, for the asparagus. Cooking time will depend on the thickness of the fish.

NOTES

MAKE YOUR OWN
Bread Crumbs 71

IF YOU HAVE MORE TIME
Thicker asparagus are also terrific broiled, but they take a bit longer. If you have an extra 5 to 10 minutes, use the thicker ones and cook up some white rice while you're at it.

SIDES

Green Salad 911

Couscous 910

Fennel Salad with Capers and Dill 917

SPEED SERVES 4

Salmon with Fresh Salsa

Both wild salmon and tomatoes are in season during summer—and you've also got your grill out. Perfect. But the broiler also makes quick and delicious work of this dish. And there are lots of variations to consider.

Ingredients

3 medium ripe tomatoes (about 1 pound)

1 small onion

1 fresh hot green chile (like jalapeño)

1 bunch fresh cilantro

2 limes

Salt and pepper

4 thick salmon steaks or fillets (1 ½ pounds)

2 tablespoons olive oil

Prep | Cook

1. Prepare a grill or turn the broiler to high; put the rack 4 inches from the heat.

   Core and chop the tomatoes; put them in a medium bowl.

   Trim, peel, and chop the onion; add it to the bowl.

   Trim and mince the chile; add it to the bowl.

   Chop ½ cup cilantro and add it to the bowl.

   Halve the limes; squeeze the juice into the bowl. Sprinkle with salt and pepper and stir.

2. When the grill or broiler is hot, brush the salmon with 2 tablespoons olive oil and sprinkle with salt and pepper.

3. Grill or broil, carefully turning about halfway through the cooking, for no more than 10 minutes for medium to medium-well and less if you like your salmon closer to medium-rare, about 7 minutes.

4. Top the salmon with the salsa and serve.

VARIATIONS

Any Grilled or Broiled Fish Steaks or Thick Fillets with Fresh Salsa
Skip the salmon and try striped bass, halibut, bluefish, grouper, monkfish, or any other thick fish fillets or steaks. Cooking time will depend on the thickness of the fish.

Any Broiled Thin Fish Fillets with Fresh Salsa
Instead of salmon, use any thin fish fillets. Use the broiler (they are too delicate for the grill). Time under the broiler will be 90 seconds to 2 minutes; rarely more. Do not turn; the fillets are so thin it's not necessary. The fish is ready when it becomes opaque and the tip of a knife flakes the thickest part easily.

NOTES

EVEN FASTER
Instead of making the salsa as described in Step 1, use 1 cup Fresh Tomato Salsa (page 145).

IF YOU HAVE MORE TIME
Let the salsa marinate for 15 to 20 minutes before serving.

SALMON TEMPERATURE
It used to be more common to cook salmon until it was dry and flaky. (Maybe a more fitting word is crumbly. Even worse: chalky.) But salmon tastes a lot better when you remove it from the heat when it's slightly soft and dark pink in the middle. (It's welcome news when cooking something properly means cooking it for less time.) To know when it's done, just peek into the middle of the fish with a paring knife. If it looks too rare, keep cooking and checking until it reaches a texture you like.

SIDES

Warm Flour Tortillas 907

Mexican Street Corn 932

Sweet Potato Fries 963

Jícama and Radish Salad 918

SPEED ◔ SERVES 4

Pan-Seared Tuna with Ginger-Scallion Snow Peas

This dish takes advantage of two ingredients that cook very quickly in a screaming-hot skillet: fresh tuna and snow peas. If you're going to make a side, start it first.

Ingredients

3 tablespoons soy sauce, plus more to taste

3 tablespoons vegetable oil

1 ½ pounds fresh tuna

1 inch fresh ginger

2 garlic cloves

1 pound snow peas

4 scallions

Salt and pepper

Sesame seeds for garnish (optional)

Prep | Cook

1. Put a large skillet over high heat. Combine 3 tablespoons soy sauce and 2 tablespoons vegetable oil in a small bowl. Put the tuna on a plate and rub all over with the soy marinade.

2. When the skillet is very hot, add the tuna (saving the leftover marinade) and cook, turning once, until it's browned on both sides but still raw in the center, 3 or 4 minutes per side.
   Peel 1 inch ginger and 2 garlic cloves; mince them together.

3. When the tuna is done, remove it from the skillet. Add 1 tablespoon vegetable oil to the skillet, followed by the snow peas, garlic and ginger, remaining tuna marinade, and a splash of water.

4. Cook, stirring frequently, until the snow peas are tender and glossy and the liquid has mostly evaporated, 3 to 5 minutes.
   Trim and chop the scallions.

5. When the snow peas are tender, taste and adjust the seasoning, adding salt and pepper and more soy sauce if desired. Serve with the tuna, garnished with the scallions and with sesame seeds if you like.

VARIATIONS

Pan-Seared Tuna with Tomatoes and Olives
Substitute 3 tablespoons lemon juice and 2 teaspoons chopped fresh thyme leaves for the soy sauce and olive oil for vegetable. Use chopped or cherry tomatoes instead of the snow peas, ½ cup chopped olives instead of the ginger, and garnish with parsley instead of scallions and sesame seeds.

Pan-Seared Halibut with Garlicky Watercress or Spinach
Use thick halibut fillets instead of tuna (you'll want to cook them for a little longer, until they are just cooked through in the center). Substitute 3 tablespoons lemon juice for the soy sauce and olive oil for vegetable. Increase the garlic to 4 cloves, skip the ginger, and use watercress or spinach instead of snow peas (sauté until wilted). Garnish with chopped nuts or toasted bread crumbs instead of the scallions and sesame seeds.

NOTES

IF YOU HAVE MORE TIME
Let the tuna marinate in the soy sauce and vegetable oil mixture for 15 minutes or so.

MAKING THE SUSHI GRADE
You may have heard the phrase *sushi grade* used to describe fish that is fit to consume raw; in fact there's no such designation. The FDA does require that any fish served raw be frozen before consumption to kill parasites. As with buying any seafood, the best way to go about it is to find a source that you trust. If you say you want fish you can eat raw, the fishmonger should be able to steer you in the right direction, and chances are that reputable ones will have strict standards for their "sushi grade" fish beyond just the freezing requirement.

SIDES

White Rice 941

Quinoa 945

Sesame Noodles 949

Scallion Pancakes 940

Fish Groups

Most recipes in this chapter call for specific kinds of fish. But in almost every case any fish of a similar kind will work equally well. Take, for example, Sole (or Other Thin Fish Fillets) with Glazed Carrots (page 560). The title of this recipe tells you that if you can't find (or don't like) sole, you can choose any thin fish fillet to take its place.

This list is a primer on the different groups of fish referred to throughout the chapter and the fish that are in them. There's some overlap among the groups because some fish are sold in various forms—fillets or steaks, for example—or in fillets of varying thickness. Referring to these groups will instantly broaden your fish-cooking repertoire and ensure that you'll wind up with something that fits the cooking method you choose. (This list does not take sustainability into account; see page 587 for a note on that and resources you can use to inform your choices. And see page 596 for cooking whole fish.)

Thick White Fish Fillets

The fish on this list are white, mild flavored, and tender; they should be at least an inch thick but could even reach 2 inches. The thickness gives you some flexibility in the kitchen; you can broil or grill these fillets, roast them, fry them, or sear them in a skillet long enough to form a nice crust without overcooking.

- Atlantic pollock, also known as *Boston bluefish* (wild, and not to be confused with Alaskan pollock, which is similar to cod).
- Sea bass, also known as *black sea bass*; mild-flavored.
- Carp, a flavorful, meaty freshwater fish.
- Catfish, freshwater fish and a favorite in the South; at its best, mild flavored and similar to snapper. Wild is better than farmed.
- Cod, the North Atlantic standard, prized for its mild flavor and tenderness.
- Grouper, meaty and delicious.
- Halibut, when cut as fillets usually quite thick and meaty; do not undercook.
- Monkfish, dense fleshed, with meat that's more similar to lobster than that of other fish. Do not undercook.

- Pacific pollock, also known as *Alaskan pollock*, much like cod.
- Red snapper and other snappers, mild and meaty.
- Salmon, always better wild than farm raised.
- Striped bass, very meaty and rich; wild is far better than farmed. Do not undercook.
- Turbot, a close relative of halibut; farmed is increasingly common and pretty good.
- Whiting, very tender fleshed and mild.

Thin White Fish Fillets

The fish in this group, less than an inch thick and sometimes as little as ¼ inch, cook extremely quickly, yielding (usually) mild-flavored and delicate fillets. Don't overcook and take care when turning.

- Catfish
- Flatfish of any type: flounder, fluke, sole, dab, plaice, and so on. All are sweet and mild flavored.
- Haddock, similar to cod but usually smaller.
- Ocean perch (also known as *rockfish*), similar to haddock.
- Red snapper or other snappers.
- Sea bass
- Tilapia, almost all farmed, inexpensive and not usually very flavorful.
- Trout, distinctively flavored and mostly farmed.
- Whiting

Fish Steaks

Big fish can be cut into steaks, some with bones, others without. All are great for grilling, broiling, roasting, and pan-cooking, and their near-uniform thickness means they cook pretty evenly. Some of the most common fish steaks (like tuna, swordfish, and salmon) are best when they're cooked to medium or even medium-rare, so take care not to let them overcook by checking them frequently.

- Cod
- Grouper
- Halibut
- Mako, shark, with mild-flavored and extremely meaty flesh (do not undercook).
- Monkfish (works well in steak recipes).
- Salmon
- Swordfish, among the best; rich and meaty.
- Tuna, also among the best and good at every stage from raw to cooked through.

Oily Fish

These are on the lower end of the food chain, the fish that are eaten by the bigger fish above.

- Anchovies, soft and delicious when fresh.
- Bluefish, strong and distinct—you love it or you hate it, but in any case it's superb with acidic ingredients.
- Mackerel, milder than you might have been led to believe—think of it as small tuna.
- Mahi-mahi, sturdy and mild.
- Salmon
- Sardines, tender and meaty when perfectly fresh.
- Trout

SPEED SERVES 4

Tuna Poke with Daikon and Peanuts

Poke (pronounced *POKE-ay*) is a traditional Hawaiian dish of cubed raw fish—salty, spicy, and nearly addictive. It's often served with cashews and seaweed; this is a spin on that, using peanuts and daikon radish.

Ingredients

⅓ cup peanuts

2 tablespoons sesame seeds

1 ½ pounds fresh tuna

½ small daikon radish, or other radishes, or white turnips (about 8 ounces)

5 scallions

1 lemon

¼ cup mayonnaise

3 tablespoons soy sauce

2 teaspoons sesame oil

Sriracha

Prep | Cook

1. Put a small skillet over medium-high heat.

   Chop ⅓ cup peanuts.

2. Put the peanuts and 2 tablespoons sesame seeds in the skillet. Cook, shaking the pan occasionally until lightly toasted and fragrant, 3 to 5 minutes.

   Cut the tuna into ½-inch chunks. Put it in a large bowl.

   Peel and chop the daikon; add it to the bowl.

   Trim and chop the scallions; add them to the bowl.

   Halve the lemon; refrigerate 1 half for another use.

3. Squeeze the lemon juice into a small bowl and stir in ¼ cup mayonnaise, 3 tablespoons soy sauce, 2 teaspoons sesame oil, and Sriracha to taste.

4. Pour the dressing over the tuna and sprinkle with the toasted peanuts and sesame seeds. Toss to combine, taste and adjust the seasoning, and serve.

VARIATIONS

Shrimp Poke with Radishes and Peanuts
Use peeled shrimp instead of tuna. Before Step 1, put the shrimp in a saucepan with water to cover and bring to a boil. Turn off the heat; when the shrimp turn pink all over, drain and rinse under cold water.

Tuna Poke with Kohlrabi and Cashews
Use kohlrabi instead of daikon and cashews instead of peanuts.

4 Other Fish That Make Great Poke

1. Salmon
2. Hamachi
3. Scallops
4. Yellowtail

NOTES

MAKE YOUR OWN

Mayonnaise 144

IF YOU HAVE MORE TIME
If you don't like raw tuna, you can sear the tuna in a hot skillet until crusty on the outside but still pink in the middle. Cut it into bite-sized cubes and proceed with the recipe.

SIDES

White Rice 941

Warm Flour Tortillas 907

Cucumber Salad with Soy Sauce and Mirin 915

SPEED  SERVES 4

Smoky Shrimp Scampi

Lots of garlic and olive oil, smoked paprika, parsley, and lemon juice—the best bath a shrimp could ever ask for. A perennial favorite.

Ingredients

⅓ cup olive oil, or more as needed

4 garlic cloves

1 bunch fresh parsley

1 ½ pounds peeled medium shrimp

Salt and pepper

1 ½ teaspoons smoked paprika

1 lemon

Prep | Cook

1. Put ⅓ cup olive oil in a large skillet over low heat. There should be enough olive oil to cover the bottom of the pan; don't skimp.
   Peel and mince 4 garlic cloves.
   Chop ½ cup parsley leaves.
2. Add the garlic, shrimp, a sprinkle of salt and pepper, and 1 ½ teaspoons smoked paprika to the skillet. Toss to coat. Cook until the shrimp turn pink on one side, about 2 minutes.
   Halve the lemon; refrigerate 1 half for another use.
3. When the shrimp turn pink on 1 side, turn them over and add about half of the chopped parsley. Cook until the shrimp are pink all over and cooked through, about 2 minutes more.
4. Squeeze in the lemon juice and cook for another 30 seconds. Garnish with the remaining parsley and serve.

VARIATIONS

Smoky Scallop Scampi
Use scallops in place of shrimp, but wait to add the garlic and paprika until after you've turned them in Step 3. Cook over high heat until they are nicely seared on both sides but still pearly in the middle, less than 2 minutes per side.

Smoky Squid Scampi
Substitute squid for shrimp. After adding the squid in Step 2, cook and stir them until just opaque, only a minute or two, then stir in all the parsley and the lemon juice and serve right away.

NOTES

IF YOU HAVE MORE TIME
If you've peeled your own shrimp and have shells lying around, put them in a small saucepan with water just to cover. Bring it to a bubble, then let it simmer steadily while the garlic and shrimp are cooking. Add a splash of the shrimp stock along with the lemon juice in Step 4 and let it bubble mostly away before serving. This will intensify the shrimpy flavor of the dish. (Save the rest of the stock for risotto, paella, or other dishes.)

SIDES

Warm Buttery Bread 906

Bruschetta 909

Pasta, Plain and Simple 948

Fennel Salad 917

SPEED SERVES 4

Buffalo Shrimp

Toss something in hot sauce and butter, add blue cheese, and it'll be pretty great. The lucky vehicle here is shrimp, broiled simply and served with a celery and blue cheese dressing.

Ingredients

5 celery stalks

4 ounces Gorgonzola, Maytag blue, or other flavorful blue cheese (1 cup crumbled)

2 tablespoons olive oil

2 tablespoons red wine vinegar

Salt and pepper

4 tablespoons (½ stick) butter

1 ½ pounds peeled shrimp

⅓ cup hot sauce, plus more for serving

Prep | Cook

1. Turn the broiler to high; put the rack 4 inches from the heat.

   Trim and finely chop the celery; put in a medium bowl.

   Crumble 1 cup blue cheese.

2. Add the cheese, 2 tablespoons olive oil, 2 tablespoons red wine vinegar, and a sprinkle of salt and pepper to the bowl. Stir to combine.

   Melt 4 tablespoons butter in the microwave or in a small pot over medium-low heat.

3. Put the shrimp on a rimmed baking sheet and toss with the melted butter, ⅓ cup hot sauce, and a sprinkle of salt and pepper.

4. Broil, turning once, until the shrimp are lightly browned on the outside and just cooked through, 2 or 3 minutes per side.

5. Toss the shrimp with a little more hot sauce if you like and serve with the sauce on the side.

VARIATIONS

Buffalo Shrimp with Rémoulade
Substitute 1 small celery root, grated, for the celery and ½ cup mayonnaise and 2 tablespoons Dijon mustard for the blue cheese. Omit the olive oil.

Buffalo Shrimp with Blue Cheese Slaw
Use ½ small green cabbage, shredded, instead of the celery.

Harissa Shrimp
Substitute harissa for the hot sauce, olive oil for the melted butter, and feta for the blue cheese. Add 1 teaspoon chopped fresh thyme leaves and 1 tablespoon sesame seeds to the sauce.

Buffalo Cauliflower
Works with the main recipe or any of the variations. Instead of the chicken, use 2 medium heads cauliflower, trimmed and cut into large florets. Set the oven rack 6 inches from the heat for long-distance broiling. Coat the cauliflower as described in Step 3 and spread out on 1 or 2 rimmed baking sheets. In Step 4, broil, turning the pieces once or twice, until crisp-tender and browned in places, 10 to 15 minutes. Serve with the celery and dressing.

NOTES

EVEN FASTER
Before you start making the sauce, put the butter in a large skillet over medium-high heat. When it's melted, add the shrimp and sprinkle with salt and pepper. Cook for 2 or 3 minutes per side, stirring in the hot sauce and tossing the shrimp to coat during the last minute of cooking.

SIDES

Warm Buttery Bread 906

Green Salad 911

Crisp Seasoned Pita 908

Tomato Salad 913

SPEED ◔ SERVES 4

Black Pepper Scallops and Broccoli

This Sichuan-style dish features scallop nuggets blasted with black pepper, cooked in hot oil, then tossed with crisp-tender broccoli.

Ingredients

¼ cup vegetable oil, plus more as needed

1 ½ pounds sea scallops

2 tablespoons flour

Salt and pepper

1 large head broccoli (1 ½ to 2 pounds)

1 inch fresh ginger

2 garlic cloves

½ cup chicken stock or water

2 tablespoons soy sauce

Prep | Cook

1. Put ¼ cup vegetable oil in a large skillet over low heat.

   Pat the scallops dry and cut them into quarters; put them in a bowl.

   Line a plate with paper towels.

2. Add 2 tablespoons flour, a sprinkle of salt, and lots of pepper and toss to coat.

3. Raise the heat to high; when the oil is hot, add the scallops to the skillet and cook, tossing occasionally until they are golden and crisp all over, 3 to 5 minutes.

   Break or chop the broccoli into florets and thinly slice the stems.

4. When the scallops are golden and crisp, transfer them to the paper towels with a slotted spoon. Add more oil to the skillet if it's dry, then add the broccoli and cook, stirring occasionally until it's bright green and glossy and beginning to brown, about 5 minutes.

   Peel 1 inch ginger and 2 garlic cloves; mince them both together.

5. When the broccoli is beginning to brown, add the garlic and ginger along with ½ cup stock or water and 2 tablespoons soy sauce. Continue to cook, stirring frequently, until most of the liquid has evaporated and the broccoli is tender, 3 to 5 minutes. Taste and adjust the seasoning.

6. Return the scallops to the skillet and toss to coat lightly with the sauce and heat through. Serve immediately.

VARIATIONS

Black Pepper Shrimp and Broccoli
Substitute peeled shrimp (leave them whole) for the scallops.

Black Pepper Squid and Bok Choy
Substitute squid, cut into ¼- to ½-inch pieces, for the scallops and bok choy for broccoli. Chop the bok choy stems and leaves and cook just until the stems are tender and browned and the leaves are wilted; it won't take as long as the broccoli.

NOTES

MAKE YOUR OWN
Chicken Stock 213

SHRIMP, SQUID, AND SCALLOP DONENESS
Shrimp, squid, and scallops all cook quickly, and you can use them interchangeably. There are subtle differences in timing, though: Shrimp should be cooked until they are pink all over and firm in the middle; if they're mushy or mealy, they aren't cooked enough. Whether you sear scallops to brown the outsides or cook them more slowly, you want the insides to remain slightly creamy; a translucent center is perfect. Squid are tricky: Cook them only until they turn white, which happens very quickly. (Alternatively, you can cook them for a long, long time, but that's not "fast.")

SIDES

White Rice 941

Sesame Noodles 949

Scallion Pancakes 940

Panfried Rice Noodles 951

SPEED SERVES 4

Steamed Clams with Chorizo and Cherry Tomatoes

A huge pot of steamed clams is always tempting. Flavored with chorizo and cherry tomatoes, it's especially delicious, and the liquid makes for fantastic dunking, so serve with crusty bread. See the Notes if you want to use mussels instead.

Ingredients

2 tablespoons olive oil

8 ounces smoked Spanish chorizo

4 garlic cloves

3 pounds littleneck or other small hard-shell clams

1 pint cherry tomatoes

½ cup white wine

Pepper

1 bunch fresh parsley

Prep | Cook

1. Put 2 tablespoons oil in a large skillet or a large pot over medium-high heat.

   Chop the chorizo; add it to the skillet.

   Peel and thinly slice 4 garlic cloves; add them to the skillet.

2. Cook the chorizo and garlic, stirring occasionally until the garlic is golden, 2 or 3 minutes.

   Scrub the clams.

3. When the garlic is golden, add the clams, tomatoes, ½ cup white wine, and a sprinkle of pepper.

4. Raise the heat to high, cover, and cook, shaking the skillet occasionally until the clams have opened, 8 to 10 minutes.

   Chop ⅓ cup parsley.

5. When the clams have opened, sprinkle with the parsley and serve with the broth.

VARIATIONS

Steamed Thai-Style Clams with Spinach
Substitute butter or vegetable oil for the olive oil, 2 inches minced ginger for the garlic, 1 tablespoon curry powder for the chorizo, 1 cup coconut milk for the wine and cilantro for the parsley.

Steamed Clams with Tarragon and Cream
Skip the chorizo. Use butter instead of olive oil and 2 shallots instead of garlic. Add 1/4 cup cream along with the wine and garnish with some tarragon instead of parsley.

NOTES

SWAPPING MUSSELS FOR CLAMS
You can substitute the first for the second in almost all recipes, but clams weigh a lot more so figure you'll need half as much. Mussels tend to open a bit faster than clams, but they take more effort to clean (pulling off their beards) than clams, which need just a good scrub. (Farm-raised mussels are usually sold cleaned; they need just a rinse. But wild mussels are better.) One significant benefit of mussels is that they are much less expensive.

SIDES

Garlic Bread 906

Bruschetta 909

Warm Buttery Bread 906

Pasta, Plain and Simple 948

Crisp Roasted Potatoes with Smoked Paprika 965

SPEED ◑ SERVES 4

Salmon with Gingery Greens

A pile of just-wilted greens makes a perfect bed for steaming fish, providing enough moisture to cook it through without any scorching or drying out. Here loads of ginger in the greens permeates the salmon and leaves you with a tasty side dish.

Ingredients

3 tablespoons butter

1 large bunch kale or collards (1 ½ pounds)

2 inches fresh ginger

Salt and pepper

½ cup chicken or fish stock or water

4 thick salmon steaks or fillets (1 ½ pounds)

Prep | Cook

1. Put 3 tablespoons butter in a large skillet over low heat.
   Trim and chop the greens, separating any thick stems if necessary.
2. Raise the heat to medium-high. Add any thick stems to the skillet and cook until they begin to soften, 3 or 4 minutes.
   Peel and mince 2 inches ginger.
3. Add the ginger and the leaves, a handful at a time if necessary, to the skillet and sprinkle with salt and pepper. Cook until the leaves are just wilted, 4 or 5 minutes.
4. Add ½ cup stock or water, lay the salmon on top of the greens, and sprinkle with salt and pepper.
5. Lower the heat to medium, cover, and cook for no more than 10 minutes for medium to medium-well and less if you like your salmon closer to medium-rare. Transfer to plates or a platter and serve.

VARIATIONS

Salmon with Garlicky Stewed Greens and Tomatoes
Use 4 garlic cloves instead of the ginger and 2 tomatoes, chopped, instead of the stock or water.

Salmon with Sweet and Sour Bok Choy
Substitute bok choy for the kale or collards and 2 tablespoons rice vinegar, 1 tablespoons soy sauce, and 1 tablespoon honey for the stock or water.

Salmon with Creamed Spinach
Substitute spinach for the kale or collards, 1 large shallot for the ginger, and ½ cup cream for the stock or water. Add a pinch of nutmeg to the spinach as well; the leaves will take only 2 or 3 minutes to wilt.

Salmon with Gingery Creamed Corn
An unexpectedly good combination. Substitute 4 cups fresh or frozen corn kernels for the greens. Skip Step 2 but prepare the ginger as directed. In Step 3, cook the ginger and corn in the hot butter just long enough for them to soften a little, 1 or 2 minutes. Substitute ½ cup cream for the stock or water in Step 4.

Salmon with Gingery Creamed Peas
Follow the directions for the variation above, swapping peas for the corn. Use ½ cup cream instead of the stock or water in Step 4.

NOTES

MAKE YOUR OWN

Chicken Stock 213

Fish Stock 213

SIDES

White Rice 941

Quinoa 945

Sesame Noodles 949

RECIPE-FREE

Steamed Fish

1 Choose a skillet and heat some fat.

The pan should have a tight-fitting lid and be large enough to accommodate all the vegetables and the fish, but not so big that the vegetables can't cover the bottom in a solid layer. Put 2 or more tablespoons oil or butter in the skillet over medium-high heat.

2 Prepare vegetables.

Start with aromatics, then choose one or more main vegetables. Watery vegetables like greens, zucchini, and fresh tomatoes will release liquid and help the steaming process. Starchier vegetables like potatoes will not, so you'll have to add a splash of liquid later.

3 Sauté vegetables.

For soft vegetables, cook until they are almost fully tender. In the time that it takes to steam the fish the vegetables will become soft. For vegetables you want barely tender, sauté until they're still slightly too firm to eat. Add enough water to keep them from sticking.

❹ Check your liquid level.

If vegetable juices are bubbling in the bottom of the skillet, don't add any extra liquid. Otherwise, add a splash. If you want something more like a stew, add enough liquid to make the vegetables saucy.

❺ Add your fish.

Thick fish fillets, shrimp, clams, and mussels are ideal steamed—they cook quickly, and stay moist. (This is also a great way to cook boneless chicken.) Figure 1 to 2 pounds. Lay them on top of the vegetables, sprinkle with salt and pepper, and cover the skillet.

❻ Steam, garnish, and serve.

Steam until the fish is just cooked through, carefully checking every now and then and adding more liquid if needed. When the fish is cooked, the vegetables will be too. To serve, scoop up some vegetables and fish onto a plate, then drizzle with the pan juices.

SPEED ◑ SERVES 4

Roasted Salmon with Potato Crust

Topping salmon with a thin layer of shredded potatoes and roasting it in a hot oven is as impressive as it is delicious.

Ingredients

2 or 3 medium russet or Yukon Gold potatoes (8 ounces)

4 thick salmon fillets (1 ½ pounds)

3 tablespoons olive oil

Salt and pepper

1 bunch fresh chives

Prep | Cook

1. Heat the oven to 475°F.

   Scrub the potatoes. If you're using a food processor for grating, cut them into chunks that will fit through the feed tube. Line a colander with paper towels.

2. Shred the potatoes in a food processor with a grating disk or by hand with a box grater. Put the potatoes in the colander and squeeze out as much moisture as you can.

3. Put the salmon in a baking dish or on a rimmed baking sheet, skin side down. Spread the potatoes over the top of the fish, pressing them down and covering the fish in a thin, even layer. Drizzle with 3 tablespoons olive oil and sprinkle with salt and pepper.

4. Roast until the salmon is cooked through and the potatoes are crisp, about 10 minutes.

   Chop a few tablespoons chives.

5. If the salmon cooks through before the potatoes are as crisp as you want, put the pan under the broiler until the potatoes are done to your liking. Garnish with the chives and serve.

VARIATIONS

4 Other Grated Vegetables to Use

Peel them first:

1. Sweet potatoes
2. Parsnips
3. Celery root
4. Beets

3 Other Toppings to Use for Crust

1. Coarsely ground bread crumbs
2. Pulverized rolled oats
3. Coarsely ground nuts

NOTES

IF YOU HAVE MORE TIME

If you're up for a little more maneuvering for the sake of a fried potato crust, heat a few tablespoons of olive oil in a large skillet. Press the potatoes firmly into the top of the fish. When the oil is hot, gently lay the fish in the pan, potato side down, trying to minimize the amount of potatoes that fall off. Cook until the potatoes are golden and crisp, then turn the salmon and cook on the other side just until the fish is done to your liking.

SIDES

Green Salad 911

Sautéed Greens with Garlic 924

Garlicky Mushrooms 956

Quinoa 945

SPEED ◐ SERVES 4

Sole (or Other Thin Fillets) with Glazed Carrots

Two French preparations, glazed carrots and sole cooked in butter, take turns in the skillet, both streamlined slightly to get everything on the table quickly.

Ingredients

6 tablespoons (¾ stick) butter

1 pound carrots

1 teaspoon sugar

2 sprigs fresh thyme

Salt and pepper

1 orange

Four 6-ounce fillets of sole or any other thin white fish fillets

1 bunch fresh parsley

½ cup white wine or water

Prep | Cook

1. Heat the oven to 200°F. Put 2 tablespoons butter in a large skillet over medium-low heat.

   Trim, peel, and slice the carrots into coins.

2. Raise the heat to medium-high. When the butter foams, add the carrots, 1 teaspoon sugar, 2 fresh thyme sprigs, and a sprinkle of salt and pepper. Cook, stirring occasionally until the carrots are tender, 5 to 10 minutes.

   Halve the orange.

   Sprinkle the fish with salt and pepper.

3. When the carrots are tender, transfer them to a platter, wipe out the pan, and add 2 tablespoons butter. When the butter foam subsides, add the fish and cook, in batches if necessary, until it's golden on each side, 4 or 5 minutes total. Transfer to the oven to keep warm and repeat with the remaining fish.

   Chop ¼ cup parsley.

4. Once all the fish is cooked, put it on top of the carrots. Squeeze the orange juice into the skillet and add ½ cup wine or water and a sprinkle of salt and pepper. Let the liquid reduce a bit, then stir in 2 tablespoons butter and the parsley.

5. Pour the sauce over the fish and carrots and serve.

VARIATIONS

Sole (or Other Thin Fillets) with Sesame Bean Sprouts
Substitute bean sprouts for the carrots and sauté them in 1 tablespoon butter and 1 tablespoon sesame oil until they soften slightly but retain their crunch. Substitute ¼ cup soy sauce and the juice of 2 limes for the orange juice and cilantro for the parsley.

Sole (or Other Thin Fillets) with Balsamic Radicchio
Substitute chopped radicchio for the carrots, ¼ cup balsamic vinegar mixed with ¼ cup water for the orange juice, and basil for the parsley.

Sole (or Other Thin Fillets) with Lemony Asparagus
Use asparagus instead of carrots and a lemon instead of the orange. Omit the sugar. In Step 2, cook the asparagus until they're just beginning to get tender, closer to 5 than 10 minutes. Use mint instead of parsley to finish the sauce if you'd like.

SIDES

Green Salad 911

White Rice 941

Buttered Egg Noodles 948

Warm Buttery Bread 906

SPEED ◐ SERVES 4

Swordfish (or Other Fish Steaks) with Picante Verde

This quick skillet tomatillo salsa is an ideal accompaniment to simply cooked fish. If you can find only canned tomatillos, use a 28-ounce can and include their juice. They are already softened, so just cook until they break apart and thicken a bit.

Ingredients

4 tablespoons olive oil

1 red onion

1 poblano pepper

1 pound tomatillos (5 or 6 large ones)

2 garlic cloves

1 lime

Salt and pepper

1 ½ pounds swordfish steaks or other fish steaks

Prep | Cook

1. Turn the broiler to high; put the rack 6 inches from the heat. Put 2 tablespoons olive oil in a medium skillet over medium-high heat.

   As you work, add everything to the skillet:
   Trim, peel, and chop the onion.
   Trim, core, seed, and chop the poblano.
   Husk and chop the tomatillos.
   Peel and mince 2 garlic cloves.
   Halve the lime and squeeze in the juice.

2. Sprinkle the mixture with salt and pepper and cook, stirring occasionally until the tomatillos break down and thicken the sauce, about 10 minutes.

   Pat the swordfish dry.

3. While the sauce cooks, drizzle the swordfish with 2 tablespoons olive oil and sprinkle with salt and pepper. Broil, turning about halfway through, for no more than 10 minutes; do not overcook.

4. When the tomatillos have thickened the sauce, taste and adjust the seasoning. Spoon it on top of the swordfish and serve.

VARIATIONS

Broiled Swordfish (or Other Fish Steaks) with Picante Rojo
Use tomatoes in place of the tomatillos.

Broiled Swordfish (or Other Fish Steaks) with Picante Amarilla
Substitute 2 cups chopped pineapple and 1 cup corn kernels for the tomatillos.

Broiled Swordfish (or Other Fish Steaks) with Warm Tapenade
Substitute 1 cup chopped pitted black or green olives for the tomatillos, 3/4 cup chopped dried tomatoes for the poblano, 1/4 cup capers for the onion, and an additional 2/3 cup olive oil for the lime juice.

NOTES

EVEN FASTER
Smooth Cooked Salsa
Put all the salsa ingredients in the blender and purée, adding a little water to get the machine going if necessary. Simmer the mixture in a skillet or saucepan until the swordfish is done, or 10 to 15 minutes.

SIDES

Warm Flour Tortillas 907

White Rice 941

Mexican Street Corn 932

Sautéed Sweet Potatoes with Chipotle and Lime 964

Jícama and Radish Salad 918

SPEED ◐ SERVES 4

Striped Bass (or Other Thick Fillets) and Zucchini Ribbons

Sear striped bass in a skillet to a beautiful golden brown and serve with a rustic sauce of herbs, garlic, and capers and everyone will be pleased. Serve over a bed of shaved raw zucchini ribbons and they'll be wowed.

Ingredients

1 bunch fresh parsley

1 bunch fresh mint

1 garlic clove

2 medium zucchini (1 pound)

2 tablespoons capers

5 tablespoons olive oil

1 teaspoon red wine vinegar

Salt and pepper

1 ½ pounds 1-inch-thick striped bass fillets or other thick fillets (skin on)

Prep | Cook

Strip ½ cup parsley leaves and ¼ cup mint leaves from the most tender stems.

Peel 1 garlic clove.

Trim the zucchini; shave them into ribbons with a vegetable peeler.

1. In a food processor or by hand, mince 2 tablespoons capers, the parsley, mint, and garlic and blend with 3 tablespoons olive oil, 1 teaspoon red wine vinegar, and a sprinkle of salt and pepper.

2. Put the zucchini in a large bowl and toss with about half of the herb mixture. Taste and adjust the seasoning.

3. Put 2 tablespoons olive oil in a large skillet over medium-high heat.

   Pat the fish dry. Sprinkle it with salt and pepper.

4. When the oil is hot, add the fish skin side down. Cook until the skin is browned and crisp, 4 or 5 minutes. Turn and cook until the fish is just cooked through and tender, another few minutes.

5. Divide the zucchini among 4 plates. When the fish is done, serve it on top of the zucchini, spooning the remaining herb mixture over all.

VARIATIONS

Striped Bass (or Other Thick Fillets) and Cucumber Ribbons

Substitute 1 pound cucumbers for the zucchini. When peeling off the ribbons, turn the cucumber as you work and stop when you get to the seeds.

Striped Bass (or Other Thick Fillets) and Fennel

Substitute 2 large fennel bulbs, thinly sliced, for the zucchini and fennel fronds for the mint.

SIDES

Couscous 910

Rice Pilaf 944

Bulgur with Lemon and Parsley 946

Skin-On Mashed Potatoes 961

SPEED ◐ SERVES 4

Cod (or Other Thick Fillets) and Chickpea Stew

This hearty Spanish stew of chickpeas, spinach, and cod comes together very quickly in a single skillet. Any thick white fish fillet that is sturdy enough to hold its own with the flavor and texture of chickpeas will work perfectly.

Ingredients

3 tablespoons olive oil

1 onion

3 garlic cloves

1 bunch spinach (1 pound)

2 cups cooked or canned chickpeas (one 15-ounce can)

2 teaspoons smoked paprika

Salt and pepper

½ cup stock or water

Four 6-ounce cod or other thick white fish fillets

Several sprigs fresh parsley for garnish

Prep | Cook

1. Put 3 tablespoons oil in a large skillet over medium-high heat.

   Trim, peel, and chop the onion.

   Peel and mince 3 garlic cloves.

2. Add the onion and garlic to the skillet and cook, stirring occasionally until the onion softens, 3 to 5 minutes.

   Trim off any thick stems from the spinach and chop the leaves.

   If you're using canned chickpeas, rinse and drain them.

3. When the onions soften, add 2 teaspoons smoked paprika and cook, stirring until fragrant, a minute or 2.

4. Add the spinach, a handful at a time if necessary to fit it in, and the chickpeas and sprinkle with salt and pepper. Cook, stirring, just until the spinach wilts.

5. Add ½ cup stock or water. Sprinkle the fish with salt and pepper and lay it on top of the spinach and chickpeas. Adjust the heat so the mixture bubbles steadily but not vigorously.

6. Cover the skillet and cook until a thin-bladed knife inserted into the thickest part of the fish meets little resistance, 6 to 10 minutes. Strip the parsley leaves from several sprigs and chop.

7. When the fish is done, sprinkle the parsley over everything and serve immediately.

VARIATIONS

Cod (or Other Thick Fillets) and White Bean Stew
Substitute 1 teaspoon chopped fresh rosemary for the smoked paprika, escarole for the spinach, white beans for the chickpeas, and basil for the parsley.

Cod (or Other Thick Fillets) and Fava Stew
Substitute 1 tablespoon chopped fresh tarragon for the smoked paprika and fava beans for the chickpeas. Garnish with a squeeze of lemon juice in addition to the parsley.

NOTES

MAKE YOUR OWN

Cooked Beans 496

Fish Stock 213

Chicken Stock 213

Vegetable Stock 212

EVEN FASTER
Instead of using individual fillets, cut the fish into chunks and nestle them into the chickpea and spinach mixture before covering and cooking. They'll take no more than 5 minutes.

SIDES

Bruschetta 909

Quick Brown Rice 941

Bulgur with Lemon and Parsley 946

Couscous 910

SPEED ◐ SERVES 4

Caramel-Cooked Cod (or Other Thick Fillets)

If you haven't been to Vietnam (or a good Vietnamese restaurant), this dish may sound crazy; caramel is for ice cream, not seafood! But fish in caramel sauce is a spectacular Vietnamese technique; the sauce is bittersweet and loaded with the pleasant sharpness of black pepper.

Ingredients

1 cup sugar

3 or 4 shallots

3 limes, plus more to taste

½ cup fish sauce, plus more to taste

2 bunches scallions

1 ½ pounds cod or other thick white fish fillets

1 tablespoon vegetable oil

Salt and pepper

1 bunch fresh cilantro

Rice vinegar for serving (optional)

Prep | Cook

1. Turn the broiler to high; put the rack 4 inches from heat.
2. Put a large deep skillet over medium heat and add 1 cup sugar and 1 or 2 tablespoons water. Cook, occasionally shaking the pan gently until the sugar liquefies completely, about 5 minutes.

   Trim, peel, and thinly slice the shallots.

   Halve 3 limes.

   Mix ½ cup fish sauce with ½ cup water.
3. When the sugar is all liquid, cook until it darkens slightly, another 2 or 3 minutes; remove from the heat. Carefully, and at arm's length, add the fish sauce mixture to the melted sugar. Turn the heat to medium-high and cook, stirring constantly until the caramel melts into the liquid, 1 or 2 minutes.
4. Add the shallots and cook, stirring occasionally until they soften, 3 to 5 minutes.

   Trim the scallions.

   Cut the fish into fillets as necessary to fit in the pan.

5. Put the scallions on a rimmed baking sheet, toss with 1 tablespoon vegetable oil, and sprinkle with salt and pepper. Broil, turning as necessary, until lightly charred all over, 4 or 5 minutes.

6. While the scallions broil, squeeze the lime juice into the skillet, add 1 teaspoon (or more) pepper, and lay the fish in the sauce. If the sauce does not reach at least halfway up the fish, add some water. Adjust the heat so that the poaching liquid bubbles lightly. Simmer until a thin-bladed knife inserted into the center meets little resistance, 8 to 12 minutes.

   Chop 1/4 cup cilantro.

7. When the fish is done, taste the sauce and add more fish sauce, lime juice, or pepper if necessary. Serve with the scallions, pouring the sauce over the top, garnishing with the cilantro, and passing rice vinegar at the table if you like.

VARIATIONS

Caramel-Cooked Shrimp
Substitute shrimp for the cod and carrots, cut lengthwise into quarters, for the scallions. The shrimp will take only 5 minutes or so to cook.

Caramel-Cooked Scallops
Substitute scallops for the cod and leeks, cut lengthwise into quarters, for the scallions. The scallops will take only 5 minutes or so to cook.

NOTES

EVEN FASTER
Spread a broiler-safe pan with vegetable oil. Dredge the cod in a mixture of brown sugar and lots of coarse pepper. Broil carefully with the scallions; the fish will brown quickly. Drizzle with fish sauce and lime juice.

SIDES

White Rice 941

Quinoa 945

Fire and Ice Noodles 950

Avocado with Lime and Chili Salt 920

SPEED ◐ SERVES 4

Olive Oil–Poached Halibut (or Other Thick Fillets) with Endive

Half oil-poached, half-steamed, this method gives both the halibut and the endive great silky texture, while citrus zest and thyme gently infuse them with bright and earthy flavor.

Ingredients

Olive oil for poaching

½ cup white wine

1 lemon

1 orange

3 sprigs fresh thyme

4 heads Belgian endive

Four 6-ounce halibut or other skinless thick white fish fillets

Salt and pepper

Prep | Cook

1. Put ¼ to ½ inch olive oil and ½ cup white wine in a large skillet or large pot over medium-high heat.

   Peel a few strips of lemon and orange zest and add them to the pan (refrigerate the fruit for another use).

   Add 3 thyme sprigs to the pan.

   Cut each endive head in half lengthwise.

2. When the oil begins to send up tiny bubbles, sprinkle the fish with salt and pepper and add it to the pan. Put the endive around the fish (and on top if you run out of room). Adjust the heat so the mixture bubbles gently but steadily.

3. Cover the pan and cook, turning the fish halfway through and occasionally splashing everything with the oil, until a thin-bladed knife inserted into the thickest part of the fish meets little resistance, 15 to 20 minutes. (Since the fish will be soft, you still want the inner parts of the endive to be a bit crunchy.)

4. When the fish is done, discard the citrus peels and thyme sprigs. Serve the fish and endive with a little of the poaching liquid if you like, sprinkling with salt and pepper as needed.

VARIATIONS

Butter-Poached Halibut (or Other Thick Fillets) with Peas
Substitute melted butter for all or some of the olive oil and 3 cups fresh peas for the endive. If you use frozen peas, just add them to the skillet about 5 minutes before the fish is done.

NOTES

OIL POACHING MEETS STEAMING
Poaching fish (or anything) in olive oil is a luxurious cooking method that keeps the food incredibly moist and infuses it with loads of flavor but typically requires enough oil to submerge whatever it is you're cooking. If you combine oil poaching with steaming, you save both money and time: Cover the fish about halfway with oil, then cover the skillet so the fish steams from the top while the oil cooks it from below. Add a safety net in the form of some white wine. The liquid helps prevent the oil from browning the fish (which you don't want in the case of poaching) and lets you bring the oil to a slightly higher temperature, which allows the fish to cook a little faster.

SIDES

Bruschetta 909

Quinoa 945

Crisp Roasted Potatoes 965

Refried White Beans with Rosemary 938

Pasta, Plain and Simple 948

SPEED ◑ SERVES 4

Blackened Catfish (or Other Thick Fillets) with Green Beans

Here's blackened catfish, with green beans sizzled in what's left of the delicious cooked spice mixture when the fish is done.

Ingredients

3 tablespoons butter, plus more as needed

1 tablespoon paprika

2 teaspoons dried oregano

½ teaspoon cayenne

½ teaspoon sugar

Salt and pepper

1 ½ pounds catfish or other thick white fish fillets

1 pound green beans

¼ cup almonds

Prep | Cook

1. Heat the oven to 200°F. Put 2 tablespoons butter in a large ovenproof skillet over medium-low heat.
2. Combine 1 tablespoon paprika, 2 teaspoons oregano, ½ teaspoon cayenne, ½ teaspoon sugar, and some salt and pepper in a small bowl. Rub the spice mixture all over the fish.
3. When the butter foams, raise the heat to medium-high and add the fish (in 2 batches if necessary, adding more butter as needed). Cook, turning once, until the fish is nicely blackened on both sides and cooked through, about 4 minutes per side.
   Trim and chop the green beans into 2-inch lengths.
4. When the fish is done, transfer it to the oven to keep it warm. Add 1 tablespoon butter and the green beans to the skillet and sprinkle with salt and pepper.

5. Cook, stirring occasionally until they are just tender and beginning to brown in spots, 3 to 5 minutes, or longer if you like them softer. Chop 1/4 cup almonds.

6. When the green beans are done, put the catfish on top, sprinkle with the almonds, and serve.

VARIATIONS

Dijon Catfish with Green Beans

Skip the spices and instead coat the fish with a mixture of 2 tablespoons Dijon mustard, 1 tablespoon lemon juice, a sprinkle of salt, and lots of pepper. The fish won't blacken in the same way, but the mustard coating will get crusty and brown.

NOTES

MAKE YOUR OWN

Spice Blends 758

BLACKENED ANYTHING

Blackening adds a ton of flavor in a very short time. It consists of coating a piece of fish, chicken, meat, tofu, or anything else in a mixture of spices and dried herbs and cooking it at high heat until the spices turn dark and crusty (just shy of burning). As they toast, the spices take on a deeper, more complex flavor, a transformation that happens in a matter of minutes.

To do this, mix your spices in a bowl, sprinkle them generously on the fish (or whatever), and rub them into the flesh, shaking off any excess spices before cooking over high heat. (You can also blacken on a baking sheet in the broiler, which gives you room to cook a larger batch.)

The blackening technique usually brings to mind Cajun flavors, but the spices that you use can come from anywhere. And you don't need to make mixtures; even a single spice—like cumin or smoked paprika—or a premade mixture—like five-spice powder or curry powder—can make a huge difference.

SIDES

White Rice 941

Creamy Polenta 947

Skin-On Mashed Potatoes 961

Sautéed Sweet Potatoes 964

French Fries 963

SPEED ◐ SERVES 4

Miso-Glazed Catfish (or Other Thick Fillets) and Mushrooms

Catfish is often deep-fried—at least on the Mississippi—but it roasts well too. The miso glaze was made famous in a dish with black cod but is delicious on anything.

Ingredients

1 ½ pounds button, cremini, or shiitake mushrooms

4 thick catfish or other thick white fish fillets (1 ½ pounds)

2 tablespoons vegetable oil

¼ cup sugar

1 cup miso, preferably dark

½ cup mirin or ¼ cup honey mixed with ¼ cup water

4 scallions

Prep | Cook

1. Heat the oven to 450°F.

   Trim and quarter the mushrooms. (If you're using shiitakes, discard the stems.)

2. Put the catfish in a roasting pan and scatter the mushrooms around it; drizzle everything with 2 tablespoons vegetable oil. Roast, turning the fish once and stirring the mushrooms occasionally until the fish is nearly cooked through and the mushrooms are lightly browned, 10 to 15 minutes.

3. Combine ¼ cup sugar, 1 cup miso, and ½ cup mirin (or ¼ cup honey mixed with ¼ cup water) in a small saucepan over low heat. Bring almost to a boil, stirring occasionally to combine, then turn off the heat.

   Trim and chop the scallions.

4. When the fish is nearly cooked through and the mushrooms are lightly browned, generously baste both with the miso glaze and cook until the fish is done and the glaze is slightly caramelized but not burned, another 5 minutes or so.

5. Garnish with the scallions and serve with the remaining glaze on the side.

VARIATIONS

Miso-Glazed Fish Fillets and Carrots

Substitute sliced carrots for the mushrooms.

Hoisin-Glazed Fish Fillets and Shiitakes

Substitute ½ cup soy sauce for the sugar, ½ cup hoisin for the miso, and rice vinegar for the mirin. Use all shiitake mushrooms.

Teriyaki-Glazed Fish Fillets and Sweet Potatoes

Use ½ cup soy sauce instead of the sugar and 1 tablespoon minced ginger, 1 clove garlic, minced, and ¼ cup chopped scallion instead of the miso. Substitute thinly sliced sweet potatoes for the mushrooms.

NOTES

EVEN FASTER

Substitute thin fish fillets for thick and thinly slice the mushrooms instead of quartering them. Halve the cooking time.

FISH ROASTS

Most pieces of fish can be cooked in a skillet or under the broiler in a matter of minutes. But big steaks and fillets—especially the triangular fillets from large round fish like swordfish—may be thick enough to qualify as roasts, and you can cook them as such, either by roasting them in a hot oven from beginning to end—as in this recipe—or by searing them on one side in an ovenproof skillet and finishing them in the oven or under the broiler. It's still very quick, usually taking 15 to 20 minutes.

SIDES

White Rice 941

Fire and Ice Noodles 950

Sautéed Sweet Potatoes with Ginger and Soy 964

Cucumber Salad with Soy Sauce and Mirin 915

Stir-Fried Bok Choy 927

SPEED ◐ SERVES 4

Fish Kebabs over Bulgur Pilaf

Somewhere between a pilaf and a tabbouleh, this minty, Mediterranean-inspired bulgur is a simple and satisfying bed for grilled or broiled fish kebabs.

Ingredients

1 lemon

1 large bunch fresh mint

1 small red onion

3/4 cup green olives

1/4 cup olive oil, plus more for brushing the fish

Pepper

1 cup bulgur

Salt

1 1/2 pounds fish steaks

Prep | Cook

1. Bring 2 1/2 cups water to a boil. If you're using wooden skewers, soak them in water.
2. Prepare a grill or turn the broiler to high; put the rack 4 inches from the heat.

   Halve the lemon; squeeze the juice into a medium bowl.

   Strip 1 cup mint leaves from the stems, chop, and add them to the bowl.

   Trim, peel, and chop the onion. Pit 3/4 cup olives if necessary and chop them. Add both to the bowl.

   Add 1/4 cup olive oil and plenty of pepper to the bowl and stir to combine.
3. Put 1 cup bulgur in a large bowl with a large pinch of salt. Pour the boiling water over it and cover with a plate. Finely ground bulgur will become tender in 10 to 15 minutes, medium 15 to 20, and coarse 20 to 25.
4. Cut the fish into large chunks and thread them onto skewers. Brush the fish with a little olive oil and sprinkle with salt and pepper.
5. Grill or broil, turning as each side browns, until the fish is tender but not dry, about 2 minutes per side or 5 minutes total.

6. When the bulgur is tender, drain it in a strainer, pressing out any excess water with a spoon, and return it to the bowl.

7. Spoon some of the mint and olive mixture over the kebabs and stir the rest into the bulgur. Taste and adjust the seasoning and serve the kebabs over the bulgur.

VARIATIONS

Fish Kebabs over Italian-Style Bulgur Pilaf
Substitute parsley for the mint and ½ cup raisins plus ½ cup pine nuts for the olives. If you like, grate a little Parmesan into the bulgur after you stir in the sauce.

Shrimp Kebabs over Tomato Bulgur
Use mint, basil, or parsley for the herb and 2 large ripe chopped tomatoes instead of the olives. Substitute 1 ½ pounds peeled large shrimp for the fish steaks. In Step 5 the shrimp will take as little as half the cooking time to become just pink and opaque, so figure 1 or 2 minutes a side.

Chicken Kebabs over Seasoned Bulgur
Works for the main recipe or any of the variations. Use boneless, skinless chicken thighs instead of the fish steaks. They'll take longer to cook, 8 to 12 minutes a side.

NOTES

TWO SKEWERS, ONE KEBAB
Whether you are making kebabs with fish, meat, or vegetables, inserting two skewers through each kebab will make them a lot easier to turn on the grill or in the broiler, which will give them a better chance of cooking evenly. What often happens when you use just one skewer is that once whatever you're cooking heats up, it begins to shrink a bit, and all of a sudden the hole that you made with the skewer is wider than the skewer itself. So when you go to turn the kebabs, the food just spins around on the skewer, vastly reducing your chances of browning every side evenly. Using two parallel skewers may take a few extra minutes on the threading end but will ultimately make cooking a lot easier by keeping your ingredients locked in place.

SIDES

Green Salad 911

Bruschetta 909

Tomato Salad 913

Fennel Salad 917

SPEED ◑ SERVES 4

Malaysian-Style BBQ Fish with Cool Cucumbers

Use this salty, sweet, and spicy sauce on any kind of seafood you like. Grilling and broiling are the best methods, as they perfectly caramelize the sauce.

Ingredients

2 large cucumbers

2 tablespoons rice vinegar

Salt

1 garlic clove

1 inch fresh ginger

1 fresh hot green chile (like serrano)

3 tablespoons fish sauce

3 tablespoons soy sauce

3 tablespoons honey

1 ½ pounds any thick fish fillets or steaks

1 tablespoon vegetable oil

1 tablespoon sesame oil

1 bunch fresh cilantro

1 lime

Prep | Cook

1. Prepare a grill or turn the broiler to high; put the rack 4 inches from the heat.

   Trim the cucumbers and peel if you like; cut them in half lengthwise and scoop out the seeds with a spoon. Slice them and put them in a medium bowl.

2. Toss the cucumbers with 2 tablespoons rice vinegar and a sprinkle of salt. Put the bowl in the freezer to chill.

   Peel 1 garlic clove and 1 inch ginger; trim the chile. Mince everything together.

3. Put the garlic, ginger, and chile in a small saucepan along with 3 tablespoons each fish sauce, soy sauce, and honey. Bring to a bubble and cook until slightly thickened, a minute or 2.

4. Rub the fish with 1 tablespoon each vegetable and sesame oil. Grill or broil, turning about halfway through and basting with the sauce for the last few minutes, for no more than 10 minutes. You want the sauce to caramelize and form a crust on the fish but not for the sugars to burn.

   Chop ½ cup cilantro.

   Cut the lime into wedges.

5. When the fish is cooked, remove the cucumbers from the freezer; taste and adjust the seasoning. Scatter the cilantro on top of the fish and serve with the lime wedges, cucumbers, and any extra sauce on the side.

VARIATIONS

Malaysian-Style BBQ Fish with Cool Watermelon
Replace 1 cucumber with 2 cups cubed watermelon.

Mustard-Glazed Fish with Crisp Apples
Skip the BBQ sauce and omit the sesame and vegetable oil. Instead, whisk together 1 tablespoon olive oil, ½ cup mayonnaise, ⅓ cup Dijon mustard, and 1 tablespoon chopped fresh dill; rub on the fish before grilling or broiling. Substitute apples for the cucumbers, cider vinegar for the rice vinegar, dill for the cilantro, and lemon for the lime.

Hoisin-Glazed Fish with Cool Radishes
Substitute 2 cups halved radishes for the cucumbers, ¼ cup ketchup for the honey, and hoisin sauce for the fish sauce. Reduce the soy sauce to 1 tablespoon and add 1 tablespoon rice vinegar.

NOTES

EVEN FASTER
Use thin fish fillets (broiled; don't bother turning them), shrimp, or scallops instead of steaks or thick fillets. Keep a close eye on them; they'll cook in 5 minutes.

SIDES

White Rice 941

Fire and Ice Noodles 950

Ripe Plantains 960

SPEED ◐ SERVES 4

Poached Fish in Creamy Tomato Broth

Sautéed aromatic vegetables, tomato paste, stock, and cream join to form a fast and flavorful broth for poaching fish that simmers into a beautifully balanced sauce.

Ingredients

3 tablespoons butter

3 carrots

3 celery stalks

2 medium onions

Salt and pepper

2 garlic cloves

1 tablespoon tomato paste

2 cups fish, chicken, or vegetable stock

½ cup cream

1 ½ pounds fish steaks or thick fillets

Several sprigs fresh parsley for garnish

Prep | Cook

1. Put 3 tablespoons butter in a large skillet over medium heat.

   Trim, peel, and cut the carrots into chunks; add to the skillet.

   Trim and cut the celery into chunks; add to the skillet.

   Trim, peel, and cut the onion into chunks; add to the skillet.

2. Sprinkle the vegetables with salt and pepper and cook, stirring occasionally until they soften, 5 to 10 minutes.

   Peel and thinly slice 2 garlic cloves.

3. When the vegetables soften, stir in the garlic and 1 tablespoon tomato paste. Cook, stirring until the tomato paste darkens slightly, a minute or 2.

4. Add 2 cups stock and ½ cup cream and nestle the fish into the vegetables. Bring the mixture to a boil, then adjust the heat so it simmers gently but steadily. Cover and cook until the fish is just cooked through, 5 to 10 minutes.

   Strip the parsley leaves from several sprigs and chop.

5. When the fish is done, transfer it to a platter or bowls. If you like, turn the heat to high and continue cooking until the liquid reduces further and the vegetables get softer.

6. Serve the fish with the vegetables and some of the broth, garnished with the parsley.

VARIATIONS

Fish Steaks Poached in Soy Broth
Swap ¼ cup soy sauce for the cream.

Fish Steaks Poached in Coconut Milk
Substitute 1 inch fresh ginger, minced, for the tomato paste and 1 cup coconut milk for 1 cup of the stock. If you can find coconut cream, substitute it for the regular cream.

NOTES

MAKE YOUR OWN

Fish Stock 213

Chicken Stock 213

Vegetable Stock 212

EVEN FASTER
Cut the vegetables into smaller pieces and use thin fish fillets, shrimp, scallops, or squid if you like. It will cook in about half the time.

SIDES

Pasta, Plain and Simple 948

White Rice 941

Garlic Bread 906

Green Salad 911

SPEED ◑ SERVES 4

Panfried Trout with Bacon and Leeks

Campfire food without the campfire. Use a large cast-iron skillet if you have one, return the leeks and bacon to the pan, and take the whole thing right to the table for serving.

Ingredients

4 slices bacon

2 medium leeks

Salt and pepper

1 cup cornmeal

2 whole trout, gutted

2 tablespoons butter

1 bunch fresh parsley

1 lemon

Prep | Cook

1. Put a large skillet over medium-high heat.

   Chop 4 slices bacon.

2. Add the bacon to the skillet and cook, stirring occasionally until nearly crisp, 5 to 10 minutes.

   Trim and slice the leeks.

3. When the bacon is nearly crisp, add the leeks, sprinkle with salt and pepper, and cook until the leeks soften, 3 to 5 minutes.

   Put 1 cup cornmeal in a shallow dish big enough to hold the fish. Sprinkle the trout with salt and pepper and dredge them on both sides in the cornmeal.

4. When the leeks are soft, remove them and the bacon with a slotted spoon, leaving any bacon fat behind.

5. Add 2 tablespoons butter to the skillet, then the trout. Cook, turning once, until both sides are nicely browned and the interior of the fish turns white, 8 to 12 minutes.

   Chop ¼ cup parsley.

   Cut the lemon into wedges.

6. When the trout is browned and the interior is white, serve (1 fish for 2 people) with the leeks and bacon, garnished with the parsley and lemon wedges.

VARIATIONS

Panfried Trout with Bacon and Brussels Sprouts
Use 1 pound Brussels sprouts, halved, instead of the leeks. They'll take a few extra minutes to become tender.

Panfried Trout with Chorizo and Red Onions
Substitute 4 to 8 ounces chopped fresh Mexican chorizo for the bacon and 2 red onions for the leeks.

Panfried Soft-Shell Crabs with Bacon and Leeks
Substitute 4 soft-shell crabs for the trout. Cook until they are golden brown on the outside, no more than 5 minutes.

NOTES

EVEN FASTER
As soon as the bacon renders a little fat, spoon a tablespoon or 2 into another skillet and cook the trout while the bacon and leeks finish cooking.

SIDES

Warm Buttery Bread 906

Creamy Polenta with Parmesan 947

Green Salad 911

Mexican Street Corn 932

SPEED ◐ SERVES 4

Mediterranean Mackerel with Mint

Mint lightens everything it touches, and mackerel is a strongly flavored fish that benefits from some levity. Put the two together along with cumin, tomatoes, onions, and peppers and you've got something wonderful, especially when served on a bed of couscous. Or try one of the sides options on the opposite page.

Ingredients

3 tablespoons olive oil

1 yellow onion

1 sweet Italian long pepper (any type)

1 bunch fresh parsley

1 bunch fresh mint

1 tablespoon cumin

¼ teaspoon red chile flakes

Salt and pepper

One 28-ounce diced tomatoes

1 ½ pounds skin-on mackerel fillets

Prep | Cook

1. Heat 2 tablespoons olive oil in a large skillet over medium heat.
   Peel and chop the onion. Trim, core, seed, and chop the pepper. Add both to the skillet.
2. Turn the heat up to medium-high and cook until the vegetables soften, about 5 minutes.
   Chop 1 cup each parsley and mint leaves.
3. Turn on the broiler and put a cast-iron or other ovenproof skillet 6 inches from the heat.
4. When the onion and pepper are soft, add 1 tablespoon cumin, ¼ teaspoon red chile flakes, and a sprinkle of salt and pepper. Cook until soft and fragrant, about 3 minutes. Add the parsley and mint leaves and the tomatoes with their juice, stirring to combine. Reduce the heat to low, cover, and simmer.
5. Remove the hot skillet from the oven and add the mackerel fillets, skin side up. Return to the oven and broil until the flesh flakes with a fork, no more than 10 minutes.
6. Taste and adjust the seasoning. Spoon the tomato mixture into bowls, top with the mackerel fillets, and serve.

NOTES

IF YOU HAVE MORE TIME

If you prefer whole mackerel to fillets (or that's all you can find), feel free to substitute 2 pounds of them here, keeping in mind that they will take a few minutes longer to cook.

OILY FISH

Fish like mackerel, sardines, and bluefish are indeed "oily," "fatty," and "fishy." But these are all desirable attributes in seafood, meaning that it has plenty of flavor and will stay moist during cooking. (Not to mention that fish oil is good for you.) The other great thing about these kinds of fish is that they are generally among the most sustainable of all seafood. They are abundant, cheap, and you can eat them with a clear conscience.

SIDES

Couscous 910

Bulgur with Lemon and Parsley 946

Steamed Tender Vegetables 954

Peas with Bacon and Onion 934

Crisp Roasted Potatoes 965

TECHNIQUE

Cooking Seafood

Because fish cooks so quickly, it's important not to lose track of it while multitasking. If you err on the side of cutting and peeking often, you'll turn out perfectly cooked fish regularly. For fish that you want to cook through, the easiest way to determine doneness is simply to poke the center with a skewer or thin-bladed knife; when it penetrates without resistance, the fish is done. (If you want fish that's less than fully cooked, you have to peek.) Here are some guidelines for buying sustainable fish, cooking it, and recognizing doneness.

Type of Seafood	Cooking Suggestions
WHITE FILLETS LESS THAN ½ INCH THICK	The look of the exterior is a solid indication of whether the middle is cooked through; when it's opaque, the inside will be just about done. In any case, it will finish cooking by the time it gets to the table. Take care not to overcook.
WHITE FILLETS BETWEEN ½ AND 1 INCH	These shouldn't be cooked for any longer than 8 minutes total. To check, use a thin-bladed knife to peek between the flakes of the fish; if most of the translucence is gone and the fish is tender, it's done.
THICKER WHITE FILLETS AND STEAKS	A good guideline is about 8 minutes per inch of thickness. Begin checking after 7 minutes of cooking time per inch. Use a thin-bladed knife to gently open the fish at its thickest part and peek inside; if it's nearly opaque, stop cooking; the fish will finish cooking on the way to the table.
SWORDFISH	Swordfish is at its most moist if you stop cooking when just a little translucence remains in the center; cook it to the well-done stage if you prefer, but get it off the heat quickly or it will be dry.
TUNA AND SALMON	Tuna is typically best when still red to pink in the center. Likewise, salmon is best when it's still slightly orange in the center, not pale pink (see Salmon Temperature, page 539).

Type of Seafood	Cooking Suggestions
OTHER OILY FISH	Start with the nick-and-peek technique. When they are very nearly white throughout (or dark pink in the case of salmon—see Salmon Temperature, page 539), remove them from the heat.
MAKO, MONKFISH, HALIBUT, AND STRIPED BASS	Judge doneness not only by appearance but also by tenderness; sometimes they are tender just before the translucence disappears, other times just after. It will be a matter of just a minute or two.
SHELLFISH	Shrimp, squid, and scallops all cook quickly, and you can use them interchangeably. There are subtle differences in cooking times, though: Shrimp should be cooked until they are pink all over and firm in the middle; if they're mushy or mealy, they aren't cooked enough. Whether you sear scallops to brown the outsides or cook them more slowly, you want the insides to remain slightly creamy; a translucent center is perfect. Squid are tricky: cook them only until they turn white, which happens very quickly. (Alternatively, you can cook them for a long, long time, but that's not "fast.") Clams and mussels are done when all (or almost all) of the shells have opened.

Sustainable Seafood

Buying seafood was always more complicated than cooking it, and now the situation is worse than ever. Fish comes to our supermarket from all over the world. Some is wild, and some is farmed; some is abundant, and some is depleted; some is caught in ways that protect the environment, and some is caught in ways that destroy it. To make a long story short, it is hard to grasp all these things when we're staring at the fish counter trying to decide what to make for dinner. The lists of what's sustainable and what isn't change all the time as fish stocks are depleted and then built back up or as farming methods change. Many fish are considered endangered one year and just fine to eat the next, and nothing in print can keep up with that, so I want to point you to two invaluable resources to help you purchase fish with confidence and a clear conscience.

The Monterey Bay Aquarium:
http://www.montereybayaquarium.org/cr/seafoodwatch.aspx

Blue Ocean Institute's Seafood Guide
http://blueocean.org/seafoods/

SPEED ◑ SERVES 4

Stir-Fried Shrimp with Tomato, Eggs, and Scallions

Scrambled eggs with shrimp and soy sauce is a fantastic dish all by itself and only gets better when you weave in tomatoes and scallions. This is well on its way to being shrimp fried rice, so if you cook up a pot of white rice or noodles on the side, you'll have everything you need.

Ingredients

2 tablespoons butter

6 eggs

Salt and pepper

1 tablespoon vegetable oil

1 tablespoon sesame oil

1 inch fresh ginger

2 garlic cloves

1 pound peeled shrimp

2 or 3 medium ripe tomatoes

4 scallions

Soy sauce for serving

Prep | Cook

1. Put 2 tablespoons butter in a large skillet over medium-high heat.

   Crack the eggs into a medium mixing bowl, sprinkle with salt and pepper, and beat.

2. When the butter starts to sizzle, add the eggs. Cook, stirring frequently and scraping the sides with a heatproof rubber spatula until they begin to curdle.

3. If some parts of the eggs are drying out, remove the skillet from the heat and continue stirring until the cooking slows down a bit. Then return to the heat. When the eggs are creamy, soft, and still a bit runny, transfer them to a plate and wipe out the skillet.

4. Put 1 tablespoon vegetable oil and 1 tablespoon sesame oil in the skillet over medium heat.

   Peel 1 inch ginger and 2 garlic cloves; mince them together.

5. Turn the heat up to medium-high. Add the ginger and garlic and the shrimp and sprinkle with salt and pepper. Cook, stirring occasionally until the shrimp are just starting to turn pink, 2 or 3 minutes.

   Core and chop the tomatoes; add them to the skillet as you go.

6. Cook until the tomatoes release some of their liquid, another 2 or 3 minutes.

   Trim and chop the scallions.

7. When the tomatoes release some liquid, stir the scrambled eggs back into the skillet along with the scallions. Toss to combine and serve, passing soy sauce at the table.

VARIATIONS

Stir-Fried Shrimp with Tomato, Eggs, and Basil

Substitute 2 tablespoons olive oil for the vegetable and sesame oils, ½ teaspoon red chile flakes for the ginger, and ½ cup chopped fresh basil for the scallions. Instead of passing soy sauce at the table, pass more olive oil or even some grated Parmesan.

Stir-Fried Shrimp with Shiitakes, Eggs, and Cilantro

Swap 2 cups sliced shiitake mushrooms for the tomatoes. Before adding the ginger, garlic, and shrimp in Step 5, stir-fry the shiitakes until they begin to get tender and lightly browned, 3 to 5 minutes. Swap ½ cup chopped fresh cilantro for the scallions.

NOTES

EVEN FASTER

A little less saucy than the main recipe. Start by stir-frying the ginger, garlic, and shrimp for a minute or 2, then pour in the beaten eggs and scramble them. Stir in the chopped tomatoes and cook for a minute or 2, then garnish with the scallions and serve.

SIDES

White Rice 941

Sesame Noodles 949

Panfried Rice Noodles 951

SPEED SERVES 4

Shrimp and Cauliflower with Rustic Romesco

Instead of making this Catalan nut and red pepper sauce in the food processor, I add all the romesco ingredients to a stir-fry of cauliflower and shrimp, which infuses the dish with all the right flavors but leaves the texture rough and rustic.

Ingredients

¼ cup almonds

2 thick slices any rustic bread (a little stale is fine)

1 medium head cauliflower (1 to 1 ½ pounds)

3 tablespoons olive oil

Salt and pepper

2 garlic cloves

1 cup roasted red peppers

1 pound peeled shrimp

1 teaspoon smoked paprika

2 tablespoons sherry vinegar

1 bunch fresh parsley

Prep | Cook

1. Put a large skillet over medium-high heat.

   Chop ¼ cup almonds.

   Chop 2 thick slices bread into large crumbs.

2. Add the almonds and bread crumbs to the skillet and cook, shaking the pan frequently until they are fragrant and toasted, 3 to 5 minutes.

   Trim and break or chop the cauliflower into small florets.

3. When the almonds and bread crumbs are toasted, transfer them to a bowl and wipe out the skillet. Add 3 tablespoons olive oil.

4. When the oil is hot, add the cauliflower and sprinkle with salt and pepper. Cook, stirring occasionally it's lightly browned, 3 to 5 minutes.

   Peel and mince 2 garlic cloves.

   Chop 1 cup roasted red peppers.

5. When the cauliflower is lightly browned, stir in the garlic, peppers, shrimp, 1 teaspoon smoked paprika, 2 tablespoons sherry vinegar, and 1/4 cup water. Cover and cook, shaking the skillet once or twice, until the shrimp is cooked through and the cauliflower is just tender, another 3 or 4 minutes.

   Chop 1/2 cup parsley.

6. When the shrimp and cauliflower are done, stir in the parsley, almonds, and bread crumbs. Taste and adjust the seasoning and serve hot, warm, or at room temperature.

VARIATIONS

Squid and Cauliflower with Rustic Romesco
Substitute sliced squid for the shrimp. Add it to the skillet just for the last minute of cooking.

Shrimp and Cauliflower Curry
Substitute cashews for the almonds, 1 inch fresh ginger for the garlic, tomatoes for the peppers, 1 cup coconut milk for the vinegar and water, and 1 tablespoon curry powder for the smoked paprika. Garnish with cilantro instead of the parsley.

NOTES

MAKE YOUR OWN
Roasted Red (or Other Large) Peppers 417

SIDES

Bruschetta 909

Couscous 910

Bulgur with Lemon and Parsley 946

Green Salad 911

SPEED ◐ SERVES 4

Seared Scallops in Tomato Sauce with Basil and Chiles

If you're tempted to use two skillets to make this dish go faster, resist. Searing the scallops and then building the tomato sauce in the same skillet infuses the sauce with that great briny sweetness of the scallops as it cooks. Add some pasta or bread to sop it all up.

Ingredients

3 tablespoons olive oil

1 ½ pounds sea scallops

Salt and pepper

1 or 2 fresh hot green chiles (like serrano)

1 small red onion

½ cup white wine or water

One 28-ounce can diced tomatoes

1 bunch fresh basil

Prep | Cook

1. Put 3 tablespoons olive oil in a large skillet over medium-high heat.

   Pat the scallops dry.

2. When the oil is hot, add the scallops and sprinkle with salt and pepper. Cook, turning once, until the scallops are nicely browned on both sides, 2 or 3 minutes per side.

   Trim and thinly slice 1 or 2 chiles.

   Trim, peel, halve, and thinly slice the onion.

3. Transfer the browned scallops to a plate and add the chile and onion to the skillet. Cook, stirring occasionally until the onion softens, 3 to 5 minutes.

4. Add ½ cup white wine or water and let it bubble until nearly evaporated. Add the tomatoes with their juice and a sprinkle of salt and pepper. Adjust the heat so the mixture bubbles steadily but not vigorously and cook, adding a splash of liquid if it gets too dry, until the tomatoes begin to break down, about 10 minutes.

   Strip ¼ cup basil leaves from the stems and chop.

5. When the tomatoes begin to break down, return the scallops and any juices to the skillet. Cook, gently tossing the scallops in the sauce, for another minute or 2. Stir in the basil and serve.

VARIATIONS

Seared Scallops in Tomato-Basil Sauce
Substitute 4 garlic cloves, minced, for the chile and yellow onion for red.

Seared Scallops in Curried Tomato Sauce
Add 1 inch ginger, minced, along with the chile and onion and 1 tablespoon curry powder along with the tomatoes. Substitute cilantro for the basil (or use some of each).

Seared Squid in Any of These Tomato Sauces
To use squid in any of these sauces, cut the bodies into thin rings (and any tentacles into halves) and stir them into the sauce for the last 2 minutes of cooking. No need to sear them first.

Seared Shrimp in Any of These Tomato Sauces
To use shrimp in any of these sauces, cook them for just 2 or 3 minutes total at the beginning, then stir them into the sauce for the last few minutes of cooking.

NOTES

IF YOU HAVE MORE TIME
This dish is also wonderful with fresh tomatoes. Chop about a pound and use them instead of canned.

SIDES

Warm Buttery Bread 906

Bruschetta 909

Pasta, Plain and Simple 948

Couscous 910

Creamy Polenta 947

Green Salad 911

SPEED SERVES 4 TO 6

Fish and Chips with Tartar Sauce

It may seem like a tall order to make fried fish, French fries, and tartar sauce in under 45 minutes. But smart multitasking makes it a quick and relatively stress-free production.

Ingredients

Peanut oil for deep frying

2 pounds russet or Yukon Gold potatoes

Salt and pepper

1 egg

2 ½ cups flour

¾ cup beer

4 thick white fish fillets (about 1 ½ pounds)

1 lemon

2 sweet pickles or ¼ cup capers

1 cup mayonnaise

1 tablespoon Dijon mustard

Prep | Cook

1. Heat the oven to 400°F. Put 2 inches of peanut oil in a large pot over medium-high heat. (Use an oil thermometer clipped to the side if you have one.)

   Halve the potatoes lengthwise and cut them into wedges about ⅛ inch thick.

2. Put the potatoes on a rimmed baking sheet, drizzle with 3 or 4 tablespoons oil, sprinkle with salt and pepper, and toss to coat. Roast (it's okay if the oven isn't completely heated yet) undisturbed for the first 15 minutes, then turn as necessary until they are crisp on the outside and tender, another 15 to 20 minutes.

   Crack the egg into a medium bowl and add 1 cup flour, ¾ cup beer, and a sprinkle of salt and pepper. Whisk; the batter should be fairly thin (a little lumpy is fine).

   Put 1 ½ cups flour in a shallow bowl and stir in a sprinkle of salt and pepper.

   Line a baking sheet with paper towels.

3. When the oil reaches 350°F (or a drop of batter added to the oil bubbles vigorously but doesn't turn brown right away), you're ready to cook the fish. One piece at a time, dredge the fillets in the flour, shake off any excess, then dip in the batter, shaking off excess batter as well. Working in batches to avoid crowding the

pot, carefully put the fish into the oil. Adjust the heat as necessary. If the oil starts to smoke, remove it from the heat immediately to cool.

4. Fry the fish, turning once or twice, until it's lightly browned and a skewer or thin-bladed knife passes through each piece with little resistance, no more than 5 minutes unless the fish is especially thick. As the fish is done, transfer it to the paper towels with a slotted spoon.

   Cut the lemon into wedges. Chop 2 pickles or 1/4 cup capers; put them in a small bowl.

5. Add 1 cup mayonnaise, 1 tablespoon Dijon, and a sprinkle of salt and pepper to the bowl; stir to combine.

6. When the fish and potatoes are done, serve them with the tartar sauce and lemon wedges.

VARIATIONS

Fish and Chips with Smoked Paprika Aïoli
Substitute 2 teaspoons lemon juice for the pickles and 3 garlic cloves, minced, for the Dijon. Whisk constantly and slowly drizzle in 1/4 cup olive oil. Season to taste with salt, pepper, and smoked paprika.

Fish and Chips with Curried Yogurt Sauce
Substitute 1 tablespoon curry powder for the pickles, yogurt for the mayonnaise, and lime juice for the Dijon. Replace the lemon wedges with lime.

Fish and Chips with Vinegar-Shallot Sauce
Use 1/3 cup malt vinegar and 1/3 cup water instead of the mayonnaise, 2 sliced shallots for the pickles, and sugar instead of the Dijon.

NOTES

MAKE YOUR OWN
Mayonnaise 144

IF YOU HAVE MORE TIME
Instead of making the chips as described in Steps 1 and 2, use French Fries (page 963).

SIDES

Green Salad 911

Broiled Cherry Tomatoes 931

Fennel Salad 917

Warm Buttery Bread 906

Succotash 933

SPEED SERVES 4

Roasted Trout (or Other Whole Fish) with Fennel and Orange

Consider this recipe a template for roasting whole fish of all sizes; the main variable will be the cooking time, and the only limiting factor will be the size of your pan. Be forewarned, though: Big fish will take a while. All the more time for a side dish.

Ingredients

2 large fennel bulbs

1 orange

4 whole trout, gutted

Olive oil

Salt and pepper

1 cup stock, white wine, or water

Prep | Cook

1. Heat the oven to 450°F.

   Trim the fennel and cut it into thick slices, saving the fronds.

   Cut the orange into thin slices.

   Cut 3 or 4 parallel diagonal gashes in both sides of the trout, almost down to the bone.

2. Grease a roasting pan with a little olive oil and add the fennel. Drizzle with a little more oil and sprinkle with salt and pepper.

3. Put the trout on top of the fennel. Rub the fish with some more oil, sprinkle inside and out with salt and pepper, and stuff with the fennel fronds. Drizzle the fish with some oil and lay the orange slices on top.

4. Roast the fish until the skin browns and crisps, 15 to 20 minutes. Lift the fish out of the pan and add 1 cup stock, wine, or water, scraping up any browned bits and stirring the fennel.

5. Return the fish to the pan and continue to roast until the fish is opaque on the inside but still juicy, another 15 minutes or so, depending on the size. Add more liquid to the pan if it looks too dry. Serve with the pan juices, fennel, and orange.

VARIATIONS

Roasted Trout (or Other Whole Fish) with Carrots and Lime

Substitute 1 pound carrots, cut into chunks, for the fennel and 3 limes for the orange. Stuff the fish with chopped dill.

NOTES

MAKE YOUR OWN

Fish Stock 213

Chicken Stock 213

Vegetable Stock 212

IF YOU HAVE MORE TIME

Roasted Larger Fish

Roast a larger fish (about 3 pounds) such as grouper or haddock, which will feed four. The cooking time will be longer: Start checking after 30 minutes.

SERVING WHOLE FISH

If you've cooked one or two larger fish for people to share, remove the meat from the bones and put some on everyone's plate. The slits that you made across the fish before cooking will help you with this. The meat between the slits is all above the bones, so just use a large spoon to remove it in the largest chunks that you can. Once you've removed those meatiest parts of the fish—which should be plenty for people to start with—you can use a fork and your finger to pull the skeleton out of the fish, which will free up some more meat for you to dish out. This usually turns into a finger-food situation, which is fine.

SIDES

Rice Pilaf 944

Warm Buttery Bread 906

Boiled Potatoes 954

Shrimp Simmered in Dal

The beloved stewed lentils of India are a fantastic accompaniment to shrimp as well as a fine cooking medium. Instead of broiling or sautéing the shrimp separately, I nestle them in the lentils at the end of their cooking time. Serve with rice or flatbread.

Ingredients

2 tablespoons vegetable oil

1 small onion

1 garlic clove

1 inch fresh ginger

1 tablespoon curry powder

2 cups coconut milk (one and a half 15-ounce cans)

1 cup dried red lentils

1 bunch fresh cilantro

1 ½ pounds peeled shrimp

Salt and pepper

Prep | Cook

1. Put 2 tablespoons oil in a medium saucepan with a lid over medium-high heat.

   Trim, peel, and chop the onion.

2. Add the onion to the pan and cook, stirring occasionally until it softens, 3 to 5 minutes.

   Peel 1 garlic clove and 1 inch ginger; mince them together.

3. When the onion softens, add the garlic and ginger and 1 tablespoon curry powder. Cook, stirring until they're fragrant, a minute or 2.

4. Add 2 cups coconut milk, ½ cup water, and 1 cup red lentils. Bring to a boil, then adjust the heat so the mixture bubbles gently but steadily. Partially cover and cook, undisturbed, adding more liquid if the mixture gets too dry, until the lentils are nearly tender and beginning to break down, 20 to 25 minutes.

   Chop ½ cup cilantro.

5. When the lentils are nearly tender, nestle in the shrimp and sprinkle with salt and pepper. Cook, turning once, until the shrimp are pink and just cooked through, 3 or 4 minutes per side.

6. By the time the shrimp are cooked, the lentils should be tender and saucy. Taste and adjust the seasoning, garnish with the cilantro, and serve.

VARIATIONS

Shrimp Simmered in Buttery Lentils with Tarragon
Omit the ginger and curry powder. Replace the coconut milk with a mixture of water and chicken stock. Right before adding the shrimp, stir in 2 tablespoons chopped fresh tarragon leaves and 2 to 4 tablespoons butter.

Shrimp Simmered in Thai Coconut Lentils
Substitute 1 tablespoon Thai red curry paste for the curry powder. Garnish with lime wedges along with the cilantro.

Salmon Simmered in Dal
Use salmon, cut into a few fillets or large chunks, instead of the shrimp.

NOTES

MAKE YOUR OWN

Curry Powder 758

DEVEINING SHRIMP

The shrimp recipes in this book don't say anything about deveining. That's because it just isn't necessary. The "vein" of the shrimp is a dark line running down the outside curve, which is the animal's intestinal track.

Most people don't even notice it once it's cooked—and if you're buying it already peeled, the vein is often already removed—but if you want to remove it, just cut a shallow slit all the way down the curve with a paring knife, then use the tip of the knife and your fingers to pull out the vein. Some running water can help things along as well. It's not hard to do, but when you have 30 shrimp to devein it certainly adds some time to your prep work.

SIDES

White Rice 941

Noodles with Curry and Coconut Milk 949

Crisp Roasted Potatoes 965

Cucumber Raita 916

SPEED  SERVES 4

Baked Potato and Crab Cakes

Think part crab cake, part croquette. It's a perfect blend of crabmeat and potatoes, baked in the oven. Double or triple the recipe and you've got party food.

Ingredients

¼ cup vegetable oil

8 ounces russet potatoes (about 2 medium potatoes)

2 scallions

1 small red bell pepper

1 pound cooked lump crabmeat

1 egg

¼ cup mayonnaise

1 tablespoon Dijon mustard

3 tablespoons bread crumbs, or as needed

Salt and pepper

About 1 cup flour for dredging

1 lemon

Prep | Cook

1. Heat the oven to 375°F. Put ¼ cup vegetable oil on a rimmed baking sheet and put it in the oven.

   Peel the potatoes if you like; grate them by machine or hand and put them in a large bowl.

   Trim and chop the scallions; add them to the bowl.

   Trim, core, seed, and chop the bell pepper; add it to the bowl.

2. Pick through the crabmeat, discarding any pieces of shell or cartilage. Add it to the bowl. Crack the egg into the bowl and add ¼ cup mayonnaise, 1 tablespoon Dijon, 3 tablespoons bread crumbs, and a sprinkle of salt and pepper.

3. Stir to combine. Divide the mixture into 8 to 10 equal portions and shape them into cakes, squeezing out excess liquid and adding more bread crumbs if needed to hold their shape. Put 1 cup flour in a shallow dish and gently dredge the cakes on both sides.

4. Put the cakes on the baking sheet and cook, turning once halfway through, until they are golden on both sides and the potatoes are tender, about 15 minutes.

   Cut the lemon into wedges.

5. When the cakes are golden and the potatoes are tender, serve with the lemon wedges.

VARIATIONS

Baked Sweet Potato and Chipotle Crab Cakes

Substitute sweet potatoes for russets and 1 chipotle in adobo, chopped, for the Dijon. Serve with lime wedges.

Baked Celery Root and Crab Cakes

Substitute peeled celery root for the potatoes, 1/4 cup chopped red onion for the scallions, and 2 celery stalks for the bell pepper.

NOTES

MAKE YOUR OWN

Mayonnaise 144

Bread Crumbs 71

IF YOU HAVE MORE TIME

Breaded Baked Potato and Crab Cakes

After dredging the cakes in the flour, dredge them in beaten eggs, then the bread crumbs. Panfry the cakes in a large skillet for about 5 minutes per side. Ideally, you'll be able to do this in 2 batches. If you really need speed, use 2 skillets at the same time.

SIDES

Fresh Tomato Salsa 145

Green Salad 911

Fennel Salad 917

Coleslaw 923

Creamed Spinach 936

SPEED SERVES 4

Scallop and Corn Pan Broil

Once the oven is heated and the corn is shucked, this one-pan broil takes only as long as the scallops need to brown and cook through, which is, like, five minutes. While that happens, you chop up some scallions, chiles, and cilantro to add freshness at the end.

Ingredients

6 ears fresh corn

1 pint cherry tomatoes

1 ½ pounds sea scallops

¼ cup olive oil

Salt and pepper

4 scallions

1 fresh hot green chile (like serrano)

1 bunch fresh cilantro

1 lime

Prep | Cook

1. Turn the broiler to high; put the rack 4 inches from the heat.

   Shuck the corn and strip all of the kernels off the cob with a sharp paring knife.

2. Put the corn, tomatoes, and scallops on a rimmed baking sheet; drizzle with ¼ cup olive oil, sprinkle with salt and pepper, toss, and spread them out in a single layer.

3. Put the pan under the broiler and cook until the tops of the scallops and corn are lightly browned, 2 or 3 minutes.

   Trim and chop the scallions.

   Trim and mince the chile.

4. When the scallops and corn are browned, stir the corn and turn the scallops. Cook until the other sides of the scallops are lightly browned, another 2 or 3 minutes.

   Chop ¼ cup cilantro.

   Cut the lime into wedges.

5. When the scallops are browned all over, remove the baking sheet from the oven and stir in the scallions, chile, and cilantro. Taste and adjust the seasoning and serve with the lime wedges.

VARIATIONS

Scallop and Kale Pan Broil
Substitute 1 bunch kale, chopped, for the corn, 1/4 cup chopped black olives for the chiles, 1 small red onion for the scallions, parsley for the cilantro, and lemon for the lime.

Scallop and Green Bean Pan Broil
Substitute 1 pound green beans for the corn, 1/4 cup chopped almonds for the chiles, 1 shallot for the scallions, parsley for the cilantro, and lemon for the lime.

Sausage and Corn Pan Broil
Or try this method with either of the first two variations. Instead of the scallops, cut 1 1/2 pounds hot or sweet Italian sausage into 1-inch chunks. In Step 2, spread the sausage on the baking sheet by itself and broil, turning the pieces once or twice, until they start to brown, 3 to 5 minutes. Move them to one side, then add the corn and tomatoes to the pan and proceed with the recipe.

SIDES

Bruschetta 909

Garlic Bread 906

Quinoa 945

Rice Pilaf 944

SPEED SERVES 4

Mussel and Vegetable Pan Roast with Saffron Aïoli

Pan roast is code for throw some vegetables, shellfish, and liquid in a roasting pan, toss it in the oven, and come back when everything is done. This version with mussels, potatoes, corn, and tomatoes—kind of a one-pot clambake—is ideal in summer.

Ingredients

1 pound new potatoes

3 tablespoons olive oil

Salt and pepper

4 ears fresh corn

2 pounds mussels

8 ounces andouille, kielbasa, linguiça, or other smoked sausage

½ cup beer, white wine, or water

1 pint cherry tomatoes

1 small garlic clove

1 lemon

Pinch of saffron

½ cup mayonnaise

1 bunch fresh parsley

Prep | Cook

1. Heat the oven to 400°F.

   Cut the potatoes into halves or quarters.

2. Put the potatoes in a large roasting pan; toss with 2 tablespoons olive oil and a sprinkle of salt and pepper. When the oven is hot, roast, stirring once or twice until the potatoes are lightly browned, about 20 minutes.

   Husk the corn and cut each ear into thirds.

   Scrub and debeard the mussels; discard any that don't close when you press the shell together.

   Cut the sausage into chunks.

3. When the potatoes are lightly browned, stir in ½ cup beer, white wine, or water, scraping any browned bits from the bottom of the pan. Add the tomatoes, corn, mussels, and sausage.

4. Continue roasting until the mussels open and the potatoes are tender, another 15 minutes or so.

   Peel and mince 1 small garlic clove; put it in a small bowl.

   Grate 1 teaspoon lemon zest into the bowl; refrigerate the fruit for another use.

5. Add a pinch of saffron to the bowl along with 1 tablespoon hot water. Let the mixture sit for a few minutes, then stir in ½ cup mayonnaise and a sprinkle of salt and pepper.

   Chop ¼ cup parsley.

6. When the mussels are open and the potatoes are tender, divide the pan roast among 4 shallow bowls or serve it on a platter, garnished with parsley, with the aïoli on the side for drizzling and dipping.

VARIATIONS

Mussel and Vegetable Pan Roast with Coconut Curry
Omit the aïoli. Substitute 1 tablespoon curry powder for the sausage, coconut milk for the beer, and cilantro for the parsley.

Mussel and Vegetable Pan Roast with Spicy Tomato Broth
Skip the aïoli and use hot Italian sausage. Use 1 cup crushed tomatoes instead of the beer and add 1 teaspoon red chile flakes with the vegetables in Step 3. Garnish with basil instead of parsley.

Shrimp and Vegetable Pan Roast with Saffron Aïoli
Substitute large unpeeled shrimp for the mussels. Give the rest of the vegetables a head start and add the shrimp with about 10 minutes left in the cooking.

NOTES

MAKE YOUR OWN

Mayonnaise 144

EVEN FASTER
Parboil the whole potatoes while the oven heats, about 10 minutes, then add everything to the roasting pan at the same time once the oven is hot.

PRYING OPEN MUSSELS AND CLAMS
Many people will tell you that those mussels or clams that don't open during cooking should be tossed, but I prefer to be a bit more selective. Pry open these stragglers with a butter knife; if they look or smell spoiled, or you're worried about them for any reason, by all means chuck 'em; but if they seem just as good as the rest, eat them (I do).

SIDES

Warm Buttery Bread 906

Green Salad 911

Quinoa 945

Buttered Egg Noodles 948

Roasted Sweet Potatoes 416

Chicken

Broiled Chicken Breasts with Avocado Salsa 612

Chicken with Creamy Spinach-Cashew Sauce 614

Breaded Cutlets with Pan Sauce 616

Fastest Chicken Parm 618

Prosciutto-Crusted Chicken with Endive 620

Tapenade-Crusted Chicken with Eggplant 622

Poached Chicken and Asparagus with Lemon Aïoli 624

Moroccan-Spiced Chicken Cutlets with Chickpeas and Dried Fruit 626

Chicken with Creamed Spinach 628

Chicken Marsala with Lots of Mushrooms 630

Stir-Fried Chicken and Kale 632

Stir-Fried Chicken and Broccoli with Black Bean Sauce 634

Sesame Chicken and Snow Peas 638

Chile-Rubbed Chicken with Corn and Scallions 640

Chicken and Cauliflower Curry with Apricots 642

Provençal Chicken 644

Chicken Stroganoff 646

Charred Chicken and Pita with Gyro Fixings 648

Jerk Chicken and Onions 650

Chicken and Peppers with Black Bean "Mole" 652

Thai Peanut Chicken with Crisp Cabbage and Bean Sprouts 654

Chicken and Chard Gratin 656

Chicken and Chile Fundido 658

Chicken and Ricotta Sausage over Broccoli Rabe 660

Korean-Style Chicken and Vegetable Pancakes 662

Braised and Glazed Chicken and Leeks 664

Turkey Burgers 666

Seared Duck Breast with Fruit Sauce 668

Chicken, Vegetables, and Noodles in Soy Broth 670

Cornmeal Fried Chicken 672

Crisp Baked Chicken Tenders 674

Oven-Fried Chicken with Roasted Corn 676

Honey-Ginger-Soy-Roasted Chicken and Celery 678

Chicken and Tomato Packages 680

Chicken and Green Beans 682

Collard-Wrapped Chicken 684

Split Whole Chicken and Vegetables 686

Za'atar Wings and Eggplant with Yogurt-Harissa Sauce 690

Chicken and Sweet Potato Adobo 692

Chicken and Dumplings with Lots of Peas 694

Arroz con Pollo 696

Chicken and Spinach Meat Loaf 698

Roast Turkey with Sage Sausage Stuffing 700

Red Wine–Braised Turkey 702

Chicken

Americans buy and eat more chicken than any other meat, and no wonder: It cooks quickly and takes well to an almost infinite range of treatments. This chapter focuses on speedy, efficient chicken cookery, resulting in a richly varied collection of recipes that guarantees this ubiquitous weeknight dinner is anything but same old, same old.

A combination of simple seasoning strategies and cooking techniques will enhance chicken's unique advantages and minimize its challenges. For starters, you can be more assertive than you think with flavorings. The meat has a relatively mild taste, but unlike seafood it's not delicate. The recipes here give you permission to treat chicken like a blank canvas and sprinkle it liberally with spices and herbs before, during, and after cooking if you like—especially salt and pepper.

By far the most common mistake people make is to overcook chicken. The fastest cuts are also the leanest and the quickest to dry out, and the thickness and sizes vary wildly. So check the interior frequently—the easiest way is to nick with a knife and peek—and remove pieces from the heat as they're done.

Many of the recipes use boneless cuts of chicken, fast to cook and easy to eat and handle. I rely especially on boneless, skinless thighs; while they take a minute or two longer to cook than breasts, the extra flavor and juiciness (they've got more fat) justifies a few more minutes at the stove. But you can also cook bone-in parts in 30 to 45 minutes. And although this is the "chicken" chapter, I've included recipes for turkey and duck.

Chapter Highlights

Chicken 101 Useful notes on chicken labels and safety. Chicken Lingo (page 610).

Roast Your Own Chicken The starting point for all kinds of quick meals. Make a habit of roasting one while you're doing something else. Whole Roast Chicken (page 688).

Saucy Vegetables When you've finished sautéing chicken cutlets, you can use the hot skillet to cook up vegetables and a sauce. Vegetable Pan Sauce (page 631).

Full Steam Ahead You don't need to own a steamer (I don't); just make one out of a couple bowls or plates. Rigging a Fast Steamer (page 685).

Bubble, Bubble, Broil and Bubble For fast flavor, broil chicken briefly to brown it, then simmer in flavorful sauce. Broiling and Bubbling (page 653).

The Butterfly Effect Here's how to cook a whole chicken in less than an hour. Butterflying a Chicken (page 687).

Free-Form Meat Loaf Less fussy than using a loaf pan, and you get better browning too. Shaping Meat Loaf (page 699).

Quick Braising Braising offers more time flexibility than you might think, and it's an ideal method for improvisation—not just with chicken, but with meat and vegetables too. Recipe-Free Braised Meat (page 763).

Hot Pan, Fast Dinner Stir-fries are a staple of any fast kitchen. Here's an all-purpose map to making your own. Recipe-Free Stir-Fry (page 636).

Turkey the Rest of the Year When cut up, turkey is both fast and easy and worth enjoying year-round. Turkey Parts (page 703).

Instant Thanksgiving A roast turkey dinner in 45 minutes. Roast Turkey with Sage Sausage Stuffing (page 700).

Ground Rules Ground chicken gets exciting. Korean-Style Chicken and Vegetable Pancakes (page 662), Chicken and Chile Fundido (page 658), Chicken and Ricotta Sausage over Broccoli Rabe (page 660).

For the Kids A hassle-free method for crisp chicken fingers in the oven. Crisp Baked Chicken Tenders (page 674).

Duck! There's only one duck recipe in this chapter, but it's one you'll use again and again. Seared Duck Breast with Fruit Sauce (page 668).

INGREDIENT

Chicken Lingo

You may already know your way around a bird, but to sum it all up, the keys to great chicken dishes are buying well, cooking safely, and keeping it moist. Get these points sorted out and a lifetime of delicious chicken awaits.

Type of Chicken	What's the Story?
NATURAL	The term *natural* means nothing when applied to chicken. It's not a designation that's regulated by the federal government or anyone else, so it's entirely up to the producer to label a bird natural or not, and why wouldn't they when there are no repercussions for calling a chicken that's been pumped with antibiotics "natural"? Ignore it.
FREE-RANGE	A meaningful but still misleading label. *Free-range* evokes images of chickens roaming around in a field, but the designation means only that the birds have access to outdoor space. This doesn't mean they go there. And the label says nothing of the chickens' diet or living conditions. A free-range label is no guarantee of a humanely raised or flavorful bird, but it's a bit of a starting place.
ORGANIC	Organic certification doesn't paint a full picture of how chickens are raised, but at least it's a term that's defined and regulated by the U.S. Department of Agriculture. To receive this certification producers must at least provide the chickens with some amount of mobility, never give them antibiotics or other drugs, nor feed them genetically modified organisms. This doesn't guarantee that a chicken will taste incredible or be free of salmonella, but it is the only way we can know for sure that it was raised decently.
HERITAGE OR LOCAL	Neither of these terms is regulated in any way, but they are generally used to describe breeds of chickens that have superior flavor and texture or birds that have been raised in a healthy and responsible way—although they're not necessarily organic. These are the kinds of chickens that you'll find at farmers' markets, specialty butchers, or high-end supermarkets. They are usually superior and are priced accordingly.

Piecing Out

Popularity comes with benefits. You can buy chicken any way you want it: whole bird, quartered, cut into eight or sixteen pieces, or all—or a combination—of parts like thighs or wings. And almost all cuts come bone-in or bone out, with or without skin. Each has pros and cons in the fast kitchen.

A whole bird takes close to an hour to cook. And though it's easy enough, that timeframe does not merit the "fast" moniker. But when you want to pull together leisurely sides or don't mind butchering a chicken yourself, it's usually the best buy in terms of quality and price. And for precooked meat to use in salads or sandwiches, it's a great way to go. (See the master recipes on page 688.)

For the ideal combination of flavor, juiciness, and speed, bone-in chicken parts are best: They're undeniably convenient and cook more quickly than whole birds. I use them in some recipes here, and there's another master recipe on page 689.

Cutlets made from thighs, breasts, and tenderloins (or "tenders") are by far the most convenient and fast-cooking. But without the flavor and protection of bone and skin, the meat can become lackluster and dry quickly during cooking. Fortunately both challenges are easily overcome with confident seasoning and a watchful eye. (And helpful recipes!)

Chicken Safety and Doneness

Food safety is particularly important when it comes to chicken, since an unnervingly high percentage of birds routinely contain the bacteria salmonella. The way to kill salmonella (theoretically) is to cook the chicken until it is fully done, which you ensure in two ways. The most reliable way to know whether chicken is cooked through is by using a quick-read thermometer (this works best on larger bone-in chicken parts or whole chickens). Insert the thermometer into a few places in the breast and/or thigh, avoiding the bones. The government officially recommends cooking chicken to 165°F, which almost certainly guarantees dried-out white meat. To ensure that chicken is both safe and not overcooked, I remove the chicken from the heat after it reaches 155° to 160°F on a quick-read thermometer and let it continue to rise those last few degrees while it rests on the cutting board.

The other way to check for doneness is simply to make a small cut into the chicken and take a peek. For bone-in pieces, cut right down to the bone, while for boneless chicken make sure you can see the middle of the thickest part. The meat should be opaque; the tiniest trace of pink in the meat is okay since it will continue to cook as you get it to the table, but you shouldn't see any traces of red, and the juices that spill out of the meat should run clear.

SPEED SERVES 4

Broiled Chicken Breasts with Avocado Salsa

Garlic burns easily under the broiler; to impart its flavor without having charred bits, broil whatever you're making first—in this case chicken—then rub the exterior with a cut clove, as you would with bruschetta. Halving the chicken breasts first speeds up cooking and gets you more surface area for the garlic and the avocado salsa topping.

Ingredients

4 boneless, skinless chicken breasts (about 2 pounds)

2 tablespoons olive oil

2 teaspoons paprika

Salt and pepper

2 garlic cloves

2 avocados

1 small red onion

1 cup cherry tomatoes

1 lime

Several sprigs fresh cilantro for garnish

Prep | Cook

1. Turn the broiler to high; put the rack 4 inches from the heat.

   Cut each chicken breast in half horizontally to make 2 thin cutlets. Press down on each with the heel of your hand to flatten.

2. Put the cutlets on a rimmed baking sheet, rub with 2 tablespoons olive oil, and sprinkle with 2 teaspoons paprika and some salt and pepper.

3. Broil, turning once, until lightly browned on both sides and just cooked through, 2 to 5 minutes per side.

   Peel and halve 2 garlic cloves.

   Halve and pit the avocados, cut the flesh into cubes, and scoop it out of the skin into a medium bowl.

   Trim, peel, and chop the onion; add it to the bowl.

4. Rub the browned cutlets all over with the raw garlic and put them on plates or a platter. Discard what's left of the garlic.

   Halve 1 cup cherry tomatoes; add them to the bowl.

   Halve the lime.

   Chop several sprigs cilantro.

5. Squeeze the lime juice into the salsa and sprinkle with salt and pepper. Spoon the salsa over the top of the chicken, garnish with the cilantro, and serve.

VARIATIONS

Broiled Chicken Breasts with Peach Salsa
Substitute peaches for the avocados.

Broiled Chipotle Chicken Breasts with Watermelon Salsa
Instead of using paprika, rub the cutlets with 2 tablespoons chopped chipotle chiles in adobo sauce. Use 2 cups cubed watermelon instead of the avocado.

Broiled Curried Chicken Breasts with Pineapple Salsa
Swap curry powder for the paprika and 2 cups chopped pineapple for the avocado. Add ¼ cup chopped mint to the salsa.

Herb-Rubbed Chicken Breasts with Peas and Parmesan
Use dried herbes de Provence instead of paprika, 2 cups warmed peas instead of avocado, ½ cup grated Parmesan in place of onion, and lemon instead of lime.

NOTES

EVEN FASTER
Instead of making the salsa in Steps 3 through 5, use 1 cup Fresh Tomato Salsa (page 145) and add chopped avocado.

SIDES

White Rice 941

Warm Flour Tortillas 907

Jícama and Radish Salad 918

Mexican Street Corn 932

SPEED ◑ SERVES 4

Chicken with Creamy Spinach-Cashew Sauce

This is a classic Indian preparation, achieving a delicious creaminess in almost no time.

Ingredients

Two 10-ounce packages frozen spinach

2 tablespoons vegetable oil

2 pounds boneless, skinless chicken thighs

Salt and pepper

1 cup cream

1 ½ cups unsalted cashews

2 garlic cloves

1 inch fresh ginger

1 teaspoon garam masala

Several sprigs fresh cilantro for garnish

Prep | Cook

Thaw the spinach in the microwave; put it in a blender.

1. Put 2 tablespoons vegetable oil in a large skillet over medium-high heat.

   Chop the chicken into large chunks.

2. Add the chicken to the skillet, sprinkle with salt and pepper, and cook, stirring occasionally until the chicken just loses its pink color, 3 to 5 minutes.

3. Add 1 cup cream, 1 ½ cups cashews, ¾ cup water, and a sprinkle of salt and pepper to the blender. Turn the machine on and blend until it becomes a smooth sauce.

   Peel 2 garlic cloves and 1 inch ginger; mince them together.

4. When the chicken loses its pink color, add the garlic, ginger, and 1 teaspoon garam masala. Cooking, stirring frequently until fragrant, about a minute.

5. Pour the sauce into the skillet. Adjust the heat so the mixture simmers gently but steadily and cook, stirring occasionally until the sauce thickens slightly and the chicken is cooked through, 4 to 6 minutes.

   Chop several sprigs cilantro.

6. Taste and adjust the seasoning, garnish with the cilantro, and serve immediately.

VARIATIONS

Chicken with Coconut-Spinach-Cashew Sauce
Use coconut milk in place of cream.

Chicken with Creamy Scallion-Peanut Sauce
Substitute 1 cup chopped scallions for the spinach and peanuts for the cashews.

NOTES

IF YOU HAVE MORE TIME
Toast the cashews in a dry skillet before adding to the blender.

SIDES

White Rice 941

Crisp Seasoned Pita 908

Cucumber Raita 916

SPEED  SERVES 4

Breaded Cutlets with Pan Sauce

Always popular and simple to make. A lot of different side dishes will complement these cutlets, or you can incorporate vegetables right into the sauce.

Ingredients

4 boneless, skinless chicken breasts (about 2 pounds)

2 tablespoons olive oil, plus more as needed

2 cups flour

2 cups bread crumbs

2 eggs

Salt and pepper

1 bunch fresh parsley

1 lemon

½ cup white wine

½ cup chicken stock

2 tablespoons butter

Prep | Cook

1. Heat the oven to 200°F.

   Cut each chicken breast in half horizontally to make 2 thin cutlets. Press down on each with the heel of your hand to flatten.

2. Put 2 tablespoons olive oil in a large skillet over medium heat.

3. Set up 3 shallow bowls for dredging; fill one with 2 cups flour, one with 2 cups bread crumbs, and crack the eggs into the last bowl and beat them. Season all with salt and pepper.

4. Dredge the chicken cutlets one at a time in flour, then egg, then bread crumbs. As you finish each cutlet, put it in the skillet (you'll need to work in batches). Raise the heat to medium-high.

5. Cook the cutlets, rotating them occasionally and adjusting the heat so they sizzle but don't burn, until they are browned, 3 or 4 minutes. Turn and cook on the other side until browned and cooked through, another 3 or 4 minutes.

6. As each piece is done, transfer it to the oven to keep warm; continue cooking the remaining cutlets, adding more oil to the skillet as needed.

   Chop ¼ cup parsley leaves.

   Halve the lemon.

7. When all the cutlets are cooked and warming in the oven, add ½ cup wine to the skillet; cook, scraping the bottom of the pan until it is reduced by about half, a minute or 2.

8. Add ½ cup chicken stock along with any juices that have accumulated around the chicken; cook until the sauce thickens a bit, another 2 or 3 minutes.

9. Stir in 2 tablespoons butter, squeeze in the lemon juice, and stir in the parsley. Cook, swirling the pan to melt the butter. Taste and adjust the seasoning, pour the sauce over the cutlets, and serve.

VARIATIONS

Spicy Breaded Cutlets with Pan Sauce
Add 2 teaspoons chili powder to the flour; substitute lime for lemon and cilantro for parsley.

Parmesan-Breaded Cutlets with Balsamic Pan Sauce
Add ½ cup grated Parmesan to the bread crumbs; stir in 1 tablespoon vinegar just before adding the butter at the end.

Breaded Cutlets with Mushroom Pan Sauce
Cook ½ cup chopped mushrooms and 1 chopped shallot in the skillet until softened, about 3 minutes. Then add the wine and proceed as directed.

5 Ways to Flavor Pan Sauce
Add any of the following to the pan sauce in Step 9:

1. Minced garlic, ginger, or chiles
2. Chopped fresh rosemary, sage, thyme, or oregano
3. Chopped capers, olives, or anchovies
4. Pinch of saffron
5. Curry powder, chili powder, or other dried spices

NOTES

MAKE YOUR OWN

Bread Crumbs 71

Chicken Stock 213

EVEN FASTER
Skip the eggs and bread crumbs and just dredge the cutlets in the flour before cooking.

SIDES

Green Salad 911

Sautéed Greens with Garlic 924

Tomato Salad 913

Creamy Polenta 947

Garlic Bread 906

Skin-On Mashed Potatoes 961

Pasta, Plain and Simple 948

SPEED ◐ SERVES 4

Fastest Chicken Parm

This take on the classic couldn't be easier: Instead of dredging and panfrying, just stack the ingredients in two stages on a baking sheet and broil. Done this way, the tomatoes get lightly roasted and the bread crumbs stay nice and crunchy. (For eggplant like this, see the Variations.)

Ingredients

5 tablespoons olive oil

3 medium ripe tomatoes

4 boneless, skinless chicken breasts (about 2 pounds)

Salt and pepper

8 ounces fresh mozzarella cheese

2 ounces Parmesan cheese (½ cup grated)

1 bunch fresh basil

1 cup bread crumbs

Prep | Cook

1. Turn the broiler to high; put the rack 6 inches from the heat. Put 2 tablespoons olive oil on a rimmed baking sheet and spread it around; put the baking sheet in the broiler.

   Core and slice the tomatoes.

   Cut the chicken breasts in half horizontally to make 2 thin cutlets for each breast. Press down on each with the heel of your hand to flatten.

2. Carefully remove the baking sheet from the broiler. Put the chicken cutlets on the sheet and sprinkle with salt and pepper. Top with the tomatoes, and broil one one side only until the chicken is no longer pink in the center, rotating the pan if necessary for even cooking, 5 to 10 minutes.

   Grate the mozzarella and Parmesan.

   Strip 16 to 20 basil leaves from the stems.

   Combine the bread crumbs, mozzarella, and Parmesan in a small bowl.

3. When the chicken is cooked through, remove the baking sheet from the broiler. Lay the basil leaves on top of the tomatoes, sprinkle with the bread crumb and cheese mixture, and drizzle with 3 tablespoons olive oil.

4. Return to the broiler, and cook until the bread crumbs and cheese are browned and bubbly, 2 to 4 minutes. Serve immediately.

VARIATIONS

Cubano Chicken

Use sliced dill pickles instead of the tomatoes and Swiss cheese instead of the mozzarella. Omit the basil. Before putting the pickles on top of the chicken in Step 2, spread a little Dijon mustard on the cutlets. Instead of the Parmesan, mix ½ cup chopped ham into the bread crumb and Swiss topping.

Chicken Melt

Use Gruyère cheese instead of the mozzarella and 1 tablespoon fresh thyme leaves instead of the basil. Omit the Parmesan. Before putting the tomatoes on top of the chicken in Step 2, spread a little Dijon mustard over the cutlets.

Fastest Eggplant Parm

Instead of the chicken, slice about 2 pounds large eggplant crosswise 1 inch thick. After the pan heats in Step 2, spread out the eggplant slices—but not the tomatoes—and turn to coat them in some oil and sprinkle with salt and pepper. Broil until softened and browned in places, about 3 to 5 minutes. Flip the eggplant, then top with the tomatoes and proceed with the recipe from the end of Step 2.

NOTES

MAKE YOUR OWN

Bread Crumbs 71

EVEN FASTER

Spread about 2 cups Tomato Sauce (page 296) on the cutlets instead of sliced tomatoes.

SIDES

Pasta, Plain and Simple 948

Garlic Bread 906

Warm Buttery Bread 906

Green Salad 911

Chopped Salad 912

SPEED ◐ SERVES 4

Prosciutto-Crusted Chicken with Endive

Pounding a slice of prosciutto into the top of a boneless, skinless chicken breast is a tasty way to keep the meat moist. The Parmesan helps the prosciutto adhere to the meat and boosts the flavor even more, while the wrapper forms a crisp crust.

Ingredients

4 boneless, skinless chicken breasts (about 2 pounds)

4 ounces Parmesan cheese (1 cup grated)

Salt and pepper

8 slices prosciutto

4 tablespoons olive oil, plus more as needed

4 heads Belgian endive (1 to 1 ½ pounds)

1 lemon

Prep | Cook

1. Heat the oven to 200°F.

   Cut the chicken breasts in half horizontally to make 2 thin cutlets for each breast.

   Grate 1 cup Parmesan.

2. Sprinkle the cutlets with salt and pepper and half of the Parmesan. Lay a slice of prosciutto over each cutlet, folding over any edges around the sides.

3. Put a large piece of plastic wrap over the cutlets and bang on them a few times with the bottom of a large skillet to flatten them a bit and get the prosciutto to stick.

4. Put 2 tablespoons olive oil in the large skillet and put it over medium-high heat. When it's hot, add the cutlets prosciutto side down (you'll need to work in batches). Cook until the prosciutto is crisp, 4 to 6 minutes, then turn and cook until the chicken is cooked through, another 2 or 3 minutes.

5. As each piece is done, transfer it to the oven to keep warm; continue cooking the remaining cutlets, adding more oil to the skillet as needed.

   Trim and chop the endive.

6. When all the cutlets are cooked and warming in the oven, add 2 tablespoons oil to the skillet. Add the endive and a sprinkle of salt and pepper; cook, stirring occasionally until it's lightly browned and just tender but still with some crunch, 3 to 5 minutes.

   Cut the lemon into wedges.

7. Sprinkle ½ cup Parmesan over the endive and toss. Serve with the cutlets, garnished with the lemon wedges.

VARIATIONS

Prosciutto-Crusted Chicken with Kale
Substitute 1 bunch kale, chopped, for the endive; sauté until it just wilts, 4 or 5 minutes.

Bacon-Crusted Chicken with Apples
Substitute thin-cut bacon strips for the prosciutto; to cover the chicken, either cut 8 slices bacon in half or use 16 slices (2 per cutlet). Substitute cheddar for the Parmesan and sliced apples for the endive: Sauté them until they are tender and nicely browned, 5 to 10 minutes.

SIDES

Bruschetta 909

Garlic Bread 906

Pasta, Plain and Simple 948

Refried White Beans with Rosemary 938

Tomato Salad 913

SPEED ◐ SERVES 4

Tapenade-Crusted Chicken with Eggplant

Olive tapenade isn't just a great dip; it also works as an intensely flavorful paste for seasoning chicken or other meats. Spread on chicken breasts, it turns into an irresistible, briny crust under the broiler. Spoon any leftovers onto the eggplant.

Ingredients

1 large or 2 medium eggplant (about 2 pounds)

8 tablespoons olive oil, plus more as needed

Salt and pepper

8 ounces black olives

1 garlic clove

1 tablespoon capers

3 or 4 anchovy fillets

4 boneless, skinless chicken breasts (about 2 pounds)

Several sprigs fresh parsley for garnish

Prep | Cook

1. Turn the broiler to high; put the rack 4 inches from the heat.

   Trim and slice the eggplant into 1-inch rounds and put them on a rimmed baking sheet.

2. Drizzle the eggplant with 4 tablespoons olive oil and sprinkle with salt and pepper. Broil, turning once or twice and brushing with more oil if it looks dry, until nicely browned and cooked through, 10 to 12 minutes total.

   Pit 8 ounces black olives if necessary; put them in a food processor.

   Peel and chop 1 garlic clove; add it to the food processor.

3. Add 1 tablespoon capers, 3 or 4 anchovy fillets, 2 tablespoons oil, and a sprinkle of pepper to the food processor. Pulse, adding oil if necessary, until the mixture becomes a thick paste.

   Cut the chicken breasts in half horizontally to make 2 thin cutlets for each breast. Press down on each with the heel of your hand to flatten.

4. When the eggplant is done, transfer it to a platter. Put the chicken on the baking sheet, drizzle with 2 tablespoons oil, and sprinkle with pepper. Broil until the top is lightly browned, 2 to 5 minutes.
   Strip the parsley leaves from several sprigs and chop.

5. When the cutlets are browned, flip them and carefully spread a layer of tapenade over the top of each. Continue broiling until the tapenade becomes slightly crusty and the chicken cooks through, another 2 to 5 minutes.

6. Put the chicken on top of the eggplant, garnish with the parsley and a drizzle of oil if you like, and serve.

VARIATIONS

Pesto-Crusted Chicken with Eggplant

Substitute 1 cup loosely packed fresh basil leaves for the olives, 1 tablespoon pine nuts or chopped walnuts for the capers, and ¼ cup grated Parmesan for the anchovies.

Puttanesca-Crusted Chicken with Fennel

Use fennel, cut into thick slices, instead of the eggplant. Broil, turning or tossing once or twice, until the fennel is nicely browned and tender, 10 to 12 minutes. Substitute 1 cup dried tomatoes for half of the olives. Add ¼ cup grated Parmesan if you like.

SIDES

Green Salad 911

Bruschetta 909

Couscous 910

Quinoa 948

SPEED ◐ SERVES 4

Poached Chicken and Asparagus with Lemon Aïoli

Two techniques in one pot: While the chicken poaches in herb-seasoned water, asparagus steams on top. Both pair well with a simple garlic and lemon mayo.

Ingredients

4 boneless, skinless chicken breasts (about 2 pounds)

3 sprigs fresh thyme

1 large bunch asparagus (1 pound)

1 garlic clove

1 lemon

½ cup mayonnaise

Salt and pepper

Prep | Cook

1. Put the chicken, 2 cups water, and 3 sprigs thyme in a large pot over high heat.

2. When the liquid boils, lower the heat so it bubbles steadily but not vigorously and turn the chicken. Cover and cook until the chicken is opaque and just cooked through, 12 to 15 minutes.

   Trim the asparagus.

3. About 7 minutes after you covered the chicken, add the asparagus and re-cover the pot: By the time the chicken is cooked through, the asparagus will be tender but still have a little crunch, 5 to 8 minutes. If one finishes before the other, remove it first.

   Peel and mince 1 garlic clove; add it to a small bowl.

   Halve the lemon; squeeze the juice into the bowl.

4. Add ½ cup mayonnaise and a sprinkle of salt and pepper to the bowl; stir to combine.

5. When the chicken and asparagus are done, put the asparagus on a platter. Cut the chicken on the bias into long diagonal slices and add them to the platter.

6. Sprinkle the chicken and asparagus with a little salt and pepper and spoon the aïoli over the top or serve it on the side.

VARIATIONS

Poached Chicken and Snap Peas with Curry Aïoli
Use 1/4 teaspoon whole cumin seeds, 2 cardamom pods, 1 teaspoon coriander seeds, and 1/4 teaspoon mustard seeds instead of the thyme and snap peas instead of the asparagus. The peas will take just a few minutes to cook, so add them closer to the end. Add 1 tablespoon curry powder to the aïoli.

Poached Chicken and Carrots with Lemon-Soy Aïoli
Substitute 1 tablespoon orange juice and 1 tablespoon soy sauce for the thyme and carrots (thin ones or halved lengthwise) for the asparagus. The carrots take longer to cook than the asparagus, so add them to the pan as soon as you're done prepping them. Add 2 teaspoons soy sauce to the aïoli.

Poached Chicken Cutlets and Red Peppers with Smoked Paprika Aïoli
Replace the asparagus with red peppers, cut into thick slices; they'll take a little less time to cook. Add 2 teaspoons smoked paprika to the aïoli.

Chinese-Style Poached Chicken and Bok Choy
Substitute 1 inch ginger, sliced, and a few fresh basil sprigs for the thyme and chopped bok choy for the asparagus. Instead of the aïoli, serve with a mixture of soy sauce, sesame oil, minced ginger, and chopped fresh basil.

NOTES

MAKE YOUR OWN
Mayonnaise 144

SIDES

Warm Buttery Bread 906

Skin-On Mashed Potatoes 961

White Rice 941

Quinoa 945

Moroccan-Spiced Chicken Cutlets with Chickpeas and Dried Fruit

It takes forever to make a tagine, but you can infuse all the same warm Moroccan flavors into this simple two-step sauté and get it done in a flash.

Ingredients

2 tablespoons olive oil, plus more as needed

4 boneless, skinless chicken breasts (about 2 pounds)

2 teaspoons cumin

1 teaspoon coriander

½ teaspoon cinnamon

¼ teaspoon cayenne

Salt and pepper

2 cups cooked or canned chickpeas (one 15-ounce can)

1 cup dried apricots

¼ cup red wine vinegar

Several sprigs fresh parsley for garnish

Prep | Cook

1. Heat the oven to 200°F. Put 2 tablespoons olive oil in a large skillet over medium-low heat.

   Cut the chicken breasts in half horizontally to make 2 thin cutlets for each breast. Press down on each with the heel of your hand to flatten.

2. Combine 2 teaspoons cumin, 1 teaspoon coriander, ½ teaspoon cinnamon, ¼ teaspoon cayenne, and a sprinkle of salt and pepper in a small bowl. Rub the spices all over the chicken.

3. Raise the heat to medium-high and add the cutlets to the skillet (you'll need to work in batches). Cook the cutlets, rotating them occasionally and adjusting the heat so they sizzle but don't burn, until the spices are nicely browned, 3 or 4 minutes. Turn and cook on the other side until the chicken is cooked through, another 3 or 4 minutes.

4. As each piece is done, transfer it to the oven to keep warm; continue cooking the remaining cutlets, adding more oil to the skillet as needed.

   If you're using canned chickpeas, rinse and drain them.

   Chop 1 cup dried apricots.

5. When all the cutlets are cooked and warming in the oven, add ¼ cup red wine vinegar to the skillet, scraping up the browned bits from the bottom. Add the chickpeas and apricots, sprinkle with salt and pepper, and cook, stirring occasionally until warmed through, 3 or 4 minutes.

   Strip the parsley leaves from several sprigs and chop.

6. When the chickpeas and apricots are warm, stir in most of the parsley, taste, and adjust the seasoning. Serve with the chicken, garnished with the remaining parsley and a drizzle of olive oil.

VARIATIONS

BBQ-Spiced Chicken Cutlets with Pinto Beans and Ham
Substitute chili powder for the coriander and paprika for the cinnamon. Use pinto beans instead of chickpeas and replace red wine vinegar with cider vinegar and the apricots with 1 cup chopped smoked ham or other cooked smoked pork.

Smoked Paprika-Spiced Chicken Cutlets with White Beans and Dried Tomatoes
Substitute 1 tablespoon smoked paprika for the spices, white beans for the chickpeas, sherry vinegar for the red wine vinegar, and 1 cup chopped dried tomatoes for the dried apricots.

NOTES

MAKE YOUR OWN

Cooked Beans 496

SIDES

Couscous 910

Cucumber Raita 915

Tahini Slaw 923

SPEED ◐ SERVES 4

Chicken with Creamed Spinach

Creamed spinach goes with everything, but the leanness of the chicken breast highlights the richness of the spinach like nothing else. A lovely old combination.

Ingredients

4 boneless, skinless chicken breasts (about 2 pounds)

4 tablespoons (½ stick) butter, plus more as needed

2 tablespoons olive oil, plus more as needed

1 cup flour

Salt and pepper

1 ½ pounds spinach

1 garlic clove

¾ cup cream

¼ teaspoon nutmeg

Prep | Cook

1. Heat the oven to 200°F.

   Cut the chicken breasts in half horizontally to make 2 thin cutlets for each breast. Press down on each with the heel of your hand to flatten.

2. Put 2 tablespoons butter and 2 tablespoons olive oil in a large skillet over medium-high heat.

   Put 1 cup flour in a shallow bowl; sprinkle with salt and pepper.

3. Dredge the chicken cutlets one at a time in the flour. As you finish each, put it in the skillet (you'll need to work in batches).

4. Cook the cutlets, rotating them occasionally and adjusting the heat so they sizzle but don't burn, until browned on the bottom, 3 or 4 minutes. Turn and cook on the other side until browned and cooked through, another 3 or 4 minutes.

5. As each piece is done, transfer it to the oven to keep warm; continue cooking the remaining cutlets, adding more fat to the skillet as needed.

   Trim off any thick stems from the spinach and finely chop the leaves.

   Peel and mince 1 garlic clove.

6. When all the cutlets are cooked and warming in the oven, add ¾ cup cream, 2 tablespoons butter, the garlic, ¼ teaspoon nutmeg, and a sprinkle of salt and pepper to the skillet. Reduce the heat to medium.

7. Add the spinach to the pan, a handful at a time if necessary to fit.

8. Cook, stirring occasionally until the spinach is completely wilted and tender and the cream has reduced and thickened to the consistency you like, 5 to 10 minutes. Taste and adjust the seasoning and spoon onto plates.

9. Cut the chicken on the bias into long diagonal slices, fan them out over the spinach, and serve.

VARIATIONS

Seared Chicken with Curried Creamed Spinach
Replace the garlic with ½ inch ginger, minced, and the nutmeg with 1 tablespoon curry powder.

Seared Chicken with Creamed Onions
Substitute 1 pound onions, thinly sliced, for the spinach. Before adding the cream, sauté the onions in a little butter until soft. Then add the remaining ingredients and cook until the onions are very tender and the cream has reduced and thickened to the consistency you like.

NOTES

EVEN FASTER
Cook the creamed spinach in a separate saucepan while you cook the chicken.

SIDES

Crisp Roasted Potatoes 965

Skin-On Mashed Potatoes 961

Garlicky Mushrooms 956

SPEED ◐ SERVES 4

Chicken Marsala with Lots of Mushrooms

Chicken Marsala is a favorite that doesn't need much in the way of tweaking. This version increases the mushrooms. Their earthiness balances the sweet sauce brilliantly.

Ingredients

4 boneless, skinless chicken breasts (about 2 pounds)

4 tablespoons (½ stick) butter, plus more as needed

2 tablespoons olive oil, plus more as needed

1 cup flour

Salt and pepper

1 ½ pounds button, cremini, or shiitake mushrooms

Several sprigs fresh parsley for garnish

¾ cup Marsala

1 cup chicken or beef stock

Prep | Cook

1. Heat the oven to 200°F.

   Cut the chicken breasts in half horizontally to make 2 thin cutlets for each breast. Press down on each with the heel of your hand to flatten.

2. Put 2 tablespoons butter and 2 tablespoons olive oil in a large skillet over medium-high heat.

   Put 1 cup flour in a shallow bowl; sprinkle with salt and pepper.

3. Dredge the chicken cutlets one at a time in the flour and add to the skillet (you'll need to work in batches).

4. Cook the cutlets, rotating them occasionally and adjusting the heat so they sizzle but don't burn, until browned on the bottom, 3 or 4 minutes. Turn and cook on the other side until browned and cooked through, another 3 or 4 minutes.

5. As each piece is done, transfer it to the oven to keep warm; continue cooking the remaining cutlets, adding more fat to the skillet as needed.

   Trim and slice the mushrooms. (If you're using shiitakes, discard the stems.)

6. When all of the cutlets are in the oven, add more fat to the skillet if it's dry, then add the mushrooms. Sprinkle with salt and pepper and cook, stirring occasionally until the mushrooms are tender and the pan is beginning to dry out, 8 to 12 minutes.

   Strip the parsley leaves from several sprigs and chop.

7. Add ¾ cup Marsala and 1 cup stock to the mushrooms; raise the heat to high and let the liquid bubble away until it thickens into a sauce. Stir in 2 tablespoons butter, taste, and adjust the seasoning.

8. Pour the sauce over the cutlets, garnish with the parsley, and serve.

VARIATIONS

7 Other Liquids to Use in Place of Marsala:

1. Red or white wine
2. Beer
3. Apple cider
4. Cognac (about ½ cup)
5. Half water, half soy sauce
6. Coconut milk
7. Crushed tomatoes

NOTES

MAKE YOUR OWN

Fast Chicken Stock 213

Beef Stock 212

EVEN FASTER

Sauté the mushrooms in a separate skillet while you cook the chicken.

VEGETABLE PAN SAUCE

The easiest way to turn a dish like this into a meal is to cook a vegetable in the same pan you used to cook the chicken. Remove the chicken from the skillet when it's done, then add a little more oil to the pan, followed by some chopped vegetables like zucchini, mushrooms, kale, or whatever you think makes sense. When the vegetables are tender, either remove them and make the sauce or leave them in the skillet and build the pan sauce right around them.

SIDES

Buttered Egg Noodles 948

Pasta, Plain and Simple 948

Creamy Polenta 947

Skin-On Mashed Potatoes 961

Green Salad 911

SPEED ◑ SERVES 4

Stir-Fried Chicken and Kale

It might not be a common green used in stir-fries, but kale takes well to high-heat preparations. The leaves wilt quickly but remain chewy and acquire wonderful singed brown spots (especially in a cast-iron skillet) that deepen their earthy flavor.

Ingredients

4 tablespoons vegetable oil

1 ½ pounds boneless, skinless chicken thighs or breasts

Salt and pepper

1 inch fresh ginger

2 garlic cloves

4 scallions

1 ½ pounds kale (1 large bunch)

2 tablespoons soy sauce

Sesame oil for serving

Prep | Cook

1. Put 2 tablespoons vegetable oil in a large skillet over medium-high heat.

   Thinly slice the chicken or chop it into small pieces.

2. Add the chicken to the skillet, sprinkle with salt and pepper, and cook, stirring occasionally until it loses its pink color and is cooked through, 5 to 10 minutes.

   Peel 1 inch ginger and 2 garlic cloves; mince them together.

   Trim and chop the scallions; separate the white and light green parts from the dark green tops.

   Rinse and trim the kale, cutting out any thick stems. Cut the leaves into thin ribbons.

3. When the chicken is done, add the ginger, garlic, and white and light green parts of the scallions. Cook, stirring until fragrant, about a minute. Transfer the chicken mixture to a bowl.

4. Add 2 tablespoons oil to the skillet. Add the kale, a handful at a time if necessary to fit it in, and sprinkle with salt and pepper. Cook until the leaves wilt and begin to brown slightly, 5 or 6 minutes.

5. Return the chicken mixture to the skillet; add 2 tablespoons soy sauce and stir to coat. Taste and adjust the seasoning, garnish with the scallion tops, and serve, passing sesame oil at the table.

VARIATIONS

Stir-Fried Chicken and Collards with Dried Chiles
Swap collards for kale. Mince 3 or 4 dried red chiles and add them along with the ginger in Step 3.

Stir-Fried Chicken and Chard and Citrus
Substitute chard for kale. Add 1 teaspoon each grated lemon and orange zest along with the ginger in Step 3. Add a little of the citrus juice along with the soy sauce in Step 5.

NOTES

IF YOU HAVE MORE TIME
If you want to include the kale stems, slice them thinly and give them a 1- or 2-minute head start in the skillet before adding the leaves.

SIDES

White Rice 941

Sesame Noodles 949

Scallion Pancakes 940

SPEED ◐ SERVES 4

Stir-Fried Chicken and Broccoli with Black Bean Sauce

The secret to the delicious black bean sauce you get in Chinese restaurants is fermented black beans—beans that have been salted for so long they break down. They add a deep, earthy flavor and deliver a little kick of salt.

Ingredients

2 tablespoons fermented black beans

2 tablespoons rice wine or white wine

2 tablespoons soy sauce

1 teaspoon sugar

4 tablespoons vegetable oil

1 ½ pounds boneless, skinless chicken thighs or breasts

Salt and pepper

1 inch fresh ginger

4 garlic cloves

3 scallions

1 medium head broccoli (1 to 1 ½ pounds)

1 tablespoon sesame oil

Prep | Cook

1. Combine 2 tablespoons fermented black beans, 2 tablespoons rice wine or white wine, 2 tablespoons soy sauce, and 1 teaspoon sugar in a small bowl.

2. Put 2 tablespoons vegetable oil in a large skillet over medium-high heat.

   Thinly slice the chicken or chop it into small pieces.

3. Add the chicken to the skillet, sprinkle with salt and pepper, and cook, stirring occasionally, until it loses its pink color and is cooked through, 5 to 10 minutes.

   Peel 1 inch ginger and 4 garlic cloves; mince them together.

   Trim and chop the scallions, separating the white and light green bottoms from the dark green tops.

   Trim the broccoli; break or chop it into small florets.

4. When the chicken is done, add the ginger, garlic, and white and light green parts of the scallions to the skillet. Cook, stirring until fragrant, about a minute. Transfer the chicken mixture to a bowl.

5. Add 2 tablespoons oil to the skillet. Add the broccoli and cook, stirring occasionally until it browns slightly, 3 or 4 minutes. Add ¼ cup water, cover the skillet, and cook until the broccoli is just tender, another 3 or 4 minutes.
6. When the broccoli is just tender, remove the lid and let the remaining water mostly bubble away. Return the chicken to the skillet and add the fermented black bean mixture, tossing to coat everything with the sauce.
7. Drizzle with 1 tablespoon sesame oil, taste, and adjust the seasoning. Garnish with the scallion tops and serve.

VARIATIONS

Stir-Fried Chicken and Broccoli with Tomato-Soy Sauce
Increase the soy sauce to 3 tablespoons. Substitute 1 tablespoon tomato paste for the fermented black beans and red wine for the rice wine.

Stir-Fried Chicken and Cauliflower with Orange–Black Bean Sauce
Add 2 tablespoons orange juice to the fermented black bean mixture and skip the sugar. Substitute cauliflower for the broccoli.

NOTES

EVEN FASTER
Prepare the broccoli in a separate skillet while you cook the chicken. When both are cooked, add the broccoli to the skillet with the chicken and stir in the black bean sauce.

SIDES

White Rice 941

Sesame Noodles 949

Fire and Ice Noodles 950

Panfried Rice Noodles 951

Scallion Pancakes 940

Stir-Fry

1 Pick a game plan.

Stir-frying goes so fast that it's often advantageous to prep ingredients before you start. If you decide to prep as you go, make sure you're starting with the ingredients that will take a little longer to cook, like chicken thighs and broccoli, not shrimp and snow peas.

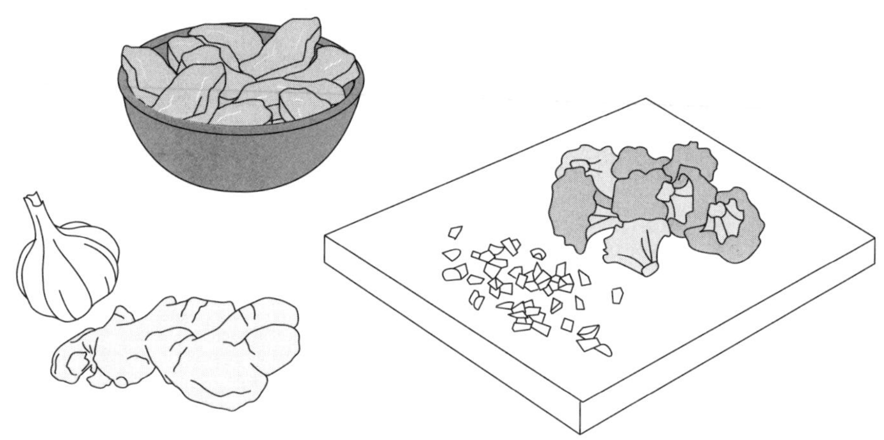

2 Cook the first wave.

Put a film of vegetable oil, like peanut or grapeseed, in a large skillet over high heat. When it's hot, add chopped or sliced meat or tofu (if using seafood, hold off until you add the vegetables) and cook, stirring once or twice to brown everything in places.

3 Add aromatics.

Garlic, ginger, and/or chiles are the norm, but shallots, anchovies, leeks, and rosemary are also good—the flavors needn't be ones traditionally associated with this technique. Stir constantly until fragrant, then remove everything from the skillet.

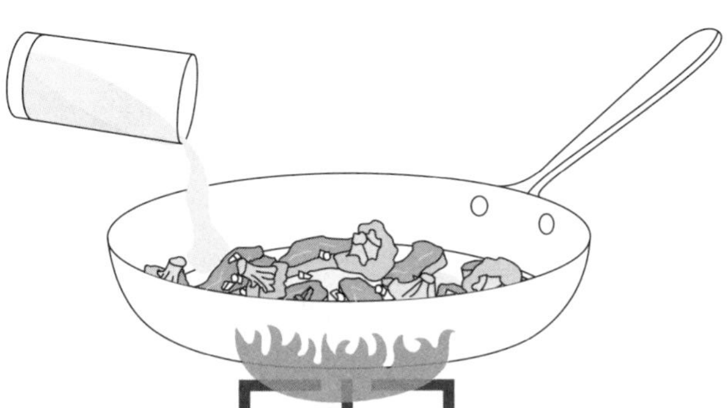

4 Cook vegetables (and seafood).

Add more oil if necessary. Quick-cooking vegetables—like snow peas and bean sprouts—or seafood—like shrimp or squid—need only a few minutes. Firmer vegetables like broccoli will cook faster if you add a small splash of water.

5 Combine, sauce, and serve.

Return everything to the skillet and add a small splash of liquid to make a sauce, anything from soy sauce or fish sauce to lemon juice or tomato sauce (or more water). Add any final seasonings like herbs or a drizzle of sesame oil. Toss, taste, and serve.

SPEED ◐ SERVES 4

Sesame Chicken and Snow Peas

The trick to cooking the thick, sweet sauces associated with American Chinese food is cornstarch. For sesame chicken, the restaurant favorite, it's a must.

Ingredients

3 tablespoons sesame seeds

4 tablespoons vegetable oil

1 ½ pounds boneless, skinless chicken thighs or breasts

Salt and pepper

1 inch fresh ginger

2 garlic cloves

1 lemon

2 tablespoons cornstarch

1 pound snow peas

3 tablespoons soy sauce

2 teaspoons honey

Prep | Cook

1. Put 3 tablespoons sesame seeds in a large skillet over medium-high heat. Cook, shaking the pan frequently until the seeds are lightly browned and fragrant, 2 or 3 minutes. Transfer them to a small bowl.

2. Put 2 tablespoons vegetable oil in the skillet over medium-high heat.

   Slice the chicken or cut it into small chunks.

3. Add the chicken to the skillet, sprinkle with salt and pepper, and cook, stirring occasionally until the chicken loses its pink color and is cooked through, 6 to 8 minutes.

   Peel 1 inch ginger and 2 garlic cloves; mince them together.

   Halve the lemon.

   Whisk together 2 tablespoons cornstarch and ⅓ cup water in a small bowl.

4. Transfer the cooked chicken to a bowl. Add 2 tablespoons oil to the skillet along with the ginger, garlic, and snow peas. Cook, stirring occasionally until the snow peas are slightly tender but still have some crunch, 2 or 3 minutes.

   Add the lemon juice, 3 tablespoons soy sauce, and 2 teaspoons honey to the cornstarch mixture and whisk to combine.

5. When the snow peas are slightly tender, return the chicken to the skillet. Add the cornstarch mixture and most of the sesame seeds (save some for garnish).

6. Cook, stirring until the chicken and snow peas are coated in a thick sauce. Taste and adjust the seasoning, garnish with the remaining sesame seeds, and serve.

VARIATIONS

Sesame Beef and Broccoli
Swap beef sirloin for the chicken and chopped broccoli for the snow peas. Stir-fry the broccoli until just tender, sprinkling a little water to speed the cooking, 6 to 8 minutes, then add the garlic and ginger and cook for another minute before returning the chicken to the skillet.

Cumin Lamb with Green Peppers
Substitute cumin seeds for the sesame seeds, lamb shoulder or loin for the chicken, sliced green bell peppers for the snow peas, and 2 limes for the lemon.

NOTES

IF YOU HAVE MORE TIME
Chinese-American-style sesame chicken involves frying the chicken and tossing it in the sauce. To do this, dredge the chicken in cornstarch and shallow- or deep-fry it until golden brown and cooked through. Let it drain on paper towels while you cook the snow peas, then return it to the skillet as directed in Step 5.

SIDES

White Rice 941

Sesame Noodles 949

Scallion Pancakes 940

SPEED ◐ SERVES 4

Chile-Rubbed Chicken with Corn and Scallions

The simple skillet stir-fry gets a lot out of its ingredients in a short amount of time. Chicken with a spiced cornmeal coating becomes crunchy and smoky, while corn kernels develop an earthy char. Serve with warm tortillas or something more unexpected from the opposite page.

Ingredients

5 tablespoons vegetable oil

½ cup cornmeal

2 teaspoons chili powder

2 teaspoons cumin

Salt and pepper

1 ½ pounds boneless, skinless chicken thighs or breasts

4 ears fresh corn

6 scallions

1 lime

1 bunch fresh cilantro

4 ounces queso fresco (1 cup crumbled)

Hot sauce for serving

Prep | Cook

1. Put 2 tablespoons vegetable oil in a large skillet over medium-low heat.
2. Combine ½ cup cornmeal, 2 teaspoons chili powder, 2 teaspoons cumin, 1 teaspoon salt, and ¼ teaspoon pepper in a large bowl.

   Thinly slice the chicken or chop it into small pieces.
3. Add the chicken to the cornmeal mixture and toss to coat. Raise the heat to medium-high.
4. Add half of the chicken to the skillet, shaking off excess coating. Cook, stirring occasionally until the chicken is cooked through and its coating is crisp, 5 to 10 minutes. Transfer to a plate. Add another 2 tablespoons oil and cook the second batch.

   Husk the corn and strip the kernels off the cobs.

   Trim and chop the scallions.
5. When the second batch of chicken is cooked and crisp, transfer it to the plate.

6. Add 1 tablespoon oil to the skillet. Add the corn and scallions and sprinkle with salt and pepper. Cook, shaking the pan occasionally and keeping the corn in as much of a single layer as possible, until the kernels are well browned on at least one side, 5 to 10 minutes.

   Halve the lime.

   Chop 1/4 cup cilantro.

7. When the corn is browned, return the chicken to the skillet and cook, tossing, to heat it through. Taste and adjust the seasoning.

8. Squeeze in the lime juice; crumble 1 cup queso fresco and sprinkle over the top. Garnish with the cilantro and serve, passing hot sauce at the table.

VARIATIONS

Curry-Rubbed Stir-Fried Chicken with Corn and Red Onion

Substitute 1 tablespoon curry powder for the chili powder and cumin and 1 large red onion for the scallions. Skip the queso fresco and garnish with lime, cilantro, mint, and 1/4 cup chopped cashews.

NOTES

MAKE YOUR OWN

Chili Powder 758

EVEN FASTER

Stir-fry the corn and scallions in a separate skillet while you cook the chicken.

SIDES

Warm Corn Tortillas 907

White Rice 941

Refried Beans 938

Chile-Cumin Black Beans 937

Ripe Plantains 960

SPEED ◑ SERVES 4

Chicken and Cauliflower Curry with Apricots

Inspired by tandoori: Yogurt-marinated chicken thighs and cauliflower char under the broiler while you prepare a creamy curry sauce brightened by dried apricots.

Ingredients

1 cup yogurt

4 tablespoons vegetable oil

Salt and pepper

1 small head cauliflower (1 ½ pounds)

1 ½ pounds boneless, skinless chicken thighs

1 onion

2 garlic cloves

1 inch fresh ginger

1 cup dried apricots

1 tablespoon curry powder

One 15-ounce can coconut milk

½ cup cream

1 bunch fresh cilantro

Prep | Cook

1. Turn the broiler to high; put the rack 6 inches from the heat.
2. Combine 1 cup yogurt, 2 tablespoons vegetable oil, and a sprinkle of salt and pepper in a large bowl.

   Trim the cauliflower and break or chop it into small florets and add them to the bowl.

   Cut the chicken into large chunks; add them to the bowl.
3. Toss the chicken and cauliflower to coat, then spread them out on a rimmed baking sheet. Broil, turning once or twice, until they are brown in spots and cooked through, 10 to 15 minutes.
4. Put 2 tablespoons oil in a large skillet or large pot over medium-high heat.

   Trim, peel, and chop the onion.
5. Add the onion to the skillet and cook, stirring occasionally until it softens, 3 to 5 minutes.

   Peel 2 garlic cloves and 1 inch ginger; mince them together.

   Chop 1 cup dried apricots.

6. When the onion is soft, add the garlic, ginger, 1 tablespoon curry powder, and a sprinkle of salt and pepper. Cook, stirring until fragrant, a minute or 2.

7. Add the coconut milk, ½ cup cream, and the apricots and stir. Adjust the heat so the mixture bubbles steadily but not vigorously and cook until the liquid reduces into a creamy sauce, 2 or 3 minutes.

   Chop ¼ cup cilantro.

8. When the chicken and cauliflower are done, add them to the sauce and stir to coat. Cook for a minute or 2 to combine the flavors. Taste and adjust the seasoning, garnish with the cilantro, and serve.

VARIATIONS

Chicken and Cauliflower Curry with Tomatoes
Substitute cherry tomatoes, halved, for the apricots.

Chicken and Eggplant Green Curry
Skip the apricots. Substitute eggplant, cut into small chunks, for the cauliflower and 2 tablespoons green curry paste for the curry powder.

NOTES

MAKE YOUR OWN
Curry Powder 758

IF YOU HAVE MORE TIME
Let the chicken and cauliflower marinate in the yogurt for up to a day. The longer they marinate, the more tender and flavorful they will be.

To give a deeper flavor to the sauce, cook the onions slowly over medium heat until they are dark brown, 10 to 15 minutes.

SIDES

White Rice 941

Crisp Seasoned Pita 908

Cucumber Raita 916

SPEED ◐ SERVES 4

Provençal Chicken

I'm a sucker for the flavors of Provence: olives, capers, garlic, and tomatoes. They are the makings of this hearty country stew.

Ingredients

4 tablespoons olive oil

1 ½ pounds boneless, skinless chicken thighs

Salt and pepper

2 large zucchini

3 medium ripe tomatoes (1 pound)

½ cup black olives

2 tablespoons capers

4 garlic cloves

2 sprigs fresh thyme

½ cup chicken stock, white wine, or water

Several sprigs fresh basil for garnish

Prep | Cook

1. Put 2 tablespoons olive oil in a large skillet or large pot over medium-high heat.

   Cut the chicken into large chunks.

2. Add the chicken to the skillet, sprinkle with salt and pepper, and cook, stirring occasionally until it loses its pink color and is nearly cooked through, 6 to 8 minutes.

   Trim and chop the zucchini. Core and chop the tomatoes.

   Pit ½ cup olives if necessary; chop 2 tablespoons capers.

3. When the chicken is nearly cooked through, transfer it to a bowl.

4. Add 2 tablespoons oil to the skillet. Add the zucchini, sprinkle with salt and pepper, and cook, stirring occasionally until lightly browned, 4 or 5 minutes.

   Peel and mince 4 garlic cloves.

   Strip the thyme leaves from 2 sprigs.

5. When the zucchini is lightly browned, add the tomatoes, olives, capers, garlic, thyme, ½ cup stock, wine, or water, and lots of pepper. Scrape any browned bits from the bottom of the pan, then return the chicken the pan.

6. Adjust the heat so the mixture bubbles steadily but not vigorously and cook, stirring once or twice, until the tomatoes thicken a bit and the chicken finishes cooking, 5 to 10 minutes.

   Strip the basil leaves from several sprigs and chop.

7. When the tomatoes have thickened and the chicken is cooked, taste and adjust the seasoning. Garnish with the basil and serve.

VARIATIONS

Provençal Chicken with Goat Cheese
For a creamier, richer dish, stir 1/4 cup goat cheese into the skillet along with the basil.

Creamy Provençal Chicken
Also creamy, but less tangy than the first variation. Stir 1/4 cup (or a little more) cream or crème fraîche into the skillet along with the basil.

NOTES

MAKE YOUR OWN

Chicken Stock 213

SIDES

Warm Buttery Bread 906

Red Wine and Rosemary Quinoa 945

Buttered Egg Noodles 948

Skin-On Mashed Potatoes 961

Green Salad 911

SPEED ◑ SERVES 4

Chicken Stroganoff

It doesn't get much more comforting than stroganoff, the rich mushroom and sour cream sauce that's more commonly simmered with beef (see the variation) than chicken. Either way you get one of those amazing dishes that tastes like it's been cooking forever.

Ingredients

3 tablespoons butter

1 onion

1 ½ pounds button or cremini mushrooms

Salt and pepper

1 ½ pounds boneless, skinless chicken thighs

1 medium ripe tomato

1 cup chicken stock

1 tablespoon Dijon mustard

1 bunch fresh dill

½ cup sour cream

Prep | Cook

1. Put 3 tablespoons butter in a large skillet over medium heat.

   Trim, peel, and chop the onion. Trim and slice the mushrooms.

2. Add the onions and mushrooms to the skillet, sprinkle with salt and pepper, and raise the heat to medium-high. Cook, stirring occasionally until the onion is very soft but not browned, about 10 minutes.

   Cut the chicken into large chunks.

   Core and chop the tomato.

3. When the onion is very soft, add the chicken to the skillet, sprinkle with salt and pepper, and cook, stirring occasionally for a minute or 2.

4. Add the tomato, 1 cup chicken stock, and 1 tablespoon Dijon. Adjust the heat so the mixture bubbles steadily but not vigorously and cook, stirring occasionally until the chicken is cooked through, 5 to 10 minutes.

   Strip ¼ cup dill leaves from the stems and chop.

5. When the chicken is cooked, stir in ½ cup sour cream and turn off the heat. Taste and adjust the seasoning, stir in the dill, and serve immediately.

VARIATIONS

Beef Stroganoff
Substitute beef tenderloin for the chicken; it'll probably take about the same amount of time to cook.

Pork Stroganoff
Use boneless pork loin instead of the chicken. Substitute 1 tablespoon chopped fresh sage (or 1 teaspoon dried) for the dill.

Curried Chicken and Mushrooms
Swap 1 tablespoon curry powder for the Dijon; add it to the skillet along with the chicken in Step 3. Use cilantro instead of dill and yogurt instead of sour cream.

Chicken Paprikash
Replace the Dijon with 1 tablespoon paprika; add it to the skillet along with the chicken in Step 3.

NOTES

MAKE YOUR OWN

Chicken Stock 213

SIDES

Buttered Egg Noodles 948

White Rice 941

Steamed Tender Vegetables 954

Skin-On Mashed Potatoes 961

SPEED ◑ SERVES 4

Charred Chicken and Pita with Gyro Fixings

Gyros—those meaty, saucy loose wraps—have a tendency to fall apart when you eat them, so here you don't bother assembling them in the first place. Serve everything on a platter and let people make sandwiches, scoop up bites with the toasted pita, or devour as they like.

Ingredients

2 pounds boneless, skinless chicken thighs

3 tablespoons olive oil

1 teaspoon cumin

½ teaspoon turmeric

Salt and pepper

1 lemon

¼ cup yogurt

¼ cup mayonnaise

½ head iceberg lettuce

2 medium ripe tomatoes

1 small red onion

Four 6- to 8-inch pitas (with or without pockets)

Prep | Cook

1. Turn the broiler to high; put the rack 4 inches from the heat.
2. Put the chicken on a rimmed baking sheet; drizzle it with 2 tablespoons olive oil and sprinkle with 1 teaspoon cumin, ½ teaspoon turmeric, and some salt and pepper. Toss to coat the chicken in the oil and spices.
3. When the broiler is hot, cook the chicken, turning once, until lightly charred on both sides and just cooked through, 6 to 8 minutes per side.

   Halve the lemon and squeeze the juice into a medium bowl.
4. Add ¼ cup yogurt, ¼ cup mayonnaise, and a sprinkle of salt and pepper to the bowl. Stir to combine.

   Chop ½ head of lettuce; add it to the bowl.

   Core and chop the tomatoes; add them to the bowl.

   Trim, peel, halve, and thinly slice the onion; add it to the bowl.
5. Toss the vegetables with the dressing, taste, and adjust the seasoning.

6. Rub the pitas with 1 tablespoon oil. Sprinkle with salt and pepper.
7. When the chicken is lightly charred and cooked through, transfer it to a cutting board.
8. Put the pitas on a clean baking sheet and broil, turning once, until browned or even slightly charred on both sides, 2 to 5 minutes total.
9. Slice or chop the chicken and put on plate or a platter. Add the pitas. Serve with the chopped salad over the top or on the side.

VARIATIONS

Charred Chicken and Tortillas with Taco Fixings
Substitute chili powder for the turmeric, flour tortillas for the pita, lime for the lemon, and ½ cup crumbled queso fresco and a dash of hot sauce for the yogurt.

Charred Chicken and Crusty Bread with Hero Fixings
Use 1 teaspoon oregano instead of the cumin and turmeric, thick slices of crusty bread for the pita, 2 tablespoons red wine vinegar for the lemon juice, and 3 tablespoons olive oil for the mayonnaise and yogurt. If you have any olives or spicy pickled peppers lying around, throw some of those into the salad as well.

NOTES

MAKE YOUR OWN
Mayonnaise 144

SIDES

Rice Pilaf 944

Couscous 910

Hummus 939

Refried White Beans with Rosemary 938

SPEED ◐ SERVES 4

Jerk Chicken and Onions

In addition to being easy and insanely flavorful, this jerk dish will remind you of all the worthy and underused spices in your pantry. Once the marinade comes together, all you have to do is toss it with a mess of chicken and sliced onions and broil away, which gives you an uninterrupted stretch to whip up a side.

Ingredients

1 garlic clove

½ inch fresh ginger

1 teaspoon dried thyme

2 teaspoons allspice

½ teaspoon cayenne

1 ½ teaspoons paprika

1 ½ teaspoons sugar

3 tablespoons olive oil

Salt and pepper

2 large onions

1 ½ pounds boneless, skinless chicken thighs

Prep | Cook

1. Turn the broiler to high; put the rack 6 inches from the heat.

   Peel 1 garlic clove and ½ inch ginger; mince them together and put them in a small bowl.

2. Add to the bowl 1 teaspoon dried thyme, 2 teaspoons allspice, ½ teaspoon cayenne, 1 ½ teaspoons paprika, 1 ½ teaspoons sugar, 3 tablespoons olive oil, and a sprinkle of salt and pepper. Stir into a paste.

   Trim, peel, halve, and slice the onions.

3. Put the onions and chicken on a rimmed baking sheet. Rub the spice paste onto everything (getting your hands messy is the best way). Spread everything in a single layer.

4. Broil, turning the chicken once and tossing the onions occasionally, until the chicken is browned and cooked through and the onions are browned and tender, 12 to 16 minutes total. Serve hot or warm.

VARIATIONS

Five-Spice Chicken and Scallions
Substitute 2 tablespoons five-spice powder for the jerk spices, vegetable oil for the olive oil, and 2 or 3 bunches scallions, trimmed, for the onions.

Za'atar Chicken and Onions
Substitute 2 tablespoons za'atar for the jerk spices.

Lemon-Pepper Chicken and Onions
Use 1 ½ tablespoons grated lemon zest and lots of pepper instead of the jerk spices.

SIDES

White Rice 941

Ripe Plantains 960

Ripe Plantains with Cinnamon and Cumin 960

Crunchy Okra 959

SPEED ◐ SERVES 4

Chicken and Peppers with Black Bean "Mole"

There are many versions of mole, the classic Mexican sauce, many of them notorious for including upward of thirty ingredients, taking hours to make and years to perfect. My solution is a black bean sauce that retains the deep, earthy flavors of the original. It's legit.

Ingredients

3 bell peppers (any color)

8 bone-in, skin-on chicken thighs

2 tablespoons vegetable oil

Salt and pepper

2 cups cooked or canned black beans (one 15-ounce can)

2 ounces bittersweet or semisweet chocolate

1 garlic clove

¾ cup almonds or peanuts or a combination

1 teaspoon cumin

1 teaspoon chili powder

½ teaspoon cinnamon

2 cups chicken stock or water

1 lime

Several sprigs fresh cilantro for garnish

Sour cream (optional)

Prep | Cook

1. Turn the broiler to high; put the rack 4 inches from the heat.

   Core, seed, and quarter the peppers.

2. Put the peppers and chicken (skin side up) on a rimmed baking sheet. Drizzle with 2 tablespoons vegetable oil and sprinkle with salt and pepper. Broil until the chicken and peppers are nicely browned on 1 side, 6 to 12 minutes, depending on your broiler.

   If you're using canned beans, rinse and drain them. Put the beans in a blender.

   Roughly chop 2 ounces chocolate and add it to the blender.

   Peel and crush the garlic clove and add it to the blender.

3. Add to the blender ¾ cup nuts, 1 teaspoon cumin, 1 teaspoon chili powder, ½ teaspoon cinnamon, 2 cups stock or water, and a sprinkle of salt and pepper.

4. Blend until smooth.

5. Transfer the sauce to a large skillet or saucepan. Bring it to a boil, then adjust the heat so that it bubbles gently but steadily.

6. Add the browned chicken and peppers to the sauce along with any juices from the baking sheet. Cover the pan and simmer, tossing once or twice, until the chicken is cooked through, 12 to 15 minutes.

   Cut the lime into wedges.

   Chop several sprigs cilantro.

7. When the chicken is cooked, taste the sauce and adjust the seasoning. Garnish with the cilantro and serve with the lime wedges and a dollop of sour cream if you like.

VARIATIONS

Chicken and Peppers with Pumpkin Seed Mole
Use hulled pumpkin seeds instead of the nuts.

Chicken and Peppers with Tomatillo Sauce
Replace the black beans with 2 cups chopped tomatillos. Omit the chocolate.

NOTES

MAKE YOUR OWN

Cooked Beans 496

Chili Powder 758

Chicken Stock 213

IF YOU HAVE MORE TIME
Let the chicken simmer in the sauce for 30 to 60 minutes, adding an extra splash of liquid if the sauce gets too thick. The chicken will become more tender and the sauce more complex.

BROILING AND BUBBLING
The broiler is perfect for getting some nice color on bone-in chicken parts, but once the meat is browned, the broiler doesn't impart any extra flavor. Often I'll brown chicken well under the broiler, then let it finish cooking in a sauce on the stovetop, where it soaks up additional flavor. Almost any sauce fits the bill—this mole, Tomato Sauce (page 296), or Barbecue Sauce (page 145), for example. Bone-in chicken pieces or fattier cuts of meat that won't overcook as they simmer are ideal for this method, but since the sauce adds so much moisture, even leaner cuts like chicken breast or pork tenderloin will remain pretty tender.

SIDES

Warm Tortillas 907

White Rice 941

Jícama and Radish Salad 918

Sautéed Sweet Potatoes with Chipotle and Lime 964

Avocado with Lime and Chili Salt 920

SPEED ◐ SERVES 4

Thai Peanut Chicken with Crisp Cabbage and Bean Sprouts

Whole boneless thighs get the brush-and-broil treatment with a peanut sauce that you can whip up just in time to slather on chicken as it finishes cooking. Crisp stir-fried cabbage and bean sprouts provide a light, refreshing bed for the tender chicken.

Ingredients

1 garlic clove

½ inch fresh ginger

½ cup peanut butter

2 tablespoons soy sauce

1 ½ pounds boneless, skinless chicken thighs

4 tablespoons vegetable oil

Salt and pepper

1 small Savoy or green cabbage (1 pound)

8 ounces bean sprouts (1 ½ to 2 cups)

3 scallions

Prep | Cook

1. Turn the broiler to high; put the rack 6 inches from the heat.

   Peel 1 garlic clove and ½ inch ginger; mince them together and put them in a medium bowl.

   Add ½ cup peanut butter, 2 tablespoons soy sauce, and ¼ cup hot water. Stir, adding more hot water if necessary, until the sauce is smooth. Reserve half of the sauce in a separate bowl for serving.

2. Rub the chicken with 2 tablespoons vegetable oil and sprinkle with salt and pepper. Broil, turning once and brushing with the peanut sauce, until the sauce is caramelized and the chicken is cooked through, 6 to 8 minutes per side.

3. Put 2 tablespoons oil in a large skillet over medium-high heat.

   Trim, core, and quarter the cabbage. Cut each quarter crosswise into thin ribbons.

4. Add the cabbage and bean sprouts to the skillet, sprinkle with salt and pepper, and cook, stirring occasionally until they are slightly softened but still crunchy, 2 to 4 minutes.

   Trim and chop the scallions.

5. When the cabbage and bean sprouts are slightly softened, put them on a platter. When the chicken is done, put the pieces on top of the vegetables. Drizzle with the reserved peanut sauce, garnish with the scallions, and serve.

VARIATIONS

Herby Chicken Thighs with Crisp Cabbage and Fennel

Instead of the peanut sauce, brush the chicken with a mixture of 1 garlic clove, minced, 1 tablespoon chopped fresh rosemary, 2 teaspoons chopped fresh oregano, ¼ cup olive oil, 2 tablespoons balsamic vinegar, and a sprinkle of salt and pepper. Use 1 fennel bulb, trimmed and thinly sliced, instead of the bean sprouts.

BBQ Chicken Thighs with Crisp Cabbage and Red Onion

Use barbecue sauce instead of the peanut sauce and 1 large red onion, thinly sliced, instead of the bean sprouts.

NOTES

EVEN FASTER

Shred the cabbage as finely as you can and leave it and the bean sprouts raw. Toss with vegetable oil, salt, and pepper.

SIDES

White Rice 941

Fire and Ice Noodles 950

Bulgur with Corn 946

Sesame-Soy Black Beans 937

SPEED ◐ SERVES 4

Chicken and Chard Gratin

What starts as a simple stir-fry ends up as a bubbly, crisp, and rich gratin.

Ingredients

3 tablespoons olive oil, plus a little more for drizzling

1 ½ pounds boneless, skinless chicken thighs or breasts

Salt and pepper

2 garlic cloves

1 ½ pounds chard

4 to 8 ounces Gruyère cheese (1 to 2 cups grated)

2 thick slices any rustic bread (a little stale is fine)

Prep | Cook

1. Put 3 tablespoons olive oil in a large ovenproof skillet over medium-high heat. Turn the broiler to high; put the rack 6 inches from the heat.

   Chop the chicken into chunks.

2. Add the chicken to the skillet, sprinkle with salt and pepper, and cook, stirring occasionally until it just loses its pink color, 3 or 4 minutes.

   Peel and mince 2 garlic cloves.

   Trim the chard, cutting out any thick stems. Chop the leaves.

   Grate 1 to 2 cups Gruyère.

3. When the chicken is no longer pink, add the garlic, chard, and another sprinkle of salt and pepper. Cook, stirring occasionally until the chard leaves are just wilted, 3 or 4 minutes.

   Tear 2 slices bread into pieces and put them in a food processor; pulse into coarse crumbs (you should have about 1 cup).

4. When the chard is just wilted, sprinkle the Gruyère and bread crumbs over the top and drizzle with a little more olive oil. Broil until the cheese is bubbly and the bread crumbs are browned and crisp, 2 to 5 minutes. Serve immediately.

VARIATIONS

Mexican-Style Chicken and Chard Gratin

Add a minced fresh hot green chile along with the garlic, substitute cheddar or Jack cheese for the Gruyère, and use 2 cups tortilla chips instead of bread (pulse them into coarse crumbs).

Chicken and Broccoli Rabe Gratin

Substitute broccoli rabe for the chard and mozzarella for the Gruyère. If you like, stir ½ cup Tomato Sauce (page 296) into the skillet once the chard is wilted. Grate a little Parmesan over the top before broiling.

Chicken and Chard Gratin with Blue Cheese and Walnuts

Substitute crumbled blue cheese for the Gruyère and 1 cup chopped walnuts for the bread crumbs. (Walnuts can burn easily under the broiler, so keep an eye on them; if the blue cheese isn't fully melted by the time the nuts are brown, that's fine.)

5 Other Great Dishes to Turn into Gratins

A nice alternative to serving over rice or noodles: Top any of these with cheese and/or bread crumbs and run under the broiler until toasted and bubbly.

1. White Beans with Sausage, Greens, and Garlic (page 480)
2. Scrambled Broccoli with Parmesan and Lemon (page 442)
3. Quick-Stewed Green Beans with Bacon (page 450)
4. Pan-Seared Corn and Pork (page 454)
5. Smoky Shrimp Scampi (page 546)

NOTES

EVEN FASTER

Instead of making crumbs in Step 3, use Bread Crumbs (page 71) you already have on hand.

SIDES

Green Salad 911

Skin-On Mashed Potatoes 961

Quinoa 945

Buttered Egg Noodles 948

Chicken and Chile Fundido

The queso fundido you usually encounter in restaurants consists mostly of melted cheese with scant amounts of toppings and is eaten as an appetizer or snack. But if you load it up with vegetables (like the one on page 418) and/or meat (like this one), it becomes a meal.

Ingredients

3 tablespoons vegetable oil

1 medium onion

1 pound ground chicken

3 garlic cloves

3 poblano peppers

2 medium ripe tomatoes

1 teaspoon cumin

1 teaspoon chili powder

Salt and pepper

8 ounces Jack or Oaxaca cheese (2 cups grated)

Several sprigs fresh cilantro for garnish

Prep | Cook

1. Heat the oven to 450°F. Put 3 tablespoons oil in a large ovenproof skillet over medium-high heat.

   Trim, peel, and chop the onion.

2. Add the chicken and onion to the skillet.

   Peel and mince 3 garlic cloves; add them to the skillet.

   Core, seed, and slice the poblanos; core and chop the tomatoes. Add them to the skillet.

3. Add 1 teaspoon cumin, 1 teaspoon chili powder, and a sprinkle of salt and pepper. Cook, stirring occasionally until the chicken is browned and the vegetables are soft, 8 to 12 minutes.

   Grate 2 cups Jack or Oaxaca cheese.

4. When the chicken is browned and the vegetables are soft, taste and adjust the seasoning. Stir in half of the cheese so it's incorporated and sprinkle the other half over the top.

5. Bake until the cheese is bubbly, 5 to 10 minutes.

   Chop several sprigs cilantro.

6. When the cheese is bubbly, garnish with the cilantro and serve immediately.

VARIATIONS

Smoky Lamb and Sweet Potato Fundido
Substitute ground lamb for ground chicken, 1 pound sweet potatoes, peeled and grated, for the poblanos, and 1 tablespoon chopped chipotle chiles in adobo for the chili powder.

Chicken and Roasted Red Pepper Skillet Bake
Use olive oil instead of vegetable oil, 1 cup chopped roasted red peppers instead of the poblanos, and mozzarella instead of the Jack or Oaxaca cheese.

NOTES

MAKE YOUR OWN
Chili Powder 758

MEXICAN CHEESES
There are both melting and non-melting kinds. The most famous melter is queso Oaxaca, a pearly white, mild variety that's stretched and pulled into a ball; mozzarella is the best substitute, with Jack cheese close behind. Of the nonmelting cheeses, queso fresco is the most common and the most useful; it's crumbly and slightly salty, perfect for sprinkling on tacos or over salads, beans, or rice. If you can't find it, feta and ricotta salata are excellent proxies. Salty cotija cheese is a lot like queso fresco when it is fresh, but as it ages and hardens it's perfect for grating; you can always use Parmesan instead.

SIDES

Warm Tortillas 907

White Rice 941

Chile-Cumin Black Beans 937

Ripe Plantains 960

Jícama and Radish Salad 918

SPEED ◐ SERVES 4

Chicken and Ricotta Sausage over Broccoli Rabe

Store-bought chicken sausages tend to be unexciting. Better to season ground chicken yourself and fry it up in crispy patties. Here ricotta adds fat to the lean chicken and garlicky broccoli rabe provides a luscious and colorful bed for the juices.

Ingredients

4 tablespoons olive oil

1½ pounds broccoli rabe

4 garlic cloves

Several sprigs fresh basil

Salt and pepper

2 ounces Parmesan cheese (½ cup grated)

½ cup ricotta cheese

1 ½ pounds ground chicken

Prep | Cook

1. Put 2 tablespoons olive oil in a large skillet over low heat.

   Trim and chop the broccoli rabe, keeping thick stems separate.

2. Raise the heat to medium-high. Add any chopped stems to the skillet and cook until they begin to soften, 3 or 4 minutes.

   Peel and mince 4 garlic cloves; add half to the skillet and put the other half in a large bowl.

   Strip the basil leaves from several sprigs, chop, and add to the garlic in the bowl.

3. Add the broccoli rabe leaves to the skillet, a handful at a time if necessary to fit them in, and sprinkle with salt and pepper. Cook until they're just wilted, 3 or 4 minutes. Transfer to a platter and cover with aluminum foil to keep warm.

   Grate ½ cup Parmesan and add to the garlic and basil.

4. Add ½ cup ricotta, the ground chicken, and a sprinkle of salt and pepper to the bowl. Mix gently with your hands to combine. Put 2 tablespoons oil in the skillet over medium-high heat.

5. Gently shape the meat into 4 patties, adding them to the skillet as you go. Cook, turning once, until the burgers are nicely browned on both sides and the chicken is just cooked through, 4 or 5 minutes per side.

6. Serve the patties on top of the broccoli rabe.

VARIATIONS

Chicken and Feta Sausage over Sautéed Spinach
Use spinach instead of the broccoli rabe, mint instead of the basil, ¼ cup chopped kalamata olives instead of the Parmesan, and crumbled feta in place of the ricotta. The spinach will take a little less time to wilt than the broccoli rabe.

Chicken and Blue Cheese Sausage over Sautéed Kale
Substitute kale for the broccoli rabe, tarragon for the basil, and crumbled blue cheese for the ricotta. The kale will take a little more time to wilt than the broccoli rabe.

Maple-Chicken-Apple Sausage over Sautéed Collards
Substitute collard greens for the broccoli rabe, sage for the basil, 1 tablespoon maple syrup for the Parmesan, and ¼ cup chopped dried apples for the ricotta. The collards will take a little more time to wilt than the broccoli rabe.

NOTES

EVEN FASTER
The flatter the patties, the faster they'll cook.

SIDES

Garlic Bread 906

Bruschetta 909

Pasta, Plain and Simple 948

Caprese Salad 922

SPEED ◐ SERVES 4 TO 6

Korean-Style Chicken and Vegetable Pancakes

Korean pa jun are a delicious take on scallion pancakes: fluffy, crisp, and loaded with all sorts of vegetables. Add ground chicken to the mix and dinner is served.

Ingredients

4 tablespoons vegetable oil, plus more as needed

8 ounces ground chicken

Salt and pepper

2 eggs

2 cups flour

4 scallions

1 carrot

1 small zucchini

1 tablespoon rice vinegar

3 tablespoons soy sauce

1 teaspoon sugar

Prep | Cook

1. Heat the oven to 200°F. Put 1 tablespoon oil in a large skillet (preferably nonstick) over medium-high heat. When it's hot, add the chicken, sprinkle with salt and pepper, and cook until browned, 5 to 10 minutes.

2. Crack the eggs into a medium bowl; add 2 cups flour and 1 ½ cups water and whisk to form a smooth batter.

   Trim and chop the scallions; add them to the batter.

   Trim and peel the carrot; trim the zucchini. Grate both and add to the batter.

3. When the chicken is browned, add it to the batter and wipe out the skillet. Stir the batter to incorporate all the ingredients.

4. Put 3 tablespoons oil in the skillet and return it to medium-high heat. Ladle half of the batter into the skillet and spread it out into a circle (if the first pancake is too thick, stir a little water into the remaining batter).

5. Cook, adjusting the heat so the pancake sizzles but doesn't burn, until the bottom is browned, about 3 minutes. Flip and cook until the other side is browned, about 2 minutes.

6. If the pancake is crisp but still not cooked in the middle, turn the heat to medium-low and cook, flipping once, until cooked through. Transfer the pancake to the oven to keep warm and repeat with the remaining batter, adding more oil to the skillet if needed.

   Combine 1 tablespoon rice vinegar, 3 tablespoons soy sauce, and 1 teaspoon sugar in a small bowl.

7. When the pancakes are done, cut them into wedges and serve with the dipping sauce.

VARIATIONS

Korean-Style Chicken and Vegetable Cornmeal Pancakes
Replace ½ cup of the flour with ½ cup cornmeal.

Garlic-Rosemary Chicken and Vegetable Pancakes
Use 2 garlic cloves, minced, and 1 tablespoon minced rosemary instead of the scallions. For the dipping sauce, combine 3 tablespoons olive oil, 1 tablespoon lemon juice, and a sprinkle of salt and pepper. If you like, grate a little Parmesan over the pancakes while they're still warm.

NOTES

EVEN FASTER
Cook the pancakes in two skillets at the same time.

SIDES

Stir-Fried Bok Choy 927

Cucumbers with Peanut Vinaigrette 953

White Rice 941

Fire and Ice Noodles 950

Cold Sesame Noodles 949

Braised and Glazed Chicken and Leeks

If you braise meat and vegetables in very little liquid, there's enough to generate steam for cooking but not so much that you need to spend time reducing it into a sauce at the end. Just open the pot, toss in a little butter, and you're all set.

Ingredients

1 tablespoon olive oil

8 bone-in chicken thighs (about 2 pounds)

Salt and pepper

2 leeks

¼ cup white wine

½ cup chicken stock or water

Several sprigs fresh parsley for garnish

1 tablespoon butter

Prep | Cook

1. Put 1 tablespoon olive oil in a large skillet or large pot over medium-high heat.

   Pat the chicken thighs dry.

2. When the oil is hot, add the chicken skin side down (in batches if necessary) and sprinkle with salt and pepper. Cook, undisturbed, until the skin is nicely browned, about 10 minutes, then transfer the chicken to a plate.

   Trim the leeks and halve them lengthwise; cut them into 2-inch pieces.

3. When all the chicken is browned and on the plate, drain all but 1 tablespoon of the fat from the pan. Add ¼ cup wine and ½ cup stock or water to the skillet, scraping any browned bits from the bottom. Add the leeks and sprinkle with salt and pepper.

4. Return the chicken to the pot and adjust the heat so the mixture bubbles gently. Cover and simmer until the chicken is cooked through and the leeks are tender, 15 to 20 minutes.

   Strip the parsley leaves from several sprigs and chop.

5. Uncover the pot and transfer the chicken to a platter. Add 1 tablespoon butter to the pot and stir to melt. Pour the leeks and sauce over the chicken. Garnish with the parsley and serve.

VARIATIONS

Braised and Glazed Chicken with Onions and Soy
Substitute vegetable oil for the olive oil, 1 large onion, sliced, for the leeks, soy sauce for the white wine, and cilantro for the parsley. Go easy on the salt.

Braised and Glazed Chicken and Brussels Sprouts
Use 12 ounces Brussels sprouts instead of the leeks.

NOTES

MAKE YOUR OWN
Chicken Stock 213

EVEN FASTER
Use boneless, skinless chicken thighs and brown well on one side.

SIDES

Buttered Egg Noodles 948

Skin-On Mashed Potatoes 961

Warm Buttery Bread 906

Quinoa 945

SPEED  SERVES 4

Turkey Burgers

Since ground turkey is so mild and lean, it needs help. Bring these burgers to life by incorporating a sofrito, a cooked-down mixture of green pepper, onions, garlic, and tomato paste that contributes flavor and moisture, turning dry turkey burgers into something that can compete with the best.

Ingredients

4 tablespoons vegetable oil, plus more as needed

1 green bell pepper

1 large onion

2 garlic cloves

1 tablespoon tomato paste

1 ½ pounds ground turkey

Salt and pepper

4 buns for serving (optional)

Prep | Cook

1. Put 2 tablespoons oil in a large skillet over medium heat.
   Core, seed, and chop the pepper.
   Trim, peel, and chop the onion.
   Peel 2 garlic cloves. Chop all of them together; it's okay if the pieces are uneven as long as they're small.
2. Raise the heat to medium-high and add the vegetables and 1 tablespoon tomato paste. Cook, stirring occasionally until the vegetables soften and the tomato paste darkens, 3 to 5 minutes.
3. Put the turkey in a large bowl. When the vegetables are ready, add them to the turkey. Sprinkle with salt and pepper and mix gently with your hands to incorporate the sofrito.
4. Wipe out the skillet, add 2 tablespoons oil, and return the pan to medium-high heat.
5. Gently shape the meat into 4 patties, adding them to the skillet as you go. Cook, turning once, until the burgers are nicely browned on both sides and the turkey is just cooked through, 4 or 5 minutes per side.

6. While the burgers cook, toast buns if you're using them. Serve the burgers on the buns or plain, with your favorite condiments.

VARIATIONS

10 Ways to Flavor Turkey Burgers

Add any of the following to the sofrito as it cooks:

1. 2 teaspoons smoked paprika
2. 1 teaspoon cumin and 1 teaspoon chili powder
3. Pinch of saffron
4. 2 teaspoons curry powder
5. 2 teaspoons chopped fresh rosemary, sage, thyme, or oregano (or 1 teaspoon dried)
6. 1 tablespoon chopped capers
7. A few minced anchovy fillets
8. 2 teaspoons harissa, Sriracha, or Worcestershire
9. ½ cup grated Parmesan cheese (stir it into the turkey mixture)
10. ½ cup chopped nuts or dried fruit

NOTES

EVEN FASTER

Remember, the thinner the patties, the faster they'll cook.

IF YOU HAVE MORE TIME

Grind your own turkey by pulsing pieces in the food processor until they're minced but not puréed. Dark meat will be richer, but you could also add some skin to the work bowl. (The same suggestions apply to chicken.)

SIDES

Green Salad 911

Chopped Salad 912

Tomato Salad 913

German-Style Potato Salad 962

Coleslaw 923

SPEED ◐ SERVES 4

Seared Duck Breast with Fruit Sauce

Duck breasts are low maintenance and high flavor. You don't even need to oil the pan; they cook in their own delicious fat until the skin is irresistibly crisp.

Ingredients

4 boneless duck breasts

Salt and pepper

1 shallot

1 cup cherries or blackberries (or a combination)

1 tablespoon butter

Prep | Cook

1. To score the duck skin, make a few slices across each breast, cutting down into the fat but not the meat (about 1/4 inch deep). Sprinkle both sides with salt and pepper.

2. Put the breasts skin side down in a large skillet over medium-low heat. Cook, undisturbed, until much of the fat has rendered and the skin is crisp, 8 to 12 minutes.

   Trim, peel, and chop the shallot.

   Pit the cherries if you're using them. Chop the cherries or berries.

3. When the duck skin is crisp, turn the breasts and cook until the duck is done, 2 to 4 minutes for medium-rare (about 130°F on a quick-read thermometer or rosy pink in the middle if you cut into it and peek). Transfer the breasts to a plate and tent with aluminum foil to keep warm.

4. Pour off all but 1 tablespoon of the rendered duck fat (save it in the fridge for roasting potatoes if you want) and put the skillet over medium heat. Add the shallot and cook for a minute, then stir in the fruit and sprinkle with salt and pepper.

5. Cook, stirring occasionally until the fruit breaks down and the mixture gets saucy, 5 to 10 minutes. Stir in 1 tablespoon butter and any juices that have accumulated around the duck; taste and adjust the seasoning.

6. Slice the duck if you like and spoon the sauce over the top or serve it on the side.

VARIATIONS

4 Other Fruits to Use for Seared Duck Breast with Fruit Sauce

1. Mango
2. Blueberries
3. Raspberries
4. Peaches

6 Ways to Flavor Fruit Sauce

As the sauce cooks, add any of the following to taste:

1. Minced fresh ginger
2. Minced chile
3. Chopped chipotle chiles in adobo
4. Whole black peppercorns
5. Vanilla bean (seeds scraped out of the pod)
6. Chopped fresh rosemary

NOTES

EVEN FASTER

Once the duck renders some fat, spoon a tablespoon of it into a small skillet or saucepan. Put it over medium heat and make the fruit sauce in there while the duck cooks. Let the duck rest for 5 minutes before serving.

SIDES

Skin-On Mashed Potatoes 961

Roasted Squash 416

Crisp Roasted Potatoes 965

Brussels Sprouts with Bacon 958

Green Salad 911

Chicken, Vegetables, and Noodles in Soy Broth

This dish is inspired by white-cut chicken, a Chinese preparation where a whole chicken is simmered in broth and served at room temperature with soy sauce. The dish begs for noodles, so I've built them right in, cooking them in the broth as soon as the chicken is done.

Ingredients

2 inches fresh ginger

5 scallions

2 pieces star anise

2 tablespoons sugar

⅓ cup soy sauce, plus more for serving

2 carrots

1 large onion

3 to 4 pounds bone-in chicken parts

8 ounces Chinese egg noodles

Prep | Cook

Cut 2 inches ginger into coins (don't bother to peel).

Trim the scallions.

1. Put the ginger and scallions in a large pot, along with 2 pieces star anise, 2 tablespoons sugar, ⅓ cup soy sauce, and 6 cups water. Bring to a boil.

   Trim, peel, and slice the carrots.

   Trim, peel, halve, and thickly slice the onion.

2. When the liquid comes to a boil, add the chicken, return the liquid to a boil, then adjust the heat so that it bubbles steadily. Add the carrots and onion and cover the pot.
3. Simmer until the chicken is cooked through and the carrots and onion are tender, 15 to 20 minutes. When they're done, transfer them to a platter. Pull or slice the chicken from the bones, leaving the pieces in large chunks.
4. Bring the liquid to a boil and add the noodles. Fresh noodles will be done in just a few minutes; dried will take a bit longer.

5. When the noodles tender but not mushy, divide them among 4 shallow bowls. Add some chicken and vegetables, ladle some broth over the top (leaving the scallions and ginger behind), and serve, passing more soy sauce at the table if you like.

VARIATIONS

Chicken, Vegetables, and Noodles in Miso Broth
Omit the soy sauce and substitute 1 piece kombu (seaweed) for the star anise and mirin for the sugar. After the noodles are cooked and in the bowls, stir 1/4 cup miso into the broth until it dissolves.

Boiled Chicken, Vegetables, and Noodles in Coconut Curry Broth
Swap 1 cinnamon stick for the star anise, salt to taste for the sugar, and 1 tablespoon curry powder or Indian curry paste for the soy sauce. Use 3 cups coconut milk in place of 3 cups of the water.

NOTES

EVEN FASTER
For a very fast (though slightly less flavorful) spin, use boneless chicken and tender vegetables like snow peas or chopped greens. Simmer until the chicken is cooked through, then remove and add the noodles.

IF YOU HAVE MORE TIME
White-Cut Chicken with Noodles
Use a whole chicken instead of parts. Simmer for about 20 minutes, then turn off the heat and leave it in the pot until it is cooked through, another 10 minutes or so.

SIDES

Cucumbers with Peanut Vinaigrette 953

Ginger-Orange Bean Sprouts 919

Stir-Fried Bok Choy 927

SPEED SERVES 4

Cornmeal Fried Chicken

You can make real fried chicken in under 45 minutes. Dredging the chicken in a paper bag speeds prep and cleanup. From then on, the hot oil does all the work.

Ingredients

Vegetable oil for frying

½ cup buttermilk

Cayenne or hot sauce

Salt and pepper

1 cup cornmeal

1 cup flour

3 pounds chicken parts

Prep | Cook

1. Put ½ inch vegetable oil in a large skillet over medium-high heat.
   Put ½ cup buttermilk in a large bowl along with a pinch of cayenne or a few dashes of hot sauce and a generous sprinkle of salt and pepper.
   Put 1 cup cornmeal, 1 cup flour, and another generous sprinkle of salt and pepper in a large paper bag.
2. Add the chicken parts to the buttermilk and toss to coat each piece. Transfer them to the paper bag, roll the top so that it's sealed, and shake, holding the top of the bag so it stays closed, until the chicken is fully coated.
3. Test the oil by adding a pinch of flour; it will sizzle when the oil is ready. Carefully add the chicken pieces skin side down. It's okay if it's a tight fit; just keep adjusting the heat so the chicken sizzles but doesn't burn.
4. Cover and cook until the skin is browned and the pieces release easily from the skillet, 5 to 10 minutes. Turn the chicken and cook, uncovered, until the other side is nicely browned, 5 to 10 minutes.

5. Continue to cook, uncovered, turning every few minutes and transferring the pieces to paper towels as they finish cooking (smaller pieces will be done first), until all the chicken is cooked through, another 5 to 10 minutes. The chicken is done when it registers between 155° and 160°F on a quick-read thermometer or when its juices run clear and there are no traces of pink in the meat. Serve hot, warm, or at room temperature.

VARIATIONS

Coconut-Curried Fried Chicken
Replace half of the buttermilk with coconut milk and add 1 tablespoon curry powder to the liquid.

Korean Fried Chicken
In a large bowl, combine 3 garlic cloves, minced, 1 inch ginger, minced, 3 tablespoons soy sauce, 3 tablespoons gochujang (Korean red chile paste), 1 tablespoon rice vinegar, 1 teaspoon sesame oil, and 1 tablespoon honey. The mixture should be the consistency of a vinaigrette; add a splash of water to thin it if necessary. When the chicken is fried, add it to the bowl and toss gently to coat with the sauce.

7 Other Seasonings to Add to the Buttermilk Mixture

1. 1 teaspoon chili powder
2. 1 teaspoon cumin
3. 1 teaspoon smoked paprika
4. 2 teaspoons chopped fresh rosemary or sage
5. 1 tablespoon soy sauce
6. 1 teaspoon minced garlic, ginger, or chiles
7. 2 teaspoons maple syrup or honey

NOTES

IF YOU HAVE MORE TIME
Let the chicken sit in the buttermilk overnight before dredging and frying.

SIDES

Skin-On Mashed Potatoes 961

Coleslaw 923

Peach, Blue Cheese, and Tarragon Salad 922

Broiled Cherry Tomatoes 931

Mexican Street Corn 932

SPEED SERVES 4

Crisp Baked Chicken Tenders

I am obsessed with this method of making chicken tenders. Instead of fussy dredging and frying, you toss the chicken in a pile of homemade bread crumbs and bake. The crumbs become this irresistibly crunchy topping, while the chicken stays moist. Dead easy.

Ingredients

1 ½ pounds chicken tenders

Olive oil

Salt and pepper

2 ounces Parmesan cheese (½ cup grated)

4 thick slices any rustic bread (a little stale is fine)

1 lemon

Several sprigs fresh parsley for garnish

Prep | Cook

1. Heat the oven to 375°F. Put the chicken tenders on a rimmed baking sheet or in a 9 × 13-inch baking dish. Rub with a little olive oil and sprinkle with salt and pepper.

   Grate ½ cup Parmesan and put into a medium bowl.

2. Tear 4 slices bread into pieces, put in a food processor, and pulse into crumbs (you should have about 1 ½ cups).

3. Add the bread crumbs and a sprinkle of salt and pepper to the Parmesan and toss to combine. Scatter the mixture over the chicken and drizzle generously with oil.

4. When the oven is hot, bake the chicken, undisturbed, until the bread crumbs are golden and crisp and the chicken is cooked through, 20 to 25 minutes.

   Cut the lemon into wedges.

   Strip the parsley leaves from several sprigs and chop.

5. When the crumbs are crisp and the chicken is cooked, garnish with the parsley and serve with the lemon wedges, spooning extra crumbs on top if you like.

VARIATIONS

Mustard-Pretzel Chicken Tenders
Rub the chicken with a mixture of 1 tablespoon Dijon mustard and 1 tablespoon olive oil and use 1 ½ cups ground pretzels instead of the bread crumbs.

Chipotle Chicken Tenders
Swap cotija cheese for the Parmesan or just leave it out. Rub the chicken with 1 tablespoon chopped chipotle chiles in adobo and 1 tablespoon olive oil and use 1 ½ cups ground tortilla chips instead of the bread crumbs.

Miso-Cashew Chicken Tenders
Omit the Parmesan. Rub the chicken with 1 tablespoon miso and 1 tablespoon vegetable oil and use 1 ½ cups ground cashews instead of the bread crumbs.

Peanut-Coconut Chicken Tenders
Omit the Parmesan. Substitute 2 tablespoons peanut butter mixed with 1 tablespoon warm water for the olive oil and shredded unsweetened coconut for the bread crumbs.

Sesame Chicken Tenders
Skip the Parmesan. Rub the chicken with 1 tablespoon tahini and 1 tablespoon olive oil and use 1 ½ cups sesame seeds instead of the bread crumbs.

NOTES

EVEN FASTER
Instead of making the bread crumbs as described in Step 2, use Bread Crumbs (page 71) you already have on hand.

SIDES

Skin-On Mashed Potatoes 961

Rice Pilaf 944

Creamed Spinach 936

Green Salad 911

SPEED  SERVES 4

Oven-Fried Chicken with Roasted Corn

A homemade TV dinner: retro and awesome.

Ingredients

1 egg

¼ cup milk

Salt and pepper

2 cups corn flakes (or other plain flaked cereal)

2 sprigs fresh rosemary

4 tablespoons (½ stick) butter

4 boneless, skinless chicken breasts (about 2 pounds)

4 ears fresh corn

Prep | Cook

1. Heat the oven to 375°F.

   Crack the egg into a shallow bowl or dish. Add ¼ cup milk and a sprinkle of salt and pepper to the bowl and beat.

   Put 2 cups corn flakes in a large bowl and crush them with your hands or the bottom of a heavy glass.

   Strip the rosemary leaves from 2 sprigs and chop. Add to the corn flakes along with a sprinkle of salt and pepper and toss.

2. Melt 4 tablespoons butter in the microwave; drizzle half on a rimmed baking sheet and spread it around.

3. Cut the chicken breasts in half horizontally to make 2 thin cutlets for each breast. Press down on each with the heel of your hand to flatten.

4. Dip the cutlets in the egg mixture, then dredge them in the seasoned corn flakes. Put them on the baking sheet, leaving some room for the corn if you can.

   Husk the corn; put it on the baking sheet next to the chicken.

5. Drizzle the remaining butter over the chicken and corn. Bake, turning once, until the chicken is cooked through and the corn is lightly browned, 15 to 20 minutes. Serve hot or warm.

VARIATIONS

Pecan Oven-Fried Chicken with Roasted Corn
Substitute coarsely ground pecans for the corn flakes.

Wheaty Oven-Fried Chicken with Roasted Corn
Use crumbled shredded wheat or wheat flakes instead of corn flakes.

Oven-Fried Pork Chops with Roasted Corn
Use 1-inch-thick boneless pork loin chops instead of the chicken in the main recipe or any of the variations.

SIDES

Skin-On Mashed Potatoes 961

Green Salad 911

Smashed Peas 935

Garlicky Mushrooms 956

SPEED SERVES 4

Honey-Ginger-Soy Roasted Chicken and Celery

This dish is highly adaptable. The bed of vegetables can be anything you like. Try fennel or carrots instead of celery. The method is perfect and timeless.

Ingredients

6 tablespoons olive oil

1 bunch celery

Salt and pepper

3 to 4 pounds bone-in chicken parts

1 lemon

1 inch fresh ginger

¼ cup soy sauce

1 tablespoon honey

Several sprigs fresh cilantro for garnish

Prep | Cook

1. Heat the oven to 450°F. Drizzle the bottom of a roasting pan or rimmed baking sheet with 4 tablespoons olive oil.

   Trim and chop the celery into large chunks.

2. Put the celery in the roasting pan, toss with the oil, and sprinkle with salt and pepper.

3. Put the chicken parts on top of the celery, skin side up, drizzle with 2 tablespoons oil, and sprinkle with salt (not too much) and pepper. Roast for 15 minutes.

   Halve the lemon; squeeze the juice into a small bowl.

   Peel 1 inch ginger; grate or finely mince it and add it to the bowl.

4. Add ¼ cup soy sauce and 1 tablespoon honey to the bowl. Taste and adjust the seasoning.

5. After the chicken has roasted for 15 minutes, start basting occasionally with the soy mixture and the pan drippings, rotating the pan whenever you do and lowering the heat if the chicken starts to burn.

6. Continue to roast and baste until the chicken is browned and cooked through (its juices will run clear and there will be no traces of pink in the meat) and the celery is lightly browned and tender, 30 minutes total.

   Chop several sprigs cilantro.

7. When the chicken is done, garnish with the cilantro. Serve the chicken and the celery with some of the pan drippings and any extra basting sauce spooned over the top.

VARIATIONS

Maple-Chile-Beer Roasted Chicken and Peppers
Substitute 4 large bell peppers, thickly sliced, for the celery. Swap lime for the lemon, 1 fresh hot green chile, minced, for the ginger, maple syrup for the honey, and ½ cup beer for the soy sauce. Garnish with scallions instead of the cilantro.

Dijon-Garlic-Cider Roasted Chicken and Carrots
Replace the celery with 1 pound carrots, cut into ¼-inch slices. Swap 2 garlic cloves for the ginger, mustard for the honey, and ½ cup apple cider for the soy sauce. Garnish with chopped fresh tarragon instead of the cilantro.

NOTES

EVEN FASTER
Roasting and basting chicken parts on a bed of vegetables is faster and more flavorful than roasting a whole bird and has become my roasting method of choice for that reason. But there is an even faster way: While the oven heats up, put a few tablespoons of oil in the roasting pan and set it on 2 burners over medium heat. Sauté the chicken, skin side down, until the skin is nicely browned, about 10 minutes. Remove the chicken, add the celery, and put the chicken skin side up on top. With this head start, the roasting time will be reduced. Start basting after 10 minutes and check the chicken for doneness after 20.

SIDES

Sesame Noodles 949

White Rice 941

Scallion Pancakes 940

Chicken and Tomato Packages

Cooking in individual foil packages not only makes for incredibly moist chicken and vegetables, but it's also a fun way to serve a meal. And there are practically no dishes to wash when you're done. For when you have time to be more elegant, see the Notes.

Ingredients

3 medium ripe tomatoes

½ cup black olives

2 garlic cloves

8 boneless, skinless chicken thighs (1 ½ to 2 pounds)

4 tablespoons olive oil

Salt and pepper

4 sprigs fresh thyme

Prep | Cook

1. Heat the oven to 425°F.

   Core and chop the tomatoes; put them in a medium bowl.

   Pit ½ cup black olives if necessary; add to the bowl.

   Peel and mince 2 garlic cloves; add to the bowl.

2. Cut aluminum foil into 4 rectangles each about 12 × 18 inches; fold each in half crosswise to crease, then reopen.

3. Spoon the tomato mixture onto 1 half of the rectangle as close to the center as you can. Top each with 2 chicken thighs, drizzle with 1 tablespoon olive oil, sprinkle with salt and pepper, and top with a sprig of thyme.

4. Fold over and seal the packages, rolling the edges tightly to completely enclose the filling.

5. Put the packages on a rimmed baking sheet and put it in the oven. Bake until the chicken is cooked through and the tomatoes are tender and saucy, 25 to 30 minutes (open up 1 package to check).

6. Open the packages carefully and serve hot or warm right in the packages or on plates with the juices poured over.

VARIATIONS

Chicken, Tomato, and Feta Packages

Substitute oregano for the thyme and add a sprinkle of feta to each package.

Chicken and Potato Packages

Heartier. Replace some of the tomatoes with very thin slices of potato, peeled if you like.

NOTES

PARCHMENT PACKAGES

For speed and ease, aluminum foil is the undisputed champ for this technique. But if you're after elegance and gorgeous browned edges, use parchment paper. The assembly process is the same, although you must be more diligent about crimping the paper's edges, since it doesn't self-seal like foil. Tightly roll each side of the open edges, pressing down to form a tight seal so the moisture can't escape. For rounded packages, fold the rectangle in half and cut it around as if you were making one half of a heart. Fill as usual, then crimp the rounded open edge by folding overlapping pleats all the way to the point.

SIDES

Skin-On Mashed Potatoes 961

Creamy Polenta 947

Couscous 910

Bruschetta 909

SPEED  SERVES 4

Chicken and Green Beans

You can't go wrong with well-browned meat simmered in a little bit of liquid and a good amount of vegetables. This one features a rich—and substantial—mustard cream sauce.

Ingredients

1 tablespoon olive oil

8 bone-in chicken thighs (about 2 pounds)

Salt and pepper

2 shallots

½ cup chicken stock or water

½ cup white wine

1 pound green beans

Several sprigs fresh tarragon

2 tablespoons Dijon mustard

½ cup cream

Prep | Cook

1. Put 1 tablespoon olive oil in a large skillet or large pot over medium-high heat.

   Pat the chicken thighs dry.

2. When the oil is hot, add the chicken skin side down and sprinkle with salt and pepper. Cook, undisturbed, until the skin is nicely browned, about 10 minutes.

   Trim, peel, and chop the shallots.

3. When the chicken skin is nicely browned, turn the thighs and spoon out all but about 1 tablespoon of fat. Add the shallots. Cook until the shallots soften slightly, then add ½ cup stock or water and ½ cup white wine.

4. Adjust the heat so the mixture bubbles gently but steadily. Cover and cook until the chicken is just cooked through, 10 to 15 minutes.

   Trim the green beans.

5. When the chicken is cooked, add the green beans on top and sprinkle with salt and pepper. Cover and cook until the green beans are just tender but still retain some crunch, 6 to 8 minutes.

   Strip the tarragon leaves from several sprigs and chop.

6. Transfer the chicken and green beans to a platter. Add 2 tablespoons Dijon, ½ cup cream, and the tarragon to the skillet and adjust the heat so the liquid bubbles steadily.
7. Cook, stirring frequently until the sauce thickens to the consistency that you like. Taste and adjust the seasoning, pour the sauce over the chicken and green beans, and serve.

VARIATIONS

Chicken and Green Bean Sauté with Mustard and Soy
Skip the cream and replace 2 tablespoons of the wine with 2 tablespoons soy sauce.

Veal and Mushroom Sauté with Mustard and Cream
Substitute 1 ½ pounds veal shoulder or breast, cut into 1 ½-inch cubes, for the chicken. Brown the veal very well on one side before turning and adding the shallots. Use mushrooms, halved, in place of green beans and add them to the skillet along with the shallots. The veal will take a little longer to become tender than the chicken.

Lamb and Carrot Sauté with Mustard and Miso
Use 1 ½ pounds lamb shoulder, cut into 1 ½-inch cubes, instead of the chicken. Brown the lamb very well on one side before turning and adding the shallots. Replace the green beans with carrots, cut into coins, and add them about halfway through the cooking. Swap ¼ cup miso for the cream and cilantro for the tarragon. The lamb will take a little longer to become tender than the chicken.

NOTES

EVEN FASTER
Use boneless thighs instead of bone-in. Brown them very well on one side before turning and adding the shallots. They will cook through in 10 to 15 minutes.

SIDES

Warm Buttery Bread 906

French Fries 963

Panfried Corn and Onions 933

Bulgur with Lemon and Parsley 946

SPEED SERVES 4

Collard-Wrapped Chicken

Collard leaves make a delicious and sturdy wrapper for steaming chicken. The seasonings flavor the chicken from inside their little packages, and the meat stays moist. If you don't own a steamer, don't worry; see the Notes.

Ingredients

1 bunch collards

Ice cubes

1 inch fresh ginger

2 garlic cloves

1 or 2 fresh hot chiles (like serrano or Thai)

¼ teaspoon cinnamon

⅛ teaspoon allspice

⅛ teaspoon cloves

1 tablespoon vegetable oil

Salt and pepper

4 boneless, skinless chicken breasts (about 2 pounds)

Prep | Cook

1. Rig a steamer and bring the water to a boil.

   Trim the collards. Pull out 6 to 8 of the biggest leaves, depending on their size, and slice out the thick stems that run through the middle, keeping the leaves intact. If there are any left over, refrigerate for another use.

2. When the water boils, adjust the heat so it simmers gently. Add the collard leaves to the steamer, cover, and cook until they are pliable, 2 or 3 minutes.

   Prepare a large bowl of ice water for the collards.

3. When the collards are pliable, carefully drop them into the ice bath to cool. Turn the heat under the steamer to low.

   Peel 1 inch ginger and 2 garlic cloves; trim 1 or 2 chiles. Mince everything together and put in a small bowl.

4. Add ¼ teaspoon cinnamon, ⅛ teaspoon allspice, and ⅛ teaspoon cloves to the bowl; add 1 tablespoon vegetable oil, ½ teaspoon salt, and ¼ teaspoon pepper and stir to combine.

5. Pat the collard leaves dry with paper towels and lay them out on a cutting board or the counter. If 1 leaf is big enough to wrap a chicken breast, fantastic; if not, overlap 1 ½ or 2 leaves.

6. Put each chicken breast on top of a collard wrapper and rub with some of the spice paste. Wrap the chicken in the collard leaves, folding in the sides like a burrito.

7. Put the packages in the steamer, adding more water if necessary, and bring the liquid to a simmer. Cover and cook until the chicken is opaque and just cooked through, 15 to 20 minutes (you'll need to pierce one with a thin-bladed knife to check).

8. Remove the packages from the steamer and let cool for a minute or 2. Serve them whole or cut them in half or into thick slices.

VARIATIONS

Cabbage-Wrapped Miso Chicken
Use cabbage leaves instead of collards, ¼ cup miso paste instead of the cinnamon, allspice, and cloves, and sesame oil instead of the vegetable oil.

Collard-Wrapped BBQ Chicken
Instead of the spice paste, use ⅓ cup Barbecue Sauce (page 145).

NOTES

EVEN FASTER
Lay a few raw collard leaves in the steamer; rub the chicken all over with the spice paste and put them on top. Lay more collard leaves over the top and steam.

RIGGING A FAST STEAMER
Simply turn a shallow bowl or 2 or 3 ramekins upside down in a large pot with a tight-fitting lid and put a plate right side up on top. Make sure it's stable. Add an inch or so of water. The plate becomes your steaming rack.

SIDES

White Rice 941

Ripe Plantains 960

Skin-On Mashed Potatoes 961

SPEED  SERVES 4

Split Whole Chicken and Vegetables

The fastest way to cook a whole chicken. Flattening out the bird and broiling it gives you the added bonus of an even layer of skin that gets more uniformly crisp than if you roasted the chicken whole. It's really one of the greatest methods ever. If you have a butcher who will butterfly a chicken for you, request it. If not, see the Notes.

Ingredients

2 garlic cloves

2 sprigs fresh rosemary

1 lemon

2 tablespoons olive oil, plus more for garnish

Salt and pepper

1 whole chicken (3 to 4 pounds)

1 ½ pounds mixed vegetables (bell peppers, onions, asparagus, mushrooms, eggplant, or zucchini)

Prep | Cook

1. Turn the broiler to high; put the rack 6 inches from the heat.

   Peel and mince 2 garlic cloves; put them in a small bowl.

   Strip the rosemary leaves from 2 sprigs, mince, and add them to the bowl.

   Halve the lemon and squeeze the juice into the bowl.

2. Add 1 tablespoon olive oil and a sprinkle of salt and pepper to the bowl. Stir to combine.

   Butterfly the chicken if necessary.

3. Rub the garlic and herb mixture all over the chicken, tucking some under the skin as well. Put the chicken skin side down on a rimmed baking sheet. Loosely cover the exposed areas of the baking sheet with pieces of foil to prevent smoking. Transfer the chicken to the broiler and cook skin side down, undisturbed, for 15 minutes.

   Trim the vegetables and chop or slice as necessary.

4. Remove the foil pieces and reserve. Scatter the vegetables around the chicken, drizzle with 1 tablespoon oil, sprinkle with salt and pepper, and return to the broiler.

5. Turn the vegetables occasionally, leaving the chicken alone, until they are tender and browned, 10 to 15 minutes. When the vegetables are just tender, transfer them to a platter. Replace the foil.

6. Broil the chicken until the skin is browned, another 5 to 10 minutes. Check for doneness (a quick-read thermometer should register 155° to 160°F or the juices will run clear when you pierce a piece close to the bone). If the chicken still needs a few more minutes, cook it skin side down until done, then skin side up for just another minute or 2 to make sure the skin is crisp.

7. Let the chicken rest for 5 minutes, then cut it up and add it to the platter with the vegetables. Drizzle with the pan juices and serve.

VARIATIONS

Grilled Split Whole Chicken and Vegetables

Takes longer but is quite a treat. Heat a charcoal or gas grill, with the fire built up on one side so part of the grill is cool; put the rack 6 inches from the heat. Put the chicken skin side up on the cool side of the grill, cover, and cook, turning once, until most of the fat renders, about 20 minutes total. Continue to cook, turning once or twice, until the chicken is cooked through, another 30 minutes. Cut the vegetables into large pieces. Move the chicken to the hot part of the grill and cook, turning frequently, until nicely browned. (While the chicken is on the cool side of the grill, cook the vegetables on the hot side.)

NOTES

BUTTERFLYING A CHICKEN

To butterfly a chicken (also known as *spatchcocking*), put it on a cutting board with the breasts facing up. The backbone (which is what you are removing) is now resting against the cutting board. Use a heavy knife to cut on each side of that backbone, from the front to the rear. Those two cuts will free the backbone enough that you can cut it out with the tip of a knife or (better yet) pull it out with your hands. Now you should be able to open the chicken like a book and lay it flat.

SIDES

Rice Pilaf 944

Bulgur with Lemon and Parsley 946

Quinoa 945

Skin-On Mashed Potatoes 961

Hummus 939

Roast Chicken

A whole roast chicken stashed in your refrigerator makes for great repurposing throughout the week. It takes about an hour (for faster methods ideal for immediate eating, you can roast it in parts, page 689, or butterflied, page 687), but that's almost all unattended time. Get into the habit of roasting a bird when you happen to be home doing something else—it's faster than a trip to the market, and the results will be much better.

Whole Roast Chicken

1 Heat the Oven and Skillet

Heat the oven to 450°F. Put a heavy ovenproof skillet (preferably cast iron) on a rack set low in the oven while it heats up.

2 Rub the Chicken

Trim any excess fat from a 3- to 4-pound chicken, rub it with olive oil, and sprinkle with salt and pepper.

3 Roast

When the oven is hot, carefully put the chicken, breast side up, in the heated skillet. Roast, undisturbed, for 40 to 50 minutes; the chicken is done when a thermometer inserted into the thickest part of the thigh registers 155° to 165°F on a quick-read thermometer or when its juices run clear and there are no traces of pink in the meat.

4 Rest and Store (or Eat)

Transfer the chicken to a platter and let it rest for at least 5 minutes. If you're serving the chicken right away, quarter it or cut it into parts and serve with some of the pan juices spooned over the top. To store in the fridge, let the chicken cool to room temperature, then cut it into parts or leave it whole. Store in a freezer bag or tightly sealed container for up to a week.

VARIATIONS

8 Ways to Flavor Any Roast Chicken

1. **Herbs:** Start cooking the chicken without any olive oil. Halfway through, spoon a mixture of ¼ cup olive oil and 2 tablespoons chopped fresh parsley, basil, cilantro, or dill or 1 tablespoon rosemary, sage, thyme, or oregano over the chicken.
2. **Lemon:** Halve a lemon and put it in the chicken's cavity during roasting. Squeeze the juice from the cooked lemon over the chicken before serving or storing.
3. **Chinese Style:** Substitute vegetable oil for the olive oil. Make a mixture of ¼ cup soy sauce, 2 tablespoons honey, 1 teaspoon minced garlic, and 1 teaspoon minced ginger; spoon or brush it over the chicken about halfway through cooking.
4. **Cumin and Orange:** Make a mixture of 2 tablespoons orange juice, 2 tablespoons honey, 1 teaspoon minced garlic, and 2 teaspoons cumin; spoon or brush it over the chicken about halfway through cooking.
5. **Chile-Lime:** Make a mixture of 3 tablespoons lime juice, 1 teaspoon minced fresh hot green chile, chopped fresh cilantro, and 2 tablespoons vegetable oil; spoon or brush it over the chicken about halfway through cooking.
6. **Honey-Mustard:** Combine 3 tablespoons Dijon mustard and 2 tablespoons honey and brush it over the chicken for the last 5 to 10 minutes of cooking.
7. **Curry:** Substitute vegetable oil for the olive oil. Combine ½ cup coconut milk and 2 tablespoons curry powder and brush it over the chicken for the last 5 to 10 minutes of cooking.
8. **Wine and Garlic:** Put ½ cup white wine and a few crushed garlic cloves in pan for basting the chicken as it roasts.

Roast Chicken Parts

1 Heat the Oven and Pan

Heat the oven to 450°F. Put 4 tablespoons butter or olive oil in a large roasting pan and put the pan in the oven until the oil is hot or the butter melts, just a few minutes.

2 Coat the Chicken

Carefully remove the pan from the oven and add about 3 pounds cut-up chicken parts (any combination you like). Roll the pieces in the fat to coat them all over, and turn them skin side up with as much space in between them as possible. Sprinkle with salt and pepper and put the pan back in the oven.

3 Roast

Roast the chicken, undisturbed, until the skin is crisp and the chicken is cooked through, 30 to 45 minutes. When the chicken is ready you'll see clear juices if you make a small cut in the meat near the bone; a thermometer will register between 155° to 165°F. Remove pieces from the pan as they are ready.

4 Rest and Store (or Eat)

Skim the excess fat from the pan juices if necessary and spoon the juices over the chicken if you're eating it right away. To store in the fridge, separate the chicken and juices and cool to room temperature before chilling. Store both in freezer bags or tightly sealed containers for up to a week.

SPEED SERVES 4

Za'atar Wings and Eggplant with Yogurt-Harissa Sauce

Buffalo wings go to Beirut. Za'atar is a spice blend containing thyme, sumac, and sesame seeds that's ubiquitous in the Middle East.

Ingredients

1 small garlic clove

1 lemon

1 cup yogurt

1 tablespoon harissa

Salt and pepper

1 large or 2 medium eggplant (about 2 pounds)

3 pounds chicken wings

¼ cup olive oil

2 tablespoons ground sumac

1 tablespoon dried thyme

2 teaspoons sesame seeds

Prep | Cook

1. Heat the oven to 450°F.

   Peel and mince 1 small garlic clove; put it in a medium bowl.

   Halve the lemon; squeeze the juice into the bowl.

2. Add 1 cup yogurt, 1 tablespoon harissa, and a sprinkle of salt and pepper to the bowl. Stir to combine, taste and adjust the seasoning, and refrigerate.

   Trim the eggplant and cut it in half lengthwise, then slice into ½-inch-thick half-moons. Put them on a rimmed baking sheet or in a roasting pan.

   If the wings aren't already divided into 2 pieces, cut them through the center joint to separate the flat from the drumette. (If you like, cut off the wing tips and save them for stock; otherwise, just leave them on.) Put the wings on another rimmed baking sheet.

3. Drizzle the wings and eggplant with ¼ cup olive oil and sprinkle with salt and pepper.

4. Put both pans in the oven and roast, turning once or twice (when the wings are ready to turn, they will release easily from the pan), rotating pans, and spooning off excess fat from the wings, until the wings are browned and the eggplant is browned and tender, 25 to 30 minutes.

   Mix together 2 tablespoons sumac, 1 tablespoon dried thyme, and 2 teaspoons sesame seeds in a small bowl.

5. When the wings and eggplant are browned and cooked, sprinkle with the spice blend and toss. Roast for another 3 to 5 minutes to toast the spices.

6. Divide the wings and eggplant among 4 plates and serve with the yogurt sauce on the side or drizzle over the top.

VARIATIONS

Hot Wings and Brussels Sprouts with Yogurt–Blue Cheese Sauce
Substitute ½ cup crumbled blue cheese for the harissa, halved Brussels sprouts for the eggplant, and a few tablespoons hot sauce for the thyme and sesame seeds.

Cumin Wings and Eggplant with Yogurt-Tahini Sauce
Swap 1 tablespoon tahini for the harissa, 1 tablespoon cumin for the thyme, and 1 teaspoon paprika for the sesame seeds.

SIDES

Tahini Slaw 923

Carrot Salad with Raisins 914

Couscous 910

Watermelon, Feta, and Mint Salad 922

Roasted Red Pepper Hummus 939

SPEED SERVES 4

Chicken and Sweet Potato Adobo

The national dish of the Philippines is a contender for the best chicken dish, period. The salty, tangy, and spicy sauce is that good. White rice is ideal for soaking up the sauce.

Ingredients

2 garlic cloves

1 pound sweet potatoes

8 bone-in chicken thighs (about 2 pounds)

½ cup soy sauce

½ cup rice or white wine vinegar

2 bay leaves

½ teaspoon pepper

2 dried chipotle chiles (or 1 canned chipotle chile in adobo)

Prep | Cook

Peel and mince 2 garlic cloves; put them in a large pot.

Peel the sweet potatoes and cut them into 1-inch cubes.

1. Add the chicken to the pot along with the sweet potatoes, ½ cup soy sauce, ½ cup vinegar, 2 bay leaves, ½ teaspoon pepper, 2 dried chipotle chiles (or 1 canned chipotle chile), and 1 ¼ cups water.
2. Cover and bring to a boil, then reduce the heat so the mixture simmers gently. Cook, covered, turning the chicken once or twice, until it's cooked through and the sweet potatoes are tender, about 30 minutes.
3. While the chicken cooks, turn the broiler to high; put the rack 4 inches from the heat. Line a rimmed baking sheet with foil.
4. When the chicken and sweet potatoes are cooked, transfer them to the sheet with a slotted spoon; spoon off some of the fat from the liquid. Bring the liquid to a boil and cook until it is reduced to about 1 cup, 5 to 10 minutes.
5. Pat the chicken dry and broil with the sweet potatoes, turning once, until brown and crisp on both sides, 3 to 5 minutes per side.

6. If you used dried chipotle chiles, remove them from the finished sauce. Serve the chicken with the sweet potatoes on the side and the sauce poured over the top.

VARIATIONS

Curried Chicken and Potatoes, Adobo Style
Substitute 1 inch fresh ginger for the garlic, russet or Yukon Gold potatoes for the sweet potatoes, 2 tablespoons curry paste or powder for the vinegar, coconut milk for the water, and 1 fresh hot green chile for the chipotle.

NOTES

IF YOU HAVE MORE TIME
Marinate the chicken (not the sweet potatoes) in the liquid for up to 3 hours before adding the sweet potatoes and boiling.

SIDES

White Rice 941

Stir-Fried Bok Choy 927

Peas with Ginger 934

Smashed Curried Peas 935

SPEED SERVES 4

Chicken and Dumplings with Lots of Peas

Comfort in a bowl. Making your own biscuit dough is worth it for this dish, but see Even Faster for a nonbiscuit shortcut.

Ingredients

6 cups chicken stock

1 large onion

2 medium carrots

1 celery stalk

1 ½ pounds boneless, skinless chicken thighs or breasts

4 sprigs fresh thyme

Salt and pepper

1 cup flour, plus more as needed

1 ½ teaspoons baking powder

½ teaspoon baking soda

3 tablespoons butter (keep it in the fridge)

½ cup yogurt or buttermilk

3 cups frozen peas

Prep | Cook

1. Put 6 cups chicken stock in a large pot and bring to a boil.

   Trim, peel, and chop the onion; add it to the pot.

   Trim, peel, and slice the carrots and chop the celery; add them to the pot.

   Chop the chicken and add it to the pot.

2. Add 4 sprigs thyme, a sprinkle of salt, and lots of pepper to the pot. When it boils, adjust the heat so the mixture simmers gently but steadily. Cook until the vegetables are tender and the chicken is cooked through, 5 to 10 minutes.

3. Combine 1 cup flour, ¼ teaspoon salt, 1 ½ teaspoons baking powder, and ½ teaspoon baking soda in a food processor. Cut up 3 tablespoons cold butter and add to the food processor.

4. Pulse a few times to blend the butter into the flour mixture. Add ½ cup yogurt or buttermilk and pulse until the mixture just forms a ball. Sprinkle a little flour onto your cutting board, turn out the dough, and knead it 10 times.

5. When the chicken and vegetables are done, transfer them to a bowl with a mesh strainer or slotted spoon (fish out the thyme). Adjust the heat so the stock bubbles gently and never boils.

6. Drop about 8 heaping tablespoons of biscuit dough into the stock and cover. Cook, adjusting the heat to maintain a gentle bubble, until the dumplings are puffed and cooked through (a toothpick will come out clean), 12 to 15 minutes.

7. Nestle the chicken and vegetables underneath the dumplings and add 3 cups frozen peas. Cook until the peas are warmed through, a minute or 2, taste and adjust the seasoning, and serve.

VARIATIONS

Chipotle Chicken and Dumplings with Beans
Substitute 1 or 2 chopped chipotle chiles in adobo for the thyme and cooked or canned black beans or pinto beans for the peas.

Chicken and Egg Noodles with Lots of Peas
Swap 1 pound egg noodles for the dumplings. Boil in the stock until tender but not mushy.

NOTES

MAKE YOUR OWN
Chicken Stock 213

EVEN FASTER
Chicken and Bread Stew
To thicken the stew without having to make biscuit dough, tear off pieces of rustic bread (3 or 4 cups) and add them to the pot when the chicken and vegetables are done (no need to remove them from the pot). Let the bread soften, but serve before it totally disintegrates. Alternatively, put the pieces of bread in the bottom of the bowls and pour the soup right on top.

SIDES

Green Salad 911

Chopped Salad 912

Tender Vegetables 954

Arroz con Pollo

The absolute essentials for great arroz con pollo are rice, chicken, and onions. Everything else boosts those ingredients. Chicken stock adds flavor, but water works fine; saffron (as usual) is optional. If you don't use saffron but want that yellow color, add a few pinches of turmeric.

Ingredients

3 cups chicken stock or water

3 tablespoons olive oil

1 large onion

2 red bell peppers

2 garlic cloves

Salt and pepper

1 ½ cups short-grain rice

Pinch of saffron (optional)

1 chicken, cut up, or any combination of parts (3 to 4 pounds)

1 bunch fresh parsley

1 lime

Prep | Cook

1. Put 3 cups stock or water in a small pot over medium-high heat. Put 3 tablespoons olive oil in a large skillet or large pot over medium-high heat.

   Trim, peel, and chop the onion; add it to the skillet.

   Core, seed, and chop the peppers. Peel and mince 2 garlic cloves. Add them to the skillet.

2. Sprinkle the vegetables with salt and pepper and cook, stirring occasionally until they soften, 3 to 5 minutes.

3. When the vegetables are soft, add 1 ½ cups rice and cook, stirring, until it's coated with oil, a minute or 2. Stir in a pinch of saffron if you're using it.

4. Nestle the chicken pieces into the rice and sprinkle with a little more salt and pepper. Pour in the warmed stock and bring the mixture to a boil.

5. Adjust the heat so the mixture bubbles gently but steadily. Cover and cook until all the liquid is absorbed and the chicken is cooked through, 20 to 25 minutes.

   Chop ¼ cup parsley leaves.

   Cut the lime into wedges.

6. When the liquid is absorbed and the chicken is cooked, taste the rice and adjust the seasoning. Garnish with the parsley and serve with the lime wedges.

VARIATIONS

Smoky Arroz con Pollo
Add 1 or 2 chopped chipotle chiles in adobo instead of the saffron.

Curried Rice and Chicken
Omit the saffron. Add 1 inch fresh ginger, minced, and 1 tablespoon curry powder along with the onions, peppers, and garlic. Garnish with cilantro instead of parsley.

NOTES

MAKE YOUR OWN
Chicken Stock 213

IF YOU HAVE MORE TIME
To deepen the flavor of the dish, let the onions, peppers, and garlic cook over medium heat until they are very soft and nearly melting, 15 to 20 minutes.

SIDES

Chile-Cumin Black Beans 937

Tomato Salad 913

Avocado with Lime and Chili Salt 920

Ripe Plantains 960

SPEED SERVES 4 TO 6

Chicken and Spinach Meat Loaf

You might think ground chicken isn't fatty enough for meat loaf, but the spinach adds moisture and tenderness. Don't skip the nutmeg here; it's wonderful.

Ingredients

Salt

1 small bunch spinach (about 12 ounces)

1 cup bread crumbs

½ cup milk

2 pounds ground chicken

½ teaspoon nutmeg

Pepper

2 ounces Parmesan cheese (½ cup grated)

1 garlic clove

1 egg

2 tablespoons olive oil

Prep | Cook

1. Put an inch of water and a sprinkle of salt in a large pot; bring to a boil. Heat the oven to 425°F.

   Trim any thick stems from the spinach.

2. When the water boils, add the spinach leaves, cover, and cook, stirring once or twice, until the spinach is wilted. Run the spinach under cold water to cool it, squeeze dry, and chop into large pieces.

3. Put the spinach in a large bowl along with 1 cup bread crumbs, ½ cup milk, the ground chicken, ½ teaspoon nutmeg, and 2 teaspoons salt and ½ teaspoon pepper.

   Grate ½ cup Parmesan and add to the bowl. Peel and mince 1 garlic clove; add it to the bowl.

   Crack the egg into the bowl.

4. Grease a rimmed baking sheet with 1 tablespoon olive oil. Gently mix together the ingredients in the bowl with your hands, turn it out onto the baking sheet, and shape it into a roughly 8 × 5-inch loaf. Drizzle with 1 tablespoon olive oil and rub to coat the loaf all over.

5. Bake until the loaf is nicely browned and firm, 30 to 35 minutes (a quick-read thermometer inserted into the center should read between 160° and 165°F).

6. Let cool for a few minutes before slicing and serving.

VARIATIONS

Chicken and Chard Meat Loaf
Substitute chard for the spinach and 1/4 cup ricotta for 1/4 cup of the Parmesan.

Moroccan-Spiced Turkey and Spinach Meat Loaf
Substitute ground turkey for the chicken, use a mixture of 1 teaspoon cumin, 1 teaspoon coriander, and 1/2 teaspoon cinnamon instead of the nutmeg, and use 1/2 cup golden raisins instead of the Parmesan.

Pork and Bok Choy Meat Loaf
Omit the Parmesan. Substitute bok choy for the spinach, ground pork for the chicken, and a pinch of red chile flakes for the nutmeg. Serve with white or brown rice and pass soy sauce at the table.

NOTES

MAKE YOUR OWN
Bread Crumbs 71

EVEN FASTER
Use 8 ounces frozen spinach instead of fresh.

The flatter you form the loaf, the faster it will cook.

SHAPING MEAT LOAF
I've always preferred making free-form meat loaves to packing them into loaf pans. Not only are they fast and easy to shape by hand, but they brown on three sides instead of just on the top, and the fat is allowed to run off, rather than being trapped in the loaf pan next to the meat. Another benefit is that since you're not constricted by the volume of a loaf pan, you can make the meat loaf as tall or as flat as you like. If you're short on time, press the loaf a bit flatter and it will cook through faster.

SIDES

Creamy Polenta 947

Skin-On Mashed Potatoes 961

Tomato Salad 913

Caprese Salad 922

Bruschetta 909

SPEED SERVES 6

Roast Turkey with Sage Sausage Stuffing

For this fast riff on Thanksgiving dinner, the whole bird is replaced by a quick-roasted butterflied turkey breast. In place of crisp skin I crust the turkey in a sausage stuffing that gets golden and crisp as the meat finishes roasting.

Ingredients

One 3-pound boneless, skin-on turkey breast

3 tablespoons olive oil

Salt and pepper

3 tablespoons butter

8 ounces sage or Italian pork sausage

2 sprigs fresh sage

6 to 8 slices any rustic bread

2 eggs

1 cup chicken stock

Prep | Cook

1. Heat the oven to 450°F.

   Remove and discard the turkey skin. To butterfly the breast, cut horizontally partway through so it opens like a book, creating a fairly even thickness of about 1 inch.

2. Put the opened turkey breast on a rimmed baking sheet, rub with 1 tablespoon oil, and sprinkle with salt and pepper. Flip it over and repeat with oil and salt and pepper. Break 1 tablespoon butter into bits and scatter on top. When the oven is hot, roast the turkey for 30 minutes.

3. Put 1 tablespoon oil in a large skillet over medium-high heat.

   Remove the sausage meat from the casings.

   Strip the leaves from 2 sage sprigs and chop.

4. Add the sausage to the skillet and cook, stirring occasionally until the sausage is browned, 5 to 10 minutes, adding the sage for the last minute or 2.

   Cut 6 to 8 slices bread into small cubes and put them in a large bowl (you should have 4 to 5 cups of cubes).

   Mix 2 eggs into the bowl.

5. When the sausage is browned, add it to the bowl along with a sprinkle of salt and pepper and ¼ cup chicken stock. Mix well to combine; you want the bread to absorb the moisture. If it needs more liquid, add up to another ¼ cup stock.

   Melt 2 tablespoons butter in the microwave or on the stove.

6. After the turkey has roasted for 30 minutes, gently pack the stuffing on top of the breast to cover (it's okay if some falls off). Drizzle on the melted butter and return to the oven to finish roasting for 15 minutes. It's done when the turkey is firm to the touch, white or very pale pink inside, and 160° to 165°F on a quick-read thermometer.

7. When the turkey and stuffing are cooked, transfer it all to a cutting board, add ½ cup stock to the baking sheet, and stir to scrape up any browned bits from the bottom.

8. To serve, transfer the stuffing to a platter, slice the turkey and put on top, then drizzle the pan juices over all.

VARIATIONS

5 Ways to Flavor Stuffing

Add during the last few minutes of cooking:

1. 1 tablespoon minced garlic, ginger, or chiles
2. 2 teaspoons cumin, smoked paprika, or curry powder
3. 1 tablespoon chopped chipotles in adobo
4. ¼ cup chopped scallions
5. ¼ cup chopped dried fruit

NOTES

MAKE YOUR OWN

Chicken Stock 213

EVEN FASTER

Instead of using bread as described in Step 4, use Bread Crumbs (page 71) you have on hand.

SIDES

Brussels Sprouts with Bacon 958

Simmered Squash 955

Tender Vegetables 954

Skin-On Mashed Potatoes 961

SPEED SERVES 4

Red Wine–Braised Turkey

With their dark, rich meat and somewhat coarse texture, turkey thighs are reminiscent of pork. Substitute them for chicken parts or pork in any braise.

Ingredients

2 tablespoons olive oil

2 to 4 bone-in turkey thighs (about 3 pounds)

Salt and pepper

1 cup red wine

1 cup chicken stock

3 sprigs fresh thyme

1 large onion

2 carrots

2 celery stalks

1 garlic clove

Several sprigs fresh parsley for garnish

Prep | Cook

1. Put 2 tablespoons olive oil in a large pot over medium-high heat.

   Remove and discard the turkey skin. Pat the turkey thighs dry.

2. When the oil is hot, add the turkey thighs and sprinkle with salt and pepper. Add 1 cup wine, 1 cup chicken stock, and 3 sprigs thyme. Cover the pot and bring to a boil. When the mixture boils, adjust the heat so that it bubbles gently. Cook, turning the thighs once, for 30 minutes.

   Trim, peel, and chop the onion and carrots.

   Trim and chop the celery.

   Peel and crush 1 garlic clove.

3. After 30 minutes, add the vegetables and sprinkle with salt and pepper. Cover and continue to cook until the turkey thighs are fully cooked and the vegetables are tender, about 10 minutes more; they should reach 155° to 160°F on a quick-read thermometer.

   Strip the parsley leaves from several sprigs and chop.

4. When the turkey thighs are cooked and the vegetables are tender, transfer them all to a platter. Boil the remaining liquid until it reduces into a thick sauce, 3 or 4 minutes.

5. Pour the sauce over the turkey and vegetables, garnish with the parsley, and serve.

VARIATIONS

White Wine–Braised Turkey and Celery Root
Use 2 to 3 cups chopped celery root instead of the carrots and celery and white wine instead of red.

Cider-Braised Turkey and Squash
Substitute 2 to 3 cups chopped winter squash for the carrots and celery and apple cider for the red wine.

NOTES

EVEN FASTER
Use 1 ½ pounds boneless, skin-on turkey breast instead of thighs. Cut it into 2-inch chunks. Chop the vegetables into smaller pieces; the turkey and vegetables will be cooked in about 20 minutes.

IF YOU HAVE MORE TIME
Brown the turkey thighs on both sides, remove them from the pot, and cook the vegetables until they're lightly browned, 5 to 10 minutes. Then return the thighs and proceed as directed.

TURKEY PARTS
Obviously, supermarkets start packing their shelves with turkey in the run-up to Thanksgiving, but you can reliably find a few different turkey parts in the stores year-round. Boneless breast is one of them, and it is a fantastic way to get roast turkey on the table in less than 45 minutes. Another useful cut is bone-in thigh, which is meaty, flavorful, and wonderful for braising (as in this recipe). As with whole turkeys, the size of the parts can vary significantly; I've seen breasts that weigh 7 pounds and thighs that weigh 3. For some reason I tend to prefer them on the smaller end, but if you have a crowd to feed, go big.

SIDES

Skin-On Mashed Potatoes 961

Buttered Egg Noodles 948

Warm Buttery Bread 906

Creamy Polenta 947

Meat

BEEF

Seared Steak with Mustard Spinach 708

Thai-Style Steak, Lettuce, and Herb Wraps 710

Stir-Fried Beef with Skillet Kimchi 712

Caramel Stir-Fried Beef and Green Beans 716

Steak and Vegetables with Chimichurri 718

Soy-Marinated Flank Steak and Cherry Tomatoes 722

Beef and Mushroom Kebabs with Spicy Peanut Sauce 724

The Better Burger 726

Sloppy Joes 728

Stir-Fried Beef and Broccoli with Scallions and Ginger 730

Veal Scaloppini with Lemon and Capers 732

Braised Veal with Peas 734

Curry-Braised Beef and Eggplant 738

Pan-Roasted Beef Tenderloin with Potatoes 740

Skillet Meat Loaf 742

Steak and Potato Enchiladas 744

Beef Stew 746

PORK

Stir-Fried Pork with Edamame and Scallions 748

Seared Pork Chops with Apples and Onions 750

BBQ Baby Back Ribs 752

Pork Souvlaki with Zucchini 754

Spice-Rubbed Pork with Pineapple Salsa 756

Five-Spice Pork Meatballs with Bok Choy 760

Homemade Chorizo with Pinto Beans 762

Maple-Glazed Ham Steaks with Collards 764

Braised Pork with Cabbage and Beer 766

Browned and Braised Sausage and Endive 768

Bangers and Mash 770

Pork Tenderloin with Butternut Purée 772

Porchetta-Style Pork Loin with Parsnips 776

Pork Stew and Dumplings 778

Pork and Onion Carnitas 780

Pork, White Bean, and Kale Stew 782

Provençal Braised Pork and Fennel 784

Moroccan-Style Braised Pork with Couscous and Grapes 786

LAMB

Lamb Chops with Balsamic Couscous 788

Stir-Fried Lamb and Green Peppers with Cumin 790

Seared Miso Lamb Chops with Carrots 792

Lamb and Rice with Dried Fruit 794

Herb-Rubbed Leg of Lamb with Chopped Greek Salad 798

Lamb and Bulgur Meatballs in Tomato Sauce 800

Meat

The appeal of meat is easy to understand. It's flavorful, filling, fast, and easy to prepare. For many of us, meat has moved from the center of the plate to the side, from a two- or three-time daily habit to a treat, which means it's more important than ever that when we do eat meat we thoroughly enjoy it. Part of that means buying higher-quality meat, and part of it means being sure you cook it well.

These recipes are designed to help you get the most out of meat in the shortest amount of time, covering a range of cooking methods from super-fast stir-frying to relatively languid braising. Some cooking methods and cuts of meat are typically associated with quick cooking, while tricks like slicing pork or lamb shoulder thin for quick braising or browning cubes of meat thoroughly on just one or two sides as opposed to every surface show how to save time while still developing good flavor. You'll even find some long-cooking classics, like porchetta and leg of lamb, reimagined so that you can get them on the table in 45 minutes or less.

Chapter Highlights

A Method to the Meatiness Systems for speed: The Fastest Cuts of Meat (page 714).

Fire It Up Put your grill or broiler to work using whatever ingredients are on hand. Broiling and Grilling (page 720).

Try a Little Tenderloin Do-it-yourself deli meats: fantastic. Homemade Cold Cuts (page 774).

Homemade Spice Blends They'll speed your cooking and make everything taste better. Spice Blends (page 758).

Marinate on It Preseasoning food doesn't mean slow. Marinades and "Rub-in-ades" (page 796).

Let It Sit Letting meat sit for a few minutes after cooking is time well spent. Give It a Rest (page 741).

Chop Talk These cuts of pork and lamb are fast, easy, and delicious. Boneless vs. Bone-In Pork Chops (page 751), Lamb Chops (page 789).

Skillet Stir-Fries No, you actually don't need a wok. Wok the Other Way (page 731).

Big Meat Two classic roasts reworked for the fast kitchen. Porchetta-Style Pork Loin with Parsnips (page 776), Herb-Rubbed Leg of Lamb with Chopped Greek Salad (page 798).

Mexican Chorizo Fresh chorizo isn't much harder to make than burgers. Homemade Chorizo with Pinto Beans (page 762).

One-Pot Meals Comfort food can be homey or exotic: your choice. Pork Stew and Dumplings (page 778), Moroccan-Style Braised Pork with Couscous and Grapes (page 786).

Grind Your Own Pulsing chunks of any meat in the food processor will always produce better ground meat than any you can buy. You decide which cut to use. You control how much fat to include. You determine the coarseness of the grind. And it's easy. The only inconvenience is cleaning the machine when you're done, and I almost always consider that a good trade-off. See the pork meatballs on page 760 for a demonstration.

Drop, Don't Roll Perhaps you reserve meatballs for special occasions because you don't want the fuss of rolling them out. So why bother? It's much easier to drop seasoned ground meat from a spoon, just like you do cookie dough. This technique works whether you cook them in the oven or on the stove and, since you won't over-handle them, they'll remain tender. Some examples are on page 760, 800, and 890.

SPEED  SERVES 4

Seared Steak with Mustard Spinach

Skillet, steak, spinach; the simplicity of this dish is phenomenal.

Ingredients

1 ½ pounds beef rib-eye, sirloin, or strip steak (about 1 inch thick)

Salt and pepper

1 tablespoon olive oil

1 ½ pounds spinach

1 shallot

1 tablespoon Dijon mustard

¼ cup white wine

Prep | Cook

1. Put a large skillet over high heat. Pat the steaks dry with a paper towel and sprinkle both sides with salt and pepper. Cut the steaks as needed to fit in the skillet.
2. When the skillet is very hot, add 1 tablespoon olive oil and swirl it around. Add the steaks and cook, turning once, until browned on both sides but still a bit pinker inside than you like it, 5 or 6 minutes per side.

   Trim and chop the spinach, discarding any thick stems.

   Trim, peel, and mince the shallot.
3. When the steaks are done, transfer them to a cutting board. Lower the heat to medium-high. Carefully add the shallot, 1 tablespoon Dijon, and ¼ cup wine, followed immediately by the spinach.
4. Sprinkle with salt and pepper and cook, stirring occasionally until the spinach is wilted and coated with the mustard, 2 or 3 minutes. Taste and adjust the seasoning. Slice the steak and serve with the spinach.

VARIATIONS

Seared Steak with Lemon Spinach
Replace the mustard with 2 tablespoons lemon juice.

Seared Steak with Creamy Spinach
Use 1/4 cup cream instead of the mustard. Add a pinch of nutmeg to the spinach while it cooks if you like.

Seared Steak with Parmesan Spinach
Omit the mustard and use 4 smashed garlic gloves instead of the shallots. After the spinach and garlic cook in Step 4, drizzle with another tablespoon olive oil and sprinkle with 1/2 cup grated Parmesan cheese. Toss until it melts a little before serving.

Seared Steak with Garlicky Chard
Skip the mustard. Swap chard (keep the stems) for the spinach, red wine for white, and 2 garlic cloves for the shallots. Before adding the chard leaves to the skillet, sauté the chopped stems by themselves to soften a bit, 3 or 4 minutes.

SIDES

Warm Buttery Bread 906

Couscous 910

Skin-On Mashed Potatoes 961

Sautéed Sweet Potatoes 964

SPEED SERVES 4

Thai-Style Steak, Lettuce, and Herb Wraps

A fresh, light Thai dish everyone loves. Make a quick dipping sauce while the steak grills. Then lay out herbs and lettuce leaves and let everyone assemble wraps at the table.

Ingredients

1 ½ pounds beef flank or skirt steak

Salt and pepper

2 limes

1 fresh hot red chile (like Thai bird; optional)

2 tablespoons peanuts

¼ cup fish sauce

1 tablespoon brown sugar

1 head Boston lettuce

1 bunch fresh mint

1 bunch fresh cilantro

1 bunch fresh Thai or regular basil

Prep | Cook

1. Prepare a grill or turn the broiler to high; put the rack 4 inches from the heat. Blot the steak dry with a paper towel and sprinkle with salt and pepper.
2. Grill or broil the steak, turning as necessary, until it is charred on both sides but still a bit pinker inside than you like it, 5 to 10 minutes total.

   Halve the limes and squeeze the juice into a small bowl.

   Trim and mince the chile if you're using it; chop 2 tablespoons peanuts; add both to the bowl.
3. Add ¼ cup fish sauce and 1 tablespoon brown sugar to the bowl. Stir to combine; taste and adjust the seasoning.
4. When the steak is done, transfer it to a cutting board.

   Remove the leaves from the head of lettuce, leaving them intact.

   Strip about ½ cup each mint leaves, cilantro leaves, and Thai or regular basil leaves from their stems.

5. Thinly slice the steak against the grain. Put it on a serving platter with the lettuce and herbs.

6. Serve with the dipping sauce on the side. To eat, put the steak and herbs in the lettuce leaves, roll, and dip in the sauce.

VARIATIONS

Italian-Style Steak, Lettuce, and Herb Wraps
Substitute lemon juice for lime, 1/4 teaspoon red chile flakes for the fresh chile, 1 minced garlic clove for the peanuts, and olive oil for the fish sauce. Omit the brown sugar; season the dipping sauce with salt and pepper. Use 1 cup halved cherry tomatoes instead of the mint, 1/2 cup shaved Parmesan instead of the cilantro, and regular basil in place of Thai.

Mexican-Style Steak, Lettuce, and Herb Wraps
Swap 1 minced garlic clove for the peanuts and 2 tablespoons vegetable oil plus 2 tablespoons chopped chipotle chiles in adobo for the fish sauce. Omit the fresh chile and brown sugar; season the dipping sauce with salt. Replace the mint with 1 cup corn kernels and the basil with 1/2 cup thinly sliced red onion.

SIDES

White Rice 941

Sesame Noodles 949

Cucumber Salad with Hot Sauce and Lime Juice 915

Fire and Ice Noodles 950

SPEED SERVES 4

Stir-Fried Beef with Skillet Kimchi

An easy stir-fry takes on bright, lively flavor thanks to spicy kimchi seasonings.

Ingredients

4 tablespoons vegetable oil, plus more as needed

1 ½ pounds beef sirloin, flank, or rib-eye steak

Salt and pepper

1 medium Napa cabbage

1 inch fresh ginger

4 garlic cloves

½ teaspoon red chile flakes

1 teaspoon sugar

2 tablespoons rice vinegar

1 tablespoon gochujang (Korean red pepper paste) or Sriracha (optional)

Prep | Cook

1. Put 2 tablespoons vegetable oil in a large skillet over medium-high heat.

   Slice the beef as thinly as you can.

2. Add half of the beef to the skillet, sprinkle with salt and pepper, turn the heat to high, and cook, stirring occasionally until it's lightly browned, 3 to 5 minutes. Transfer to a bowl and repeat with the remaining beef, adding more oil as necessary.

   Core, trim, and chop the cabbage.

   Peel 1 inch ginger and 4 garlic cloves; mince them together.

3. Transfer the second batch of cooked beef to the bowl. Add 2 tablespoons oil to the skillet along with the ginger and garlic. Cook, stirring until fragrant, 30 seconds to a minute.

4. Add the cabbage, ½ teaspoon red chile flakes, 1 teaspoon sugar, and a sprinkle of salt and pepper. Cook, stirring occasionally until the cabbage is tender but still has some crunch, 6 to 8 minutes.

5. Add 2 tablespoons rice vinegar to the skillet along with 1 tablespoon gochujang or Sriracha if you're using it and stir.

6. Return the beef to the skillet and toss to coat everything in the sauce and heat the beef through. Taste and adjust the seasoning and serve immediately.

VARIATIONS

Stir-Fried Pork with Skillet Sauerkraut
Substitute pork loin for the beef and green cabbage, thinly sliced, for the Napa. Omit the ginger and substitute caraway seeds for the red chile flakes. Use white or cider vinegar instead of the rice vinegar; omit the gochujang and add 1 tablespoon Dijon if you want a mustardy bite.

SIDES

Carrot Salad with Cilantro and Lime 914

Edamame Succotash 933

White Rice 941

Scallion Pancakes 940

Panfried Rice Noodles 951

The Best Fast Cuts of Meat

There are enough different cuts of meat to make your head spin, but when I need to throw together a quick meal I find myself turning to the same ones time and again. These go-to cuts, along with smart substitutes, take well to various cooking methods and cook quickly; they're the ones called for most often in this chapter.

Cut of Meat	Notes	Cuts to Substitute	Recipes
BEEF SIRLOIN, RIB-EYE, FLANK STEAK	Pan-sear, grill, or broil whole steaks or thinly slice for stir-frying. Rib-eye is the most tender and flavorful (it's also the priciest). For my money, it's better to splurge on rib-eye for a showstopping steak than for a sliced-up stir-fry, where the chew of sirloin and flank are an asset. Colder meat is easier and faster to slice thinly for stir-frying; if you have a few minutes to spare, pop it in the freezer before slicing.	Strip steak, skirt steak, and beef tenderloin. Other than rib-eye, skirt is my favorite, but best thinly sliced either before or after cooking. Tenderloin (aka *filet mignon*) is the most tender, most expensive, and least flavorful, since it has so little fat.	Caramel Stir-Fried Beef and Green Beans (page 716); Steak and Vegetables with Chimichurri (page 718); Soy-Marinated Flank Steak and Cherry Tomatoes (page 722)
BEEF CHUCK	From a harder-working group of muscles—therefore loaded with fat and flavor but also a bit tough—chuck is a wonderful middle ground between fast and slow cooking. If you slice or cut it into small pieces, it's good for quick braises and stews: It cooks without drying out but isn't so tough that it takes hours to become tender enough to eat. For even faster cooking, chop it finely in the food processor to make ground meat.	Brisket, round, beef shoulder roast, short ribs, and shanks; all will take longer to get tender than chuck.	Curry-Braised Beef and Eggplant (page 738); The Better Burger (page 726); Beef Stew (page 746)

Cut of Meat	Notes	Cuts to Substitute	Recipes
PORK SHOULDER	Pork shoulder is an incredibly versatile addition to the fast kitchen. Like beef chuck, it's fatty and flavorful and useful in much the same way: Thinly slice it for quick braises, grind it in the food processor for meatballs, or char cubes under the broiler. Sliced very thin, it's wonderful in stir-fries and is considerably less expensive than other cuts.	Pork butt is actually the top section of the shoulder; what's called *pork shoulder* is the bottom section. I use the cuts interchangeably. You might also come across country-style pork ribs, which are ribs cut from the section of the shoulder closest to the loin. Cut the meat as you would pork shoulder, and if you're braising, throw the bone into the pot for extra flavor.	Pork Souvlaki with Zucchini (page 754); Five-Spice Pork Meatballs with Bok Choy (page 760); Provençal Braised Pork and Fennel (page 784); Pork and Onion Carnitas (page 780)
LAMB CHOPS	Even double-thick chops cook in a flash. They are perfect for pan-searing, broiling, and grilling and come from all different parts of the animal, offering varying degrees of tenderness, flavor, bone, and price (for a quick rundown of the different types of lamb chops, see page 789).	Boneless leg or shoulder sliced into steaks or cutlets.	Lamb Chops with Balsamic Couscous (page 788); Seared Miso Lamb Chops with Carrots (page 792)
GROUND MEAT	It pays to have ground meat of one kind or another in your freezer or fridge. It's not only essential for burgers, meatballs, and meat loaves but can be the base of lightning-quick stir-fries or pasta sauces. To speed up the already fast cooking, break up the chunks of ground meat with the edge of a spoon as you stir it.	Grind your own beef chuck, pork shoulder, or lamb shoulder by pulsing it in the food processor or just use bulk sausage meat.	Lamb and Bulgur Meatballs in Tomato Sauce (page 800); Skillet Meat Loaf (page 742); Sloppy Joes (page 728)

SPEED SERVES 4

Caramel Stir-Fried Beef and Green Beans

Beef braised in caramel flavored with fish sauce is a staple of Vietnamese clay pot cooking. The sauce also works terrifically in quick skillet dishes, bubbling down to a sweet-salty coating for beef and green beans in minutes.

Ingredients

1 ½ pounds beef sirloin, flank, or rib-eye steak

½ cup sugar

3 shallots

½ inch fresh ginger

1 fresh hot green chile (like serrano)

1 pound green beans

3 tablespoons fish sauce

Pepper

Several sprigs fresh cilantro for garnish

Prep | Cook

1. Put the beef in the freezer. Put ½ cup sugar in a large skillet over medium-low heat. Cook, shaking the pan occasionally until the sugar becomes liquid and darkens slightly, 5 to 7 minutes.

   Trim, peel, and thinly slice 3 shallots. Peel ½ inch ginger and trim the chile; mince them together.

   Trim the green beans.

2. When the sugar melts and darkens slightly, remove it from the heat and carefully add ¼ cup water and 3 tablespoons fish sauce. Stir in a good amount of pepper and return the skillet to medium heat.

3. Add the shallots, ginger, chile, and green beans. Cook, stirring occasionally for 2 minutes.

   Remove the beef from the freezer and slice it as thinly as you can.

4. Add the steak to the skillet and cook, stirring occasionally until it's cooked through and the caramel has thickened and coated the beef and green beans, 3 to 5 minutes.

   Chop several sprigs cilantro.

5. Taste and adjust the seasoning. Garnish with the cilantro and serve immediately.

VARIATIONS

Orange Caramel Stir-Fried Pork and Green Beans
Swap pork loin for the beef and freshly squeezed orange juice for the fish sauce. You'll need to add a little salt.

Soy Caramel Stir-Fried Beef and Peppers
Swap soy sauce for the fish sauce and bell peppers (I like green ones here) for the green beans.

SIDES

White Rice 941

Panfried Rice Noodles 951

Warm Tortillas 907

Tomato Salad with Sesame and Soy 913

Daikon Salad with Fish Sauce, Lime, and Peanuts 918

SPEED ◐ SERVES 4

Steak and Vegetables with Chimichurri

Chimichurri, the addictive fresh herb sauce ubiquitous in Argentina, is known as a sidekick for steak, but more often than not I eat it with vegetables. Here you don't have to choose.

Ingredients

1 ½ pounds beef sirloin, rib-eye, or strip steaks

Salt and pepper

8 ounces portobello mushrooms

1 pound Yukon Gold potatoes

1 large onion

2 red bell peppers

¾ cup olive oil, plus more as needed

1 bunch fresh parsley

1 bunch fresh cilantro

3 garlic cloves

2 tablespoons sherry vinegar

½ teaspoon red chile flakes (optional)

Prep | Cook

1. Turn the broiler to high; put the rack 4 inches from the heat. Blot the steaks dry with a paper towel and sprinkle with salt and pepper.

   Trim the mushrooms.

   Peel the potatoes if you like and cut them into thin rounds.

   Trim, peel, and slice the onion into rounds.

   Core, seed, and quarter the peppers.

2. Toss the vegetables with ¼ cup olive oil and sprinkle with salt and pepper. Put the steaks and vegetables on a rimmed baking sheet or 2.

3. Broil, turning as necessary, until the steaks are charred on both sides but still a bit pinker inside than you like them and the vegetables are tender and lightly charred, 5 to 10 minutes for the steak and a little longer for the vegetables.

   Strip 2 cups parsley leaves from the stems and pull 1 cup cilantro sprigs from the bunch.

   Peel and mince 3 garlic cloves.

4. Put the herbs, garlic, ½ cup oil, 2 tablespoons sherry vinegar, ½ teaspoon red chile flakes if you're using them, and some salt and pepper in a food processor. Process until smooth, scraping down the sides as necessary. Taste and adjust the seasoning.

5. When the steaks are done, transfer them to a cutting board and let them rest while you finish cooking the vegetables. Slice the steak and serve it on a platter alongside the vegetables, with the chimichurri spooned over everything.

VARIATIONS

Pork Chops and Vegetables with Chimichurri
Chops are completely untraditional—but excellent—with this sauce. Instead of the steaks, use 1 ½ pounds boneless pork chops, each about 1 inch thick. Cook them with the vegetables as described in Step 3 until firm but still a little pink inside, 10 to 15 minutes total, depending on their thickness.

Chicken Cutlets and Vegetables with Chimichurri
Substitute boneless, skinless chicken thighs for the steaks. They'll take 10 to 15 minutes total cooking time in Step 3.

4 Other Vegetables to Try

1. Asparagus
2. Eggplant
3. Zucchini
4. Winter squash (thinly sliced)

NOTES

EVEN FASTER
To simplify things, cook just one vegetable, about 2 pounds total.

SIDES

Creamy Polenta 947

Skin-On Mashed Potatoes 961

White Rice 941

Quinoa 945

Bruschetta 909

Broiling and Grilling

The broiler is the most underappreciated kitchen appliance. Like a grill flipped on its head, it provides direct heat for searing food quickly. You can control the speed at which it cooks by moving the rack closer to or farther away from the heat. Unlike pan-searing, which also provides a quick burst of heat, broiling spreads heat over a large area, allowing you to sear big batches of food at once. There's a lot of broiling in this book, so here's a quick primer:

Getting to Know Your Broiler

Some broilers boast intense and powerful heat, while others are weak. One way to see what kind of firepower you're dealing with is to broil a slice of bread about 4 inches away from the heat. If the top turns crusty and dark brown in about a minute, your broiler is pretty powerful; if it takes 3 minutes or longer, you've got a wimpy one. I try to give time ranges to account for all kinds of broilers, so if yours is strong, lean toward shorter cooking times, and if it's weak, broil for longer or move the food closer to the heat—sometimes as close as possible.

The Broiler Rack

If your broiler is a drawer that pulls out from under your oven, it likely comes with a rack that looks like a small baking pan. The broiler pan is perfectly fine to cook on, but I prefer the larger surface area of baking sheets.

Heating Broilers

Broilers may be gas flames or electric coils, located in a separate drawer beneath the oven or inside the oven at the very top. No matter what kind you have, it's important to let it run for 5 minutes before you start cooking; this time allows the roof of the broiler and the inside air temperature to heat up, which enables faster and more even cooking. Generally, turn on the broiler when you start a recipe; that way by the time the food is ready to broil, the heat will be raring to go.

Controlling the Heat

Some broilers have heat settings that you can control with the turn of a knob, but most don't. (Even those that claim to often don't.) The one fail-safe way to adjust the heat during cooking is to change the position of the rack. Say you're cooking vegetables that are getting singed on the outside but are still crunchy in the middle: Move them farther away from the heat. Or if a steak isn't getting the kind of char you want, move it closer.

If a food is charring too quickly, another option is to cover the pan loosely with aluminum foil, which will slow the browning while continuing to cook the food. Unlike an oven, a broiler doesn't lose most of its effectiveness when you open the door, so don't be shy about checking on the progress of your food often and turning food or adjusting the rack position as needed.

Long-Distance and Regular Broiling

Most foods that you're going to broil—tender vegetables, seafood, or steaks, chops, or chicken pieces an inch or less thick—benefit from being positioned close to the heat, about 4 inches away. Then there's something I call "long-distance broiling," which means putting the rack farther away from the heat—about 6 inches—so that food cooks more slowly. This is best for thicker pieces of meat or vegetables that take longer to cook; if you put them too close to the heat, they'll burn on the outside before cooking through in the middle. While it's obviously not as fast as regular broiling, it is a wonderful and quicker alternative to roasting.

Moving the Kitchen Outside

Gas Grilling

A broiler is just like a gas grill turned upside down; both use direct heat to cook foods quickly and impart a slightly smoky char. And they're interchangeable when it comes to timing too, which is why a handful of recipes here give you the option of either. But there's one significant difference that needs to be accounted for: The broiler is in your kitchen, and the grill is outside. The flow of prepping and cooking on which these recipes are based is much smoother when you don't have to run back and forth from the kitchen to the backyard. If you're lucky enough to have a gas grill positioned right outside of your kitchen—of if you're cooking with a friend and can share tasks—then use it in place of the broiler whenever you like. But I'm not counting on it, so any recipe here that calls for grilling takes those outside trips into account.

Charcoal Grilling

Grilling over charcoal provides deeper flavor and better char than grilling over gas, and the cooking itself is quick, but charcoal grilling, overall, is too slow to call "fast," simply because it takes too much time to get the coals going. However, if you account for heating time, you can use a charcoal grill for any of the grilling recipes in this book.

Multitasking

If you're into cooking outdoors big-time, then you'll want to start bringing out pots and pans and using the grill as a stove. Nothing is stopping you. In fact, you can use these recipes to give it a try.

SPEED ◐ SERVES 4

Soy-Marinated Flank Steak and Cherry Tomatoes

Soy sauce is a classic marinade for steak; its savoriness—or umami—also pairs wonderfully with sweet cherry tomatoes. The just-burst tomatoes and an extra drizzle of the marinade provide all the sauce that steak needs.

Ingredients

3 garlic cloves

1 inch fresh ginger

⅓ cup soy sauce

Pepper

1 ½ pounds flank steak

2 pints cherry tomatoes

1 tablespoon vegetable oil

2 scallions

Prep | Cook

1. Turn the broiler to high; put the rack 4 inches from the heat.

   Peel 3 garlic cloves and 1 inch ginger; mince them together.

2. Put the garlic and ginger in a large dish or freezer bag; add ⅓ cup soy sauce and a sprinkle of pepper. Add the steak and tomatoes and toss to coat; let them marinate for 5 minutes.

3. Put a large skillet over high heat. Remove the steak from the marinade, letting any liquid drip off, and pat dry with a paper towel. Cut the steak in half if necessary to fit it into the skillet.

4. When the skillet is very hot, add 1 tablespoon vegetable oil and swirl it around. Add the steak and cook, turning it once, until browned on both sides but still a bit pinker inside than you like it, 3 to 5 minutes per side.

5. Remove the tomatoes from the marinade and put them on a rimmed baking sheet. Broil, shaking the pan occasionally until they're charred in spots and starting to burst, 4 to 6 minutes.

6. Pour the marinade into a small saucepan and bring it to a boil. Let boil gently for 5 minutes.

   Trim and chop the scallions.

7. When the steak is done, transfer it to a cutting board. When the tomatoes are lightly charred, put them on a platter or divide them among 4 plates. Pour any accumulated juices into the simmering marinade.

8. Slice the steak and drizzle it and the tomatoes with some of the marinade. Garnish with the scallions and serve.

VARIATIONS

Mustard-Marinated Flank Steak and Cherry Tomatoes
Omit the ginger. Substitute 2 tablespoons red wine vinegar, 2 tablespoons Dijon mustard, and 1 tablespoon olive oil for the soy sauce.

Soy-Marinated Flank Steak and Green Beans
Swap 1 pound green beans for the tomatoes. Broil, tossing once or twice, until they're browned and just tender but still have some crunch, 5 to 10 minutes.

Chipotle-Marinated Flank Steak and Asparagus
Substitute 1 bunch asparagus, cut into 3-inch pieces, for the tomatoes, 1 tablespoon lime juice for the ginger, and 3 tablespoons chopped chipotle chiles in adobo for the soy sauce. Broil the asparagus, tossing once or twice, until they're browned and just tender but still have some crunch, 5 to 10 minutes.

NOTES

EVEN FASTER
Skip marinating. Prepare the soy sauce mixture while the steak and tomatoes cook, then spoon it over as a sauce.

IF YOU HAVE MORE TIME
Let the steak and tomatoes marinate in the refrigerator for up to a few hours.

SIDES

Warm Tortillas 907

White Rice 941

Panfried Rice Noodles 951

Scallion Pancakes 940

SPEED ◐ SERVES 4

Beef and Mushroom Kebabs with Spicy Peanut Sauce

Chile-tinged peanut sauce adds kick and helps the beef char beautifully in the broiler.

Ingredients

20 button mushrooms

1 ½ pounds beef sirloin

2 tablespoons vegetable oil

Salt and pepper

1 garlic clove

½ inch fresh ginger

1 fresh hot green chile (like serrano)

¼ cup peanut butter

1 tablespoon soy sauce

1 tablespoon rice vinegar

2 teaspoons sesame oil

Several sprigs fresh cilantro for garnish

Prep | Cook

If you're using wooden skewers, soak them in water. Turn the broiler to high; put the rack 4 inches from the heat.

Trim 20 button mushrooms, leaving them whole.

Cut the beef into 1 ½-inch chunks.

1. Thread the mushrooms and the beef onto separate skewers. Rub with 2 tablespoons vegetable oil and some salt and pepper.

2. Put just the mushroom kebabs in the broiler and cook, turning once, until they are tender and browned on 2 sides, 10 to 15 minutes.

   Peel 1 garlic clove and ½ inch ginger and trim the chile; mince everything together and put in a small bowl.

3. Add ¼ cup peanut butter, 1 tablespoon soy sauce, 1 tablespoon rice vinegar, and 2 teaspoons sesame oil to the bowl. Stir to combine, adding a little hot water to thin the sauce bit. Pour a little of the sauce into a small bowl to save for later.

4. After you turn the mushrooms, put the beef kebabs in the broiler alongside the mushrooms. Cook, basting everything with some of the remaining sauce and turning the kebabs as they brown, until the sauce is caramelized, the mushrooms are tender, and the beef is just cooked through, 5 to 10 minutes more; cut a piece of beef to check for doneness after about 5 minutes.

   Chop several sprigs cilantro.

5. When the mushrooms and beef are done, spoon the reserved peanut sauce over the top, garnish with the cilantro, and serve.

VARIATIONS

Beef and Onion Kebabs with Mustard-Rosemary Sauce
Swap 5 small onions, quartered, for the mushrooms, 1 tablespoon chopped fresh rosemary for the ginger and chile, ¼ cup Dijon mustard for the peanut butter, lemon juice for the rice vinegar, and olive oil for the sesame oil. Omit the soy sauce and garnish with parsley instead of cilantro.

NOTES

EVEN FASTER
Don't skewer; just broil the beef and mushrooms on a rimmed baking sheet.

SIDES

White Rice 941

Sesame Noodles 949

Scallion Pancakes 940

Stir-Fried Bok Choy 927

SPEED ◑ SERVES 4

The Better Burger

A burger is all about the texture and flavor of the meat, so if there's one dish that rewards spending the time to grind your own beef, this is it. The no-frills recipe here benefits from a side or two. See the list of options opposite.

Ingredients

1 ½ pounds boneless beef sirloin (not too lean) or chuck

Salt and pepper

4 hamburger buns

Prep | Cook

1. Prepare a charcoal or gas grill with the rack 4 inches from the heat or put a large skillet over medium-low heat.

   Cut the beef into chunks; put them in the food processor.

   Pulse until the beef is coarsely ground; transfer to a bowl and sprinkle with salt and pepper.

2. Lightly shape the beef into 4 patties; sprinkle both sides with salt and pepper.

3. If you're cooking in a skillet, raise the heat to medium-high. Grill or pan-cook the burgers, turning once, until they're cooked as you like—3 minutes per side for very rare and another minute per side for each increasing stage of doneness.

4. Serve on buns, with whatever condiments you like.

VARIATIONS

The Better Pork and Scallion Burger
Substitute boneless pork shoulder for the beef and add 1/4 cup chopped scallions along with the salt and pepper. Cook until the pork is just cooked through, about 5 minutes per side.

The Better Lamb and Red Onion Burger
Substitute boneless lamb shoulder for the beef and add 1/4 cup chopped red onion along with the salt and pepper. Keep it rare.

NOTES

EVEN FASTER
Use preground meat. Not as good, of course, but at least twice as fast.

THE BETTER CHEESEBURGER
Add cheese immediately after you flip the burgers. The surface that you put the cheese on needs to be quite hot so the cheese melts before the burgers overcook. Or make them diner style: Add the cheese, put a small splash of water in the skillet, then quickly put a lid on top. The steam melts the cheese in a flash.

SIDES

French Fries 963

German-Style Potato Salad 962

Coleslaw 923

Green Salad 911

Tomato Salad 913

SPEED  SERVES 4

Sloppy Joes

Bad sloppy Joes are terrible. Good ones are a game-changer: homemade meat sauce on a bun, here with some vegetables added for good measure.

Ingredients

2 tablespoons olive oil

1 onion

2 celery stalks

1 medium zucchini

2 bell peppers

3 garlic cloves

12 ounces ground beef

1 teaspoon chili powder

1 teaspoon cumin

Salt and pepper

One 14-ounce can diced tomatoes

¼ cup ketchup

1 teaspoon Worcestershire sauce

1 teaspoon soy sauce

4 hamburger buns

Prep | Cook

1. Put 2 tablespoons olive oil in a large skillet or large pot over medium-high heat.

   Trim, peel, and chop the onion; add it to the skillet.

   Trim and chop the celery stalks and the zucchini; add them to the skillet.

   Core, seed, and chop the bell peppers; add them to the skillet.

2. Cook, stirring occasionally until the vegetables soften, 5 to 10 minutes.

   Peel and mince 3 garlic cloves.

3. When the vegetables are soft, add the garlic, beef, 1 teaspoon chili powder, 1 teaspoon cumin, and a sprinkle of salt and pepper. Cook, stirring occasionally until the meat loses its pink color, 8 to 12 minutes.

4. Stir in the tomatoes, ¼ cup ketchup, 1 teaspoon Worcestershire, and 1 teaspoon soy sauce. Bring the mixture to a simmer and cook, stirring occasionally and adding a splash of water if the pan gets too dry, until the mixture is thick and the flavors come together, 10 to 15 minutes.

5. Taste and adjust the seasoning and serve on buns.

VARIATIONS

Chinese-Style Sloppy Joes
Substitute ground pork for the beef, 1 inch ginger, minced, for the chili powder, 1 minced fresh hot green chile for the cumin, ¼ cup hoisin for the ketchup, and an extra teaspoon of soy sauce for the Worcestershire.

Moroccan-Style Sloppy Joes
Use red onion instead of yellow, ½ cup chopped dried apricots instead of the celery, ground lamb instead of the beef, 1 teaspoon coriander and ½ teaspoon cinnamon instead of the chili powder, and 2 teaspoons chopped fresh oregano or 1 teaspoon dried instead of the Worcestershire and soy sauce. If you have harissa, replace 2 tablespoons of the ketchup with it.

NOTES

MAKE YOUR OWN

Chili Powder 758

EVEN FASTER
Brown the beef in a separate skillet with the spices and garlic while the vegetables soften; when it's browned, add the vegetables to the skillet with the beef; proceed from Step 4.

IF YOU HAVE MORE TIME
For a deeper flavor, simmer the mixture for anywhere between 15 minutes and an hour, adding liquid to the pan if it gets too dry.

SIDES

Green Salad 911

White Rice 941

Warm Tortillas 907

Coleslaw 923

SPEED ◑ SERVES 4

Stir-Fried Beef and Broccoli with Scallions and Ginger

This Chinese take-out staple takes less time to make at home than it does to be delivered, and takeout can't compete with fresh-from-the-skillet flavor.

Ingredients

4 tablespoons vegetable oil

1 ½ pounds beef sirloin, flank, or rib-eye steak

Salt and pepper

1 inch fresh ginger

2 garlic cloves

1 medium head broccoli (1 to 1 ½ pounds)

4 scallions

1 tablespoon sesame oil

1 tablespoon hoisin sauce

Prep | Cook

1. Put 2 tablespoons vegetable oil in a large skillet over medium-high heat.

   Slice the beef as thinly as you can.

2. Add the beef to the skillet, sprinkle with salt and pepper, and cook, stirring occasionally until it's lightly browned, 3 to 5 minutes.

   Peel 1 inch ginger and 2 garlic cloves; mince them together.

   Trim the broccoli and break or chop it into small florets.

3. When the beef is lightly browned, add the ginger and garlic. Cook, stirring until fragrant, about a minute. Transfer the beef mixture a bowl.

4. Add 2 tablespoons oil to the skillet. Add the broccoli and cook, stirring occasionally until it browns slightly, 3 or 4 minutes. Add ¼ cup water, cover the skillet, and cook until the broccoli is just tender, another 3 or 4 minutes.

   Trim and chop the scallions.

5. When the broccoli is just tender, remove the lid and let the remaining water mostly evaporate. Return the beef to the skillet along with the scallions, 1 tablespoon sesame oil, and 1 tablespoon hoisin sauce.

6. Toss to coat to coat everything with the sauce and heat the beef through. Taste and adjust the seasoning and serve.

VARIATIONS

Stir-Fried Pork and Broccoli with Chiles
Swap pork loin for the beef and add 1 or 2 minced fresh hot green chiles along with the ginger and garlic.

Stir-Fried Beef and Asparagus with Scallions and Ginger
Swap 1 large bunch asparagus, cut into 2-inch lengths, for the broccoli; it will take a little less time to become tender.

NOTES

WOK THE OTHER WAY
Many people believe the only way to cook good stir-fries at home is with a wok; it isn't so. What makes woks so effective in Chinese restaurants is the intense burners that fit under them, burners the size of the one under your hot water heater, which allow you to stir-fry ingredients in a matter of seconds. You'll never get a pan that hot at home. But a cast-iron skillet—which gets quite hot and holds the heat well—is as good as you're going to get, so there's no reason to buy a wok, especially if storage space is an issue.

SIDES

White Rice 941

Sesame Noodles 949

Cucumber Salad with Soy Sauce and Mirin 915

Panfried Rice Noodles 951

Scallion Pancakes 940

SPEED ◐ SERVES 4

Veal Scaloppini with Lemon and Capers

Sautéed veal cutlets with white wine, lemon, and capers is old-school Italian-American restaurant food. Like chicken with an extra jolt of richness, the veal soaks up the tangy sauce and is as supple and juicy as can be.

Ingredients

1 tablespoon olive oil, plus more as needed

2 tablespoons butter, plus more as needed

2 cups flour

Salt and pepper

1 ½ to 2 pounds veal cutlets

2 garlic cloves

1 lemon

2 tablespoons capers

1 bunch fresh parsley

½ cup white wine

Prep | Cook

1. Heat the oven to 200°F. Put 1 tablespoon olive oil and 1 tablespoon butter in a large skillet over medium-high heat.
2. Put 2 cups flour in a shallow bowl; season with salt and pepper. Sprinkle the cutlets with salt and pepper and dredge one at a time in the flour, shake off the excess, and put in the skillet (you'll need to work in batches).
3. Cook the cutlets, rotating them occasionally and adjusting the heat so they sizzle but don't burn, until they are browned, 3 or 4 minutes. Turn and cook on the other side until browned and cooked through, another 3 or 4 minutes.
4. As each piece is done, transfer it to the oven to keep warm; continue cooking the remaining cutlets, adding more oil and/or butter to the skillet as needed.

   Peel and mince 2 garlic cloves. Halve the lemon.

   Chop 2 tablespoons capers and ¼ cup parsley.

5. When all the cutlets are cooked and warming in the oven, add ½ cup white wine to the skillet; cook, scraping the bottom of the pan, until it is reduced by about half, a minute or 2.

6. Add the garlic, capers, and parsley; squeeze in the lemon juice and add 1 tablespoon butter and any juices that have accumulated around the veal.

7. As the sauce bubbles, quickly dip each piece of veal into the skillet to coat with the sauce; put them on a platter, pour the remaining sauce over the top, and serve.

VARIATIONS

Veal Scaloppini with Peas and White Wine
Instead of capers, add ½ cup fresh or frozen peas.

Chicken Cutlets with Lemon and Capers
Swap 4 boneless, skinless chicken breasts for the veal. Cut each breast in half horizontally to make 2 thin cutlets. Press down on each with the heel of your hand to flatten a bit.

Veal Marsala
Make Chicken Marsala with Lots of Mushrooms (page 630) using 1 ½ to 2 pounds veal cutlets instead of the chicken.

NOTES

A WORD ON VEAL
For a long time it was nearly impossible to find veal that had been raised under humane conditions, but that's changing. Look for veal that is labeled *cage-free* or *free-range*; as always, a butcher, farmer, or supermarket that you trust is your best bet.

SIDES

Creamy Polenta 947

Skin-On Mashed Potatoes 961

Garlic Bread 906

Green Salad 911

SPEED ◐ SERVES 4

Braised Veal with Peas

Brimming with fresh flavor, this quick and simple braise is a perfect dish for spring. Veal sirloin and leg will yield more tender chunks of meat, while fattier breast will have more flavor and chew. If you can get your hands on fresh shelled peas, even better.

Ingredients

1 tablespoon olive oil

2 tablespoons butter

1 ½ pounds veal sirloin, leg, or breast

Salt and pepper

1 pound shallots

½ cup white wine or water

Several sprigs fresh tarragon for garnish

2 cups fresh or frozen peas

Prep | Cook

1. Put 1 tablespoon olive oil and 2 tablespoons butter in a large skillet or saucepan over medium-high heat.

   Cut the veal into 1-inch chunks.

2. Add the veal to the skillet, sprinkle with salt and pepper, and cook undisturbed until nicely browned on the bottom, about 5 minutes.

   Trim, peel, and quarter the shallots.

3. When the veal is browned on the bottom, add the shallots and cook, stirring occasionally until they soften slightly, 2 or 3 minutes. Add ½ cup white wine or water.

4. Adjust the heat so that the mixture bubbles gently but steadily. Cover and cook until the veal is tender and cooked through, 15 to 20 minutes.

   Strip the tarragon leaves from several sprigs and chop them.

5. When the veal is tender, stir in 2 cups peas and cook, stirring occasionally until they heat through, 2 or 3 minutes. Sir in the tarragon, taste and adjust the seasoning, and serve.

VARIATIONS

Soy-Braised Veal with Edamame
Add 1 inch fresh ginger, minced, along with the shallots and substitute ¼ cup soy sauce for ¼ cup of the wine, edamame for the peas, and 2 scallions for the tarragon.

Braised Veal with Garlic and White Beans
Add 3 garlic cloves, thinly sliced, along with the shallots and swap cooked white beans for the peas.

NOTES

EVEN FASTER

Stir-Fried Veal with Shallots and Peas
Cut the veal into thin slices and stir-fry it in a large skillet with the oil and butter until lightly browned, 3 to 5 minutes. Remove and stir-fry the shallots, sliced instead of quartered, until lightly browned and tender, 3 to 5 minutes. Return the veal to the skillet along with the peas and ¼ cup white wine. Cook, stirring occasionally until the peas are warmed through, 2 or 3 minutes. Stir in the tarragon, taste and adjust the seasoning, and serve.

IF YOU HAVE MORE TIME
Use a tougher cut of veal (like the shoulder) and braise, adding more liquid as needed, until it is fall-apart tender, up to 3 hours. At that point the shallots will melt into the sauce; if you prefer them to stay intact, add them closer to the end of cooking.

SIDES

Buttered Egg Noodles 948

Rice Pilaf 944

Warm Buttery Bread 906

Creamy Polenta 947

Braised Meat

1 Pick a cut of meat.

For braising you want the tougher (and cheaper) cuts that become tender when simmered in liquid, usually for a long time. To speed things up, cut or slice them into pieces no thicker than 1 inch. Beef chuck and pork or lamb shoulder are perfect for this technique.

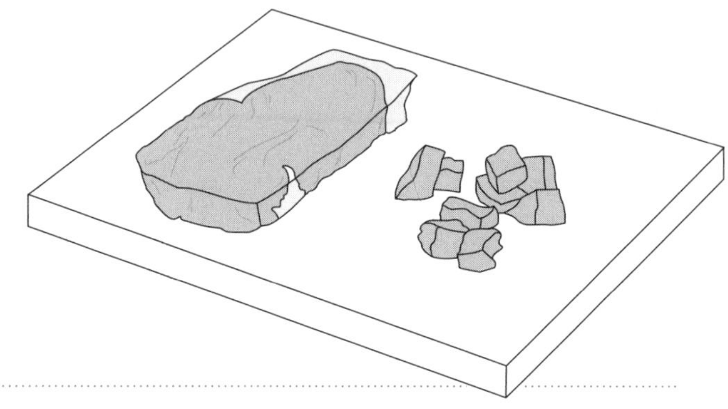

2 Brown, baby, brown.

Start by browning meat well in fat in a large pot. If you are short on time, just brown it really well on one side. (I skip this flavor-building step altogether if I'm really in a hurry; the stew will still be good.)

3 Add vegetables.

Remove the meat from the pot and brown any vegetables on their own to get the most flavor. (These are typically aromatics, but you can also include root vegetables at this point.) Again, if you're in a rush, just stir the vegetables into the pot with the meat.

❹ Add liquid.

Add water, stock, juice, booze—whatever you want the stew to taste like—scraping up any browned bits with a wooden spoon. Return the meat to the pot, making sure there is enough liquid to barely cover the ingredients. Bring to a boil, then reduce to a gentle bubble and cover.

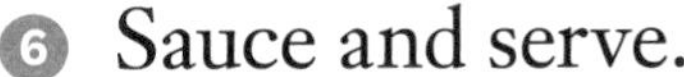

❺ Cook until tender.

Getting fall-apart-tender meat can take a long time, but with smaller pieces you can still develop excellent flavor and tenderness in less than an hour.

❻ Sauce and serve.

Once the meat is tender, check the liquid. If it's too thin, transfer the meat to a platter, skim off some of the fat if you like, and boil until the liquid thickens into a sauce. If there's no liquid left, add a splash more. Garnish and serve.

SPEED SERVES 4

Curry-Braised Beef and Eggplant

The silky texture that eggplant develops as it becomes tender gives this Thai-style curry a wonderful richness and warmth in a fairly short amount of time. Browning the beef and vegetables at the beginning develops great flavor in the pot, but you can skip it if you're in a pinch (see Even Faster on the opposite page).

Ingredients

4 tablespoons vegetable oil

1 ½ pounds boneless beef chuck

Salt and pepper

1 onion

1 large or 2 medium eggplant

1 bunch fresh Thai basil or sweet basil

2 tablespoons red or green curry paste or curry powder

One 15-ounce can coconut milk

1 lime

1 small bunch fresh cilantro

Prep | Cook

1. Put 2 tablespoons vegetable oil in a large pot over medium-high heat.

   Cut the beef into 1-inch chunks.

2. Add the meat to the pan and sprinkle with salt and pepper. Cook, undisturbed, until well browned on one side, 2 or 3 minutes.

   Trim, peel, and chop the onion. Trim the eggplant and cut into 1-inch cubes.

3. Transfer the beef to a plate with a slotted spoon. Add 2 tablespoons oil and then the onion and eggplant to the pot; cook, stirring occasionally until the vegetables begin to soften, 5 to 10 minutes.

   Strip 1 cup basil leaves from the stems and chop.

4. Stir 2 tablespoons curry paste or powder into the eggplant and cook until fragrant, 1 to 2 minutes. Add the coconut milk, basil, and beef with any juices. Bring to a boil, reduce the heat so the mixture bubbles gently but steadily, and cover.

5. Cook, adding a splash of water if the skillet gets dry, until the beef and eggplant are tender, 10 to 15 minutes.
   Cut the lime into wedges. Chop 1/4 cup cilantro.

6. When the beef and eggplant are tender, add more liquid if the skillet is dry; taste and adjust the seasoning. Garnish with the cilantro and serve with the lime wedges.

VARIATIONS

Curry-Braised Beef and Potatoes
Instead of eggplant, use 3 large potatoes, cut into ½-inch cubes.

Braised Beef and Eggplant with Tomato-Yogurt Sauce
Omit the basil and curry paste or powder. Add 3 cloves garlic, minced, along with the onion and eggplant. Swap one 15-ounce can diced tomatoes plus ½ cup Greek yogurt for the coconut milk. Use lemon instead of lime and parsley instead of cilantro.

NOTES

MAKE YOUR OWN
Curry Powder 758

EVEN FASTER
Skip the browning; put all the ingredients except the lime and cilantro in the pot, bring to a simmer, and cover. Cook, stirring once or twice, until the beef and vegetables are tender, 15 to 20 minutes.

The smaller you cut the beef and eggplant, the faster they will cook.

IF YOU HAVE MORE TIME
Brown the beef on all sides.

SIDES

White Rice 941

Sesame Noodles 949

Quinoa 945

Cucumber Salad 915

SPEED SERVES 4

Pan-Roasted Beef Tenderloin with Potatoes

Beef tenderloin roasted in a sizzling oven gets a crackly crust while maintaining luscious, rosy flesh. It's a roast as decadent as it is fast, with time to make crisp potatoes alongside.

Ingredients

2 pounds russet or Yukon Gold potatoes

1 ½ pounds beef tenderloin in 1 piece

4 tablespoons olive oil

Salt and pepper

Prep | Cook

1. Heat the oven to 500°F; put a roasting pan in the oven while it heats up.

   Peel the potatoes if you like and cut them into 1-inch chunks.

2. Pat the beef dry with a paper towel; rub it with 1 tablespoon olive oil and sprinkle with salt and pepper.

3. When the oven is hot, carefully remove the roasting pan. Put the beef in the middle and scatter the potatoes around it. Drizzle the potatoes with 3 tablespoons oil and sprinkle with salt and pepper.

4. Roast, turning the beef once and stirring the potatoes occasionally until the beef is somewhere between rare and medium-rare (120°to 125°F), 20 to 25 minutes. Transfer the beef to a cutting board.

5. If the potatoes still need a little more time to become tender and crisp, continue roasting while the beef rests. Thickly slice the beef and serve it with the potatoes, with any accumulated juices spooned over the top.

VARIATIONS

Pan-Roasted Beef Tenderloin with Chile Sweet Potatoes

Substitute sweet potatoes for regular potatoes and toss with 2 teaspoons chili powder or smoked paprika when you add them to the roasting pan.

Pan-Roasted Pork Tenderloin with Celery Root

Substitute 1 ½ pounds pork tenderloin for the beef and celery root for the potatoes. Since pork tenderloin is smaller than beef, it will roast faster; cook until it reaches 145°F, 15 to 20 minutes.

NOTES

GIVE IT A REST

When cooking thicker cuts of meat like steaks, chops, and roasts, don't slice the meat immediately after cooking. If you slice too soon, the hot juices, which have become concentrated in the cool center, will spill out, leaving your cutting board wet and your meat dry. To prevent this, let the meat sit on a plate or cutting board for 5 to 10 minutes. During that time the outer edges of the meat will cool a bit and reabsorb some of the juices that have retreated into the center.

SIDES

Green Salad 911

Creamed Spinach 936

Garlicky Mushrooms 956

Sautéed Greens with Garlic 924

SPEED SERVES 4 TO 6

Skillet Meat Loaf

Flattening out meat loaf to cook it in a skillet not only reduces cooking time but also dramatically increases the surface area to maximize crunch. It's faster *and* better.

Ingredients

1 tablespoon olive oil

1 cup bread crumbs

½ cup milk

1 pound ground beef

1 pound ground pork

Salt and pepper

2 ounces Parmesan cheese (½ cup grated)

1 garlic clove

1 egg

¼ cup ketchup

Prep | Cook

1. Heat the oven to 425°F. Grease a large skillet (preferably cast iron) with 1 tablespoon olive oil and put it in the oven while it heats and you prepare the meat loaf.
2. Combine 1 cup bread crumbs, ½ cup milk, the ground beef and ground pork, and a sprinkle of salt and pepper in a large bowl.

   Grate ½ cup Parmesan and add to the bowl. Peel and mince 1 garlic clove and add it to the bowl.

   Crack the egg into the bowl.
3. Gently mix the ingredients together with your hands, then carefully pack the mixture into the skillet. Drizzle ¼ cup ketchup on top.
4. Bake until the loaf is firm (a quick-read thermometer inserted into the center should read 160°F), 15 to 20 minutes.
5. Turn the broiler to high and put the rack 4 inches from the heat. Broil the meat loaf until the top is brown and crisp, 2 to 5 minutes.
6. Let cool for a few minutes before slicing into wedges. Serve hot, warm, or at room temperature.

VARIATIONS

Skillet BBQ Meat Loaf
Omit the Parmesan; brush the top with barbecue sauce instead of ketchup.

Skillet Chipotle Meat Loaf
Swap 1 teaspoon cumin and 1 teaspoon chopped chipotle chiles in adobo (or to taste) for the Parmesan; brush the top with a bit of the adobo sauce instead of the ketchup.

Blue Cheese Skillet Meat Loaf
Substitute ½ cup crumbled blue cheese or Gorgonzola for the Parmesan and skip the ketchup.

Skillet Miso Meat Loaf
Substitute ½ cup any miso for the Parmesan and 1 inch peeled and minced ginger for the garlic. Omit the ketchup.

Skillet Lamb Meat Loaf with Harissa Glaze
Substitute ground lamb for the beef and pork and crumbled feta for the Parmesan. Brush the top with ¼ cup harissa thinned with a little water if you can find it. Otherwise stick with the ketchup.

NOTES

MAKE YOUR OWN
Bread Crumbs 71

SIDES

Skin-On Mashed Potatoes 961

Creamy Polenta 947

Two-Step Broccoli 926

Asparagus Gratin 929

Sautéed Greens with Garlic 924

Steak and Potato Enchiladas

There's much to do in this recipe—sautéing potatoes and steak, simmering sauce, rolling tortillas—but it all happens fairly quickly. And when you pull those smoky, cheesy enchiladas from the broiler, you'll be pleased you put in the work.

Ingredients

1 ½ pounds sirloin or flank steak

3 tablespoons vegetable oil, plus more as needed

2 ½ pounds russet or Yukon Gold potatoes

Salt and pepper

One 28-ounce can crushed tomatoes

3 canned chipotle chiles in adobo

2 garlic cloves

4 scallions

4 to 8 ounces Jack cheese (1 to 2 cups grated)

Eight 10-inch flour tortillas

Several sprigs fresh cilantro for garnish

Sour cream for serving

Prep | Cook

1. Turn the broiler to high; put the rack 6 inches from the heat. Put the steak in the freezer.

2. Put 2 tablespoons vegetable oil in a large skillet over medium-low heat.

   Peel the potatoes; shred them in a food processor with a grating disk or by hand with a box grater.

3. Put the potatoes in the skillet, sprinkle with salt and pepper, and raise the heat to medium-high. Cook, stirring occasionally until they soften, 8 to 10 minutes. Add more oil as needed.

4. Put the tomatoes in a small saucepan over medium heat.

   Chop 3 chipotles in adobo; peel and mince 2 garlic cloves. Add them to the saucepan.

5. Bring the tomato mixture to a bubble, then reduce the heat and let it simmer gently, adding a splash of water if it gets too thick.

   Remove the steak from the freezer and slice it as thinly as you can without shredding it.

6. When the potatoes have begun to soften, continue to cook, stirring more frequently, until they are tender but not mushy, 2 or 3 minutes. Remove them from the skillet and wipe it out.

7. Add 1 tablespoon oil to the skillet, followed by the steak. Sprinkle with salt and pepper and cook, stirring once or twice, until it's lightly browned, 3 to 5 minutes.

   Trim and chop the scallions.

   Grate 1 to 2 cups Jack cheese.

8. When the steak is lightly browned, return the potatoes to the skillet, add the scallions, and stir to combine. Taste and adjust the seasoning.

9. Spread a thin layer of tomato sauce into the bottom of a 9 × 13-inch baking dish. Divide the potato mixture among 8 tortillas, roll them tightly, and put them in the baking dish. Spread the rest of the sauce over the top and sprinkle with the cheese.

10. Broil until the cheese is bubbly and browned, 3 to 5 minutes.

    Chop several sprigs cilantro.

11. Divide the enchiladas among 4 plates, sprinkle with the cilantro, and serve with a dollop of sour cream.

VARIATIONS

Pork and Sweet Potato Enchiladas
Use pork loin or shoulder instead of the steak and sweet potatoes instead of russet or Yukon Gold.

Smoky Steak and Potato Enchiladas
Substitute 1 teaspoon each smoked paprika and cumin for the chipotles.

SIDES

White Rice 941

Chile-Cumin Black Beans 937

Jícama and Radish Salad 918

Ripe Plantains 960

SPEED ◔ SERVES 4

Beef Stew

It's impossible to replicate the fall-apart tenderness of long-simmered meat quickly, but this shortcut stew has all the deep flavor of browned beef and is given extra body with a sprinkling of flour. The result: a hearty bowl in less than 45 minutes.

Ingredients

2 tablespoons olive oil

1 ½ pounds boneless beef chuck or round

Salt and pepper

2 pounds russet or Yukon Gold potatoes

2 large carrots

3 celery stalks

2 tablespoons flour

2 sprigs fresh thyme

3 cups chicken or beef stock or water

Several sprigs fresh parsley for garnish

1 cup frozen peas

Prep | Cook

1. Put 2 tablespoons oil in a large pot over medium-high heat.

   Cut the beef into 1-inch chunks.

2. Put the beef in the pot, sprinkle with salt and pepper, and cook, turning once, until well browned on 2 sides, 8 to 10 minutes.

   Peel the potatoes if you like. Trim and peel the carrots and trim the celery; cut them all into ½-inch chunks.

3. When the beef is browned, add 2 tablespoons flour to the pot and cook, stirring until the flour is absorbed into the fat, about 2 minutes. Add 2 thyme sprigs and 3 cups stock or water. Bring to a boil. Add the potatoes, carrots, and celery; then adjust the heat so the mixture bubbles gently but steadily.

4. Cover and cook, stirring occasionally and adding more liquid if the mixture gets too dry, until the beef and vegetables are tender, 25 to 30 minutes.

   Strip the parsley leaves from several sprigs and chop them.

5. When the beef and vegetables are tender, stir in 1 cup peas and cook until they're warmed through. Taste and adjust the seasoning. Divide among 4 bowls, garnish with the parsley, and serve immediately.

VARIATIONS

Beef Carbonnade with Mushrooms
Swap 1 pound chopped cremini or button mushrooms for the carrots and celery. Omit the flour and substitute 1 ½ cups dark beer for the stock or water. If you like, stir in 1 tablespoon Dijon mustard before serving.

Lamb or Pork Stew
Substitute lamb or pork shoulder for the beef.

Beef, Lamb, or Pork Stew with Root Vegetables
Works with any of the cuts from the main recipe or the variations. Use parsnips instead of carrots and 12 ounces celery root instead of the celery. Cut everything into ½-inch chunks.

NOTES

MAKE YOUR OWN

Chicken Stock 213

Beef Stock 212

EVEN FASTER
The smaller the pieces of beef, the faster they will become tender.

IF YOU HAVE MORE TIME

Thicker Beef Stew
Brown 2-inch chunks of beef on all sides, then remove from the pot and brown some large chunks of chopped carrots, celery, and onions. Add the flour and cook it for 2 minutes before returning the beef to the pot along with the herbs and stock. Simmer until the meat and vegetables are very tender, even falling apart if you like, 45 to 90 minutes.

SIDES

Buttered Egg Noodles 948

Skin-On Mashed Potatoes 961

Creamy Polenta 947

Warm Buttery Bread 906

SPEED ◔ SERVES 4

Stir-Fried Pork with Edamame and Scallions

Edamame add vibrant color and a fresh flavor to stir-fries. Add them right out of the freezer bag toward the end: Their moisture will loosen up any flavors stuck to the bottom of the pan.

Ingredients

2 tablespoons vegetable oil

1 ½ pounds boneless pork loin

Salt and pepper

1 inch fresh ginger

2 garlic cloves

6 scallions

3 cups frozen shelled edamame

1 lemon

1 tablespoon soy sauce

Prep | Cook

1. Put 2 tablespoons vegetable oil in a large skillet over medium-high heat.

   Slice the pork as thinly as you can.

2. Add the pork to the skillet, sprinkle with salt and pepper, and cook, stirring occasionally until lightly browned, 3 to 5 minutes.

   Peel 1 inch ginger and 2 garlic cloves; mince them together.

   Trim and chop the scallions; separate the white and light green bottoms from the dark green tops.

3. Add the ginger, garlic, and scallion bottoms to the pork. Cook, stirring until fragrant, about a minute.

4. Add 3 cups edamame and a sprinkle of salt and pepper. Cook, stirring occasionally until they are heated through, 2 or 3 minutes.

   Halve the lemon.

5. Squeeze in the lemon juice and add 1 tablespoon soy sauce; toss to coat. Stir in the scallion tops, taste and adjust the seasoning, and serve.

VARIATIONS

Stir-Fried Pork with Peas and Shallots
Swap olive oil for vegetable, 3 minced shallots for the garlic and ginger, peas for the edamame, and Dijon mustard for the soy sauce.

Stir-Fried Pork with Onions and Black Beans
Instead of scallions, chop 1 medium onion and add it in Step 3; use black beans instead of edamame. Garnish with cilantro.

Stir-Fried Pork with Corn and Scallions
Substitute 1 minced fresh hot green chile for the ginger, corn kernels for the edamame, lime for the lemon, and 1 tablespoon chopped chipotle chiles in adobo for the soy sauce.

SIDES

White Rice 941

Sesame Noodles 949

Soy Slaw 923

Panfried Rice Noodles 951

Scallion Pancakes 940

SPEED ◐ SERVES 4

Seared Pork Chops with Apples and Onions

Pork chops, apples, and onions make one of the greatest flavor combinations. Rarely do so few ingredients taste like so much.

Ingredients

2 tablespoons olive oil

Four 1-inch-thick pork chops (1 ½ to 2 pounds)

Salt and pepper

3 medium apples

1 large onion

½ cup chicken stock or water, plus more as needed

Several sprigs fresh parsley for garnish

1 tablespoon butter

Prep | Cook

1. Put 2 tablespoons olive oil in a large skillet over medium-high heat.

   Pat the pork chops dry with a paper towel and sprinkle with salt and pepper.

2. When the oil is hot, add the chops and raise the heat to high. Cook until the chops are nicely browned on the bottom, 3 to 5 minutes.

   Core and slice the apples. Trim, peel, halve, and slice the onion.

3. When the chops are nicely browned on the bottom, turn them and scatter the apples and onion around (and on top if necessary). Sprinkle with salt and pepper and cook, tossing them occasionally until the apples and onion soften, 3 to 5 minutes.

4. Add ½ cup stock or water and scrape up any browned bits from the bottom of the pan. Bring to a boil; then adjust the heat so the mixture simmers. Cover the skillet and cook until the chops are tender and cooked through, 5 to 10 minutes.

   Strip the parsley leaves from several sprigs and chop them.

5. When the chops are tender and cooked through, transfer them to a platter. If the skillet is dry, add a splash of stock or water to make it slightly saucy and scrape up any browned bits from the bottom of the pan.

6. Stir in 1 tablespoon butter and the parsley. Taste and adjust the seasoning, pour the apples and onions on top of the pork, and serve immediately.

VARIATIONS

Seared Pork Chops with Fennel
Swap 3 medium fennel bulbs for the apples and onions.

Seared Pork Chops with Brussels Sprouts
Substitute 1 pound halved Brussels sprouts for the apples and onions. Brown the pork chops well on both sides, then remove them from the skillet, add the Brussels sprouts, and sauté until lightly browned, about 5 minutes. Add the stock, return the chops to the skillet, and proceed from the rest of Step 4.

NOTES

MAKE YOUR OWN
Chicken Stock 213

EVEN FASTER
If you can find smoked pork chops, which taste like ham, all you need to do is brown them and soften the apples and onions. Simmer for a few minutes to make the mixture saucy if you like, but they're already cooked.

BONELESS VS. BONE-IN PORK CHOPS
Chops that still have the bone may take an extra few minutes to cook, but the bone adds flavor and keeps the meat moister. When given a choice, I always opt for bone-in chops that are at least an inch thick. Many supermarket chops are quite skinny, which greatly increases your chances of overcooking them. Thicker chops with the bone give you a much better shot at hitting the rosy-pink sweet spot.

SIDES

Skin-On Mashed Potatoes 961

Green Salad 911

Skillet Stuffing 952

Couscous 910

SPEED ◐ SERVES 4

BBQ Baby Back Ribs

Baby back ribs are the meaty bones from the loin that are attached to pork chops. They cook much faster than their counterpart spareribs. A long-distance run in the broiler yields crusty, saucy, finger-licking barbecue in a hurry.

Ingredients

Salt

1 tablespoon sugar

2 teaspoons cumin

Pepper

1 tablespoon plus 2 teaspoons chili powder

1 tablespoon paprika

2 or 3 pounds baby back ribs (2 or 3 slabs)

1 garlic clove

1 cup ketchup

¼ cup red wine or water

2 tablespoons wine vinegar

1 teaspoon soy sauce

Prep | Cook

1. Turn the broiler to high; put the rack 6 inches from the heat.
2. Combine 1 ½ teaspoons salt, 1 tablespoon sugar, 2 teaspoons cumin, 1 teaspoon pepper, 2 teaspoons chili powder, and 1 tablespoon paprika in a small bowl. Rub the spice mixture all over the ribs and place them on a broiler pan or baking sheet.
3. Broil the ribs, turning as necessary, until both sides of the slabs are browned, 8 to 12 minutes.
   Mince 1 garlic clove; put it in a small saucepan.
4. Add to the saucepan 1 cup ketchup, ¼ cup red wine or water, 2 tablespoons wine vinegar, 1 teaspoon soy sauce, 1 tablespoon chili powder, and a sprinkle of salt and pepper. Bring to a simmer and cook, stirring occasionally while the ribs broil.
5. When the ribs are browned on both sides, start basting with the barbecue sauce. Cook, turning as necessary, until the exterior is nicely caramelized, 7 to 12 minutes.
6. Cut the slabs into individual ribs if you like and serve with the remaining sauce on the side.

VARIATIONS

BBQ Ginger-Hoisin Baby Back Ribs
Swap five-spice powder for the paprika, ½ cup hoisin sauce for ½ cup of the ketchup, rice vinegar for the wine vinegar, and 1 tablespoon minced ginger for the chili powder. Just put the ginger in the sauce; no need to rub any on the ribs.

BBQ Maple-Dijon Baby Back Ribs
Replace the ketchup with ¼ cup Dijon mustard. Add 2 tablespoons maple syrup to the sauce.

NOTES

MAKE YOUR OWN
Chili Powder 758

EVEN FASTER
Instead of making the barbecue sauce as described in Step 4, use about 1 ½ cups Barbecue Sauce (145) if you have some in the fridge.

IF YOU HAVE MORE TIME
For fall-off-the-bone tender ribs, bake them in a 275°F oven until they are as tender as you like, up to a few hours. Baste them with the sauce, then broil or roast at 500°F until the sauce browns.

SIDES

Coleslaw 923

Chile-Cumin Black Beans 937

German-Style Potato Salad 962

Watermelon, Feta, and Mint Salad 922

French Fries 963

SPEED ◐ SERVES 4

Pork Souvlaki with Zucchini

An intense Greek-style marinade gives chunks of pork and zucchini plenty of punch before broiling—no skewers necessary. There's minimal checking and turning, so use the downtime to make a side like rice pilaf or toasted pita.

Ingredients

2 lemons

1 small bunch fresh mint

3 garlic cloves

2 large zucchini

1 ½ pounds boneless pork shoulder

¼ cup olive oil, plus more for garnish (optional)

¼ cup red wine

½ cup Greek yogurt

1 tablespoon dried oregano

Salt and pepper

Several sprigs fresh parsley for garnish

Prep | Cook

1. Turn the broiler to high; put the rack 4 inches from the heat.

   Halve the lemons and squeeze the juice into a large bowl.

   Strip ½ cup mint leaves from the stems, chop, and add them to the bowl.

   Peel and mince 3 garlic cloves; add them to the bowl.

   Trim the zucchini, cut it into 1-inch chunks, and add it to the bowl.

   Cut the pork shoulder into 1-inch chunks and add it to the bowl.

2. Add to the bowl ¼ cup olive oil, ¼ cup red wine, ½ cup Greek yogurt, 1 tablespoon oregano, and a sprinkle of salt and pepper. Toss to combine.

3. Put the zucchini on 1 side of a rimmed baking sheet and broil for 2 minutes.

4. Add the pork to the other side of the baking sheet. Cook, turning everything once, until the zucchini is tender and browned, 6 to 10 minutes, and the pork is nicely browned on 2 sides and just cooked through, 5 to 10 minutes (cut into a piece to check for doneness after about 5 minutes).

5. Remove each ingredient as it is done, leaving the other to finish if need be. Transfer the food to a platter as it finishes cooking.

   Strip the parsley leaves from several sprigs and chop them.

6. Once all the pork and zucchini are on the platter, drizzle with a little extra oil if you like, garnish with the parsley, and serve.

VARIATIONS

Broiled Jerk Pork with Pineapple

Instead of the yogurt marinade, use the spice paste from Jerk Chicken and Onions (page 650). Substitute 1 small pineapple, cut into 1-inch chunks, for the zucchini.

Broiled Pork Paprikash with Red Peppers

Use only 1 lemon. Swap parsley for the mint, sour cream for the yogurt, and paprika for the oregano. Use 3 or 4 large red bell peppers, sliced, instead of the zucchini.

NOTES

IF YOU HAVE MORE TIME

Marinate the pork for at least a few hours or overnight; it will become more tender. Add the zucchini to marinate for the last 30 minutes.

SIDES

Rice Pilaf 944

Crisp Seasoned Pita 908

White Rice 941

Bulgur with Lemon and Parsley 946

SPEED ◐ SERVES 4

Spice-Rubbed Pork with Pineapple Salsa

Pork tenderloin is a perfect cut for this kind of broiling because the outside browns in the time it takes to cook through. A spice rub heightens the smoky char, while a fast pineapple salsa—made in the same skillet—adds sweetness.

Ingredients

1 teaspoon cumin

½ teaspoon chili powder

½ teaspoon paprika

Salt and pepper

1 pork tenderloin (1 ½ pounds)

1 small pineapple

1 small red onion

1 small bunch fresh cilantro

2 limes

1 tablespoon vegetable oil

Prep | Cook

1. Turn the broiler to high; put the rack 6 inches from the heat.

   Combine 1 teaspoon cumin, ½ teaspoon chili powder, ½ teaspoon paprika, and some salt and pepper in a small bowl.

2. Rub the mixture all over the tenderloin. Put it in a large ovenproof skillet and broil, turning periodically, until browned all over and cooked through (a quick-read thermometer inserted into the center should read 145°F), 10 to 15 minutes.

   Peel, core, and chop the pineapple into ½-inch chunks. Trim, peel, and chop the onion. Chop ¼ cup cilantro. Halve the limes.

3. When the pork is done, transfer it to a plate and tent with aluminum foil.

4. Put 1 tablespoon vegetable oil in the skillet and set it over medium-high heat. When hot, add the pineapple and onion; sprinkle with salt and pepper. Cook until they begin to soften, 3 to 5 minutes.

5. Add the cilantro, squeeze in the lime juice, and add any meat juices to the skillet. Taste and adjust the seasoning. Slice the pork and serve with the salsa.

VARIATIONS

Curry-Rubbed Pork Tenderloin with Mango Salsa
Substitute 1 teaspoon curry powder for the chili powder and paprika and 2 ripe mangoes for the pineapple.

Paprika-Rubbed Pork Tenderloin with Peach and Tomato Salsa
Swap 2 teaspoons smoked paprika for the cumin, chili powder, and paprika and 2 peaches and 2 tomatoes for the pineapple.

NOTES

MAKE YOUR OWN
Chili Powder 758

EVEN FASTER
Add the pineapple and onion to the pan with the pork right after chopping them. Stir them occasionally as the pork broils and make a raw salsa with the same ingredients.

Garnish with the lime juice and cilantro and serve with the salsa.

SIDES

Warm Tortillas 907

White Rice 941

Refried Beans 938

Mexican Street Corn 932

MASTER RECIPE

Spice Blends

A big reward for 10 minutes of work, especially when you taste how much these mixtures enhance your food: The flavors that come from toasting and grinding your own spices blow store-bought blends out of the water. These yield about ¼ cup—enough to store and use for weeks or even months. And once you commit to buying the first round of whole spices, you'll have them on hand to make new batches whenever you run out.

Chili Powder

1 Toast the Spices

Put the following in a small skillet: 2 tablespoons ground ancho or other mild dried chile, ½ teaspoon cayenne, ½ teaspoon black peppercorns, 2 teaspoons cumin seeds, 2 teaspoons coriander seeds, and 1 tablespoon dried oregano (Mexican if you can find it). Turn the heat to medium and toast the spices, shaking the pan occasionally until the mixture is fragrant, 3 to 5 minutes.

2 Grind and Store

Let the spices cool, then transfer them to a spice or coffee grinder and grind until they become a coarse powder. Store in a tightly covered opaque container for up to several weeks.

Mild Curry Powder

1 Toast the Spices

Put the following in a medium skillet: ¼ teaspoon nutmeg pieces, 1 teaspoon cardamom seeds, 3 cloves, one 3-inch cinnamon stick, 1 teaspoon black peppercorns, 2 tablespoons cumin seeds, ¼ cup coriander seeds, and 2 bay leaves. Turn the heat to medium and toast the spices, shaking the pan occasionally, until the mixture is lightly browned and fragrant, 2 or 3 minutes. Add 1 teaspoon ground fenugreek and cook for another minute.

2 Grind and Store

Let the spices cool, then transfer them to a spice or coffee grinder and grind until they become a coarse powder. Store in a tightly covered opaque container for up to several months.

Hot Curry Powder

1 Toast the Spices

Put the following in a medium skillet: 2 small dried Thai or other hot chiles, 1 tablespoon black peppercorns, 1 tablespoon coriander seeds, 1 teaspoon cumin seeds, and 1 teaspoon fennel seeds. Turn the heat to medium and toast the spices, shaking the pan occasionally until the mixture is lightly browned and fragrant, 2 or 3 minutes. Add 1 teaspoon ground fenugreek, 1 tablespoon ground turmeric, and 1 tablespoon ground ginger; cook for another minute.

2 Grind and Store

Let the spices cool, then transfer them to a spice or coffee grinder and grind until they become a coarse powder. At this point if you want a little extra kick, add a pinch of cayenne. Store in a tightly covered opaque container for up to several months.

Five-Spice Powder

1 Toast the Spices

Put the following in a medium skillet: 1 tablespoon Sichuan peppercorns or black peppercorns, 6 star anise, 1 ½ teaspoons whole cloves, one 3-inch stick cinnamon, and 2 tablespoons fennel seeds. Turn the heat to medium and toast the spices, shaking the pan occasionally until the mixture is lightly browned and fragrant, 2 or 3 minutes.

2 Grind and Store

Let the spices cool, then transfer them to a spice or coffee grinder and grind until they become a coarse powder. Store in a tightly covered opaque container for up to several months; use to add an exotic kick to stir-fries, soups, pilafs, or sauces.

Toasting Dried Chiles

The best way to bring out the smoky flavor of dried chiles is to toast them first. Just a few minutes on each side in a dry skillet over medium heat will do the trick, and you'll be able to smell them getting toasty. But unless the chile is really featured prominently in a dish, I usually don't bother with toasting.

Five-Spice Pork Meatballs with Bok Choy

Grinding your own meat doesn't seem like a shortcut, but once the food processor is in use you can use it for everything—no mincing by hand.

Ingredients

4 tablespoons vegetable oil

1 large head bok choy (1 ½ pounds)

2 scallions

1 inch fresh ginger

1 bunch fresh cilantro

Salt and pepper

1 pound boneless pork shoulder

1 teaspoon five-spice powder or more pepper

½ cup bread crumbs

1 egg

Soy sauce for serving

Prep | Cook

1. Put 2 tablespoons vegetable oil in a large skillet over medium-high heat.

   Trim the bok choy; cut the leaves into wide ribbons and thinly slice the stems.

2. Add the stems to the skillet and cook, stirring occasionally until they start to soften, 3 to 5 minutes.

   Trim and chop the scallions.

   Peel and chop 1 inch ginger.

   Pull ¼ cup cilantro sprigs from the bunch.

3. When the bok choy stems start to soften, add the leaves and a sprinkle of salt and pepper to the skillet. Cook, stirring occasionally until the leaves wilt and the stems are nearly tender but still have some crunch, 3 or 4 minutes.

   Cut the pork shoulder into 1-inch chunks.

4. When the bok choy is done, transfer to a platter and cover to keep warm.

5. Put the scallions, ginger, and cilantro in a food processor and pulse until finely chopped. Add the pork, 1 teaspoon five-spice powder, and ½ cup bread crumbs, and crack in the egg. Sprinkle with salt and pepper. Pulse, scraping down the sides of the bowl as necessary, until the pork is ground and the mixture combined.

6. Wipe out the skillet, add 2 tablespoons oil, and return the skillet to medium-high heat.

7. Use 2 spoons to roughly shape meatballs and drop them into the skillet as you go; cook, turning occasionally until they are browned all over and cooked through, 8 to 10 minutes. Serve with the bok choy and pass soy sauce at the table.

VARIATIONS

Mustard-Herb Pork Meatballs with Broccoli Rabe
Swap broccoli rabe for bok choy, ¼ cup chopped onion for the scallions, 1 teaspoon chopped fresh rosemary or thyme for the five-spice powder, 2 teaspoons Dijon mustard for the ginger, and parsley for the cilantro.

Chorizo Meatballs with Chard
Use fresh Mexican chorizo instead of pork. Substitute chard for bok choy, ¼ cup chopped onions for the scallions, 1 teaspoon smoked paprika for the five-spice powder, 3 garlic cloves for the ginger, and parsley for the cilantro.

Lamb and Feta Meatballs with Kale
Use lamb shoulder instead of pork. Swap kale for the bok choy, ¼ cup chopped onion for the scallions, 1 teaspoon chopped rosemary or thyme for the five-spice powder, ¼ cup crumbled feta for the ginger, and mint leaves for the cilantro.

NOTES

MAKE YOUR OWN
Bread Crumbs 71

EVEN FASTER
Use preground pork instead of grinding your own. Finely chop the scallions, ginger, and cilantro before mixing them into the pork by hand.

IF YOU HAVE MORE TIME
If you prefer rounder meatballs, roll them by hand.

SIDES

White Rice 941

Sesame Noodles 949

Scallion Pancakes 940

Tomato Salad with Sesame and Soy 913

SPEED ◐ SERVES 4

Homemade Chorizo with Pinto Beans

Unlike Spanish chorizo, which is cured until dried, Mexican-style chorizo is a fresh sausage: essentially spiced pork you cook in a skillet. That means you can whip up a batch from scratch in no time, cooking it loose for tacos or shaping patties for chorizo burgers.

Ingredients

2 garlic cloves

1 ½ pounds boneless pork shoulder

1 teaspoon cumin

1 teaspoon chili powder

¼ teaspoon cayenne

Pinch of cinnamon

Pinch of cloves

1 teaspoon cider vinegar

Salt and pepper

2 tablespoons vegetable oil

1 large onion

2 cups cooked or canned pinto beans (one 15-ounce can)

1 lime

1 small bunch fresh cilantro

Prep | Cook

Peel 2 garlic cloves. Pulse in the food processor until minced.

Cut the pork into 2-inch chunks.

1. Add the pork to the food processor along with 1 teaspoon cumin, 1 teaspoon chili powder, ¼ teaspoon cayenne, a pinch each of cinnamon and cloves, 1 teaspoon cider vinegar, and a sprinkle of salt and pepper. Pulse the mixture until the pork is coarsely ground but not puréed.

2. Put 2 tablespoons vegetable oil in a large skillet over medium-high heat.

   Trim, peel, and chop the onion.

3. When the oil is hot, add the chorizo mixture and the onion. Cook, stirring occasionally until the chorizo is cooked through and crisp, 5 to 10 minutes.

   If you're using canned beans, rinse and drain them.

   Cut the lime into wedges; chop ¼ cup cilantro.

4. When the chorizo is crisp, stir in the beans and cook, stirring occasionally until they heat through. Taste and adjust the seasoning, garnish with the cilantro, and serve with the lime wedges.

VARIATIONS

Homemade Spanish-Style Chorizo with Chickpeas
The flavor of cured Spanish chorizo, made fresh: Swap 1 tablespoon smoked paprika for the chili powder, cayenne, cinnamon, and cloves and sherry vinegar for the cider vinegar. Use olive oil instead of vegetable oil. Swap chickpeas for the pinto beans, lemon for the lime, and parsley for the cilantro.

Homemade Italian Sausage with White Beans
Omit the cumin, chili powder, cayenne, cinnamon, and cloves; instead use 1 tablespoon fennel seeds and 1/4 teaspoon red chile flakes. Substitute red wine vinegar for the cider vinegar. Use olive oil instead of vegetable oil. Replace the pinto beans with white beans, lime with lemon, and cilantro with basil.

NOTES

MAKE YOUR OWN

Chili Powder 758

Cooked Beans 496

EVEN FASTER
Use preground pork rather than grinding your own.

SIDES

Warm Tortillas 907

White Rice 941

Jícama and Radish Salad 918

Avocado with Hot Sauce and Cilantro 920

Ripe Plantains 960

SPEED ◐ SERVES 4

Maple-Glazed Ham Steaks with Collards

Smoked ham steaks are a great addition to your fast-cooking pantry; they're flavorful and, because they're precooked, they can be turned into a meal without much effort. Here a tangle of sliced collards soaks up caramelized bits of maple-mustard glaze as the collards wilt.

Ingredients

2 tablespoons vegetable oil

¼ cup maple syrup

1 tablespoon cider vinegar

1 teaspoon Dijon mustard

1 ½ pounds smoked ham steaks

Salt and pepper

1½ pounds collard greens

½ cup beer or chicken stock

Prep | Cook

1. Put 2 tablespoons vegetable oil in a large skillet over medium-high heat.

2. Combine ¼ cup maple syrup, 1 tablespoon cider vinegar, and 1 teaspoon Dijon in a small bowl. Brush the glaze on 1 side of the ham steaks and sprinkle with salt and pepper.

3. Add the ham to the skillet glaze side down, brush the tops with glaze, and sprinkle with salt and pepper. Cook, turning and brushing with glaze periodically until the ham is nicely caramelized on both sides, 4 to 6 minutes.
   Trim the collards and slice them into thin ribbons.

4. When the ham is caramelized, transfer it to a cutting board and lightly tent with foil to keep warm. Add ½ cup beer or chicken stock to the skillet, stirring to scrape up any browned bits from the bottom.

5. Add the collards and sprinkle with salt and pepper. Cover and cook, stirring occasionally until they just wilt, 4 or 5 minutes.

   Cut the ham into thick slices.

6. When the collards are wilted, taste and adjust the seasoning and divide them among 4 plates. Lay the ham slices over the top or on the side and serve.

VARIATIONS

BBQ-Glazed Ham Steaks with Collards
Swap ¼ cup barbecue sauce for the maple syrup, vinegar, and mustard.

Honey-Mustard-Glazed Ham Steaks with Kale
Swap 3 tablespoons honey for the maple syrup and kale for the collards.

NOTES

MAKE YOUR OWN
Chicken Stock 213

EVEN FASTER
If you have room in your skillet, add the beer and collards to the ham steaks after you flip them the first time. Cover and simmer until the collards wilt.

SMOKED PORK STEAKS
If you can't find smoked ham steaks or smoked pork chops, just have the deli counter slice some extra-thick pieces of smoked sandwich ham.

SIDES

White Rice 914

Creamy Polenta 947

Skin-On Mashed Potatoes 961

Chile-Cumin Black Beans 937

Coleslaw 923

SPEED ◑ SERVES 4

Braised Pork with Cabbage and Beer

It's hard to go wrong with pork, cabbage, and beer. Here the pork is thinly sliced and the cabbage shredded to get them as tender as possible during their quick simmer.

Ingredients

2 tablespoons vegetable oil

1 ½ pounds boneless pork shoulder

Salt and pepper

1 onion

1 Savoy or green cabbage (about 1 ½ pounds)

1 teaspoon caraway seeds

1 teaspoon mustard seeds

1 cup beer

2 tablespoons red wine vinegar or cider vinegar

Prep | Cook

1. Put 2 tablespoons vegetable oil in a large skillet or large pot over medium-high heat.

   Thinly slice the pork.

2. Add the pork to the skillet, sprinkle with salt and pepper, and cook, stirring occasionally until it is lightly browned, 3 to 5 minutes.

   Trim, peel, halve, and slice the onion.

3. Add the onion and cook, stirring occasionally until it softens, 3 to 5 minutes.

   Trim, core, and shred the cabbage.

4. Add the cabbage along with 1 teaspoon caraway seeds, 1 teaspoon mustard seeds, 1 cup beer, 2 tablespoons vinegar, and a sprinkle of salt and pepper. Bring the mixture to a boil, then adjust the heat so that it bubbles steadily.

5. Cook, stirring occasionally and adding more liquid if the mixture gets too dry, until the cabbage is tender and the liquid has reduced into a sauce, 8 to 12 minutes. Taste and adjust the seasoning and serve.

VARIATIONS

Braised Pork with Red Cabbage and Red Wine
Substitute red onion for yellow, red cabbage for Savoy, 2 sprigs fresh rosemary for the caraway and mustard seeds, and red wine for the beer. Use red wine vinegar.

Braised Pork with Celery and White Wine
Choose a sweetish white (like Riesling) for a surprisingly amazing sauce. Use 1 bunch celery instead of the cabbage; reserve the leaves to chop for garnish. (And fennel is always a good substitute for celery.)

NOTES

IF YOU HAVE MORE TIME
Use larger chunks of pork shoulder and simmer until they begin to fall apart, up to a couple of hours. By that point the cabbage will be meltingly tender: quite nice.

SIDES

German-Style Potato Salad 962

Skin-On Mashed Potatoes 961

Warm Buttery Bread 906

Skillet Stuffing 952

Quinoa 945

SPEED ◑ SERVES 4

Browned and Braised Sausage and Endive

The near-perfect combination of fatty sausage and bitter endive needs very little embellishment; as the endive cooks and mingles with the sausage, it turns sweet and rich but holds just enough of its edge to balance the flavor of the pork.

Ingredients

2 tablespoons olive oil

1 ½ pounds hot or sweet Italian sausage links

4 heads endive (1 to 1 ½ pounds)

1 lemon

2 ounces Parmesan cheese (½ cup grated)

Salt and pepper

½ cup chicken stock, white wine, or water

Prep | Cook

1. Put 2 tablespoons olive oil in a large skillet over medium heat. When it's hot, add the sausages and cook, turning occasionally until nicely browned all over, 10 to 12 minutes.

   Trim and chop the endive.

   Grate the lemon zest and ½ cup Parmesan (refrigerate the fruit for another use).

2. When the sausage is browned, remove it from the skillet; add the endive and a sprinkle of salt and pepper. Cook, stirring occasionally until the endive is lightly browned, 6 to 8 minutes.

3. Return the sausages to the pan along with ½ cup stock, wine, or water. Adjust the heat so the mixtures bubbles steadily but not vigorously; partially cover the pan and cook 3 to 5 minutes.

4. Add the lemon zest and Parmesan to the skillet and stir. Taste and adjust the seasoning and serve.

VARIATIONS

10 Other Vegetables to Use

1. Radicchio
2. Escarole
3. Kale
4. Brussels sprouts
5. Bell peppers
6. Onions
7. Mushrooms
8. Broccoli
9. Broccoli rabe
10. Leeks

NOTES

MAKE YOUR OWN

Chicken Stock 213

EVEN FASTER

Slice the sausages or crumble them into the pan before cooking. When they're lightly browned, add the endive and proceed as directed.

SIDES

Pasta, Plain and Simple 948

Garlic Bread 906

Skin-On Mashed Potatoes 961

Refried White Beans with Rosemary 938

SPEED ◐ SERVES 4

Bangers and Mash

This British meat and potatoes staple often uses the rendered sausage fat as the base of a gravy. You can mash the potatoes right in the skillet that you used to cook the sausage.

Ingredients

Salt

4 to 6 medium russet or Yukon Gold potatoes (2 pounds)

2 tablespoons olive oil

1 ½ pounds whole sausage links (preferably flavored with sage)

½ cup milk, plus more as needed

4 tablespoons (½ stick) butter

1 teaspoon cider vinegar

1 teaspoon dry mustard

Pepper

Prep | Cook

1. Fill a large pot with about an inch of water; add a pinch of salt and turn the heat to high.

   Halve the potatoes lengthwise and cut them into thin slices, dropping them into the pot as you go.

2. Cover and boil until the potatoes are tender and just breaking apart, 15 to 20 minutes.

3. While the potatoes cook, put 2 tablespoons olive oil in a large skillet over medium heat. When it's hot, add the sausages and cook, turning occasionally until nicely browned all over and cooked through, 10 to 15 minutes. Remove them from the skillet and cover with foil to keep warm.

4. When the potatoes are tender, drain them well and transfer them to the skillet. Add ½ cup milk, 4 tablespoons butter, 1 teaspoon vinegar, 1 teaspoon dry mustard, and a sprinkle of pepper.

5. Mash with a potato masher or fork, adding more milk if needed. Taste and adjust the seasoning and serve alongside the sausages.

VARIATIONS

8 Other Vegetables to Mash

Peel before boiling:

1. Turnips
2. Rutabagas
3. Parsnips
4. Celery root
5. Sweet potatoes
6. Beets
7. Winter squash
8. Kohlrabi

NOTES

SAUSAGE DONENESS

Most sausages will cook through in 10 to 15 minutes over medium heat, but since thickness can vary, instead of relying on time the best way to know is to slice into one. It should be firm to the touch, and the juices that spill out should be clear, not pink.

SIDES

Sautéed Greens with Garlic 924

Green Salad 911

Creamed Spinach 936

Tomatoes with Fried Bread Crumbs 930

Smashed Peas 935

SPEED SERVES 4

Pork Tenderloin with Butternut Purée

Lean pork tenderloins can always benefit from a little extra seasoning, which is why I often stuff them with slivers of garlic; here a creamy squash purée adds an automatic side dish.

Ingredients

1 medium butternut squash (1 ½ pounds)

2 garlic cloves

Salt

1 pork tenderloin (1 ½ pounds)

2 tablespoons olive oil

Pepper

½ cup sour cream

Prep | Cook

1. Heat the oven to 400°F.

   Cut the squash in half crosswise, peel and trim it, and scoop out and discard the seeds. Chop it into roughly ¾-inch cubes.

   Peel 2 garlic cloves.

2. Transfer the squash and 1 of the garlic cloves to a medium pot with water to cover and a pinch of salt; bring to a boil and cook until the squash is soft enough to purée, 12 to 15 minutes.

   Thinly slice the remaining garlic clove.

   Cut slits all over the pork with the tip of a paring knife; stuff each slit with a garlic sliver.

3. Put 2 tablespoons olive oil in large ovenproof skillet over medium-high heat. When it's hot, add the pork and sprinkle with salt and pepper. Cook until nicely browned on the bottom, about 5 minutes, then turn the tenderloin and transfer the skillet to the oven. Roast until the pork is cooked through with a hint of pink in the middle (145°F), about 15 minutes.

4. When the squash is tender, drain it well, reserving some cooking water. Transfer the squash to a food processor, along with ½ cup sour cream and a sprinkle of salt and pepper, and purée until smooth, adding a splash of cooking water if needed to make a smooth purée. Taste and adjust the seasoning.

5. When the pork is done, transfer it to a plate, cover with aluminum foil, and let it rest for 5 minutes. Slice and serve with the squash and any accumulated meat juices.

VARIATIONS

Pork Tenderloin with Sweet Potato Purée
Swap sweet potatoes for squash and stuff the pork with ½ inch fresh ginger, thinly sliced, instead of the garlic. Use 2 tablespoons molasses instead of the sour cream.

Pork Tenderloin with Parmesan Mashed Potatoes
Use russet or Yukon Gold potatoes instead of squash and add ¼ cup grated Parmesan along with the sour cream. Instead of puréeing the potatoes in the food processor, mash them in the pot with a potato masher.

NOTES

A FAST ROAST
Pork tenderloin is one of the fastest-roasting cuts of meat (it also broils quickly; see page 774). It has almost no fat, so for the meat to stay tender and juicy you want to leave it slightly pink in the center: 145°F internal temperature is the highest I'd let it get before taking it out of the oven, but you can even remove it close to 140°F, as the temperature will rise a bit as it rests.

SIDES

Green Salad 911

Quinoa 945

Rice Pilaf 944

Sautéed Greens with Garlic 924

Warm Buttery Bread 906

Homemade Cold Cuts

Needless to say, having cooked meats on hand makes whipping up a meal fast and easy. Most deli meats are fine for sandwiches but not much else. Cooked beef, pork, and turkey breast or tenderloins (a part of the breast), however, are a fantastic alternative (as is a roast chicken—see page 688). You can slice them thinly for sandwiches, cut them into thick slices or chunks, or leave them whole for use in any number of recipes. All of these take little time to cook and are seasoned minimally so the meat can be used in dishes of any flavor. Stored in an airtight container or wrapped tightly with plastic wrap, these meats will keep in the fridge for several days.

Roast Turkey Tenderloin

1 Season and Cook

Heat the oven to 400°F. Rub 2 or 3 turkey tenderloins (about 2 pounds) with olive oil and sprinkle them all over with salt and pepper. Roast until a quick-read thermometer in the center reads 155° to 160°F on a quick-read thermometer, 30 to 40 minutes.

2 Rest

No matter what you're doing with it, let the meat rest for about 5 minutes. If you're eating it right away, slice and serve. If you're storing it in the fridge to use throughout the week, let it cool completely, then wrap and refrigerate whole, cutting off pieces as you need them.

Broiled Chicken Breast

1 Heat the Broiler

Turn the broiler to high and put the rack 3 or 4 inches from the heat.

2 Season and Cook

Figure 1 ½ pounds of boneless, skinless chicken breasts will get you 4 to 6 servings. Rub the pieces with olive oil and sprinkle all over with salt and pepper. Broil, turning as necessary to brown all sides.

3 Rest

Remove the breasts as they are done: The center should no longer be pink but still be juicy. Let them cool a bit before slicing. Or let them come to room temperature then wrap and refrigerate them for later.

Roasted Beef Tenderloin

1 Trim and Season

Heat the oven to 450°F. Choose a piece of beef tenderloin that's at least 2 pounds, pat the meat dry, rub it with olive oil, and sprinkle it all over with salt and pepper. Put on a rack set in a roasting pan or on a rimmed baking sheet.

2 Roast

Roast, undisturbed, for 20 minutes, then check the temperature with a quick-read thermometer. When the meat measures 125°F on a quick-read thermometer in a few places, it will be medium-rare; if you prefer it rare, or know you plan to cook the meat further as you use it throughout the week, remove it at 120°F. Transfer the meat to a cutting board.

3 Rest

No matter what you're doing with it, let the meat rest for about 5 minutes. If you're eating it right away, slice and serve. If you're storing it in the fridge to use throughout the week, let it cool completely, then wrap and refrigerate it whole, cutting off pieces as you need them.

Broiled Pork Tenderloin

1 Heat the Broiler

Turn the broiler to high and put the rack 3 or 4 inches from the heat.

2 Season and Cook

Rub the tenderloins (you should roast at least 2 pounds in a batch to make it worth your while) with olive oil and sprinkle all over with salt and pepper. Broil, turning the meat and rotating the pan as necessary to brown all sides, 3 to 8 minutes total, depending on the thickness of the pieces. If the meat starts to scorch, move the rack farther from the heat. Cook until the pork is almost cooked through but still slightly pink in the very center, 10 to 15 minutes (a quick-read thermometer in the center should read no more than 145°F).

3 Rest

No matter what you're doing with it, let the meat rest for about 10 minutes. If you're eating it right away, slice and serve. If you're storing it in the fridge to use throughout the week, let it cool completely, then wrap and refrigerate whole, cutting off pieces as you need them.

SPEED ◕ SERVES 4

Porchetta-Style Pork Loin with Parsnips

Porchetta is a traditional Italian roast of pork wrapped in fat and flavored with garlic and fennel seed. Here a quicker-cooking piece of butterflied loin gets the same flavor treatment, turning crusty and dark in a hot oven. I've listed ingredients rather than specific quantities, and assume you'll similarly season to your own taste with salt and pepper.

Ingredients

1 boneless pork loin (2 pounds)

2 garlic cloves

1 lemon

4 tablespoons olive oil

1 tablespoon fennel seeds

½ teaspoon red chile flakes

Salt and pepper

1 ½ pounds parsnips

½ cup white wine

Prep | Cook

1. Heat the oven to 450°F.

   To butterfly the pork loin, use a long, sharp knife to cut the meat lengthwise almost in half. Open it up like a book and flatten it out with your hands. Put the pork in a large roasting pan.

   Peel and mince 2 garlic cloves.

   Grate the lemon zest, refrigerating the fruit for another use.

2. Rub the pork all over with 2 tablespoons olive oil, the garlic, the lemon zest, 1 tablespoon fennel seeds, ½ teaspoon red chile flakes, and some salt and pepper.

   Trim and peel the parsnips; cut them into 1 ½- to 2-inch chunks and scatter them around the pork.

3. Drizzle the parsnips with 2 tablespoons oil and sprinkle with salt and pepper. Pour ½ cup white wine in the bottom of the pan and put it in the oven.

4. Cook, turning the pork and parsnips once or twice and stirring the parsnips 3 or 4 times until both are browned and tender and the pork has just a hint of pink in the middle, 30 to 35 minutes. (A quick-read thermometer inserted into the pork should read 145°F.)

5. When the pork and parsnips are done, transfer the pork to a cutting board and let it rest for 5 minutes. Cut it into slices and serve with the parsnips.

VARIATIONS

Pernil-Style Pork Loin with Plantains

Substitute an orange for the lemon, dried oregano for the fennel seeds, and cumin for the red chile flakes. Use ripe plantains, peeled and cut into chunks, instead of the parsnips and beer or stock instead of wine.

NOTES

IF YOU HAVE MORE TIME

After rubbing the pork, let it sit in the refrigerator for an hour or 2 (or overnight) before roasting. Bring it back to room temperature before you put it in the oven.

SIDES

Garlic Bread 906

Warm Buttery Bread 906

Pasta, Plain and Simple 948

SPEED ◕ SERVES 4

Pork Stew and Dumplings

This chile-tinged pork stew turns into a hearty meal with the addition of masa—tamale-like—dumplings that simmer right in the broth.

Ingredients

2 tablespoons olive oil

1 ½ pounds boneless pork shoulder

Salt and pepper

1 large onion

2 poblano peppers

3 garlic cloves

1 cup masa harina

½ teaspoon baking powder

1 tablespoon vegetable oil

4 cups chicken or beef stock or water

1 lime

Several sprigs fresh cilantro for garnish

Prep | Cook

1. Put 2 tablespoons olive oil in a large pot over medium-high heat.

   Thinly slice the pork shoulder.

2. Add the pork shoulder to the pot, sprinkle with salt and pepper, and cook, stirring occasionally until it is lightly browned, 3 to 5 minutes.

   Trim, peel, and chop the onion. Trim, core, and chop the poblanos. Peel and mince 3 garlic cloves.

3. When the pork is lightly browned, add the onion, poblanos, and garlic, sprinkle with salt and pepper, and cook, stirring occasionally until they soften, 6 or 7 minutes.

4. Meanwhile, combine 1 cup masa harina, ½ teaspoon baking powder, ½ teaspoon salt and a sprinkle of pepper, and 1 tablespoon vegetable oil in a medium bowl. Stir to combine into a coarse meal, then slowly add 1 cup warm water, incorporating it as you go, until the mixture forms a thick dough.

5. When the vegetables are soft, add 4 cups stock or water to the pot. Bring the mixture to a boil, then adjust the heat so that it simmers gently but steadily. Cover and cook until the pork and vegetables are tender and cooked through, 10 to 15 minutes.

6. When the pork and vegetables are tender, uncover the pot and drop small dollops of dough into the bubbling liquid. Cover and cook until the dumplings puff up a bit and are tender, 3 to 5 minutes.

   Cut the lime into wedges. Chop several sprigs cilantro.

7. When the dumplings are tender, divide the stew among 4 bowls. Garnish with the cilantro and serve with the lime wedges.

VARIATIONS

Chicken Stew and Dumplings
Swap boneless, skinless chicken thighs for the pork shoulder.

NOTES

MAKE YOUR OWN

Chicken Stock 213

Beef Stock 212

IF YOU HAVE MORE TIME
Cut the pork into 1 ½-inch chunks and simmer them until they shred apart, up to 2 hours. Pull the meat apart slightly before adding the dumplings to the pot.

SIDES

Warm Tortillas 907

Sautéed Sweet Potatoes with Chipotle and Lime 964

Jícama and Radish Salad 918

Chile-Cumin Black Beans 937

SPEED SERVES 4

Pork and Onion Carnitas

This version preserves the spirit of slow-cooked carnitas but cuts way down on the time. Instead of braising large chunks of pork, you chop the meat into small pieces that become crisp without needing to braise long enough to fall apart. Warm tortillas are a must.

Ingredients

1 ½ pounds boneless pork shoulder

2 tablespoons vegetable oil, plus more as needed

1 ½ cups beer (one 12-ounce bottle or can)

2 onions

2 garlic cloves

1 teaspoon cumin

¼ teaspoon cayenne

Salt and pepper

4 radishes

1 lime

Several sprigs fresh cilantro for garnish

Prep | Cook

1. Chop the pork into ½-inch pieces. Put them in a large skillet or pot with 2 tablespoons vegetable oil and 1 ½ cups beer. Turn the heat to high.

   Trim, peel, halve, and slice the onions; add them to the pan.

   Peel and mince 2 garlic cloves; add them to the pan.

2. Add 1 teaspoon cumin, ¼ tablespoon cayenne, and a sprinkle of salt and pepper. When the mixture boils, adjust the heat so it bubbles steadily but not vigorously.

3. Cover and cook, adding a splash of liquid if the pan gets dry, until the pork is tender and the onions are very soft, about 20 minutes.

   Trim and chop the radishes. Cut the lime into wedges.

   Chop several sprigs cilantro.

4. When the pork and onions are tender, uncover the pan and turn the heat to high. Cook, stirring occasionally until the liquid evaporates and the pork and onions brown and crisp in the rendered fat, 8 to 12 minutes (add a little more oil if the pan looks dry).

5. Taste and adjust the seasoning and serve garnished with the radishes, lime wedges, and cilantro.

VARIATIONS

Pork and Corn Carnitas

Omit the onions. Once you uncover the pot to start evaporating the liquid in Step 4, stir in 3 cups corn kernels. Let them brown in the rendered fat along with the pork.

Moroccan-Style Pork and Onion Carnitas

Substitute ½ teaspoon cinnamon for the cayenne and add ½ cup chopped dried apricots to the braising mixture. Omit the radishes; swap lemon for the lime and mint for the cilantro.

NOTES

EVEN FASTER

Chop the pork in the food processor.

IF YOU HAVE MORE TIME

Cut the pork into 2-inch chunks and simmer slowly until it shreds apart, for up to a few hours. Pull the pork apart with a fork, then proceed with the crisping in Step 4.

SIDES

Warm Tortillas 907

White Rice 941

Jícama and Radish Salad 918

Chile-Cumin Black Beans 937

Avocado with Lime and Chili Salt 920

Ripe Plantains 960

SPEED ◕ SERVES 4

Pork, White Bean, and Kale Stew

Stewing already cooked beans coaxes them into falling apart and becoming wonderfully creamy. Paired with browned, fatty pork and earthy wilted kale, this is perfect for a cold day.

Ingredients

2 tablespoons olive oil, plus more for garnish

1 ½ pounds boneless pork shoulder

Salt and pepper

3 garlic cloves

1 small bunch kale

3 cups cooked or canned white beans (one and a half 15-ounce cans)

2 sprigs fresh rosemary

¼ teaspoon red chile flakes

1 ½ cups chicken stock or water

2 ounces Parmesan cheese (½ cup grated; optional)

Prep | Cook

1. Put 2 tablespoons olive oil in a large pot or Dutch oven over medium-high heat.

   Cut the pork into ½-inch pieces.

2. Add the pork to the pot, sprinkle with salt and pepper, and cook, stirring occasionally until nicely browned, 8 to 10 minutes.

   Peel and thinly slice 3 garlic cloves. Trim and chop the kale.

   If you're using canned beans, rinse and drain them.

3. When the pork is nicely browned, add the garlic, kale, beans, 2 rosemary sprigs, ¼ teaspoon red chile flakes, 1 ½ cups stock or water, and a sprinkle of salt and pepper. Stir to combine.

4. Bring the mixture to a boil, then adjust the heat so it simmers gently but steadily. Cover and cook, stirring occasionally and adding more liquid if the mixture gets too dry, until the beans have broken down a bit, the kale is wilted, and the pork is tender, 25 to 30 minutes. Fish out the rosemary sprigs.

5. Taste and adjust the seasoning, adding a splash of liquid if you want to make it soupier. Divide among 4 bowls, grate ½ cup Parmesan and sprinkle over the top if you like, drizzle with a little extra oil, and serve.

VARIATIONS

Pork, Black Bean, and Collard Stew

For the last few minutes of browning, sprinkle the pork with 1 teaspoon cumin and 1 teaspoon chili powder. Substitute collards for the kale, black beans for white, oregano for the rosemary, and queso fresco for the Parmesan.

NOTES

MAKE YOUR OWN

Cooked Beans 496

Chicken Stock 213

EVEN FASTER

White Bean Chili

Use ground pork instead of cubes of shoulder. As soon as the beans break down a bit and thicken the stew, 10 to 15 minutes, it's done. Alternatively, use chunks or slices of Italian sausage.

IF YOU HAVE MORE TIME

The longer you simmer the stew (up to 3 hours), the more tender the pork will become and the more the beans will break down. If you prefer that some of them hold their shape, add half of the beans closer to the end of cooking.

SIDES

Warm Buttery Bread 906

Garlic Bread 906

Tomato Salad 913

Broiled Cherry Tomatoes 931

Pasta, Plain and Simple 948

SPEED  SERVES 4

Provençal Braised Pork and Fennel

A rustic dish with the big flavors of southern France.

Ingredients

3 tablespoons olive oil

1 ½ pounds boneless pork shoulder

Salt and pepper

2 large fennel bulbs

3 garlic cloves

¼ cup Niçoise or kalamata olives

3 sprigs fresh thyme

2 or 3 anchovy fillets

1 tablespoon capers

1 cup white wine

One 15-ounce can diced tomatoes or 2 large tomatoes

Several sprigs fresh basil for garnish

Prep | Cook

1. Put 3 tablespoons olive oil in a large skillet over medium-high heat.

   Thinly slice the pork.

2. Add the pork to the skillet, sprinkle with salt and pepper, and cook, stirring occasionally until it is lightly browned, 3 to 5 minutes.

   Trim and thinly slice the fennel.

3. When the pork is lightly browned, add the fennel, sprinkle with salt and pepper, and cook, stirring occasionally until it softens, 3 to 5 minutes.

   Peel 3 garlic cloves. Pit ¼ cup olives if necessary. Strip the thyme leaves from 3 sprigs.

   Chop the garlic, olives, and thyme, along with 2 or 3 anchovies and 1 tablespoon capers.

4. Add the garlic mixture; cook and stir until fragrant, a minute or 2. Add 1 cup white wine and let it bubble for a minute.

   Core and chop the tomatoes if you're using fresh ones.

5. Add the canned or fresh tomatoes to the pan. Bring the mixture to a boil, adjust the heat so that it simmers gently but steadily, and cook, stirring occasionally until the tomatoes break down and begin to thicken the sauce, 10 to 15 minutes. Add more liquid if the pan gets too dry.

   Strip the basil leaves from several sprigs and chop them.

6. When the tomatoes break down, taste and adjust the seasoning, garnish with the basil, and serve.

VARIATIONS

Provençal Chicken and Fennel
Replace the pork with boneless, skinless chicken thighs, cut into large chunks.

Moroccan Lamb and Fennel
Substitute 1 teaspoon cumin and ½ teaspoon cinnamon for the capers. Add them along with the garlic mixture in Step 4.

NOTES

IF YOU HAVE MORE TIME
Cut the pork into 1 ½-inch chunks. After adding the tomatoes, cover the pot and simmer until the pork falls apart easily, up to 3 hours. Add more liquid if the mixture gets too dry.

SIDES

Garlic Bread 906

Warm Buttery Bread 906

Skin-On Mashed Potatoes 961

White Rice 941

Couscous 910

SPEED SERVES 4

Moroccan-Style Braised Pork with Couscous and Grapes

With warm spice, sweet grapes and onions, and tangy vinegar, this Moroccan-scented pork stew hits every part of your taste buds.

Ingredients

2 tablespoons olive oil

1 ½ pounds boneless pork shoulder

Salt and pepper

1 teaspoon cumin

1 teaspoon coriander

½ teaspoon cinnamon

1 large red onion

1 tablespoon tomato paste

1 tablespoon harissa (optional)

1 cup white wine

1 ½ cups red grapes

1 cup chicken or vegetable stock or water

2 tablespoons red wine vinegar

1 cup couscous

1 bunch fresh parsley

Prep | Cook

1. Put 2 tablespoons olive oil in a large skillet or large pot over medium-high heat.

   Cut the pork into ½-inch pieces.

2. Add the pork to the pot along with a sprinkle of salt and pepper, 1 teaspoon cumin, 1 teaspoon coriander, and ½ teaspoon cinnamon. Cook, stirring occasionally until the spices are nicely browned but not burned, 3 to 5 minutes.

   Trim, peel, halve, and slice the onion.

3. When the pork is browned, add 1 tablespoon tomato paste and 1 tablespoon harissa if you're using it and cook, stirring occasionally until they darken slightly, a minute or 2.

4. Add 1 cup white wine, scraping any browned bits from the bottom of the pot. Add the onion, 1 ½ cups grapes, 1 cup stock or water, and 2 tablespoons red wine vinegar.

5. Bring the mixture to a boil, then adjust the heat so it simmers gently but steadily. Cover and cook, stirring occasionally and adding more liquid if the mixture gets too dry, until the pork is nearly tender, 20 to 25 minutes.

6. Stir in 1 cup couscous, turn off the heat, and cover the pot. Let it steep until tender, 5 to 10 minutes.

   Chop 1/4 cup parsley.

7. When the couscous is tender, fluff it a bit with a fork and taste and adjust the seasoning. Stir in the parsley and serve.

VARIATIONS

Curried Pork with Couscous and Spinach
Swap 1 tablespoon curry powder or garam masala for the cumin, coriander, and cinnamon. Omit the harissa. Use coconut milk instead of the wine, 3 cups chopped spinach instead of the grapes, and lime juice instead of the vinegar. Garnish with cilantro.

Moroccan Braised Lamb with Couscous and Olives
Replace the pork shoulder with lamb shoulder and the grapes with 1 cup pitted black or green olives.

NOTES

MAKE YOUR OWN

Chicken Stock 213

Vegetable Stock 212

IF YOU HAVE MORE TIME
The longer you simmer the pork (up to 2 hours), the more tender it will become.

SIDES

Carrot Salad with Raisins 914

Tomato Salad with Olive Oil and Yogurt 913

Tahini Slaw 923

SPEED ◔ SERVES 4

Lamb Chops with Balsamic Couscous

A double-thick lamb rib chop takes longer to cook than a single, but since you can fit all four chops in the skillet at once, you end up saving time. Plus, those meaty chops are easier to keep rare or medium-rare, so they burst with juice.

Ingredients

2 tablespoons balsamic vinegar

2 tablespoons olive oil

4 double-thick lamb rib chops (about 1 ½ pounds)

Salt and pepper

1 ½ cups chicken stock or water

1 cup couscous

2 medium ripe tomatoes

1 bunch fresh mint

Prep | Cook

1. Put a large skillet over medium-high heat. Combine 2 tablespoons balsamic vinegar and 2 tablespoons olive oil in a large bowl. Add the lamb chops and toss to coat.

2. When the skillet is hot, sprinkle the bottom with salt and pepper and add the lamb chops. (Reserve the marinade.) Sprinkle the tops with salt and pepper and cook, turning a couple of times, until they are nicely browned on both sides and medium-rare in the middle, 4 or 5 minutes per side.

3. When the lamb is done, transfer the chops to a plate and cover with aluminum foil to keep them warm. Add 1 ½ cups chicken stock or water to the skillet, along with the reserved marinade and a sprinkle of salt. Boil for about 1 minute.

4. Stir in 1 cup couscous, then turn off the heat. Cover the skillet and let the couscous steep for about 5 minutes.

   Core and chop the tomatoes. Strip ¼ cup mint leaves from the stems and chop them.

5. When the couscous is tender, add the tomatoes and mint and fluff it with a fork. Taste and adjust the seasoning and drizzle with any accumulated meat juice. Serve the couscous alongside or underneath the lamb.

VARIATIONS

Lamb Chops with Soy-Ginger Couscous
Swap soy sauce for the balsamic and cilantro for the mint. Add 1 tablespoon minced ginger to the skillet along with the couscous in Step 4.

Lamb Chops with Pomegranate Couscous
Omit the balsamic. Substitute ½ cup unsweetened pomegranate juice for ½ cup of the stock.

NOTES

MAKE YOUR OWN
Chicken Stock 213

EVEN FASTER
While the lamb cooks, put the couscous in a medium pot with 1 ½ cups water or stock, the remaining balsamic and oil mixture, and a pinch of salt. Bring to a boil, then turn off the heat, cover, and steep for 5 minutes.

IF YOU HAVE MORE TIME
Lamb Chops with Balsamic Bulgur
Use bulgur instead of couscous and increase the amount of stock or water to 2 ½ cups.

LAMB CHOPS
Lamb rib chops (which are what I call for in this chapter) are the most tender and fastest to cook. Loin chops (tender but bonier) and shoulder chops (a bit tougher) are more flavorful and cheaper as well. Loin and shoulder chops take slightly longer to cook than a single rib chop (and a few minutes less than a double), but the cooking times are close enough that you can substitute them as you like.

SIDES

Green Salad 911

Crisp Seasoned Pita 908

Carrot Salad with Olives and Rosemary 914

Cucumber Salad 915

Tomato Salad with Olive Oil and Yogurt 913

SPEED SERVES 4

Stir-Fried Lamb and Green Peppers with Cumin

Stir-fried lamb with cumin is a traditional dish from Mongolia; the flavor is eye-opening. Red chile flakes provide the heat, while green peppers cool the smoke and spice.

Ingredients

4 tablespoons vegetable oil

1 ½ pounds boneless lamb shoulder

2 teaspoons cumin

1 teaspoon red chile flakes, or to taste

Salt and pepper

1 inch fresh ginger

2 garlic cloves

3 green bell peppers

3 scallions

1 teaspoon soy sauce

Prep | Cook

1. Put 2 tablespoons vegetable oil in a large skillet over medium-high heat.

   Slice the lamb as thinly as you can.

2. Add the lamb to the skillet, sprinkle with 2 teaspoons cumin, 1 teaspoon red chile flakes or to taste, and a sprinkle of salt and pepper. Cook, stirring occasionally until the spices and lamb are nicely browned but not burned, 3 to 5 minutes.

   Peel 1 inch ginger and 2 garlic cloves; mince them together.

   Core, seed, and thinly slice the peppers.

3. When the lamb is browned, add the ginger and garlic. Cook, stirring until fragrant, about a minute. Transfer the lamb mixture to a bowl.

4. Add 2 tablespoons oil to the skillet. Add the peppers and cook, stirring occasionally until they are lightly browned and just tender but still have a little crunch, 3 to 5 minutes.

   Trim and chop the scallions.

5. When the peppers are done, return the lamb to the skillet and add 1 teaspoon soy sauce and the scallions. Toss everything to combine, taste and adjust the seasoning, and serve.

VARIATIONS

Stir-Fried Lamb and Leeks with Cumin
Swap 3 medium leeks, sliced, for the peppers.

Stir-Fried Lamb and Green Peppers with Curry
Use curry powder instead of the cumin.

NOTES

IF YOU HAVE MORE TIME
Before beginning, heat 2 teaspoons cumin seeds and 2 or 3 small dried red chiles in a dry skillet until lightly toasted, 3 or 4 minutes; grind them in a spice grinder. Use these spices to sprinkle on the lamb in Step 2.

SIDES

White Rice 941

Fire and Ice Noodles 950

Sesame Noodles 949

Panfried Rice Noodles 951

Scallion Pancakes 940

SPEED ◑ SERVES 4

Seared Miso Lamb Chops with Carrots

The sweet-saltiness of lamb, carrots, and miso is both unfamiliar and wonderful.

Ingredients

4 double-thick lamb rib chops (about ½ pound)

2 tablespoons vegetable oil

Salt and pepper

1 pound carrots

3 scallions

¼ cup chicken stock, white wine, or water

2 tablespoons any miso

1 teaspoon soy sauce

Prep | Cook

1. Put a large skillet over medium-high heat. Rub the lamb chops with 1 tablespoon vegetable oil and sprinkle all over with salt and pepper.
2. When the skillet is hot, add the chops. Cook, turning once, until they are nicely browned on both sides and medium-rare in the middle, 4 or 5 minutes per side.

   Trim, peel, and thinly slice the carrots.
3. When the chops are done, transfer them to a platter and cover with aluminum foil to keep them warm. Add 1 tablespoon oil to the skillet.
4. When the oil is hot, add the carrots and cook, stirring occasionally until they are lightly browned and just tender, 5 to 10 minutes.

   Trim and chop the scallions.
5. Add ¼ cup stock, wine, or water, 2 tablespoons miso, and 1 teaspoon soy sauce. Stir, scraping up any browned bits from the bottom of the skillet and coating the carrots with the sauce.
6. Taste and adjust the seasoning and serve the carrots over the lamb chops, garnished with the scallions.

VARIATIONS

Pan-Seared Miso Lamb Chops with Sweet Potatoes
Substitute grated sweet potatoes for the carrots.

Pan-Seared Dijon Lamb Chops with Parsnips
Swap parsnips for the carrots, 2 tablespoons chopped fresh tarragon for the scallions, Dijon mustard for the miso, and cider or red wine vinegar for the soy sauce.

NOTES

MAKE YOUR OWN
Chicken Stock 213

EVEN FASTER
Cook the carrots in a separate skillet while you sear the lamb chops.

SIDES

White Rice 941

Bulgur with Lemon and Parsley 946

Sesame Noodles 949

Cucumber Salad with Soy Sauce and Mirin 915

SPEED ◐ SERVES 4

Lamb and Rice with Dried Fruit

Pilaf perfection. Between chunks of tender, browned lamb, sweet dried fruit, and an earthy Moroccan spice mix, rice never had it so good.

Ingredients

3 tablespoons olive oil

1 ½ pounds boneless lamb shoulder

Salt and pepper

1 onion

2 garlic cloves

1 cup dried apricots or dates or a combination

1 teaspoon cumin

1 teaspoon coriander

¼ teaspoon cinnamon

¼ teaspoon cayenne

1 ½ cups long-grain rice

3 cups chicken stock or water

1 bunch fresh parsley

Prep | Cook

1. Put 3 tablespoons olive oil in a large skillet or large pot over medium-high heat.

   Cut the lamb into 1-inch chunks.

2. Add the lamb to the pan, sprinkle with salt and pepper, and cook undisturbed until it's nicely browned on the bottom, about 5 minutes.

   Trim, peel, and chop the onion.

   Peel and mince 2 garlic cloves.

   Chop 1 cup apricots or dates or a combination.

3. Add the onion, garlic, and dried fruit to the pan, along with 1 teaspoon cumin, 1 teaspoon coriander, ¼ teaspoon cinnamon, and ¼ teaspoon cayenne. Cook, stirring occasionally until the onion begins to soften and the spices are fragrant, 2 or 3 minutes.

4. Add 1 ½ cups rice and cook, stirring occasionally, until glossy and coated with the spices, 2 or 3 minutes. Add 3 cups chicken stock or water and bring to a boil.

5. When the mixture boils, adjust the heat so it bubbles steadily but not vigorously. Cover and cook until the rice is tender and the liquid is absorbed, 10 to 20 minutes.

   Strip 1/4 cup parsley leaves from the stems and chop them.

6. When the rice done, stir in the parsley. Taste and adjust the seasoning and serve.

VARIATIONS

Lamb and Rice with Green Olives
Replace the dried fruit with pitted green olives.

Pork and Rice with Pinto Beans
Swap pork shoulder, thinly sliced, for the lamb and 1 cup cooked or canned pinto beans for the dried fruit. Swap 1 teaspoon chili powder for the coriander and cilantro for the parsley.

NOTES

MAKE YOUR OWN
Chicken Stock 213

IF YOU HAVE MORE TIME
Brown the lamb all over instead of on just one side.

SIDES

Green Salad 911

Crisp Seasoned Pita 908

Tomato Salad with Olive Oil and Yogurt 913

Carrot Salad with Raisins 914

Flavor Before Cooking

These are my go-to seasoning combinations that you can use not only on meat but chicken, fish, tofu, and vegetables as well. The first chart is for typical wet marinades, whereas the second lists what I've come to call "rub-in-ades," which flavor the ingredients faster than wetter marinades and can help develop a lovely crust. The charts offer two different options for every base ingredient; I've listed combinations of ingredients rather than specific quantities, and also assume you'll similarly season to your own tastes as you do with salt and pepper.

Marinades

Toss or submerge the meat in these mixtures before cooking or use them to drizzle over the finished dish like a sauce (or do both, but boil the marinade briefly before drizzling if it's come into contact with raw meat). These should be thin and liquid. You can marinate for a long time or just a little. Even a 10-minute bath will give your ingredients more flavor.

Base Ingredient	Seasonings Option 1	Seasonings Option 2
SOY SAUCE	Minced garlic, minced ginger, sesame oil	Lime juice, minced fresh hot chile
OLIVE OIL	Lemon juice, minced garlic	White wine, minced anchovies, red chile flakes
COCONUT MILK	Fish sauce, lime juice, basil, mint	Curry powder, minced ginger
RED WINE	Orange zest, cinnamon stick, whole cloves	Rosemary, minced garlic
ORANGE JUICE	Tarragon, dill, minced shallot	Chopped chipotle chiles in adobo, lime juice

Rub-in-ades

Rub all over the meat or other ingredient before cooking; if you're using a high-heat cooking method like pan-searing or grilling, steer clear of minced garlic (it will burn and turn bitter). These should be the consistency of a thick paste.

Base Ingredient	Seasonings Option 1	Seasonings Option 2
SMOKED PAPRIKA	Olive oil, lemon zest	Sherry vinegar, tomato paste
GROUND CUMIN AND CORIANDER	Cinnamon, allspice, olive oil	Chili powder, cayenne, vegetable oil
DIJON MUSTARD	Minced garlic, rosemary, olive oil	Soy sauce, honey
YOGURT	Tahini, lemon juice, cumin	Chopped chipotle chiles in adobo, lime juice
CHOPPED FRESH PARSLEY	Olive oil, grated Parmesan, lemon zest	Minced olives, minced capers, olive oil
TOMATO PASTE	soy sauce, brown sugar, minced scallion	olive oil, oregano, grated Parmesan
CURRY POWDER	coconut milk, minced garlic, minced ginger	lime juice, minced chiles
PEANUT BUTTER	soy sauce, minced ginger, sesame oil	chopped chipotle chiles in adobo, lime juice, cumin
MINCED OLIVES	minced anchovies, chopped capers, olive oil	tomato paste, lemon juice, olive oil
MISO (ANY KIND)	honey, minced ginger	orange juice, rosemary

SPEED SERVES 6 TO 8

Herb-Rubbed Leg of Lamb with Chopped Greek Salad

Butterflied leg of lamb is affordable, widely available, tender, and easy to cook. Even its uneven thickness is a bonus, yielding meat from rare to medium-well, so there's something for everyone. The best part: It cooks this way in about 30 minutes.

Ingredients

1 garlic clove

3 sprigs fresh rosemary or 2 teaspoons dried

3 sprigs fresh oregano or 2 teaspoons dried

1 lemon

One 3- to 4-pound butterflied leg of lamb

6 tablespoons olive oil

Salt and pepper

4 medium cucumbers

4 large ripe tomatoes

1 red onion

1 cup kalamata olives

4 ounces feta cheese (1 cup crumbled)

2 tablespoons red wine vinegar

Prep | Cook

1. Turn the broiler to high; put the rack 6 inches from the heat.

   Peel 1 garlic clove; strip the leaves from 3 sprigs each of rosemary and oregano if you are using fresh herbs. Mince everything together (crumble in the dried herbs if you're using them) and put in a small bowl.

   Halve the lemon and squeeze the juice into the bowl.

   If the lamb is tied, remove the string and unroll it.

2. Add 3 tablespoons olive oil and a sprinkle of salt and pepper to the bowl. Put the lamb in a roasting pan or on a rimmed baking sheet and rub the garlic and herb mixture all over it.

3. Broil, turning as necessary until it is nicely browned (even a little charred) on both sides, 20 to 30 minutes; the internal temperature at the thickest part will be about 125°F; this will give you some lamb that is quite rare and some that is nearly well-done.

   Trim the cucumbers and peel them if you like; cut them in half lengthwise and scoop out the seeds with a spoon. Chop them and put them in a large bowl.

Core and chop the tomatoes; trim, peel, halve, and thinly slice the onion. Add them to the bowl.

Pit 1 cup olives if necessary; add them to the bowl.

Crumble 1 cup feta and add to the bowl.

4. When the lamb is done, transfer it to a cutting board to rest for 5 minutes. Drizzle the salad with 2 tablespoons red wine vinegar, 3 tablespoons oil, and sprinkle with salt and pepper. Toss.

5. Thinly slice the lamb and serve it with the salad.

VARIATIONS

Moroccan Spice-Rubbed Leg of Lamb with Shredded Carrot Salad

For the lamb rub, combine ¼ cup yogurt, 2 tablespoons olive oil, 1 teaspoon cumin, 1 teaspoon coriander, ½ teaspoon cinnamon, ½ teaspoon paprika, a sprinkle of salt and pepper, 1 minced garlic clove, and the juice of a lemon. For the salad, combine 1 ½ pounds grated carrots, 1 sliced red onion, ½ cup chopped pitted olives, ½ cup raisins, 2 tablespoons red wine vinegar, 3 tablespoons olive oil, and a sprinkle of salt and pepper.

NOTES

IF YOU HAVE MORE TIME

After rubbing the lamb, let it marinate in the refrigerator for at least an hour or up to overnight. Return the meat to room temperature before broiling.

SIDES

Crisp Seasoned Pita 908

Rice Pilaf 944

White Rice 941

Bulgur with Lemon and Parsley 946

Couscous 910

SPEED SERVES 4

Lamb and Bulgur Meatballs in Tomato Sauce

The Middle Eastern and North African tradition of making meatballs with lamb and grains is a fantastic way to stretch a small amount of meat while keeping it moist.

Ingredients

½ cup bulgur

Salt

4 tablespoons olive oil

1 red onion

1 teaspoon cumin

¼ cup raisins

¼ cup pine nuts

One 28-ounce can diced tomatoes

Pepper

1 pound ground lamb

1 egg

1 bunch fresh mint

Prep | Cook

1. Bring 1 ¼ cups water to a boil. Put ½ cup bulgur in a large bowl with a large pinch of salt. Pour the boiling water over all and cover with a plate.
2. Put 2 tablespoons olive oil in a large skillet over medium-high heat.

   Trim, peel, and chop the onion.
3. Add the onion to the skillet and cook, stirring occasionally until softened, 3 to 5 minutes. Add 1 teaspoon cumin, ¼ cup raisins, and ¼ cup pine nuts. Cook, stirring until the cumin is fragrant and the pine nuts are lightly toasted, 2 or 3 minutes.
4. Add the tomatoes and their juice and a sprinkle of salt and pepper. Adjust the heat so the mixture simmers and cook, stirring occasionally until the tomatoes break down and thicken the sauce, 10 to 15 minutes.
5. Strain the bulgur, pressing out any excess water with a spoon (it's okay if it's not fully tender), and return it to the bowl. Add the lamb, crack the egg into the bowl, and sprinkle with salt and pepper. Put 2 tablespoons oil in a large skillet over medium-high heat.

6. Gently combine the meatball mixture and use 2 spoons to start dropping rounds of the mixture into the skillet. Cook in batches, turning occasionally until the meatballs are browned all over, 8 to 10 minutes. Transfer them to a plate as they finish cooking and repeat with the next batch.

   Strip 1/4 cup mint leaves from the stems and chop them.

7. When all the meatballs are browned, drop them into the tomato sauce and toss gently to coat. Simmer gently until the meatballs are cooked through, about 5 minutes. Garnish with the mint and serve hot or warm.

VARIATIONS

Chicken and Bulgur Meatballs with Provençal Tomato Sauce
Substitute 1 yellow onion for the red, 3 minced garlic cloves for the cumin, 1/4 cup chopped olives for the pine nuts, and 1 tablespoon each chopped anchovies and capers for the raisins. Swap ground chicken for the lamb and basil for the mint.

Beef and Bulgur Meatballs in Chipotle Tomato Sauce
Use 2 tablespoons chopped chipotle chiles in adobo instead of the pine nuts, ground beef instead of the lamb, and cilantro in place of the mint. If you have some queso fresco, crumble some over the top as well.

NOTES

EVEN FASTER
Form the lamb and bulgur mixture into patties instead of balls. Once they're browned and cooked through, spoon the tomato sauce over the top and serve.

SIDES

Smashed Peas 935

Stuffed Portobellos 957

Avocado with Lemon and Salt 920

Seared Broccoli or Cauliflower 925

Breakfast

FRUIT, GRAINS, TOAST, AND CEREAL

Loaded Muesli 806

Fruit, Yogurt, and Graham Cracker Parfait 808

Piña Colada Smoothie 810

Broiled Grapefruit with Almond–Brown Sugar Crunch 812

Toast with Toasted Almond Butter and Strawberries 814

Breakfast Bruschetta 816

Sautéed Apples and Bananas with Honey-Yogurt Sauce 818

Apricot-Cinnamon Couscous 820

No-Bake Fruit and Cereal Bars 822

Maple-Orange Oatmeal with Caramelized Pecans 824

Honey-Cheddar Grits with Sage 826

EGGS

Roasting-Pan French Toast 830

Tortilla French Toast 832

Omelet for Two 834

Fried Eggs with Chimichurri 836

Scrambled Eggs with Smoked Salmon and Dill 838

Goat Cheese and Spinach Scrambled Eggs 840

Tortilla Scramble 842

Chipotle Black Beans with Fried Eggs 846

Broiled Eggs 848

Fast Florentine 850

Fried Eggs with Mushrooms and Leeks 852

Eggs and Steak with Peppers and Onions 854

Classic Breakfast Burritos 856

MEATS, PANCAKES, AND WAFFLES

Pork 'n' Greens Breakfast Patties 858

Smoky Two-Potato and Ham Hash 860

Prosciutto and Drop Biscuits 862

Jalapeño-Scallion Johnnycakes 864

Banana-Coconut Pancakes 866

Orange-Ricotta Pancakes 868

Cheddar Waffles with Bacon Maple Syrup 870

Breakfast

Most days, breakfast is the fastest meal that we cook and eat. While it might be lovely to hang around the stove every morning flipping pancakes or tending to eggs, I like the hectic pace of a typical weekday morning—it's a welcome test of our fast cooking reflexes, because it usually must be prepared while juggling getting out of the house.

This time crunch can lead to the kind of morning meltdown that ends in eating junk food on the run, but it can just as easily produce tasty, easy, and incredibly fast breakfasts from the pantry, things you'll want to make and eat every day. This chapter includes plenty of recipes that are quick enough for a weekday, as well as many others that you'll want to save for the weekend. And if you've never tried eating breakfast for dinner, there are a lot of dishes here that will make you a convert.

As tempting as it often is to grab breakfast at work or on the road, or skip it altogether, making breakfast at home—even if it's as simple as oatmeal—is a satisfying and healthy way to start the day.

Chapter Highlights

Homemade Cereal, Muesli, or Granola Each takes just minutes, and you know exactly what's in them. Loaded Muesli (page 806).

Yogurt Here's what you need to know about buying the perfect accompaniment to your homemade cereal. Yogurt (page 809).

New Takes on Toast Recipes that take advantage of one of the fastest and easiest breakfast foods on earth. Toast with Toasted Almond Butter and Strawberries (page 814), Breakfast Bruschetta (page 816).

Raising the Bar You'll never need to buy breakfast bars in the supermarket again. No-Bake Fruit and Cereal Bars (page 822).

Grains for Breakfast We eat oats for breakfast all the time, so why not spice things up with some different grains? Start with Apricot-Cinnamon Couscous (page 820).

Eggs in a Nutshell A quick rundown of what you need to know about eggs, including how to decipher confusing labels. Eggs in a Nutshell (page 828).

Broiling Breakfast Two of my favorite breakfasts can be cooked hassle-free in the broiler. Broiled Grapefruit with Almond–Brown Sugar Crunch (page 812), Broiled Eggs (page 848).

Poached Eggs, No Water A skillet filled with vegetables, greens, or thick sauce is a wonderfully forgiving place to poach eggs. Fast Florentine (page 850).

Try Grits A staple in the South, but we'd all be wise to keep some in our kitchens at all times. Honey-Cheddar Grits with Sage (page 826).

Breakfast for a Crowd The easiest breakfast dishes to cook for a lot of people. Loaded Muesli (page 806), No-Bake Fruit and Cereal Bars (page 822), Roasting-Pan French Toast (page 830), Broiled Eggs (page 848), Scrambled Eggs with Smoked Salmon and Dill (page 838), Goat Cheese and Spinach Scrambled Eggs (page 840).

Breakfast Burger Making your own breakfast sausage is no harder than making a hamburger. Pork 'n' Greens Breakfast Patties (page 858).

Pancake Pointers A few simple suggestions will get you flipping with ease. See the Note A Few Tips for Cooking Pancakes (page 867).

SPEED | SERVES 2

Loaded Muesli

Muesli purists insist on an overnight soaking in milk or yogurt for maximal nutritional benefit and a pleasant creaminess. Try it that way, but if you're like me, you'll probably just mix it together at the last minute. Soaked or not, the muesli itself is fast to make and leagues better than boxed cereal. You can even make larger batches; see the Notes.

Ingredients

½ cup raisins or chopped dried fruit

3 cups rolled oats

1 cup any nuts and seeds

½ cup shredded unsweetened coconut

½ teaspoon cinnamon

Salt

Yogurt or milk for serving

Prep | Cook

Measure ½ cup raisins or other dried fruit, chopping up any larger items.

1. Combine the fruit, 3 cups rolled oats, 1 cup nuts and seeds, ½ cup coconut, ½ teaspoon cinnamon, and a sprinkle of salt.

   Taste and adjust the seasoning. Serve with yogurt or milk or store in sealed containers (it will last pretty much indefinitely).

VARIATIONS

Ginger-Clove Muesli
Substitute ¼ cup chopped crystallized ginger for the raisins and cloves for the cinnamon.

Apricot-Cardamom Muesli
Use chopped dried apricots for the fruit; use cardamom instead of cinnamon.

12 Different Dried Fruits and Seeds to Use

1. Cranberries
2. Cherries
3. Currants
4. Golden raisins
5. Apricots
6. Mangoes
7. Apples or pears
8. Pineapple
9. Sunflower seeds
10. Pumpkin seeds
11. Sesame seeds
12. Flaxseeds

NOTES

IF YOU HAVE MORE TIME

Granola
Combine the muesli ingredients, minus the dried fruit, and ¼ to ½ cup honey or maple syrup. Spread on a rimmed baking sheet and bake at 350°F, stirring occasionally until browned, about 30 minutes. Stir in the fruit and cool completely before storing.

Big Batch Muesli or Granola
This is a perfect recipe to make a big batch of on the weekend. Just multiply the quantities as many times as you like, adjusting here and there to suit your tastes. It takes a bit more time to pull together a large batch, but once it's done you have breakfast ready for the entire week, or more. Both muesli and granola keep for weeks in the fridge.

SIDES

Pick-a-Fruit Salad 921

SPEED SERVES 2

Fruit, Yogurt, and Graham Cracker Parfait

Sometimes just putting a few ingredients together is all you need or want; this is "assembling," rather than "cooking," but don't let that bother you. In this case something creamy, something crunchy, and something juicy combine to produce something delicious and kind of pretty.

Ingredients

4 large graham crackers

2 cups berries or any other fruit

2 cups yogurt

Prep | Cook

Crumble 4 graham crackers with your fingers or chop them with a chef's knife.

Hull strawberries or peel and chop any other fruit as needed to get 2 cups.

1. Divide the fruit, 2 cups yogurt, and the graham crackers between 2 squat glasses, layering them in that order until you use everything up. Serve.

VARIATIONS

12 Ways to Flavor Parfaits

Mix any of the following into the graham crackers:

1. Chopped nuts or whole seeds
2. Chopped dried fruit
3. Dried spices like cardamom, cinnamon, or ginger

Toss any of the following with the fruit:

4. Citrus juice
5. Chopped fresh basil or mint
6. Lemon or orange liqueur
7. Balsamic vinegar

Stir any of the following into the yogurt:

8. Honey or maple syup
9. Cocoa powder
10. Small splash of coffee
11. Vanilla extract
12. Jam or jelly

NOTES

EVEN FASTER

In a hurry? Forget layering the ingredients. Just stir everything together.

IF YOU HAVE MORE TIME

Warm Fruit, Graham Cracker, and Yogurt Parfait

Cook the fruit with a tablespoon or so of brown sugar in a small skillet over medium heat until it's soft and juicy. Layer as directed.

YOGURT

There are probably a hundred different varieties of yogurt in most supermarkets. Look for labels that say "live, active cultures" (or something similar) and try to avoid anything with gelatin, gums, or stabilizers. You can get pretty much any flavor imaginable, but I much prefer to buy plain yogurt and *make* any flavor imaginable by stirring in various ingredients. For any recipe in this book that calls for yogurt you can use either full-fat, low-fat, or nonfat, but as always, the full-fat version will give you the richest flavor. Greek-style yogurt is thicker than regular yogurt, and I use it often.

SPEED ◔ SERVES 2 TO 4

Piña Colada Smoothie

Smoothies make for endlessly variable breakfasts, and not much is faster than throwing a bunch of stuff into the blender.

Ingredients

1 medium pineapple

2 bananas

One 14-ounce can coconut milk

Ice cubes

Water or orange juice, if needed

Prep | Cook

Cut the top and bottom off the pineapple; stand it upright and slice around the outside to remove the skin. Still cutting from top to bottom, slice around the core; you'll have at least 4 pieces. Discard the core and chop the flesh. Refrigerate half for another use.

Peel and chop the bananas.

1. Put the pineapple, bananas, coconut milk, and a few ice cubes in a blender.

2. Blend until completely smooth, adding some water or orange juice to thin it out if necessary, and serve. Leftovers will keep for a day or 2 in the fridge.

VARIATIONS

Red Smoothie
Replace the coconut milk with 1 ½ cups yogurt and the pineapple and banana with 4 cups combined strawberries and watermelon.

Orange Smoothie
Substitute 1 cup yogurt and ½ cup orange juice for the coconut milk and 4 cups combined chopped cantaloupe and mango for the pineapple and banana.

Green Smoothie
Substitute 1 ½ cups soy milk for the coconut milk and 4 cups combined chopped avocado and green grapes for the pineapple and banana.

Blueberry and Tofu Smoothie
Swap 1 cup silken tofu and ½ cup soy milk for the coconut milk and 4 cups blueberries for the pineapple and banana.

Strawberry and Almond Milk Smoothie
Use 1 ½ cups almond milk in place of coconut milk and 4 cups strawberries instead of pineapple and banana.

Peach-Raspberry Smoothie
Replace the coconut milk with 1 ½ cups yogurt and the pineapple and banana with 4 cups combined chopped peaches and raspberries.

Apple-Ginger Smoothie
Substitute 4 cups chopped apples and 2 teaspoons minced fresh ginger for the pineapple and banana.

Cantaloupe and Basil Smoothie
Substitute 1 ½ cups yogurt for the coconut milk and 4 cups chopped cantaloupe and ¼ cup chopped fresh basil for the pineapple and banana.

SPEED SERVES 4

Broiled Grapefruit with Almond–Brown Sugar Crunch

A halved grapefruit is a classic breakfast and—obviously—pretty fast. (Nor do you need a recipe for it.) Here's an even better version where you make an almond crumble with butter and brown sugar and caramelize it under the broiler. The sweet, crunchy topping is a wonderful match for the sour grapefruit.

Ingredients

2 grapefruits

¼ cup almonds

1 tablespoon packed brown sugar

1 tablespoon cold butter

Prep | Cook

1. Turn the broiler to high; put the rack 4 inches from the heat.
   Halve the grapefruits. Put them on a baking sheet.
   Chop ¼ cup almonds.
2. Combine the almonds with 1 tablespoon packed brown sugar and 1 tablespoon cold butter. Roughly mash everything together with your fingers or a fork to make a crumbly mixture.
3. Sprinkle the almond mixture over the grapefruit halves and broil until the tops are bubbly and browned, 2 to 5 minutes. Serve immediately.

VARIATIONS

Broiled Grapefruit with Pecan-Honey Crunch
Use pecans instead of almonds and honey instead of brown sugar.

Broiled Grapefruit with Soy–Brown Sugar Glaze
Omit the almonds and butter. Mix the brown sugar with 2 teaspoons soy sauce and brush the mixture on top of the grapefruits.

Broiled Pineapple with Coconut Crunch
Substitute 4 thick pineapple rounds for the grapefruit and shredded unsweetened coconut for the almonds.

NOTES

EVEN FASTER

Grapefruit Brûlée
If you happen to have a kitchen torch lying around, these are excellent candidates for browning. Instead of broiling, apply the torch flame to the almond mixture until it starts to bubble a bit and turn brown.

Broiled Grapefruit
Skip the butter and almonds. Just sprinkle the grapefruits with the brown sugar and broil until the sugar bubbles and browns.

IF YOU HAVE MORE TIME

To coat even more of the fruit with topping, butter a piece of foil and put it on a rimmed baking sheet. Peel and segment the grapefruit, spread the pieces on the foil-lined baking sheet, sprinkle with the almond mixture, and broil.

SPEED SERVES 4

Toast with Toasted Almond Butter and Strawberries

It's amazing how simple it is to make nut butter at home. All you do is give some nuts a whirl in the food processor with a little water. It may take a minute or two for the mixture to get creamy, but the food processor does the work while you do something else.

Ingredients

1 cup almonds

2 cups strawberries

4 thick slices rustic whole wheat bread

Salt

Prep | Cook

1. If you don't have a toaster, heat the oven to 400°F.
2. Put 1 cup almonds in a large dry skillet over medium heat. Cook, shaking the skillet occasionally, until lightly browned and fragrant, 3 to 5 minutes.

   Hull and slice 2 cups strawberries.
3. Toast 4 thick slices of bread in the toaster (or on a baking sheet in the oven, turning once) until it's as dark as you like.
4. Transfer the toasted almonds to a food processor; add a sprinkle of salt. Grind to the consistency of coarse meal.
5. Add 2 tablespoons water. Process until creamy, 1 or 2 minutes. Add more water, 1 tablespoon at a time, and process until smooth and spreadable. Taste and adjust the seasoning.
6. Spread the toast generously with almond butter. Top with sliced strawberries and serve. Refrigerate leftover almond butter in a sealed container for up to a month.

VARIATIONS

Toast with Rich Toasted Almond Butter and Strawberries
Use softened butter instead of water (in the main recipe or any of the following variations).

Toast with Toasted Pecan Butter and Peaches
Replace the almonds with pecans and the strawberries with 2 large or 3 medium peaches, pitted and sliced.

Toast with Toasted Walnut Butter and Apples
Substitute walnuts for the almonds and 1 large or 2 medium apples, cored and sliced, for the strawberries.

Toast with Toasted Cashew Butter and Blueberries
Substitute cashews for the almonds, blueberries for the strawberries, and lemon juice for the water.

SPEED  SERVES 4

Breakfast Bruschetta

Bruschetta is most often toasted bread rubbed with garlic and drizzled with olive oil, but why not give it a sweet twist? In this version, suitable for breakfast—or even dessert—you rub the toasted bread with butter instead of garlic, drizzle it with diluted honey instead of olive oil, and top it with chopped strawberries and peaches. An instant fruit crisp.

Ingredients

8 thick slices any rustic bread (a little stale is fine)

1 cup strawberries

2 medium peaches

Several sprigs fresh mint

3 tablespoons honey

2 tablespoons butter

Prep | Cook

1. Turn the broiler to high; put the rack 4 inches from the heat.
2. Put 8 thick slices of bread on a baking sheet and broil, turning once, until browned on both sides, 2 to 5 minutes.

   Hull and chop 1 cup strawberries.

   Pit and chop the peaches.

   Strip the mint leaves from several sprigs and chop.
3. Combine the strawberries, peaches, and mint in a small bowl.
4. Put 3 tablespoons honey in a liquid measuring cup and add enough warm water to thin it a bit, 2 or 3 tablespoons.
5. When the bread is browned, spread each slice with a bit of butter, then drizzle with the thinned honey. Top each slice with the fruit and serve.

VARIATIONS

Maple-Banana Breakfast Bruschetta

Use 2 cups chopped bananas instead of strawberries and peaches and maple syrup in place of honey.

Mango-Lime Breakfast Bruschetta

Use 2 cups chopped mango instead of the strawberries and peaches and the juice of 1 lime instead of the warm water.

Ricotta-Honey Breakfast Bruschetta

Substitute ½ cup ricotta for the butter.

Middle Eastern Breakfast Bruschetta

Omit the honey. Swap 1 cup chopped tomato and 1 cup chopped cucumber for the strawberries and peaches and toss with the juice of ½ lemon and some chopped fresh mint. Swap ½ cup hummus for the butter.

Maple-Bacon Breakfast Bruschetta

Substitute 1 cup crumbled cooked bacon (about 6 slices) for the strawberries and peaches and maple syrup for the honey.

Egg and Chive Breakfast Bruschetta

Omit the fruit and honey. Scramble 4 eggs until they are just set (they should still be a bit runny). Stir in ¼ cup chopped chives and top the buttered toast with the egg mixture. See Scrambled Eggs with Smoked Salmon and Dill (page 838) for instructions on scrambling eggs.

NOTES

EVEN FASTER

Toast and Fruit Salad

Think of this as fruity panzanella: Increase the fruit to 4 cups and reduce the bread to 4 slices. Spread the butter on both sides of the bread before broiling. When the bread is toasted, chop it up into cubes and put it in a large bowl. Thin the honey with lemon, lime, or orange juice and mix it with the fruit. Add the fruit and honey mixture to the bread and toss. Sprinkle with a little salt if you like and garnish with chopped fresh mint.

SPEED ◔ SERVES 4

Sautéed Apples and Bananas with Honey-Yogurt Sauce

Warm caramelized apples are a classic topping for pancakes and arguably way more delicious than the pancakes themselves. Why, then, not eat them without the pancakes? It's much faster and easier and, with sliced bananas and a cool yogurt sauce, feels like a proper breakfast.

Ingredients

4 tablespoons (½ stick) butter

1 pound apples (about 3 medium)

1 tablespoon packed brown sugar

½ teaspoon cinnamon

3 bananas

1 cup Greek yogurt

2 tablespoons honey

Prep | Cook

1. Put 4 tablespoons butter in a large skillet over low heat.
   Peel, core, and thinly slice 1 pound apples.
2. Add the apples, 1 tablespoon packed brown sugar, and ½ teaspoon cinnamon to the pan and turn the heat to medium-high. Cook, stirring occasionally until the apples are tender and nicely browned, 5 to 10 minutes.
   Peel and slice the bananas.
   Stir together 1 cup Greek yogurt and 2 tablespoons honey.
3. Add the bananas to the cooked apples and toss. Divide the fruit mixture among 4 bowls, top each with a dollop of the yogurt sauce, and serve.

VARIATIONS

7 Ways to Flavor Yogurt

Stir any of the following (alone or in combination) into the yogurt instead of the honey:

1. 2 tablespoons maple syrup
2. 2 teaspoons grated citrus zest
3. 1 teaspoon vanilla extract
4. 1 tablespoon bourbon or rum
5. 1 tablespoon chopped fresh mint or basil
6. 1 teaspoon cardamom, allspice, or nutmeg
7. 1/4 cup chopped nuts

NOTES

IF YOU HAVE MORE TIME

Use 2 tablespoons of the butter to cook the apples. When they are done, transfer them to a bowl, add the remaining 2 tablespoons butter to the skillet, and cook the bananas, stirring occasionally until they are golden all over. Add them to the apples and toss.

SPEED SERVES 2 TO 4

Apricot-Cinnamon Couscous

Steeping couscous in cider—or other flavorful liquids—is a fantastic and unexpected way to infuse it with a lot of flavor in the short time that it cooks.

Ingredients

1 cup couscous

1 tablespoon packed brown sugar

1 cinnamon stick or ¼ teaspoon ground

Salt

1 ½ cups apple cider

½ cup dried apricots

Prep | Cook

1. Put 1 cup couscous, 1 tablespoon packed brown sugar, 1 cinnamon stick (or ¼ teaspoon ground), a sprinkle of salt, and 1 ½ cups apple cider in a medium pot over high heat.
   Chop ½ cup dried apricots.
2. Add the apricots to the pot. When the cider comes to a boil, cover the pot and turn off the heat.
3. Let the couscous steep for about 5 minutes. Fish out the cinnamon stick if you're using it, fluff the couscous with a fork, taste and adjust the seasoning, and serve.

VARIATIONS

Cranberry-Ginger Couscous
Use honey in place of brown sugar, 1 teaspoon minced fresh ginger (or 1/4 teaspoon dried) instead of cinnamon, cranberry juice instead of apple cider, and dried cranberries instead of apricots.

Orange-Clove Couscous
Substitute honey for the brown sugar, 1/4 teaspoon cloves for the cinnamon, orange juice for the apple cider, and chopped walnuts (stirred in right before serving) for the apricots.

Tomato-Garlic Couscous
Swap 1 tablespoon olive oil for brown sugar, 1 garlic clove, minced, for cinnamon, tomato juice for apple cider, and 1/4 cup chopped fresh basil (stirred in right before serving) for apricots.

Pineapple-Cardamom Couscous
Skip the sugar. Substitute ground cardamom for the cinnamon, pineapple juice for the apple cider, and dried pineapple for the dried apricots.

SIDES

Pick-a-Fruit Salad 921

SPEED ◑ SERVES 8

No-Bake Fruit and Cereal Bars

These fruit and cereal bars come together so quickly that you can make and set them in less than 30 minutes, with a little help from the freezer. They're also better and better for you than any granola or energy bar you can buy.

Ingredients

4 cups muesli, granola, small puffed rice, crumbled shredded wheat, or any other ready-to-eat breakfast cereal

3 cups dried fruit

¼ cup vegetable oil

Fruit juice or water

Prep | Cook

Put ½ cup of the cereal in a food processor and pulse until finely chopped. Transfer to a bowl.

1. Add 3 cups dried fruit and ¼ cup vegetable oil to the food processor. Purée until the fruit is smooth and sticky, adding just enough juice or water to keep the machine running and scraping down the sides of the bowl as necessary.
2. Transfer the fruit mixture to a large bowl and stir the remaining 3 ½ cups cereal into it by hand until it's well incorporated and broken up a bit.
3. Line an 8- or 9-inch square baking pan with plastic wrap. Spread the fruit mixture evenly into the pan and press it down. Sprinkle with the chopped cereal and lightly press it down; shake off any excess cereal that doesn't stick to the top.
4. Put the pan in the freezer until the bars are set, 15 to 20 minutes. Turn them out of the pan, remove the plastic wrap, and cut them into squares. Serve or store in the refrigerator for several days.

VARIATIONS

6 Ways to Flavor No-Bake Fruit and Cereal Bars

Add any of the following to the food processor along with the dried fruit:

1. ½ cup nuts or shredded unsweetened coconut (if it's not already in the cereal)
2. 1 teaspoon cinnamon, allspice, nutmeg, or cloves
3. 2 tablespoons honey, maple syrup, or peanut butter
4. 1 teaspoon vanilla extract
5. 1 tablespoon cocoa powder
6. 2 teaspoons grated citrus zest

NOTES

MAKE YOUR OWN

Loaded Muesli 806

IF YOU HAVE MORE TIME

Put the bars in the refrigerator to firm up instead of the freezer. It will probably take an hour or so.

DRIED FRUIT IN THE FOOD PROCESSOR

If you think that putting dried fruit in the food processor will result in a sticky glob you're exactly right. But sometimes that's just what you want. In the case of these breakfast bars, the sticky insides of the dried fruit are what binds everything together. You can apply this technique to other dishes as well: If you pulse dried fruit and nuts in the food processor, roll them into balls, and dust them in cocoa powder, you've got bonbons. On the savory end of things you can mix some of that sticky dried fruit with ground meat to make meatballs or burgers; the fruit not only helps bind them but also supplies flavor and moisture.

SPEED ◑ SERVES 2

Maple-Orange Oatmeal with Caramelized Pecans

You've got to do something while oatmeal cooks and, even though that time is minimal, you might as well take full advantage of it. Here I make a sweet, rich maple-pecan topping.

Ingredients

1 cup rolled oats

1 cup milk

Salt

1 orange

2 tablespoons butter

¾ cup pecans

2 tablespoons maple syrup, plus more for drizzling

Prep | Cook

1. Put 1 cup rolled oats, 1 cup milk, 1 ¼ cups water, and a sprinkle of salt in a medium saucepan over high heat.

   Grate the zest from the orange and add it to the pot; refrigerate the remaining fruit for another use.

2. When the liquid comes to a boil, turn the heat to low and cook, stirring occasionally until the liquid is just absorbed, 8 to 12 minutes.

3. Put 2 tablespoons butter in a medium skillet over medium heat.

4. When the butter starts to sizzle, add ¾ cup pecans and 2 tablespoons maple syrup. Cook, stirring frequently and adjusting the heat so the syrup doesn't burn, until the pecans are coated and caramelized, 3 or 4 minutes. Turn off the heat.

5. When the oatmeal is done, divide it between 2 bowls. Top with the pecan mixture, drizzle with a little more maple syrup if you like, and serve.

VARIATIONS

Maple-Ginger Oatmeal with Caramelized Walnuts
Use walnuts instead of pecans and ½ inch minced fresh ginger instead of orange zest.

Honey-Lemon Oatmeal with Caramelized Pine Nuts
Substitute pine nuts for the pecans, honey for the maple syrup, and lemon for the orange.

Peanut and Jelly Oatmeal
Omit the orange. Substitute peanuts for the pecans and jelly (any kind you like, plus a splash of water) for the maple syrup.

Oatmeal with Soy Sauce and Scallions
One of my favorite savory breakfasts. Skip the nuts and go straight to the oatmeal. Cook the oatmeal in 2 ¼ cups water or a combination of water and stock; divide it between the bowls and garnish with soy sauce and chopped fresh scallions. A little Sriracha and/or sesame oil is great too.

NOTES

EVEN FASTER
Don't caramelize the pecans, but chop them up. Stir the butter and maple syrup into the oatmeal when it's done and top with chopped nuts.

SPEED ◑ SERVES 2 TO 4

Honey-Cheddar Grits with Sage

Grits are the oatmeal of the South. Most of the rest of the country overlooks them, which is too bad, because they are fast, tasty, and versatile. Make basic grits with a pat of butter and a pinch of salt and you'll understand all the fuss. Or if you have time, try this gussied-up version, which is infused with sage and finished with cheese and a swirl of honey.

Ingredients

1 ¼ cups milk

1 cup grits, preferably stone-ground

1 sprig fresh sage

2 ounces cheddar cheese (½ cup grated)

1 tablespoon honey, or to taste

Salt and pepper

Prep | Cook

1. Put 1 ¼ cups milk and 1 ¼ cups water in a small saucepan over medium-high heat.
2. When the liquid comes to a boil, turn the heat to low and slowly whisk in 1 cup grits, trying to eliminate any lumps.
3. Add 1 sprig fresh sage, cover, and cook, stirring occasionally and adding more liquid if the grits become too thick, until all the liquid is absorbed and the grits are creamy, 10 to 15 minutes.
   Grate ½ cup cheddar cheese.
4. When the grits are done, remove and discard the sage and stir in the cheddar until it melts. Stir in 1 tablespoon honey and a sprinkle of salt and pepper. Taste and adjust the seasoning and serve immediately.

VARIATIONS

Maple-Almond Grits
Omit the sage. Replace the cheddar with ¼ cup chopped almonds and the honey with maple syrup.

Parmesan Grits with Rosemary
Swap rosemary for the sage, Parmesan for the cheddar, and olive oil for the honey.

Soy-Orange Grits with Ginger
Substitute 1 inch fresh ginger, sliced into coins, for the sage, 1 tablespoon grated orange zest for the cheddar, and soy sauce for the honey.

Classic Buttery Grits
Omit the sage and cheddar. Swap 2 tablespoons butter for the honey.

NOTES

TOPPING GRITS
Anything you can stir into polenta will go equally well with grits. Try any of these.

1. Sautéed Greens with Garlic (page 924)
2. Garlicky Mushrooms (page 956)
3. Crunchy Okra (page 959)
4. Broiled Cherry Tomatoes (page 931)
5. Fajita Peppers and Onions (page 928)
6. Arugula with Fried Eggs and Shaved Parmesan (page 50)
7. Charred Brussels Sprout Salad with Walnuts and Gorgonzola (page 126)
8. Shrimp Gumbo (page 260)
9. Beef and Butter Bean Chili (page 272)
10. Collard Greens Stewed with Smoked Pork (page 268)
11. Fast Feijoada (page 504)
12. Provençal Chicken (page 644)
13. Sloppy Joes (page 728)
14. Homemade Chorizo with Pinto Beans (page 762)

SIDES

Green Salad 911

Warm Tortillas 907

Pick-a-Fruit Salad 921

Eggs in a Nutshell

Eggs are among our most versatile and popular ingredients, beloved not only at the breakfast table but also for lunch and snacks. They're essential to many of our favorite desserts, and quite often the perfect thing to cook when you're not sure what to make. And the best thing? They're the most satisfying food that you can cook in less than 3 minutes. Simply having them in your fridge is a major step toward fast cooking.

Buying Eggs

The slowest thing about eggs is buying them. Eggs come not only in multiple sizes and colors but with all kinds of labels and grades as well, some of which can be helpful and others needlessly confusing—see What Egg Labels Mean (or Don't), opposite, for decoding advice. The ideal situation is to buy eggs that are produced locally. And with more and more farmers' markets popping up, and even regular people starting to raise hens in their backyards, they're becoming easier to find. For the recipes in this book, buy large or extra-large eggs; needless to say, the fresher the better.

Storing Eggs

Strangely enough, the door of the fridge is the worst place to store them because it is often too warm. Keep them where it's nice and cool, usually the bottom, toward the back.

Checking Eggs for Freshness

Fresh eggs feature firm yolks that sit high on a mound of whites. An older egg is runnier, with a flatter yolk; those are still fine to eat (unless, of course, they smell rotten).

Cracking Eggs

Cracking an egg is fast. Fishing out tiny pieces of shell from the bowl is not. To keep bits of shell out of the egg, smack the side sharply on a hard flat surface instead of on the lip of the bowl.

Runny Yolks

There are few foods more luxurious and satisfying than an egg with an oozing yolk. Also, a runny yolk is a lot faster to produce than a hard one. But is it safe? The danger of salmonella in eggs is slim, but not nonexistent. If you are concerned for any reason, make sure to use properly stored eggs, rinse the shells before cracking, and cook them thoroughly. Salmonella is killed in eggs when you maintain their temperature at 160°F—firm yolks—for 1 minute or 140°F—runny yolks—for 5 minutes.

What Egg Labels Mean (Or Don't)

Knowing what the labels on eggs mean (or don't mean) will help you get in, get eggs, and get out.

Type of Egg	Description
CAGE-FREE	The hens aren't in cages, but they're probably not outside either.
HORMONE-FREE	It's illegal to raise hens using hormones. That's not to say that there aren't producers who do it, but any claim about hormone-free eggs is like saying "we obey the law."
FREE-RANGE	The hens have access to the outdoors, but that doesn't mean they actually go outside—10,000 hens in a barn with a two-foot door could be called free-range. Plus, the USDA applies the term *free-range* only to meat chickens, not laying hens, so there is no official standard for "free-range" eggs.
NATURAL	There are no standards for "natural" eggs. An egg producer's putting a "natural" label on a carton is the equivalent of my putting one on the front of this book. In other words, it's meaningless.
VEGETARIAN-FED	In theory this would mean that there are no animal by-products in the feed that the hens eat, but *vegetarian-fed* is not a term that is regulated or enforced.
PASTURED	Again, this is not a regulated standard, but it refers to hens that are raised out on pasture. They forage for seeds and insects and are typically fed grain as well, which may or may not be organic. Pastured eggs typically come from small farms, so you are less likely to see that label in the supermarket.
ORGANIC (CERTIFIED ORGANIC)	This is a label that actually means something: The hens are raised without cages and with access to the outdoors; are fed organic, all-vegetarian diets; and are raised without antibiotics, pesticides, or insecticides. The eggs aren't irradiated (treated with radiation to kill pathogens). It's worth noting, however, that a small farm that isn't certified organic may very well treat its hens better than a large farm that is.
CERTIFIED HUMANE, OR ANIMAL WELFARE APPROVED	These are certifications granted by independent organizations whose inspection standards are approved by the USDA. They guarantee a certain (comparatively high) standard of living for the animals on a given farm, often ensuring a minimum amount of space, fresh air, fresh water, food, and limited stress.

SPEED SERVES 4

Roasting-Pan French Toast

What slows French toast down is cooking it in batches in a skillet. While not everyone owns a griddle, most have a roasting pan. Set it over two burners and you can cook eight slices in one go. If you decide to go the skillet route or are making several batches, keep finished slices warm in a 200°F oven on a baking sheet lined with a rack to keep them crisp.

Ingredients

2 eggs

1 cup milk

1 tablespoon sugar

1 teaspoon vanilla extract

Salt

4 tablespoons (½ stick) butter, plus more as needed

8 slices bread

Maple syrup for serving (optional)

Prep | Cook

1. Set a roasting pan on 2 burners over medium-low heat.
2. Crack 2 eggs into a large, shallow bowl or dish. Add 1 cup milk, 1 tablespoon sugar, 1 teaspoon vanilla, and a sprinkle of salt; whisk to combine.
3. Add 4 tablespoons butter to the roasting pan and swirl it around. Raise the heat to medium.
4. Dip 8 slices bread, 1 slice at a time, into the egg mixture, soaking it well and coating both sides. Put each slice in the roasting pan as you finish.
5. Cook, turning once and adding more butter if the toast starts to stick, until browned on both sides, 3 to 5 minutes per side. Serve with maple syrup if you like.

VARIATIONS

Cinnamon-Orange French Toast
Add 1 teaspoon cinnamon and 1 teaspoon grated orange zest to the custard.

Rosemary-Parmesan French Toast
Omit the sugar, vanilla, and maple syrup. Add 1 teaspoon minced fresh rosemary and ¼ cup grated Parmesan to the custard. Drizzle with olive oil.

SIDES

Pick-a-Fruit Salad 921

SPEED SERVES 2

Tortilla French Toast

Flour tortillas aren't an obvious choice for French toast, but when you think about how good they are griddled in butter, like quesadillas, using them this way starts to make sense. Stuffed with ricotta and strawberries, rolled into hand-held packages, and sprinkled with cinnamon sugar, they're hard to resist. Ditto the variations.

Ingredients

Butter

1 egg

½ cup milk

½ teaspoon vanilla extract

Salt

4 large flour tortillas

1 teaspoon cinnamon

1 teaspoon sugar

1 cup strawberries

1 cup ricotta cheese

Prep | Cook

1. Heat the oven to 200°F. Put 1 teaspoon butter in a large skillet over low heat.

2. Crack 1 egg into a baking pan large enough to hold the tortillas. Add ½ cup milk, ½ teaspoon vanilla, and a sprinkle of salt and whisk to combine.

3. Dip a tortilla into the egg mixture, coating both sides, and put in the skillet. Raise the heat to medium and cook, turning once and adding another teaspoon of butter when the skillet gets too dry, until golden and crisp on both sides but still pliable, 1 or 2 minutes per side.

   Mix together 1 teaspoon cinnamon and 1 teaspoon sugar in a small bowl.

4. As each tortilla is done, sprinkle it with some cinnamon sugar, put on a baking sheet or a piece of aluminum foil, and transfer to the warm oven. Continue with 3 more tortillas.

   Hull and slice 1 cup strawberries.

5. Spread $1/4$ cup ricotta over each tortilla and top with the strawberries. Roll up each tortilla, sprinkle the outsides with more cinnamon sugar, and serve hot or warm.

VARIATIONS

Jam-Filled Tortilla French Toast

Omit the strawberries, ricotta, cinnamon, and sugar. Spread the cooked tortillas with a thin layer of any jam right before rolling. Sprinkle the outsides with a little powdered sugar.

Mexican Tortilla French Toast

Better to eat with a knife and fork. Skip the strawberries, ricotta, cinnamon, and sugar. Swap a dash of hot sauce for the vanilla. Spread the cooked tortillas with a thin layer of salsa, sour cream, and/or guacamole right before rolling. Top with chopped scallions and a little queso fresco.

NOTES

EVEN FASTER

If you happen to have two skillets large enough to hold the tortillas, this process will go twice as fast.

SIDES

Pick-a-Fruit Salad 921

SPEED SERVES 2

Omelet for Two

Omelets are miraculous. Take a pantry staple, add whatever other ingredients you have at hand—leftover vegetables or meat, cheese, beans—and you end up with a dish that is much more than the sum of its parts. A couple of tips: Make sure the heat is high enough and add the cheese toward the end when the eggs have nearly set, so it doesn't burn.

Ingredients

5 eggs

2 tablespoons milk or cream (optional)

Salt and pepper

2 ounces Gruyère cheese (½ cup grated)

3 tablespoons butter

Prep | Cook

1. Crack the eggs into a medium mixing bowl. Add 2 tablespoons milk or cream if you're using it and a sprinkle of salt and pepper. Whisk until the egg yolks and whites are thoroughly combined. Grate ½ cup Gruyère.

2. Put a medium skillet (preferably nonstick) over medium heat. After about a minute, add 2 tablespoons butter and swirl it around. When the foam subsides, add the eggs and cook, undisturbed, for 30 seconds.

3. Push the edges of the eggs toward the center with a heatproof rubber spatula, tipping the pan so the uncooked eggs in the center slide out to the perimeter.

4. When the eggs are becoming firm enough that they no longer slide under the omelet, scatter the cheese on top. Continue cooking until the omelet is mostly cooked but still runny in the center, about 3 minutes total.

5. Fold the omelet in half or into thirds and slide it out of the pan onto a plate. Rub the top with 1 tablespoon butter, cut it in half, and serve immediately.

VARIATIONS

9 Ways to Flavor an Omelet

Add any of the following to the eggs before beating:

1. Up to ¼ cup chopped fresh parsley, basil, or dill
2. Up to 1 tablespoon chopped fresh rosemary, sage, thyme, or oregano
3. Up to 1 tablespoon soy sauce (go easy on the salt)
4. Up to 1 tablespoon Dijon mustard
5. Dash of hot sauce

Add any of the following to the omelet shortly before folding it up:

6. ½ cup any cooked meat, seafood, or vegetables
7. ½ cup chopped tomato
8. ½ cup any cooked grains or beans
9. ½ cup chopped fresh fruit or 2 tablespoons jam

SIDES

Warm Buttery Bread 906

Green Salad 911

Tomato Salad 913

Garlicky Mushrooms 956

Crisp Roasted Potatoes 965

SPEED SERVES 2

Fried Eggs with Chimichurri

Chimichurri, the bright and spicy Argentine herb sauce, is traditionally served with grilled steak. But it's one of those condiments that makes everything better, including simple fried eggs. Plus it's fast; a few whirls in the food processor while the eggs cook and it's ready to go.

Ingredients

1 bunch fresh parsley

1 bunch fresh cilantro

2 garlic cloves

1 tablespoon butter

4 eggs

¼ cup olive oil

2 tablespoons red wine vinegar

¼ teaspoon red chile flakes

Salt and pepper

Prep | Cook

Chop ½ cup parsley leaves and ½ cup cilantro.

Peel 2 garlic cloves. Put the herbs and garlic in a food processor.

1. Put a large skillet over medium heat. After about 1 minute, add 1 tablespoon butter and swirl it around. When the butter foam subsides, crack the eggs into the skillet and cook until the whites are no longer translucent, 2 or 3 minutes.

   Add ¼ cup olive oil, 2 tablespoons red wine vinegar, ¼ teaspoon red chile flakes, and a sprinkle of salt and pepper to the food processor.

2. When the egg whites are no longer translucent, turn the heat to low and sprinkle with salt and pepper.

   Purée the herb mixture, stopping to scrape down the sides as necessary. Taste and adjust the seasoning.

3. The eggs are done when the whites are completely firm and the yolks are as runny as you like them, just another few minutes. Spoon some of the chimichurri over the top, and serve immediately. Store any leftover sauce in the fridge, covered, for a few days.

VARIATIONS

Fried Eggs with Pesto
Replace the parsley and cilantro with 1 cup fresh basil leaves, the red wine vinegar with pine nuts, and the red chile flakes with 1/4 cup grated Parmesan.

Fried Eggs with Romesco
Substitute 1/2 cup chopped roasted red peppers for the parsley and cilantro, sherry vinegar for the red wine vinegar, and 1/4 cup almonds for the red chile flakes.

NOTES

COOKING FRIED EGGS EVENLY
Sometimes when you crack an egg into a skillet it will spread out thin, but other times it will set up very high—that's the sign of a good, fresh egg but it can make it harder to cook the whites evenly. To get a tall egg to finish cooking quickly you can either cut through some of the uncooked parts of the white with a paring knife or cover the skillet and cook for a minute or 2 longer. Alternatively, take your time; even a fried egg is as firm or as runny as you like it in no more than 10 minutes.

SIDES

Warm Buttery Bread 906

Chile-Cumin Black Beans 937

Warm Tortillas 907

Green Salad 911

Broiled Cherry Tomatoes 931

Crisp Roasted Potatoes 965

SPEED SERVES 2

Scrambled Eggs with Smoked Salmon and Dill

Soft scrambled eggs are the perfect canvas for the classic combination of smoked salmon and dill. For extra creaminess, see the cream cheese variation.

Ingredients

1 bunch fresh dill

4 ounces smoked salmon

2 tablespoons butter

1 tablespoon milk or cream (optional)

4 eggs

Salt and pepper

Prep | Cook

Strip 1/4 cup dill leaves from the stems and chop.

Slice or chop 4 ounces smoked salmon into 1-inch pieces.

1. Put 2 tablespoons butter and 1 tablespoon milk or cream if you're using it in a medium skillet. Crack 4 eggs into the skillet and turn the heat to medium-high.
2. Cook, stirring constantly with a whisk. Be gentle so the eggs don't foam, but consistent so they don't stick. If they are getting stuck to the bottom of the pan, turn the heat down.
3. When the eggs have formed loose curds, stir in the dill and smoked salmon. Continue cooking for another minute to warm through.
4. Taste, season with salt and pepper, and serve immediately.

VARIATIONS

Scrambled Eggs with Salmon, Cream Cheese, and Dill
Swap 2 tablespoons softened cream cheese for the milk or cream.

Scrambled Eggs with Prosciutto and Basil
Use basil instead of dill and prosciutto instead of smoked salmon.

Scrambled Eggs with Chorizo and Parsley
Substitute parsley for the dill and chopped smoked chorizo for the smoked salmon.

Scrambled Eggs with Ham and Tarragon
Replace the dill with tarragon and the smoked salmon with sliced ham.

Scrambled Eggs with Smoked Trout and Dill
Instead of smoked salmon, use smoked trout.

NOTES

IF YOU HAVE MORE TIME
Scramble the eggs over ultra-low heat, breaking curds up as they form. This can take up to a half hour, but the results are incredible.

SCRAMBLING EGGS
Scrambled eggs very much lend themselves to fast cooking, because if you don't get them off the heat quickly they'll overcook. And unless you like your eggs firm, there is no good reason to cook them any other way but soft and runny. The optional milk or cream helps prevent overcooking and adds richness.

SIDES

Bruschetta 909

Warm Tortillas 907

Green Salad 911

Tomato Salad with Olive Oil and Yogurt 913

Crisp Roasted Potatoes 965

SPEED SERVES 2

Goat Cheese and Spinach Scrambled Eggs

Scrambled eggs are creamy on their own but become exponentially so with the addition of soft goat cheese, its subtle tang tempered by the earthy spinach.

Ingredients

1 small bunch spinach (about 8 ounces)

3 tablespoons butter

Salt and pepper

4 eggs

1 sprig fresh rosemary

4 ounces goat cheese

Prep | Cook

Trim any thick stems from the spinach and chop the leaves.

1. Put 2 tablespoons butter in a medium skillet over medium-high heat.
2. When the butter starts to sizzle, add the spinach, sprinkle with salt and pepper, and cook, stirring occasionally until wilted, 2 or 3 minutes.

   Crack the eggs into a medium mixing bowl, sprinkle with salt and pepper, and beat.

   Strip the rosemary leaves from 1 sprig and chop.
3. When the spinach is wilted, add 1 tablespoon butter to the skillet and swirl it around. Add the eggs and cook, stirring frequently and scraping the sides with a heatproof rubber spatula until they begin to curdle.
4. Stir in the rosemary and 4 ounces goat cheese. If some parts of the eggs are drying out, remove the skillet from the heat and continue stirring until the cooking slows down a bit. Then return to the heat.

5. When the eggs are creamy, soft, and still a bit runny, they're done, no more than 10 minutes total. Taste and adjust the seasoning and serve immediately.

VARIATIONS

Feta and Spinach Scrambled Eggs

Substitute oregano for the rosemary and feta for the goat cheese. If you like, stir in a handful of chopped tomato when you add the oregano and feta.

Ricotta and Spinach Scrambled Eggs

Use ¼ cup chopped fresh parsley or basil instead of rosemary and ricotta in place of goat cheese.

Parmesan and Kale Scrambled Eggs

Substitute kale for the spinach and ½ cup grated Parmesan for the goat cheese. Allow a few extra minutes for the kale to wilt before adding the eggs.

NOTES

EVEN FASTER

Start the eggs right away and add the spinach along with the rosemary and goat cheese; the spinach will wilt as the eggs finish cooking. The spinach will be chewier this way, more like a vegetable and less like a sauce.

SCRAMBLED EGGS FOR A CROWD

Unlike fried or poached eggs, scrambled eggs are not much harder to make for a crowd than for just a few people. It takes a little extra time to crack, beat, and cook the eggs, a skillet big enough to hold them all, and some more of whatever ingredients you're stirring in. Other than that the process is the same, and the results don't suffer a bit. Just make sure to stir often; with a thick layer of eggs it's harder to see the curds on the bottom of the skillet that are getting firm, and you run the risk of sticking or even scorching.

SIDES

Bruschetta 909

Warm Buttery Bread 906

Warm Tortillas 907

Broiled Cherry Tomatoes 931

Green Salad 911

Crisp Roasted Potatoes 965

SPEED SERVES 2

Tortilla Scramble

Admittedly, frying your own tortillas is not faster than buying chips, but they'll be better than anything you'll find in the store. So see Even Faster if this seems too much for you. Either way you do it, crisp tortillas add phenomenal texture to soft scrambled eggs. With all the colorful ingredients and garnishes in this dish, I like to take the skillet right to the table.

Ingredients

2 corn tortillas

1 medium onion

¼ cup vegetable oil

2 poblano chiles

Salt and pepper

1 ripe tomato

1 avocado

2 scallions

4 eggs

2 ounces queso fresco (½ cup crumbled)

Prep | Cook

Line a plate with paper towels.

Cut the tortillas in half, stack, and cut into ½-inch-wide strips.

Trim, peel, and slice the onion.

1. Put ¼ cup vegetable oil in a medium skillet over medium heat.

   Core, seed, and slice the poblanos.

2. When the oil is hot (toss in a bit of tortilla; it will sizzle), add the tortilla strips. Cook, stirring constantly until they are golden brown and crisp, 1 or 2 minutes. Transfer the strips to the paper towels with a slotted spoon and sprinkle with salt.

3. Raise the heat to medium-high. Add the onion and poblanos to the skillet, sprinkle with salt and pepper, and cook, stirring occasionally, until they soften and begin to brown, 5 to 10 minutes.

   Core and chop the tomato.

   Halve and pit the avocado, scoop out the flesh, and chop.

   Trim and chop the scallions.

   Crack the eggs into a medium bowl, sprinkle with salt and pepper, and beat.

4. Add the eggs to the skillet and cook, stirring frequently and scraping the sides with a heatproof rubber spatula until they begin to curdle, 3 to 5 minutes.

5. Stir in the tomato and tortilla strips. If some parts of the eggs are drying out, remove the skillet from the heat and continue stirring until the cooking slows down a bit. Then return to the heat.

6. When the eggs are creamy, soft, and still a bit runny, they're done, just another minute or 2. Sprinkle with the avocado and scallions and sprinkle ½ cup crumbled queso fresco over the top. Serve immediately.

VARIATIONS

Pita Scramble
Use olive oil in place of vegetable oil and 1 pita pocket, split around the equator and cut into strips, instead of tortillas. Substitute red onion for yellow, red bell peppers for the poblanos, ½ cup chopped kalamata olives for the avocado, ¼ cup chopped fresh parsley for the scallions, and feta for the queso fresco.

French Bread Scramble
Substitute 2 tablespoons butter and 2 tablespoons olive oil for the vegetable oil, 1 cup crusty bread cubes for the tortillas, 2 large shallots for the onion, ½ cup chopped ham for the poblanos, 2 tablespoons capers for the avocado, 2 tablespoons chopped fresh tarragon for the scallions, and goat cheese for the queso fresco.

Chicken Tortilla Scramble
Add 2 chopped boneless, skinless chicken thighs along with the onion and poblanos.

NOTES

EVEN FASTER
Instead of frying your own tortillas, crumble in store-bought tortilla chips. Reduce the amount of oil you use to just a couple of tablespoons.

SIDES

Chile-Cumin Black Beans 937

Warm Tortillas 907

Avocado with Lime and Chili Salt 920

Mexican Street Corn 932

Sautéed Sweet Potatoes with Chipotle and Lime 964

Scrambles

1 Heat the pan.

Put a few tablespoons of oil, butter, or a combination in a large skillet over low heat. The fat will heat up very slowly, so you'll have plenty of time to pick out and prep a few ingredients.

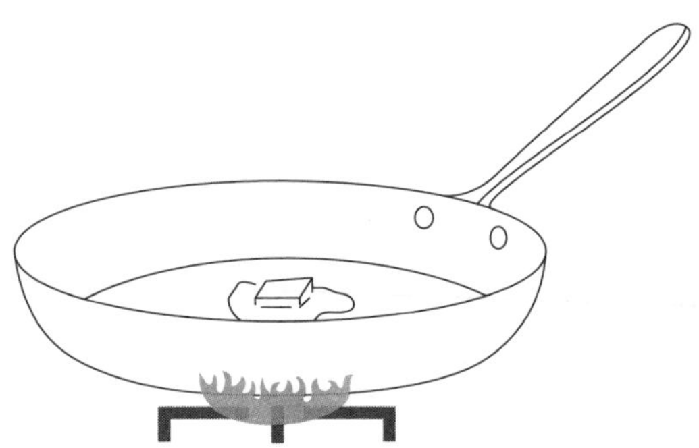

2 Choose ingredients to sauté.

Think about chopped raw or cooked vegetables and greens; raw or cooked bits of meat, poultry, or seafood; cubes of bread or chopped tortillas; or cooked grains and beans. Use whatever you have handy and figure 1 cup per egg.

3 Sauté.

Raw vegetables should be softened and raw greens wilted; raw meat, poultry, and seafood should be cooked all the way through, while bread and tortillas should be cooked until golden and crisp. Precooked ingredients just need to be warmed.

4 Prepare eggs (or tofu).

Beat a few eggs with salt and pepper or open a package of soft or silken tofu (or beat the two together). Either one adds creaminess to the dish and binds everything together. One egg per person will do just fine.

5 Stir in the eggs or tofu.

Once your ingredients are ready, add the eggs or tofu and cook, stirring often with a rubber sspatula. (Tofu will break up into small, scrambled-egg-like curds as you stir it.) Cook and stir over medium-low heat until everything is hot and all the ingredients are combined.

6 Season and serve.

Add an extra burst of flavor with chopped fresh herbs or scallions, citrus zest, Parmesan, soy sauce, sesame oil, or hot sauce. Serve right away.

SPEED SERVES 2 TO 4

Chipotle Black Beans with Fried Eggs

Chipotle chiles (smoked jalapeños) in adobo sauce have an intense heat and a smokiness that works wonders on black beans. That's why nearly every restaurant with a brunch—Mexican or not—has something like this on its menu. The home-cooked version is almost always better.

Ingredients

2 tablespoons vegetable oil

1 small onion

2 garlic cloves

2 chipotle chiles in adobo, with their sauce to taste

4 cups cooked or canned black beans (two 15-ounce cans)

4 scallions

Salt and pepper

½ cup chicken or vegetable stock or water

1 tablespoon butter

4 eggs

Prep | Cook

1. Put 2 tablespoons vegetable oil in a medium skillet over medium heat.

   Trim, peel, and chop the onion.

2. When the oil is hot, add the onion and cook, stirring occasionally until softened, 3 to 5 minutes.

   Peel and mince 2 garlic cloves.

   Chop 2 chipotles.

   If you're using canned beans, rinse and drain them.

   Trim and chop the scallions.

3. When the onion is soft, add the garlic and chipotles (include some of the adobo sauce if you like) and cook, stirring for a minute. Add the beans, a sprinkle of salt and pepper, and ½ cup stock or water. Adjust the heat so the mixture bubbles gently.

4. Put a large skillet over medium heat. After about 1 minute, add 1 tablespoon butter and swirl it around. When the butter foam subsides, crack the eggs into the skillet.

5. When the egg whites are no longer translucent, just a minute, turn the heat to low and sprinkle the eggs with salt and pepper.

6. The eggs are done when the whites are completely firm and the yolks are as runny as you like them, just another few minutes. Meanwhile, taste the beans and adjust the seasoning. Serve the eggs on top of the beans, garnished with the scallions.

VARIATIONS

Tahini Chickpeas with Fried Eggs
Substitute olive oil for vegetable, red onion for yellow, 1 teaspoon cumin for the chipotle chiles, chickpeas for the black beans, a handful of chopped fresh parsley for the scallions, and ¼ cup tahini for ¼ cup of the stock. If you like, roughly mash the chickpeas in the skillet with a potato masher.

BBQ Bacon Pinto Beans with Fried Eggs
Replace the onion with 4 slices chopped bacon, the chipotles with 1 teaspoon each paprika, chili powder, and brown sugar, the black beans with pinto beans, the scallions with a handful of chopped cilantro, and ¼ cup of the stock with ¼ cup ketchup.

White Beans and Zucchini with Fried Eggs
Substitute olive oil for vegetable, 4 cups grated zucchini and 2 cups white beans for the black beans, a handful of chopped fresh parsley for the scallions, and the juice of 1 lemon for ¼ cup of the stock.

NOTES

MAKE YOUR OWN

Cooked Beans 496

Chicken Stock 213

Vegetable Stock 212

CHIPOTLES IN ADOBO
Chipotles in adobo come in small cans, but even so you'll rarely use the whole thing in one go. If you don't know when you'll use them next, transfer the chipotles and their adobo sauce to a small glass jar and keep them in the fridge for a few weeks or longer in the freezer. If you freeze them, store them in separate servings.

SIDES

Warm Tortillas 907

Avocado with Lime and Chili Salt 920

Tomato Salad 913

Jícama and Radish Salad 918

Broiled Cherry Tomatoes 931

Sautéed Sweet Potatoes with Chipotle and Lime 964

SPEED ◔ SERVES 6

Broiled Eggs

You've probably never broiled an egg before, but if you're cooking for a crowd, this is the best way to make sure all your eggs finish at the same time. The key to making it work is to position them as far away from the heat as you can so they'll cook all the way through before the top gets too firm. The muffin tin helps keep each egg in place, and the uniform shape allows them to cook evenly and at the same rate.

Ingredients

2 tablespoons butter

12 eggs

Salt and pepper

Prep | Cook

1. Turn the broiler to high; put the rack 6 inches from the heat. Grease a 12-cup muffin tin with 2 tablespoons butter.
2. Carefully crack 1 egg into each of the cups.
3. Put the muffin tin in the oven and broil until the eggs are just set (the yolks should still be slightly runny), 6 to 8 minutes.
4. Gently remove each egg from the muffin tin. Sprinkle with salt and pepper and serve.

VARIATIONS

7 Ways to Flavor Broiled Eggs

Sprinkle about 1 tablespoon of any of the following on each of the eggs before baking:

1. Grated cheese
2. Goat cheese or cream cheese
3. Chopped olives or capers (use only a teaspoon)
4. Chopped prosciutto, crumbled cooked bacon, or ham
5. Chopped mushrooms, onions, or bell peppers
6. Chopped tomato
7. Chopped raw spinach leaves or other tender greens

NOTES

IF YOU HAVE MORE TIME

Baked Eggs

Bake the eggs in a 350°F oven until just set, 15 to 20 minutes.

SIDES

Warm Buttery Bread 906

Crisp Roasted Potatoes 965

Green Salad 911

SPEED ◐ SERVES 2

Fast Florentine

Typical eggs Florentine consist of sautéed spinach and a poached egg on top of an English muffin with Mornay (cheese) sauce over all. Cooking all of those components separately takes a while, and I'm not convinced that the dish is any better because of it. Here I cook everything except the English muffin in the same skillet, wilting the spinach in the cheese sauce, then poaching the eggs right in the spinach, which is actually better than poaching in water because the spinach cradles the eggs.

Ingredients

3 tablespoons butter

1 tablespoon flour

1 cup milk

2 ounces Gruyère cheese (½ cup grated)

1 garlic clove

2 medium bunches spinach (1 ½ pounds)

Pinch of nutmeg

Salt and pepper

2 English muffins

4 eggs

Prep | Cook

1. Put 2 tablespoons butter and 1 tablespoon flour in a medium skillet over medium heat. Cook, stirring occasionally until the flour is incorporated into the butter, a minute or 2.
2. Add 1 cup milk, whisking to break up any lumps.

   Grate ½ cup Gruyère.

   Peel and mince 1 garlic clove.
3. Add the Gruyère and garlic to the skillet, whisking constantly to incorporate the cheese.

   Trim any thick stems from the spinach and chop the leaves.
4. Add the spinach to the skillet (in batches if necessary) along with a pinch of nutmeg and a sprinkle of salt and pepper. Cook, stirring occasionally until the spinach wilts into the sauce, 3 or 4 minutes.

   Split and toast 2 English muffins. Spread with 1 tablespoon butter.

5. Make 4 indentations in the spinach mixture and carefully crack 1 egg into each of them. Sprinkle the eggs with salt and pepper, cover the skillet, and cook just until the whites are set and the yolks have filmed over but are still runny, about 5 minutes.

6. When the eggs are cooked, carefully scoop them along with some spinach mixture on top of the English muffins and serve immediately.

VARIATIONS

Eggs Poached in Mushrooms
Substitute Parmesan for the Gruyère, 1 ½ pounds sliced mushrooms for the spinach, and 1 teaspoon chopped fresh rosemary for the nutmeg. Cook the mushrooms in the butter until soft, 6 to 8 minutes, before sprinkling in the flour. If the pan is too dry by the time you're ready to add the flour, add a little more butter first.

Eggs Poached in Creamy Tomato Sauce
Use Parmesan instead of the Gruyère, one 28-ounce can crushed tomatoes instead of the spinach, and ¼ teaspoon red chile flakes instead of the nutmeg.

SIDES

Broiled Cherry Tomatoes 931

Garlicky Mushrooms 956

Sweet Potato Fries 963

Crisp Roasted Potatoes 965

SPEED ◐ SERVES 2

Fried Eggs with Mushrooms and Leeks

There's not much better than a soft egg yolk oozing over a pile of meaty, caramelized mushrooms. The eggs cook in just a few minutes, but you can't rush the mushrooms or they won't develop the deep, earthy flavor that makes them so good.

Ingredients

4 tablespoons olive oil

1 medium leek

1 pound button, cremini, or shiitake mushrooms

Salt and pepper

1 garlic clove

Several sprigs fresh parsley

2 ounces Parmesan cheese (½ cup grated)

¼ cup white wine or water

4 eggs

Prep | Cook

1. Put 3 tablespoons olive oil in a large skillet over medium-high heat.

   Trim the leek and slice the white and light green parts only.

2. When the oil is hot, add the leek.

   Trim and quarter the mushrooms. (If you're using shiitakes, discard the stems.)

3. Add the mushrooms to the skillet, sprinkle with salt and pepper, and cook, stirring occasionally until tender and well browned, 8 to 10 minutes.

   Peel and mince 1 garlic clove.

   Strip the parsley leaves from several sprigs and chop.

   Grate ½ cup Parmesan.

4. Stir ¼ cup white wine or water into the skillet and let the liquid mostly bubble away. Stir in the garlic and parsley, taste and adjust the seasoning, and divide between 2 plates.

5. Wipe out the skillet and return it to medium heat. After about 1 minute, add 1 tablespoon olive oil and swirl it around.

6. Crack 4 eggs into the skillet and cook until the whites are no longer translucent, 2 or 3 minutes. Turn the heat to low and sprinkle the eggs with salt and pepper.
7. The eggs are done when the whites are completely firm and the yolks are as runny as you like them, just another few minutes. Remove the eggs from the skillet and serve on top of the mushrooms and leeks, garnished with the Parmesan and parsley.

VARIATIONS

Fried Eggs with Creamy Mushrooms and Leeks
Especially luxurious. Swap the white wine for cream.

Fried Eggs with Mushrooms and Poblanos
Use 2 poblano peppers, cut into strips, instead of the leek, cilantro instead of parsley, beer in place of white wine, and Jack cheese rather than Parmesan.

Fried Eggs with Tomatoes and Leeks
Substitute 2 cups chopped tomato for the mushrooms and 1 teaspoon chopped fresh thyme for the parsley. Cook the tomato until it releases some of its juice and the mixture thickens slightly.

NOTES

EVEN FASTER
Fry the eggs in a separate skillet while the mushrooms are cooking.

SIDES

Warm Buttery Bread 906

Tomato Salad 913

Crisp Roasted Potatoes 965

SPEED ◑ SERVES 2 TO 4

Eggs and Steak with Peppers and Onions

Thinner cuts of steak, like skirt and flank, cook very quickly in a screaming-hot skillet (keep a fan close by; it gets a little smoky). With peppers and onions steaks makes for a classic combination (think fajitas). I like to add a fried egg on top to make it more breakfasty.

Ingredients

1 medium onion

2 bell peppers

2 tablespoons olive oil

Salt and pepper

1 pound skirt or flank steak

1 tablespoon vegetable oil

2 scallions

1 tablespoon butter

4 eggs

Prep | Cook

Trim, peel, and slice the onion.

1. Put the onion in a large skillet over medium-high heat. Cover and cook, undisturbed, until the onion is dry and starting to brown, 5 to 7 minutes.

   Core, seed, and slice the bell peppers.

2. Uncover the skillet and stir in 2 tablespoons olive oil. Add the peppers, sprinkle with salt and pepper, and cook, stirring occasionally until the vegetables are soft, 5 to 10 minutes.

3. While the vegetables cook, put another large skillet over high heat. Pat the steak dry with a paper towel and sprinkle both sides with salt and pepper. Cut the steak in half if needed to fit in the skillet. When the skillet is very hot, add 1 tablespoon vegetable oil and swirl it around.

4. Add the steak and cook, turning once, until browned on both sides but still one shade pinker inside than you like it, 3 to 5 minutes per side.

   Trim and chop the scallions.

5. Check on the peppers and onion; if they're soft, turn off the heat.

6. When the steak is done, transfer it to a cutting board, carefully rinse and wipe out the skillet, and put it over medium heat. After about 1 minute, add 1 tablespoon butter and swirl it around. When the butter foam subsides, crack 4 eggs into the skillet.

7. When the egg whites are no longer translucent, after 1 minute, turn the heat to low and sprinkle the eggs with salt and pepper.

8. Thinly slice the steak against the grain. Divide the steak among 2 or 4 plates and lay some of the peppers and onion on top.

9. The eggs are done when the whites are completely firm and the yolks are as runny as you like them, just another few minutes. Top each plate with an egg or 2, garnish with the scallions, and serve immediately.

VARIATIONS

Spicy Eggs and Steak with Mushrooms and Onions
Use 1 pound sliced mushrooms instead of the bell peppers. Add a sprinkle of cayenne whenever you use salt and pepper.

Smoky Eggs and Shrimp with Tomatoes
Substitute 2 large, ripe tomatoes for the bell peppers and 1 pound peeled shrimp for the steak. Cook the tomatoes with the onion until they release some of their juice and the mixture thickens slightly. Broil the shrimp until pink all over and just cooked through, 1 to 3 minutes. Add a sprinkle of smoked paprika wherever you use salt and pepper.

SIDES

Bruschetta 909

Sautéed Greens with Garlic 924

Buttery Egg Noodles 948

Peas with Parmesan 934

SPEED SERVES 4

Classic Breakfast Burritos

Small details can make a huge difference between delicious homemade dishes and mediocre fast or frozen food. The keys to my breakfast burritos are simple: Keep the eggs creamy and soft, make your own refried beans, and lightly char the tortillas right before rolling. Rest assured this won't take longer than a trip to the drive-through.

Ingredients

6 slices bacon

1 small onion

1 large russet potato

1 ½ cups cooked or canned pinto beans (one 15-ounce can)

Salt and pepper

2 garlic cloves

Several sprigs fresh cilantro

4 eggs

2 tablespoons vegetable oil

Pinch of cayenne

4 ounces Jack cheese (1 cup grated)

1 lime

4 large flour tortillas

Prep | Cook

1. Put a large skillet over medium heat.

   Chop 6 slices bacon into 1-inch pieces.

2. Add the bacon to the skillet. Cook, stirring occasionally, until crisp, 5 to 10 minutes.

   Trim, peel, and chop the onion.

   Scrub the potato, peel it if you like, and grate it.

   If you're using canned beans, rinse and drain them.

3. Add the onion and potato to the skillet and sprinkle with salt and pepper. Cook, stirring occasionally, until the potato is lightly browned and almost tender, 5 to 10 minutes.

   Peel and mince 2 garlic cloves.

   Chop several sprigs cilantro.

   Crack the eggs into a medium mixing bowl, sprinkle with salt and pepper, and beat.

4. Stir the eggs into the skillet. Cook, stirring frequently and scraping down the sides with a heatproof rubber spatula.

5. When the eggs are creamy, soft, and still a bit runny, they're done. It shouldn't take more than 10 minutes. Taste and adjust the seasoning and transfer the mixture to a bowl or plate. Wipe out the skillet.

6. Put 2 tablespoons vegetable oil in the skillet. When it's hot, add the beans, garlic, a pinch of cayenne, and a sprinkle of salt and pepper. Cook, mashing the beans with a potato masher until they're partly broken up. Continue to mash until the beans are mostly broken down, about 5 minutes.

   Grate 1 cup Jack cheese. Halve the lime.

7. If the bean mixture is too thick, stir in a splash of water until it's the consistency you like.

8. Put each tortilla (one at a time) directly over a gas burner and cook, turning once, until lightly charred on both sides. (If you have an electric range, broil them.)

9. Fill each tortilla with the beans and the egg mixture. Top with the cheese, cilantro, and a squeeze of lime. Roll up and serve.

VARIATIONS

Sweet Potato and Chorizo Breakfast Burritos
Use 8 ounces fresh Mexican chorizo instead of bacon and sweet potato instead of russet. Remove the chorizo from its casing and cook until browned and slightly crisp.

Italian Breakfast Burritos
Substitute prosciutto for the bacon, white beans for pinto, basil for the cilantro, red chile flakes for the cayenne, Parmesan for the Jack cheese, olive oil for the vegetable oil, and lemon for the lime. Cook the prosciutto in 2 tablespoons olive oil and keep an eye on the time; it will be faster.

NOTES

MAKE YOUR OWN
Cooked Beans 496

EVEN FASTER
Fry the beans in a separate skillet or saucepan while the eggs cook.

SPEED ◐ SERVES 4

Pork 'n' Greens Breakfast Patties

Once you see how easy it is to make your own breakfast sausages, you'll be hooked. And once you see how delicious kale cooked in sausage fat is, you'll be in trouble.

Ingredients

2 tablespoons olive oil

2 or 3 sprigs fresh sage or ½ teaspoon dried

1 ½ pounds ground pork

Pinch of nutmeg

Salt and pepper

1 bunch kale (1 pound)

Prep | Cook

1. Put 2 tablespoons olive oil in a large skillet over low heat.

   Strip the leaves from 2 or 3 sage sprigs and chop them if you're using fresh.

2. Put 1 ½ pounds ground pork in a bowl along with the chopped sage or ½ teaspoon dried, a pinch of nutmeg, and a sprinkle of salt and pepper. Mix the seasonings into the pork.

3. Raise the heat to medium-high. Break off a very small piece of the sausage mixture, flatten it, and fry it in the skillet until cooked through. Taste it and adjust the seasoning as necessary.

4. Shape the sausage mixture into 4 patties and cook, turning as necessary until they're browned and crisp on both sides and cooked through, 8 to 12 minutes total.

   Trim and chop the kale.

5. Transfer the cooked sausages to a plate. Add the kale to the skillet, sprinkle with salt and pepper, and cook, stirring occasionally until it's just wilted, 4 or 5 minutes. Serve immediately with the sausage patties.

VARIATIONS

Spicy Breakfast Patties with Sautéed Apples
Replace the sage with ½ teaspoon cayenne, the nutmeg with 1 teaspoon minced garlic, and the kale with 1 pound apples, sliced. Cook the apples until slightly softened and lightly browned; you still want them to be a little crisp.

Italian Breakfast Patties with Sautéed Fennel
Substitute 1 tablespoon fennel seeds for the sage, 1 teaspoon minced garlic for the nutmeg, and 1 pound fennel, thinly sliced, for the kale. Cook the fennel until slightly softened and lightly browned.

Chorizo with Sautéed Peppers
Swap 1 tablespoon chili powder, 2 teaspoons garlic powder, 1 teaspoon cumin, and ½ teaspoon cayenne for the sage and nutmeg and 4 thinly sliced bell peppers for the kale. Cook the peppers until soft, about 5 minutes.

NOTES

EVEN FASTER
It's a treat to sauté the kale in the pork fat left over from frying the sausage, but you can always cook the greens first, while you're making the sausage mix.

The thinner the patties, the faster they'll cook.

IF YOU HAVE MORE TIME
Breakfast patties are best when they incorporate a decent amount of fat, so if you have the time, grind cubes of pork shoulder in the food processor instead of using preground pork.

SIDES

Hummus 939

Creamy Polenta 947

Crisp Roasted Potatoes 965

SPEED  SERVES 4

Smoky Two-Potato and Ham Hash

Grating potatoes allows them to cook as fast as possible and develop the maximum amount of crisp exterior, which is what hash is about. Supplementing regular potatoes with sweet potatoes adds a perfect sweetness to balance the smoky ham and paprika.

Ingredients

3 tablespoons olive oil

One 8-ounce piece ham

1 small onion

2 or 3 medium russet or Yukon Gold potatoes (1 pound)

2 medium sweet potatoes (1 pound)

1 teaspoon smoked paprika

Salt and pepper

Several sprigs fresh parsley for garnish

Prep | Cook

1. Put 1 tablespoon olive oil in a large skillet over low heat.
   Cut the ham into small chunks or slices.

2. When the oil is hot, add the ham and cook, stirring occasionally until it's lightly browned, 8 to 10 minutes.
   Trim and peel the onion and add it to the ham.
   Trim the potatoes and peel them if you'd like.
   Trim and peel the sweet potatoes. Grate both (together is fine) with the large holes on a box grater or in a food processor.

3. Transfer the potato mixture to a colander and press to squeeze out as much moisture as you can. Toss with 1 teaspoon smoked paprika and a sprinkle of salt and pepper right in the colander.

4. When the ham is lightly browned, add 2 tablespoons olive oil to the skillet and swirl it around. Add the potato mixture to the skillet, spread it out, and press it down with a spatula.

5. Raise the heat to medium-high and cook, shaking the skillet occasionally, until the bottom of the potatoes becomes crisp, 6 to 8 minutes.

6. Turn the potatoes with a spatula (in pieces is fine). Continue to cook, adjusting the heat if necessary until the second side is browned, 6 to 8 minutes more.

   Strip the parsley leaves from several sprigs and chop.

7. When the potatoes are browned, cut or divide the hash into 4 pieces, garnish with the parsley, and serve.

VARIATIONS

Potato and Chorizo Hash
Substitute Spanish smoked chorizo for the ham and use 2 pounds russet or Yukon Gold potatoes; omit the sweet potatoes.

Sweet Potato and Tofu Hash
Use 1 tablespoon sesame oil in place of 1 tablespoon of the olive oil, 8 ounces extra-firm tofu instead of ham, 1 tablespoon minced fresh ginger rather than paprika, and 4 scallions in place of parsley. Use 2 pounds sweet potatoes; omit the regular potatoes. Drizzle with soy sauce at the table if you like.

Celery Root and Prosciutto Hash
Swap prosciutto for the ham, 2 pounds celery root for the regular and sweet potatoes, and 1 tablespoon grated lemon zest for the paprika.

NOTES

EVEN FASTER
Don't precook the ham. Chop it into small pieces, toss with the raw potatoes and onions, and add everything to the skillet together.

SIDES

Green Salad 911

Chile-Cumin Black Beans 937

Warm Tortillas 907

SPEED ◐ MAKES 12 OR MORE BISCUITS

Prosciutto and Drop Biscuits

There are different ways to make biscuits, and while none is especially time-consuming, the drop method saves you the fuss of rolling and cutting the dough. Fill them with prosciutto while they're hot from the oven and you've got a fantastic breakfast sandwich.

Ingredients

2 cups flour, plus more if needed

1 teaspoon salt

¼ teaspoon pepper

1 tablespoon baking powder

1 teaspoon baking soda

4 tablespoons (½ stick) cold butter, plus a little more for greasing the pan

1 cup buttermilk, plus more if needed

6 slices prosciutto or country ham

Prep | Cook

1. Heat the oven to 450°F.
2. Put 2 cups flour, 1 teaspoon salt, ¼ teaspoon pepper, 1 tablespoon baking powder, and 1 teaspoon baking soda into a food processor. Pulse to combine.
3. Cut 4 tablespoons butter into ½-inch cubes, add to the food processor, and pulse until the bits of butter are the size of peas.
4. Add 1 cup buttermilk and pulse just until the mixture forms a ball. (If it seems very sticky and wet, pulse in more flour, a tablespoon at a time, until the dough comes together. If it's too dry, do the same with buttermilk.)
5. Grease a baking sheet with butter and drop tablespoons of the dough onto the sheet. Bake the biscuits until golden brown, 7 to 9 minutes.

   Cut the prosciutto slices in half lengthwise.
6. When the biscuits are done, cut them in half across the equator and fold a piece of prosciutto in the middle. Serve hot or warm.

VARIATIONS

10 Fillings for Biscuit Sandwiches

Swap any of the following for the prosciutto:

1. Cooked ham, Canadian bacon, salami, or smoked chorizo
2. Cooked bacon or sausage
3. Scrambled Eggs (page 838) or Fried Eggs (page 836)
4. Sautéed Greens with Garlic (page 924)
5. Ripe tomato slices
6. Grated cheddar, Gruyère, Parmesan, or Jack cheese
7. Sliced fresh fruit
8. Butter and jam
9. Peanut butter or Nutella
10. Hummus (page 939), pesto (page 284), or Tomato Sauce (page 296)

NOTES

IF YOU HAVE MORE TIME

Classic Prosciutto Biscuits

Prettier and slightly flakier. Once the dough comes together, turn it out onto a lightly floured surface and knead it 10 times. It should still stick slightly to your hands. Press the dough into a ¾-inch-thick rectangle and cut it into 2-inch rounds with a biscuit cutter or small glass. Put on the baking sheet and bake as directed.

SIDES

Green Salad 911

Fennel Salad 917

Tomato Salad 913

SPEED ◐ SERVES 4

Jalapeño-Scallion Johnnycakes

Johnnycakes are pancakes made with cornmeal instead of flour, loaded with corn kernels and pretty much any seasonings you like—in this case, jalapeño and scallions. Just be patient and let the cornmeal hydrate for a few minutes so that it becomes a supple batter.

Ingredients

1 ½ cups fine or medium-grind cornmeal

Salt

1 jalapeño chile

3 scallions

2 ears fresh corn (about 1 cup corn kernels)

½ cup milk, plus more if needed

2 tablespoons vegetable oil, plus more for frying

Maple syrup for serving (optional)

Prep | Cook

1. Put 1 ½ cups water in a small saucepan over high heat. Heat the oven to 200°F.

2. Combine 1 ½ cups cornmeal and 1 teaspoon salt in a large mixing bowl. When the water comes to a boil, stir it into the cornmeal. Let the mixture sit until the cornmeal absorbs the water and softens, 5 to 10 minutes.

   Trim and mince the jalapeño.

   Trim and chop the scallions.

   Shuck the corn and cut 1 cup kernels from the cobs.

3. When the cornmeal has softened, put a large skillet over medium heat. Stir ½ cup milk into the cornmeal; the batter should be spreadable but still thick. If it's too dry, add milk, a tablespoon at a time. Stir in the corn kernels, the jalapeño, the scallions, 2 tablespoons vegetable oil, and a sprinkle of salt.

4. Add a thin film of vegetable oil to the skillet. When the oil is hot, spoon the batter into the skillet, working in batches and making any size pancakes you like.

5. Cook until the bottoms are golden brown and bubbles appear and burst on the top, 3 to 5 minutes. Flip and cook until the second sides are golden, another 3 to 5 minutes.

6. As you finish, transfer the cooked cakes to the oven to keep them warm. Continue making johnnycakes until you've used up all the batter. Serve warm, with maple syrup if you like.

VARIATIONS

Jalapeño-Cheddar Johnnycakes
Substitute ½ cup grated cheddar for the scallions.

Honey-Walnut Johnnycakes
Use 2 tablespoons honey instead of jalapeño and ½ cup chopped walnuts instead of scallions.

Bacon Johnnycakes
Omit the jalapeño. Swap ½ cup crumbled cooked bacon for the scallions.

Parmesan Johnnycakes
Substitute ½ teaspoon red chile flakes for the jalapeño and ¼ cup chopped fresh parsley and ½ cup grated Parmesan for the scallions.

NOTES

EVEN FASTER
Use 1 cup thawed frozen corn kernels instead of fresh.

Get a second skillet going on the stovetop so you can cook two batches at once.

SIDES

Green Salad 911

Chile-Cumin Black Beans 937

Avocado with Hot Sauce and Cilantro 920

Sautéed Sweet Potatoes with Chipotle and Lime 964

SPEED ◐ SERVES 4

Banana-Coconut Pancakes

I've come to love pancakes that carry a little oomph in texture and flavor. Adding cooked grains is a good way to do this (see the Variation), but coconut and bananas create something special, sweet and savory, with real texture. The batter comes together very quickly too.

Ingredients

2 cups flour

2 teaspoons baking powder

½ teaspoon salt

½ cup shredded unsweetened coconut

1 tablespoon sugar

2 eggs

One 15-ounce can coconut milk

2 bananas

Butter for cooking

Maple syrup for serving (optional)

Prep | Cook

1. Heat the oven to 200°F.
2. In a large mixing bowl, combine 2 cups flour, 2 teaspoons baking powder, ½ teaspoon salt, ½ cup coconut, and 1 tablespoon sugar.
3. Crack the eggs into a medium bowl and beat. Stir in the coconut milk. Gently stir the wet ingredients into the dry. Mix only enough to moisten the flour (don't worry about lumps).
4. Put a large skillet over medium-low heat.
   Peel and slice the bananas; gently fold them into the batter.
5. Put a tablespoon or so of butter into the skillet and swirl it around.
6. When the butter foam subsides, ladle the batter into the skillet, working in batches and making any size pancakes you like, spreading the batter with the bottom of the ladle. Cook until the bottoms are golden brown and bubbles appear in the center, 2 to 4 minutes.
7. Flip and cook, adjusting the heat so that the bananas don't burn, until the second sides are lightly browned, another few minutes.

8. As the pancakes are done, put them on a baking sheet and transfer to the warm oven. Continue cooking, adding a little more butter for each batch, until you've used up all the batter. Serve warm, with maple syrup if you like.

VARIATIONS

Banana–Chocolate Chip Pancakes
Substitute ½ cup chocolate chips for the shredded coconut and whole milk for the coconut milk.

7 Ingredients to Stir into Pancake Batter
Add any of the following ingredients to the batter:

1. Up to 1 cup cooked grains, like rice, couscous, quinoa, or barley
2. Up to 1 cup fresh berries or chopped fruit
3. Up to 1 cup chopped nuts, dried fruit, or granola
4. 2 teaspoons grated orange or lemon zest
5. 2 teaspoons minced fresh or crystallized ginger
6. ¼ cup cocoa powder
7. Up to 1 cup crumbled cooked bacon

NOTES

A FEW TIPS FOR COOKING PANCAKES

1. Use a nonstick skillet if you have one.
2. Leave room between the pancakes so they're easier to flip.
3. The edges of the pancakes will set first; it's not until bubbles appear in the center that they're ready to flip.
4. Warm the maple syrup (on the stove or in the microwave) before serving.

SIDES

Pick-a-Fruit Salad 921

SPEED ◐ SERVES 4 TO 6

Orange-Ricotta Pancakes

Ricotta and sour cream stiffen pancake batter a bit more than milk and produce incredibly light and fluffy cakes with a little more heft than normal pancakes. Orange zest brightens them up, as does lemon (see the Variation).

Ingredients

2 cups flour

½ teaspoon baking soda

½ teaspoon salt

2 eggs

1 cup ricotta cheese

1 cup sour cream

1 tablespoon honey, plus more for serving (optional)

1 orange

Butter for cooking

Prep | Cook

1. Heat the oven to 200°F.
2. In a large bowl, combine 2 cups flour, ½ teaspoon baking soda, and ½ teaspoon salt.
3. Crack the eggs into a medium bowl and beat. Stir in 1 cup ricotta, 1 cup sour cream, and 1 tablespoon honey.
4. Put a large skillet over medium-low heat.
   Grate 1 tablespoon zest from the orange; then halve it.
5. Add the orange zest to the wet ingredients and squeeze in the juice. Gently stir the wet ingredients into the dry. Mix only enough to moisten the flour (don't worry about lumps).
6. Put a tablespoon or so of butter into the skillet and swirl it around. When the butter foam subsides, ladle the batter into the skillet, working in batches and making any size pancakes you like. Cook until the bottoms are golden brown and bubbles appear in the centers of the pancakes, 2 to 4 minutes.

7. Flip and cook, adjusting the heat so that the pancakes don't burn, until the second sides are lightly browned, another few minutes.

8. As you finish, transfer the cooked pancakes to the oven to keep them warm. Continue cooking, adding a little more butter for each batch, until you've used up all the batter. Serve warm, with honey if you like.

VARIATIONS

Lemon-Ricotta Pancakes

Swap a lemon for the orange. If you like, add 1/4 cup poppy seeds to the batter.

NOTES

LEAVING LUMPS

One thing that slows a lot of pancake cooks down is painstakingly trying to get rid of all the little lumps of flour that are left after they mix the wet ingredients into the dry ones. Turns out, feverishly whisking the batter to get rid of lumps does you a double disservice: It takes up time, and it results in a tougher pancake. You want all pancakes to be a bit fluffy, not dense. So don't worry about the lumps; they'll disappear as the pancakes cook.

SIDES

Pick-a-Fruit Salad 921

SPEED SERVES 4 TO 6

Cheddar Waffles with Bacon Maple Syrup

An addictive mix of sweet and savory. The waffles bake up crisp and rich like grilled cheese sandwiches, only with the classic flavors of breakfast on top.

Ingredients

Vegetable oil

6 slices bacon

4 ounces sharp cheddar cheese (1 cup grated)

2 cups flour

1 tablespoon baking powder

¼ teaspoon salt

2 eggs

1 cup milk

¾ cup maple syrup

Pepper

Prep | Cook

1. Heat the oven to 200°F. Brush a waffle iron lightly with oil and heat it. Put a medium skillet over medium-high heat.

   Chop 6 slices bacon into ½-inch pieces.

2. Add the bacon to the skillet and cook, stirring occasionally, until crisp, 5 to 10 minutes.

   Grate 1 cup cheddar and add to a large bowl.

3. Add 2 cups flour, 1 tablespoon baking powder, and ¼ teaspoon salt to the bowl and stir to combine.

4. Crack 2 eggs into a medium bowl; add 1 cup milk and whisk until smooth. Gently stir the wet ingredients into the dry, mixing only enough to moisten the flour. (The batter will be thick and lumpy.)

5. When the bacon is crisp, add ¾ cup maple syrup to the skillet along with a generous sprinkle of pepper and turn the heat as low as you can.

6. When the iron is hot, spread enough batter onto the iron to barely cover it. Close the top and bake until the waffles are well browned, crisp, and cooked through, 3 to 5 minutes, depending on your iron.

7. As the waffles are done, transfer them to the oven to keep them warm. Continue cooking, brushing a little more oil on the iron each time, until you've used up all the batter.

8. Serve the waffles with the bacon maple syrup on top.

VARIATIONS

Molasses Waffles with Ginger Maple Syrup
Omit the cheddar. Substitute 2 tablespoons molasses for 2 tablespoons of the milk and 1 tablespoon minced fresh ginger for the bacon. No need to cook the ginger first in Step 2; just combine it in a small saucepan with the syrup and warm it over medium-low heat while you make the waffles.

Corn Waffles with Blueberry Maple Syrup
Substitute 1 cup fresh or thawed frozen corn kernels for the cheddar and ½ cup fresh blueberries for the bacon. Cook the blueberries in a little butter in Step 2 until they start to soften and give up their juice, then add the maple syrup.

SIDES

Pick-a-Fruit Salad 921

Appetizers

Rosemary Popcorn 876

Spiced Cashews with Bacon 877

No-Cook Spanish Skewers 878

Panfried Olives 879

Broiled Radishes with Soy 880

Edamame with Chili Salt 881

Raw Veggies with Romesco 882

Endive Spears with Olives 883

Pinzimonio 884

Goat Cheese Truffles 885

Prosciutto-Wrapped Pears 886

Greek Pita Pizzas 887

Bagel Chips with Smoked Salmon 888

Crab Toast 889

Peel-and-Eat Shrimp 892

Skewerless Chicken Satay 893

Tortillas Rojas 894

Roasted Nuts with Ginger, Soy, and Honey 895

Warm-Pickled Cucumber Spears 896

Green Beans with Onion Dip 897

Hard-Boiled Eggs with Dijon Mayo 898

Parmesan Crisps 899

Quesadillas with Pico de Gallo 900

Pizza Wedges 901

Appetizers

Anything that primes your appetite could be called an *appetizer.* Soups count, and so do salads. But we have separate chapters in this book for those things, so what you'll find here is more accurately described as finger foods or snacks, "fancier" dishes that you'd be likely to eat at a cocktail party as well as casual ones that you might munch in front of the TV.

With the ascendance of the "small plates" craze, these kinds of dishes are no longer required to be the precursors to a more substantial meal: Sometimes, eaten three or four at a time—or combined with a salad or a side—they *are* the meal. That's good news for the home cook, because, for the most part, these dishes don't take very long to cook. None of the recipes in this chapter takes more than 30 minutes, and more than half of them can be made in 15.

Finger foods sound a little fussy (especially when you call them *hors d'oeuvres*), while snacks are all too often synonymous with junk. But when you make your own versions, neither of those things is the case. Something that I (and many others) would call "elegant" can be as simple as a ball of goat cheese coated in bread crumbs (page 885), while a basic snack like popcorn can be elevated far beyond the level of junk (page 876).

Chapter Highlights

Finger Sandwiches Any sandwich cut into small pieces makes a fine appetizer. See Sandwiches (page 128).

A New Spin on Nuts Elevating the bar snack to new heights. Spiced Cashews with Bacon (page 877), Roasted Nuts with Ginger, Soy, and Honey (page 895).

Crudités Raw vegetables with an addictive dip remain one of the best and easiest kinds of appetizers I know. Raw Veggies with Romesco (page 882), Green Beans with Onion Dip (page 897).

So Simple, So Good Easy appetizers that will turn heads. Panfried Olives (page 879), Broiled Radishes with Soy (page 880), Parmesan Crisps (page 899).

A Dip by Another Name Lots of things that go by other names can double as dips. Hummus (page 939) and Pinzimonio (page 884) are as useful on a cocktail tray as Onion Dip (page 897) and Romesco (page 882).

Speed Demons An equally delicious, faster version of deviled eggs. Hard-Boiled Eggs with Dijon Mayo (page 898).

Chips in Salsa You might not think to drench your chips in salsa, but it works. Tortillas Rojas (page 894).

Pickles on the Fly How to make something in 30 minutes that usually takes 3 days. Warm-Pickled Cucumber Spears (page 896).

No Heat, No Problem Appetizers sans cooking. No-Cook Spanish Skewers (page 878), Endive Spears with Olives (page 883), Prosciutto-Wrapped Pears (page 886), Bagel Chips with Smoked Salmon (page 888).

Many More Appetizers For lots more recipes that you could serve as appetizers, see the Sides chapter (page 902).

SPEED  SERVES 4

Rosemary Popcorn

Microwave popcorn is undeniably a "convenience" food, but really, so is regular popcorn. It takes only a few minutes longer to cook and pop kernels in a pot, and the result is real food—no preservatives, really good oil. Add a little rosemary and you may never go back.

Ingredients

2 tablespoons vegetable oil

½ cup popping corn

3 sprigs fresh rosemary

2 tablespoons olive oil

Salt

Prep | Cook

1. Put 2 tablespoons vegetable oil in a large pot over medium heat. Add 3 corn kernels and cover the pot.
2. When the 3 kernels pop, add ½ cup kernels, cover, and, holding the lid in place, shake the pot.
3. Cook, shaking occasionally until the popping stops, about 5 minutes.

   Strip the leaves from 3 rosemary sprigs and chop.
4. When the popping stops, transfer the popcorn to a large bowl and toss with the rosemary, 2 tablespoons olive oil, and a sprinkle of salt. Serve immediately.

VARIATIONS

7 Ways to Flavor Popcorn

Toss with the popcorn instead of the rosemary:

1. 1 teaspoon cumin, curry powder, chili powder, or smoked paprika
2. 2 tablespoons chopped fresh parsley, cilantro, or basil
3. 1 tablespoon grated citrus zest
4. ¼ cup grated Parmesan cheese
5. ½ cup dried fruit (chopped if necessary)
6. ½ cup chopped nuts
7. 1 tablespoon honey or maple syrup

SPEED ◔ SERVES 4

Spiced Cashews with Bacon

Sautéing nuts in rendered bacon fat is luxurious—and much faster than roasting.

Ingredients

4 slices bacon

2 cups unsalted cashews

1 teaspoon curry powder

Salt

Prep | Cook

1. Put a large skillet over medium heat.
   Chop 4 slices bacon into ½-inch pieces.
2. Add the bacon to the skillet. Cook, stirring occasionally until crisp, 5 to 10 minutes.
3. Transfer the bacon to a paper towel with a slotted spoon; keep the rendered fat in the pan.
4. Add 2 cups cashews, 1 teaspoon curry powder, and a sprinkle of salt to the skillet. Cook, stirring frequently and adjusting the heat to prevent burning if necessary, until the nuts are lightly browned, 3 to 5 minutes.
5. Stir the bacon back into the nuts. Let the mixture cool for a few minutes before serving.

VARIATIONS

Spiced Peanuts with Bacon
Substitute peanuts for the cashews and ½ teaspoon cayenne for the curry powder.

Spiced Almonds with Bacon
Substitute almonds for the cashews and cumin for the curry powder.

Pecans with Bacon and Brown Sugar
Substitute pecans for the cashews and brown sugar for the curry powder.

NOTES

MAKE YOUR OWN

Curry Powder 758

SPEED ◔ SERVES 4

No-Cook Spanish Skewers

A tapas tray on a stick. Each ingredient already had a ton of work and time put into it by somebody else, so all you have to do is a little assembly. Rounded toothpicks are best here.

Ingredients

8 ounces smoked Spanish chorizo

8 ounces manchego cheese

1 cup dried apricots

A few pinches of smoked paprika

Prep | Cook

Cut 8 ounces chorizo and 8 ounces manchego into small cubes (you should have about a cup of each).

Slice 1 cup dried apricots into halves.

1. Thread 1 or 2 pieces each of the chorizo, manchego, and apricots onto toothpicks, alternating ingredients until you use them all.
2. Sprinkle the skewers with a few pinches of smoked paprika; serve within a few hours.

VARIATIONS

No-Cook Salami Skewers
Substitute cured Italian salami for the chorizo, fresh mozzarella for the manchego, dried tomatoes (soaked in a little warm water until soft) for the apricots, and red chile flakes for the smoked paprika.

No-Cook Ham Skewers
Swap thick-cut smoked ham for the chorizo, cheddar for the manchego, dried apples for the apricots, and pepper for the smoked paprika.

No-Cook Olive Skewers
Use 1 cup whole pitted green olives instead of the chorizo, fresh mozzarella instead of the manchego, 1 cup crusty bread cubes in place of the apricots, and pepper instead of the smoked paprika. Drizzle with a little olive oil if you like.

SPEED ◔ SERVES 4

Panfried Olives

No, it's not as fast as eating olives right out of the jar. But sizzling olives in a skillet with rosemary and garlic—which doesn't take long—is well worth the time.

Ingredients

3 tablespoons olive oil

2 garlic cloves

2 sprigs fresh rosemary

1 pound olives, preferably a combination of black and green

Pepper

Prep | Cook

1. Put 3 tablespoons olive oil in a large skillet over the lowest possible heat.

   Peel and thinly slice 2 garlic cloves; add them to the skillet.

   Strip the leaves from 2 rosemary sprigs, chop, and add to the skillet.

   Pit the olives if necessary; blot them dry with a paper towel.

2. Add the olives to the skillet, sprinkle with pepper, and raise the heat to medium. Cook, stirring occasionally until the olives have softened slightly and browned in spots, 3 to 5 minutes.

3. Serve hot, warm, or at room temperature.

VARIATIONS

Panfried Olives with Chile and Mint
Substitute 1 fresh hot red chile (like Thai) for the garlic; keep the seeds if you like spice. Use 2 tablespoons chopped fresh mint instead of the rosemary; don't stir it in until the very end.

Panfried Olives with Shallots and Thyme
Use a small shallot in place of the garlic and thyme instead of the rosemary.

SPEED SERVES 4

Broiled Radishes with Soy

Spicy when raw, radishes mellow under the broiler. The Chinese-style dressing adds wonderful dimensions of flavor.

Ingredients

¼ cup sesame oil

2 tablespoons soy sauce

1 teaspoon honey

1 pound radishes

Prep | Cook

1. Turn the broiler to high; put the rack 4 inches from the heat.
2. In a large bowl, whisk together ¼ cup sesame oil, 2 tablespoons soy sauce, and 1 teaspoon honey.

   Trim the radishes; halve them and add them to the bowl.
3. Toss the radishes to coat them with the dressing. Put them cut side up on a rimmed baking sheet, leaving any excess dressing in the bowl.
4. Broil until the tops of the radishes are golden brown or even slightly charred, 2 to 5 minutes, depending on your broiler.
5. Serve warm or at room temperature, with any extra dressing for dipping if you like.

VARIATIONS

Broiled Radishes with Olive Oil and Lemon

Skip the dressing. Toss the radishes with ¼ cup olive oil, 2 teaspoons grated lemon zest, and salt.

NOTES

EVEN FASTER

Serve the radishes raw, tossed with the dressing, or with the dressing on the side for dipping.

SPEED ◔ SERVES 4

Edamame with Chili Salt

Boiled or steamed in-shell edamame with salt is a classic Japanese snack and about as simple as it gets. Here a dash of chili powder adds heat, a touch of sweetness, and a deep red color to the salt. If you can find only shelled edamame, no problem; they're just as tasty and still big enough to pick up with your fingers like nuts (use about 1 pound).

Ingredients

Salt

1 teaspoon chili powder

1 ½ pounds edamame in their pods (fresh or frozen)

Prep | Cook

1. Bring a medium pot of water to a boil and salt it.
   Stir together 1 teaspoon chili powder and 1 teaspoon salt.
2. When the water boils, add the edamame and cook until tender and warmed through, 3 to 5 minutes, depending on the beans. Drain well, toss with the chili salt, and serve hot or warm.

VARIATIONS

Microwaved Edamame
Put the beans in a covered microwave-safe dish with ¼ cup water. Cook on high, checking and stirring every minute or so until they're hot and plump.

NOTES

MAKE YOUR OWN

Chili Powder 758

SPEED  SERVES 4

Raw Veggies with Romesco

Romesco is a traditional Spanish sauce that's made by blending tomatoes, garlic, vinegar, olive oil, and almonds—which thicken everything else nicely. Usually you just throw everything in the food processor raw, but I like to give the tomatoes and almonds a little char first. It's worth the effort, but you can skip it.

Ingredients

3 garlic cloves

1 cup cherry tomatoes

2 tablespoons almonds

1 ½ pounds assorted vegetables (for eating raw)

2 tablespoons sherry vinegar

⅓ cup olive oil

½ teaspoon smoked paprika or chili powder

Salt and pepper

Prep | Cook

1. Put a large skillet over medium heat.
   Crush and peel 3 garlic cloves.

2. When the skillet is hot, add the garlic, the cherry tomatoes, and 2 tablespoons almonds. Cook, shaking the skillet occasionally so the almonds don't burn, until the tomatoes are a bit charred and the almonds and garlic are lightly browned, 4 to 6 minutes.
   Trim, peel, and seed the vegetables that need it and cut them into pieces you can use for dipping. Put them on a platter.

3. Transfer the charred tomatoes, almonds, and garlic to a food processor. Add 2 tablespoons sherry vinegar, ⅓ cup olive oil, ½ teaspoon smoked paprika or chili powder, and a sprinkle of salt and pepper.

4. Process until the mixture is thick and relatively smooth but still has some crunch from the almonds. Taste and adjust the seasoning.

5. Transfer the romesco to a serving bowl and serve with the vegetables alongside for dipping.

SPEED | SERVES 4

Endive Spears with Olives

My grown-up version of ants on a log. Ten times better than the original.

Ingredients

2 heads Belgian endive

½ cup black olives

4 ounces blue cheese (1 cup crumbled)

1 teaspoon olive oil

Pepper

Prep | Cook

Trim the endive and separate into individual leaves.

Pit ½ cup olives if necessary and chop them up a bit.

Crumble 1 cup blue cheese and put in a small bowl.

1. Add the olives, 1 teaspoon olive oil, and a sprinkle of pepper to the blue cheese; stir to combine.
2. Spoon about a tablespoon of the filling into each endive spear, spreading the mixture from end to end.
3. Serve immediately or refrigerate for a few hours and bring back to room temperature before serving.

VARIATIONS

Endive Spears with Basil
Substitute ricotta for the blue cheese and ½ cup chopped fresh basil for the olives. Add some salt to the mixture as well.

Endive Spears with Prosciutto
Use 4 ounces chopped prosciutto instead of the olives.

NOTES

IF YOU HAVE MORE TIME

Broiled Endive Spears with Blue Cheese and Black Olives
Put the filled endive spears on a baking sheet and run under the broiler for a minute or 2, just until the cheese is a bit melted and the edges of the endive are slightly charred. Try it with either of the variations as well.

SPEED  SERVES 4

Pinzimonio

Pinzimonio may sound complicated, but what could be simpler than dipping raw vegetables in gently warmed seasoned olive oil?

Ingredients

2 or more garlic cloves

⅓ cup olive oil

Salt and pepper

2 carrots

2 celery stalks

1 large cucumber

Prep | Cook

Peel and mince 2 garlic cloves.

1. Combine the garlic, ⅓ cup olive oil, and a sprinkle of salt and pepper in a small saucepan over medium-low heat.

2. Cook, swirling the pot occasionally until the garlic is puffed and fragrant; remove from the heat as soon as it starts to turn golden.

   Trim and peel the carrots. Trim the celery. Trim and peel the cucumber, cut it in half lengthwise, and scoop out the seeds with a spoon.

   Cut all the vegetables into sticks and put them on a platter.

3. Put the warm oil in a small bowl next to the platter of vegetables and serve.

SPEED SERVES 4

Goat Cheese Truffles

We think of truffles as dessert—little balls of chocolate rolled around in cocoa powder, or something along those lines. But there's no rule saying they can't be savory too.

Ingredients

2 tablespoons olive oil

2 thick slices any rustic bread (a little stale is fine)

Salt and pepper

8 ounces soft goat cheese

Prep | Cook

1. Put 2 tablespoons olive oil in a large skillet over low heat.

   Tear 2 thick slices of bread into pieces and put them into a food processor. Pulse into coarse crumbs; you need 1 cup.

2. Raise the heat to medium. Add the bread crumbs to the skillet, sprinkle with a little salt and some pepper, and stir gently to coat in the oil. Cook, stirring frequently until the crumbs are golden and crisp, 6 or 7 minutes. Shake the pan every minute or so to keep the crumbs from burning.

   Break off pieces of the goat cheese with your fingers and roll them into sixteen 1-inch balls.

3. When the crumbs are crisp, pour them into a shallow bowl.

4. Roll the goat cheese balls in the bread crumbs to coat lightly, pressing the crumbs into the cheese a bit if needed to make them stick. Put them on a plate and serve.

VARIATIONS

Nutty Goat Cheese Truffles

Substitute 1 ½ cups walnuts, almonds, pecans, or pistachios for the bread. Toast them whole in a dry skillet over medium heat until lightly browned, 3 to 5 minutes. Then pulse them in the food processor until finely chopped. Add salt and pepper to taste.

SPEED SERVES 4

Prosciutto-Wrapped Pears

Classy, elegant, and easy: A piece of fruit wrapped in a piece of prosciutto is about as simple as an appetizer gets, and it's perfect for entertaining. (If you have kids, let them do it.)

Ingredients

2 large pears

1 tablespoon sherry vinegar or red wine vinegar

Salt and pepper

8 slices prosciutto

Prep | Cook

Core the pears and cut each one into 8 wedges; put them in a medium bowl.

1. Add 1 tablespoon vinegar, a sprinkle of salt, and plenty of pepper to the bowl and toss to coat.

   Cut 8 slices of prosciutto in half lengthwise.

2. Wrap each piece of prosciutto around a wedge of pear and serve immediately.

VARIATIONS

Prosciutto-Wrapped Cantaloupe
Use ½ small cantaloupe, cut into wedges, instead of the pears. Substitute a pinch of smoked paprika for the pepper.

Ham-Wrapped Apples
Swap apples for the pears, cider vinegar for the sherry or red wine vinegar, and thinly sliced smoked ham for the prosciutto.

Prosciutto-Wrapped Tomatoes
Use 2 large ripe tomatoes, cut into wedges, instead of pears and balsamic instead of sherry or red wine vinegar.

SPEED SERVES 4

Greek Pita Pizzas

The key to successfully broiling and topping bread is to give the foundation a head start before adding ingredients. Just make sure not to pile the ingredients on too high after flipping.

Ingredients

4 small pitas (preferably pocketless)

Olive oil

½ cup kalamata olives

3 sprigs fresh oregano or 1 teaspoon dried

4 ounces feta cheese (1 cup crumbled)

Prep | Cook

1. Turn the broiler to high; put the rack 4 inches from the heat.
2. Brush both sides of 4 pitas with a little olive oil and put them on a baking sheet.

   Pit ½ cup olives if necessary and chop them up a bit.

   If you're using fresh oregano, strip the leaves from 3 sprigs and chop.

   Crumble 1 cup feta.
3. When the broiler is hot, put the baking sheet under the broiler and cook until the tops of the pita are lightly charred, 1 to 3 minutes.
4. Flip each pita over and top the untoasted side with the feta, olives, and oregano. Cook until the cheese just starts to bubble, another 2 to 5 minutes.
5. Let the pitas cool for a minute or 2, drizzle with a little more olive oil, cut into wedges, and serve.

SPEED  SERVES 4

Bagel Chips with Smoked Salmon

This recipe transforms the irresistible brunch combination of bagels and lox into a light, elegant, and very fast hors d'oeuvre. Buy the simplest bagel chips you can find (the best are found in bagel shops); they should contain only bagels, oil, and salt, with minimal preservatives. Or make your own—see below.

Ingredients

1 small cucumber

½ cup crème fraîche

16 store-bought plain bagel chips (8 ounces)

4 ounces smoked salmon

Pepper

Prep | Cook

Trim the cucumber, peel if necessary, and thinly slice.

1. Spread ½ cup crème fraîche on 16 bagel chips.
2. Lay the cucumber slices on top of the crème fraîche, then lay the smoked salmon over the top, breaking it into smaller pieces so you have enough for all of the chips. Sprinkle with pepper. Serve.

VARIATIONS

Bagel Chips with Prosciutto, Tomato, and Ricotta
Swap 1 ripe tomato, chopped, for the cucumber, ricotta for the crème fraîche, and prosciutto for the smoked salmon.

NOTES

IF YOU HAVE MORE TIME

Homemade Bagel Chips
Slice 1 bagel crosswise into rounds as thin as possible: ⅛ inch is ideal if you can manage it. Brush both sides lightly with olive oil and put on a baking sheet. Bake at 300°F, turning once, until crisp, 10 to 15 minutes (start checking them at 5 minutes and remove any that are already brown). Cool completely before storing for up to a few days. These will be bigger than the ones usually found in stores; either keep them whole before adding the topping or break them in half.

SPEED ◔ SERVES 4 TO 8

Crab Toast

Cooked crabmeat is an incredibly useful fast ingredient, with a wonderful sweet, briny flavor.

Ingredients

1 bunch fresh dill

1 lemon

1 cup lump crabmeat (about 8 ounces)

2 tablespoons mayonnaise

2 teaspoons Dijon mustard

Salt and pepper

4 thick slices any rustic bread

Olive oil

Prep | Cook

1. Turn the broiler to high; put the rack 6 inches from the heat.

   Strip 3 tablespoons dill from the stems; chop 2 tablespoons and put in a medium bowl. Save what's left for garnish.

   Grate 2 teaspoons lemon zest into the bowl; refrigerate the fruit for another use.

   Pick through 1 cup crabmeat, discarding any pieces of shell or cartilage you find. Add it to the bowl.

2. Add 2 tablespoons mayonnaise, 2 teaspoons Dijon, and a sprinkle of salt and pepper to the bowl. Stir to combine.

3. Drizzle both sides of 4 thick slices of bread with olive oil. Broil the bread, turning once, until lightly browned on both sides, 2 to 5 minutes total.

4. Spread the crab mixture on the bread, pressing it down lightly with your fingers. Cut each slice of bread crosswise into 2 or 3 pieces, garnish with the remaining dill, and serve.

VARIATIONS

Curried Crab Toast

Substitute cilantro for the dill and add ½ teaspoon curry powder to the dressing.

NOTES

MAKE YOUR OWN

Mayonnaise 144

Cocktail Meatballs

We all know that meatballs are a go-to combo with spaghetti (see page 320), but they're even more useful as appetizers. Freeing the meatball from the confines of pasta and tomato sauce allows you to experiment with flavor combinations that you may have never tried before. The master recipe is spiked with a teriyaki sauce; see the variations for some easy seasoning and dipping sauce adjustments. You can even mix, shape, and bake them in batches large enough to feed a crowd. (Figure the quantities here make 4 main or 8 appetizer servings. The cooked meatballs will keep in the fridge for a couple days or the freezer for several months.) Either way, just pop them, covered, into a 300°F oven until they're hot, whip up the dipping sauce, and serve warm or at room temperature.

Beef Teriyaki Meatballs

1 Heat the Oven

Heat the oven to 450°F; grease a rimmed baking sheet with 1 tablespoon vegetable oil.

2 Make the Sauce

In a small saucepan over high heat, combine ½ cup soy sauce and ½ cup mirin (or ¼ cup honey and ¼ cup water), 1 inch minced fresh ginger, 1 minced garlic clove, and 4 chopped scallions. Bring to a bubble, then remove the sauce from the heat.

3 Mix and Drop (or Roll)

Put 1 pound ground beef, 1 beaten egg, half the teriyaki sauce, and some pepper in a large bowl; combine gently. Scoop out rounded tablespoons of the mixture and drop them onto the baking sheet as you go. Or, roll them between your palms to make balls.

4 Bake and Serve

Bake, turning the meatballs only as necessary to prevent burning, until they're lightly browned, 8 to 12 minutes. Put the meatballs on a platter with the remaining teriyaki sauce on the side for dipping.

Lamb and Rosemary Meatballs with Yogurt Sauce Use ground lamb instead of beef and skip the teriyaki sauce. Instead, stir together 1 cup Greek yogurt, 1 minced garlic clove, 2 teaspoons minced fresh rosemary, 1/4 cup chopped fresh mint, the juice of 1 lemon, salt, and pepper (don't cook it). Stir half of that into the meat and egg mixture. Bake the meatballs as directed, serving the remaining yogurt sauce on the side for dipping.

Chipotle Beef Meatballs Omit the teriyaki sauce. Add 1 chopped chipotle chile in adobo with some of its sauce directly to the ground beef and egg mixture. Add 1 minced garlic clove, the juice of 1 lime, 1/4 cup chopped scallions, and some salt and pepper. Bake the meatballs as directed and sprinkle with crumbled queso fresco before serving (no dipping sauce here unless you want to put out a bowl of salsa).

Curry Pork Meatballs Use ground pork instead of beef. Skip the teriyaki sauce. Instead add the minced garlic and ginger directly to the ground pork and egg mixture, along with 1/4 cup chopped fresh cilantro, 1 tablespoon curry powder, the juice of 1 lime, and some salt and pepper. Bake as directed. While the meatballs cook, warm 3/4 cup apricot jam with 1/4 cup cider vinegar and use that as the dipping sauce.

Chicken and Basil Meatballs Use ground chicken (or turkey) instead of beef. Omit the teriyaki sauce. Add 1/4 cup chopped fresh basil, 1 minced garlic clove, 1/2 cup freshly grated Parmesan, 1/4 cup bread crumbs, 1/4 cup milk, and some salt and pepper directly to the chicken and egg mixture. Bake the meatballs as directed. Grate a little Parmesan over the top before serving with warmed tomato sauce (page 296) on the side for dipping.

Swedish Meatballs Substitute ground pork for half of the beef. Omit the teriyaki sauce. Add 1/4 teaspoon allspice, 1/4 teaspoon nutmeg, some salt, and lots of pepper directly to the ground meat and egg mixture. Bake the meatballs as directed. For the sauce: Sauté 1 chopped medium onion in 3 tablespoons butter over medium heat until soft, 3 to 5 minutes. Stir in 3 tablespoons flour and cook, stirring frequently, until the flour and butter form a paste and it turns light brown, another 3 to 5 minutes. Add 1 cup beef broth and cook, stirring constantly until it thickens into the consistency of gravy. Stir in 1/4 cup cream, taste and adjust the seasoning, and pour on top of the meatballs (or serve on the side for dipping).

SPEED  SERVES 4

Peel-and-Eat Shrimp

Grilling or broiling shrimp with their shells on saves you time on peeling and imparts more flavor while protecting them from getting overcooked. Plus it's fun to peel at the table before dipping into a seasoned mayo. (For more ideas about flavoring the dip, see page 144.) If you prefer, you can skip the dipping sauce and just serve the shrimp with lemon wedges.

Ingredients

1 cup mayonnaise

2 teaspoons seasoning: curry powder, chili powder, cumin, coriander, paprika, smoked paprika, or Old Bay

Salt and pepper

1 ½ pounds any size shell-on shrimp

1 tablespoon olive oil

Prep | Cook

1. Prepare a grill or turn the broiler to high; put the rack 4 inches from the heat.

   Put 1 cup mayonnaise, 2 teaspoons seasoning, and a sprinkle of salt and pepper in a serving bowl; stir to combine.

2. Put the shrimp on a rimmed baking sheet and toss with 1 tablespoon olive oil and a sprinkle of salt and pepper.

3. When the grill or broiler is hot, cook the shrimp, turning once, until they're lightly charred on the outside and just cooked through, 3 or 4 minutes per side.

4. Serve with the mayonnaise for dipping, letting people peel the shrimp at the table.

NOTES

MAKE YOUR OWN

Mayonnaise 144

Curry Powder 758

Chili Powder 758

VARIATIONS

Boiled Peel-and-Eat Shrimp

Instead of heating the broiler, bring a large pot of water to boil and salt it. Cook the shrimp until just pink, 2 to 5 minutes depending on the size.

SPEED SERVES 4

Skewerless Chicken Satay

This is better than the satay at most Thai restaurants, and you'll never miss the skewer.

Ingredients

6 boneless, skinless chicken thighs (about 18 ounces)

1 lime

1 garlic clove

½ inch fresh ginger

1 tablespoon soy sauce

1 tablespoon rice vinegar

1 teaspoon cumin

1 teaspoon chili powder

2 tablespoons sugar

¼ cup peanut butter

Prep | Cook

1. Turn the broiler to high; put the rack 4 inches from the heat. Put the chicken in the freezer.

   Halve the lime; squeeze the juice into a large bowl.

   Peel 1 garlic clove and ½ inch fresh ginger. Mince them together and add them to the bowl.

2. Add 1 tablespoon soy sauce, 1 tablespoon rice vinegar, 1 teaspoon cumin, 1 teaspoon chili powder, and 2 tablespoons sugar to the bowl. Whisk to combine. Divide the marinade in half, reserving half for making the dipping sauce.

3. Remove the chicken thighs from the freezer, cut them into thin slices, and add to 1 portion of the marinade; toss to coat.

4. Line a rimmed baking sheet with foil; using tongs, transfer the chicken to the foil, discarding the marinade left behind. Spread out the chicken so it overlaps as little as possible.

5. When the broiler is hot, cook the chicken, turning as necessary, until lightly charred all over, 6 to 8 minutes.

6. While the chicken cooks, whisk ¼ cup hot water and ¼ cup peanut butter into the reserved portion of marinade until smooth.

7. Pour the sauce into a serving bowl. When the chicken is done, let it cool for a minute or 2, transfer it to a platter, and serve with the peanut sauce for dipping.

SPEED  SERVES 4

Tortillas Rojas

The quick blended salsa here is a keeper you'll make again and again.

Ingredients

One 9-ounce bag tortilla chips

1 tablespoon vegetable oil

1 fresh hot green chile (like serrano)

2 garlic cloves

One 14-ounce can diced tomatoes

Salt

Several sprigs fresh cilantro

1 lime

Dash of hot sauce (optional)

4 ounces queso fresco (1 cup crumbled)

Prep | Cook

1. Heat the oven to 300°F. Spread the tortilla chips on a rimmed baking sheet; put them in the oven to warm.
2. Put 1 tablespoon vegetable oil into a small saucepan over medium heat.

   Trim the chile and seed it if you like. Peel 2 garlic cloves. Mince the chile and garlic together.
3. Add the chile and garlic to the pan and cook, stirring frequently until fragrant, 15 to 30 seconds.
4. Add the tomatoes and their juice to the pan, sprinkle with salt, and raise the heat to medium-high. Cook, stirring once or twice, until the tomatoes start to break apart, 5 to 8 minutes.

   Chop several sprigs cilantro. Cut the lime into wedges.
5. Blend the tomatoes until smooth, starting the machine on low to avoid splashing. Taste and adjust the seasoning, adding a dash of hot sauce if you like.
6. Put the warmed chips in a large bowl. Add a few spoonfuls of the salsa gradually, tossing constantly so the chips are evenly coated. Reserve the remaining salsa.
7. Put the chips on a platter; crumble 1 cup queso fresco on top of the chips. Garnish with cilantro and lime wedges and serve immediately with the remaining salsa.

SPEED ◐ SERVES 4 TO 6

Roasted Nuts with Ginger, Soy, and Honey

This salty, sticky-sweet, and spicy recipe blows store-bought nuts out of the water.

Ingredients

1 inch fresh ginger

2 tablespoons honey

2 teaspoons soy sauce

Vegetable oil

2 cups any unsalted raw nuts

Salt and pepper

Prep | Cook

1. Heat the oven to 350°F. Put a large skillet over medium-low heat. Peel and mince 1 inch fresh ginger.
2. Add 2 tablespoons honey, 2 teaspoons soy sauce, and the ginger to the skillet. Bring to a simmer.
3. Grease a rimmed baking sheet with vegetable oil.
4. Add 2 cups nuts to the skillet. Sprinkle with salt and pepper and toss to coat.
5. Spread the nuts evenly on the baking sheet. Roast, shaking occasionally, until lightly browned, 10 minutes. Let the nuts cool for a few minutes before serving.

VARIATIONS

Roasted Nuts with Smoked Paprika and Lemon
Skip the honey. Substitute 2 teaspoons grated lemon zest for the ginger, 1 teaspoon smoked paprika for the soy sauce, and olive oil for the vegetable oil.

Sweet and Salty Roasted Nuts, Thai Style
Use 1 fresh hot green chile (like serrano) in place of the ginger, fish sauce for the soy sauce, and brown sugar for the honey. Add 2 teaspoons grated lime zest.

SPEED ◐ SERVES 4

Warm-Pickled Cucumber Spears

Steeping vegetables in hot brine infuses them with lots of flavor in little time. They pick up a great tang from the vinegar and retain their crunch. Kirby cucumbers make the best pickles if you can find them, but the small Persian cukes and even English cukes also work well.

Ingredients

½ cup red wine vinegar

1 bay leaf

1 teaspoon salt

½ teaspoon sugar

3 medium cucumbers (1 to 1 ½ pounds)

1 bunch fresh dill

Prep | Cook

1. Put ½ cup red wine vinegar, 1 bay leaf, 1 teaspoon salt, ½ teaspoon sugar, and 2 cups water in a large pot over high heat.

   Trim the cucumbers; cut them into thick spears.

   Strip 2 tablespoons dill leaves from the stems and chop.

2. When the liquid comes to a boil, add the cucumbers and dill; cover and turn off the heat.

3. Let the cucumbers sit for 10 to 15 minutes; Serve warm or at room temperature. To store, let the cucumbers cool a bit, then submerge them in the brine and refrigerate. They'll keep for about a week and pickle further in the fridge.

VARIATIONS

Warm-Pickled Bell Peppers
Substitute 1 pound red or yellow bell peppers, thickly sliced, for the cucumbers and 1 teaspoon dried oregano for the dill.

Warm-Pickled Zucchini
Replace the cucumbers with 1 pound zucchini. Add 2 teaspoons grated lemon zest to the pot along with the dill.

Warm-Pickled Carrots
Use 1 pound carrots, cut into sticks, instead of cucumbers and 1 tablespoon cumin seeds instead of dill.

SPEED ◐ SERVES 4

Green Beans with Onion Dip

Most onion dips feature caramelized onions, which are super but can take an hour to cook. Onions that are cooked more quickly, just until some charred spots start to appear, get very sweet with a hint of pleasing bitterness—and you can't beat those crisp edges.

Ingredients

¼ cup olive oil

2 large onions

Salt and pepper

1 bunch fresh chives

1 cup sour cream

½ cup Greek yogurt

1 pound green beans

Prep | Cook

1. Put ¼ cup olive oil in a large skillet over medium-high heat.
   Trim, peel, halve, and thinly slice the onions.
2. When the oil is hot, add the onions and a sprinkle of salt and pepper. Cook, stirring occasionally until they begin to brown, 4 or 5 minutes.
   Chop 2 tablespoons chives; put them in a medium bowl.
3. Add 1 cup sour cream, ½ cup Greek yogurt, and a sprinkle of salt and pepper to the bowl. Stir to combine and transfer the mixture to the fridge.
4. When the onions begin to brown, lower the heat to medium and cook, stirring a little more frequently, until they are shriveled, dry, and just starting to char, 10 to 15 minutes.
   Trim the green beans; put them on a platter or in a bowl.
5. When the onions are just starting to char, transfer them to paper towels with a slotted spoon and let them cool for a few minutes. Chop the onions and stir them into the sour cream and yogurt mixture. Taste and adjust the seasoning.
6. Transfer to a serving bowl and serve with the green beans alongside for dipping.

SPEED ◐ SERVES 4

Hard-Boiled Eggs with Dijon Mayo

All the flavors of deviled eggs without the hassle. Not sure why I never thought of this before now, but . . . they're beauties. (For more ways to flavor the mayo, see page 144.)

Ingredients

4 eggs

Ice cubes

2 tablespoons mayonnaise

2 teaspoons Dijon mustard

½ teaspoon paprika, plus more for garnish

Salt and pepper

Prep | Cook

1. Fill a medium saucepan about two-thirds full with water and gently submerge 4 eggs. Bring to a boil, turn off the heat, and cover. Set a timer: Large to extra-large eggs will cook in 9 minutes.

   Fill a large bowl with ice water.

   Put 2 tablespoons mayonnaise, 2 teaspoons Dijon, ½ teaspoon paprika, and a sprinkle of salt and pepper in a small bowl. Stir to combine.

2. When the eggs are done, transfer them to the ice water with a slotted spoon. Leave them submerged for at least 1 minute.

3. Crack and peel the eggs, transfer them to a cutting board, and halve them lengthwise.

4. Sprinkle the eggs with a little salt and dollop about 1 teaspoon of the mayonnaise mixture on top of each. Garnish with a small dusting of paprika and serve.

VARIATIONS

Hard-Boiled Eggs with Curry Mayo
Substitute curry powder for the paprika.

NOTES

MAKE YOUR OWN
Mayonnaise 144

SPEED ◑ SERVES 4

Parmesan Crisps

Many believe that the best part of a grilled cheese sandwich is the bit of cheese that oozes out and browns directly on the skillet. Well, these crisps are that part. Use a nonstick skillet if you have one. Note: This will work only with Parmesan that has been grated into large or long pieces, not the kind that's finely ground like a powder.

Ingredients

12 ounces Parmesan cheese (3 cups grated)

Pepper

Prep | Cook

1. Put a large skillet (preferably nonstick) over medium-low heat.
   Grate 3 cups Parmesan into a large bowl; add plenty of pepper and toss.

2. Mound ¼ cup of the Parmesan in the skillet. Flatten it into a 3- to 4-inch circle and cook until the cheese is fully melted and browning around the edges, about a minute.

3. Flip the crisp over with a metal spatula and cook on the other side, adjusting the heat as necessary to prevent burning, until golden brown on the bottom, another minute or so.

4. Transfer to a paper towel and repeat the process with the rest of the cheese. Serve at room temperature.

VARIATIONS

Rosemary-Parmesan Crisps
Add 2 teaspoons minced fresh rosemary to the Parmesan along with the pepper.

Spicy Cheddar Crisps
Use cheddar cheese instead of Parmesan and ½ teaspoon cayenne instead of pepper.

SPEED  SERVES 4 TO 8

Quesadillas with Pico de Gallo

Cooking quesadillas in the broiler lets you make four at once, as opposed to the one or two that you can fit in a skillet. And that leaves you time to whip up fresh pico de gallo.

Ingredients

1 large ripe tomato

1 fresh hot green chile (like jalapeño)

1 small onion

Several sprigs fresh cilantro

1 lime

Salt and pepper

6 scallions

4 ounces cheddar cheese (1 cup grated)

Four 6-inch flour tortillas

1 tablespoon vegetable oil

Sour cream for garnish

Prep | Cook

1. Turn the broiler to high; put the rack 6 inches from the heat.

   Core and chop the tomato; put it in a medium bowl.

   Trim the chile, remove the seeds if you'd like, and mince it; add it to the bowl.

   Trim, peel, and finely chop the onion; add it to the bowl.

   Chop several sprigs cilantro and add to the bowl.

   Halve the lime; squeeze the juice into the bowl.

2. Add a sprinkle of salt and pepper to the bowl and stir to combine.

   Trim and chop the scallions.

   Grate 1 cup cheddar cheese.

3. Brush 1 side of the tortillas with 1 tablespoon vegetable oil; put them oil side down on a rimmed baking sheet.

4. Sprinkle the cheese and scallions evenly over the tortillas. Broil until the cheese melts, then carefully fold the tortillas in half.

5. Continue to cook, turning once, until the tortillas are golden and crisp on both sides, 2 to 5 minutes total.

6. Cut the quesadillas in half if you like and serve with the pico de gallo and some sour cream.

SPEED ◐ SERVES 4

Pizza Wedges

Remember those miniature pizza bagels that you cook in the microwave and eat as a snack? These are not that much slower, and they're a hundred times more flavorful.

Ingredients

8 ounces fresh mozzarella cheese

Four 8-inch flour tortillas

4 tablespoons tomato paste

Olive oil

Salt and pepper

Prep | Cook

1. Heat the oven to 450°F.

   Thinly slice 8 ounces fresh mozzarella.

2. Put the tortillas in a single layer on 1 or 2 baking sheets. Put a tablespoon of tomato paste on each tortilla and spread it out toward the edges.
3. Lay the mozzarella slices on the tortillas, drizzle each tortilla with olive oil, and sprinkle with salt and pepper.
4. Put them in the oven (even if it's not fully heated yet), and bake, checking once or twice, until the cheese is bubbly and brown and the tortillas are crisp, 5 to 10 minutes.
5. Cut into wedges and serve.

VARIATIONS

Pesto Pizza Wedges
Use pesto instead of tomato paste.

Salsa and Jack Pizza Wedges
Swap 1 cup shredded Jack cheese for the mozzarella and salsa for the tomato paste.

Fig and Gorgonzola Pizza Wedges
Substitute 1 cup crumbled Gorgonzola for the mozzarella and fig jam for the tomato paste. Add slices of pear on top of the jam, cover with Gorgonzola, then add arugula.

Sides

Garlic Bread 906

Warm Flour Tortillas 907

Crisp Seasoned Pita 908

Bruschetta 909

Couscous 910

Green Salad 911

Chopped Salad 912

Tomato Salad 913

Carrot Salad with Raisins 914

Cucumber Salad 915

Cucumber Raita 916

Fennel Salad 917

Jícama and Radish Salad 918

Ginger-Orange Bean Sprouts 919

Avocado with Lemon and Salt 920

Pick-a-Fruit Salad 921

Caprese Salad 922

Coleslaw 923

Sautéed Greens with Garlic 924

Seared Broccoli or Cauliflower 925

Two-Step Broccoli 926

Stir-Fried Bok Choy 927

Fajita Peppers and Onions 928

Asparagus Gratin 929

Tomatoes with Fried Bread Crumbs 930

Broiled Cherry Tomatoes 931

Mexican Street Corn 932

Succotash 933

Peas with Bacon and Onion 934

Smashed Peas 935

Creamed Spinach 936

Chile-Cumin Black Beans 937

Refried Beans 938

Hummus 939

Scallion Pancakes 940

White Rice 941

Rice Pilaf 944

Quinoa 945

Bulgur with Lemon and Parsley 946

Creamy Polenta 947

Pasta, Plain and Simple 948

Sesame Noodles 949

Fire and Ice Noodles 950

Panfried Rice Noodles 951

Skillet Stuffing 952

Cucumbers with Peanut Vinaigrette 953

Tender Vegetables 954

Simmered Squash 955

Garlicky Mushrooms 956

Stuffed Portobellos 957

Brussels Sprouts with Bacon 958

Crunchy Okra 959

Ripe Plantains 960

Skin-On Mashed Potatoes 961

German-Style Potato Salad 962

French Fries 963

Sautéed Sweet Potatoes 964

Crisp Roasted Potatoes 965

Sides

When I was growing up in the fifties and sixties, the only acceptable definition of a "meal" in my house—and many others—was a piece of meat served with both a starch and a vegetable on the same plate. The way we eat has changed a lot since then, mostly for the better. Certainly the way you assemble meals is a lot less rigid.

"Sides" have become way more important, and sometimes, as in the case of tapas and many vegetarian meals, there is no more "center of the plate." If you're after the traditional starch and vegetable, there's plenty here to mix and match; all the "mains" in the book offer suggestions.

But you might want to use the sides in this chapter—which includes many simple two- or three-ingredient salads—as appetizers. You might not always feel the need to fuss with another dish, or you'll be inspired to make a whole meal of them. You decide what sides you put on the table when. This flexibility helps you make the most efficient use of your kitchen time.

After all, you almost never cook sides in a vacuum. There's always something else on the stove or in the oven, so timing can become a potential point of stress, especially when you're in a hurry. But recipes like these dovetail with your kitchen choreography. You attend to them periodically, but they need not dominate your activity. And almost none need to be served piping hot—some aren't even cooked—which means they can sit around for a bit while you wrap up the main recipe.

Chapter Highlights

A Side of Bread Why overthink it? Sometimes the only side you need. Warm Buttery Bread (page 906), Crisp Seasoned Pita (page 908), Bruschetta (page 909).

Instant Flatbread You don't have to cook Mexican food or wrap anything to enjoy this simple, traditional accompaniment. Warm Flour Tortillas (page 907).

Beyond Salt and Pepper There is a world of flavors in your kitchen. Seasoning Sides (page 942).

Fewer Ingredients, Less Prep, Less Time Discover the virtues of prepping one or two ingredients instead of four or five. Pick-a-Fruit Salad (page 921).

Sides in the Microwave The microwave can be the perfect place to cook side dishes. Warm Flour Tortillas (page 907), Creamy Polenta (page 947), Two-Step Broccoli (page 926).

Your New "Knife" For vegetable ribbons, use your peeler. Simmered Squash (page 955).

Potatoes in a Hurry Shortcuts to crispness. Crisp Roasted Potatoes (page 965), Sautéed Sweet Potatoes (page 964).

Canned Beans, Transformed Chile-Cumin Black Beans (page 937), Refried Beans (page 938).

Homemade Hummus Try serving a spoonful as a bed for simply cooked meat, fish, chicken, or vegetables. Hummus (page 939).

Cook Sides Simultaneously All of the recipes in this chapter are designed to be cooked while you prepare the main dish. It's easy to coordinate the timing: The chapter is organized with the fastest sides first. Once you decide what you want to make—each main dish offers several suggestions—use the clock icon at the top of the recipe to give you an idea when to start. And when in doubt, you can always start the side dish first. If it's done before the rest of the meal, it's rarely a big deal; just let it hang out until you're ready to eat.

Mix and Match Almost all of the recipes in this book offer variations to help you change ingredients and flavor profiles; they're an important way to keep your menus exciting, so I hope you incorporate them into your repertoire. It's easy to adjust the sides accordingly: Use the suggestions after the main dishes to help you locate alternatives in this chapter and quickly find the ideal side—either a main recipe or its variation—that complements your meal.

SPEED SERVES 4

Garlic Bread

Crisp-crusted bread turns lots of recipes into a complete meal.

Ingredients

4 tablespoons (½ stick) butter, or to taste

4 garlic cloves

Several sprigs fresh parsley

1 loaf any rustic unsliced bread (about 1 pound)

1 tablespoon olive oil

Salt and pepper

Prep | Cook

1. Heat the oven to 375°F. Put 4 tablespoons (more or less) butter in a dish near the oven to soften. Or soften in the microwave on low for 10 to 40 seconds.

   Peel and mince 4 garlic cloves.

   Strip the leaves from several parsley sprigs and chop.

   Cut thick slices downward into the bread without going all the way through, leaving the pieces connected at the bottom.

2. When the butter is soft, mix in the garlic, parsley, 1 tablespoon olive oil, and some salt and pepper. Spread a little between the slices of bread. Wrap the loaf in aluminum foil so that the bottom and sides are covered but the top is open.

3. Bake the bread directly on the oven rack until the crust is crackling crisp, 10 to 15 minutes.

4. Remove the bread from the oven; serve the whole loaf and let everyone break off pieces or finish slicing through the bottom crust to separate it.

VARIATIONS

Warm Buttery Bread
Skip the seasonings and just add plain softened butter to the cuts you've made in the bread.

SPEED SERVES 4

Warm Flour Tortillas

Many if not most Mexican dishes deserve a stack of steaming tortillas on the side, but flour tortillas—which are really just flat bread—go with other styles of cooking too.

Ingredients

Eight 10-inch flour tortillas

Prep | Cook

1. Heat the oven to 375°F.

   Stack 8 flour tortillas and wrap in aluminum foil.

2. Bake the tortilla package directly on the oven rack until the tortillas are steaming hot, 5 to 10 minutes. Keep them wrapped in the foil until you're ready to serve.

VARIATIONS

Warm Corn Tortillas
Use 12 small corn tortillas instead of the flour ones here.

Microwaved Tortillas
Wrap the tortillas in a damp paper towel and put them on a microwave-safe plate. Microwave on high for 15 to 20 seconds.

Fried Tortillas
Never greasy if you do it like this. Heat 1/4 inch vegetable oil in a skillet large enough to hold a tortilla over medium-high heat. When hot but not smoking, add a tortilla and cook, turning once, until golden brown and crisp on both sides, 1 to 2 minutes per side. Add more oil to the pan as necessary. Drain on paper towels.

Charred Tortillas
If you have a gas stove, turn as many burners as you have free to high. Put the tortillas directly on the flame and cook, carefully turning with tongs, until they're lightly charred around the edges on both sides, 30 seconds to a minute per side. This will keep you busy, so pay attention.

SPEED SERVES 4

Crisp Seasoned Pita

There's something about pita that begs to be cooked over an open flame until lightly charred. The classic Middle Eastern topping is za'atar, a mixture of thyme, sumac, toasted sesame seeds, marjoram, oregano, and salt that you can buy at Middle Eastern or spice stores.

Ingredients

Four 6- to 8-inch pitas

4 teaspoons olive oil

Salt and pepper

Prep | Cook

1. Prepare a grill or turn the broiler to high; put the rack 4 inches from the heat.

   Drizzle the pitas with olive oil (about ½ teaspoon per side) and rub them all over with your fingers. Sprinkle salt and pepper over all and if broiling spread them out on a baking sheet.

2. Grill or broil the pitas, turning once, until browned (even slightly charred) on both sides, 2 to 5 minutes total.

3. Stack the pitas and cut into halves or wedges if you like, wrap in a towel, and serve warm.

VARIATIONS

8 Ways to Season Pita

Sprinkle a pinch over each along with the salt and pepper:

1. Cumin
2. Curry powder (page 758)
3. Smoked paprika
4. Chili powder (page 758)
5. Chopped fresh (or dried) rosemary or oregano
6. Sesame seeds
7. Fresh or dried thyme
8. Za'atar

SPEED SERVES 4 TO 8

Bruschetta

Good bread, toasted and rubbed with fresh garlic, then showered in olive oil. Stop there and you'll be happy, or see the list that follows for other toppings.

Ingredients

1 loaf any rustic unsliced bread (about 1 pound)

2 garlic cloves

¼ cup olive oil, or more to taste

Salt and pepper

Prep | Cook

1. Prepare a grill or turn the broiler to high; put the rack 4 inches from the heat.

   Cut the bread into slices about 1 inch thick. If broiling, put them on a rimmed baking sheet.

   Peel and halve 2 garlic cloves.

2. Grill or broil the bread, turning once, until golden on both sides but still soft in places, 2 to 5 minutes total.

3. Rub the tops of the bread with the cut side of the garlic.

4. Spread them out and drizzle ¼ cup olive oil over all; sprinkle with salt and pepper and add more olive oil if you like. Serve warm.

ADDITIONS

10 Easy Bruschetta Toppings

Top each slice of bread with a tablespoon or 2 of the following:

1. Grated Parmesan cheese
2. Chopped fresh tomatoes with chopped fresh basil
3. Mashed white beans (with salt and pepper)
4. Canned tuna (with salt and pepper)
5. Ricotta, sliced mozzarella, or crumbled feta cheese
6. Pesto (page 284)
7. Olive tapenade (page 622)
8. Hummus (page 939)
9. Tomato Salsa (page 145)
10. Smashed Peas (page 935)

SPEED ◔ SERVES 4

Couscous

Plain couscous is a cook's—and eater's—dream: It's almost as easy as boiling water, takes just over 5 minutes, requires almost no watching, and is delicious with a wide variety of main dishes. For the whole wheat and Israeli versions, see the Variations.

Ingredients

1 cup couscous

Salt

Prep | Cook

1. Put 1 cup couscous in a medium saucepan; add 1 ½ cups water and a big pinch of salt.
2. Bring just to a boil, cover, and remove from the heat. Let it steep for about 5 minutes; fluff with a fork, taste and add more salt if you like, and serve.

VARIATIONS

Whole Wheat Couscous
Use whole wheat couscous instead of white; let it steep for about 10 minutes.

Israeli Couscous
Chewy and more pastalike; also known as *pearl couscous*. Use Israeli couscous along with 2 cups water. When the water boils, reduce the heat so it bubbles gently but steadily and cook, stirring occasionally until the water almost evaporates and the couscous is barely tender, 2 to 5 minutes or more. (The cooking time varies a lot depending on the size and brand, so taste it a couple times.) Then cover, let sit, and fluff as directed.

Seasoning Couscous
Anything you can stir into cooked rice you can also stir into cooked couscous. See the list on page 355 for ideas.

SPEED SERVES 4

Green Salad

The side that goes with more dishes than any other. Add other ingredients as you have the time and inclination; see the list below for options. For information about how to rinse, dry, and store greens, see page 49. I usually use sherry vinegar, but any will work.

Ingredients

1 large head romaine lettuce

⅓ cup olive oil

2 tablespoons any vinegar or lemon juice

Salt and pepper

Prep | Cook

Trim the lettuce and tear the leaves into bite-sized pieces (you should have about 6 cups).

1. Put the leaves in a large bowl, drizzle with ⅓ cup olive oil and 2 tablespoons vinegar, and sprinkle with salt and pepper.
2. Toss gently, lifting from the bottom to coat with dressing. Taste and adjust the seasoning, then serve right away.

VARIATIONS

Green Salad with Sesame-Soy Dressing
Substitute 3 tablespoons vegetable oil and 2 tablespoons sesame oil for olive oil and use rice vinegar.

12 Other Greens to Use (Alone or in Combination)

1. Iceberg lettuce
2. Boston lettuce
3. Green or red leaf lettuce
4. Spinach
5. Arugula
6. Endive
7. Radicchio
8. Watercress
9. Frisée
10. Dandelion greens
11. Beet greens
12. Escarole

SPEED  SERVES 4

Chopped Salad

Basically any vegetable that you would eat raw is fair game here, but use the ingredient list as a guideline for making the most versatile salad ever while cleaning out your produce drawer.

Ingredients

1 medium head romaine lettuce

1 large carrot

2 celery stalks

1 small cucumber

1 medium red bell pepper

1 small red onion

3 tablespoons olive oil

1 tablespoon sherry or red wine vinegar

Salt and pepper

Prep | Cook

Trim and chop the lettuce; put it in a large bowl.

Trim and peel the carrot. Trim the celery. Peel the cucumber; cut it in half lengthwise and scoop out the seeds with a spoon.

Core and seed the bell pepper. Trim and peel the onion.

Chop the vegetables, adding them to the bowl as you go.

1. Drizzle the salad with 3 tablespoons olive oil, 1 tablespoon vinegar, and a sprinkle of salt and pepper.
2. Toss gently, lifting from the bottom to coat with dressing. Taste and adjust the seasoning and serve right away.

10 Ways to Turn Chopped Salad into a Meal

Add about 2 cups of the following (alone or in combination):

1. Cold pasta, soba, udon, or rice noodles
2. Chopped or sliced cooked meat, chicken, seafood, or tofu
3. Canned tuna
4. Cooked or canned beans
5. Edamame, lima beans, peas (thawed if frozen)
6. Fresh or frozen corn kernels
7. Chopped peanuts or other nuts (you'll need only 1 cup)
8. Chopped hard-boiled eggs
9. Fresh or toasted Bread Crumbs (page 71)
10. Cooked grains, like rice, bulgur, or quinoa

SPEED ◔ SERVES 4

Tomato Salad

This combination—juicy, ripe tomatoes with basil and olive oil—is an absolute no-brainer. But salt the tomatoes and they'll be even better.

Ingredients

5 or 6 medium ripe tomatoes (2 pounds)

Salt

1 bunch fresh basil

3 tablespoons olive oil

Pepper

Prep | Cook

Core the tomatoes and cut into wedges or large chunks.

1. Put the tomatoes in a large bowl; sprinkle with salt.

   Strip about ½ cup basil leaves from the stems and tear them into the bowl.

2. Add 3 tablespoons olive oil and lots of pepper; toss. Taste and adjust the seasoning and serve.

VARIATIONS

Tomato Salad with Olive Oil and Yogurt
Substitute 1/4 cup chopped fresh parsley for basil. Add 3 tablespoons plain yogurt.

Tomato Salad with Sesame and Soy
An excellent combination. Don't salt the tomatoes in Step 1. Substitute 1/4 cup chopped scallions or shallots for the basil and 1 tablespoon sesame oil and 2 tablespoons soy sauce for the olive oil. Taste, then add salt and pepper.

Jícama Salad with Chiles
Substitute 1 pound peeled and grated jícama for the tomatoes, chopped fresh chiles or red chile flakes to taste for the basil, and 1 tablespoon toasted sesame oil and the juice of 2 limes for the olive oil.

Grape Salad with Mint
Instead of the tomatoes, use 1 ½ pounds red or green seedless grapes; substitute ¼ cup chopped fresh mint for the basil. Add 1 tablespoon red or white wine vinegar.

SPEED SERVES 4

Carrot Salad with Raisins

Add cumin to the classic American picnic salad to give it a Moroccan twist.

Ingredients

½ cup raisins

3 tablespoons olive oil

2 tablespoons cider vinegar

1 teaspoon cumin

Salt and pepper

4 to 6 large carrots (1 ½ pounds)

Prep | Cook

1. Put ½ cup raisins, 3 tablespoons olive oil, 2 tablespoons cider vinegar, 1 teaspoon cumin, and a sprinkle of salt and pepper in a large bowl.

   Trim and peel the carrots; slice them into thin coins by hand or machine, or grate them.

2. Add the carrots to the bowl and toss. Taste and adjust the seasoning and serve.

VARIATIONS

Carrot Salad with Olives and Rosemary
Substitute ½ cup chopped olives for the raisins, sherry or red wine vinegar for the cider vinegar, and 1 teaspoon minced fresh rosemary for the cumin.

Carrot Salad with Soy Sauce and Scallions
Use ½ cup chopped scallions in place of the raisins and 1 tablespoon each sesame oil, vegetable oil, and soy sauce instead of olive oil. Use rice vinegar instead of cider vinegar. Garnish with toasted sesame seeds if you like.

Carrot Salad with Cilantro and Lime
Use ¼ cup hulled pumpkin seeds instead of the raisins and the juice of 1 lime in place of vinegar. Add 1 teaspoon chili powder and ½ cup chopped fresh cilantro to the dressing.

SPEED ◔ SERVES 4

Cucumber Salad

It never hurts to dress cucumbers up a bit. If you have time to make these before you start the main dish, the result is a quick, fresh pickle.

Ingredients

3 medium cucumbers (1 to 1 ½ pounds)

3 tablespoons olive oil

2 tablespoons sherry vinegar or red wine vinegar

Salt and pepper

Prep | Cook

Trim the cucumbers, peel if necessary, cut them in half lengthwise, and scoop out the seeds with a spoon. Cut them into small chunks or slices and put them in a large bowl.

1. Add 3 tablespoons olive oil, 2 tablespoons vinegar, and a sprinkle of salt and pepper and toss. Taste and adjust the seasoning and serve.

VARIATIONS

Cucumber Salad with Soy Sauce and Mirin
Substitute soy sauce for the olive oil and mirin for the vinegar.

Cucumber Salad with Dijon Mayo
Replace the olive oil with mayonnaise and the vinegar with Dijon mustard.

Cucumber Salad with Hot Sauce and Lime Juice
Use mayonnaise instead of olive oil and the juice of 1 lime instead of vinegar; add a few dashes of your favorite hot sauce (Sriracha is great here).

Cucumber Salad with Sour Cream and Dill
Substitute sour cream for the olive oil and ¼ cup chopped fresh dill for the vinegar.

NOTES

EVEN FASTER
If you have Vinaigrette (page 70) in the fridge, use it instead of making the dressing as described in Step 1.

SPEED SERVES 4

Cucumber Raita

This classic Indian yogurt sauce is a cooling accompaniment to all sorts of spicy dishes, whether they feature chicken, meat, seafood, vegetables, legumes, or rice.

Ingredients

2 medium cucumbers

1 garlic clove

1 lemon

1 ½ cups yogurt

Salt and pepper

Prep | Cook

Trim the cucumbers, peel if necessary, cut them in half lengthwise, and scoop out the seeds with a spoon. Chop the cucumbers into small or large pieces, depending on how chunky you want the sauce. Add them to a medium bowl.

Peel and mince 1 garlic clove; add it to the bowl.

Halve the lemon; squeeze the juice into the bowl.

1. Add 1 ½ cups yogurt and a sprinkle of salt and pepper to the bowl. Stir to combine. Taste and adjust the seasoning and serve right away or refrigerate for up to 1 day.

VARIATIONS

8 Other Vegetable Raitas

Use the following alone or in combination (about 3 cups):

1. Tomatoes
2. Bell peppers
3. Grated carrots
4. Grated beets
5. Grated celery root
6. Daikon or other radish
7. Fennel
8. Tomatillos

5 Ways to Flavor Raita

Stir in any of the following (alone or in combination):

1. Up to ½ cup chopped fresh parsley, cilantro, or mint
2. Up to 1 teaspoon cumin, curry powder, chili powder, or cinnamon
3. Up to ½ cup chopped pistachios
4. Hot sauce to taste
5. 2 teaspoons minced fresh hot chile or ginger

SPEED SERVES 4

Fennel Salad

Thinly sliced fennel dressed in citrus juice, olive oil, salt, and pepper is one of my favorite salads, and shaved Parmesan adds just the right richness. Celery is equally good this way; see the first Variation.

Ingredients

1 large or 2 small fennel bulbs (1 pound)

1 lemon

3 tablespoons olive oil

Salt and pepper

Prep | Cook

Trim the fennel, saving a few of the fronds for garnish. Thinly slice the fennel by hand or machine and put it in a large bowl.

Grate the lemon zest and add the zest to the bowl; cut the fruit in half and squeeze in the juice.

1. Add 3 tablespoons olive oil and a sprinkle of salt and pepper and toss. Taste and adjust the seasoning and serve.

VARIATIONS

Celery Salad
Substitute 1 pound celery, thinly sliced, for the fennel or use a combination.

Fennel Salad with Olives
Use an orange instead of the lemon. Add ½ cup chopped green or black olives.

Fennel Salad with Capers and Dill
Substitute mayonnaise for the olive oil. Add 2 tablespoons capers and ¼ cup chopped fresh dill.

Fennel Salad with Caraway Seeds
Use 2 tablespoons cider vinegar instead of the lemon zest and juice. Add 2 teaspoons caraway seeds.

NOTES

EVEN FASTER
If you have Vinaigrette (page 70) in your fridge, use it instead of making the dressing as described in Step 1, omitting the lemon.

SPEED SERVES 4

Jícama and Radish Salad

Jícama and radish have similar textures, both crisp with a slight burst of juice, but the mild jícama benefits from the spicy edge of radish. If you have only one or the other, make this anyway. A crumble of feta or queso fresco is a bonus here.

Ingredients

2 medium jícama (1 pound)

4 to 6 radishes (8 ounces)

2 limes

1 teaspoon honey

½ teaspoon chili powder

Salt

1 bunch fresh cilantro

Prep | Cook

Peel and quarter the jícama. Trim and halve the radishes. Slice them both thinly by hand or machine and put them in a large bowl.

Halve the limes and squeeze the juice into the bowl.

1. Add 1 teaspoon honey, ½ teaspoon chili powder, and a sprinkle of salt.

   Chop ½ cup cilantro and add it to the bowl.

2. Toss the salad well to distribute the honey and chili powder. Taste and adjust the seasoning and serve.

VARIATIONS

Jícama and Radish Salad with Dried Cranberries and Cinnamon
Substitute 1 orange for the limes, ¼ teaspoon cinnamon for the chili powder, and mint for the cilantro. Add ½ cup dried cranberries.

Daikon Salad with Fish Sauce, Lime, and Peanuts
Instead of the jícama and radishes, use 1 ½ pounds daikon. Omit the chili powder and add ½ cup chopped peanuts and 2 teaspoons fish sauce.

SPEED SERVES 4

Ginger-Orange Bean Sprouts

The only way to cook bean sprouts so that they don't lose their crunch—their best feature—is *very* quickly. They get a flash of heat and no more.

Ingredients

2 tablespoons vegetable oil

1 inch fresh ginger

1 pound bean sprouts (about 4 cups)

Salt and pepper

1 orange

1 tablespoon soy sauce

2 teaspoons sesame oil

Prep | Cook

1. Put 2 tablespoons vegetable oil in a large skillet over high heat.

   Peel and mince 1 inch fresh ginger.

2. Add the ginger to the skillet and cook, stirring until fragrant, about 30 seconds.

3. Add the bean sprouts and sprinkle with salt and pepper. Toss to coat in the oil; cook, stirring occasionally until they barely begin to soften, 1 to 2 minutes.

   Halve the orange.

4. Squeeze the orange juice into the skillet; add 1 tablespoon soy sauce and 2 teaspoons sesame oil; turn off the heat and toss.

5. Taste and adjust the seasoning, adding more salt or soy sauce if necessary, and serve.

VARIATIONS

Olive Oil and Rosemary Bean Sprouts
Omit the soy sauce and sesame oil. Substitute olive for vegetable oil, 1 tablespoon minced garlic for the ginger, and a lemon for the orange. Add 1 teaspoon chopped fresh rosemary with the lemon juice.

Scallion-Miso Bean Sprouts
Use 3 chopped scallions in place of the orange and 1 tablespoon miso paste thinned with a small splash of water instead of soy sauce.

SPEED SERVES 4

Avocado with Lemon and Salt

Not long ago avocados were exotic; now they're commonplace. But there's nothing common about how delicious and beautifully textured they are.

Ingredients

2 medium avocados (about 1 pound)

Salt

1 lemon

Prep | Cook

Halve and pit the avocados; scoop out the flesh in one piece, thinly slice, and fan the slices out on a plate. Sprinkle with salt.

Halve the lemon.

1. Squeeze the lemon juice over the avocado slices and serve.

VARIATIONS

Avocado with Lime and Chili Salt
Substitute lime for lemon and mix a little chili powder into the salt before sprinkling.

Avocado with Rice Vinegar and Peanuts
Use 2 teaspoons rice vinegar instead of lemon juice. Garnish with 2 tablespoons finely chopped peanuts.

Avocado with Hot Sauce and Cilantro
Replace lemon with lime. Garnish with hot sauce to taste and some chopped fresh cilantro.

Avocado with Soy Sauce and Sesame Seeds
Substitute 2 tablespoons soy sauce for the lemon juice and 1 tablespoon sesame seeds for the salt.

SPEED SERVES 4

Pick-a-Fruit Salad

Limiting the types of fruits you use cuts down on prep time, although of course you can go to town if you like. See the list that follows for additional seasoning options.

Ingredients

1 medium pineapple (or 1 ½ pounds peaches or nectarines, apples, pears, bananas, fresh figs, kiwi, apricots, or melon)

2 cups strawberries (or any other berries)

1 lemon

Salt or sugar as you like

Prep | Cook

Cut the top and bottom off the pineapple; stand it upright and slice around the outside to remove the skin.

Still cutting from top to bottom, slice around the core; you'll have 3 or 4 large pieces. Discard the core, chop the flesh, and put it in a large bowl. (Or trim, peel, and cut the other fruit as necessary.)

Hull 2 cups strawberries. Cut them into quarters if they're big or into halves if they're small; add them to the bowl.

Halve the lemon and squeeze the juice into the bowl.

1. Gently stir the fruit, sprinkle with salt or sugar, taste and adjust the seasoning, and serve.

10 More Ways to Flavor Fruit Salad

Add any of the following in addition to or instead of the lemon:

1. Lime juice
2. ¼ cup chopped fresh basil or mint
3. Up to 2 teaspoons brown sugar, honey, or maple syrup
4. ¼ cup chopped toasted nuts or shredded coconut
5. 2 tablespoons lemon or orange liqueur
6. 2 teaspoons poppy seeds
7. Pepper
8. 2 tablespoons balsamic vinegar
9. Minced fresh chile to taste
10. ½ teaspoon vanilla extract

SPEED  SERVES 4

Caprese Salad

Witness one of the most popular combinations of our time; then use this recipe as a model.

Ingredients

1 small head romaine

4 or 5 medium ripe tomatoes (1 ½ pounds)

8 ounces fresh mozzarella cheese

1 bunch fresh basil

Salt and pepper

2 tablespoons olive oil

2 tablespoons balsamic vinegar

Prep | Cook

Trim the lettuce, pull off the whole leaves, and lay them on a platter to form a bed.

Core the tomatoes; slice crosswise into ½-inch rounds.

Cut 8 ounces fresh mozzarella crosswise into slices about the same thickness.

Strip about ½ cup basil leaves from the stems.

1. Alternating, overlap the tomato slices, mozzarella slices, and basil leaves on top of the lettuce.
2. Sprinkle with salt and lots of pepper; drizzle with 2 tablespoons olive oil and 2 tablespoons balsamic vinegar and serve.

VARIATIONS

Peach, Blue Cheese, and Tarragon Salad
Substitute 2 pounds peaches for the tomatoes, crumbled blue cheese for the mozzarella, 2 tablespoons fresh tarragon for the basil, and red wine vinegar for balsamic.

Watermelon, Feta, and Mint Salad
Use 2 pounds watermelon instead of the tomatoes, crumbled feta for the mozzarella, fresh mint for the basil, and lime juice for the balsamic.

Plum, Manchego, and Parsley Salad
Substitute 2 pounds plums for the tomatoes, shaved manchego cheese for the mozzarella, parsley for the basil, and sherry vinegar for balsamic.

SPEED ◔ SERVES 4

Coleslaw

Choose a slightly pliable cabbage—like Napa or Savoy—for a crisp-tender slaw. Use everyday red or green cabbage when you want more crunch.

Ingredients

1 large lemon, plus more as needed

¼ cup mayonnaise

2 tablespoons olive oil, plus more as needed

Salt and pepper

4 scallions

1 small head any cabbage (1 pound)

2 large carrots

Prep | Cook

Halve the lemon and squeeze the juice into a large bowl.

1. Add ¼ cup mayonnaise and 2 tablespoons olive oil and sprinkle generously with salt and pepper. Whisk well to combine.

Trim and slice the scallions; add them to the bowl.

Trim, core, and quarter the cabbage. Trim and peel the carrots.

Shred the cabbage and carrots in a food processor with a grating disk or by hand with a knife or box grater; transfer to the bowl.

2. Stir the vegetables into the dressing. Taste and adjust the seasoning, adding more lemon juice or olive oil if needed, and serve immediately or refrigerate for up to a day.

VARIATIONS

Soy Slaw
Substitute 1 tablespoon each sesame oil and vegetable oil for the olive oil and add 2 tablespoons soy sauce. Garnish with sesame seeds.

Tahini Slaw
Replace 2 tablespoons of the mayonnaise with 2 tablespoons tahini. Add 1 teaspoon cumin if you like.

No-Mayo Slaw
Omit the mayonnaise and increase the olive oil to ⅓ cup. Substitute 2 tablespoons red wine vinegar for the lemon juice.

NOTES

MAKE YOUR OWN

Mayonnaise 144

SPEED SERVES 4

Sautéed Greens with Garlic

The same drill works with any greens. The only thing that varies is the cooking time: Sturdier leaves—like kale—take longer to soften than tender leaves like spinach.

Ingredients

3 tablespoons olive oil

1 ½ pounds spinach, kale, collards, chard, or broccoli rabe

Salt and pepper

2 garlic cloves

Prep | Cook

1. Put 3 tablespoons olive oil in a large skillet over low heat.

   Trim and chop the greens, keeping any thick stems separate (discard any thick spinach stems).

2. Raise the heat to medium-high. Add any chopped stems to the skillet and cook until they begin to soften, 3 or 4 minutes. Add the leaves, a handful at a time if necessary to fit them in, and sprinkle with salt and pepper.

3. Cook until they're just wilted, 2 to 3 minutes for spinach, 3 or 4 minutes for chard and broccoli rabe, 4 or 5 minutes for kale and collards.

   Peel and mince 2 garlic cloves; add them to the skillet as soon as you're done.

4. When the greens are wilted, taste and adjust the seasoning and serve hot or at room temperature.

VARIATIONS

4 Ways to Flavor Greens

Add any of the following along with or instead of the garlic:

1. Minced fresh hot chile or red chile flakes to taste
2. 2 teaspoons sesame oil (use vegetable oil instead of olive oil)
3. ½ cup grated Parmesan cheese
4. ½ cup chopped cooked bacon, sausage, or ham

SPEED ◔ SERVES 4

Seared Broccoli or Cauliflower

A screaming-hot pan works wonders on florets of broccoli or cauliflower, which crisp and brown as they soften. (Broccoli rabe works too and cooks even faster.)

Ingredients

3 tablespoons olive oil

1 medium head broccoli or cauliflower (1 to 1 ½ pounds)

2 garlic cloves

½ teaspoon red chile flakes (optional)

Salt and pepper

Prep | Cook

1. Put 3 tablespoons olive oil in a large skillet over medium heat.
   Trim the broccoli or cauliflower; break or chop into small florets.
2. Add the broccoli or cauliflower to the skillet and raise the heat to high. Cook undisturbed until the florets brown, 3 to 5 minutes.
   Peel and mince the garlic.
3. When the florets are brown on the bottom, turn and sear on the other side, another 2 or 3 minutes.
4. Add the garlic to the skillet along with ½ teaspoon red chile flakes if you're using them and a sprinkle of salt and pepper. Cook, stirring or shaking the pan occasionally until the broccoli or cauliflower is nearly tender and the garlic is fragrant, 1 or 2 minutes.
5. Add ¾ cup water and scrape any browned bits off the bottom of the skillet, then lower the heat to medium.
6. Cook, stirring occasionally until the broccoli or cauliflower is fully tender and the liquid bubbles away, 2 to 4 minutes. Taste and adjust the seasoning and serve hot, warm, or at room temperature.

SPEED SERVES 4

Two-Step Broccoli

Broccoli and cheddar is a classic of the microwave age—and still a great dish if you make it yourself (see the variation). But I've always preferred this vegetable with Parmesan. And yes, you can still use the microwave!

Ingredients

1 large head broccoli (1 ½ pounds)

4 ounces Parmesan cheese (1 cup grated)

Salt and pepper

Prep | Cook

1. Turn the broiler to high; put the rack 4 inches from the heat.
   Trim the broccoli; break or chop into small florets.
2. Put the broccoli in a microwave-safe dish, add 2 tablespoons water, and cover. Cook on high, checking once or twice, until it's barely tender, 3 to 5 minutes.
   Grate 1 cup Parmesan cheese.
3. When the broccoli is tender, transfer it to a broiler-safe pan, sprinkle with salt and pepper, and top with the Parmesan. Broil until the cheese bubbles and browns, just a minute or 2. Serve hot or at room temperature.

VARIATIONS

Broccoli and Cheddar
Substitute cheddar for the Parmesan.

Broccoli and Toasted Almonds
Use ½ cup chopped almonds instead of the cheese in Step 3; broil until they darken but don't burn.

SPEED ◔ SERVES 4

Stir-Fried Bok Choy

A two-for-one side dish. You get the crunchy white stems, which get a head start in the skillet while you prepare everything else, and the tender green leaves, which finish quickly.

Ingredients

3 tablespoons vegetable oil

1 large head bok choy (1 ½ pounds)

2 garlic cloves

1 fresh hot green chile (like Thai)

Salt and pepper

1 lime

1 tablespoon soy sauce, plus more to taste

Prep | Cook

1. Put 3 tablespoons vegetable oil in a large skillet over medium heat.
   Trim the bok choy; cut (or pull) the leaves from the stems. Thinly slice the stems.

2. Add the stems to the skillet and raise the heat to medium-high. Cook, stirring occasionally until they start to soften, 3 to 5 minutes.
   Cut the leaves into wide ribbons.
   Peel 2 garlic cloves and trim the chile; mince both together.

3. Add the leaves, garlic, chile, a little salt, and some pepper to the skillet. Cook, stirring occasionally until the leaves wilt and the stems are nearly tender but still have some crunch, 3 or 4 minutes.
   Halve the lime.

4. Squeeze the lime juice into the pan with 1 tablespoon soy sauce and stir. Taste and adjust the seasoning; add more soy sauce if you like and serve.

VARIATIONS

Stir-Fried Bok Choy with Olives and Lemon
Omit the soy sauce. Substitute olive oil for the vegetable oil, ¼ cup chopped olives for the chile, and a lemon for the lime.

SPEED SERVES 4

Fajita Peppers and Onions

The sizzle of fajitas making their way to your table on a scorching-hot cast-iron plate is about as enticing a sound as you'll hear in a restaurant, and it's easy to replicate at home.

Ingredients

3 tablespoons vegetable oil

2 medium onions

3 medium bell peppers (any color)

2 teaspoons cumin

Salt and pepper

Prep | Cook

1. Put 3 tablespoons vegetable oil in a large skillet over medium heat.

   Trim, peel, halve, and slice the onions; add them to the skillet.

   Core, seed, and slice the peppers; add them to the skillet.

2. Raise the heat to high and cook, stirring frequently, until the vegetables are as tender and brown as you like, 5 to 10 minutes.

3. Sprinkle with the cumin and some salt and pepper and cook, stirring, for a minute. Taste and adjust the seasoning and serve.

VARIATIONS

Fajita Poblanos and Scallions

For the peppers, use 1 pound poblano chiles. Instead of the onion, trim 2 bunches scallions and cut into 2-inch pieces.

SPEED SERVES 4

Asparagus Gratin

Crisp-tender vegetables topped with a crunchy, savory Parmesan-laced crust. For a fast vegetable dish, this cannot be beat.

Ingredients

1 large bunch or 2 medium bunches asparagus (1 ½ to 2 pounds)

2 tablespoons olive oil

Salt and pepper

3 thick slices any rustic bread (a little stale is fine)

4 ounces Parmesan cheese (1 cup grated; optional)

Prep | Cook

1. Turn the broiler to high; put the rack 6 inches from the heat.

   Trim the asparagus.

2. Put the asparagus on a rimmed baking sheet, toss with 2 tablespoons olive oil, and sprinkle with salt and pepper. Broil until lightly browned on the top side, 4 or 5 minutes.

   Chop 3 slices bread into cubes. Transfer to a food processor and pulse until they become coarse crumbs. (You should have about 1 ½ cups.)

   Grate 1 cup Parmesan cheese if you're using it.

3. When the tops of the asparagus are brown, turn them, sprinkle with the bread crumbs and Parmesan, and broil until the thickest parts can be pierced with a knife and the bread crumbs and cheese are golden and crisp, 4 or 5 minutes more. Serve hot or warm.

VARIATIONS

Eggplant Gratin

Use eggplant instead of asparagus. Don't bother to peel it. If the eggplant is large, cut it crosswise into slices less than 1 inch thick; if you're using the long slender kind, split them in half lengthwise. You'll need to turn them at least once during cooking in Steps 2 and 3.

SPEED ◔ SERVES 4

Tomatoes with Fried Bread Crumbs

Fried Green Tomatoes meets *A Year in Provence*: This spin on *tomates provençales* tops raw slices of tomato with crisp bread crumbs fried in a skillet. With the southern-hospitality-sized portions you might have leftovers, which is fine since they're good cold too.

Ingredients

¼ cup olive oil, plus more for garnish

4 thick slices any rustic bread (a little stale is fine)

Salt and pepper

5 or 6 medium ripe tomatoes (2 pounds)

Prep | Cook

1. Put ¼ cup olive oil in a large skillet over low heat.

   Chop 4 slices bread into cubes. Transfer to a food processor and pulse into coarse crumbs. (You should have about 2 cups.)

2. Raise the heat to medium-high. Add the bread crumbs to the skillet, sprinkle with salt and pepper, and stir gently to coat in the oil. Cook, stirring frequently and adjusting the heat to avoid burning, until the crumbs are golden and crisp, 5 to 7 minutes. Shake the pan every minute or so to keep the crumbs from burning.

   Core the tomatoes; slice crosswise into rounds ¼ to ½ inch thick. Lay the tomatoes on a platter and sprinkle with salt.

3. When the bread crumbs are crisp, sprinkle over the tomatoes, drizzle with a little more olive oil, and serve.

VARIATIONS

Tomatoes with Parsley Bread Crumbs
Just before topping the tomatoes, stir ½ cup chopped fresh parsley into the crumbs.

Tomatoes with Parmesan Bread Crumbs
Stir ½ cup grated Parmesan cheese into the crumbs before topping the tomatoes.

SPEED ◔ SERVES 4

Broiled Cherry Tomatoes

Run ripe cherry tomatoes under the broiler to char them lightly and concentrate their sweetness—nothing short of amazing.

Ingredients

1 ½ pounds cherry tomatoes

2 tablespoons olive oil

Salt and pepper

Prep | Cook

1. Turn the broiler to high; put the rack 4 inches from the heat.
   Rinse and dry the tomatoes.
2. Put the tomatoes on a rimmed baking sheet. Add 2 tablespoons olive oil and a sprinkle of salt and pepper and toss.
3. Broil, shaking the pan occasionally, until the tomatoes are charred in spots and just starting to burst, 4 to 6 minutes. Let them cool for a minute or 2 before serving, drizzled with any pan juices.

VARIATIONS

5 Ways to Flavor Broiled Tomatoes

Add any of the following when the tomatoes come out of the broiler:

1. ¼ cup chopped fresh parsley, cilantro, basil, or mint
2. 1 teaspoon chopped fresh rosemary, thyme, or oregano
3. 1 teaspoon minced garlic
4. ¼ cup cream
5. ¼ cup grated Parmesan or crumbled feta, blue cheese, or goat cheese

SPEED SERVES 4

Mexican Street Corn

A fantastic street food, usually served on a stick. But at home there's no need for that.

Ingredients

4 ears fresh corn

1 lime

2 tablespoons mayonnaise

¼ teaspoon chili powder, or more to taste

Salt and pepper

Prep | Cook

1. Prepare a grill or turn the broiler to high; put the rack 4 inches from the heat.

   Husk the corn. If broiling, put it on a rimmed baking sheet.

   Halve the lime.

2. Grill or broil the corn, turning as necessary, until all the sides are charred in places, 5 to 8 minutes total.

   Squeeze the lime juice into a small bowl and add 2 tablespoons mayonnaise, ¼ teaspoon chili powder, and a sprinkle of salt and pepper. Stir to combine, taste, and adjust the seasoning, adding more chili powder if you like.

3. When the corn is done, remove it from the grill or broiler and spread each ear all over with some of the mayonnaise mixture. Serve hot.

VARIATIONS

Mexican Street Corn with Cheese
After spreading the mayonnaise mixture on the corn, sprinkle the ears all over with crumbled cotija cheese or queso fresco.

Mediterranean Corn
Substitute lemon for the lime, olive oil for the mayonnaise, and red chile flakes for the chili powder. If you like, garnish with a sprinkle of grated Parmesan.

SPEED SERVES 4

Succotash

This winning combination takes advantage of two of the best frozen foods: corn and lima beans. When you have both handy, this dish comes together in no time.

Ingredients

3 tablespoons butter

1 medium red bell pepper

1 ½ cups frozen corn kernels

1 cup frozen lima beans

Salt and pepper

2 scallions

Prep | Cook

1. Put 3 tablespoons butter in a medium skillet over medium heat.

   Core, seed, and chop the pepper; add it to the skillet.

2. Cook the pepper, stirring once or twice until it begins to soften, 2 or 3 minutes.

3. Add 1 ½ cups corn and 1 cup lima beans and sprinkle with salt and pepper. Cook, stirring occasionally until both are hot all the way through, 3 to 4 minutes.

   Trim and chop the scallions; add them to the pan and stir.

4. When the succotash is hot, taste and adjust the seasoning and serve hot or at room temperature.

VARIATIONS

Edamame Succotash
Substitute 2 tablespoons vegetable oil and 1 tablespoon sesame oil for the butter and frozen edamame for the lima beans.

Panfried Corn and Onions
Use 3 cups corn kernels and skip the scallions. Use 1 large onion instead of the bell pepper; add it to the skillet once the butter melts in Step 1. Cook, stirring occasionally, until golden, 5 to 10 minutes; then add the corn.

NOTES

EVEN FASTER
For extra speed, skip the bell pepper and scallions.

SPEED SERVES 4

Peas with Bacon and Onion

A quick warming with cooked bacon and onions keeps frozen peas firm and vibrant green while turning them into an elegant, delicious side.

Ingredients

1 tablespoon olive oil

4 slices bacon

1 medium onion

3 cups frozen peas

Salt and pepper

Prep | Cook

1. Put 1 tablespoon olive oil in a medium skillet over medium heat.
   Chop 4 slices bacon; add them to the skillet.
   Trim, peel, and chop the onion; add it to the skillet.
2. Cook, stirring occasionally until the bacon is crisp and the onion is soft and brown, 5 to 10 minutes.
3. Stir in 3 cups peas and sprinkle with salt and pepper. Cook, stirring occasionally until the peas are hot all the way through, 3 or 4 minutes. Taste and adjust the seasoning and serve.

VARIATIONS

Peas with Prosciutto and Mint
Increase the olive oil to 2 tablespoons. Substitute thin prosciutto slices for the bacon and use red onion instead of yellow. Stir in 1/4 cup chopped fresh mint just before serving.

Peas with Parmesan
Omit the bacon and increase the olive oil to 2 tablespoons. Cook the onion by itself; then add the peas. Stir in up to 1/2 cup grated Parmesan cheese just before serving.

Peas with Ginger
Skip the bacon and use 2 tablespoons butter instead of the olive oil. Mince 1 inch fresh ginger and add it to the butter once it's melted in Step 1. Cook and stir until fragrant, just a minute or 2; then stir in the peas.

SPEED ◔ SERVES 4

Smashed Peas

Warmed in stock with some butter until soft, then mashed up a bit, these bright and tasty peas are nothing like the dreary gray mush of the past.

Ingredients

¾ cup chicken or vegetable stock

2 tablespoons butter

3 cups frozen peas

Salt and pepper

Prep | Cook

1. Put ¾ cup stock, 2 tablespoons butter, 3 cups peas, and a sprinkle of salt and pepper in a medium saucepan over medium-high heat.
2. Bring to a boil and cook, stirring occasionally until some of the liquid evaporates and the peas heat through and become tender, 3 to 4 minutes.
3. Mash the peas with a potato masher or fork; leave them chunky if you like or keep mashing for a smoother consistency. Taste and adjust the seasoning and serve.

VARIATIONS

Smashed Curried Peas
Substitute coconut milk for stock. In Step 1, cook 1 tablespoon curry powder in the butter for 30 seconds or so before adding the other ingredients.

Smashed Tomato Peas
Perfect for when you have a little leftover Tomato Sauce (page 296). Instead of the stock, use ½ cup tomato sauce mixed with ¼ cup water.

NOTES

MAKE YOUR OWN

Chicken Stock 213

Vegetable Stock 212

SPEED SERVES 4

Creamed Spinach

Cooking spinach directly in cream is a bit unorthodox, but here efficiency tastes great.

Ingredients

¾ cup cream

2 tablespoons butter

¼ teaspoon nutmeg, or to taste

Salt and pepper

2 medium bunches spinach (1 ½ to 2 pounds)

Prep | Cook

1. Put ¾ cup cream, 2 tablespoons butter, ¼ teaspoon nutmeg, and a sprinkle of salt and pepper in a medium saucepan over medium heat.

   Trim off any thick stems from the spinach and chop the leaves.

2. Add the spinach to the pot, a handful at a time until it all fits.

3. Cook, stirring occasionally until the spinach is completely wilted and tender and the cream has reduced and thickened to the consistency you like, 5 to 10 minutes. Taste and adjust the seasoning and serve.

VARIATIONS

Long-Cooked Buttery Spinach

As rich as with the cream but with more spinach flavor. Omit the cream and nutmeg. Put lots of butter (an entire stick wouldn't be too much) in a large skillet over medium-low heat. When it's melted, add the spinach and a sprinkle of salt and pepper. Cook, stirring occasionally, until the spinach is completely wilted and tender, 10 to 15 minutes.

Tahini Creamed Spinach

Substitute ½ cup tahini and ¼ cup water for the cream, olive oil for the butter, and 1 teaspoon cumin for the nutmeg.

Chile-Cumin Black Beans

Warming the cumin in oil before adding the beans maximizes its flavor.

Ingredients

3 tablespoons olive oil

2 teaspoons cumin

2 garlic cloves

1 fresh hot green chile (like jalapeño)

3 cups cooked or canned black beans (one-and-a-half 15-ounce cans)

Salt and pepper

Prep | Cook

1. Put 3 tablespoons olive oil and 2 teaspoons cumin in a large skillet over medium heat.

   Peel 2 garlic cloves; trim the chile. Mince them together and add them to the skillet.

   If you're using canned beans, rinse and drain them.

2. Let the cumin, garlic, and chile sizzle in the oil until the mixture is fragrant and the garlic turns light brown, 1 or 2 minutes.

3. Add the beans and a sprinkle of salt and pepper. Cook, stirring occasionally until the beans are warmed all the way through, 2 or 3 minutes. Taste and adjust the seasoning and serve.

VARIATIONS

Sesame-Soy Black Beans
Omit the cumin; go light on the salt. Swap 1 tablespoon each sesame oil and vegetable oil for the olive oil. Add 1 tablespoon soy sauce when you add the beans.

Black Beans with Tomato and Feta
Add 1 cup halved cherry tomatoes when you add the garlic and chile. Garnish with ¼ cup crumbled feta cheese.

Lentils with Smoked Paprika and Garlic
Substitute smoked paprika for the cumin, ½ teaspoon red chile flakes for the fresh chile, and lentils for the black beans.

SPEED  SERVES 4

Refried Beans

Refried beans are traditionally cooked in lard, but oil works just fine. That said, if you happen to have any lard or bacon drippings in your fridge or freezer, now's the time to use it.

Ingredients

⅓ cup vegetable oil

2 cups cooked or canned pinto, black, or pink beans (one 15-ounce can)

1 small yellow onion

½ teaspoon cumin

½ teaspoon chili powder

¼ teaspoon cayenne

Salt and pepper

Prep | Cook

1. Put ⅓ cup vegetable oil in a large skillet over medium-high heat.
   If you're using canned beans, rinse and drain them.
   Trim, peel, and chop the onion.
2. When the oil is hot, add the beans and cook, mashing them with a potato masher until they're partly broken up.
3. Add the onion, ½ teaspoon cumin, ½ teaspoon chili powder, ¼ teaspoon cayenne, and a sprinkle of salt and pepper. Cook, continuing to mash, until the beans are mostly broken down and the onion is lightly cooked, 3 to 5 minutes.
4. If the mixture is too thick, stir in a splash of bean cooking liquid or water until it's the consistency that you like. Taste and adjust the seasoning and serve.

VARIATIONS

Refried White Beans with Rosemary
Substitute olive oil for the vegetable oil and use white beans. Substitute 2 teaspoons minced fresh rosemary for the cumin, chili powder, and cayenne.

NOTES

MAKE YOUR OWN

Cooked Beans 496

Chili Powder 758

SPEED SERVES 4

Hummus

If you use canned chickpeas, you can make hummus yourself in less time than it would take to go to a store and buy it, and the results are infinitely better.

Ingredients

2 garlic cloves

1 lemon

2 cups cooked or canned chickpeas (one 15-ounce can)

½ cup tahini

¼ cup olive oil, plus more as needed

1 tablespoon cumin or paprika

Salt and pepper

Prep | Cook

Peel and chop 2 garlic cloves. Put them in a food processor or blender.

Halve the lemon; squeeze the juice into the machine.

If you're using canned chickpeas, rinse and drain them.

1. Add the chickpeas, ½ cup tahini, ¼ cup olive oil, 1 tablespoon cumin or paprika, and a sprinkle of salt and pepper to the food processor or blender.
2. Let the machine run, adding water, chickpea cooking liquid, or olive oil as necessary until the purée is as smooth as you like. Taste and adjust the seasoning and serve.

VARIATIONS

Roasted Red Pepper Hummus
Add 2 roasted red peppers to the food processor before puréeing.

NOTES

MAKE YOUR OWN

Cooked Beans 496

SPEED ◐ SERVES 4

Scallion Pancakes

Certainly a bit more work than plain rice, but crisp, chewy, tender, flaky, and addictive, especially with a quick dipping sauce. Fantastic with stir-fries.

Ingredients

1 egg

¾ cup flour, plus more as needed

3 tablespoons soy sauce

½ teaspoon sesame oil

Vegetable oil for frying

6 scallions

1 tablespoon mirin or 1 ½ teaspoons honey with 1 ½ teaspoons water

Prep | Cook

1. Combine the egg, ½ cup water, ¾ cup flour, 1 tablespoon soy sauce, and ½ teaspoon sesame oil in a large bowl. Whisk until smooth. The mixture should have the consistency of thin pancake batter; if it doesn't, add water or flour as necessary.
2. Put a thin film of vegetable oil in a large skillet (preferably nonstick) over medium heat.

   Trim and chop the scallions.
3. Stir the scallions into the batter.
4. When the oil is hot, pour half of the batter into the skillet and spread it into a thin layer with a spatula.
5. Cook, undisturbed, until the edges crisp and the batter sets, 2 to 4 minutes; adjust the heat so the pancake sizzles but doesn't burn.

   Whisk together 2 tablespoons soy sauce and 1 tablespoon mirin (or 1 ½ teaspoons honey mixed with 1 ½ teaspoons water) in a small bowl.
6. Flip the pancake with a broad spatula and cook the other side for another minute or 2. Transfer to a cutting board. Repeat with the remaining batter, adding more oil to the pan if necessary. Cut the pancakes into wedges and serve with the dipping sauce.

SPEED ◑ SERVES 4

White Rice

What is there to say about a pot of rice other than that it's among the most useful dishes in the history of civilization? It's also a blank canvas; see the list that follows for stir-ins.

Ingredients

1 ½ cups long-grain white rice

Salt

Prep | Cook

1. Put 1 ½ cups rice in a medium saucepan; add a big pinch of salt and water to cover by an inch. Bring to a boil, then adjust the heat so the mixture bubbles steadily but not vigorously; cover.
2. Cook, undisturbed, until small craters appear on the surface, 10 to 15 minutes. Tip the pot to see if any liquid remains. If so, cover and keep cooking until the rice is dry, checking every minute or 2. If the rice is done but not all the water has boiled off, drain off the water and return the rice to the pan.
3. Turn off the heat and keep the pan covered. The rice will stay warm for another 10 to 15 minutes. Fluff with a fork and serve.

VARIATIONS

Quick Brown Rice
Use short-grain brown rice. In Step 2, cook for 20 to 25 minutes.

7 Stir-Ins
Before fluffing the rice, add any of the following:

1. 1 or more tablespoons butter or olive oil
2. 1 tablespoon chopped fresh herbs
3. ½ cup grated or crumbled cheese
4. 1 cup cooked beans, peas, or lentils
5. ½ cup chopped scallions
6. ½ cup tomato sauce or salsa
7. ½ to 1 teaspoon ground spices

Seasoning Sides

I've compiled key seasonings and their best uses in a single table here. Use this as your go-to guide. If you keep some or most of these on hand, you'll be able to customize your sides so you'll never find them boring.

What to Add	When to Add It
CHOPPED FRESH MILD HERBS	Like parsley, cilantro, basil, dill, and mint. To keep these herbs fresh and vibrant, add them to cooked dishes only for the last few seconds of cooking or even after they're done.
CHOPPED FRESH STRONG HERBS	Like rosemary, thyme, sage, and oregano. Unlike milder herbs, heat helps bring out the flavor in these oilier herbs. Mix with a little oil or butter and spread on breads before warming in the oven or add to cooked greens, vegetables, beans, and starches anytime during cooking. If you want to flavor salads or raw vegetables, mix them into the dressing.
DRIED HERBS AND SPICES	These are strong, so start with about one-third of what you'd use fresh. Cook and use them as you would fresh, except you probably won't use them much for garnishing.
CITRUS ZEST	Immediately perks up hot or cold dishes, but it's powerful, so be judicious. Make a little zest a part of dressings, add it to sautéed greens, vegetables, and beans as they cook, or simply toss with (almost) anything before serving.
BUTTER AND OIL	Butter is best with hot foods; oil is more versatile for drizzling on salads or cold dishes. Use either on cooked greens, vegetables, beans, or starches. Add right after cooking so the residual heat melts the butter or warms the oil, and toss to coat.
VINEGAR, SOY SAUCE, FISH SAUCE, AND HOT SAUCE	All of these pack a punch. Include them in dressings; add to sautéed greens, vegetables, and beans as they cook; or simply use them as condiments and drizzle them over anything hot or cold before serving.
MINCED GARLIC, GINGER, AND CHILES	For salads or raw vegetables, mix small amounts into the dressing. For sautéed greens, vegetables, and beans, add them to the skillet either at the beginning if you're cooking them gently or for the last few minutes if you're afraid they'll burn; you can use more in these instances. For starches, add them for the last few minutes of cooking so they soften with some heat.

What to Add	When to Add It
CHOPPED TOMATOES, ONIONS, AND SCALLIONS	Add them toward the end of the cooking to keep their flavor and texture fresh. Or use them as a garnish (onion should be chopped finely).
NUTS, SEEDS, AND DRIED FRUIT	Toasting nuts and seeds in oil or a dry skillet intensifies their flavor, but you can also keep them raw. Dried fruit can be added raw or after steeping in warm liquid until it plumps. Either way, toss into almost any dish before serving.
CHOPPED OLIVES AND CAPERS, AND MASHED ANCHOVIES	You can use these cured foods as is, but a little heat infuses their flavor into the dish (especially true for anchovies). Add them to dressings, to sautéed greens, vegetables, and beans during cooking, or stir them into starches immediately after cooking. Mashed together with a little olive oil, any will make a great condiment to spread on bread.
PREPARED SAUCES AND CONDIMENTS	See Pesto (page 285), Tomato Sauce (page 296), Fresh Salsa (page 145), Smooth Cooked Salsa (page 563), Olive Tapenade (page 622), and Hummus (page 939). All are versatile companions for all kinds of sides. Spread them on any bread; add some to dressings; stir into sautéed greens, vegetables, and beans during cooking; or stir into starches with a fork immediately after cooking. Or garnish with a spoonful before serving.
PARMESAN CHEESE	Rich, nutty, and incredibly versatile. Shave or grate over salads and raw vegetables and it will stay intact, or grate and stir into cooked dishes while they're still warm and it will become buttery and creamy.
COOKED AND CRUMBLED BACON, SAUSAGE, OR OTHER CHOPPED CURED MEAT	I'm a big fan of using pork as a garnish instead of a main component. Full-flavored, already cooked, smoked or cured meats (like ham, salami, or prosciutto) can be added to salads before serving, to sautéed greens, vegetables, and beans for the last few minutes of cooking, and to starches just before serving.

Seasoning During Cooking

When you're cooking, you have two choices: You can add seasonings while cooking aromatics or heating oil or at the end of cooking while the dish is hottest, right before serving. The residual heat in the food improves the flavor of pretty much anything you add and infuses it into the dish. If you want the sharpest flavor of a seasoning, wait to add it as a garnish just before serving.

Seasoning to Taste

As with salt and pepper, the most accurate seasoning is done to taste. For some ingredients, like strong herbs, dried spices, and citrus zest, a little goes a long way. For others, like fresh mild herbs, there's really no limit to how much you might want to use. My suggestion: Add a little at a time, taste, and add more if it's not enough. You can always keep adding, but you can't take it away.

SPEED ◐ SERVES 4

Rice Pilaf

Cook rice in fat with some other ingredients, add liquid and seasonings, and you end up with something magical; you'll never buy boxed pilaf again.

Ingredients

3 tablespoons butter or olive oil

1 medium onion

1 ½ cups long-grain white rice

Salt and pepper

1 tablespoon curry, chili, or five-spice powder; or large pinch saffron (optional)

2 ½ cups any stock or water

Several sprigs fresh parsley for garnish

Prep | Cook

1. Put 2 tablespoons butter or olive oil in a large skillet over medium-high heat.

   Trim, peel, and chop the onion.

2. When the butter is sizzling or the oil is hot, add the onion and cook, stirring occasionally until it starts to soften, 3 to 5 minutes.

3. Add 1 ½ cups rice, turn the heat down to medium, and cook, stirring frequently until the rice is glossy and starting to color slightly, 3 to 5 minutes.

4. Sprinkle with salt and pepper and add the spices if you're using them. Add 2 ½ cups stock or water and bring to a boil. Adjust the heat so the mixture bubbles steadily. Stir, cover, and cook undisturbed until small craters appear, 10 to 15 minutes. Tip the pot to see if any liquid remains. If so, cover and keep cooking until the rice is dry, checking every minute or 2.

   Strip the parsley leaves from several sprigs and chop.

5. Turn off the heat and keep covered. The rice will stay warm for another 10 to 15 minutes. Add the parsley and 1 tablespoon butter or olive oil, fluff with a fork, and serve.

SPEED ◑ SERVES 4

Quinoa

Despite the good press it's been getting, high-protein, high-fiber quinoa is still way underused. This tiny grain has wonderful grassy flavor and a texture that pops like caviar. It also gets you some of the nuttiness of brown rice but cooks in half the time.

Ingredients

1 ½ cups quinoa

Salt and pepper

2 tablespoons olive oil or butter

Prep | Cook

Rinse and drain 1 ½ cups quinoa.

1. Put the quinoa in a medium saucepan; add a big pinch of salt, a sprinkle of pepper, and water to cover by about an inch. Bring to a boil, then adjust the heat so it bubbles gently.
2. Cover and cook undisturbed until small craters appear, 15 to 20 minutes. Tip the pan to see if any liquid remains. If so, cover and keep cooking until the quinoa is dry, checking every minute.
3. Turn off the heat and keep the pan covered. The quinoa will stay warm for another 10 to 15 minutes. Add 2 tablespoons olive oil or butter, fluff with a fork, and serve.

VARIATIONS

Quinoa Cooked in Stock
Substitute chicken, vegetable, beef, or fish stock for some or all of the water.

Red Wine and Rosemary Quinoa
Substitute 1 cup red wine for 1 cup water and add up to 1 tablespoon minced fresh rosemary when you add the liquid.

Seasoning Quinoa
Anything you can stir into cooked rice you can also stir into cooked quinoa. See the list on page 941 for ideas.

SPEED ◐ SERVES 4

Bulgur with Lemon and Parsley

Since bulgur is partially cooked cracked whole wheat, all you need to do is pour boiling water over it and go back to doing other prep.

Ingredients

1 cup bulgur (common medium grind is best here)

Salt

1 lemon

1 bunch fresh parsley

¼ cup olive oil

Pepper

Prep | Cook

1. Bring 2 ½ cups water to a boil.
2. Put 1 cup bulgur in a large bowl with a large pinch of salt. Pour the boiling water over all and cover with a plate. Finely ground bulgur will take 10 to 15 minutes to become tender, medium 15 to 20, and coarse 20 to 25.

   Grate the lemon zest, then cut the fruit in half.

   Chop ½ cup parsley.
3. When the bulgur is tender, pour it into a strainer and press out any excess water with a spoon; return it to the bowl.
4. Stir in the lemon zest, parsley, ¼ cup olive oil, and a sprinkle of salt and pepper; squeeze in the lemon juice. Taste and adjust the seasoning and serve.

VARIATIONS

Bulgur with Corn
Substitute lime zest and juice for the lemon and cilantro for the parsley; add 1 cup corn kernels (thawed frozen kernels are fine) along with the rest of the ingredients in Step 4.

Bulgur with Dried Cranberries and Orange
Substitute orange zest and juice for the lemon and mint for the parsley; add ½ cup dried cranberries in Step 4.

SPEED ◐ SERVES 4

Creamy Polenta

Serve polenta soft and creamy or make it ahead of the meal (see the Variation).

Ingredients

½ cup milk

Salt

1 cup medium cornmeal

4 ounces Parmesan cheese (1 cup grated; optional)

1 tablespoon butter or olive oil, or more to taste

Pepper

Prep | Cook

1. Put ½ cup milk, 2 cups water, and a big pinch of salt in a medium saucepan and bring to a boil.
2. When the liquid comes to a boil, add 1 cup cornmeal in a steady stream, whisking constantly to prevent lumps. Adjust the heat so the mixture simmers and cook, whisking frequently until the mixture is creamy and the grains are soft, 10 to 15 minutes. If the mixture becomes too thick, whisk in more water or milk (unless you intend to cook it a second time, as in the Variation, in which case you want it thick).

   Grate 1 cup Parmesan cheese if you're using it.
3. When the polenta is done, stir in 1 tablespoon butter or olive oil, the Parmesan, and lots of pepper. Taste and adjust the seasoning and serve immediately.

VARIATIONS

Grilled, Broiled, or Panfried Polenta

Use the butter or oil to grease a rimmed baking sheet. Make sure the cooked polenta is thick. Pour the cooked polenta into the prepared pan and let it cool until firm; it will likely firm up in as little as 10 minutes but will be easier to handle if you can wait longer. Cut the polenta into slices, brush them with more olive oil, sprinkle with salt and pepper, and grill, broil, or panfry, turning once, until brown on both sides.

SPEED  SERVES 4

Pasta, Plain and Simple

A warm bowl of pasta is about as comforting as it gets. Like rice, it can always be served under something saucy. (See the list below for more seasoning ideas.)

Ingredients

Salt

1 pound any pasta

2 tablespoons olive oil or butter, or more to taste

Salt and pepper

Prep | Cook

1. Bring a stockpot of water to a boil and salt it.
2. When the water boils, add the pasta and stir occasionally. Start tasting after 5 minutes.
3. When the pasta is tender but not mushy, drain it. Return the pasta to the pot, stir in 2 tablespoons olive oil or butter, and add a sprinkle of salt and pepper. Serve hot or warm.

VARIATIONS

Buttered Egg Noodles

Use any egg noodles instead of the pasta and toss with butter while still warm.

5 Ways to Flavor Plain Pasta

Stir in any of the following along with the olive oil or butter:

1. 1 to 2 tablespoons minced fresh rosemary, thyme, oregano, or sage
2. ½ cup chopped fresh parsley or basil
3. 1 teaspoon grated lemon zest
4. Up to 1 cup grated Parmesan cheese
5. 1 cup chopped fresh tomatoes

Sesame Noodles

Everyone loves sesame noodles—they're packed with flavor and just as good cold as hot.

Ingredients

Salt

4 scallions

12 ounces soba or udon noodles

¼ cup soy sauce

2 tablespoons sesame oil

1 tablespoon peanut oil

Prep | Cook

1. Bring a stockpot of water to a boil and salt it.
   Trim and chop the scallions.

2. When the water boils, add the noodles and stir occasionally. Start tasting after 3 minutes.

3. When the noodles are tender but not mushy, drain them. Return the noodles to the pot and stir in the scallions, ¼ cup soy sauce, 2 tablespoons sesame oil, and 1 tablespoon peanut oil. Serve hot or warm.

VARIATIONS

Cold Sesame Noodles
After draining the noodles, rinse them under cold water until completely cool and drain well. Transfer the noodles and the remaining ingredients to a big bowl for tossing. You can keep the cold sesame noodles at room temperature, covered, for up to a few hours or refrigerate them.

Noodles with Curry and Coconut Milk
Use ½ cup chopped fresh cilantro instead of the scallions and ¼ cup coconut milk instead of the oils. Add 1 teaspoon curry powder along with the soy sauce and coconut milk.

SPEED ◐ SERVES 4

Fire and Ice Noodles

Since you don't need much water to steep glass noodles—also known as *mung bean threads*—this bracing and spicy dish comes together more quickly than pasta. You can even make it up to several hours ahead and serve straight from the fridge.

Ingredients

Salt

1 large cucumber

4 ounces glass noodles

1 tablespoon any Asian red chile sauce (like Sriracha), or more to taste

1 tablespoon peanut oil

1 teaspoon fish or soy sauce, or more to taste

Prep | Cook

1. Bring a medium saucepan of water to a boil and salt it.
   - Trim the cucumber, peel if necessary, cut it in half lengthwise, and scoop out the seeds with a spoon.
   - Grate the cucumber; put it in a strainer and press out as much liquid as possible. Put the dried cucumber in a large bowl in the freezer to chill quickly.
2. When the water boils, add the noodles, cover, and remove from the heat. Steep until tender but not mushy, 10 to 15 minutes.
3. Meanwhile, add 1 tablespoon (or more) chile sauce to the cucumbers along with 1 tablespoon peanut oil, 1 teaspoon fish or soy sauce, and a sprinkle of salt. Stir until they're coated with dressing and return them to the freezer.
4. Drain the noodles, rinse them under cold water until cool, and drain well. Cut the noodles with scissors or a knife right in the strainer so the strands are manageable.
5. Add the noodles to the cucumber mixture and toss to combine. Taste and adjust the seasoning, adding more fish or soy sauce if you like, and serve.

SPEED ◐ SERVES 4

Panfried Rice Noodles

When you can't decide between a soft side dish like noodles and a crisp one like scallion pancakes, my shortcut method—browning only one side—gives you both textures.

Ingredients

Salt

12 ounces rice vermicelli

3 tablespoons vegetable oil

Soy sauce for drizzling

Prep | Cook

1. Bring a medium saucepan of water to a boil and salt it. When the water comes to a boil, add the noodles, stir once or twice, turn off the heat, and let them steep until they're not quite fully tender, 3 to 5 minutes.
2. Put a medium skillet (preferably nonstick) over medium heat.
3. When the noodles are done, drain well, shaking off as much excess water as you can. Toss with 2 tablespoons vegetable oil.
4. When the skillet is hot, add 1 tablespoon oil and swirl. Then spread the noodles out in it as evenly as possible.
5. Cook undisturbed until the bottom side is golden and crisp, 5 to 10 minutes. Slide the noodles out onto a cutting board or large plate, cut into wedges, drizzle with soy sauce, and serve.

VARIATIONS

Panfried Pasta
Use angel hair pasta instead of the rice noodles and olive oil instead of vegetable oil. Boil the noodles in a stockpot of salted water until not quite fully tender; start tasting after 3 minutes.

Panfried Udon
Substitute udon noodles for the rice noodles. Boil the noodles in a stockpot of salted water until not quite fully tender; start tasting after 3 minutes.

SPEED ◐ SERVES 8

Skillet Stuffing

I've never understood why we don't eat this simple combination of bread, butter, and vegetables more often. With this quick-broil method, there's no excuse not to.

Ingredients

4 tablespoons (½ stick) butter

1 small onion

Salt and pepper

1 loaf rustic bread or corn bread (about 1 pound)

4 celery stalks

3 sprigs fresh sage

2 cups chicken or vegetable stock

Prep | Cook

Turn the broiler to high; put the rack 6 inches from the heat.

1. Put 4 tablespoons butter in a large ovenproof skillet over medium heat.

   Trim, peel, and chop the onion.

2. When the butter foams, add the onion and a sprinkle of salt and pepper. Cook, stirring occasionally until the onion softens, 3 to 5 minutes.

   Tear the bread into chunks and pulse it into coarse crumbs in a food processor or cut it into small cubes by hand (or crumble the corn bread). You'll end up with 8 to 10 cups.

   Trim and chop the celery.

3. When the onion is soft, add the bread, sprinkle with salt and pepper, and toss gently to coat the bread in the butter.

4. Add the celery and cook, stirring occasionally until the bread begins to color and the celery softens, 3 to 5 minutes.

   Strip the sage leaves from 3 sprigs and chop.

5. Stir the sage into the skillet along with 2 cups stock; toss gently to coat the bread in the stock, pressing the bread into the skillet as it softens. Transfer the skillet to the broiler and cook, watching to make sure it doesn't burn, until the top is golden and crisp, 2 to 5 minutes. Serve hot or warm.

SPEED ◐ SERVES 4

Cucumbers with Peanut Vinaigrette

Cooking fast doesn't mean compromising on taste and texture. Salting cucumbers, however briefly, works like magic to ensure firm texture and concentrated flavor.

Ingredients

3 medium cucumbers (1 to 1½ pounds)

1 teaspoon salt, plus more if needed

2 tablespoons vegetable oil

2 tablespoons sesame oil

2 tablespoons rice vinegar

2 tablespoons peanut butter

Prep | Cook

Trim the cucumbers, peel if necessary, cut them in half lengthwise, and scoop out the seeds with a spoon. Cut them into small chunks or slices and put them in a colander.

Sprinkle with 1 teaspoon salt, toss to coat, and let sit as long as you can: 10 to 25 minutes.

1. Combine 2 tablespoons each vegetable oil, sesame oil, rice vinegar, and peanut butter in a large bowl. Whisk to combine, adding a small splash of water to make the dressing pourable.
2. Pat the cucumbers dry with paper towels, add them to the bowl with the dressing, and toss. Taste and adjust the seasoning and serve.

VARIATIONS

Carrots with Curry Vinaigrette
Substitute carrots for the cucumbers, ⅓ cup olive oil for the vegetable and sesame oils, sherry or red wine vinegar for the rice vinegar, and 1 teaspoon curry powder for the peanut butter.

Salted Cabbage with Sesame Vinaigrette
Substitute shredded cabbage for the cucumbers, ⅓ cup olive oil for the vegetable and sesame oils, the juice of 1 lemon for the rice vinegar, and tahini for the peanut butter. Add pepper.

SPEED ◑ SERVES 4

Tender Vegetables

Boiled vegetables never go out of style. Nothing could be more basic and reliably delicious.

Ingredients

Salt

2 pounds broccoli (or other vegetables; see the list that follows)

2 tablespoons butter or olive oil

Pepper

Prep | Cook

1. Bring a large pot of water to a boil and salt it.
   Trim the broccoli or other vegetables; cut as needed into pieces.
2. When the water boils, add the broccoli or other vegetables. Cook until just tender when pierced, 5 to 10 minutes.
3. Drain the vegetables; return them to the pot.
4. Add 2 tablespoons butter or olive oil and a sprinkle of salt and pepper; stir to coat the vegetables. Taste and adjust the seasoning and serve hot, at room temperature, or chilled.

VARIATIONS

Timing for 10 Other Vegetables

1. Any peas (3 minutes)
2. Spinach (3 minutes)
3. Green beans (4 to 6 minutes)
4. Asparagus (4 to 6 minutes)
5. Cauliflower florets (10 to 12 minutes)
6. Kale or collards (10 minutes)
7. Sweet potato (15 to 20 minutes)
8. Potato cubes (25 to 30 minutes)
9. Winter squash (25 to 30 minutes)
10. Root vegetables (25 to 30 minutes)

Steamed Tender Vegetables
Fill the pot with only 2 inches of water and bring to a boil. Add the vegetables as directed; adjust the heat so the water bubbles steadily, cover the pot, and steam the vegetables until tender.

SPEED ◐ SERVES 4

Simmered Squash

Bite-sized pieces of winter squash braise quickly to become tender and brightly colored, with a sweet-and-earthy taste that goes with most main dishes.

Ingredients

3 cups chicken or vegetable stock or water

Salt

3 garlic cloves

1 medium butternut squash (1 ½ pounds)

2 tablespoons olive oil

Pepper

Prep | Cook

1. Put 3 cups stock or water in a large pot over medium-high heat. If you are using water, add a large pinch of salt.

   Peel and smash 3 garlic cloves; add them to the pot.

   Cut the squash in half crosswise; trim and peel it, and scoop the seeds out with a spoon.

   Cut the squash into 1-inch chunks, adding it to the pot as you go.

2. Stir the squash, cover, and cook until the pieces are tender but not falling apart, 4 to 8 minutes.
3. Fish out the garlic if you like and transfer the squash mixture to a serving bowl with a slotted spoon.
4. Add 2 tablespoons olive oil and a splash of the cooking liquid. Toss, taste, and add salt as needed and lots of pepper; serve.

VARIATIONS

Simmered Squash in Coconut Milk
Substitute 2 cups coconut milk for 2 cups of the stock or water and vegetable oil for olive. If you like, add a fresh hot chile, trimmed and halved, along with the garlic.

NOTES

MAKE YOUR OWN

Chicken Stock 213

Vegetable Stock 212

SPEED ◐ SERVES 4

Garlicky Mushrooms

Mushrooms sautéed with garlic are irresistible alone or over any kind of noodles or rice.

Ingredients

¼ cup olive oil

1 ½ pounds button, cremini, or shiitake mushrooms

Salt and pepper

2 garlic cloves

1 bunch fresh parsley

¼ cup dry white wine or water

Prep | Cook

1. Put ¼ cup olive oil in a large skillet over medium-low heat.

   Trim and slice the mushrooms. (If you're using shiitakes, discard the stems.) Add them to the skillet as you work.

2. Sprinkle the mushrooms with salt and pepper and raise the heat to medium. Cook, stirring occasionally, until the mushrooms are tender and the pan is beginning to dry out, 10 to 15 minutes.

   Peel and mince 2 garlic cloves.

   Chop ¼ cup parsley.

3. When the pan is dry, add ¼ cup wine or water and scrape any browned bits off the bottom. Let most of the liquid bubble away, then stir in the garlic and parsley and cook for another minute. Taste and adjust the seasoning and serve at any temperature.

VARIATIONS

Garlicky Fresh and Dried Mushrooms
Takes more time but works well with longer-cooking main dishes. Soak about ½ cup dried porcini mushrooms in hot water to cover until soft, 15 to 20 minutes. Lift the mushrooms out, saving the soaking liquid but being careful to leave the dirt behind. Chop the porcini and cook them along with the fresh mushrooms. Add some of the soaking liquid instead of or along with the wine.

SPEED ◐ SERVES 4

Stuffed Portobellos

Yes, they're a good proxy for meat, but they're also just good. Period.

Ingredients

4 large portobello mushrooms

1 small shallot

4 sprigs fresh thyme or 1 teaspoon dried

⅓ cup olive oil

Salt and pepper

2 medium tomatoes

4 ounces feta cheese (1 cup crumbled)

Prep | Cook

1. Turn the broiler to high; put the rack 4 inches from the heat.

   Trim the stems from the mushrooms; rinse and pat dry. Put them top side up on a rimmed baking sheet.

   Trim, peel, and mince the shallot; put it in a small mixing bowl.

   If you're using fresh thyme, strip the leaves from 4 sprigs and chop them. Add them (or 1 teaspoon dried thyme) to the bowl.

   Add ⅓ cup olive oil and a sprinkle of salt and pepper and stir.

2. Brush the tops of the mushrooms with half of the oil mixture and broil until they begin to brown, 5 to 8 minutes.

   Core and chop the tomatoes.

3. When the mushrooms are brown on top, flip them, brush with the remaining oil mixture, and cook until the second side is brown, another 5 to 8 minutes.

   Put the tomatoes in the mixing bowl you used for the oil mixture; crumble 1 cup feta, add, and toss.

4. Spoon the tomato and feta mixture into the mushrooms and broil until the cheese is hot and slightly melted, 1 or 2 minutes. Serve hot or at room temperature.

SPEED ◐ SERVES 4

Brussels Sprouts with Bacon

Adding a little water lets you cook Brussels sprouts whole and keeps them vibrant green. Reduces chopping time too.

Ingredients

2 tablespoons olive oil

6 slices bacon

1 ½ pounds Brussels sprouts

Salt and pepper

Prep | Cook

1. Put 2 tablespoons olive oil in a large skillet over medium heat.
   Chop 6 slices bacon; add them to the skillet.
   Trim the Brussels sprouts.

2. Cook the bacon, stirring occasionally, until it releases some fat and crisps in places, 3 to 5 minutes.

3. Add the Brussels sprouts to the partially cooked bacon, along with a sprinkle of salt and pepper and ½ cup water.

4. Cover and cook, checking once or twice and adding small amounts of water as needed, until the Brussels sprouts are a little shy of tender, 6 to 10 minutes, depending on their size.

5. Remove the cover and raise the heat to high. Cook, resisting the urge to stir too much, until the liquid evaporates and the Brussels sprouts become brown and crisp in places. Taste and adjust the seasoning and serve hot or warm.

VARIATIONS

Brussels Sprouts with Chorizo
Substitute 4 ounces fresh Mexican chorizo for the bacon.

Brussels Sprouts with Sausage
Use 4 ounces chopped hot or sweet Italian sausage instead of bacon.

SPEED ◐ SERVES 4

Crunchy Okra

Talk about a quick and easy preparation of a classic southern ingredient. The intermittent char gives the okra a deeper flavor and reduces sliminess, so if you've found okra a turnoff before, you might give this method a try.

Ingredients

1 ½ pounds okra

3 tablespoons olive oil

Salt and pepper

Prep | Cook

1. Heat the oven to 500°F.
   Trim the okra.
2. Put the okra on a rimmed baking sheet; toss with 3 tablespoons olive oil and a sprinkle of salt and pepper.
3. Roast, shaking the pan occasionally until the okra is browned in spots and tender, 5 to 10 minutes. Serve hot, warm, or at room temperature.

VARIATIONS

Fried Okra

Put an inch or 2 of vegetable oil in a large skillet over medium heat. If the okra is small, cut it in half lengthwise; if it's big, cut it crosswise on a diagonal into thick slices. Dip the okra in buttermilk, then in a mixture of cornmeal, a pinch of cayenne, and salt and pepper. When the oil is hot (a pinch of the cornmeal mixture should sizzle immediately but not burn), fry the okra until golden and crisp, 3 to 5 minutes. Transfer them to paper towels with a slotted spoon and sprinkle immediately with salt and pepper. If you're cooking in batches, keep them warm in a 200°F oven while you fry the rest.

SPEED ◑ SERVES 4

Ripe Plantains

Ripe plantains are soft and sweet. But watch 'em: Once they brown, they can burn easily.

Ingredients

3 tablespoons vegetable oil

3 large or 4 medium ripe (yellow-black or black) plantains

2 limes

¼ teaspoon chili powder

Salt

Prep | Cook

1. Put 3 tablespoons vegetable oil in a large skillet over medium heat.

   Trim both ends from the plantains, cut them crosswise into 3 sections, score the peels with a knife, and strip away the skins. Cut each section crosswise into 1-inch pieces.

2. Add the plantains to the skillet and cook, turning as necessary and adjusting the heat so they don't burn, until they are deep golden and very tender, 10 to 15 minutes.

   Halve the limes.

3. When the plantains are ready, sprinkle with ¼ teaspoon chili powder and some salt and squeeze the limes over all. Serve hot or warm.

VARIATIONS

Ripe Plantains with Cinnamon and Cumin
Substitute ¼ teaspoon cinnamon and ¼ teaspoon cumin for the chili powder.

Ripe Plantains with Smoked Paprika
Substitute olive oil for vegetable, 2 teaspoons sherry vinegar for the lime juice, and smoked paprika for the chili powder.

NOTES

MAKE YOUR OWN

Chili Powder 758

SPEED ◐ SERVES 4

Skin-On Mashed Potatoes

Mashed potatoes don't take much longer than it does to prep and cook the potatoes, so leaving the skins on and slicing them thinly puts you well ahead of the game.

Ingredients

Salt

4 to 6 medium russet or Yukon Gold potatoes (2 pounds)

4 or more garlic cloves

½ cup milk, plus more as needed

4 tablespoons (½ stick) butter

Pepper

Prep | Cook

1. Fill a large pot with about an inch of water; add a big pinch of salt and turn the heat to high.

   Scrub the potatoes, halve them lengthwise, and cut them into thin slices, dropping them into the pot as you go.

   Peel 4 (or more) garlic cloves; add them to the pot.

2. Once you've added the potatoes and garlic to the pot, cover and cook (letting the water boil the whole time) until the potatoes are tender and just breaking apart, 15 to 20 minutes.

3. Drain the potatoes well and return them to the pot.

4. Add ½ cup milk, 4 tablespoons butter, and some salt and pepper. Mash with a potato masher or fork, adding more milk if needed. Taste and adjust the seasoning and serve.

VARIATIONS

5 More Ways to Flavor Mashed Potatoes

Stir in any of the following in Step 4:

1. 1 or more tablespoons Dijon or coarsely ground mustard
2. ½ cup chopped fresh parsley, basil, or dill
3. 1 tablespoon chopped fresh oregano, rosemary, thyme, or a mixture
4. 1 cup grated Parmesan, cheddar, Gruyère, or other melting cheese
5. ½ cup cream or buttermilk instead of the milk

SPEED ◐ SERVES 4

German-Style Potato Salad

I have nothing against mayonnaise, but this is my favorite kind of potato salad. Dressed with olive oil, vinegar, and Dijon while still warm, the potatoes absorb loads of flavor.

Ingredients

2 pounds new or fingerling potatoes

Salt

1 bunch fresh parsley

1 medium red onion

½ cup olive oil

3 tablespoons red wine vinegar

1 tablespoon Dijon mustard

Pepper

Prep | Cook

Scrub the potatoes and cut them in half.

1. Put the potatoes in a medium pot with water to cover. Add a big pinch of salt and turn the heat to high.

2. Cook until the potatoes are just tender, 10 to 15 minutes.

   Chop ½ cup parsley and put it in a large mixing bowl.

   Trim, peel, and chop the onion. Add it to the bowl.

3. Add ½ cup olive oil, 3 tablespoons vinegar, 1 tablespoon Dijon, and a sprinkle of salt and pepper to the bowl. Stir to combine, taste, and adjust the seasoning.

4. When the potatoes are just tender, drain them well and add them to the bowl. Toss to combine. Taste and adjust the seasoning and serve warm.

VARIATIONS

Chipotle Potato Salad
Substitute cilantro for the parsley, 3 scallions for the onion, the juice of 1 lime for the vinegar, and 2 chopped chipotle chiles in adobo with some of their sauce for the Dijon.

Tahini-Lemon Potato Salad
Use the juice of 1 lemon instead of vinegar and ¼ cup tahini instead of Dijon.

Classic Potato Salad
Swap mayonnaise for olive oil. Add chopped celery and red bell pepper if you like.

SPEED ◑ SERVES 4

French Fries

Conventional wisdom says you have to fry French fries twice. That does work beautifully (see the Variation), but there's another, easier way. Bonus: I learned this from my mother.

Ingredients

Vegetable oil for deep frying

2 pounds starchy ("baking") potatoes

Salt and pepper

Prep | Cook

1. Put at least 1 ½ to 2 inches of oil in a deep pot over medium-high heat.

   Scrub the potatoes and cut them into whatever frylike shape you want.

   Lay out some paper towels for the cooked fries.

2. Put the fries in the pot and cook undisturbed while the oil comes to a boil. (Don't leave the pot unattended.)

3. Continue to cook, stirring occasionally and adjusting the heat so the oil bubbles enthusiastically, until the fries are golden and crisp, a total of 20 to 25 minutes from the time you put them in the pot. Drain the fries on the paper towels, immediately sprinkle with salt and pepper, and serve hot.

VARIATIONS

Double-Fried French Fries
You have the advantage here of doing the first stage ahead of time. Heat the oil to 300°F, then add the potatoes and fry for 5 to 10 minutes, depending on how thick they are. Drain and let them cool completely. Raise the oil temperature to 350°F and cook the potatoes until golden and crisp, just a few minutes more.

Sweet Potato Fries
Substitute sweet potatoes for regular potatoes. They will be tender and start to burn faster, so watch them.

SPEED ◑ SERVES 4

Sautéed Sweet Potatoes

This is one of my favorite ways to cook sweet potatoes, even without the time savings. I've served these at Thanksgiving with great success.

Ingredients

3 tablespoons olive oil

2 ½ pounds sweet potatoes

Salt and pepper

Prep | Cook

1. Put 3 tablespoons olive oil in a large skillet over medium-low heat.
   Peel the sweet potatoes; shred them in a food processor with a grating disk or by hand with a box grater.

2. Put the sweet potatoes in the skillet, sprinkle with salt and pepper, and raise the heat to medium-high.

3. Cook, stirring occasionally until they begin to brown, 8 to 10 minutes. Continue to cook, stirring a bit more frequently until they are tender but not mushy, 2 or 3 minutes. Taste and adjust the seasoning and serve hot or warm.

VARIATIONS

Sautéed Sweet Potatoes with Garlic and Sage
Cook 3 whole garlic cloves and a handful of fresh sage leaves in the oil while you grate the sweet potatoes.

Sautéed Sweet Potatoes with Chipotle and Lime
Add 1 or 2 (or more!) chopped chipotle chiles in adobo, to taste, to the skillet along with the sweet potatoes. Squeeze the juice of 1 lime over the sweet potatoes before serving.

Sautéed Sweet Potatoes with Ginger and Soy
Cook 1 inch fresh ginger, minced, in the oil while you grate the sweet potatoes. Drizzle at least 2 tablespoons soy sauce over the sweet potatoes before serving.

SPEED ◔ SERVES 4

Crisp Roasted Potatoes

With a couple of easy tricks, you can roast potatoes in less than 45 minutes. And the tricks aren't complicated: It's just a matter of using your oven and broiler to their greatest effect.

Ingredients

2 pounds any potatoes

3 tablespoons olive oil

Salt and pepper

Prep | Cook

1. Heat the oven to 500°F.

   Scrub the potatoes (don't bother to peel) and halve them. Cut each half into ½-inch-thick half-moons. Put them on a rimmed baking sheet as you go.

2. Toss the potatoes with 3 tablespoons oil and a sprinkle of salt and pepper; spread them out in an even layer.

3. Transfer them to the oven (whether it's fully heated or not) and cook undisturbed until the potatoes are tender in the middle and golden in spots on the bottom, 25 to 30 minutes.

4. Turn on the broiler; put the rack 4 inches from the heat. Transfer the potatoes to the broiler and cook, rotating the baking sheet as necessary, until the tops are brown and crisp, 3 to 5 minutes. Serve hot or warm.

VARIATIONS

4 Ways to Season the Potatoes

Toss any of the following with the cooked potatoes:

1. 1 teaspoon any dried spices
2. ¼ cup chopped fresh parsley, cilantro, basil, dill, or chives
3. 1 tablespoon chopped fresh rosemary, thyme, oregano, or sage
4. 1 teaspoon grated citrus zest

Dessert

Caramelized Honey-Orange Bananas 970

Fruity Shaved Ice 971

Broiled Peaches with Brown Sugar 972

Watermelon Soup with Fresh Herbs 973

Fruit Sorbet 974

Black and White Milkshakes 975

Orange Cream Sundaes 976

Almond Cookie Dough 977

Chocolate Chip Cookie Squares 980

Molasses Whoopie Pies 981

Salted Chocolate Peanut Butter Balls 982

Coconut Oatmeal Cookies 983

Chocolate-Covered Pretzels 986

Molten Chocolate Cake 987

Chocolate-Orange Pudding 990

Individual Tiramisus 991

Chocolate Custard Soup 992

Pumpkin Mousse 993

Lemon S'mores 994

Skillet Fruit Crisp 995

Berry Fool 996

Sautéed Apple Crunch 997

Pecan-Bourbon Brownies 998

Chocolate Peanut Brittle 999

Chocolate Chunk Banana Cupcakes 1000

Peach Cobbler Under the Broiler 1001

Apple Crumble Under the Broiler 1002

Key Lime Crumble 1003

Dessert

No matter how simple, dessert is always festive; it keeps guests lingering and chatting—and children from dining and dashing.

There are a lot of ways to satisfy a sweet tooth, and they needn't be elaborate or time-consuming. Often the simplest things do the trick, and this chapter shows how just a little effort can turn out desserts that are welcome, impressive, and delicious.

And desserts need not rely on baking. In fact, the majority of the recipes in this chapter don't involve the oven at all, exploring a range of cold and no-cook dishes and quick desserts made on the stovetop or under the broiler. (Of course if you're really short on time, prepare a fruit bowl. An apple or a clementine enjoyed over coffee can be as satisfying as a chocolate cake.)

Those recipes that do involve baking have been reconceived to streamline processes. Chocolate chip cookies are baked as bars—saving the step of shaping individual mounds of dough—and taste even better hot out of the oven.

You may be tempted to skip the sweets—or to buy something from your local bakery. But if you give yourself 15 minutes to half an hour to make your own, you'll be glad you made the effort.

Chapter Highlights

Baking Ingredients What you need to stock your baking pantry. Dessert Staples (page 978).

Sweet, Sweet Sauce A homemade sauce can turn any dessert into a special treat. Dessert Sauces (page 988).

Quick Cake The most versatile cakes you've ever made. Cake Without a Mix (page 984).

Broiled Desserts Classic desserts that can be made under the broiler in no time. Peach Cobbler Under the Broiler (page 1001), Apple Crumble Under the Broiler (page 1002), Skillet Fruit Crisp (page 995), Sautéed Apple Crunch (page 997).

No-Bake Cookies Skip the oven and go for the dough; it's a favorite anyway. Almond Cookie Dough (page 977), Salted Chocolate Peanut Butter Balls (page 982).

Wonderful Whipped Cream It's fast and luxurious, not only as a topping but also as the base for simple desserts. Berry Fool (page 996), Individual Tiramisus (page 991).

Liquid Dessert Desserts you can sip with a straw or slurp with a spoon. Watermelon Soup with Fresh Herbs (page 973), Black and White Milkshakes (page 975).

Easy Electric Even if you rarely bake, a hand-held electric mixer will save you a ton of time and hassle—in fact, it might get you to bake more often.

SPEED SERVES 4

Caramelized Honey-Orange Bananas

Decadent—and almost no work. Honey and orange juice add complexity; an optional splash of rum (see the Variation) takes the dish to the limit.

Ingredients

4 tablespoons (½ stick) butter

¼ cup packed brown sugar

2 tablespoons honey

¼ cup orange juice

4 ripe bananas

Prep | Cook

1. Put 4 tablespoons butter, ¼ cup packed brown sugar, 2 tablespoons honey, and ¼ cup orange juice in a medium skillet over medium heat. Cook, stirring frequently, until the mixture begins to thicken and darken, about 10 minutes.

   Peel and slice the bananas.

2. Add the bananas and cook until warm and coated with caramelized sauce. Serve immediately.

VARIATIONS

Caramelized Maple-Rum Bananas
Instead of the honey, use 3 tablespoons maple syrup. In place of the orange juice, use 3 tablespoons rum.

Caramelized Chile-Lime Bananas
Use ¼ cup lime juice instead of the orange juice and add 1 teaspoon chili powder.

SPEED SERVES 4

Fruity Shaved Ice

All it takes to make delicious shaved ice is a food processor with a grating attachment and a bag of frozen fruit. Serve it in bowls or, if you really want to be authentic, in little paper cups.

Ingredients

1 pound frozen fruit (any combination)

½ lemon

¼ cup sugar, plus more as needed

Prep | Cook

1. Turn on the food processor fitted with the grating disk. Push the fruit through the feed tube a few pieces at a time. Transfer to a mixing bowl.

   Squeeze the lemon half into a small bowl and add ¼ cup sugar. Stir to dissolve.

2. Add the mixture to the shaved fruit ice and stir gently to combine. Taste and add more sugar if necessary. Serve immediately.

VARIATIONS

5 Frozen Fruits to Use for Shaved Ice

1. Strawberries
2. Raspberries
3. Pineapple
4. Mangoes
5. Peaches or nectarines

NOTES

IF YOU HAVE MORE TIME

Start with fresh fruit. You can use fruits not usually found frozen, like melons and pears. Cut into chunks if necessary to fit through the feed tube and freeze the finished ice mixture overnight.

SPEED SERVES 4

Broiled Peaches with Brown Sugar

Broiling peaches with a bit of butter and sugar caramelizes their natural sugars and beautifully chars the tops. That space where the pit used to be is just begging for vanilla ice cream.

Ingredients

4 ripe peaches

2 tablespoons butter

¼ cup packed brown sugar

Prep | Cook

1. Turn the broiler to high; put the rack 4 inches from the heat.
   Halve the peaches and remove the pits.
   Chop 2 tablespoons butter into bits and put them in a small mixing bowl.

2. Add ¼ cup packed brown sugar to the butter and mix them together with your fingers. Put the peaches cut side up on a rimmed baking sheet and sprinkle them with the sugar mixture.

3. Broil until the tops are lightly charred, 2 to 5 minutes. Serve warm.

VARIATIONS

5 Other Fruits to Broil

1. Apples
2. Pears
3. Apricots
4. Grapefruit
5. Pineapple (cut into rings)

Additions to the Butter and Sugar Mixture

1. 2 tablespoons chopped nuts
2. ½ teaspoon cinnamon, cardamom, cloves, or nutmeg
3. 1 tablespoon chopped candied ginger

SPEED SERVES 4

Watermelon Soup with Fresh Herbs

Drink this refreshing purée for breakfast and it's a smoothie; eat it with a spoon for dessert and it's a slightly sweet and bright-tasting soup.

Ingredients

2 pounds seedless watermelon

1 lemon

3 tablespoons honey

Several sprigs fresh basil or mint for garnish

Prep | Cook

Peel the watermelon and cut the flesh into rough chunks; put them in a blender.

Halve the lemon and squeeze the juice into the blender.

1. Add 3 tablespoons honey to the blender. Blend, adding a small splash of water if necessary to get the machine going, until the watermelon is liquefied.

   Strip the basil or mint leaves from several sprigs and chop.

2. Taste the purée and adjust the seasoning. Put the purée in the freezer for 10 minutes to chill.
3. Pour into 4 bowls or glasses, garnish with the herbs, and serve.

VARIATIONS

5 Other Fruits to Make into Soup

1. Cantaloupe
2. Peaches
3. Cherries
4. Strawberries
5. Mangoes

NOTES

EVEN FASTER

Skip freezing the purée and pour into bowls directly after puréeing.

SPEED SERVES 4

Fruit Sorbet

A revelation: The method is easy, and the result is better than most store-bought sorbets.

Ingredients

1 pound any frozen berries, stone fruit, or other frozen fruit

½ cup yogurt, crème fraîche, or silken tofu

¼ cup sugar

Prep | Cook

1. In a food processor, combine the fruit, ½ cup yogurt, crème fraîche, or tofu, ¼ cup sugar, and 1 or 2 tablespoons water.
2. Process, stopping to scrape down the sides as necessary, until just puréed and creamy. If the fruit does not break down completely, add water through the feed tube, 1 tablespoon at a time. Be careful not to overprocess or the sorbet will liquefy. Serve immediately.

VARIATIONS

Chocolate-Fruit Sorbet
Add ½ cup chopped chocolate to the mixture before processing.

NOTES

IF YOU HAVE MORE TIME
Let the sorbet harden in the freezer and allow 10 to 15 minutes for it to soften before serving.

SPEED ◔ SERVES 4

Black and White Milkshakes

A diner classic. Only for this version I put the vanilla on the bottom and chocolate on the top for a fancier presentation.

Ingredients

1 pint vanilla ice cream

1 cup milk

½ cup chocolate syrup

Prep | Cook

1. Put 1 cup vanilla ice cream and ½ cup milk in a blender. Blend until thick and smooth, then pour the shake into 4 glasses, filling them halfway.
2. Add 1 cup ice cream, ½ cup milk, and ½ cup chocolate syrup to the blender. Blend as before. Pour the chocolate shake on top of the vanilla and serve.

VARIATIONS

Black and White Mocha Milkshakes
Add 3 tablespoons brewed espresso along with the chocolate syrup in Step 2.

Salty Chocolate Shakes
Use chocolate ice cream instead of vanilla, skip the chocolate syrup, and add a teaspoon of salt (or to taste). Blend everything all at once.

Spicy Chocolate Shakes
Replace the vanilla ice cream with chocolate, skip the chocolate syrup, and add a pinch of cayenne. Blend everything all at once.

Boozy Black and White Milkshakes
Add 1 or more tablespoons rum or bourbon along with the chocolate syrup in Step 2.

Fruit Milkshakes
Substitute 1 cup fresh or frozen fruit for the chocolate syrup. Blend everything all at once.

SPEED ◐ SERVES 4

Orange Cream Sundaes

A simple orange syrup poured over vanilla cream re-creates the tangy-on-creamy flavor of the retro Creamsicle. Other combinations work too—see the Variations.

Ingredients

1 quart vanilla ice cream

2 cups orange juice

½ cup sugar

Prep | Cook

Take the ice cream out of the freezer to soften.

1. Put 2 cups orange juice and ½ cup sugar in a large skillet over high heat. Cook, stirring occasionally until the mixture is reduced by half and thickens into a syrup, 10 to 15 minutes. Transfer to a dish and put it in the freezer to cool, about 10 minutes.

2. Scoop 1 cup vanilla ice cream into each of 4 bowls and drizzle the orange syrup over the top.

VARIATIONS

Applejack Sundaes
Replace the orange juice with apple cider and add 2 tablespoons bourbon. Reduce the sugar by ¼ cup.

Cranberry-Port Sundaes
Great for fall. Omit the orange juice. Add 2 cups cranberries, ½ cup port wine, and the zest of a lemon to the skillet along with the sugar, bring to a boil, then let bubble gently but steadily until the cranberries break apart and thicken the sauce, 15 to 20 minutes. Taste and add more sugar if necessary. Serve warm over the ice cream.

NOTES

EVEN FASTER
If you don't mind some melted ice cream, don't bother to chill the syrup.

SPEED ◐ MAKES 24 COOKIES

Almond Cookie Dough

Some people like raw cookie dough better than the finished cookies, so why fight it?

Ingredients

1 cup almonds

¾ cup dried apricots

¼ cup sugar

½ teaspoon vanilla extract

2 tablespoons butter

¼ cup flour

⅛ teaspoon salt

½ cup powdered sugar

1 lemon

Prep | Cook

1. In a food processor, combine 1 cup almonds, ¾ cup dried apricots, ¼ cup sugar, ½ teaspoon vanilla, 2 tablespoons butter, ¼ cup flour, ⅛ teaspoon salt, and 1 tablespoon water. Process until the mixture forms a stiff, chunky dough. If necessary, add more water, a tablespoon at a time, until the dough comes together.
2. Pinch off rounded-tablespoon-size pieces of the dough, roll them into balls, and put them on a baking sheet or the counter; press your thumb into the center of each to make an indentation.
3. Put ½ cup powdered sugar in a small bowl.
   Halve the lemon.
4. Squeeze 2 teaspoons of the juice into the bowl and whisk to form a glaze. Fill each indentation in the dough and serve.

VARIATIONS

Chocolate Cookie Dough
Use ½ cup chopped chocolate or chocolate chips instead of the apricots.

Coconut Cookie Dough
Add ½ cup shredded unsweetened coconut along with the other ingredients in Step 1 and use lime juice instead of lemon.

Dessert Staples

A dessert is only as good as its ingredients. This is especially true here, where recipes are pared down to their essentials. Here's what an ideal dessert pantry contains.

Ingredient	Description
BUTTER	Opt for unsalted, which is typically fresher than salted, has a sweet, creamy taste, and lets you control the amount of salt in a dish. If you do buy salted butter, you can leave out the salt that is often called for in recipes.
FLOUR	Use unbleached all-purpose flour for baking.
GRANULATED SUGAR	All recipes here calling for sugar refer to granulated, the most common type.
BROWN SUGAR	White sugar with molasses added, resulting in deeper flavor and added moisture. Dark brown sugar has more molasses than light, thus its more intense flavor and darker color, but you can use them interchangeably. To keep brown sugar from hardening after you open the box, wrap the sugar tightly in a plastic bag and store in the fridge.
POWDERED SUGAR	Also known as *confectioners' sugar, icing sugar,* and *10x sugar,* this is regular sugar ground into a powder and mixed with a little cornstarch so that it doesn't cake and clump. It's perfect for dusting over desserts: Put some in a mesh strainer, hold it over the dessert, and tap on the sides.
CHOCOLATE	From darkest and most bitter to lightest and sweetest: unsweetened, bittersweet, semisweet, dark, and milk. Chocolate bars for baking typically note their percentage of cacao on the package; the higher the number, the darker the chocolate (meaning less sugar). This book calls for bittersweet and semisweet. White chocolate is not technically chocolate since it doesn't contain any cocoa solids.
COCOA POWDER	Like powdered sugar, sprinkle it over desserts for a fancy touch.
FLOUR	Use unbleached all-purpose flour for baking.

Ingredient	Description
BAKING POWDER AND BAKING SODA	These leavening agents produce carbon dioxide in baked goods, causing them to rise.
EGGS	Essential for both sweet and savory cooking; read all about them on page 828.
FROZEN FRUIT	If you keep frozen fruit in the house, a smoothie or sorbet is easy to make.
HEAVY CREAM	Essential for whipped cream (obviously) and also caramel and butterscotch sauces (page 989).
NUTS	In most baking, walnuts, almonds, hazelnuts, and pecans are most common, but peanuts, pistachios, and pine nuts are also excellent.
DRIED FRUIT	Small pieces are perfect for stirring into cookie dough; you can dip whole dried fruits like apricots or mangoes in melted chocolate for a bittersweet treat.
SHREDDED UNSWEETENED COCONUT	Stir it into cookie dough, add it to crisp or crumble toppings, or toast it in a skillet until lightly browned and sprinkle it on top of ice cream.
ROLLED OATS	A must not only for oatmeal cookies but also for crisp and crumble toppings. Whatever you don't use for dessert you can eat for breakfast.
PHYLLO DOUGH	These finicky sheets of dough are usually part of time-consuming, labor-intensive recipes, but I simply cut them into shreds and bake them until golden and crisp. The result is a crisp, easy topping for cooked fruit (see page 997) or ice cream.
HONEY AND MAPLE SYRUP	Use them as alternative sweeteners to sugar or just stir them into yogurt, whipped cream, or mascarpone cheese and use as a topping for fresh fruit.
VANILLA EXTRACT	Vanilla not only makes chocolate taste better (go figure), but it's that hidden ingredient that rounds out the flavor of all sorts of doughs and batters. Plus, you'll want it on hand for pancakes and French toast.
BAKING SPICES	The seasonings for pumpkin pie—cinnamon, nutmeg, cloves, and ginger—are also useful in cookies, sautéed fruit, other pies, crumbles, and crisps.

SPEED ◑ MAKES 9 SQUARES

Chocolate Chip Cookie Squares

The fastest way to have warm chocolate chip cookies from scratch is to bake them as bars.

Ingredients

1 stick unsalted butter, plus more for greasing the pan

1 cup flour, plus more for the pan

¼ cup plus 2 tablespoons granulated sugar

¼ cup plus 2 tablespoons packed brown sugar

1 egg

¼ teaspoon baking soda

¼ teaspoon salt

1 teaspoon vanilla extract

4 ounces semisweet or bittersweet chocolate

Prep | Cook

1. Heat the oven to 375°F. Grease a 9-inch square baking pan with butter, then sprinkle with flour and shake out the excess.
   Put 1 stick butter in a large microwave-safe bowl and microwave it for a few seconds to soften it.
2. Add to the butter ¼ cup plus 2 tablespoons granulated sugar and ¼ cup plus 2 tablespoons packed brown sugar. Beat with an electric mixer until creamy, then crack in the egg and beat until well blended.
3. Add 1 cup flour, ¼ teaspoon baking soda, ¼ teaspoon salt, and 1 teaspoon vanilla. Beat just to combine.
   Chop 4 ounces chocolate; stir it into the dough.
4. Scrape the dough into the prepared pan and press it into a thin, even layer. Bake until the edges are golden brown and a toothpick inserted into the center comes out relatively clean but not dry, with a few crumbs clinging to it, 10 to 12 minutes.
5. Let cool for 5 minutes, then cut into squares. Serve warm.

SPEED ◐ SERVES 4

Molasses Whoopie Pies

So much like real whoopie pies that I have to fill them with cream cheese frosting.

Ingredients

1 ½ sticks unsalted butter

4 ounces cream cheese

¼ cup packed brown sugar

¼ cup molasses

1 egg

1 ½ cups flour

1 teaspoon baking soda

¼ teaspoon salt

½ teaspoon cinnamon

¼ teaspoon ginger

1 ½ teaspoons vanilla extract

1 ½ cups powdered sugar

Prep | Cook

1. Heat the oven to 400°F.

   Cut up 1 stick butter, put it in a large microwave-safe bowl, and soften it in the microwave for just a few seconds. Put ½ stick butter and 4 ounces cream cheese in a medium bowl.

2. Add ¼ cup packed brown sugar to the softened butter. Beat with an electric mixer until creamed and fluffy, then add ¼ cup molasses and beat until combined. Crack in the egg and beat until well blended.

3. Add 1 ½ cups flour, 1 teaspoon baking soda, ¼ teaspoon salt, ½ teaspoon cinnamon, ¼ teaspoon ginger, and 1 teaspoon vanilla. Beat gently until the dough is just combined and soft enough to handle.

4. Scoop 16 rounded-tablespoon-sized balls onto an ungreased baking sheet; press with your fingers to evenly flatten a little. They won't spread as they bake.

5. Bake until puffed and set but not browned, 7 or 8 minutes. Transfer to a rack to cool for 5 minutes.

   Beat the butter and cream cheese with an electric mixer until fully creamed, about 1 minute. Add 1 ½ cups powdered sugar and ½ teaspoon vanilla. Beat until creamy.

6. Spread a dollop on the bottom sides of 8 cookies and sandwich a second cookie on top.

SPEED MAKES 36 BALLS

Salted Chocolate Peanut Butter Balls

Like a Reese's peanut butter cup rolled into a ball, these no-bake morsels just need a little blast of cold air from the freezer to firm up.

Ingredients

2 tablespoons butter

4 ounces semisweet or bittersweet chocolate

1 cup peanut butter

1 cup powdered sugar, plus more as needed

Salt (the flaky kind is best here)

Prep | Cook

1. Put 2 tablespoons butter in a medium microwave-safe bowl.
   Chop 4 ounces chocolate; add it to the bowl.
2. Microwave the mixture, checking and stirring occasionally until the butter and chocolate melt, a minute or 2.
3. Add 1 cup peanut butter and stir until it's evenly incorporated. Blend in 1 cup powdered sugar and stir until the mixture is smooth.
4. Put a piece of wax or parchment paper on a rimmed baking sheet. Use 2 teaspoons to drop 1-inch balls of dough onto the sheet. Sprinkle the tops with a little salt.
5. Put the baking sheet in the freezer and freeze just until the balls firm up a bit, 10 to 15 minutes. Serve.

VARIATIONS

Chocolate Almond Butter Balls
Use almond butter instead of peanut butter.

NOTES

IF YOU HAVE MORE TIME
Before freezing, roll each ball in finely chopped peanuts or grated unsweetened coconut.

SPEED ◑ MAKES 36 TO 48 COOKIES

Coconut Oatmeal Cookies

One of the simplest of all cookies, here with coconut.

Ingredients

1 stick unsalted butter

½ cup granulated sugar

½ cup packed brown sugar

2 eggs

1 ½ cups flour

1 cup rolled oats

1 cup shredded unsweetened coconut

½ teaspoon cinnamon

2 teaspoons baking powder

Salt

½ cup milk

½ teaspoon vanilla or almond extract

Prep | Cook

1. Heat the oven to 375°F.

   Put 1 stick butter in a large microwave-safe mixing bowl and microwave it for a few seconds to soften it.

2. Add ½ cup granulated sugar and ½ cup packed brown sugar to the butter. Beat with an electric mixer until creamy, then crack in the eggs, one at a time, and beat until well blended.

3. Add 1 ½ cups flour, 1 cup rolled oats, 1 cup shredded coconut, ½ teaspoon cinnamon, 2 teaspoons baking powder, a pinch of salt, ½ cup milk, and ½ teaspoon vanilla or almond extract. Beat just to combine.

4. Drop tablespoon-size mounds of dough 3 inches apart on ungreased baking sheets. Bake until lightly browned, 12 to 15 minutes. Let cool for a few minutes and serve warm.

VARIATIONS

Nutty Coconut Oatmeal Cookies
Add in ½ cup any nut butter in Step 2 and ½ cup chopped walnuts or pecans in Step 3.

Dried Fruit Oatmeal Cookies
Add 1 cup dried cranberries, blueberries, chopped dried apricots, chopped dates, or raisins in Step 3.

NOTES

IF YOU HAVE MORE TIME
Let the cookies cool completely on a rack after they come out of the oven.

Cake Without a Mix

Homemade mini pound cakes are festive, delicious, and easy to vary. Plus, they love to be loaded up with toppings—think whipped cream, frosting, fruit, or chocolate sauce. They keep for several days, and if you bake them as cupcakes, you can have your cake in less than half the usual time. This recipe makes 12 cupcakes.

Classic Pound Cupcakes

1 Cream the Butter and Sugar

Heat the oven to 375°F and grease 12 muffin cups (in one or more tins) with butter or line them with paper cups. Soften—without melting— 2 sticks butter on low in the microwave (unless it's soft already). Put the butter and 1 cup sugar in a large bowl. Beat with an electric mixer until creamy.

2 Add the Yolks

Separate 5 eggs, letting the whites fall into a clean mixing bowl, and add the yolks to the creamed butter and sugar. Add 2 teaspoons vanilla extract to the yolks and beat until well blended.

3 Add the Dry Ingredients

Add 2 cups flour, 1½ teaspoons baking powder, and a pinch of salt to the bowl; mix by hand until just combined.

4 Beat the Whites

Using clean beaters and a clean bowl, beat the egg whites until they hold soft peaks. Fold half of them into the batter with a rubber spatula until streaks no longer appear, then gently fold in the remaining egg whites the same way.

5 Bake

Pour the batter into the prepared muffin tins, filling each cup three-quarters full. Bake for 12 to 15 minutes, until the cupcakes are puffed and golden and a toothpick inserted into the center comes out with just a few crumbs clinging to it. Transfer the pan (or pans) to a cooling rack; turn out the cupcakes as soon as they're cool enough to handle, 10 minutes or so.

6 Add Toppings

Top the cupcakes (or any of the variations) with powdered sugar or whipped cream or drizzle with any of the following sauces: Chocolate Sauce (page 988); Creamy Caramel Sauce (page 989); Butterscotch Sauce (page 989); Raw Fruit Sauce (page 989); Vanilla Custard Sauce (page 988).

Citrus Pound Cupcakes Reduce the vanilla to 1 teaspoon. Add the zest and juice of 1 lemon or lime (or 1/2 orange) to the yolk mixture in Step 2.

Spice Pound Cupcakes Add 1/2 teaspoon each cinnamon, allspice, and ginger and 1/4 teaspoon each nutmeg and cloves with the dry ingredients.

Chocolate Pound Cupcakes Add 1/2 cup cocoa powder with the dry ingredients. If you like, add 1 cup chocolate chips to the batter after folding in the egg whites.

Almond Pound Cupcakes Reduce the vanilla to 1 teaspoon and add 1 teaspoon pure almond extract.

Poppy Pound Cupcakes Add 1/4 cup poppy seeds with the dry ingredients. (This is especially nice with the lemon juice and zest from the first variation.)

Ginger Pound Cupcakes Add 1 teaspoon ground ginger with the dry ingredients and fold in 1 tablespoon minced crystallized ginger after folding in the egg whites.

Polenta Pound Cupcakes Substitute 1 cup cornmeal for 1 cup of the flour.

Yogurt Pound Cupcakes Even more moist: Substitute 3/4 cup yogurt for half of the butter.

Nutty Pound Cupcakes Substitute 1 cup any finely ground nut meal or nut flour for half of the flour.

SPEED ◑ SERVES 4

Chocolate-Covered Pretzels

Melt, dip, freeze, and devour.

Ingredients

12 ounces bittersweet, semisweet, or white chocolate

4 cups large, thin salted pretzel twists

Prep | Cook

1. Put an inch or so of water in a small saucepan and bring it to a boil.
   Chop 12 ounces chocolate.
2. Put the chocolate in a bowl that you can set over the saucepan without the bottom touching the water. Adjust the heat so the water simmers and set the bowl on top.
3. Melt the chocolate, stirring frequently until it's completely smooth. Turn off the heat.
   Line a rimmed baking sheet with wax paper or foil.
4. When the chocolate is melted, dip in the pretzels, one at a time, but quickly, tapping to shake off any excess chocolate, and put them on the rack. When done, put the sheet in the freezer until the chocolate hardens, 10 to 15 minutes.

VARIATIONS

5 Other Things to Dip in Melted Chocolate

1. Fresh fruit
2. Dried fruit
3. Cookies
4. Graham crackers
5. Angel food or pound cake (page 984)

NOTES

EVEN FASTER

Put the melted chocolate in a bowl, scatter the pretzels around it, and let everyone dip and eat right away. Messy but fun.

SPEED SERVES 4

Molten Chocolate Cake

A four-star dessert that bakes in less than 10 minutes.

Ingredients

1 stick unsalted butter, plus more for greasing the pan

4 ounces bittersweet or semisweet chocolate

4 eggs

¼ cup sugar

2 teaspoons flour, plus more for dusting the pan

Prep | Cook

1. Heat the oven to 450°F.

   Put 1 stick butter in a medium bowl and melt it in the microwave. Chop 4 ounces chocolate.

2. Add the chocolate to the melted butter and stir until it's melted.

3. In a separate bowl, crack in 2 eggs. Separate 2 more eggs and add the yolks (discard the whites or refrigerate and save for another use). Add ¼ cup sugar and beat or whisk the mixture until it's light and thick, about 1 minute. Add the egg mixture and 2 teaspoons flour to the chocolate mixture and beat to combine.

4. Butter four 4-ounce ramekins and dust them with flour. Tap to shake out the excess flour and divide the batter among them.

5. When the oven is hot, bake the cakes until they are slightly puffy and the tops are barely set, 7 to 9 minutes. They should still jiggle when you shake them. After a minute, put a plate over each ramekin and invert the ramekin onto the plate. Wait 10 seconds and remove the ramekin from each cake. Serve immediately.

VARIATIONS

Molten White Chocolate Cake
Use white chocolate.

Mexican Molten Chocolate Cake
Add ½ teaspoon cinnamon and ½ teaspoon cayenne along with the flour in Step 3.

MASTER RECIPE

Dessert Sauces

A homemade sauce can instantly turn an everyday—and even store-bought—dessert into a special treat. The sauces here come together in a flash and can be made in advance to use over the course of a few days.

Chocolate Sauce

1 Melt Chocolate with Butter

In a small saucepan, combine 4 ounces chopped semisweet or bittersweet chocolate, 4 tablespoons (½ stick) butter, ¼ cup sugar, ¼ cup water, and a pinch of salt. Cook over very low heat until the chocolate melts and the mixture is smooth.

2 Add Vanilla

Stir in 1 teaspoon vanilla extract and serve immediately, keep warm over hot water or refrigerate for up to a week; rewarm before using.

Vanilla Custard Sauce

1 Heat Milk

Put 2 cups milk in a small saucepan over medium heat until it steams. Let it cool for 5 minutes.

2 Cook the Custard

Once the milk has cooled somewhat, separate 4 eggs and add the yolks (discard the whites or save for another use) and ½ cup sugar and whisk to combine. Cook over medium heat, whisking pretty constantly, until the mixture thickens and coats the back of a spoon (175° to 180°F on a quick-read thermometer).

3 Strain and Cool

Pass the sauce through a strainer into a bowl and let it cool slightly. Then stir in 1 teaspoon vanilla extract and serve warm or cold or refrigerate for up to 3 days.

Creamy Caramel Sauce

1 Dissolve the Sugar

Combine 2 cups sugar, 1 cup cream, and 2 tablespoons butter in a broad saucepan or deep skillet over medium-low heat. Cook, swirling the pan occasionally until the sugar dissolves, 3 to 5 minutes.

2 Darken the Sugar

Continue to cook until the sugar darkens to a caramel color and the temperature reaches 245°F on a candy thermometer, about 15 minutes. Add more cream if the sauce is too thick. Serve immediately or refrigerate for up to a week; rewarm before using.

Butterscotch Sauce

1 Melt Butter in Cream

Put ¾ cup cream and 6 tablespoons (¾ stick) butter, cut into pieces, in a small saucepan over medium-low heat. Cook, stirring occasionally until the butter melts.

2 Add Sugar

Stir in ¾ cup brown sugar and a pinch of salt. Cook, stirring frequently until the mixture is thick and shiny, 5 to 10 minutes. Taste and add more sugar if you like. Serve immediately or refrigerate for up to a week; rewarm before using.

Raw Fruit Sauce

1 Prep the Fruit

Trim, pit, and chop soft fruits—like peaches, nectarines, cherries, and mangoes—as needed to get 2 cups.

2 Purée

Put the fruit in a blender and blend, adding a splash of water if necessary to get the machine going. If you're using raspberries or blackberries and prefer a smooth purée, pour it through a strainer to remove the seeds.

3 Sweeten

Stir in powdered sugar to taste; thin the sauce to your desired consistency with water or orange or lemon juice. Serve immediately or refrigerate for up to 2 days.

SPEED ◐ SERVES 4 TO 6

Chocolate-Orange Pudding

Using silken tofu is the easiest and fastest way to make, well, silken pudding.

Ingredients

¾ cup sugar

8 ounces bittersweet or semisweet chocolate, plus 1 ounce for garnish

1 orange

14 to 16 ounces silken tofu

1 teaspoon vanilla extract

Prep | Cook

1. Put ¾ cup water and ¾ cup sugar in a small saucepan and bring it to a boil. After it boils, stir it so the sugar crystals dissolve, then remove from the heat.

   Chop 8 ounces chocolate.

2. Put the chocolate in a bowl that you can set over the saucepan without the bottom touching the water. Adjust the heat so the water simmers and set the bowl on top. Stir the chocolate frequently until it's melted and completely smooth.

   Grate 1 tablespoon orange zest (refrigerate the fruit for another use).

3. In a blender, combine the melted chocolate, the sugar syrup from the saucepan, the silken tofu, orange zest, and 1 teaspoon vanilla. Blend, stopping as necessary to scrape down the sides, until the mixture is completely smooth.

4. Divide the mixture among ramekins or servings bowls and freeze them until the pudding firms up a bit, 15 to 20 minutes. To serve, shave 1 ounce chocolate over the tops using a vegetable peeler.

VARIATIONS

Chocolate-Banana Pudding
Replace the orange zest with 1 ripe banana.

White Chocolate–Orange Pudding
Use white chocolate instead of dark.

SPEED ◑ SERVES 4

Individual Tiramisus

Quick tiramisus assembled right in the serving bowls. For a boozy version, see the Variations.

Ingredients

Instant coffee or espresso powder

20 ladyfingers

1 cup cream

½ cup mascarpone cheese

1 cup powdered sugar

Cocoa powder for dusting

Prep | Cook

1. Brew 1 cup instant coffee or espresso. Dip 20 ladyfingers in the coffee and lay them in the bottom of 4 shallow bowls.
2. Beat 1 cup cream in a medium bowl using an electric mixer until it holds soft peaks.
3. Put ½ cup mascarpone and 1 cup powdered sugar in a separate bowl. Beat with the electric mixer until the sugar is fully incorporated; start slow so it doesn't fly everywhere.
4. Gently fold the mascarpone mixture into the whipped cream and spread it on top of the ladyfingers. Dust some cocoa powder over the top and serve.

VARIATIONS

Boozy Individual Tiramisus
Add 2 tablespoons crème de cacao, crème de menthe, or Marsala to the coffee.

SPEED ◐ SERVES 4

Chocolate Custard Soup

The classic custard sauce crème anglaise makes a delicious dessert soup. If you're having a party, serve this in shot glasses.

Ingredients

3 ounces bittersweet or semisweet chocolate

2 cups milk

1 teaspoon vanilla extract

½ cup sugar

4 eggs

Prep | Cook

Chop 3 ounces chocolate.

1. Combine 2 cups milk, 1 teaspoon vanilla, ½ cup sugar, and the chocolate in a small saucepan. Separate the eggs and add the yolks (discard the whites or refrigerate them and save for another use); whisk well.
2. Cook over medium heat, whisking constantly until the mixture thickens enough to coat the back of a spoon. Don't let it boil.
3. Pour the custard into small bowls and serve as a soup.

VARIATIONS

Vanilla Custard Soup
Omit the chocolate.

Chocolate-Almond Custard Soup
Add 1 teaspoon almond extract in Step 1.

7 Ways to Garnish Chocolate Custard Soup

1. Shaved chocolate
2. Berries or chopped fruit
3. Chopped fresh mint
4. Grated orange zest
5. Chopped nuts
6. Crumbled cake, cookies, or graham crackers
7. Whipped cream

NOTES

IF YOU HAVE MORE TIME
If you prefer, cool the soup in the refrigerator and serve it chilled.

SPEED ◐ SERVES 4 TO 6

Pumpkin Mousse

Few desserts this decadent are also this fast. You could eat it right away if you wanted, but a quick chill in the freezer firms it up perfectly.

Ingredients

½ cup cream

4 tablespoons sugar

3 eggs

One 15-ounce can pumpkin

½ teaspoon cinnamon

¼ teaspoon nutmeg

¼ teaspoon cloves

¼ teaspoon cardamom

Prep | Cook

1. Put ½ cup cream and 2 tablespoons sugar in a medium bowl. Using an electric mixer, beat the cream until it holds soft peaks.
2. Separate the eggs and add the whites and 2 tablespoons sugar to a clean medium bowl (discard the yolks or refrigerate and save for another use). Wash and dry the beaters and beat the egg whites until they hold soft peaks.
3. Add the pumpkin, ½ teaspoon cinnamon, ¼ teaspoon nutmeg, ¼ teaspoon cloves, and ¼ teaspoon cardamom to the egg whites. Gently fold them in with a rubber spatula. Fold in the whipped cream just enough so no streaks of white remain.
4. Spoon the mousse into ramekins or small bowls and freeze for 15 minutes to chill before serving.

VARIATIONS

Chocolate Mousse
Instead of the pumpkin and spices, heat 4 ounces chopped chocolate and 2 tablespoons butter in a bowl set over simmering water until almost completely melted; then remove from the heat and stir until smooth. Fold the whipped egg whites into the chocolate, then fold in the whipped cream.

SPEED ◐ SERVES 4

Lemon S'mores

Marshmallows and chocolate aren't the only foods worth piling on graham crackers.

Ingredients

Ice cubes

2 lemons

1 ½ tablespoons cornstarch

1 cup milk

½ cup sugar

2 eggs

1 stick butter

8 large graham crackers

½ cup shredded unsweetened coconut

Prep | Cook

Put a medium metal bowl in the refrigerator. Place a couple handfuls of ice in a larger bowl and set aside.

Halve the lemons; squeeze the juice of 3 halves into a small saucepan (refrigerate the remaining half for another use).

1. Whisk 1 ½ tablespoons cornstarch into the juice until dissolved. Add 1 cup milk and ½ cup sugar. Separate the eggs, add the yolks (discard the whites or refrigerate them and save for another use), and whisk well. Add a stick of butter to the pan.
2. Cook over medium heat, whisking until the butter melts. Switch to a rubber spatula and stir until the mixture starts to thicken, after about 6 minutes. Continue cooking for another 5 minutes.
3. Pour the hot curd through a mesh strainer into the chilled bowl from the refrigerator. Add some cold water to the bowl of ice and cradle the medium bowl inside it. Stir the curd for 5 minutes to cool. Let sit in the water bath for another 5 minutes to thicken.
4. Spoon the thickened lemon curd onto 8 graham crackers and sprinkle with ½ cup shredded coconut. Serve immediately.

VARIATIONS

Mounds Bar S'mores
Skip the lemon curd. Melt 8 ounces dark chocolate, drizzle it over the graham crackers, and sprinkle with the coconut.

SPEED ◑ SERVES 4 TO 6

Skillet Fruit Crisp

The essence of a crisp—sweet, tender fruit and a crunchy buttery topping—done quickly on the stovetop. Soft fruit cooks faster, but you can use firm fruit like apples: Just sauté them a bit longer, but it won't take much more time.

Ingredients

6 tablespoons (¾ stick) butter

2 pounds peaches, bananas, berries, or any combination

½ cup walnuts or pecans

1 lemon

½ cup rolled oats

¼ cup shredded unsweetened coconut

⅓ cup packed brown sugar

½ teaspoon cinnamon

Salt

Prep | Cook

1. Put 1 tablespoon butter in a large skillet over medium heat.

   If you're using stone fruits, pit and slice them; if using bananas, peel and slice.

2. Add the fruit to the skillet and cook, stirring occasionally until soft, 5 or 6 minutes. Add the berries for the last few minutes of cooking or, if using all berries, cook for a little less time, 3 or 4 minutes.

3. Put 5 tablespoons butter in another large skillet over medium heat.

   Chop ½ cup nuts.

   Grate 1 teaspoon lemon zest (refrigerate the fruit for another use).

4. When the butter is melted, add the nuts, lemon zest, ½ cup rolled oats, ¼ cup shredded coconut, ⅓ cup packed brown sugar, ½ teaspoon cinnamon, and a pinch of salt; toss to coat. Cook, stirring frequently, until the topping is golden and crisp, 6 to 8 minutes.

5. When the fruit is soft, divide it among bowls. Scatter the topping over the fruit and serve.

SPEED ◐ SERVES 4

Berry Fool

Adjust the ingredients a bit to make this summery treat creamier, sweeter, or fruitier.

Ingredients

2 to 3 cups raspberries or blackberries

½ cup plus 1 tablespoon sugar

1 cup cream

Prep | Cook

1. Put about two-thirds of the berries in a small bowl and toss with ¼ cup sugar.
2. Pour 1 cup cream into a medium bowl; add 1 tablespoon sugar. Using an electric mixer, beat the cream until it holds soft peaks.
3. Save a few of the remaining berries for garnish. Put the rest in a blender with ¼ cup sugar. Purée. Pass the purée through a mesh strainer into the whipped cream, pressing it through with a spoon or rubber spatula.
4. Beat the purée into the cream, then add the sugared berries with their liquid and fold them in with a rubber spatula. Garnish with the remaining berries and serve.

VARIATIONS

Peach Fool

Instead of the berries, use 6 to 8 peaches (1 ½ pounds). Peel and slice them, then divide and prepare as described in the recipe.

NOTES

EVEN FASTER

Don't bother straining the seeds out of the purée before folding it into the whipped cream.

SPEED ◐ SERVES 4

Sautéed Apple Crunch

Crisp, buttery phyllo dough can be as convenient as it is frustrating. Instead of wrestling with fragile layers of dough, slice the lot into shreds for a crunchy topping.

Ingredients

8 tablespoons (1 stick) butter

12 sheets phyllo dough

½ cup walnuts

1 ½ pounds firm, crisp apples, like Golden Delicious

½ cup packed brown sugar

½ teaspoon cinnamon

Prep | Cook

1. Heat the oven to 375°F.

   Put 4 tablespoons butter in a small microwave-safe bowl and melt it in the microwave.

   Stack 12 phyllo sheets on top of each other and cut them into shreds; put them on a rimmed baking sheet.

   Chop ½ cup walnuts; add them to the baking sheet.

2. Drizzle the melted butter over the phyllo and nuts; toss to coat. Bake (it's okay if the oven's not fully heated), tossing occasionally until the phyllo is golden and crisp, 20 to 25 minutes.

   Core and slice the apples.

3. Put 4 tablespoons butter in a large, deep skillet over medium heat. When the butter is melted, add the apples and stir; turn the heat to low, cover, and cook for 10 minutes.

4. Add ½ cup packed brown sugar and ½ teaspoon cinnamon and raise the heat to medium. Cook, stirring frequently until the apples are tender and glazed, 10 minutes more.

5. Transfer the apples to a large, shallow serving dish. When the phyllo is crisp, scatter it and the nuts over the apples and serve.

SPEED ◕ SERVES 6

Pecan-Bourbon Brownies

Crunchy, gooey, boozy, and quick.

Ingredients

1 stick butter, plus more for greasing the pan

3 ounces unsweetened chocolate

1 cup pecans

1 cup sugar

2 eggs

½ cup flour

Salt

½ teaspoon vanilla extract

2 tablespoons bourbon

Prep | Cook

1. Heat the oven to 350°F.

   Grease an 8- or 9-inch square baking pan with butter.

   Chop 3 ounces chocolate.

2. Put 1 stick butter and the chocolate in a small saucepan over very low heat. Cook, stirring occasionally until the chocolate is just melted. Remove it from the heat and continue to stir until the mixture is smooth.

   Chop 1 cup pecans.

3. Transfer the chocolate mixture to a medium bowl and stir in 1 cup sugar. With a whisk or an electric mixer, beat in the eggs, one at a time. Gently stir in ½ cup flour, a pinch of salt, ½ teaspoon vanilla, 2 tablespoons bourbon, and the pecans.

4. Pour the batter into the prepared pan and bake until just barely set in the middle, 20 to 25 minutes. A toothpick inserted into the center should come out moist but not wet.

5. Let the brownies cool just long enough so that you can slice them, 5 to 10 minutes. Cut and serve warm.

SPEED SERVES 4 TO 6

Chocolate Peanut Brittle

Peanut brittle has a reputation for being tricky and painstaking. This recipe clears its name.

Ingredients

2 cups sugar

1 tablespoon butter

2 cups roasted unsalted peanuts

Pinch of salt

4 ounces bittersweet or semisweet chocolate

Prep | Cook

1. Put 2 cups sugar and ⅓ cup water in a small saucepan over medium heat and stir gently just to wet the sugar. Cook without stirring, swirling the pan occasionally until the sugar dissolves and starts to color, 10 to 15 minutes. Do not stir.

   Grease a rimmed baking sheet with 1 tablespoon butter.

2. Continue to cook and swirl carefully until the caramel turns deep golden but not dark brown or smoking, another 5 to 10 minutes. Remove from the heat. Stir in 2 cups peanuts and a pinch of salt and immediately spread the mixture onto the baking sheet.

3. Pour an inch of water into a small saucepan and bring it to a boil over high heat.

   Chop 4 ounces chocolate.

4. Put the chocolate in a bowl that you can set over the saucepan without the bottom touching the water. Adjust the heat so the water simmers and set the bowl on top.

5. Melt the chocolate, stirring frequently until it's smooth.

6. When the peanut brittle is slightly firm but not yet hard, drizzle the melted chocolate on top. Refrigerate until the chocolate is firm, 10 to 15 minutes. Break the brittle into pieces and serve.

SPEED MAKES 12 CUPCAKES

Chocolate Chunk Banana Cupcakes

An irresistible crust gives way to an oozing middle. The key to success is a very hot oven.

Ingredients

1 stick butter, plus more for greasing the pan

2 cups flour

½ teaspoon salt

1 ½ teaspoons baking powder

¾ cup sugar

2 eggs

3 very ripe bananas

5 ounces semisweet or bittersweet chocolate

1 teaspoon vanilla extract

Prep | Cook

1. Heat the oven to 400°F. Grease a 12-cup muffin tin with butter.
2. In a large bowl, combine 2 cups flour, ½ teaspoon salt, 1 ½ teaspoons baking powder, and ¾ cup sugar.
3. Cut up 1 stick butter and put in a medium bowl; beat with an electric mixer until creamy. Crack in the eggs. Peel the bananas and add them to the bowl, mashing them up as you drop them in. Beat until well combined.

   Chop 5 ounces chocolate.
4. Add the banana mixture to the dry ingredients and beat gently to combine. Fold in the chopped chocolate and 1 teaspoon vanilla.
5. Scoop the batter into the muffin cups so they are three-quarters full. Bake until the cupcakes are slightly crusty on the outside but still soft in the middle (the tops should leave an indent when pressed with your finger), 15 to 20 minutes. Serve warm.

VARIATIONS

Praline Banana Cupcakes
Toss ½ cup chopped walnuts or pecans with ½ cup brown sugar; sprinkle on top of the cupcakes before baking.

Banana-Rum Cupcakes
Add 1 tablespoon rum along with the vanilla in Step 4.

SPEED SERVES 6

Peach Cobbler Under the Broiler

Much faster than the original and with extra caramelization thanks to the broiler.

Ingredients

1 stick butter, plus more for greasing the pan

2 pounds fresh or frozen peaches

½ cup plus 2 tablespoons sugar

½ cup flour

½ teaspoon baking powder

Pinch of salt

1 egg

½ teaspoon vanilla extract

Prep | Cook

1. Turn the broiler to high; put the rack 6 inches from the heat.
   Grease a broiler-safe 9 × 13-inch pan with butter.
   Pit and slice the peaches if using fresh.
2. Spread the peaches in a somewhat single layer in the pan. Sprinkle with 2 tablespoons sugar. Broil until the peaches begin to soften and caramelize, 6 minutes.
   Cut 1 stick butter into small cubes.
3. In a food processor, combine ½ cup flour, ½ cup sugar, ½ teaspoon baking powder, and a pinch of salt. Pulse a few times to mix. Add the butter and process until the mixture is well blended, about 10 seconds.
4. Crack in the egg and add ½ teaspoon vanilla. Process until the egg is just combined.
5. Drop tablespoons of the batter onto the peaches. If you have an adjustable broiler, reduce the heat to low; otherwise, cover the cobbler with aluminum foil to prevent burning. Broil until the biscuit topping is cooked through and the peaches have softened slightly and caramelized in places, 8 to 12 minutes.
6. If you've covered the top and the biscuit hasn't browned, remove the foil and broil until the top is golden. Serve hot or warm.

SPEED SERVES 6

Apple Crumble Under the Broiler

Close to instant gratification.

Ingredients

1 stick cold butter, plus more for greasing the pan

2 pounds apples

½ lemon

1 teaspoon cinnamon

1 cup flour

½ cup packed brown sugar

1 teaspoon baking powder

Salt

Prep | Cook

1. Turn the broiler to high; put the rack 6 inches from the heat.
   Grease a broiler-safe 9 × 13-inch pan with butter.
   Core and slice the apples; put them in the pan. Squeeze the lemon juice over the apples.

2. Sprinkle 1 teaspoon cinnamon over the apples and toss to coat. Put the pan under the broiler and cook, stirring occasionally to give the apples a chance to start softening, 10 minutes or more.
   Cut 1 stick butter into small cubes; put them in a medium bowl.

3. Add to the bowl 1 cup flour, ½ cup packed brown sugar, 1 teaspoon baking powder, and a sprinkle of salt. Rub the mixture together with your fingers, combining the ingredients and incorporating the butter until it becomes crumbly.

4. Remove the apples from the broiler, make sure they are in an even layer, and sprinkle the crumble over the top. Turn the broiler to low. If your broiler doesn't have a low setting, move the pan a few inches farther away from the heat.

5. Broil until the topping is golden and crisp, 10 to 15 minutes. Serve hot or warm.

SPEED SERVES 4

Key Lime Crumble

A deconstructed take on the pie—buttery graham crackers crumbled on rich custard.

Ingredients

4 tablespoons (½ stick) butter

12 graham crackers

One 14-ounce can sweetened condensed milk

4 eggs

3 limes

Prep | Cook

1. Heat the oven to 350°F.

   Put 4 tablespoons butter in a medium microwave-safe bowl and melt in the microwave.

   Put 12 graham crackers in a food processor and pulse a few times until crumbly. (Or crush them with your hands.)

2. Add the cracker crumbs to the melted butter and toss to coat.

3. Put the condensed milk in a medium bowl. Separate the eggs and add the yolks to the bowl (discard the whites or refrigerate for another use). Using an electric mixer, beat until well combined.

   Halve the limes.

4. Squeeze in the lime juice one half at a time, beating as you go, until the mixture thickens slightly. Pour it into 4 ramekins or 1 pie plate and sprinkle with the graham cracker crumbs.

5. Bake until the crumbs are golden and the filling is just firm, 15 to 20 minutes. Remove and cool on a rack for 10 minutes before serving. Serve with a spoon.

VARIATIONS

Orange Pie with Gingersnap Crumble
Swap 1 or 2 oranges for the limes (about ⅓ cups juice) and 2 cups crumbled gingersnaps for the graham crackers.

Fast Navigation

Helpful ways to search for recipes.

Recipes Within Recipes

Go-to components, built into other recipes

DRESSINGS

Bacon Vinaigrette 52
Gorgonzola Dressing 54
Lemon-Dill Yogurt Dressing 62
Caper and Mustard Dressing 72
Caesar Dressing 76–77
Tahini Dressing 86
Peanut-Lime Dressing 88
Hoisin Vinaigrette 90
Basil Vinaigrette 114
Parmesan Dressing 116
Rosemary-Mayo Dressing 120
Peanut Vinaigrette 158
Warm Bacon-Dijon Dressing 174
Russian Dressing 186
Cumin Vinaigrette 914

SAUCES AND SEASONINGS

Warm Cumin Oil 64
Herb Butter 132
Hummus 140
Salmorejo 176
Fast Tomato Meat Sauce 188
Mango Chutney 194
Parsley Pesto 218
Chile-Sesame-Drizzle Sauce 250
Basil Pesto 284
Fresh Tomato Sauce 290
Fast Skillet Tomato Sauce 320
Brown Butter 328
Peanut Sauce 330
Chile Oil 334
Cilantro-Scallion Pesto 340
Fresh Tomato-Garlic Sauce 420
Fresh Apple Sauce 426
Soy Dipping Sauce 444
Tartar Sauce 594
Saffron Aïoli 604
Olive Tapenade 622
Lemon Aïoli 624
Jerk Rub 650
Yogurt-Harissa Sauce 690
Chimichurri 718
Spicy Peanut Sauce 724
Spicy Enchilada Sauce 744
BBQ Rub 752
Toasted Almond Butter 814
Honey-Yogurt Sauce 818
Bacon Maple Syrup 870
Romesco 882
Warm Garlic Oil 884
Onion Dip 897
Orange Syrup 976
Whipped Cream 993

SALSAS

Fresh Salsa 170
Skillet Tomatillo Salsa 562
Avocado Salsa 612
Skillet Pineapple Salsa 756
Salsa Roja 894
Pico de Gallo 900

OTHER COMPONENTS

Fast Caramelized Onions 84
Crisp, Crumbled Tofu 88
Poached Eggs 98
Pickled Red Onions 168
Quick Pickled Daikon, Carrot, and Cucumber 180
Charred Onions 192
Fast Caramelized Onions 258
Toasted Breadcrumbs 286
Fried Onions 372
Fast Sticky Rice 374
Masa Cake 392
Grits 398
Parmesan Toast 482
Fried Tofu 520
Glazed Carrots 560
Caper-Herb Zucchini Ribbons 564
Quick-Chilled Cucumber Pickles 578
Dal 598
Roasted Corn 676
Sautéed Spinach with Mustard 708
Skillet Kimchi 712
Butternut Squash Purée 772
Greek Salad 798
Maple-Caramelized Pecans 824
Hard-Boiled Eggs 898
Cream Cheese Frosting 981
Meringue 993
Lemon Curd 994
Skillet Crumble Topping 995

Flavor Blasts

Recipes that pack a punch quickly

Endive and Radicchio with Bacon Vinaigrette 52
Green Bean Salad with Caramelized Onions and Toasted Almonds 84

Hot and Sour Bok Choy with Mussels 112
Korean-Style Beef Soup with Rice 250
Creamy Chinese Rice with Clams 358
Curried Lentils and Rice with Fried Onions 372
Glazed Brussels Sprouts with Vietnamese Flavors 422
Hot and Sour Black Beans with Bok Choy 478
BBQ Lima Beans with Collards 514
Malaysian-Style BBQ Fish with Cool Cucumbers 578
Za'atar Wings and Eggplant with Yogurt-Harissa Sauce 690
Stir-Fried Beef with Skillet Kimchi 712
Caramel Stir-Fried Beef and Green Beans 716
Seared Miso Lamb Chops with Carrots 792
Apricot-Cinnamon Couscous 820
Maple-Orange Oatmeal with Caramelized Pecans 824
Honey-Cheddar Grits with Sage 826
Fried Eggs with Chimichurri 836
Banana-Coconut Pancakes 866
Cheddar Waffles with Bacon Maple Syrup 870
Spiced Cashews with Bacon 877

Deconstructed Recipes

Familiar ingredients and flavors, streamlined to their bare essentials

Veggie Fajita Salad 96
BLT Salad with Rosemary-Mayo Dressing 120
Open-Face Lyonnaise Sandwich 174
Big T's Meat Sauce Sub 188
Broken Wonton Soup 248
Masa and Rajas 392
Unstuffed Cabbage 424
Shrimp and Cauliflower with Rustic Romesco 590
Fastest Chicken Parm 618
Charred Chicken and Pita with Gyro Fixings 648
Fast Florentine 850
Hard-Boiled Eggs with Dijon Mayo 898

Reinvented Recipes

Classics, updated so now they're both faster and better

Steakhouse Salad 54
Crab and Celery Root Remoulade 66
Asparagus and Kale Caesar Salad 76
Curried Tofu Salad with Pecans and Golden Raisins 92
Warm Three-Bean Potato Salad 102
Broccoli Tabbouleh with Charred Tomato and Lemon 124
Broiled Cheese 134
Spanish Dip 176
Bacon and Egg Drop Soup 210
Homemade Chicken Ramen 238
American Onion Soup 258
Rice Bowl with Sausage 368
Rice and Wings 382
Quinoa Puttanesca with Fresh Mozzarella 388
Couscous Helper 400
Skillet Shepherd's Pie with Quinoa Crust 408
Bubbling Caprese 414
Cauliflower "Polenta" with Mushrooms 432
Stuffed Poblanos with Black Beans and Cheese 434
Tortilla Lasagna 466
Eggs Sukiyaki 524
Olive Oil-Poached Halibut (or Other Thick Fillets) with Endive 570
Crisp Baked Chicken Tenders 674
Oven-Fried Chicken with Roasted Corn 676
Roast Turkey Breast with Sage Sausage Stuffing 700
Skillet Meat Loaf 742
Pork and Onion Carnitas 780
Breakfast Bruschetta 816
Endive Spears with Olives 883
Tortillas Rojas 894

Twofers

Recipes that combine two favorite dishes into one main course

Greek Salad with Orzo and Shrimp 110
Miso Soup with Scallops, Soba, and Spinach 234
Chipotle Rice and Corn with Seared Beef 366
Fast Thai Sticky Rice with Meaty Vegetable Sauce 374
Warm Tabbouleh with Mussels 396
Bok Choy Pancake with Soy Dipping Sauce 444
Vegetable Flatbread with Kale and White Bean Stew 462
Braised Lentils with Salmon 512
Manchurian Tofu and Cauliflower 522
Sole (or Other Thin Fillets) with Glazed Carrots 560
Olive Oil-Poached Halibut (or Other Thick Fillets) with Endive 570
Blackened Catfish (or Other Thick Fillets) with Green Beans 572
Shrimp Simmered in Dal 598
Chicken Marsala with Lots of Mushrooms 630
Sesame Chicken and Snow Peas 638
Chicken and Chile Fundido 658
Korean-Style Chicken and Vegetable Pancakes 662

Chicken, Vegetables, and Noodles in Soy Broth 670
Chicken and Sweet Potato Adobo 692
Pork Souvlaki with Zucchini 754
Five-Spice Pork Meatballs with Bok Choy 760
Pork Tenderloin with Butternut Purée 772
Lamb Chops with Balsamic Couscous 788
Fried Eggs with Mushrooms and Leeks 852

Slow Food, Done Fast

Celebration food to enjoy every day

Broiled Cheese 134
Eggplant Parmesan Sub 156
Bánh Mì 180
Reuben with All the Trimmings 186
Big T's Meat Sauce Sub 188
Steak Sandwich with Charred Onions 192
BBQ Chopped Pork and Slaw Sandwich 196
Creamy Parsnip Soup with Parsley Pesto 218
Butternut Squash Soup with Apples and Bacon 220
Fast Pho 236
Bone-In Chicken Noodle Soup 256
American Onion Soup 258
Shrimp Gumbo 260
Beef and Butter Bean Chili 272
Mac and Cheese 280
Broiled Ziti 298
Spaghetti with Nearly Instant Bolognese 318
Spaghetti and Drop Meatballs with Tomato Sauce 320
Three-Cheese Lasagna with Fresh Noodles 326
Fast Jook with Chicken and Snow Peas 360
Three-Stir Mushroom Risotto 370
Fast Thai Sticky Rice with Meaty Vegetable Sauce 374
Pozole and Pork Chops 404
Unstuffed Cabbage 424
Stuffed Poblanos with Black Beans and Cheese 434
Skillet Spanakopita 464
Fast Feijoada 504
Fish and Chips with Tartar Sauce 594
Scallop and Corn Pan Broil 602
Chicken with Creamy Spinach-Cashew Sauce 614
Fastest Chicken Parm 618
Poached Chicken and Asparagus with Lemon Aïoli 624
Chicken and Peppers with Black Bean "Mole" 652
Chicken, Vegetables, and Noodles in Soy Broth 670
Split Whole Chicken and Vegetables 686
Chicken and Dumplings with Lots of Peas 694
Roast Turkey with Sage Sausage Stuffing 700
Skillet Meat Loaf 742
Beef Stew 746
BBQ Baby Back Ribs 752
Porchetta-Style Pork Loin with Parsnips 776
Pork Stew and Dumplings 778
Pork and Onion Carnitas 780
Herb-Rubbed Leg of Lamb with Chopped Greek Salad 798
Roasting-Pan French Toast 830
Broiled Eggs 848
Fast Florentine 850
Spiced Cashews with Bacon 877
Crab Toast 892
Skewerless Chicken Satay 893
Warm-Pickled Cucumber Spears 896

Five Ingredients or Less

Not counting salt, pepper, oil, or butter.

Watercress with Peaches, Pecans, and Blue Cheese 44
Tomato Salad with Strawberries, Feta, and Balsamic 46
Arugula with Fried Eggs and Shaved Parmesan 50
Pressed Tofu and Cucumber Salad with Hoisin Vinaigrette 90
Bulgur, Apple, and Fennel Salad 94
Raw Butternut Squash Salad with Warm Edamame 100
Tomato and Chicken Salad with Basil Vinaigrette 114
BLT Salad with Rosemary-Mayo Dressing 120
Kimchi and Snow Pea Salad with Grilled or Broiled Beef 122
Charred Brussels Sprout Salad with Walnuts and Gorgonzola 126
Radish and Herb Butter Baguette 132
Broiled Cheese 134
Peanut Butter and Banana Sandwich with Honey and Raisins 138
Tofu Sandwich with Cucumber and Hoisin Mayo 142
Tuna Sandwich with Pickles and Mustard 146
Crab Salad Sandwich 148
Broiled Ham and Gruyère with Apples 150
Sausage and Pepper Sub 178
Steak Tacos with Lots of Options 182
Steak Sandwich with Charred Onions 192
Bacon and Egg Drop Soup 210
Frozen Vegetable Soup 214
Cacio e Pepe (Cheese and Pepper) 278
Mac and Cheese 280

Pasta with Broccoli Rabe and Ricotta **282**
Pasta with Fennel, White Beans, and Stock **288**
Pasta with Greens and Eggs **300**
Pasta with Tuna and Dried Tomatoes **304**
Ricotta Dumplings with Spinach and Brown Butter **328**
Rice Bowl with Sausage **368**
Couscous Gratin with Leeks and Gruyère **390**
Couscous Paella with Chicken and Zucchini **406**
Bubbling Caprese **414**
Sweet Pepper Queso Fundido **418**
Eggplant Steaks with Fresh Tomato-Garlic Sauce **420**
Potato Rösti with Fresh Apple Sauce **426**
Squash au Gratin with Toasted Nuts **430**
Scrambled Broccoli with Parmesan and Lemon **442**
Pan-Seared Corn and Pork **454**
Roasted Spaghetti Squash with Brown Butter and Walnuts **458**
Spanish Tortilla **460**
Cauliflower Tikka with Boiled Eggs **470**
Red Beans and Cabbage in Buttery Tomato Sauce **490**
Manchurian Tofu and Cauliflower **522**
Roasted Tofu with Sesame Drizzle **528**
Salmon and Asparagus with Toasted Bread Crumbs **536**
Smoky Shrimp Scampi **546**
Buffalo Shrimp **548**
Salmon with Gingery Greens **554**
Roasted Salmon with Potato Crust **558**
Roasted Trout (or Other Whole Fish) with Fennel and Orange **596**
Prosciutto-Crusted Chicken with Endive **620**
Chicken and Chard Gratin **656**
Braised and Glazed Chicken and Leeks **664**
Seared Duck Breast with Fruit Sauce **668**
Cornmeal Fried Chicken **672**
Crisp Baked Chicken Tenders **674**
Chicken and Tomato Packages **680**
Seared Steak with Mustard Spinach **708**
The Better Burger **726**
Braised Veal with Peas **734**
Pan-Roasted Beef Tenderloin with Potatoes **740**
Seared Pork Chops with Apples and Onions **750**
Browned and Braised Sausage and Endive **768**
Bangers and Mash **770**
Pork Tenderloin with Butternut Purée **772**
Fruit, Yogurt, and Graham Cracker Parfait **808**
Piña Colada Smoothie **810**
Broiled Grapefruit with Almond-Brown Sugar Crunch **812**
Toast with Toasted Almond Butter and Strawberries **814**
Breakfast Bruschetta **816**
Apricot-Cinnamon Couscous **820**
No-Bake Fruit and Cereal Bars **822**
Maple-Orange Oatmeal with Caramelized Pecans **824**
Honey-Cheddar Grits with Sage **826**
Omelet for Two **834**
Scrambled Eggs with Smoked Salmon and Dill **838**
Goat Cheese and Spinach Scrambled Eggs **840**
Broiled Eggs **848**
Pork 'n' Greens Breakfast Patties **858**
Prosciutto and Drop Biscuits **862**
Rosemary Popcorn **876**
Spiced Cashews with Bacon **877**
No-Cook Spanish Skewers **878**
Panfried Olives **879**
Broiled Radishes with Soy **880**
Edamame with Chili Salt **881**
Endive Spears with Olives **883**
Pinzimonio **884**
Goat Cheese Truffles **885**
Prosciutto-Wrapped Pears **886**
Greek Pita Pizzas **887**
Bagel Chips with Smoked Salmon **888**
Peel-and-Eat Shrimp **892**
Roasted Nuts with Ginger, Soy, and Honey **895**
Warm-Pickled Cucumber Spears **896**
Green Beans with Onion Dip **897**
Hard-Boiled Eggs with Dijon Mayo **898**
Parmesan Crisps **899**
Pizza Wedges **901**
Caramelized Honey-Orange Bananas **970**
Fruity Shaved Ice **971**
Broiled Peaches with Brown Sugar **972**
Watermelon Soup with Fresh Herbs **973**
Fruit Sorbet **974**
Black and White Milkshakes **975**
Orange Cream Sundaes **976**
Salted Chocolate Peanut Butter Balls **982**
Chocolate-Covered Pretzels **986**
Molten Chocolate Cake **987**
Chocolate-Orange Pudding **990**
Chocolate Custard Soup **992**
Berry Fool **996**
Sautéed Apple Crunch **997**
Chocolate Peanut Brittle **999**
Key Lime Crumble **1003**

Vegetarian Main Dishes

Meatless meals are everywhere in this book.

SALADS

Watercress with Peaches, Pecans, and Blue Cheese 44
Tomato Salad with Strawberries, Feta, and Balsamic 46
Arugula with Fried Eggs and Shaved Parmesan 50
Grated Beet and Carrot Salad with Toasted Cashews 56
Puffed Rice Salad with Dates and Almonds 60
White Bean and Cucumber Salad with Yogurt and Dill 62
Chickpea and Carrot Salad with Warm Cumin Oil 64
Asparagus and Kale Caesar Salad 76
Warm Kale Salad with Pine Nuts and Balsamic Currants 80
Warm Pickled Cauliflower Salad with Roasted Red Peppers 82
Green Bean Salad with Caramelized Onions and Toasted Almonds 84
Broiled Eggplant and Zucchini Salad with Tahini Dressing 86
Cabbage with Crisp Tofu and Peanut-Lime Dressing 88
Pressed Tofu and Cucumber Salad with Hoisin Vinaigrette 90
Curried Tofu Salad with Pecans and Golden Raisins 92
Bulgur, Apple, and Fennel Salad 94
Veggie Fajita Salad 96
Warm Escarole and White Bean Salad with Poached Eggs 98
Raw Butternut Squash Salad with Warm Edamame 100
Warm Three-Bean Potato Salad 102
Broccoli Tabbouleh with Charred Tomato and Lemon 124
Charred Brussels Sprout Salad with Walnuts and Gorgonzola 126

SANDWICHES

Radish and Herb Butter Baguette 132
Broiled Cheese 134
Peanut Butter and Banana Sandwich with Honey and Raisins 138
Hummus and Vegetable Pita Pockets 140
Tofu Sandwich with Cucumber and Hoisin Mayo 142
Smoky Black Bean and Carrot Burgers152
Egg Salad Sandwich with Lots of Vegetables 154
Eggplant Parmesan Sub 156

SOUPS AND STEWS

Green Gazpacho 204
Spicy Black Bean Soup 208
Frozen Vegetable Soup 214
Provençal Tomato Soup with Fennel 216
Creamy Parsnip Soup with Parsley Pesto 218
Tomato and Bread Soup with White Beans 224
Pasta e Fagioli 226
Chickpea and Couscous Stew with Moroccan Spices 228
Fast Pho 236

PASTA AND NOODLES

Cacio e Pepe (Cheese and Pepper) 278
Pasta with Broccoli Rabe and Ricotta 282
Pasta with Pesto and Cherry Tomatoes 284
Pasta with Artichokes, Toasted Bread Crumbs, and Lemon 286
Pasta with Fennel, White Beans, and Stock 288
Spaghetti with Garlicky Fresh Tomato Sauce 290
Pasta with Spicy Eggplant and Tomato Sauce 292
Broiled Ziti 298
Pasta with Greens and Eggs 300
Orzo Risotto with Asparagus and "Poached" Eggs 324
Three-Cheese Lasagna with Fresh Noodles 326
Ricotta Dumplings with Spinach and Brown Butter 328
Noodles with Snow Peas and Chile Oil 334
Udon with Teriyaki Tofu 336
Noodles, Shrimp, and Sweet Potatoes in Curry Broth 338

RICE AND GRAINS

Rice, Beans, and Broccoli 350
Rice with Cabbage, Scrambled Eggs, and Scallions 356
Three-Stir Mushroom Risotto 370
Curried Lentils and Rice with Fried Onions 372

Quinoa Pilaf with Chickpeas and Dried Fruit 384
Smoky Bulgur with Eggplant, Dried Tomatoes, and Feta 386
Couscous Gratin with Leeks and Gruyère 390
Masa and Rajas 392

VEGETABLES

Bubbling Caprese 414
Sweet Pepper Queso Fundido 418
Eggplant Steaks with Fresh Tomato-Garlic Sauce 420
Glazed Brussels Sprouts with Vietnamese Flavors 422
Unstuffed Cabbage 424
Potato Rösti with Fresh Apple Sauce 426
Squash au Gratin with Toasted Nuts 430
Cauliflower "Polenta" with Mushrooms 432
Stuffed Poblanos with Black Beans and Cheese 434
Sweet Potato Flautas 436
Potato and Spinach Saag 438
Zucchini Fattoush 440
Scrambled Broccoli with Parmesan and Lemon 442
Bok Choy Pancake with Soy Dipping Sauce 444
Fried Fennel and Arugula 446
Roasted Spaghetti Squash with Brown Butter and Walnuts 458
Spanish Tortilla 460
Vegetable Flatbread with Kale and White Bean Stew 462
Cherry Tomato Cobbler 464
Tortilla Lasagna 466
Skillet Spanakopita 468
Cauliflower Tikka with Boiled Eggs 470

BEANS AND TOFU

Beans on Toast 476
Hot and Sour Black Beans with Bok Choy 478
Stewed White Beans and Tomatoes with Parmesan Toast 482
Stir-Fried Curried Chickpeas with Potatoes and Carrots 486
Lemony Limas with Broccoli 488
Red Beans and Cabbage in Buttery Tomato Sauce 490
Lima Bean and Cabbage Gratin with Rye Crumbs 492
White Bean and Spinach Frittata 494
Lentil and Mushroom Stew 506
Red Lentils with Toasted Cauliflower 508
Tomato-Braised Lentils and Potatoes 510
Stir-Fried Tofu and Green Beans 516
Deep-Fried Tofu with Peanut Sauce and Scallions 520
Manchurian Tofu and Cauliflower 522
Eggs Sukiyaki 524
Smoky Tofu and Black Bean Chili 526
Roasted Tofu with Sesame Drizzle 528
Braised Tofu with Tomatoes and Broccoli 530

BREAKFAST

Loaded Muesli 806
Fruit, Yogurt, and Graham Cracker Parfait 808
Piña Colada Smoothie 810
Broiled Grapefruit with Almond-Brown Sugar Crunch 812
Toast with Toasted Almond Butter and Strawberries 814
Breakfast Bruschetta 816
Sautéed Apples and Bananas with Honey-Yogurt Sauce 818
Apricot-Cinnamon Couscous 820
No-Bake Fruit and Cereal Bars 822
Maple-Orange Oatmeal with Caramelized Pecans 824
Honey-Cheddar Grits with Sage 826
Roasting-Pan French Toast 830
Tortilla French Toast 832
Fried Eggs with Chimichurri 836
Goat Cheese and Spinach Scrambled Eggs 840
Tortilla Scramble 842
Chipotle Black Beans with Fried Eggs 846
Broiled Eggs 848
Fast Florentine 850
Fried Eggs with Mushrooms and Leeks 852
Jalapeño-Scallion Johnnycakes 864
Banana-Coconut Pancakes 866
Orange-Ricotta Pancakes 868

Kitchen Notes

Tips, tricks, ingredients, and other invaluable information.

SEASONINGS

Dressing Salad on the Fly 45
Shaving Parmesan 51
More Uses for Warm Vinaigrette 53
DIY Nut Butter 139
"Blooming" Ground Spices 229
Miso 235
Plenty of Pestos 285
Storing Pesto 285
Making Chile Oil 335
Soy Sauce 337
Smoked Paprika 425
Chipotles in Adobo 847

FRUITS AND VEGETABLES

Raw Root Vegetables 57
Versatile Dill 63
The Citrus Cycle 69
Snapping Asparagus 77
Grilling Greens 79
Using Jarred Roasted Peppers 83
Salting Vegetables 91
Types of Apples 95
Two Vegetables, One Pot 103
Types of Radishes 105
Pitting Olives 111
Toasted Bread Salad 119
Kimchi 123
Broiled Bits 127
Shucking Corn 207
Peeling Butternut Squash 221
Canned Tomato Tricks 227
Frozen, Jarred, and Canned Artichokes 287
Savoy Cabbage 425
Stripping Rosemary 433
Creamy Green Sauces 439
Vegetable Pan Sauce 631

PASTA, GRAINS, AND BEANS

Finding Ramen 239
Masa Harina 241
From Rice Comes Broth 251
The Fastest Legumes 267
Pasta Cooking Times 291
Pasta with Olive Oil and Other Stuff 305
Egg Roll Wrappers and Wonton Skins 327
Fresh Pasta Options 327
Asian Noodle Dishes with Pasta 331
One-Pot Noodles 339
Substituting Brown Rice for White 351
Fermented Black Beans 359
Rice Cakes 377
Paella Rice 379
Crisp Grains 409
Impromptu Lasagnas and Gratins 467
Braising with Beans 511
Timing Bulgur 789
Big Batch Muesli or Granola 807
Topping Grits 827
A Few Tips for Cooking Pancakes 867
Leaving Lumps 869

MEAT, FISH, POULTRY, AND DAIRY

Tofu for Chicken 93
Poaching Eggs 99
Chopping Chicken 107
Chicken as Bruschetta 109
Bacon in the Microwave 121
Turning Eggs into Flower Petals 211
Seasoning with Smoked Pork 269
Steam-Poached Eggs 325
Sustainable Canned Tuna 395
Saving Shellfish Liquid 397
Eggs to the Rescue 443
Cooking with Ham 503
Salmon Temperature 539
Making the Sushi Grade 541
Shrimp, Squid, and Scallop Doneness 551
Swapping Mussels for Clams 553
Fish Roasts 575
Oily Fish 585
Serving Whole Fish 597
Deveining Shrimp 599
Prying Open Mussels and Clams 605
Mexican Cheeses 659
Butterflying a Chicken 687
Shaping Meat Loaf 699
Turkey Parts 703
A Word on Veal 733
Give It a Rest 741
Boneless vs. Bone-In Pork Chops 751
Smoked Pork Steaks 765
Sausage Doneness 771
A Fast Roast 773
Lamb Chops 789
Yogurt 809
Cooking Fried Eggs Evenly 837
Scrambling Eggs 839
Scrambled Eggs for a Crowd 841

COOKING TECHNIQUES

Cooking, Once Removed 117
One Sandwich is Faster than Four 133
Brushing vs. Spreading Butter 149
Wrap It Up 167
Open Your Mind to Opening Your Sandwich 175
Anything Tacos 183
The Time-Texture Continuum 215
Thickening with Beans 247
Chop-and-Drop Soups 253
Thickening with Cornstarch 271
Salting Pasta Water 279
Filling the Pot 281
Stock for Water 385
Braising and Glazing 423
Eating Around the Stove 449
Cooking with Beer 451
Oil Poaching Meets Steaming 571
Blackened Anything 573
Two Skewers, One Kebab 577
Broiling and Bubbling 653
Parchment Packages 681
Rigging a Fast Steamer 685
Wok the Other Way 731
Dried Fruit in the Food Processor 823

Index

Page numbers in *italics* indicate illustrations.

A

Adobo-style
- canned chipotles in adobo, 847
- chicken and sweet potato, 692–693
- curried chicken and potatoes, 693

Aïoli
- curry, 625
- lemon, 624–625
- lemon-soy, 625
- lemon-tarragon, 161
- saffron, 604–605
- smoked paprika, 595, 625

Almond(s)
- broccoli and, 926
- -brown sugar crunch, broiled grapefruit with, 812–813
- cookie dough, 977
- in maple-almond grits, 827
- salad
  - arugula with apricots, manchego, and, 45
  - charred Brussels sprouts with ricotta salata and, 127
  - green bean, with caramelized onions and, 84–85
  - puffed rice, with dates and, 60–61
- spiced, sautéed with bacon, 877
- stew, green bean, with tomatoes, olives, and, 255
- and strawberry smoothie, 811

Almond butter
- and apple sandwich, 139
- chocolate, balls, 982
- toast with strawberries and, 814–815

Almond extract, 985, 992

Anaheim peppers, 457

Ancho chiles, 457

Anchovies
- cauliflower stewed with, 269
- pasta with garlic and, 305
- seasoning with, 943

Andouille
- black-eyed pea and Southern greens soup with, 247
- rice bowl with, 369

Appetizers, 872–901. *See also* Sides
- about, 874–875
- bagel chips, 888
- broiled radishes with olive oil and lemon, 880
- broiled radishes with soy, 880
- chicken satay, skewerless, 893
- cocktail meatballs, master recipe, 890–891
- crab toast, 889
- crisps, 899
- edamame with chili salt, 881
- endive spears, 883
- goat cheese truffles, 885
- Greek pita pizzas, 887
- green beans with onion dip, 897
- ham-wrapped apples, 886
- hard-boiled eggs with curry mayo, 898
- hard-boiled eggs with Dijon mayo, 898
- no-cook skewers, 878
- nuts, roasted, 895
- nuts, spiced, 877
- panfried olives, 879
- peel-and-eat shrimp, 892
- pinzimonio, 884
- pizza wedges, 901
- prosciutto-wrapped
  - cantaloupe, 886
  - pears, 886
  - tomatoes, 886
- quesadillas with pico de gallo, 900
- raw veggies with romesco, 882
- rosemary popcorn, 876
- tortillas rojas, 894
- warm-pickled
  - bell peppers, 896
  - carrots, 896
  - cucumber spears, 896
  - zucchini, 896

Apple(s)
- about
  - prep shortcuts, *32*
  - storing, 19
  - types of, 95
- and almond butter sandwich, 139
- bacon-crusted chicken with, 620–621
- and bananas, sautéed, with honey-yogurt sauce, 818–819
- bulgur and fennel salad with, 94–95
- butternut squash soup with bacon and, 220–221
- caramelized, 818–819
- charred Brussels sprout salad with, 127
- crumble, broiled, 1002
- -ginger smoothie, 811
- ham and Gruyère sandwich, broiled, with, 150–151
- ham-wrapped, 886
- and honey-mustard baguette, 133
- mustard-glazed fish with, 579
- pork chops, seared, with onions and, 750–751
- potato rösti with apple sauce, 426–427
- pumpkin soup with pumpkin seeds and, 221
- and sauerkraut salad, with pork, 123
- sautéed, breakfast patties with, 859
- spinach with walnuts, goat cheese, and, 45
- tacos, crisp pork and, 185
- toast with walnut butter and, 815
- turkey salad sandwich with sage and, 165

Apple cider
- in applejack sundaes, 976
- -braised turkey and squash, 703
- in Dijon-garlic-cider roasted chicken and carrots, 679

Applejack sundaes, 976

Apricot(s)
- arugula with Marcona almonds, manchego, and, 45
- -cardamom muesli, 807
- chicken and cauliflower curry with, 642–643
- -cinnamon couscous, 820–821
- dried, puffed wheat salad with pistachios and, 61

Arborio rice, 352

Arroz con pollo, 696–697

Artichokes
- about, 287
- pasta with bread crumbs, lemon, and, 286–287

Arugula
- about, 49
- with apricots, Marcona almonds, and manchego, 45
- and egg salad sandwich, 155
- with eggs, fried, and shaved Parmesan, 50–51
- farro and white beans with Parmesan and, 395
- and fried fennel, 446–447
- and jícama fry salad with creamy lime sauce, 447

and pea frittata, 495
with scallops, seared, and orange dressing, 79
Asian greens, hot and sour soup with tofu and, 271
Asian noodles, 332–333
Asparagus
about, 21, 77
and beef, stir-fried, with scallions and ginger, 731
chipotle-marinated flank steak and, 723
creamy soup with rustic mint pesto, 219
gratin, 929
hot and sour beef with, 479
and kale Caesar salad, 76–77
lemony, with sole, 561
orzo risotto with eggs and, 324–325
pasta with ricotta and, 283
and poached chicken with lemon aïoli, 624–625
polenta with chicken and, 403
and salmon with toasted bread crumbs, 536–537
and scallops with toasted bread crumbs, 537
and soy-lemon edamame, 489
Avocado(es)
about, *30*
chicken, bacon, and tomato wrap with, 166–167
chipotle-avocado spread, 159
green bean salad with fresh tuna and, 74–75
green bean salad with tofu and, 75
in green gazpacho, 204–205
with hot sauce and cilantro, 920
with lemon and salt, 920
with lime and chili salt, 920
with rice vinegar and peanuts, 920
in salsa, 612–613
soup with crab and corn, 206–207
with soy sauce and sesame seeds, 920
tuna sandwich with cilantro and, 147

B

Baby back ribs, BBQ, 752–753
Bacon
about, 121, 943
in BBQ pinto beans with fried eggs, 846–847
in BLT salad with rosemary-mayo dressing, 120–121
braised cabbage, kimchi, and, 453
Brussels sprouts with, 958
chicken, avocado, and tomato wrap with, 166–167
chicken, tomato, and blue cheese wrap with, 167
-crusted chicken with apples, 621
curried rice, beans, and broccoli with, 351
in fast feijoada, 504–505
green beans, quick-stewed, with, 450–451
johnnycakes, 865
maple syrup, 870–871
in maple-bacon breakfast bruschetta, 817
panfried
soft-shell crabs with leeks and, 583
trout with Brussels sprouts and, 583
trout with leeks and, 582–583
peas with onion and, 934
risotto-style pasta with mushrooms and, 323
seafood chowder with, 231
soup
butternut squash, with apples and, 220–221
egg drop and, 210–211
egg drop and, toast in, 211
egg drop and, with greens, 211
pancetta in carbonara soup, 211
sweet potato, with pears and, 221
tomato and peach gazpacho with, 203
spiced nuts sautéed with, 877
in steakhouse salad, 55
in vinaigrettes, 52–53
white beans with greens, garlic, and, 481
Bagel chips
homemade, 888
with prosciutto, tomato, and ricotta, 888
with smoked salmon, 888
Baguettes
about, 136
apple and honey-mustard, 133
fennel and garlic butter, 133
goat cheese, peach, and pecan, 133
jícama and chile mayo, 133
radish and herb butter, 132–133
ricotta and olive, 133
Baked
chicken tenders, 674–675
crab cakes, 600–601
eggs, 849
Baking powder, 17, 979
Baking soda, 17, 979
Banana(s)
and apples, sautéed, with honey-yogurt sauce, 818–819
caramelized, 970
-chocolate chip pancakes, 867
in chocolate chunk banana cupcakes, 1000
chocolate-banana pudding, 990
-coconut pancakes, 866–867
in maple-banana breakfast bruschetta, 817
and peanut butter sandwich with honey and raisins, 138–139
praline banana cupcakes, 1000
-rum cupcakes, 1000
Bangers and mash, 770–771
Bánh mì, 180–181
Barbecue (BBQ)
baby back ribs, 752–753
bacon pinto beans with fried eggs, 846–847
black-eyed pea and sweet potato burgers, 153
cauliflower tikka with boiled eggs, 471
chicken
blackened, sandwich with pickled cucumbers, 169
collard-wrapped, 685
sandwich with peach chutney, 195
-spiced cutlets with pinto beans and ham, 627
thighs with crisp cabbage and red onion, 655
chopped pork and slaw sandwich, 196–197
fish, Malaysian-style, 578–579
-glazed ham steaks with collards, 765
lima beans with collards, 514–515
skillet meat loaf, 743
sweet potato and black-eyed pea burgers, 153
tofu and cauliflower, 523
Barbecue sauce
Chinese-style, 145
chipotle, 145
Dijon, 145
ginger-hoisin, 753
maple-Dijon, 753
master recipe, 145
Barley, pearled, 353, 355
Basil
in bubbling caprese, 414–415
in cantaloupe and basil smoothie, 811
and chicken meatballs, 891
endive spears with, 883
noodles with chicken, peppers, and, 342–343
rice with tomatoes, scrambled eggs, and, 357
scrambled eggs with prosciutto and, 839
tomato sauce with chiles and, 592–593
tomato-basil sauce, 593
in vinaigrette, 114–115
Basmati rice
about, 352

Basmati rice *(cont.)*
cooking times, 355
pilaf, recipe-free, *364–365*
Bass, striped. *See* Striped bass
Bay scallops, pasta with tomatoes and, 311
BBQ. *See* Barbecue (BBQ)
Bean(s), 472–515. *See also specific types of beans*
about
braising with, 511
dried vs. canned, 484
flavoring, 497
freezing, 484
soaking, 496–497
storing, 19, 484–485
substituting ingredients, 21
thickening with, 247
chipotle chicken and dumplings with, 695
master recipe, 496–497
in pasta e fagioli, 226–227
refried, 938
on toast, 476–477
Bean curd. *See* Tofu
Bean sprouts
ginger-orange, 919
hot and sour soup with, 271
jook with beef and, 361
noodles with beef and, 345
with olive oil and rosemary, 919
scallion-miso, 919
sole with sesame, 561
Thai coconut soup with, 253
Thai peanut chicken with crisp cabbage and, 654–655
Bean threads, 333
Beef, 708–747. *See also* Steak; Veal
about
cuts of meat, 714–715
homemade cold cuts, master recipe, 775
stock, master recipe, 212
in Big T's meat sauce sub, 188–189
burger, better, 726–727
and butter bean chili, 272–273
in cabbage, unstuffed, with ground meat, 425
carbonnade with mushrooms, 747
chipotle rice and corn with, 366–367
and eggplant, curry-braised, 738–739
hot and sour, with asparagus, 479
jook with bean sprouts and, 361
kebabs, with mushrooms and spicy peanut sauce, 724–725
kebabs, with onions and mustard-rosemary sauce, 725
kimchi and snow pea salad with, 122–123
meatballs
and bulgur, with chipotle tomato sauce, 801
chipotle, 891
and spaghetti with tomato sauce, 320–321
teriyaki, 890
noodles
with bean sprouts and, 345
with celery and, 344–345
with cilantro-scallion pesto and, 341
with onions, mint, and, 343
spaghetti and drop meatballs with tomato sauce, 320–321
pan-roasted tenderloin with chile sweet potatoes, 741
pan-roasted tenderloin with potatoes, 740–741
and potatoes, curry-braised, 739
in Reuben sandwich, 186
sesame, and broccoli, 639
skillet meat loaf, 742–743
sloppy Joes, 728–729
soup
hot and sour, with, 271
and kimchi, with rice, 251
Korean-style beef, with rice, 250–251
in pho, slow with meat, 237
and red cabbage, 245
Thai coconut, with, 252–253
stew, 746–747
stir-fried
and asparagus, with scallions and ginger, 731
and broccoli, with scallions and ginger, 730–731
caramel, with green beans, 716–717
caramel, with peppers, 717
with skillet kimchi, 712–713
stroganoff, 647
tenderloin, pan-roasted, with chile sweet potatoes, 741
tenderloin, pan-roasted, with potatoes, 740–741
teriyaki, udon with, 337
Beer
about, 451
-braised black beans and corn with chorizo, 499
-braised black beans with chicken and corn, 498–499
-braised pinto beans with chiles and sour cream, 499
braised pork with cabbage and, 766–767
in green beans, quick-stewed, with bacon, 450–451
in maple-chile-beer roasted chicken and peppers, 679
Beet(s)
gratin with toasted nuts, 431
rösti with pear sauce, 427
salad
and cabbage, 57
and carrot, with olives, mint, and lemon, 57
and carrot, with toasted cashews, 56–57
in three Bs pasta, 313
Belgian endive. *See* Endive
Bell pepper(s)
about, *30*, 457
and beef, caramel stir-fried, 717
with chicken, basil, and noodles, 342–343
in chicken, maple-chile-beer roasted, and peppers, 679
and chicken, poached, with smoked paprika aïoli, 625
and chicken, with black bean mole, 652–653
and chicken, with pumpkin seed mole, 653
crab and egg salad with, 105
eggs and steak with onions and, 854–855
fajita onions and, 928
in lamb, cumin, with green peppers, 639
and pinto beans in buttery tomato sauce, 491
with pork, cilantro, and noodles, 343
pork paprikash with, 755
queso fundido, sweet pepper, 418–419
in sausage and pepper salad with mustard dressing, 121
and sausage sub, 178–179
and sausage sub with melted mozzarella, 179
sautéed, breakfast patties with, 859
stir-fried lamb with cumin and, 791
stir-fried lamb with curry and, 791
warm-pickled, 896
Berry fool, 996
Big T's meat sauce sub, 188–189
Biscuits, drop, 862–863
Black and white milkshakes, 975
Black bean(s)
beer-braised, with chicken and corn, 498–499
beer-braised, with chorizo and corn, 499

burgers, smoky, with carrots, 152–153
burrito, with chicken, 170–171
burrito, with steak and salsa, 171
and cabbage gratin with tortilla crumbs and Jack, 493
and cabbage salad with sour cream and cilantro, 63
chile-cumin, 937
chili, tofu and, 526–527
in chipotle chicken and dumplings with beans, 695
chipotle, with fried eggs, 846–847
with chorizo, greens, and garlic, 481
and corn salad with garlic chicken, 108–109
and corn salad with shrimp, 109
in fast feijoada, 504–505
hot and sour, with bok choy, 478–479
and lamb chili, 273
mole, chicken and peppers with, 652–653
pasta with chorizo, red onions, and, 289
pork stew with collards and, 783
sauce, stir-fried chicken and broccoli with, 634–635
sauce, stir-fried chicken and cauliflower with, 635
sesame-soy, 937
soup, smoky, 209
soup, spicy, 208–209
stir-fried pork with onions and, 749
stuffed poblanos with cheese and, 434–435
and three-bean and sweet potato salad, warm, 103
with tomato and feta, 937
in tomato salsa, 145
and veggie fajita salad, 97

Black pepper
about, 15
scallops and broccoli, 550–551
shrimp and broccoli, 551
squid and bok choy, 551

Blackened
catfish or fish fillets with green beans, 572–573
chicken sandwich, BBQ, with pickled cucumbers, 169
chicken sandwich with pickled red onions, 168–169

Black-eyed pea(s)
in hoppin' John with collards, 362–363
soup, andouille, Southern greens, and, 247
and sweet potato burgers, 153
and tofu chili with collards, 527

"Blooming" ground spices, 229

BLT
salad with rosemary-mayo dressing, 120–121
wrap, chipotle, 167

Blue cheese
in Buffalo shrimp, 548–549
chicken and chard gratin with walnuts and, 657
chicken, bacon, and tomato wrap with, 167
and chicken sausage over sautéed kale, 661
endive spears with olives and, 883
endive with fried eggs and, 51
leek soup with, 259
pasta with, 279
peach and tarragon salad with, 922
skillet meat loaf, 743
slaw, Buffalo shrimp with, 549
in three Bs pasta, 312–313
watercress with peaches, pecans, and, 44–45
in yogurt-blue cheese sauce, 691

Blue Ocean Institute, 587

Blueberry(ies)
maple syrup, 871
toast with cashew butter and, 815
and tofu smoothie, 811

Boiled
eggs with cauliflower tikka, 470–471
eggs with celery root rémoulade, 67
peel-and-eat shrimp, 892

Bok choy
black beans, hot and sour, with, 478–479
chicken, Chinese-style poached, and, 625
chicken, hot and sour, with, 479
grilled or broiled, seared scallops with, 79
hot and sour, with mussels, 112–113
pancake with soy dipping sauce, 444–445
and pork meat loaf, 699
pork meatballs, five-spice, with, 761
rice with scrambled eggs, scallions and, 357
soup
hot and sour, with pork and, 270–271
miso, with tofu, soba, and, 235
peanut, Chinese-style, with tofu and, 243
squid, black pepper, 551
stir-fried, 927
sweet and sour, salmon with, 555
tuna sandwich, seared, with soy mayo and, 162–163

Bolognese-style
skillet shepherd's pie, 409
spaghetti, 318–319

Bonito flakes
in dashi, 213
in miso soup, 234–235

Boozy
black and white milkshakes, 975
pecan-bourbon brownies, 998
tiramisu, 991

Boston (butter) lettuce
about, 48
in BLT salad with rosemary-mayo dressing, 120–121
in steak, lettuce, and herb wrap, 710–711

Bourbon
in applejack sundaes, 976
in boozy black and white milkshakes, 970
in pecan-bourbon brownies, 998

Braising
about
with beans, 511
glazing and, 423
beer-braised
black beans with chicken and corn, 498–499
black beans with chorizo and corn, 499
pinto beans with chiles and sour cream, 499
cabbage, kimchi, and bacon, 453
cabbage, sauerkraut, and ham, 452–453
chicken and leeks, braised and glazed, 664–665
curry-braised beef and eggplant, 738–739
curry-braised beef and potatoes, 739
lamb, Moroccan, with couscous and olives, 787
lentils
with chicken, 513
with pork chops, 513
and potatoes, 510–511
with salmon, 512–513
meat, recipe-free, *736–737*
pork
with cabbage and beer, 766–767
with cabbage and wine, 767
with celery and wine, 767
Moroccan-style, with couscous and grapes, 786–787
Provençal, and fennel, 784–785

Braising *(cont.)*
recipe-free, *736–737*
sausage, browned, and endive, 768–769
tofu with tomatoes, 530–531
veal
with edamame, 735
with garlic and white beans, 735
with peas, 734–735
vegetables, heartier, 423
wine-braised turkey, 702–703
wine-braised white beans with cherry tomatoes and Parmesan, 499
Bratwurst
in cabbage soup with smoked sausage, 244–245
and onion sub, 179
Bread. *See also* Toasted bread
about
croutons for salads, 47, 57
storing, 137
types of, 136–137
and charred chicken, with hero fixings, 649
garlic, 906
Middle Eastern chicken and bread salad, 118–119
in tomato and bread soup
with eggplant, 225
with hearty greens, 225
with white beans, 224–225
with zucchini, 225
warm buttery, 906
Bread crumbs
fish fillets or steaks and toasted, 537
fried, 293, 930
master recipe, 71
Parmesan, 930
parsley, 930
pasta with artichokes, lemon, and, 286–287
pasta with fennel and, 287
salmon with asparagus and toasted, 536–537
scallops with asparagus and toasted, 537
Breaded
baked potato and crab cakes, 601
chicken breasts with pan sauce, 616–617
Breakfast, 802–871
about, 804–805
eggs, 828–857
fruit, grains, toast, and cereal, 806–827
meats, 858–863
pancakes and waffles, 864–871
prosciutto and drop biscuits, 862–863
scrambles, recipe-free, *844–845*
smoothies, 810–811
Brie and turkey sandwich, broiled, with tomatoes, 151
Brioche, 136
Broccoli
about, *31*
beef, sesame, and, 639
and beef, stir-fried, with scallions and ginger, 730–731
charred, yellow lentils with, 509
and cheddar, 926
chicken soup with rice and, 263
chicken, stir-fried, with black bean sauce and, 634–635
chicken, stir-fried, with tomato-soy sauce and, 635
couscous gratin with onions, cheddar, and, 391
lemony lima beans with, 488–489
and pork, stir-fried, with scallions and ginger, 730–731
rice, beans, and, 350–351
scallops, black pepper and, 550–551
scrambled, with Parmesan and lemon, 442–443
scrambled, with soy sauce and lime, 443
seared, 925
shrimp, black pepper and, 551
tabbouleh with charred tomato and lemon, 124–125
and toasted almonds, 926
tofu, braised, with tomatoes and, 530–531
two-step, 926
warm pickled salad, 83
Broccoli rabe
chicken and ricotta sausage over, 660–661
and chicken gratin, 657
pancake with ricotta dipping sauce, 445
pasta with ricotta and, 282–283
pork meatballs, mustard-herb, with, 761
and sausage sub, 179
steamed, with shrimp, 113
stewed with tons of garlic, 269
and turkey hero, 172–173
Broiled(ing)
about, 720–721
apple crumble, 1002
beef, kimchi and snow pea salad with, 122–123
chicken
about, 653
breasts, 612–613
homemade cold cuts, master recipe, 774
split whole, and vegetables, 686–687
eggs, 848–849
fish, 539, 562–563
grains, 409
grapefruit, 812–813
peaches, 972, 1001
polenta, 947
pork
curry-rubbed tenderloin with mango salsa, 757
jerk with pineapple, 755
paprika-rubbed tenderloin with peach and tomato salsa, 757
paprikash with red peppers, 755
pork tenderloin, master recipe, 775
sauerkraut and apple salad with, 123
souvlaki with zucchini, 754–755
spice-rubbed tenderloin with pineapple salsa, 756–757
sandwiches
cheese, 134–135
ham and Gruyère with apples, 150–151
prosciutto and mozzarella, with melon, 151
salami and provolone sandwich with roasted red pepper, 151
turkey and Brie, with tomatoes, 151
vegetables
bok choy with seared scallops, 79
caprese, bubbling, 414–415
cherry tomatoes, 931
eggplant, 86–87
radishes, 880
romaine with seared scallops, 78–79
with white bean dressing, 97
Broths
about, 251
coconut curry, 671
creamy tomato, 580–581
curry, 338–339
lemongrass, 339
miso, 671
soy, 581, 670–671
spicy tomato, 605
Brown butter
dumplings, ricotta, with spinach and, 328–329
roasted spaghetti squash with walnuts and, 458–459
Brown lentils, 485
Brown rice
parcooking, 351
quick, 941
stir-ins for, 941
Brown sugar
about, 978
broiled grapefruit with, 812–813

broiled peaches with, 972
pecan with bacon and, 877
Brownies, pecan-bourbon, 998
Bruschetta
breakfast, 816–817
as a side, 909
Brussels sprouts
about, 127
with bacon, 958
charred salad, 126–127
chicken, braised and glazed, with, 665
and chicken wings, hot, with yogurt-blue cheese sauce, 691
with chorizo, 958
glazed, with Vietnamese flavors, 422–423
pork chops, seared, with, 751
with sausage, 958
in three Bs pasta, 312–313
trout, panfried, with bacon and, 583
Buffalo cauliflower, 549
Buffalo shrimp, 548–549
Buffalo tofu sandwich, 143
Bulgur
about, 125, 353, 355
balsamic, lamb chops with, 789
and beef meatballs in tomato sauce, 801
and chicken meatballs in tomato sauce, 801
with corn, 946
with dried cranberries and orange, 946
and lamb meatballs in tomato sauce, 800–801
with lemon and parsley, 946
lemony, with zucchini, olives, and ricotta salata, 387
pilaf, fish kebabs over, 576–577
pilaf, recipe-free, *364–365*
salad
apple and fennel salad with, 94–95
apple and fennel salad with crisp ham and, 95
broccoli tabbouleh with tomatoes and lemon, 124–125
cauliflower tabbouleh with tomato and lime, 125
fennel and radish tabbouleh with tomato and lime, 125
warm tabbouleh with mussels, 396–397
warm tabbouleh with tuna, 397
smoky
with eggplant, dates, and feta, 387
with eggplant, dried tomatoes, and feta, 386–387
with eggplant, roasted red peppers, and manchego, 387
Burgers
better beef, 726–727
black bean and carrot, smoky, 152–153
black-eyed pea and sweet potato, 153
cheeseburgers, 727
lamb and red onion, 727
pork and scallion, 727
turkey, 666–667
white bean and zucchini, 153
Burritos
breakfast, 856–857
chicken and black bean, 170–171
shrimp and white bean, 171
steak and black bean, 170–171
Butter(y)
about
as dessert staple, 978
seasoning with, 942
spreading, 149
storing, 18
bread, warm, 906
brown butter, dumplings, ricotta, with spinach and, 328–329
brown butter, roasted spaghetti squash with walnuts and, 458–459
crab salad sandwich, 149
egg noodles, 948
garlic, 133
grits, 827
herb, 132–133
-poached halibut or fish fillets with peas, 571
ricotta dumplings with spinach and, 328–329
spinach, long-cooked, 936
tomato sauce, 490–491
Butter bean and beef chili, 272–273
Butter (Boston) lettuce
about, 48
in BLT salad with rosemary-mayo dressing, 120–121
in steak, lettuce, and herb wrap, 710–711
Butternut squash
about, *32*, 221
au gratin with toasted nuts, 430–431
butternut purée, pork tenderloin with, 772–773
risotto-style pasta with ham and, 322–323
salad
raw, with warm edamame, 100–101
raw, with warm red beans, 101
sautéed, with warm edamame, 101
simmered, 955
soup with apples and bacon, 220–221
Butterscotch sauce, 989

C

Cabbage(s)
about
grilling, 79
prep shortcuts, *31*
storing, 19
BBQ chicken thighs with crisp red onion and, 655
and black bean gratin with tortilla crumbs and Jack, 493
braised pork with beer and, 766–767
braised pork with wine and, 767
braised, with kimchi and bacon, 453
braised, with sauerkraut and ham, 452–453
and chicken stew, 265
and corned beef gratin with lima beans, 493
edamame with chicken and, 501
herby chicken thighs with crisp fennel and, 655
kimchi style, with white beans and pork, 500–501
and lima bean gratin with rye crumbs, 492–493
with pork, edamame, and miso, 501
and red beans in buttery tomato sauce, 490–491
rice with scrambled eggs, scallions, and cabbage, 356–357
salad
and beet, with rye croutons, yogurt, and dill, 47
and black bean, with sour cream and cilantro, 63
coleslaw, 923
hot and sour, with salmon, 113
with pork, crisp, and tahini-lemon dressing, 89
with sesame vinaigrette, 953
with tofu, crisp, and coconut-lime dressing, 89
with tofu, crisp, and peanut-lime dressing, 88–89
sauerkraut, preparing, 186
soup, beef and red, 245
soup with smoked sausage, 244–245
Thai peanut chicken with crisp bean sprouts and, 654–655
unstuffed, 424–425

Cabbage(s) *(cont.)*
unstuffed, with ground meat, 424–425
-wrapped miso chicken, 685
Cacio e pepe (cheese and pepper), 278–279
Caesar salad
asparagus and kale, 76–77
classic, 77
Cakes
master recipe, 984–985
Mexican molten white chocolate, 987
molten chocolate, 987
molten white chocolate, 987
Canned beans, 485
Canned tomatoes, 16, 227, 295
Canned tuna, 395
Cannellini beans
in fast cassoulet, 505
in pasta e fagioli, *226–227*
soup, sausage, kale, and, 246–247
Cantaloupe
and basil smoothie, 811
in prosciutto and mozzarella sandwich, broiled, with melon, 151
prosciutto-wrapped, 886
Caper(s)
about, 943
chicken cutlets with lemon and, 733
fennel salad with dill and, 917
and mustard dressing, 72–73
pasta with tuna and, 305
tuna sandwich with fennel, lemon, and, 147
veal scallopini with lemon and, 732–733
Caprese salad, 922
Caramel sauce, creamy, 989
Caramelized apples, 818–819
Caramelized bananas, 970
Caramelized nuts, 824–825
Caramelized onions, 84–85
Caraway seeds
cabbage and chicken stew with, 265
fennel salad with, 917
Carbonara soup, 211
Carbonnade, beef, with mushrooms, 747
Cardamom
in apricot-cardamom muesli, 807, 821
in pineapple-cardamom couscous, 821
Carnitas
pork and corn, 781
pork and onion, 780–781
pork, Moroccan-style, and onion, 781
Carrot(s)
about, *29*
and black bean burgers, smoky, 152–153
chickpeas, curried, stir-fried, with chicken and, 487
chickpeas, curried, stir-fried, with potatoes and, 486–487
glazed, sole with, 560–561
and lamb sauté with mustard and miso, 683
miso lamb chops with, 793
miso-glazed fish fillets and, 575
and poached chicken with lemon-soy aïoli, 625
roasted chicken and, 678–679
roasted whole fish with lime and, 597
salad
and beet, with olives, mint, and lemon, 57
and beet, with toasted cashews, 56–57
and chickpea, with warm cumin oil, 64–65
with cilantro and lime, 914
with curry vinaigrette, 953
with olives and rosemary, 914
with raisins, 914
shredded, 799
soy sauce and scallions, 914
soup, ginger, with crisp ham, 223
soup, Thai coconut, with, 252–253
tofu, stir-fried, with soy and mustard, 517
warm-pickled, 896
Cashew(s)
beet and carrot salad with, 56–57
miso-cashew chicken tenders, 675
spiced, sautéed with bacon, 877
in spinach-cashew sauce, 614–615
warm kale with scallions, soy currants or raisins, and, 81
Cashew butter
in cold cashew noodles, 331
toast with blueberries and, 815
Casseroles, recipe-free, *428–429*
Cassoulet
chickpea and chorizo gratin, 503
fast, 505
feijoada, fast, 504–505
white bean and ham gratin, 502–503
white bean and smoked fish gratin, 503
Catfish
blackened, with green beans, 572–573
Dijon, with green beans, 573
miso-glazed, and mushrooms, 574–575
Cauliflower
about, 21, *31*
Buffalo, 549
chicken, stir-fried, with black bean sauce and, 635
chickpea and couscous stew with, 229
curry and chicken, with apricots, 642–643
curry and chicken, with tomatoes, 643
pasta with spicy curried, 293
"polenta" with mushrooms, 432–433
salad
tabbouleh with tomato and lemon, 125
warm pickled, with prosciutto, 83
warm pickled, with roasted red peppers, 82–83
seared, 925
and shrimp with rustic romesco, 590–591
and squid with rustic romesco, 591
stewed with anchovies, 269
tikka, with boiled eggs, 470–471
toasted, with red lentils, 508–509
tofu, BBQ, and, 523
tofu, chipotle-orange, and, 523
tofu, Manchurian, and, 522–523
tofu, Moroccan-spiced, with tomatoes, 531
Celery
braised pork with wine and, 767
noodles with beef and, 344–345
noodles with tofu and, 345
roasted chicken and, 678–679
salad, 917
smoked salmon and egg salad with, 105
and tofu salad, pressed, with sesame-chile vinaigrette, 91
Celery root
and crab cakes, 601
gratin with toasted nuts, 431
hash, prosciutto and, 861
pork tenderloin, pan-roasted, with, 741
rémoulade
chicken and, 67
crab and, 66–67
with hard-boiled eggs, 67
shrimp and, 67, 549
tuna and, 67
soup, creamy, with rustic cilantro pesto, 219
wine-braised turkey and, 703
Cellophane noodles, 333
Cereal bars, no-bake fruit and, 822–823

Challah, 136
Charcoal grilling, 721
Chard
  and chicken gratin, 656–657
  and chicken meat loaf, 698–699
  chorizo meatballs with, 761
  garlicky, seared steak with, 709
  orzo risotto, with ricotta and, 325
  soup, merguez, chickpea, and, 247
  stir-fried chicken with citrus and, 633
Charred
  Brussels sprouts, 126–127
  chicken
    and crusty bread with hero fixings, 649
    and pita with gyro fixings, 648–649
    and tortillas with taco fixings, 649
  tortillas, 907
Cheat-a-little pizza, master recipe, 190–191
Cheddar
  broccoli and, 926
  on cheesy tortillas, 483
  couscous gratin with onions, broccoli, and, 391
  crisps, 899
  in honey-cheddar grits with sage, 826–827
  in jalapeño-cheddar johnnycakes, 865
  waffles with bacon maple syrup, 870–871
Cheese(s)
  blue. *See* Blue cheese
  Brie and turkey sandwich, broiled, with tomatoes, 151
  broiled cheese sandwich, 134–135
  in bubbling caprese, 415
  cacio e pepe, 278–279
  in cheeseburgers, 727
  feta. *See* Feta
  fontina and lemon zest, turkey and spinach hero with, 173
  goat cheese. *See* Goat cheese
  Gorgonzola. *See* Gorgonzola cheese
  Gruyère. *See* Gruyère
  Jack. *See* Jack cheese
  lasagna, three-cheese, 326–327
  mac and cheese, 280–281
  manchego. *See* Manchego
  Mexican, 659
  Mexican street corn with, 932
  mozzarella. *See* Mozzarella
  Parmesan. *See* Parmesan cheese
  and pepper, 278–279
  provolone and salami sandwich, broiled, with roasted red pepper, 151
  ricotta. *See* Ricotta
  ricotta salata. *See* Ricotta salata
  stuffed poblanos with black beans and, 434–435
  stuffed poblanos with corn and, 435
  Swiss cheese in Reuben sandwich, 186
  tortillas, cheesy, 483
Cheeseburgers, 727
Cherry tomato(es)
  in avocado soup with crab and corn, 207
  black beans with feta and, 937
  broccoli tabbouleh with tomato and lemon, 124–125
  broiled, 931
  cauliflower tabbouleh with tomato and lemon, 125
  cobbler, 464–465
  curried crab salad with coconut and, 93
  fennel and radish tabbouleh with tomato and lime, 125
  fish fillets or steaks with toasted bread crumbs and, 537
  kale with pine nuts, Parmesan, and, 45
  mustard-marinated flank steak and, 723
  pasta with eggs and, 301
  pasta with pesto and, 284–285
  soy-marinated flank steak and, 722–723
  steamed clams with chorizo and, 552–553
  and tofu, pressed, with soy vinaigrette, 91
  wine-braised white beans with Parmesan and, 499
Chicken, 606–703
  about
    broiling and bubbling, 653
    butterflying, 687
    checking for doneness, 611
    chopping, 107
    cooking faster, 117
    homemade cold cuts, master recipe, 774
    marinades and rubs, 796–797
    piecing out, 611
    prep shortcuts, *34*
    rigging faster steamers, 685
    rubbing garlic on, 109
    stock, master recipe, 213
    substituting ingredients, 21
    substituting tofu for, 93
    types of, 610
  bacon-crusted, with apples, 621
  BBQ thighs with crisp cabbage and red onion, 655
  beer-braised black beans with corn and, 498–499
  and blue cheese sausage over sautéed kale, 661
  braised lentils with, 513
  breasts, broiled
    with avocado salsa, 612–613
    with peach salsa, 613
    with peas and Parmesan, 613
    with pineapple salsa, 613
    with watermelon salsa, 613
  in broth with vegetables and noodles, 670–671
  in cabbage, unstuffed, with ground meat, 425
  cabbage-wrapped miso, 685
  and cauliflower curry with apricots, 642–643
  and cauliflower curry with tomatoes, 643
  chickpeas, curried, stir-fried, with carrots and, 487
  and chile fundido, 658–659
  chile-rubbed, with corn and scallions, 640–641
  collard-wrapped, 684–685
  couscous paella with zucchini and, 406–407
  with creamed onions, 629
  with creamed spinach, 628–629
  Cubano, 619
  curried and mushrooms, 647
  curried, and potatoes, adobo-style, 693
  curry-rubbed stir-fried, with corn and red onion, 641
  cutlets
    BBQ-spiced, with pinto beans and ham, 627
    breaded, with pan sauce, 616–617
    with lemon and capers, 733
    Moroccan-spiced, with chickpeas and dried fruit, 626–627
    smoked paprika-spiced, with white beans and dried tomatoes, 627
    and vegetables with chimichurri, 719
  edamame with cabbage and, 501
  and eggplant green curry, 643
  and feta sausage over sautéed spinach, 661
  five-spice, and scallions, 651
  fried, 672–673
  gratin, broccoli rabe and, 657
  gratin, chard and, 656–657
  and green beans, 682–683

Chicken *(cont.)*
herby thighs with crisp cabbage and fennel, 655
hot and sour, with bok choy, 479
jerk, and onions, 650–651
kebabs over seasoned bulgur, 577
and leeks, braised and glazed, 664–665
lemon-pepper, and onions, 651
maple-chicken-apple sausage over sautéed collards, 661
Marsala with lots of mushrooms, 630–631
masa and rajas with, 393
meat loaf with chard, 699
meat loaf with spinach, 698–699
meatballs
and basil, 891
and bulgur, with Provençal tomato sauce, 801
and spaghetti with tomato sauce, 321
miso
rice and snow peas with, 367
sandwich with pineapple chutney, 195
soup with udon, snow peas, and, 235
noodle(s)
with cilantro-scallion pesto and, 340–341
with cold cashew, 331
with cold peanut, 330–331
with cold sesame, 331
and egg noodles with peas, 695
with peppers, basil, and, 342–343
soup, bone-in, 256–257
and sweet potatoes in curry broth, 339
udon with teriyaki, 337
oven-fried, with roasted corn, 676–677
packages
with potatoes, 681
with tomato, 680–681
with tomato and feta, 681
paprikash, 647
Parmesan, fastest, 618–619
pasta
with eggplant, balsamic, and, 315
fideos with tomatoes, rosemary, and, 309
with leeks, wine, and, 315
meatballs and spaghetti, with tomato sauce, 321
with mushrooms, wine, and, 314–315
in three Bs pasta, 312–313
and peppers with black bean mole, 652–653
and peppers with pumpkin seed mole, 653
pesto-crusted, with eggplant, 623
poached
with asparagus and lemon aïoli, 624–625
with carrots and lemon-soy aïoli, 625
Chinese-style, and bok choy, 625
with red peppers and smoked paprika aïoli, 625
with snap peas and curry aïoli, 624–625
polenta with asparagus and, 403
pozole and, 405
prosciutto-crusted, with endive, 620–621
prosciutto-crusted, with kale, 621
puttanesca-crusted, with fennel, 623
rice
jook with snow peas and, 360–361
and snow peas with, 367
and thighs, 383
with vegetables and, 262–263
and wings, 382–383
and ricotta sausage over broccoli rabe, 660–661
roasted, 678–679
roasted, master recipe, 688–689
and roasted red pepper skillet bake, 659
salad
and bread, Middle Eastern, 118–119
and celery root rémoulade, 67
corn and black bean, with, 108–109
corn and edamame, with, 109
and cucumber, with dill vinaigrette, 115
curried, 93
jícama slaw with, 107
and pear, with mustard vinaigrette, 115
sandwich, 164–165
and spinach, 116–117
and tomato, 114–115, 117
and tortilla, 119
zucchini slaw with, 106–107
sandwich
bacon, avocado, and tomato wrap with, 166–167
bacon, tomato, and blue cheese wrap with, 167
BBQ, blackened, with pickled cucumbers, 168–169
BBQ, with peach chutney, 195
and black bean burrito, 170–171
blackened, with pickled red onions, 168–169
charred, 648–649
chicken melt, 619
chicken salad, 164–165
Greek wrap, 167
with mango chutney, 194–195
Parmesan sub, 157
with pineapple chutney, 195
and watermelon tacos, 185
satay, skewerless, 893
with scallion-peanut sauce, 615
sesame, and snow peas, 638–639
soup
arroz con pollo, 696–697
broken wonton, with, 249
chicken noodle, bone-in, 256–257
and egg noodles with peas, 695
homemade ramen, 238–239
hot and sour, with, 271
spicy peanut, with collards and, 242–243
spicy peanut, with spinach and, 243
tamale, 240–241
Thai coconut, with, 253
tortilla, 241
with udon, snow peas, and, 235
with vegetables and rice, 262–263
with spinach-cashew sauce, 614–615
stew
and dumplings, 779
and dumplings with beans, 695
and dumplings with peas, 694–695
and mushroom, 264–265
Provençal, 644–645
Provençal, and fennel, 785
Provençal, creamy, 645
Provençal, with goat cheese, 645
quick-stewed green beans with, 451
in white chili, 273
stir-fried
with broccoli and black bean sauce, 634–635
with broccoli and tomato-soy sauce, 635
with cauliflower and orange-black bean sauce, 635
with chard and citrus, 633

with collards and dried chiles, 633
with kale, 632–633
stroganoff, 646–647
and sweet potato adobo, 692–693
tapenade-crusted, with eggplant, 622–623
tenders, baked
chipotle, 675
crisp, 674–675
miso-cashew, 675
mustard-pretzel, 675
peanut-coconut, 675
sesame, 675
Thai peanut, with crisp cabbage and bean sprouts, 654–655
thighs and pozole, 405
thighs and rice, 383
tortilla scramble, 843
and vegetable pancakes, Korean-style, 662–663
white-cut, with noodles, 671
whole, split, and vegetables, 686–687
wings and rice, 382–383
wings, cumin, and eggplant with yogurt-tahini sauce, 691
wings, hot, and Brussels sprouts with yogurt-blue cheese sauce, 691
wings, za'atar, and eggplant with yogurt-harissa sauce, 690–691
za'atar, and onions, 651
Chickpea(s)
chicken cutlets, Moroccan-spiced, with dried fruit and, 626–627
and chorizo gratin, 503
chorizo, homemade Spanish-style, with, 763
curried
lamb stew, with tomatoes and, 255
stir-fried, with chicken and carrots, 487
stir-fried, with potatoes and carrots, 486–487
on toast, 477
in curried rice, beans, and hearty greens, 351
hummus, 939
hummus and vegetable pita pockets, 140–141
lemony, with kale, 479
quinoa pilaf with dried fruit and, 384–385
salad
and carrot, with warm cumin oil, 64–65
and cucumber, with tahini and parsley, 63
and warm greens and potato salad, 103
in warm three-bean potato salad, 102–103
soups and stews
cod or thick fillet stew, 566–567
and couscous stew, with cauliflower, 229
and couscous stew, with Moroccan spices, 228–229
lamb stew, with tomatoes and, 255
merguez, chickpea, and chard soup, 247
in pasta e fagioli, Spanish-style, 227
stir-fried
with chicken and carrots, 487
with potatoes and carrots, 486–487
with sweet potatoes, 487
tahini, with fried eggs, 846–847
Chile(s)
about
prep shortcuts, *28*
seasoning with, 942
storing, 19
substituting ingredients, 21
toasting, 759
beer-braised pinto beans with sour cream and, 499
black beans with cumin and, 937
and chicken fundido, 658–659
dried, stir-fried chicken with collards and, 633
dried, Thai, 457
gazpacho, spicy green, with lime and, 205
jícama salad with, 913
and lentil stew, 507
in maple-chile-beer roasted chicken and peppers, 679
in mayonnaise, 133
panfried olives with mint and, 879
-rubbed chicken with corn and scallions, 640–641
stir-fried pork and broccoli with, 731
sweet potatoes, pan-roasted beef tenderloin with, 741
tomato sauce with basil and, 592–593
Chile de árbol, 457
Chile oil
about, 335
noodles with snow peas and, 334–335
noodles with spinach and, 335
Chili
beef and butter bean, 272–273
lamb and black bean, 273
smoky tofu and black bean, 526–527
tofu and black-eyed peas, with collards, 527
tofu and white bean, 527
white, 273
white bean, 783
Chili powder
in chile-lime bananas, caramelized, 970
in edamame with chili salt, 881
master recipe, 758
Chili salt
avocado with, 920
edamame with, 881
Chimichurri
chicken cutlets and vegetables with, 719
fried eggs with, 836–837
pork chops and vegetables with, 719
steak and vegetables with, 718–719
Chinese egg noodle(s)
about, 332
in noodles with chicken and cilantro-scallion pesto, 340–341
soup, 249
in stir-fried noodles with beef and bean sprouts, 345
in stir-fried noodles with beef and celery, 344–345
in stir-fried noodles with tofu and celery, 345
Chinese-style
barbecue sauce, 145
couscous helper, 401
poached chicken and bok choy, 625
sesame chicken, 639
sloppy Joes, 729
soup
bone-in chicken noodle, 257
broken wonton, 248–249
peanut, with tofu and bok choy, 243
Chipotle(s)
about
in adobo, 847
in barbecue sauce, 145
description of, 457
-avocado spread, 159
beef meatballs, 891
black beans with fried eggs, 846–847
BLT wrap with, 167
broiled, chicken breasts with watermelon salsa, 613
chicken and dumplings with beans, 695
chicken tenders, 675
clams, creamy rice with, 359
-marinated flank steak and asparagus, 723
-orange tofu and cauliflower, 523
potato salad, 962

Chipotle(s) *(cont.)*
rice and corn with beef, 366–367
rice with corn and pinto beans, 367
sautéed sweet potatoes with lime and, 964
skillet meat loaf, 743
tikka, cauliflower, with boiled eggs, 471
in tofu salad with pepitas and raisins, 93
tofu sandwich with red onions and, 143
in tomato sauce, 801
Chips, fish and. *See* Fish, and chips
Chirashi, 368–369
Chive
and egg breakfast bruschetta, 817
pesto, rustic, 219
Chocolate
almond butter balls, 982
-banana pudding, 990
cake, molten, 987
chunk banana cupcakes, 1000
cookie dough, 977
-covered pretzels, 986
custard sauce, 992
as dessert staple, 978
-fruit sorbet, 974
melted, as dipping sauce, 986
milkshakes, 975
mousse, 993
-orange pudding, 990
peanut brittle, 999
pecan-bourbon brownies, 998
pound cupcakes, 985
salted, peanut butter balls, 982
in sauces, 989
white chocolate molten cake, 987
white chocolate-orange pudding, 990
Chocolate chip(s)
in banana-chocolate chip pancakes, 867
cookie squares, 980
Chop-and-drop soups, 252–253
Chopped
Greek salad, 798–799
salad, 912
Chorizo
beer-braised black beans and corn with, 499
black beans with greens, garlic, and, 481
breakfast burritos, with sweet potatoes and, 857
breakfast patties with sautéed peppers, 859
Brussels sprouts with, 958
and chickpea gratin, 503
flautas, potato and, 437
hash, potato and, 861
homemade Spanish-style, with chickpeas, 763
homemade, with pinto beans, 762–763
kidney beans with kale and, 515
masa and rajas with, 393
meatballs with chard, 761
no-cook skewers, 878
panfried trout with red onions and, 583
pasta
fideos with tomatoes, white beans, and, 309
with red onions, black beans, and, 289
with scallops, potatoes, and, 307
spaghetti with chorizo tomato sauce, 291
rice bowl with pineapple and, 369
scrambled eggs with parsley and, 839
smoked paprika in, 425
Spanish dip sandwich with, 176–177
spinach soup and, 245
steamed clams with cherry tomatoes and, 552–553
Chowder(s)
clam, 231
clam, Manhattan, 231
mussel, 231
seafood, 230–231
seafood, Manhattan, 231
seafood, with bacon, 231
shrimp and corn, 231
smoked salmon, 231
Chutney
mango, 194–195
peach, 195
pineapple, 195
Ciabatta, 136
Cilantro
about, 21, *29*
avocado with hot sauce and, 920
black bean and cabbage salad with sour cream and, 63
carrot salad with lime and, 914
deep-fried tofu with pistachio sauce and, 521
noodles with pork, peppers, and, 343
pesto, rustic, 219
shrimp, stir-fried, with shitakes, eggs, and, 589
tuna sandwich with avocado and, 147
Cinnamon
in apricot-cinnamon couscous, 820–821
jícama and radish salad with dried cranberries and, 918
-orange French toast, 831
ripe plantains with cumin and, 960
Citrus. *See also* Lemon(s); Lime(s); Orange(s)
citrus cycle, 69
prep shortcuts, *32*
Clam(s)
about
prying open, 605
saving liquid from, 397
swapping with mussels, 553
chowder, 231
chowder, seafood, 230–231
linguine with, 302–303
in red clam sauce, 303
rice, creamy, with, 358–359
spaghetti with tomato sauce and, 291
steamed
with chorizo and cherry tomatoes, 552–553
with tarragon and cream, 553
Thai-style, with spinach, 553
Clove(s)
in ginger-clove muesli, 807
in orange-clove couscous, 821
Cobb sandwich, open-face, 175
Cobbler, broiled peach, 1001
Cocktail meatballs, master recipe, 890–891
Cocoa powder, as dessert staple, 978
Coconut
about, 979
in banana-coconut pancakes, 866–867
cookie dough, 977
crunch, broiled grapefruit with, 813
oatmeal cookies, 983
in peanut-coconut chicken tenders, 675
Coconut milk
about, 17
butternut squash simmered in, 955
in coconut curry, 605
in coconut curry broth, 671
in coconut soup, Thai, 252–253
coconut-curried fried chicken, 673
in coconut-lime dressing, 89
in coconutty tomato sauce, 491
fish steaks poached in, 581
in marinades, 796
noodles with curry and, 949
in shrimp simmered in dal, 598–599
in spinach-cashew sauce, 615
Cod
caramel-cooked, 568–569
and chickpea stew, 566–567
and fava bean stew, 567
and white bean stew, 567

Cold cuts, homemade, master recipe, 774–775
Coleslaw. *See* Slaw
Collard greens
in andouille, black-eyed pea, and Southern greens soup, 247
BBQ lima beans with, 514–515
ham steaks, BBQ-glazed, with, 765
ham steaks, maple-glazed, with, 764–765
hoppin' John with, 362–363
jambalaya with, 381
peanut soup, spicy, with chicken and, 242–243
pork stew with black beans and, 783
in salmon with gingery greens, 554–555
sautéed, maple-chicken-apple sausage over, 661
stewed with smoked pork, 268–269
stir-fried chicken with dried chiles and, 633
tofu and black-eyed pea chili, 527
warm, with peaches and ham, 81
-wrapped chicken, 684–685
Condiments. *See also specific condiments*
master recipe, 144–145
seasoning techniques with, 943
storing, 17
Cookie dough, 977
Cookies and bar cookies
chocolate chip squares, 980
coconut oatmeal, 983
dried fruit oatmeal, 983
nutty coconut oatmeal, 983
pecan-bourbon brownies, 998
Coriander, in rubs, 797
Corn
about, *32,* 207
avocado soup with crab and, 206–207
beer-braised black beans with chicken and, 498–499
beer-braised black beans with chorizo and, 499
bulgur with, 946
chile-rubbed chicken with scallions and, 640–641
cobbler, cherry tomato, with, 465
creamed, salmon with, 555
curry-rubbed chicken with red onion and, 641
fideos with squid, tomatoes, and, 309
masa harina, 241
Mediterranean-style, 932
Mexican street, 932
panfried with onions, 933
pan-seared
and poblanos, 455
and pork, 454–455
and shrimp, 455
and steak, 455
in piquante amarilla, 563
and pork carnitas, 781
rice
and chipotle rice with beef, 366–367
and chipotle rice with pinto beans, 367
and tomato rice with shrimp, 367
roasted, oven-fried chicken with, 676–677
roasted, oven-fried pork chops with, 677
salad
and black bean, with garlic chicken, 108–109
and black bean, with shrimp, 109
and edamame, with ginger chicken, 109
and white bean, with garlic chicken, 109
in salsa, 171
and sausage pan broil, 603
and scallop pan broil, 602–603
and shrimp chowder, 231
stir-fried pork with scallions and, 749
stuffed poblanos with cheese and, 435
in succotash, 933
tortillas, 907
waffles with blueberry maple syrup, 871
Corned beef cabbage gratin with lima beans, 493
Cornmeal
about
cooking times, 355
description of, 353
storing, 17
fried chicken, 672–673
pancakes, chicken and vegetable, Korean-style, 663
in polenta
with chicken and asparagus, 403
with sausage and fennel, 403
with sausage and mushrooms, 402–403
shrimp over, 393
Cornstarch, thickening with, 271
Cotija cheese, 659
Couscous
about
cooking times, 355
description of, 353
seasoning, 910
balsamic, lamb chops with, 788–789
breakfast
apricot-cinnamon, 820–821
cranberry-ginger, 821
orange-clove, 821
pineapple-cardamom, 821
tomato-garlic, 821
and chickpea stew, 228–229
gratin
with leeks and Gruyère, 390–391
with mushrooms and Parmesan, 391
with onions, broccoli, and cheddar, 391
with poblanos and Jack cheese, 391
helper, 400–401
Israeli, 910
lamb, Moroccan, with olives and, 787
paella with chicken and fennel, 407
paella with chicken and zucchini, 406–407
in pasta e fagioli, Greek-style, 227
plain, 910
pomegranate, lamb chops with, 789
pork, curried, with spinach and, 787
pork, Moroccan-style, with grapes and, 786–787
salad, with fennel, oranges, and olives, 95
soy-ginger, lamb chops with, 789
whole wheat, 910
Crab
cakes, baked
with celery root, 601
with potatoes, 600–601
with sweet potatoes, 601
pasta with tomatoes and, 311
salad
and celery root rémoulade, 66–67
curried, with coconut and cherry tomatoes, 93
and egg, with bell pepper, 105
sandwich. crab salad, 148–149
soft-shell, panfried, with bacon and leeks, 583
soup
avocado, with corn and, 206–207
avocado, with daikon and, 207
gumbo, 261
toast, 889
Cracked wheat
about, 353
cooking times, 355
pilaf, recipe-free, *364–365*
Cranberry(ies)
dried, bulgur with orange and, 946
dried, jícama and radish salad with cinnamon and, 918

Cranberry(ies) *(cont.)*
-ginger couscous, 821
-port sundaes, 976
Cream cheese, scrambled eggs with smoked salmon, dill, and, 839
Creamed
corn, 555
onions, 629
peas, 555
spinach, 555, 628–629, 936
Crème anglaise, 992
Creole crab salad sandwich, 149
Crisps (cheese), 899
Crisps (sweet), skillet fruit, 995
Croque Monsieur, 150–151
Croutons
beet and cabbage salad with, 57
in Caesar salad, 76–77
master recipe, 71
tomato and strawberry panzanella, 47
Crumble
broiled apple, 1002
gingersnap, orange pie with, 1003
key lime, 1003
Cubano chicken, 619
Cucumber(s)
about, *30*
gazpacho with crisp prosciutto, 203
in green gazpacho, 204–205
Malaysian-style BBQ fish with, 578–579
with peanut vinaigrette, 953
ribbons, striped bass and, 565
salad
and chicken, with dill vinaigrette, 115
and chickpea, with tahini and parsley, 63
with Dijon mayo, 915
and edamame, with warm ginger dressing, 65
with hot sauce and lime juice, 915
lobster and egg, with tarragon and, 105
with peanut vinaigrette, 953
and salmon, with caper and mustard dressing, 72–73
and salmon, with ginger-peanut dressing, 73
shrimp and egg, with tarragon and, 105
with sour cream and dill, 915
with soy sauce and mirin, 915
and tofu, pressed, with hoisin vinaigrette, 90–91
and white bean, with yogurt and dill, 62–63
in salsa, 376–377
sandwich
in egg salad sandwich with lots of vegetables, 154–155
in hummus and vegetable pita pockets, 140–141
pickled, BBQ blackened chicken, with, 169
tofu, with hoisin mayo and, 142–143
tuna pita with feta and, 147
warm-pickled, spears, 896
Cumin (seeds)
black beans with chiles and, 937
in cumin lamb with green peppers, 639
in cumin oil, warm, chickpea and carrot salad with, 64–65
in cumin wings and eggplant with yogurt-tahini sauce, 691
ripe plantains with cinnamon and, 960
in rubs, 797
stir-fried lamb and green peppers with, 790–791
stir-fried lamb and leeks with, 791
Cupcakes
banana-rum, 1000
chocolate chunk banana, 1000
pound, master recipe, 984–985
praline banana, 1000
Currants
balsamic, raw kale salad with pine nuts and, 80–81
balsamic, warm kale salad with pine nuts and, 80–81
soy, warm kale salad with cashews, scallions, and, 81
Curry (powder)
aïoli, 625
-braised beef and eggplant, 738–739
-braised beef and potatoes, 739
broth, 338–339, 671
chicken
breasts with pineapple salsa, 613
with coconut milk, 673
and mushrooms, 647
and potatoes, adobo-style, 693
and rice, 697
salad, 93
salad sandwich with grapes, 165
stir-fried, with corn and red onion, 641
and vegetable soup with rice, 262–263
chickpea(s)
stew with lamb and tomatoes, 255
stir-fried, with chicken and carrots, 487
stir-fried, with potatoes and carrots, 486–487
on toast, 477
coconut curry, mussel and vegetable pan roast with, 605
crab salad with coconut and cherry tomatoes, 93
on crab toast, 889
creamed spinach, seared chicken with, 629
egg salad sandwich with lots of vegetables, 155
lamb, stir-fried, and green peppers with, 791
master recipes, 758–759
in mayonnaise, 898
noodles with coconut milk and, 949
pork meatballs, 891
pork with couscous and spinach, 787
rice, beans, and hearty greens, 351
-rubbed pork tenderloin with mango salsa, 757
in rubs, 797
salad dressing, 117
shrimp salad roll, 161
in smashed peas, 935
tartar sauce, 69
tofu
and cabbage with coconut-lime dressing, 89
with pecans and golden raisins, 92–93
with tomatoes and peas, 531
in vinaigrettes, 953
yogurt sauce, 595
Custard sauce
chocolate, 992
chocolate-almond, 992
vanilla, 989, 992

D

Daikon
and crab, avocado soup with, 207
salad with fish sauce, lime, and peanuts, 918
shrimp poke with peanuts and, 545
tuna poke with peanuts and, 544–545
Dal
salmon simmered in, 599
shrimp simmered in, 598–599
Dandelion greens, 49
Dashi
master recipe, 213
in miso soup, 234–235
Dates
bulgur, smoky, with eggplant, feta, and, 387
puffed rice salad with almonds and, 60–61

Deep-fried tofu
with peanut sauce and scallions, 520–521
with pistachio sauce and cilantro, 521
Dessert(s), 966–1003
about, 968–969
apple crumble, broiled, 1002
berry fool, 996
broiled apple crumble, 1002
broiled peach cobbler, 972
broiled peaches with brown sugar, 972
cakes, 987
chocolate chip cookie squares, 980
chocolate chunk banana cupcakes, 1000
cookies and bars, 977, 980, 983
crumbles, 1002–1003
cupcakes, 984–985, 1000
fruit. *See* Fruit
milkshakes, 975
mousse, 993
puddings, 990
sauces, master recipe, 988–989
sorbet, 974
staple ingredients, 978–979
sundaes, 976
tiramisu, 991
Dijon mustard. *See* Mustard
Dill
about, 63
beet and cabbage salad with yogurt and, 57
in bone-in chicken noodle soup, 257
chicken stew with, 264–265
cucumber salad with sour cream and, 915
fennel salad with capers and, 917
pasta with pesto and, 285
scrambled eggs with smoked salmon and, 838–839
scrambled eggs with smoked trout and, 839
tuna and egg salad, with radishes and, 104–105
in vinaigrettes, 115
white bean and cucumber salad with yogurt and, 62–63
Dipping sauces (savory)
for fried tofu, 521
Italian, 176
ricotta, 445
soy, 444–445
Spanish, 176
for steak, lettuce, and herb wraps, 710–711
tomato, 176
Dipping sauces (sweet), 986
Double-fried French fries, 963
Dressing(s). *See also* Vinaigrette(s)
about, 45
Caesar salad, 76–77
caper and mustard, 72–73
coconut-lime, 89
curry, 117
ginger, 79
ginger, warm, 65
ginger-peanut, 73
mustard, 72–73, 87, 121
orange, 79
paprika, warm, 65
Parmesan, 116–117
peanut-lime, 88–89
peanut-soy, 87
rosemary-mayo, 120–121
Russian, 186–187
sesame-oil, 911
tahini, 86–87
tahini-lemon, 89
warm, 65
white bean, 97
Dried beans, 16, 484–485
Dried chiles
stir-fried chicken with collards and, 633
Thai, 457
toasting, 759
Dried cranberries
bulgur with orange and, 946
jícama and radish salad with cinnamon and, 918
Dried fruit
about
as dessert staple, 979
seasoning with, 943
substituting ingredients, 21
chicken cutlets, Moroccan-spiced, with chickpeas and, 626–627
dried apricots, puffed wheat salad with pistachios and, 61
in food processor, 823
lamb and rice with, 794–795
in muesli, 807
no-bake fruit and cereal bars, 822–823
oatmeal cookies, 983
quinoa pilaf with chickpeas and, 384–385
Dried lentils, 485
Dried mushrooms, 506–507, 956
Dried tomatoes
about, 295
bulgur, smoky, with eggplant, feta, and, 386–387
chicken cutlets, smoked paprika-spiced, with white beans and, 627
pasta with tuna and, 304–305
puffed rice salad with olives and, 61
in tomato sauce, 297
Drop biscuits, prosciutto and, 862–863
Duck
breast, seared, with fruit sauce, 668–669
in fast cassoulet, 505
Dumplings
and chicken, and beans, 695
chicken stew and, 779
and chicken, with peas, 694–695
pork stew and, 778–779
ricotta, with spinach and brown butter, 328–329

E

Edamame
with chicken and cabbage, 501
with chili salt, 881
and corn salad with ginger chicken, 109
and cucumber salad with warm ginger dressing, 65
microwaved, 881
noodles with tofu, chile oil, and, 335
with pork, cabbage, and miso, 501
pork, stir-fried, with scallions and, 749–750
soy-lemon, and asparagus, 489
succotash, 933
on toast with sesame oil and scallions, 477
veal, braised, with, 735
warm, raw butternut squash salad with, 100–101
warm, sautéed butternut squash with, 101
Egg(s)
about
buying, 828
checking for freshness, 828
cooking, 443, 837, 839
cracking, 828
as dessert staple, 979
labels, 828
poaching, 99, 325
runny yolks, 828
scrambling for a crowd, 841
storing, 18, 828
turning into flower petals, 211
baked, 849
boiled
cauliflower tikka with, 470–471
with celery root rémoulade, 67
with curry mayo, 898
with Dijon mayo, 898
breakfast burritos, 856–857
broiled, 848–849
and chive breakfast bruschetta, 817
Florentine, 850–851
in French toast, roasting pan, 830–831
in French toast, tortilla, 832–833

Egg(s) *(cont.)*
fried
arugula salad with shaved Parmesan and, 50–51
BBQ bacon pinto beans, 847
with chimichurri, 836–837
with chipotle black beans, 846–847
endive salad with blue cheese and, 51
with mushrooms and leeks, 852–853
with mushrooms and poblanos, 853
with pesto, 837
with romesco, 837
spinach salad with feta and, 51
with tahini chickpeas, 847
with tomatoes and leeks, 853
with white beans and zucchini, 847
frittata, 494–495
omelet for two, 834–835
pasta
with cherry tomatoes and, 301
with greens and, 300–301
with mushrooms and, 301
poached
eggs Florentine, 850–851
in fennel, 525
lemony lima beans with spinach and, 489
in mushrooms, 851
orzo risotto with asparagus and, 324–325
in poblanos and cream, 525
in tomato sauce, 851
warm escarole and white bean salad with, 98–99
salad
and crab, with bell pepper, 105
hard-boiled, and celery root rémoulade, 67
and lobster, with cucumber and tarragon, 105
and shrimp, with cucumber and tarragon, 105
and smoked salmon, with celery, 105
and tuna, with radishes and dill, 104–105
sandwich
egg salad and arugula, 155
egg salad with lots of vegetables, 154–155
egg salad with lots of vegetables, classic, 155
egg salad with lots of vegetables, curried, 155
scrambled
with chorizo and parsley, 839
feta and spinach, 841
goat cheese and spinach, 840–841
with ham and tarragon, 839
Parmesan and kale, 841
with prosciutto and basil, 839
rice with bok choy, scallions, and, 357
rice with cabbage, scallions, and, 356–357
rice with tomatoes, basil, and, 357
ricotta and spinach, 841
with smoked salmon and dill, 838–839
with smoked trout and dill, 839
stir-fried shrimp with shitakes, cilantro, and, 589
stir-fried shrimp with tomato, basil, and, 589
stir-fried shrimp with tomato, scallions, and, 588–589
tortilla scramble, 842–843
and shrimp with tomatoes, 855
soup
carbonara soup, 211
chicken ramen, homemade, 238–239
egg drop, 210–211
and steak with mushrooms and onion, 855
and steak with peppers and onion, 854–855
sukiyaki, 524–525
in tortilla, Spanish, 460–461
Egg noodles
buttered, 948
with chicken and peas, 695
Egg roll wrappers
about, 327
in three-cheese lasagna, 326–327
Eggplant
and beef, curry-braised, 738–739
broiled
and tomato salad, with peanut-soy dressing, 87
and zucchini salad. with mustard dressing, 87
and zucchini salad, with tahini dressing, 86–87
bulgur, smoky, 386–387
chicken, pesto-crusted, with, 623
chicken, tapenade-crusted, with, 622–623
and chicken wings, cumin, with yogurt-tahini sauce, 691
and chicken wings, za'atar, with yogurt-harissa sauce, 690–691
gratin, 929
green curry, with chicken, 643
Parmesan, fastest, 619
and Parmesan sandwich, 156–157
pasta with chicken, balsamic, and, 315
pasta with tomato sauce and, 292–293
steaks with tomato-garlic sauce, 420–421
tomato and bread soup with, 225
Enchiladas
pork and sweet potato, 745
steak and potato, 744–745
Endive
about, 48
with fried eggs and blue cheese, 51
olive oil-poached halibut or fish fillets with, 570–571
prosciutto-crusted chicken with, 620–621
and radicchio with bacon vinaigrette, 52–53
sausage, browned and braised, with, 768–769
spears
with basil, 883
with blue cheese and black olives, 883
with olives, 883
with prosciutto, 883
Escarole
about, 49
and Italian sausage soup, 245
warm
in greens and chickpea potato salad, 103
and white bean salad with poached eggs, 98–99
and white bean salad with squid, 99
white beans with prosciutto and, 515
Espresso in black and white mocha milkshake, 975

F

Fajita
peppers and onions, 928
salad, steak, 97
salad, veggie, 96–97
Farro
about, 353, 355
pilaf, recipe-free, *364–365*
and white beans
with arugula and Parmesan, 395
Greek-style, 395
with tomato and fennel, 395
with tuna, 394–395
Fast kitchen
faster is better, 12–13
freezer staples, 19–20
fridge staples, 18–19

interchangeable, 21
key tools, 22–23
pantry staples, 15–17
prep shortcuts, *28–35*
setup for speed, *24–25*
shopping for speed, 14
strategies for, 26–27
Fast Rachel sandwich, 187
Fattoush
Middle Eastern chicken and bread salad, 118–119
pita, warm, with feta, 441
pita, warm, with shrimp, 441
zucchini, 440–441
Fava bean(s)
and cod or fish fillet stew, 567
in pasta e fagioli, Greek-style, 227
soup, minty, 209
Feijoada, fast, 504–505
Fennel
about, 21
cobbler, cherry tomato, with olives and, 465
couscous paella with chicken and, 407
eggs poached in, 525
farro with white beans, tomato, and, 395
fried, Parmesan, 447
fried, with arugula, 446–447
and garlic butter baguette, 133
herby chicken thighs with crisp cabbage and, 655
lamb, Moroccan and, 785
pasta
with bread crumbs, lemon and, 287
with bread crumbs, lemon, and, 287
risotto-style, with sausage and, 323
with white beans, stock, and, 288–289
polenta with sausage and, 403
Provençal braised pork and, 784–785
Provençal chicken and fennel, 785
Provençal tomato soup with, 216–217
puttanesca-crusted chicken with, 623
roasted chicken and, 678
roasted whole fish with orange and, 596–597
salad, 917
bulgur and apple, with, 94–95
with capers and dill, 917
with caraway seeds, 917
couscous and orange, with olives and, 95
with olives, 917
and radish tabbouleh with tomato and lime, 125
sautéed, breakfast patties with, 859
seared pork chops and, 751
striped bass or thick fillets and, 565
tuna sandwich with capers, lemon, and, 147
Fermented black beans, 358–359
Feta
black beans with tomatoes and, 937
bulgur, smoky, with eggplant, dates, and, 387
bulgur, smoky, with eggplant, dried tomatoes, and, 386–387
and chicken packages with tomatoes, 681
and chicken sausage over sautéed spinach, 661
eggs, scrambled, with spinach and, 841
fattoush, warm pita, with, 441
in hummus and vegetable pita pockets, 140–141
and lamb meatballs with kale, 761
Mexican cheeses and, 659
pasta
with kale, olives, and feta, 283
in pasta e fagioli, Greek-style, 227
in three Bs pasta, 313
ziti with olives and feta, 283, 299
spinach with fried eggs and, 51
tomato salad with strawberries, balsamic, and, 46–47
tomato salad with watermelon, balsamic, and, 47
tuna pita with cucumbers and, 147
and watermelon salad with mint, 922
Fideos
with chicken, tomatoes, and rosemary, 309
with chorizo, tomatoes, and white beans, 309
with shrimp, tomatoes, and peas, 308–309
with squid, tomatoes, and corn, 309
Fig(s)
Brussels sprout salad with walnuts and, 127
and Gorgonzola pizza wedges, 901
Fire and ice noodles, 950
Fish. *See also* Seafood
about
cooking, 586
fillets and steaks, 542–543
marinades and rubs, 796–797
oily, 535
roasting whole, 575
serving whole fish, 597
substituting ingredients, 21
sushi grade, 541
and chips
with curried yogurt sauce, 595
with smoked paprika aïoli, 595
with tartar sauce, 594–595
with vinegar-shallot sauce, 595
fillet(s)
with balsamic radicchio, 561
blackened, with green beans, 572–573
butter-poached, with peas, 571
and cherry tomatoes with toasted bread crumbs, 537
and chickpea stew, 566–567
and cucumber ribbons, 565
Dijon, with green beans, 573
and fava bean stew, 567
and fennel, 565
with glazed carrots, 560–561
hoisin-glazed, and shitakes, 575
hoisin-glazed, with radishes, 579
with lemony asparagus, 561
Malaysian-style BBQ, with cucumber, 578–579
Malaysian-style BBQ, with watermelon, 579
miso-glazed, and carrots, 575
miso-glazed, and mushrooms, 574–575
mustard-glazed, with apples, 579
olive oil-poached, with endive, 570–571
poached, in creamy tomato broth, 580–581
sandwich, 161
with sesame bean sprouts, 561
teriyaki-glazed, and sweet potatoes, 575
with tomato salsa, 539, 563
and white bean stew, 567
and zucchini ribbons, 564–565
and zucchini with toasted bread crumbs, 537
grilled or broiled, with fresh salsa, 539, 563
jambalaya des herbes with, 381
kebabs over bulgur pilaf, 576–577
oily, 585, 587
Provençal tomato soup with fennel and, 217

Fish *(cont.)*
roasted, whole, with carrots and lime, 597
roasted, whole, with fennel and orange, 596–597
smoked, and white bean gratin, 503
steaks
broiled, with picante amarilla, 563
broiled, with picante rojo, 563
broiled, with picante verde, 562–563
broiled, with warm tapenade, 563
and cherry tomatoes with toasted bread crumbs, 537
hoisin-glazed, with radishes, 579
Malaysian-style BBQ, with cucumber, 578–579
Malaysian-style BBQ, with watermelon, 579
mustard-glazed, with apples, 579
poached in coconut milk, 581
poached, in creamy tomato broth, 580–581
poached in soy broth, 581
and zucchini with toasted bread crumbs, 537
steamed, recipe-free, *556–557*
stock, in miso soup, 234–235
stock, master recipe, 213
Fish flakes
in dashi, 213
in miso soup, 234–235
Fish sauce
daikon salad with lime, peanuts, and, 918
seasoning with, 942
storing, 17
substituting ingredients, 21
Five-spice powder
in chicken and scallions, 651
master recipe, 759
in pork meatballs with bok choy, 760–761
Flank steak
chipotle-marinated, and asparagus, 723
mustard-marinated, and cherry tomatoes, 723
soy-marinated, and cherry tomatoes, 722–723
soy-marinated, and green beans, 723
Flatbread, vegetable, with kale and white bean stew, 462–463
Flautas
potato and chorizo, 436–437
sweet potato, 436–437
Florentine, eggs, 850–851
Flour
as dessert staple, 978
storing, 17
Focaccia, 136
Foil packages, 680–681
Fondue. *See* Queso fundido
Fontina and lemon zest, turkey and spinach hero with, 173
Fool
berry, 996
peach, 996
Freezer staples, 19–20
French bread scramble, 843
French fries, 963
French toast
roasting pan, 830–831
tortilla, 832–833
Fresno peppers, 456
Fridge staples, 18–19
Fried
bread crumbs, 293, 930
celery root tempura, 448–449
chicken, 672–673
eggs. *See* Egg(s), fried
fennel and arugula, 446–447
okra, 959
onions, curried lentils and rice with, 372–373
rice, 357
tofu, 520–523
tortillas, 907
Frisée
about, 49
in fried eggs and blue cheese, 51
Frittata
pea and arugula, 495
pinto bean and poblano, 495
white bean and spinach, 494–495
Frozen beans, 484–485
Frozen fruit
as dessert staple, 979
in fruit sorbet, 975
in fruity shaved ice, 971
Frozen vegetable soup, 214–215
Fruit. *See also* Dried fruit; *specific fruits*
about
citrus cycle, 69
prep shortcuts, *32–33*
storing, 19
and cereal bars, no-bake, 822–823
fruity shaved ice, 971
milkshakes, 975
pick-a-fruit salad, 921
raw sauce, 989
salad and toast, 817
in sauces, 668–669
skillet crisp, 995
sorbet, 974
with yogurt and graham cracker parfait, 808–809

G

Garbanzo beans. *See* Chickpea(s)
Garlic
about
prep shortcuts, *28*
seasoning with, 942
storing, 16
black beans with chorizo, greens, and, 481
bread, 906
broccoli rabe stewed with tons of, 269
croutons, 71
in Dijon-garlic-cider roasted chicken and carrots, 679
in garlic butter, 133
in garlic chicken, 108–109
garlicky chard, seared steak with, 709
in garlicky mushrooms, 956
garlicky spinach, pan-seared halibut with, 541
garlicky stewed greens and tomatoes, salmon with, 555
garlicky watercress, pan-seared halibut with, 541
greens sautéed with, 924
kidney beans with ham, greens, and, 481
lentils with smoked paprika and, 937
pasta with anchovies and, 305
-rosemary chicken and vegetable pancakes, 663
in rosemary-garlic oil, 459
sautéed sweet potatoes with sage and, 964
tomato sauce with lots of, 296
in tomato-garlic couscous, 821
in tomato-garlic sauce, 421
veal, braised, with white beans and, 735
white beans with bacon, greens, and, 481
white beans with sausage, greens, and, 480–481
Gas grilling, 721
Gazpacho
cucumber, with crisp prosciutto, 202–203
with goat cheese, 203
grapefruit, 205
green, 204–205
green, spicy, with chile and lime, 205
melon, with crisp prosciutto, 202–203
tomato and peach, with crisp bacon, 202–203
German-style potato salad, 962
Ginger
about, 16, *28*
in apple-ginger smoothie, 811
carrot soup with crisp ham and, 223
chicken, corn and edamame salad with, 109
-clove muesli, 807

in cranberry-ginger couscous, 821
gingered chicken, broken wonton soup with, 249
gingery creamed corn, salmon with, 555
gingery greens, salmon with, 554–555
gingery tofu and green beans, 517
-hoisin barbecue sauce, 753
in honey-ginger-soy roasted chicken and celery, 678–679
maple syrup, 871
in maple-ginger oatmeal with caramelized walnuts, 825
-orange bean sprouts, 919
peas with, 934
pound cupcakes, 985
roasted nuts with soy, honey, and, 895
in salad dressings
ginger, 79
ginger, warm, 65
ginger-peanut, 73
sautéed sweet potatoes with soy and, 964
-scallion snow peas, pan-seared tuna with, 540–541
seasoning with, 942
in soy-ginger couscous, lamb chops with, 789
soy-orange grits with, 827
stir-fried beef and asparagus with scallions and, 731
stir-fried beef and broccoli with scallions and, 730–731
Gingersnap crumble, orange pie with, 1003
Glass noodles, 333
Glazing(ed)
about, 423
BBQ-glazed ham steaks with collards, 765
and braised chicken and leeks, 664–665
Brussels sprouts with Vietnamese flavors, 422–423
carrots, sole with, 560–561
harissa glaze, skillet lamb meat loaf with, 743
hoisin-glazed fish with radishes, 579
hoisin-glazed fish fillets and shitakes, 575
honey-mustard-glazed ham steaks with kale, 765
maple-glazed ham steaks with collards, 764–765
miso-glazed catfish or fish fillets and mushrooms, 574–575
miso-glazed fish fillets and carrots, 575
mustard-glazed fish with apples, 579
soy-brown sugar, 813
teriyaki-glazed fish fillets and sweet potatoes, 575
Goat cheese
eggs, scrambled, with spinach and, 840–841
gazpacho with, 203
peach and pecan baguette and, 133
Provençal chicken with, 645
spinach with apples, walnuts, and, 45
truffles, 885
Golden raisins, curried tofu salad with pecan and, 92–93
Gorgonzola cheese
charred Brussels sprout salad, with walnuts and, 126–127
and fig pizza wedges, 901
roasted spaghetti squash and hazelnuts and, 459
in steakhouse salad, 54–55
Graham crackers
in key lime crumble, 1003
in lemon s'mores, 994
parfait with fruit, yogurt, and, 808–809
Grains, 384–409
about
broiling, 409
description of, 353–355
storing, 16, 20
bulgur. *See* Bulgur
cornmeal. *See* Cornmeal
couscous. *See* Couscous
cracked wheat. *See* Cracked wheat
farro. *See* Farro
grits, shrimp over, 398–399
masa and rajas, 392–393
master recipe, 354–355
millet. *See* Millet
pearled barley, 353, 355
pilaf, recipe-free, *364–365*
polenta. *See* Polenta
quinoa. *See* Quinoa
rolled oats. *See* Rolled oats
Granola
about, 807
fruit and cereal bars, no-bake, 822–823
Grape(s)
chicken salad sandwich with curry and, 165
chicken salad sandwich with rosemary and, 164–165
in green gazpacho, 204–205
Moroccan-style pork with couscous and, 786–787
salad with mint, 913
Grapefruit
broiled
with almond-brown sugar crunch, 812–813
with coconut crunch, 813
with pecan-honey crunch, 813
with soy-brown sugar glaze, 813
brûlée, 813
gazpacho, 205
Gratin
asparagus, 929
black bean and cabbage, with tortilla crumbs and Jack, 493
chicken and broccoli rabe, 657
chicken and chard, 656–657
chickpea and chorizo, 503
corned beef and cabbage, with lima beans, 493
couscous
with leeks and Gruyère, 390–391
with mushrooms and Parmesan, 391
with onions, broccoli, and cheddar, 391
with poblanos and Jack cheese, 391
eggplant, 929
lima bean and cabbage, with rye crumbs, 492–493
quinoa, with leeks and Gruyère, 391
recipe-free, 467
white bean and ham, 502–503
white bean and smoked fish, 503
Greek salad
chopped, 798–799
with orzo and shrimp, 110–111
with orzo and squid, 111
Greek-style
chicken wrap, 167
farro and white beans, 395
pasta e fagioli, 227
pita pizza, 887
pork souvlaki with zucchini, 754–755
skillet spanakopita, 468–469
Green bean(s)
about, *31*
caramel stir-fried beef and, 716–717
caramel stir-fried pork and, 717
catfish or fish fillets, blackened, with, 572–573
catfish or fish fillets, Dijon, with, 572–573
and chicken, 682–683
hoppin' John with ham and, 363
with onion dip, 897
salad
with caramelized onions and toasted almonds, 84–85
in three-bean potato salad, 102–103
with tofu and avocado, 75
with tuna and avocado, 74–75
with tuna and mango, 75

Green bean(s) *(cont.)*
and scallop pan broil, 603
soy-marinated flank steak and, 723
stew
lamb, with tomatoes and, 254–255
quick-, with bacon, 450–451
quick-, with chicken, 451
quick-, with ham, 451
quick-, with sausage, 451
quick-, with shrimp, 451
with tomatoes, olives, and almonds, 255
tofu, stir-fried, and, 516–517
Green curry, eggplant, 643
Green lentils, 485
Green smoothie, 811
Green-leaf lettuce, 48
Greens. *See also specific salad greens*
about
cooking, 117
description of, 48–49
flavoring, 924
grilling, 79
substituting ingredients, 21
washing, 49
black beans with chorizo, garlic, and, 481
breakfast patties with pork and, 858–859
creamy sauces, 439
curried rice, beans, and, 351
gingery, salmon with, 554–555
kidney beans with ham, garlic, and, 481
pasta with eggs and, 300–301
sautéed, with garlic, 924
soup
andouille, black-eyed pea, and Southern greens, 247
bacon and egg drop, with, 211
hot and sour, with tofu and, 271
tomato and bread, with, 225
and tomatoes, stewed, with salmon, 555
warm, with chickpeas and potatoes, 103
warm, with orzo and steak, 111
white beans with bacon, garlic, and, 481
white beans with sausage, garlic, and, 480–481
Grilling. *See* Broil(ed)ing
Grits
buttery, classic, 827
honey-cheddar, with sage, 826–827
maple-almond, 827
Parmesan, with rosemary, 827
shrimp over, 398–399
soy-orange, with ginger, 827
topping, 827
Grouper, roasted, 597
Gruyère
in chicken melt, 619
gratin, couscous, with leeks and, 390–391
gratin, quinoa, with leeks and, 391
and ham sandwich with apples, broiled, 150–151
turkey and kale hero with, 173
Guajillo chile, 457
Gumbo(s)
crab, 261
no-okra, 261
sausage, 261
shrimp, 260–261
tofu, 261
Gyro fixings, charred chicken and pita with, 648–649

H

Habanero peppers, 456
Haddock, roasted, 597
Halibut
about, 587
butter-poached, with peas, 571
olive oil-poached, with endive, 570–571
pan-seared, with garlicky spinach, 541
pan-seared, with garlicky watercress, 541
Ham
about, 503
BBQ-glazed steaks with collards, 765
braised cabbage with sauerkraut and, 452–453
bulgur, apple, and fennel salad with, 95
chicken cutlets, Moroccan-spiced, with pinto beans and, 627
collards, warm, with peaches and, 81
hash, smoky two-potato and, 860–861
honey-mustard-glazed steaks with kale, 765
hoppin' John with green beans and, 363
kidney beans with greens, garlic, and, 481
maple-glazed steaks with collards, 764–765
no-cook skewers, 878
prosciutto
crisp, cucumber gazpacho with, 203
crisp, melon gazpacho with, 202–203
-crusted chicken with endive, 620–621
-crusted chicken with kale, 621
curried rice, beans, and broccoli with, 351
and mozzarella sandwich, broiled, with melon, 151
warm pickled cauliflower salad with, 83
white beans with escarole and, 515
risotto-style pasta with squash and, 322–323
sandwich, and Gruyère with apples, broiled, 150–151
scrambled eggs with tarragon and, 839
soup
ginger carrot, with, 223
lentil, with, 266–267
pea, minty, with, 223
pea, sweet, with, 222–223
split pea, with, 267
stewed green beans with, 451
and white bean gratin, 502–503
-wrapped apples, 886
Hamburger buns, 136
Haricots verts. *See* Green bean(s)
Harissa
in glaze, 743
shrimp, 549
in yogurt-harissa sauce, 690–691
Hash
celery root and prosciutto, 861
potato and chorizo, 861
sweet potato and tofu, 861
two-potato and ham, 860–861
Hazelnuts, roasted spaghetti squash and Gorgonzola and, 459
Head lettuce, 48–49
Herb(s)
about
prep shortcuts, *29*
seasoning with, 942
storing, 15, 18
in bone-in chicken noodle soup, 257
in bubbling caprese, 415
butter, 132–133
in chimichurri sauce, 718–719
croutons, herbed, 71
herb-rubbed chicken breasts with peas and Parmesan, 613
in herby chicken thighs with crisp cabbage and fennel, 655
in jambalaya, 380–381
lentil soup with, 267
in mustard-herb pork meatballs with broccoli rabe, 761
-rubbed leg of lamb with chopped Greek salad, 798–799
steak wrap with lettuce and, 710–711

tartar sauce, herby, 68–69
in tomato sauce, 297
watermelon soup with fresh, 973
Hoisin
in barbecue sauce, 145
in ginger-hoisin barbecue sauce, 753
-glazed fish fillets and shitakes, 575
-glazed fish with radishes, 579
in mayonnaise, 142–143
in vinaigrettes, 90–91
Hominy, 404–405
Honey
about, 17, 979
-cheddar grits with sage, 826–827
in honey-ginger-soy roasted chicken and celery, 678–679
-lemon oatmeal with caramelized pine nuts, 825
-mustard spread, 133
-mustard-glazed ham steaks with kale, 765
-orange bananas, caramelized, 970
peanut butter and banana sandwich, with raisins and, 138–139
pecan-honey crunch, broiled grapefruit with, 813
in ricotta-honey breakfast bruschetta, 817
roasted nuts with ginger, soy, and, 895
-walnut johnnycakes, 865
-yogurt sauce, sautéed apples and bananas with, 818–819
Hoppin' John
with collards, 362–363
with green beans and ham, 363
Portuguese style, 363
Horseradish mayo, warm, 193
Hot and sour
beef with asparagus, 479
black beans and bok choy, 478–479
chicken with bok choy, 479
salad, bok choy with mussels, 112–113
salad, cabbage with salmon, 113
soup
with Asian greens and tofu, 271
with bean sprouts and beef, 271
with bok choy and pork, 270–271
with Napa cabbage and chicken, 271
Hot sauce
avocado with cilantro and, 920
cucumber salad with lime juice and, 915
in hot wings and Brussels sprouts with yogurt-blue cheese sauce, 691
seasoning with, 942
Hummus
basic recipe, 939
roasted red pepper, 939
and vegetable pita pockets, 140–141

I

Ice cream. *See* Sundaes
Iceberg lettuce, 48, 79
Interchangeable ingredients, 21
Israeli couscous, 910
Italian sausage
and escarole soup, 245
homemade, with white beans, 763
polenta
with chicken and asparagus, 403
with fennel and, 403
with mushrooms and, 402–403
soup with cannellini and kale, 246–247
soup with escarole, 245
Italian-style
breakfast burritos, 857
breakfast patties with sautéed fennel, 859
bulgur pilaf, fish kebabs over, 577
couscous helper, 401
dip sandwich, 177
steak, lettuce, and herb wrap, 711

J

Jack cheese
black bean and cabbage gratin with tortilla crumbs and, 493
on cheesy tortillas, 483
couscous gratin with poblanos and, 391
Mexican cheeses and, 659
and salsa pizza wedges, 901
stuffed poblanos with black beans and, 434–435
stuffed poblanos with corn and, 435
Jalapeño peppers
about, 456
in jalapeño-cheddar johnnycakes, 865
in jalapeño-scallion johnnycakes, 864–865
Jam or jelly
-filled tortilla French toast, 833
jelly and peanut oatmeal, 825
Jambalaya
with collards, 381
des herbes, 381
des herbes with fish, 381
des herbes with shrimp, 380–381
Japanese noodles, 333
Jasmine rice
cooking times, 355
description of, 352
Jerk
chicken and onions, 650–651
pork with pineapple, 755
Jícama
about, 21
and chile mayo baguette, 133
salad
and arugula fry, with lime sauce, 447
with chiles, 913
slaw with chopped spicy chicken, 107
Johnnycakes
bacon, 865
honey-walnut, 865
jalapeño-cheddar, 865
jalapeño-scallion, 864–865
Parmesan, 865
Jook
with beef and bean sprouts, 360–361
brown rice, with chicken and snow peas, 360–361
with chicken and snow peas, 360–361

K

Kale
about, 21
chicken and blue cheese sausage over sautéed, 661
chickpeas, lemony, with, 479
eggs, scrambled, with Parmesan and, 841
ham steaks, honey-mustard-glazed, with, 765
kidney beans with chorizo and, 515
lamb and feta meatballs with, 761
pasta with feta, olives, and, 283
pasta with lima beans and, 289
pork stew with white beans and, 782–783
prosciutto-crusted chicken with, 621
salad
and asparagus Caesar, 76–77
raw, with pine nuts and balsamic currants, 81
raw, with tomatoes, pine nuts, and Parmesan, 45
warm, with cashews, scallions, and soy currants or raisins, 81
warm, with pine nuts and balsamic currants, 80–81

Kale (cont.)
in salmon with gingery greens, 554–555
and scallop pan broil, 603
soup, sausage, cannellini, and, 246–247
stir-fried chicken and, 632–633
and turkey hero with Gruyère, 173
and white bean stew with vegetable flatbread, 463–464
and white beans, stewed, with Parmesan toast, 483
Kebabs
beef and mushroom, with spicy peanut sauce, 724–725
beef and onion, with mustard-rosemary sauce, 724–725
chicken, over seasoned bulgur, 576–577
fish, over bulgur pilaf, 576–577
Kelp (kombi)
in dashi, 213
in miso soup, 234–235
Key lime crumble, 1003
Kidney beans
with chorizo and kale, 515
with ham, greens, and garlic, 481
in warm three-bean potato salad, 102–103
Kielbasa
in cabbage soup with smoked sausage, 244–245
in fast feijoada, 504–505
Kimchi
about, 123
and beef soup with rice, 251
braised cabbage, bacon, and, 453
skillet, stir-fried beef with, 712–713
and snow pea salad with beef, 122–123
-style, white beans with pork and cabbage, 500–501
Kohlrabi, tuna poke with cashews and, 545
Kombi (kelp)
in dashi, 213
in miso soup, 234–235
Korean-style
beef soup with rice, 250–251
chicken and vegetable pancakes, 662–663
fried chicken, 673
pork soup with rice, 251

L

Lamb, 788–801
about, 715, 789
and black bean chili, 273
in cabbage, unstuffed, with ground meat, 425
and carrot sauté with mustard and miso, 683
chops
with balsamic bulgur, 789
with balsamic couscous, 788–789
Dijon, with parsnips, 793
miso, with carrots, 792–793
miso, with sweet potatoes, 793
with pomegranate couscous, 789
with soy-ginger couscous, 789
cumin, with green peppers, 639
herb-rubbed, with chopped Greek salad, 798–799
leg, herb-rubbed, with chopped Greek salad, 798–799
leg, Moroccan spice-rubbed, with shredded carrot salad, 798–799
meatballs
and bulgur, in tomato sauce, 800–801
and feta, with kale, 761
and rosemary, with yogurt sauce, 891
and spaghetti with tomato sauce, 321
Moroccan, and fennel, 785
Moroccan, with couscous and olives, 787
and red onion burger, 727
and rice with dried fruit, 794–795
and rice with green olives, 795
skillet meat loaf with harissa glaze, 743
skillet shepherd's pie with quinoa crust, 408–409
stew with root vegetables, 747
stew with tomatoes, 254–255
stir-fried
with green peppers and cumin, 790–791
with green peppers and curry, 791
with leeks and cumin, 791
and sweet potato fundido, 659
zucchini slaw with crisp ground, 107
Lasagna
recipe-free, 467
three-cheese, 326–327
tortilla, 466–467
Leek(s)
and chicken, braised and glazed, 664–665
eggs fried with mushrooms and, 852–853
eggs fried with tomatoes and, 853
gratin, couscous, with Gruyère and, 390–391
gratin, quinoa, with Gruyère and, 391
lamb, stir-fried, with cumin and, 791
panfried soft-shell crabs with bacon and, 583
panfried trout with bacon and, 582–583
pasta with chicken, wine and, 315
soup with blue cheese, 259
Legumes, cooking, 267
Lemon(s)
about, 18, 69
in aïoli, 161, 624–625
avocado with, 920
broccoli, scrambled, with Parmesan and, 442–443
in bulgur, lemony, with zucchini, olives, and ricotta salata, 387
bulgur with parsley and, 946
chicken cutlets with capers and, 733
chickpeas, lemony, with kale, 479
citrus cycle and, 69
in citrus pound cupcakes, 985
in honey-lemon oatmeal with caramelized pine nuts, 825
lemon s'mores, 994
lemony asparagus, sole with, 561
lentil soup with, 267
in lima beans
with broccoli and, 488–489
with spinach and eggs, 489
on toast with rosemary, 477
-pepper chicken and onions, 651
in pesto, 285
radishes, broiled, with olive oil and, 880
-ricotta pancakes, 869
roasted nuts with smoked paprika and, 895
in salad(s)
beet and carrot salad with, 57
broccoli tabbouleh with tomato and, 124–125
cauliflower tabbouleh with tomato and, 125
in salad dressing, 89
in sandwiches
tomato and broccoli rabe hero with mozzarella and, 173
tuna, with fennel, capers, and, 147
turkey and spinach hero with fontina and, 173
in seared steak with lemon spinach, 709

in soy-lemon edamame and asparagus, 489
stir-fried bok choy with olives and, 927
in stir-fried chicken with chard and citrus, 633
in tahini-lemon potato salad, 962
veal scallopini with capers and, 732–733
white bean soup with rosemary and, 209
Lemongrass
in broth, 339
substituting ingredients, 21
Lentil(s)
about, 485
and chicken, braised, 513
and pork chops, braised, 513
and potatoes, tomato-braised, 510–511
red, with toasted cauliflower, 508–509
and rice with fried onions, 372–373
and salmon, braised, 512–513
salmon simmered in, 599
shrimp simmered in dal, 598–599
with smoked paprika and garlic, 937
soups and stews
and beef stew with dried mushrooms, 507
and chile stew, 507
lentil soup, 266–267
and mushroom stew, 506–507
yellow, with charred broccoli, 509
Lettuce
about, 48–49
steak wrap with herbs and, 710–711
Lima bean(s)
BBQ, with collards, 514–515
in beef chili, 272–273
and cabbage gratin with rye crumbs, 492–493
corned beef and cabbage gratin with, 493
lemony, with broccoli, 488–489
lemony, with spinach and eggs, 489
limy, and poblanos, 489
pasta with kale and, 289
in succotash, 933
on toast with lemon and rosemary, 477
warm, with raw zucchini salad, 101
Lime(s)
about, 18, 69
avocado with chili salt and, 920
broccoli, scrambled, with soy sauce and, 443
carrot salad with cilantro and, 914
in chile-lime bananas, caramelized, 970
in citrus pound cupcakes, 985
cucumber salad with hot sauce and, 915
daikon salad with fish sauce, peanuts, and, 918
gazpacho, spicy green, with chile and, 205
in key lime crumble, 1003
in lima beans and poblanos, 489
in mango-lime breakfast bruschetta, 817
roasted whole fish with carrots and, 597
in salad dressings, 88–89
sauce, creamy, 447
sautéed sweet potatoes with chipotle and, 964
tabbouleh, fennel and radish, with tomato and, 125
Linguiça in fast feijoada, 504–505
Linguine with clams, 302–303
Lobster and egg salad, with cucumber and tarragon, 105
Long-grain rice, 352, 355
Loose-leaf greens, 48–49
Lyonnaise sandwich, open-face, 174–175

M

Mac and cheese, 280–281
Mackerel, Mediterranean, with mint, 584–585
Mako, cooking, 587
Malaysian-style BBQ fish, 578–579
Manchego
arugula with apricots, almonds, and, 45
bulgur, smoky, with eggplant, roasted red peppers, and, 387
plum and parsley salad with, 922
in Spanish dip sandwich, 176–177
stuffed poblanos with black beans and, 434–435
stuffed poblanos with corn and, 435
Manchurian tofu and cauliflower, 522–523
Mango(es)
about, *33*
in chutney, 194–195
-lime breakfast bruschetta, 817
in salsa, 757
tuna and green bean salad with, 75
Manhattan chowder, 231
Maple syrup
about, 17, 979
-almond grits, 827
bacon, 870–871
-bacon breakfast bruschetta, 817
-banana breakfast bruschetta, 817
blueberry, 871
ginger, 871
-ginger oatmeal with caramelized walnuts, 825
in maple-chicken-apple sausage over sautéed collards, 661
in maple-chile-beer roasted chicken and peppers, 679
in maple-Dijon barbecue sauce, 753
in maple-glazed ham steaks with collards, 764–765
in maple-rum bananas, caramelized, 970
-orange oatmeal with caramelized pecans, 824–825
Marcona almonds, arugula with apricots, manchego, and, 45
Marinades, seasoning combinations, 796
Marsala
chicken, 630–631
veal, 733
Masa and rajas, 392–393
Masa harina
about, 241
in masa and rajas, 392–393
Mascarpone, pasta with, 279
Master recipes
beans, 496–497
cakes without a mix, 984–985
cheat-a-little pizza, 190–191
cocktail meatballs, 890–891
condiments, 144–145
croutons, 71
dessert sauces, 988–989
grains, 354–355
make-ahead, 38
rice, 354–355
roast chicken, 688–689
roasted vegetables, 416–417
spice blends, 758–759
stocks, 212–213
tomato sauce, 296–297
vinaigrettes, 70–71
Mayonnaise. *See also* Aïoli
chile, 133
chipotle, 143
curry, 898
Dijon, 143, 898, 915
hoisin, 142–143
horseradish, warm, 193
master recipe, 144
in rosemary-mayo dressing, 120–121
soy, 162–163, 193

Mayonnaise *(cont.)*
tarragon, 159, 161
tomato-paprika, 161
variations for flavoring, 144
Meat. *See also* Beef; Lamb; Pork
about
marinades and rubs, 796–797
prep shortcuts, *34*
resting, 741
smoked, 269
substituting cuts of, 714–715
braising, recipe-free, *736–737*
cabbage, unstuffed, with, 425
with cold cashew noodles, 331
with cold peanut noodles, 330–331
with cold sesame noodles, 331
pho variations, 237
Meat loaf
chicken and chard, 699
chicken and spinach, 698–699
pork and bok choy, 699
shaping, 699
skillet, 742–743
turkey and spinach, 699
Meatballs
beef and bulgur, with tomato sauce, 801
beef and spaghetti with tomato sauce, 320–321
chicken and bulgur, with tomato sauce, 801
chicken and spaghetti with tomato sauce, 321
chorizo, with chard, 761
cocktail, master recipe, 890–891
lamb and bulgur, in tomato sauce, 800–801
lamb and feta, with kale, 761
lamb and spaghetti with tomato sauce, 321
pork and spaghetti with tomato sauce, 321
pork, five-spice, with bok choy, 760–761
pork, mustard-herb, with broccoli rabe, 761
turkey and spaghetti with tomato sauce, 321
Mediterranean-style
corn, 932
mackerel with mint, 932
Medium-grain rice, 352, 355
Melon. *See also* Watermelon
about, *33*
gazpacho with crisp prosciutto, 202–203
prosciutto and mozzarella sandwich, broiled, with, 151
Merguez, chickpea, and chard soup, 247
Mesclun, 49
Mexican cheeses, 659
Mexican-style
bone-in chicken noodle soup, 257
chicken and chard gratin, 657
Mexican street corn, 932
molten chocolate cake, 257
steak, lettuce, and herb wrap, 711
tortilla French toast, 833
Middle Eastern
breakfast bruschetta, 817
chicken and bread salad, 118–119
Milkshakes, 975
Millet
about, 353, 355
pilaf, recipe-free, *364–365*
Mint
beet and carrot salad with, 57
in fava bean soup, minty, 209
grape salad with, 913
mackerel, Mediterranean, with, 584–585
in minty pea soup with crisp ham, 223
noodles with beef, onions, and, 343
panfried olives with chiles and, 879
peas with prosciutto and, 934
pesto, rustic, 219
watermelon and feta salad with, 922
Mirepoix tomato sauce, 297
Mirin, cucumber salad with soy sauce and, 915
Miso
about, 235, 797
cabbage-wrapped chicken, 685
-cashew chicken tenders, 675
chicken sandwich with pineapple chutney, 195
-glazed catfish or fish fillets and mushrooms, 574–575
-glazed fish fillets and carrots, 575
lamb and carrot sauté with mustard and, 683
lamb chops, pan-seared, with carrots, 792–793
lamb chops, pan-seared, with sweet potatoes, 793
in miso broth, 671
in miso rice with snow peas and chicken, 297
pork with cabbage, edamame, and, 501
in scallion-miso bean sprouts, 919
skillet meat loaf, 743
soup
with chicken, udon, and snow peas, 235
with scallops, soba, and spinach, 234–235
with shrimp, soba, and spinach, 235
with tofu, soba, and, bok choy, 235
Molasses
waffles with ginger maple syrup, 871
whoopie pies, 981
Mole
black bean, 652–653
pumpkin seed, 653
Molten chocolate cake, 987
Monkfish, cooking, 587
Monterey Bay Aquarium, 587
Moroccan-spiced (-style)
chicken cutlets with chickpeas and dried fruit, 626–627
lamb and fennel, 785
lamb with couscous and olives, 787
lamb with shredded carrot salad, 799
pork and onion carnitas, 781
pork with couscous and grapes, 786–787
sloppy Joes, 729
tofu with tomatoes and cauliflower, 531
turkey and spinach meat loaf, 699
Mounds bar s'mores, 994
Mousse
chocolate, 993
pumpkin, 993
Mozzarella
in caprese, bubbling, 414–415
Mexican cheeses and, 659
quinoa puttanesca with, 388–389
sandwich
in Italian dip, 177
melted, sausage and pepper sub with, 179
and prosciutto, broiled, with melon, 151
tomato and broccoli rabe hero, with lemon zest and, 173
in turkey and broccoli rabe hero, 172–173
stuffed poblanos with white beans and, 435
in three-cheese lasagna, 326–327
in tomato and strawberry panzanella, 47
Muesli
apricot-cardamom, 807
fruit and cereal bars, no-bake, 822–823
ginger-clove, 807
loaded, 806–807
Multigrain bread, 136
Mung bean noodles, 333, 950
Mushroom(s)
beef carbonnade with, 747
and beef kebabs with spicy peanut sauce, 724–725
catfish, miso-glazed, and, 574–575

chicken, curried, and, 647
chicken Marsala with, 630–631
couscous gratin with Parmesan and, 391
eggs and steak with onions, 855
eggs fried with leeks and, 852–853
eggs fried with poblanos and, 853
eggs poached in, 851
in eggs sukiyaki, 524–525
fish fillets, hoisin-glazed, and, 575
fish fillets, miso-glazed, and, 574–575
garlicky, 956
in pan sauce, 617
pasta
with chicken, wine, and, 314–315
with eggs and, 301
risotto-style, with bacon and, 323
spaghetti Bolognese with, 319
"polenta," cauliflower, with, 432–433
polenta with sausage and, 402–403
portobellos, stuffed, 957
potatoes, mashed, with, 433
risotto, three-stir, 370–371
saag, spinach and, 439
shrimp, stir-fried, with eggs, cilantro, and, 589
stew
and chicken, 264–265
and lentil, 506–507
lentil and beef, with, 507
stuffed portobellos, 957
tomato sauce with, 297
and veal sauté with mustard and cream, 683
Mussel(s)
about
saving liquid from, 397
substituting ingredients, 21
swapping with clams, 553
chowder, 231
chowder, seafood, 230–231
hot and sour bok choy with, 112–113
linguine with, 303
pan roast, with vegetables and coconut curry, 605
pan roast, with vegetables and saffron aïoli, 604–605
pan roast, with vegetables and tomato broth, 605
prying open, 605
tabbouleh, warm, with, 396–397
Mustard
in barbecue sauce, 145
in chicken and green beans, 682–683
in Dijon catfish with green beans, 573
in Dijon lamb chops with parsnips, 793
Dijon mayo, cucumber salad with, 915
Dijon mayo, hard-boiled eggs with, 898
Dijon mayo, tofu sandwich with pickles and, 143
in Dijon-garlic-cider roasted chicken and carrots, 679
-glazed fish with apples, 579
-herb pork meatballs with broccoli rabe, 761
in honey-mustard baguette, 133
in honey-mustard-glazed ham steaks with kale, 765
lamb and carrot sauté with miso and, 683
lentil soup with, 267
in lentils and potatoes, tomato-and-Dijon-braised, 511
in maple-Dijon barbecue sauce, 753
-marinated flank steak and cherry tomatoes, 723
-pretzel chicken tenders, 675
-rosemary sauce, 725
in rubs, 797
in salad dressings, 72–73, 87, 121
in seared steak with mustard spinach, 708–709
tofu, stir-fried, and carrots with soy and, 517
tuna melt with pickles and, 147
tuna sandwich with pickles and, 146–147
veal and mushroom sauté with cream and, 683
in vinaigrettes, 115
Mustard greens
in andouille, black-eyed pea, and Southern greens soup, 247
in Thai sticky rice with pork and, 375

N

Napa cabbage, hot and sour soup with, 271
Niçoise style
tuna salad, 75
tuna sandwich, seared, 163
Noodles, 330–345
about, 16
Asian, 332–333
in broth with chicken and vegetables, 670–671
chicken noodle soup, 256–257
and chicken with peas, 695
Chinese egg noodles. *See* Chinese egg noodle(s)
cold cashew, 331
cold peanut, 330–331
cold sesame, 331, 949
with curry and coconut milk, 949
egg noodles, buttered, 948
fideos. *See* Fideos
fire and ice, 950
lasagna, three-cheese, 326–327
one-pot, 339
with pork. *See* Pork, noodles
ramen, 238–239, 332
rice noodles. *See* Rice noodles
soba. *See* Soba
udon. *See* Udon
white-cut chicken with, 671
Nut(s). *See also specific nuts*
about
as dessert staple, 979
seasoning with, 943
storing, 17
substituting ingredients, 21
toasting, 81, 84–85, 219
caramelized, 824–825
in goat cheese truffles, 885
making nut butters from, 139
nutty coconut oatmeal cookies, 983
pound cupcakes, 985
roasted
with ginger, soy, and honey, 895
with smoked paprika and lemon, 895
sweet and salty, Thai style, 895
spiced, sautéed with bacon, 877

O

Oatmeal
honey-lemon, with caramelized pine nuts, 825
maple-ginger, with caramelized walnuts, 825
maple-orange, with caramelized pecans, 824–825
peanut and jelly, 825
with soy sauce and scallions, 825
Oats, rolled. *See* Rolled oats
Oily fish, 585, 587
Okra
crunchy, 959
fried, 959
in gumbo, 260–261
and red beans in buttery tomato sauce, 491
Olive oil
about
infusing, 65
in marinades, 796
storing, 15
bean sprouts with rosemary and, 919

Olive oil *(cont.)*
pasta and, 305
for pinzimonio, 884
poaching in, 571
radishes, broiled, with lemon and, 880
in rosemary-garlic oil, 459
in Spanish tortilla, 460–461
tomato salad with yogurt and, 913
in warm cumin oil, 64–65
Olives
about, 943
bulgur, lemony, with zucchini, ricotta salata, and, 387
carrot salad with rosemary and, 914
cobbler, cherry tomato, with fennel and, 465
endive spears with, 883
endive spears with blue cheese and, 883
fennel salad with, 917
green bean stew with tomatoes, almonds, and, 255
lamb and rice with, 795
lamb, Moroccan, with couscous and, 787
no-cook skewers, 878
panfried, 879
pan-seared tuna with tomatoes and, 541
pasta with kale, feta, and, 283
pitting, 111
in rubs, 797
salad
beet and carrot, with, 57
couscous, fennel, and orange, with, 95
in fresh tuna, Niçoise style, 75
puffed rice, with dried tomatoes and, 61
sandwich
chicken salad, with thyme and, 165
in fresh tuna, seared, Niçoise style, 163
and ricotta baguette, 133
tuna, with, 147
stir-fried bok choy with lemon and, 927
in tomato-olive sauce, 421
ziti with feta and, 283, 299
Omelet for two, 834–835
One-pot noodles, 339
Onion(s)
about
prep shortcuts, *29*
seasoning with, 943
storing, 16
in arroz con pollo, 696–697
and beef kebabs with mustard-rosemary sauce, 725
and bratwurst sub, 179
caramelized, green bean salad with toasted almonds and, 84–85
caramelized, snow pea salad with toasted peanuts and, 85
charred, steak sandwich with, 192–193
chicken, braised and glazed, with soy and, 665
chicken, jerk, and, 650–651
chicken, lemon-pepper and, 651
chicken, za'atar, and, 651
chive pesto, rustic, 219
couscous gratin with broccoli, cheddar, and, 391
creamed, with seared chicken, 629
eggs and steak with mushrooms and, 855
eggs and steak with peppers and, 854–855
fajita peppers and, 928
fried, curried lentils and rice with, 372–373
noodles with beef, mint, and, 343
onion dip, green beans with, 897
panfried with corn, 933
peas with bacon and, 934
and pork carnitas, 780–781
pork chops, seared, with apples and, 750–751
pork, stir-fried, with black beans and, 749
red. *See* Red onion(s)
shallots in vinaigrettes, 70
soup, American, 258–259
in Spanish tortilla, 460–461
Open-face sandwiches
about, 175
Cobb, 175
Lyonnaise, 174–175
Orange(s)
about
citrus cycle, 69
in marinades, 796
storing, 18
bulgur with dried cranberries and, 946
in caramel stir-fried pork and green beans, 717
in chipotle-orange tofu and cauliflower, 523
chocolate-orange pudding, 990
in cinnamon-orange French toast, 831
-clove couscous, 821
couscous and fennel salad with olives and, 95
in ginger-orange bean sprouts, 919
in honey-orange bananas, caramelized, 970
in maple-orange oatmeal with caramelized pecans, 824–825
in orange cream sundaes, 976
in orange pie with gingersnap crumble, 1003
in orange-black bean sauce, 635
-ricotta pancakes, 868–869
roasted whole fish with fennel and, 596–597
rösti, sweet potato, with orange sauce, 427
in salad dressing, 79
smoothie, 811
in soy-orange grits with ginger, 827
in stir-fried chicken with chard and citrus, 633
white chocolate-orange pudding, 990
Orzo
risotto-style, with asparagus and eggs, 324–325
risotto-style, with chard and ricotta, 324–325
salad
Greek, with shrimp and, 110–111
Greek, with squid and, 111
green, with steak and, 111
Oven-fried
chicken with roasted corn, 676–677
pork chops with roasted corn, 677

P

Pa jun, 662–663
Packages
chicken and potato, 681
chicken and tomato, 680–681
chicken, tomato, and feta, 681
foil, 680–681
parchment, 681
Paella
about, 379
couscous, with chicken and fennel, 407
couscous, with chicken and zucchini, 406–407
shrimp and tomato, 378–379
squid and tomato, 379
Pan broil
sausage and corn, 603
scallop and corn, 602–603
scallop and green bean, 603
scallop and kale, 603
Pan roast
beef tenderloin with chile sweet potatoes, 741
beef tenderloin with potatoes, 740–741
mussel and vegetable, 604–605
pork tenderloin with celery root, 741
shrimp and vegetable, with saffron aïoli, 605
Pan sauce
balsamic, 617
breaded chicken cutlets with, 616–617

flavoring, 617
mushroom, 617
vegetable, 631
Pancakes
about, 867
banana-chocolate chip, 867
banana-coconut, 866–867
beet rösti with pear sauce, 427
bok choy, with soy dipping sauce, 444–445
broccoli rabe, with ricotta dipping sauce, 445
chicken and vegetable, Korean-style, 662–663
ingredients to stir into, 867
leaving lumps, 869
lemon-ricotta, 868–869
orange-ricotta, 868–869
potato rösti with apple sauce, 426–427
scallion, 940
sweet potato rösti with orange sauce, 427
Pancetta in carbonara soup, 211
Panfried
corn and onions, 933
olives, 879
pasta, 951
polenta, 947
rice noodles, 951
soft-shell crabs with bacon and leeks, 583
trout, 582–583
udon, 951
Pan-seared
corn
and poblanos, 455
and pork, 454–455
and shrimp, 455
and steak, 455
halibut, 541
lamb chops, miso, with carrots, 792–793
tuna with ginger-scallion snow peas, 540–541
Pantry staples, 15–17
Panzanella
shrimp, 119
tomato and strawberry, 47
Paprika. *See also* Smoked paprika
in chicken paprikash, 647
chicken stew with, 264–265
in pork paprikash, 755
-rubbed pork tenderloin with peach and tomato salsa, 757
in warm dressing, 65
Paprikash
chicken, 647
pork, 755
Parchment packages, 681
Parfaits
flavor variations, 809
fruit, yogurt, and graham cracker, 808–809
warm fruit, yogurt, and graham cracker, 809
Parmesan cheese
about
seasoning with, 943
shaving, 51
storing, 18
arugula with fried eggs and, 50–51
bread crumbs, 930
broccoli, scrambled, with lemon and, 442–443
chicken breasts, herb-rubbed, with peas and, 613
chicken, fastest, 618–619
and chicken sub, 157
couscous gratin with mushrooms and, 391
crisps, 899
eggplant, fastest, 619
and eggplant sub, 156–157
eggs, scrambled, with kale and, 841
farro and white beans with arugula and, 395
fennel fries, 447
grits with rosemary, 827
johnnycakes, 865
kale with tomatoes, pine nuts, and, 45
mashed potatoes, pork tenderloin with, 773
Mexican cheeses and, 659
in pasta e fagioli, 226–227
peas with, 934
in rosemary-Parmesan crisps, 899
in rosemary-Parmesan French toast, 831
in salad dressings, 116–117
in three-cheese lasagna, 326–327
-topped toast, 482–483
white beans on toast with sage and, 477
wine-braised white beans with cherry tomatoes and, 499
Parsley
about, *29*
bread crumbs, 930
bulgur with lemon and, 946
chickpea and cucumber salad with tahini and, 63
in pesto, 218–219
plum and manchego salad with, 922
in rubs, 797
scrambled eggs with chorizo and, 839
Parsnip(s)
about, 21
Dijon lamb chops with, 793
soup, creamy, with parsley pesto, 218–219
Pasilla chiles, 457
Pasta, 276–329
about
cooking times, 291
salting water, 279
stand-ins for fresh pasta, 327
storing, 16
with artichokes, bread crumbs, and lemon, 286–287
with asparagus and ricotta, 283
with bay scallops and tomatoes, 311
with broccoli rabe and ricotta, 282–283
cacio e pepe, 278–279
carbonara, 301
in carbonara soup, 211
with cauliflower and tomato sauce, 293
with cherry tomatoes and eggs, 301
with chicken. *See* Chicken, pasta
chorizo in. *See* Chorizo, pasta
with chorizo, red onions, and black beans, 289
with crab and tomatoes, 311
dumplings, ricotta, with spinach and brown butter, 328–329
with eggplant and tomato sauce, 292–293
with eggs. *See* Egg(s), pasta
with fennel. *See* Fennel, pasta
with feta. *See* Feta, pasta
fideos. *See* Fideos
with greens and eggs, 300–301
with kale and ricotta, 283
with kale, lima beans, and stock, 289
linguine with clams, 302–303
mac and cheese, 280–281
mushrooms in. *See* Mushroom(s), pasta
olive oil and, 305
orzo. *See* Orzo
panfried, 951
pasta e fagioli, 226–227
with pesto, 284–285
plain and simple, 948
recipe-free, *316–317*
with red onions, black beans, and stock, 287
with ricotta. *See* Ricotta, pasta
risotto style. *See* Risotto-style pasta
with sausage. *See* Sausage(s), pasta
with scallops and potatoes, 306–307
with scallops and tomatoes, 311
with shrimp. *See* Shrimp, pasta
spaghetti. *See* Spaghetti
with spinach. *See* Spinach, in pasta
with squid and tomatoes, 310–311
squid, fideos with tomatoes, corn, and, 309

Pasta *(cont.)*
three Bs, 312–313
with tomatoes. *See* Tomato(es), pasta
with tuna and dried tomatoes, 304–305
ziti, broiled, 298–299
ziti with olives and feta, 283, 299
Pea(s)
about, 21
and arugula frittata, 495
butter-poached halibut or fish fillets with, 571
chicken and dumplings with, 694–695
chicken and egg noodles with, 695
chicken breasts, herb-rubbed, with Parmesan and, 613
creamed, salmon with, 555
fideos with shrimp, tomatoes, and, 308–309
pork, stir-fried, with shallots and, 749
smashed, 935
soup
chicken, with rice and, 263
minty, with crisp ham, 223
split pea, 267
sweet, with crisp ham, 222–223
tofu, curried, with tomatoes and, 531
veal, braised, with, 734–735
veal scallopini with white wine and, 733
veal, stir-fried, with shallots and, 735
Peach(es)
broiled, with brown sugar, 972
in chutney, 195
cobbler under the broiler, 1001
fool, 996
goat cheese and pecan baguette and, 133
-raspberry smoothie, 811
salad
with blue cheese and tarragon, 922
and chicken, with tarragon vinaigrette, 115
warm collards with ham and, 81
watercress with pecans, blue cheese, and, 44–45
in salsa, 613, 757
tacos, crisp pork and, 185
toast with pecan butter and, 815
and tomato gazpacho with crisp bacon, 203
Peanut(s)
avocado with rice vinegar and, 920
daikon salad with fish sauce, lime, and, 918
and jelly oatmeal, 825
in scallion-peanut sauce, 615
soup
Chinese-style, with tofu and bok choy, 243
spicy curried, with chicken and spinach, 243
spicy, with chicken and collards, 242–243
spiced, sautéed with bacon, 877
toasted, 85
tofu, deep-fried, with scallions and peanut sauce, 520–521
tuna poke with daikon and, 544–545
in vinaigrettes, 158–159, 953
Peanut brittle, chocolate, 999
Peanut butter
about, 17
balls, salted chocolate, 982
in cold peanut noodles, 330–331
in peanut-coconut chicken tenders, 675
in rubs, 797
in salad dressings
ginger-peanut, 73
peanut-lime, 88–89
peanut-soy, 87
sandwich
and banana, with honey and raisins, 138–139
and pickle, 139
and tomato, with soy sauce, 139
in spicy peanut sauce, 724–725
in Thai peanut chicken with crisp cabbage and bean sprouts, 654–655
Pear(s)
about
prep shortcuts, *32*
storing, 19
substituting ingredients, 21
beet rösti with pear sauce, 427
charred Brussels sprout salad with, 127
and chicken salad, with mustard vinaigrette, 115
prosciutto-wrapped, 886
sweet potato soup with bacon and, 221
Pearled barley, 353, 355
Peas
with bacon and onion, 934
with ginger, 934
with Parmesan, 934
with prosciutto and mint, 934
Pecan(s)
-bourbon brownies, 998
caramelized, in maple-orange oatmeal, 825
goat cheese and peach baguette with, 133
-honey crunch, broiled grapefruit with, 813
oven-fried chicken with roasted corn, 677
sautéed with bacon and brown sugar, 877
tofu salad, curried, with golden raisins and, 92–93
watercress with peaches, blue cheese, and, 44–45
Pecan butter, toast with peaches and, 815
Peel-and-eat shrimp, 892
Pepitas and raisins, chipotle tofu salad with, 93
Peppers, hot
about, 456–457
chiles and limes, gazpacho, spicy green, with, 205
chiles in mayonnaise, 133
poblanos. *See* Poblanos
roasted, 417
Pernil-style pork loin with plantains, 777
Pesto
about, 285
chive, rustic, 219
cilantro, rustic, 219
cilantro-scallion, 340–341
-crusted chicken with eggplant, 623
fried eggs with, 836–837
lemon, 285
mint, rustic, 219
parsley, 218–219
pasta with, 284–285
pizza wedges, 901
spinach, 285
Pho
fast, 236–237
meat and seafood variations, 237
slow, with meat, 237
vegetable variations, 237
Phyllo dough
about, 979
in sautéed apple crunch, 997
spanakopita, classic, 469
spanakopita, skillet, 468
Picante amarilla, 563
Picante rojo, 563
Picante verde, 562–563
Pickle(s)
and peanut butter sandwich, 139
tofu sandwich with Dijon mayo and, 143
tuna melt with mustard and, 147
tuna sandwich with mustard and, 146–147
Pickled vegetables
in appetizers
warm-pickled bell peppers, 896
warm-pickled carrots, 896
warm-pickled cucumber spears, 896
warm-pickled zucchini, 896

in salads
warm broccoli, 83
warm cauliflower, with prosciutto, 83
warm cauliflower, with roasted red peppers, 82–83
in sandwiches
bánh mì, 180–181
BBQ blackened chicken with cucumbers, 169
blackened chicken with red onions, 168–169
Pico de gallo, quesadillas with, 900
Pie crust, quinoa, for skillet shepherd's pie, 408–409
Pilaf
about, 385
dried fruit and nut combos, 385
fish kebabs over bulgur, 576–577
lamb and rice with dried fruit, 794–795
lamb and rice with green olives, 795
pork and rice with pinto beans, 795
recipe-free, *364–365*
rice, 944
Pimentón (smoked paprika), 425
Piña colada smoothie, 810–811
Pine nuts
caramelized, in honey-lemon oatmeal, 825
kale salad
raw, with balsamic currants and, 81
raw, with tomatoes, Parmesan, and, 45
warm, with balsamic currants and, 80–81
toasting, 81, 219
Pineapple
about, *33*
-cardamom couscous, 821
in chutney, 195
jerk pork with, 755
in piquante amarilla, 563
rice bowl with chorizo and, 369
in salsa, 613, 756–757
Pinto beans
BBQ bacon, with fried eggs, 846–847
beer-braised, with chiles and sour cream, 499
chicken cutlets, BBQ-spiced, with ham and, 627
in chipotle chicken and dumplings with beans, 695
chipotle rice with corn and, 367
chorizo, homemade, with, 762–763
in pasta e fagioli, 226–227
and peppers in buttery tomato sauce, 491
and poblano frittata, 495
pork and rice with, 795
smoky, on toast, 477
and tomatoes, stewed, with cheesy tortillas, 483
in warm three-bean and sweet potato salad, 103
Pinzimonio, 884
Piquante verde, 562–563
Pistachios
pistachio sauce, deep-fried tofu with cilantro and, 521
puffed wheat salad with dried apricots and, 61
Pita pockets
about, 136
chicken
BBQ, with peach chutney, 195
charred, with gyro fixings, 648–649
curried, with mango chutney, 194–195
miso, with pineapple chutney, 195
crisp seasoned, 908
fattoush, warm, with feta, 441
fattoush, warm, with shrimp, 441
Greek pizza, 887
hummus and vegetable, 140–141
scramble, 843
tuna, with cucumbers and feta, 147
Pizza
cheat-a-little, 190–191
Greek pita, 887
with kale and white bean stew, 463
master recipe, 190–191
pizza wedges, 901
fig and Gorgonzola, 901
pesto, 901
salsa and Jack, 901
topping variations, 191
Plantains, 960
with cinnamon and cumin, 960
pernil-style pork loin with, 777
with smoked paprika, 960
Plum, manchego, and parsley salad, 922
Poached
chicken, 624–625
eggs. *See* Egg(s), poached
fish fillets or steaks, 580–581
halibut, 570–571
salmon salad, 69, 72–73
scallop salad, 69
shrimp salad, 68–69
steamed vs., 571
Poblanos
about, 457
couscous gratin with Jack cheese and, 391
eggs fried with mushrooms and, 853
eggs poached in cream and, 525
in lentil and chile stew, 507
lima beans, limy, and, 489
in masa and rajas, 392–393
pan-seared corn and, 455
and pinto bean frittata, 495
stuffed
with black beans and cheese, 434–435
with corn and cheese, 435
with white beans and mozzarella, 435
Poke
shrimp, with radishes and peanuts, 545
tuna, with daikon and peanuts, 544–545
tuna, with kohlrabi and cashews, 545
Polenta
broiled or grilled, 947
cauliflower, with mushrooms, 432–433
with chicken and asparagus, 403
creamy, 947
panfried, 947
pound cupcakes, 985
with sausage and fennel, 403
with sausage and mushrooms, 402–403
shrimp over, 393
Pomegranate couscous, lamb chops with, 789
Popcorn, 876
Poppy seeds in poppy pound cupcakes, 985
Porchetta-style pork loin with parsnips, 776–777
Pork, 748–787. *See also* Bacon; Ham; Sausage
about
boneless vs. bone-in chops, 751
cuts of meat, 715
fast roasting, 773
BBQ baby back ribs, 752–753
braising
with beer, 766–767
Moroccan-style, 786–787
with wine, 767
breakfast patties, 858–859
broiled jerk, with pineapple, 755
broiled, paprikash with red peppers, 755
cabbage, shredded, with tahini-lemon dressing and, 89
in cabbage, unstuffed, with ground meat, 425
carnitas, 780–781

Pork *(cont.)*
chops
braised lentils with, 513
in fast feijoada, 504–505
oven-fried, with roasted corn, 677
and pozole, 393
seared, with apples and onions, 750–751
seared, with Brussels sprouts, 751
seared, with fennel, 751
and vegetables with chimichurri, 719
collard greens stewed with, 268–269
and corn, pan-seared, 454–455
curried, with couscous and spinach, 787
with edamame, cabbage, and miso, 501
homemade cold cuts, master recipe, 775
meat loaf with bok choy, 699
meatballs
curry, 891
five-spice, with bok choy, 760–761
mustard-herb, with broccoli rabe, 761
and spaghetti with tomato sauce, 321
Swedish, 891
noodles
with chile oil, snow peas, and, 335
with peppers, cilantro, and, 343
udon with teriyaki, 337
pan-roasted tenderloin with celery root, 741
paprikash with red peppers, 755
pernil-style loin with plantains, 777
porchetta-style loin with parsnips, 776–777
pozole and, chops, 393
and rice with pinto beans, 795
sandwich(es)
in bánh mì, 180–181
BBQ chopped, and slaw sandwich, 196–197
in Big T's meat sauce sub, 188–189
crisp, 184–185
sloppy Joes, Chinese-style, 729
and scallion burger, 727
skillet meat loaf, 742–743
in skillet shepherd's pie with quinoa crust, 409
soup
hot and sour, with bok choy and, 270–271
Korean-style, with rice, 251
in pho, slow with meat, 237
tamale soup, 241
souvlaki with zucchini, 754–755
spaghetti and drop meatballs with tomato sauce, 321
stew
basic recipe, 747
with black beans and collards, 783
and dumplings, 778–779
Provençal braised, and fennel, 784–785
white bean chili, 783
with white beans and kale, 782–783
stir-fried
and broccoli with chiles, 731
with corn and scallions, 749
with edamame and scallions, 748–749
with onions and black beans, 749
orange caramel, with green beans, 717
with peas and shallots, 749
with skillet sauerkraut, 713
stroganoff, 647
and sweet potato enchiladas, 745
tenderloin
with butternut purée, 772–773
grilled or broiled, sauerkraut and apple salad with, 123
homemade cold cuts, master recipe, 775
pan-roasted, with celery root, 741
with Parmesan mashed potatoes, 773
spice-rubbed with pineapple salsa, 756–757
with sweet potato purée, 773
in Thai sticky rice with meaty vegetable sauce, 374–375
in Thai sticky rice with mustard greens and, 375
with white beans and cabbage, kimchi style, 500–501
Port wine in cranberry-port sundaes, 976
Potato(es). *See also* Sweet potato(es)
about, 19
bangers and mash, 770–771
and beef, curry-braised, 739
and beef tenderloin, pan-roasted, 740–741
and chicken, curried, adobo-style, 693
and chicken packages, 681
chickpeas, curried, stir-fried, with carrots and, 486–487
and crab cakes, 600–601
crust, roasted salmon with, 558–559
French fries, 963
hash, chorizo and, 861
hash, smoky two-potato and ham, 860–861
and lentils, tomato-braised, 510–511
Parmesan mashed, pork tenderloin with, 773
pasta with scallops and, 306–307
roasted, crisp, 965
salad
chipotle, 962
classic, 962
German-style, 962
tahini-lemon, 962
warm, three-bean and, 102–103
warm, with greens with chickpeas and, 103
skin-on mashed, 961
soup with rustic chive pesto, 219
in Spanish tortilla, 460–461
and steak enchiladas, 744–745
vegetable main dishes
flautas, chorizo and, 437
mashed, with mushrooms, 433
rösti with apple sauce, 426–427
saag, spinach and, 438–439
Poultry. *See* Chicken; Turkey
Pound cupcakes, master recipe, 984–985
Pozole
and chicken thighs, 405
and pork chops, 404–405
Praline banana cupcakes, 1000
Pressed tofu. *See* Tofu, pressed
Pretzels, chocolate-covered, 986
Prosciutto
bagel chips with tomato, ricotta, and, 888
crisp, cucumber gazpacho with, 203
crisp, melon gazpacho with, 202–203
-crusted chicken with endive, 620–621
-crusted chicken with kale, 621
curried rice, beans, and broccoli with, 351
and drop biscuits, 862–863
endive spears with, 883
hash, celery root and, 861
and mozzarella sandwich, broiled, with melon, 151
peas with mint and, 934
scrambled eggs with basil and, 839
warm pickled cauliflower salad with, 83

white beans with escarole and, 515
-wrapped cantaloupe, 886
-wrapped pears, 886
-wrapped tomatoes, 886
Provençal
chicken, 644–645, 785
pork and fennel, 784–785
tomato sauce, 801
tomato soup with fennel, 216–217
Provolone and salami sandwich with roasted red pepper, broiled, 151
Puddings
chocolate-banana, 990
chocolate-orange, 990
white chocolate-orange, 990
Puffed
rice salad
with dates and almonds, 60–61
with dried tomatoes and olives, 61
red beans and, 61
wheat salad, with dried apricots and pistachios, 61
Pumpkin mousse, 993
Pumpkin seed(s)
in chipotle tofu salad with raisins, 93
mole, chicken and peppers with, 653
pumpkin soup with apples and, 221
Pumpkin soup with apples and pumpkin seeds, 221
Purée(s)
butternut, 772–773
sweet potato, 773
Puttanesca
-crusted chicken with fennel, 623
eggplant, with tomato sauce, 293
quinoa, with mozzarella, 388–389
quinoa, with ricotta, 389
tomato sauce, master recipe, 297

Q

Quesadillas with pico de gallo, 900
Queso fresco
substitutions for, 659
tomato salad with tomatillos and, 47
Queso fundido
chicken and chile, 658–659
lamb and sweet potato, 659
sweet pepper, 418–419
Queso Oaxaca, 659
Quinoa
about
cooked in stock, 945
cooking times, 355
description of, 353
seasoning, 945
crust, for skillet shepherd's pie, 408–409
gratin with leeks and Gruyère, 391
pilaf, recipe-free, *364–365*
pilaf with chickpeas and dried fruit, 384–385
puttanesca with mozzarella, 388–389
puttanesca with ricotta, 389
wine and rosemary, 945

R

Radicchio
about, 48
and endive with bacon vinaigrette, 52–53
sole with balsamic, 561
in steakhouse salad, 54–55
Radish(es)
about, 105
avocado soup with crab and daikon, 207
broiled, with olive oil and lemon, 880
broiled, with soy, 880
and herb butter baguette, 132–133
hoisin-glazed fish with, 579
poke, shrimp, with peanuts and, 545
poke, tuna, with peanuts and daikon, 544–545
salad
daikon, with fish sauce, lime, and peanuts, 918
fennel tabbouleh with tomato and lime and radishes, 125
jícama and radish, 918
tuna and egg, with dill and radishes, 104–105
Raisins
carrot salad with, 914
kale, warm, with cashews, scallions and soy, 81
peanut butter and banana sandwich, with honey and, 138–139
tofu salad, chipotle, with pepitas and, 93
tofu salad, curried, with pecans and, 92–93
Raita, cucumber, 916
Ramen
about, 239, 332
chicken, homemade, 238–239
no-cook toppers, 239
Raspberries in peach-raspberry smoothie, 811
Ravioli soup, broken, 249
Raw fruit sauce, 989
Recipe-free
about, 38
braised meat, *736–737*
breakfast scrambles, *844–845*
pasta, *316–317*
pilaf, *364–365*
salads, *58–59*
soups, *232–233*
steamed fish, *556–557*
stir-fry, *636–637*
Red beans
butternut squash salad, raw, with warm, 101
and cabbage in buttery tomato sauce, 490–491
and okra in buttery tomato sauce, 491
puffed rice salad and, 61
Red cabbage and beef soup, 245
Red chile flakes
about, 457
in sesame-chile vinaigrette, 91
Red clam sauce, 303
Red lentils
about, 485
with toasted cauliflower, 508–509
Red onion(s)
BBQ chicken thighs with crisp cabbage and, 655
chicken sandwich with pickled, 168–169
curry-rubbed chicken with corn and, 641
and lamb burger, 727
panfried trout with chorizo and, 583
pasta with chorizo, black beans, and, 289
tofu sandwich with chipotle mayo and, 143
Red peppers
and poached chicken with smoked paprika aïoli, 625
pork paprikash with, 755
roasted
bulgur, smoky, with eggplant, manchego, and, 387
cauliflower salad, warm pickled, with, 82–83
and chicken, skillet bake, 659
and chickpea salad with warm paprika dressing, 65
hummus and, 939
salami and provolone sandwich, broiled, with, 151
and tomato sauce, 297
Red smoothie, 811
Red-leaf lettuce, 48
Rémoulade, celery root, 66–67, 549
Reuben sandwich, 186–187
Ribs, baby back, BBQ, 752–753
Rice, 348–383
about
cooking, 251, 355
flavoring, 355
making rice cakes, 377
parcooking, 351

Rice *(cont.)*
stir-ins for, 941
storing, 16
substituting, 351
types of, 352
in arroz con pollo, 696–697
with bok choy, scrambled eggs, and scallions, 357
with cabbage, scrambled eggs, and scallions, 356–357
with chicken. *See* Chicken, rice
with clams, creamy Chinese, 358–359
with corn. *See* Corn, rice
curried, beans, and hearty greens, 351
curried chicken and, 697
fried, 357
in hoppin' John with collards, 362–363
in jambalaya des herbes, 380–381
jook with beef and bean sprouts, 361
jook with chicken and snow peas, 360–361
Korean-style beef soup with, 250–251
Korean-style pork soup with, 251
and lamb with dried fruit, 794–795
and lamb with green olives, 795
and lentils with fried onions, 372–373
master recipe, 354–355
miso, and snow peas with chicken, 367
in paella, 378–379
pilaf, 944
pilaf, recipe-free, *364–365*
and pork with pinto beans, 795
puffed. *See* Puffed, rice salad
rice, beans, and broccoli, 350–351
rice bowl, 368–369
and salmon cakes with cucumber salsa, 376–377
sesame seeds in fried rice, 357
with shrimp. *See* Shrimp, rice
Thai sticky, with meaty vegetable sauce, 374–375
Thai sticky, with pork and mustard greens, 375
in three-stir risotto, 370–371
with tomatoes. *See* Tomato(es), rice
and trout cakes with cucumber salsa, 377
white, 941
and wings, 382–383
Rice noodles
about, 333
in noodles
with beef, onions, and mint, 343
with chicken, peppers, and basil, 342–343
with pork, peppers, and cilantro, 343
and sweet potatoes in curry broth, 338–339
panfried, 951
Rice sticks, 333, 343
Rice vinegar, avocado with peanuts and, 920
Ricotta
bagel chips with prosciutto, tomato, and, 888
and chicken sausage over broccoli rabe, 660–661
in dipping sauce, 445
eggs, scrambled, with spinach and, 841
-honey breakfast bruschetta, 817
in lemon-ricotta pancakes, 869
and olive baguette, 133
in orange-ricotta pancakes, 868–869
pasta
with broccoli rabe and, 282–283
dumplings with spinach and brown butter, 328–329
orzo risotto, with chard and, 325
with ricotta, 279
in three-cheese lasagna, 326–327
pie, deconstructed, with spinach, tomatoes, and, 469
quinoa puttanesca with, 389
Ricotta salata
bulgur, lemony, with zucchini, olives, and, 387
charred broccoli salad with almonds and, 127
Mexican cheeses and, 659
Risotto rices, 352, 355
Risotto-style pasta
with fennel and sausage, 323
with mushrooms and bacon, 323
orzo with asparagus and eggs, 324–325
orzo with chard and ricotta, 325
squash and ham, 322–323
Roasted
beef tenderloin, 775
chicken, 678–679
chicken, master recipe, 688–689
corn, 676–677
nuts, 895
potatoes, crisp, 965
red peppers. *See* Red peppers, roasted
seafood, 558–559, 575, 596–597
spaghetti squash, 458–459
tofu with sesame drizzle, 528–529
turkey, 700–701, 774
vegetables, master recipe, 416–417
Roasting pan French toast, 830–831
Rolled oats, 353, 355, 979
Romaine
about, 48
in green salad, 911
grilled or broiled, seared scallops with, 78–79
in steakhouse salad, 54–55
Romesco
fried eggs with, 837
raw veggies with, 882
rustic, shrimp and cauliflower with, 590–591
rustic, squid and cauliflower with, 591
Root vegetables. *See also specific root vegetables*
raw, 57
stew with, 747
storing, 19
Rosemary
about, 21, 433
bean sprouts with olive oil and, 919
carrot salad with olives and, 914
chicken salad sandwich with grapes and, 164–165
-garlic oil, 459
garlic-rosemary chicken and vegetable pancakes, 663
grits, Parmesan, with, 827
and lamb meatballs with yogurt sauce, 891
lima beans on toast with lemon and, 477
in mustard-rosemary sauce, 724–725
-Parmesan crisps, 899
-Parmesan French toast, 831
popcorn, 876
quinoa with wine and, 945
refried white beans with, 938
in salad dressing, 120–121
white bean soup with lemon and, 209
Rub-in-ades, seasoning combinations, 796
Rum
in banana-rum cupcakes, 1000
in boozy black and white milkshakes, 975
in maple-rum bananas, caramelized, 970
Russian dressing, 186–187
Rye bread
about, 136

beet and cabbage, with rye croutons, yogurt, and dill, 57
lima bean and cabbage gratin with rye crumbs, 492–493
in Reuben sandwich, 186

S

Saag
mushroom and spinach, 439
potato and spinach, 438–439
tofu and spinach, 439
Saffron aïoli, 604–605
Sage
brown butter, ricotta dumplings with spinach and, 328–329
honey-cheddar grits with, 826–827
in sage sausage stuffing, 700–701
sautéed sweet potatoes with garlic and, 964
turkey salad sandwich with apples and, 165
white beans on toast with Parmesan and, 477
Saimin, 332
Salad(s), 40–127
with almonds. *See* Almond(s), salad
arugula with apricots, Marcona almonds, and manchego, 45
arugula with fried eggs and shaved Parmesan, 50–51
asparagus and kale Caesar salad, 76–77
bacon steakhouse salad, 55
beet. *See* Beet(s), salad
BLT, with rosemary-mayo dressing, 120–121
bok choy, hot and sour, with mussels, 112–113
broccoli rabe, steamed, with shrimp, 113
broccoli tabbouleh with charred tomato and lemon, 124–125
broccoli, warm pickled, 83
Brussels sprouts, 126–127
bulgur. *See* Bulgur, salad
butternut squash. *See* Butternut squash, salad
cabbage. *See* Cabbage(s), salad
caprese, 922
carrot. *See* Carrot(s), salad
cauliflower. *See* Cauliflower, salad
celery, 917
chicken. *See* Chicken, salad
chickpea. *See* Chickpea(s), salad
chopped, 912
classic Caesar, 77
collards, warm, with peaches and ham, 81
corn. *See* Corn, salad
couscous, fennel, and orange with olives, 95
crab. *See* Crab, salad
cucumber. *See* Cucumber(s), salad
daikon with fish sauce, lime, and peanuts, 918
edamame and cucumber, with warm ginger dressing, 65
eggplant. *See* Eggplant, broiled
eggs. *See* Egg(s), salad
endive and radicchio with bacon vinaigrette, 52–53
endive with fried eggs and blue cheese, 51
escarole. *See* Escarole, warm
fattoush, 118–119, 440–441
fennel. *See* Fennel, salad
fish and white bean, with tomato vinaigrette, 73
fruit, 817, 921
grape, with mint, 913
Greek. *See* Greek salad
green, 911
green bean, with caramelized onions and toasted almonds, 84–85
greens, warm, chickpea, potato, and, 102–103
greens, warm, with orzo and steak, 111
hot and sour, bok choy with mussels, 112–113
hot and sour, cabbage with salmon, 113
jícama. *See* Jícama, salad
kale. *See* Kale, salad
lobster and egg, with cucumber and tarragon, 105
orzo. *See* Orzo, salad
with peaches. *See* Peach(es), salad
pick-a-fruit, 921
pickled vegetables in. *See* Pickled vegetables, in salads
pine nuts in. *See* Pine nuts
plum, manchego, and parsley, 922
puffed rice. *See* Puffed, rice salad
puffed wheat, with dried apricots and pistachios, 61
recipe-free, *58–59*
salmon. *See* Salmon, salad
sauerkraut and apple salad with pork, 123
sausage and pepper salad with mustard dressing, 121
scallops. *See* Scallop(s), salad
shrimp. *See* Shrimp, salad
slaw. *See* Slaw
snow pea and kimchi salad with beef, 122–123
snow pea, with soy-caramelized onions and toasted peanuts, 85
spinach. *See* Spinach, salad
steak. *See* Steak, salad
three-bean and potato, warm, 102–103
three-bean and sweet potato, warm, 101
tofu. *See* Tofu, salad
tomato. *See* Tomato(es), salad
tuna. *See* Tuna, salad
vegetables, broiled, with white bean dressing, 97
veggie fajita, 96–97
watercress with peaches, pecans, and blue cheese, 44–45
watermelon, feta, and mint, 922
white bean. *See* White bean(s), salad
zucchini. *See* Zucchini, salad
Salad dressings. *See* Dressing(s)
Salad greens. *See* Greens
Salade Lyonnaise, 174
Salami
no-cook skewers, 878
and provolone sandwich with roasted red pepper, broiled, 151
Salmon
about, 539, 586
and asparagus with toasted bread crumbs, 536–537
braised lentils with, 512–513
with creamed peas, 555
with creamed spinach, 555
with fresh salsa, 538–539
with garlicky stewed greens and tomatoes, 555
with gingery creamed corn, 555
with gingery greens, 554–555
and rice cakes with cucumber salsa, 376–377
roasted, with potato crust, 558–559
salad
hot and sour cabbage with, 113
poached, and cucumber salad, with caper and mustard dressing, 72–73
poached, and cucumber salad, with ginger-peanut dressing, 73
poached, with herby tartar sauce, 69
smoked salmon and egg salad with celery, 105
sandwich
with chipotle-avocado spread, 159
with peanut vinaigrette, 158–159
with tarragon mayo, 159
simmered in dal, 599
smoked salmon
bagel chips with, 888

Salmon *(cont.)*
chowder, 231
and dill, scrambled eggs with, 838–839
and egg salad with celery, 105
with sweet and sour bok choy, 555
Salmorejo, 176
Salsa
avocado, 612–613
corn, 171
cucumber, 376–377
fresh, 171
and Jack pizza wedges, 901
mango, 757
peach, 613
peach and tomato, 757
pineapple, 613, 756–757
smooth cooked, 563
tomatillo, 562–563
tomato. *See* Tomato salsa
tortillas rojas, 894
watermelon, 613
Salty(ed)
chocolate milkshake, 975
chocolate peanut butter balls, 982
and sweet, roasted nuts, Thai style, 895
Sandwiches, 128–197
about, 136–137, 167
almond butter and apple, 139
baguettes
apple and honey-mustard, 133
fennel and garlic butter, 133
goat cheese, peach, and pecan, 133
jícama and chile mayo, 133
radish and herb butter, 132–133
ricotta and olive, 133
bánh mì, 180–181
BLT wrap, chipotle, 167
broiled cheese, 134–135
Buffalo tofu, 143
burgers
better beef, 726–727
black bean and carrot, smoky, 152–153
black-eyed pea and sweet potato, 153
cheeseburgers, 727
lamb and red onion, 727
pork and scallion, 727
turkey, 666–667
white bean and zucchini, 153
chicken. *See* Chicken, sandwich
Cobb, open-face, 175
crab. *See* Crab, sandwich
egg. *See* Egg(s), sandwich
Fast Rachel, 187
fish fillet, 161
ham and Gruyère with apples, broiled, 150–151
hero
charred chicken with hero fixings, 649
tomato and broccoli rabe, 173
turkey, 172–173
homemade cold cuts, 775
Italian dip, 177
Lyonnaise, open-face, 174–175
making multiple, 133
mozzarella in. *See* Mozzarella, sandwich
open-face, 174–175
peanut butter. *See* Peanut butter, sandwich
pickled vegetables in, *See* Pickled vegetables
pita pockets. *See* Pita pockets
pizza, cheat-a-little, 190–191
pork. *See* Pork, sandwich
prosciutto and mozzarella, broiled, with melon, 151
Reuben, 186–187
salami and provolone sandwich with roasted red peppers, broiled, 151
salmon. *See* Salmon, sandwich
sausage. *See* Sausage(s), sandwich
scallop roll with lemon-tarragon aïoli, 161
shrimp. *See* Shrimp, sandwich
sloppy Joes, 728–729
Spanish dip, 176–177
spreading butter, 149
steak. *See* Steak, sandwich
subs
bánh mì, 180–181
Big T's meat sauce, 188–189
bratwurst and onion, 179
chicken Parmesan, 157
eggplant Parmesan, 156–157
sausage and broccoli rabe, 179
sausage and pepper, 178–179
vegetarian sauce, 189
tofu. *See* Tofu, sandwich
tomato. *See* Tomato(es), sandwich
turkey. *See* Turkey, sandwich
with vegetables. *See* Vegetable(s), sandwich
Saran, Suvir, 522
Satay, chicken, 893
Sauces
barbecue. *See* Barbecue sauce
black bean, 634–635
chimichurri, 718–719
coconut-spinach-cashew, 615
creamy green, 439
curried yogurt sauce, 595
dessert, 988–989
dipping. *See* Dipping sauces
fruit, 668–669
mustard cream, 682–683
mustard miso, 683
mustard soy, 683
mustard-rosemary, 724–725
orange-black bean, 635
pan, 616–617
peanut, 520–521
peanut, spicy, 724–725
pistachio, 521
red clam, 303
scallion-peanut, 615
seasoning with, 943
soy-based. *See* Soy (sauce)
spinach-cashew, 614–615
tartar, 68–69, 594–595
tomatillo, 421
tomato. *See* Tomato sauce
tomato-soy, 635
tomato-yogurt, 739
vinegar-shallot, 595
yogurt-blue cheese sauce, 691
yogurt-harissa sauce, 690–691
yogurt-tahini sauce, 691
Sauerkraut
braised cabbage with ham and, 452–453
salad with apple and pork, 123
in sandwich, Reuben, 186–187
skillet, stir-fried pork with, 713
Sausage(s). *See also* Chorizo; Italian sausage
about, 771, 943
bangers and mash, 770–771
breakfast patties, 858–859
browned and braised, with endive, 768–769
Brussels sprouts with, 958
in cabbage, unstuffed, with ground meat, 425
chicken and blue cheese, over sautéed kale, 661
chicken and feta, over sautéed spinach, 661
chicken and ricotta, over broccoli rabe, 660–661
and corn pan broil, 603
maple-chicken-apple, over sautéed collards, 661
pasta
with broccoli rabe, ricotta, and, 283
with fennel and, white beans, and, 289
risotto-style, with fennel and, 323
ziti with, 299
polenta with fennel and, 403
polenta with mushrooms and, 402–403
rice bowl with, 368–369
in sage sausage stuffing, 700–701
salad with mustard dressing, pepper and, 121

sandwich
bratwurst and onion sub, 179
and broccoli rabe sub, 179
and pepper sub, 178–179
and pepper sub with melted mozzarella, 179
soup
andouille, black-eyed pea, and Southern greens, 247
bratwurst in cabbage, with smoked sausage, 244–245
cabbage, with smoked, 244–245
cannellini, kale, and, 246–247
gumbo, 261
merguez, chickpea, and chard, 247
stewed green beans with, 451
in three-stir risotto, 371
white beans with greens, garlic, and, 480–481
Sautéed
apple crunch, 997
apples, breakfast patties with, 859
butternut squash with warm edamame, 101
collards, maple-chicken-apple sausage over, 661
fennel, breakfast patties with, 859
greens with garlic, 924
kale, chicken and blue cheese sausage over, 661
nuts with bacon, 877
peppers, breakfast patties with, 859
spinach, chicken and feta sausage over, 661
sweet potatoes, 964
Savoy cabbage, 425
Scallion(s)
about, *28*
carrot salad with soy sauce and, 914
charred, steak sandwich with soy mayo and, 193
chicken, chile-rubbed, with corn and, 640–641
chicken, five-spice, and, 651
in cilantro-scallion pesto, 340–341
edamame on toast with sesame oil and, 477
ginger-scallion snow peas, pan-seared tuna with, 540–541
in jalapeño-scallion johnnycakes, 864–865
kale, warm, with cashews, soy currants or raisins, and, 81
-miso bean sprouts, 919
oatmeal with soy sauce and, 825
pancakes, 940
-peanut sauce, 615
and pork burger, 727
rice with cabbage, scrambled eggs, and, 356–357
seasoning with, 943
stir-fried
beef and asparagus with ginger and, 731
beef and broccoli with ginger and, 730–731
pork with corn and, 749
pork with edamame and, 749–750
shrimp with tomato, eggs, and, 588–589
tofu, deep-fried, with peanut sauce and, 520–521
Scallop(s)
about, 21, 551
with asparagus and toasted bread crumbs, 537
black pepper, and broccoli, 550–551
caramel-cooked, 569
pan broil
with corn, 603
with green beans, 603
with kale, 602–603
pasta with potatoes and, 306–307
pasta with tomatoes and, 311
roll, with lemon-tarragon aïoli, 161
salad
poached, with herby tartar sauce, 69
seared, with arugula and orange dressing, 79
seared, with grilled or broiled bok choy, 78–79
seared, with grilled or broiled romaine, 78–79
scampi, smoky, 547
seared
with arugula and orange dressing, 79
with grilled or broiled bok choy, 78–79
with grilled or broiled romaine, 78–79
in tomato sauce with basil and chiles, 592–593
in tomato-basil sauce, 593
soup, miso, with soba, spinach, and, 234–235
Scallopini, veal, 732–733
Scampi
smoky scallop, 547
smoky shrimp, 546–547
smoky squid, 547
Scissors, chopping with, *35*
Scotch bonnet peppers, 456
Scrambles
broccoli, with Parmesan and lemon, 442–443
broccoli, with soy sauce and lime, 442–443
eggs. *See* Egg(s), scrambled
recipe-free, *844–845*
Sea greens
in dashi, 213, 234–235
in miso soup, 234–235
Seafood, 532–605. *See also* Fish
about
cooking, 586–587
fish fillets and steaks, 542–543
marinades and rubs, 796–797
steamed, 571
sustainable seafood, 395, 587
chowder, 230–231
chowder, Manhattan, 231
chowder with bacon, 231
pho variations, 237
steamed clams, 552–553
steamed fish, recipe-free, *556–557*
steamed salmon, 554–555
Seared
broccoli, 925
cauliflower, 925
chicken, 629
corn, 454–455
duck breast with fruit sauce, 668–669
halibut, 541
lamb chops. *See* Pan-seared lamb chops
pork chops, 750–751
scallops, 78–79, 592–593
shrimp, 593
squid, 593
steak, 708–709
striped bass or thick fillets, 564–565
tofu, 529
tuna, 162–163, 540–541
Seasoning combinations, 796–797
Serrano peppers, 456
Sesame oil
black beans with soy and, 937
edamame on toast with scallions and, 477
noodles with, 949
in roasted tofu with sesame drizzle, 528–529
in sesame vinaigrette, 953
in sesame-chile vinaigrette, 91
in sesame-oil dressing, 911
sole with sesame bean sprouts, 561
tomato salad with soy and, 913
Sesame seeds
avocado with soy sauce and, 920
in fried rice, 357
in sesame beef and broccoli, 639
in sesame chicken and snow peas, 638–639
in sesame-chile vinaigrette, 91

Shallots
about, 21
panfried olives with thyme and, 879
stir-fried pork with peas and, 749
stir-fried veal with peas and, 735
in vinaigrettes, 70
vinegar-shallot sauce, 595
Shaved ice, fruity, 971
Shellfish. *See also specific types of shellfish*
cooking, 586
saving liquid from, 397
Shepherd's pie, skillet, with quinoa crust, 408–409
Shishito peppers, 457
Shitakes
hoisin-glazed fish fillets and, 575
shrimp, stir-fried, with eggs, cilantro, and, 589
Short-grain rice, 352, 355
Shrimp
about, 551, 599
black pepper, and broccoli, 551
with blue cheese slaw, 549
Buffalo, 548–549
caramel-cooked, 569
and celery root rémoulade, 67, 549
fattoush, warm pita, with, 441
harissa, 549
kebabs over tomato bulgur, 577
with noodles
cold cashew, 330–331
cold peanut, 330–331
cold sesame, 330–331
and sweet potatoes in curry broth, 338–339
over grits, 398–399
pan roast, with vegetables and saffron aïoli, 605
pan-seared corn and, 455
pasta
fideos with tomatoes, peas, and, 308–309
with potatoes and, 307
with tomatoes and, 311
peel-and-eat, 892
poke with radishes and peanuts, 545
rice
jambalaya des herbes with, 380–381
in three-stir risotto, 371
and tomato paella, 378–379
tomato rice and corn with, 367
salad
broccoli rabe, steamed, with, 113
and celery root rémoulade, 67
corn and black bean, with, 109
and egg salad, with cucumber and tarragon, 105
Greek, with orzo and, 110–111
panzanella, 119
poached, with curried tartar sauce, 69
poached, with herby tartar sauce, 68–69
zucchini slaw with chopped spicy, 107
sandwich
bánh mì, 181
burrito with white beans and corn salsa, 171
salad roll, curried, 161
salad roll, Sriracha, 160–161
salad roll with tomato-paprika mayo, 161
scampi, smoky, 546–547
seared, in tomato sauce, 593
simmered in dal, 599
smoky eggs with tomatoes and, 855
soup
and corn chowder, 231
gumbo, 260–261
miso, with soba, spinach, and, 235
Provençal tomato, with fennel and, 217
wonton, broken, with, 249
stewed green beans with, 451
stir-fried
and cauliflower with rustic romesco, 590–591
with shitakes, eggs, and cilantro, 589
with tomato, eggs, and basil, 589
with tomato, eggs, and scallions, 588–589
tempura, celery root, with, 448–449
Shucking corn, 207
Sides, 902–965
about, 942–943
asparagus gratin, 929
avocado, 920
bean sprouts, 919
black beans, 937
broccoli, 926
broiled cherry tomatoes, 931
bruschetta, 909
Brussels sprouts, 958
bulgur, 946
butternut squash, simmered, 955
cabbage, salted, with sesame vinaigrette, 953
caprese salad, 922
carrot salad, 914, 953
celery salad, 917
chopped salad, 912
coleslaw, 923
corn, 932–933
couscous, 910
crisp seasoned pita, 908
cucumber raita, 916
cucumber salad, 915, 953
daikon salad, 918
edamame succotash, 933
egg noodles, buttered, 948
eggplant gratin, 929
fajita peppers and onions, 928
fennel salad, 917
flour tortillas, warm, 906
garlic bread, 906
garlicky mushrooms, 956
grape salad with mint, 913
green salad, 911
greens sautéed with garlic, 924
hummus, 939
jícama and radish salad, 918
jícama salad with chiles, 913
lentils with smoked paprika and garlic, 937
mushrooms, garlicky, 956
mushrooms, stuffed, 957
noodles, 949–950
okra, crunchy, 959
okra, fried, 959
panfried
pasta, 951
rice noodles, 951
udon, 951
pasta, plain and simple, 948
peach, blue cheese, and tarragon salad, 922
peas, 934–935
pick-a-fruit salad, 921
plum, manchego, and parsley salad, 922
polenta, 947
portobellos, stuffed, 957
potato(es)
crisp roasted, 965
French fries, 963
salad, 962
skin-on mashed, 961
quinoa, 945
rice, brown, 941
rice pilaf, 944
rice, white, 941
ripe plantains, 960
scallion pancakes, 940
seared broccoli, 925
seared cauliflower, 925
skillet stuffing, 952
slaw, no-mayo, 923
slaw, soy, 923
slaw, tahini, 923
spinach, creamed, 936
stir-fried bok choy, 927
stuffed portobellos, 957
succotash, 933
sweet potato fries, 963
sweet potatoes, sautéed, 964
tomato salad, 913
tomatoes with bread crumbs, 930
vegetables, tender, 954
watermelon, feta, and mint salad, 922
Silken tofu, 518

Simmered butternut squash, 955
Simmered in dal
salmon, 599
shrimp, 598–599
Singapore-style noodles with chicken, peppers, and basil, 342–343
Skillet. *See also* Seared; Stir-fried
chicken and roasted red pepper bake, 659
edamame with chicken and cabbage, 501
edamame with pork, cabbage, and miso, 501
fruit crisp, 995
kimchi, stir-fried beef with, 712–713
kimchi style, white beans with pork and cabbage, 500–501
meat loaf, 742–743
panfried soft-shell crabs with bacon and leeks, 583
panfried trout, 582–583
sauerkraut, stir-fried pork with, 713
shepherd's pie with quinoa crust, 408–409
spanakopita, 468–469
stuffing, 952
white beans with pork and cabbage, kimchi style, 500–501
Slaw
and BBQ chopped pork sandwich, 196–197
blue cheese, Buffalo shrimp with, 549
coleslaw, 923
in Fast Rachel sandwich, 187
jícama, with chopped spicy chicken, 107
no-mayo, 923
soy, 923
tahini, 923
zucchini, with chopped spicy chicken, 106–107
zucchini, with chopped spicy shrimp, 107
zucchini, with crisp ground lamb, 107
Sloppy Joes, 728–729
Smoked fish and white bean gratin, 503
Smoked paprika
about, 425
in aïoli, 595, 625
lentils with garlic and, 937
ripe plantains with, 960
roasted nuts with lemon and, 895
in rubs, 797
-spiced chicken cutlets with white beans and dried tomatoes, 627
Smoked salmon
bagel chips with, 888
chowder, 231
and dill, scrambled eggs with, 838–839
and egg salad with celery, 105
Smoked sausage, cabbage soup with, 244–245
Smoked trout, scrambled eggs with dill and, 839
Smoky black bean
burgers with carrots, 152–153
soup, 209
Smoky bulgur
with eggplant, dates, and feta, 387
with eggplant, dried tomatoes, and feta, 386–387
with eggplant, roasted red peppers, and manchego, 387
Smoky eggs and shrimp with tomatoes, 855
Smoky lamb and sweet potato fundido, 659
Smoky pinto beans on toast, 477
Smoky scallop scampi, 547
Smoky shrimp scampi, 546–547
Smoky squid scampi, 547
Smoky steak and potato enchiladas, 745
Smoky tofu and black bean chili, 526–527
Smoky two-potato and ham hash, 860–861
Smoothies, 810–811
S'mores, 994
Snap peas
about, 21
and poached chicken with curry aïoli, 625
Snow pea(s)
about, 21
ginger-scallion, pan-seared tuna with, 540–541
jook with chicken and, 360–361
and kimchi salad with beef, 122–123
and miso rice with chicken, 367
miso soup with chicken, udon, and, 235
noodles with chile oil and, 334–335
salad with soy-caramelized onions and toasted peanuts, 85
sesame chicken and, 638–639
Thai coconut soup with, 253
tofu, stir-fried, and, 517
Soba, 333
miso soup
with scallops, spinach, and, 234–235
with shrimp, spinach, and, 235
with tofu, bok choy, and, 235
in noodles with chile oil
and edamame, 335
and snow peas, 334–335
and spinach, 335
Sole
with balsamic radicchio, 561
with glazed carrots, 560–561
with lemony asparagus, 561
with sesame bean sprouts, 561
Sorbet, 974
Soup(s), 198–271
about, 215
asparagus, creamy, with rustic mint pesto, 219
avocado, with crab and corn, 206–207
avocado, with crab and daikon, 207
with bacon. *See* Bacon, soup
beef. *See* Beef, soup
black bean, 208–209
butternut squash, with apples and bacon, 220–221
cabbage, with smoked sausage, 244–245
carbonara, 211
carrot, ginger, with crisp ham, 223
carrot, Thai coconut, with, 252–253
celery root, creamy, with rustic cilantro pesto, 219
chicken. *See* Chicken, soup
Chinese-style. *See* Chinese-style, soup
chop-and-drop, 252–253
chowders. *See* Chowder(s)
with crab. *See* Crab, soup
dessert, 992
egg drop. *See* Egg(s), soup
eggs sukiyaki, 524–525
escarole and Italian sausage, 245
fava bean, minty, 209
gazpacho. *See* Gazpacho
with greens. *See* Greens, soup
gumbo. *See* Gumbo(s)
with ham. *See* Ham, soup
hot and sour. *See* Hot and sour, soup
lentil, 266–267
miso. *See* Miso, soup
parsnip, creamy, with parsley pesto, 218–219
pasta e fagioli, 226–227
with peanuts. *See* Peanut(s), soup
with peas. *See* Pea(s), soup
pho, fast, 236–237
with pork. *See* Pork, soup
potato, creamy, with rustic chive pesto, 219
pumpkin, with apples and pumpkin seeds, 221
ravioli soup, broken, 249
recipe-free, *232–233*
red cabbage and beef, 245
sausage. *See* Sausage(s), soup
shrimp. *See* Shrimp, soup

Soup(s) *(cont.)*
with spinach. *See* Spinach, soup
stocks, master recipes, 212–213
sweet potato, with pears and bacon, 221
Thai coconut soup, 252–253
with tofu. *See* Tofu, soup
with tomatoes. *See* Tomato(es), soup
vegetable, frozen, 214–215
with vegetables. *See* Vegetable(s), soup
watermelon, with fresh herbs, 973
white bean, tomato and bread, with, 224–225
white bean, with rosemary and lemon, 209
wonton. *See* Wonton soup(s)
zucchini, tomato and bread, with, 225
Sour cream
about, 21
beer-braised pinto beans with chiles and, 499
black bean and cabbage salad with cilantro and, 63
cucumber salad with dill and, 915
Southern long-grain rice, 352
Soy (sauce)
about
in marinades, 796
storing, 17
types of, 337
broth, 581, 670–671
-brown sugar glaze, broiled grapefruit with, 813
caramel stir-fried beef and peppers, 717
-caramelized onions, 85
currants or raisins, 81
in dipping sauce, 444–445
-ginger couscous, lamb chops with, 789
in honey-ginger-soy roasted chicken and celery, 678–679
-lemon edamame and asparagus, 489
in lemon-soy aïoli, 625
-marinated flank steak and cherry tomatoes, 722–723
-marinated flank steak and green beans, 723
in mayonnaise, 162–163, 193
-orange grits with ginger, 827
in peanut-soy dressing, 87
seasoning with, 942
in slaw, 923
-spiked crab salad sandwich, 149
in tomato-soy sauce, 635
in vinaigrette, 91
Soybeans. *See* Edamame
Spaghetti
with fresh tomato sauce, 290–291
and meatballs with tomato sauce, 320–321
with nearly instant Bolognese, 318–319
in pasta e fagioli, Spanish-style, 227
Spaghetti squash, roasted
with brown butter and walnuts, 458–459
with hazelnuts and Gorgonzola, 459
with rosemary-garlic oil and walnuts, 459
Spanakopita
classic, 469
skillet, 468–469
Spanish paella rice, 379
Spanish-style
chorizo, homemade, with chickpeas, 763
chorizo on skewers, no-cook, 878
dip sandwich, 176–177
pasta e fagioli, 227
Spanish tortilla, 460–461
steakhouse salad, 55
Spice(s)
about
"blooming" ground, 229
as dessert staple, 979
seasoning with, 942
storing, 15
croutons, 71
Moroccan, 228–229
nuts with bacon, 877
pound cupcakes, 985
-rubbed pork with pineapple salsa, 756–757
spice blends, master recipe, 758–759
in spicy chocolate milkshake, 975
Spinach
about, 48
-cashew sauce, 614–615
chicken and feta sausage over sautéed, 661
and chicken meat loaf, 698–699
clams, steamed, with, 553
creamed, 936
creamed, chicken with, 628–629
creamed, salmon with, 555
creamy, seared steak with, 709
in eggs Florentine, 850–851
eggs, scrambled, with feta and, 841
eggs, scrambled, with goat cheese and, 840–841
eggs, scrambled, with ricotta and, 841
in eggs sukiyaki, 524–525
garlicky, pan-seared halibut with, 541
hero, turkey and, with fontina and lemon zest, 173
in jambalaya, 381
lemon, seared steak with, 709
lima beans, lemony, with eggs and, 489
mustard, seared steak with, 708–709
in pasta and noodles
with greens and eggs, 301
noodles with chile oil and, 335
with ricotta and, 283
ricotta dumplings with brown butter and, 328–329
pesto, 285
pie, deconstructed, with tomato, ricotta, and, 469
pork, curried, with couscous and, 787
saag
mushroom and, 439
potato and, 438–439
tofu and, 439
salad
with apples, walnuts, and goat cheese, 45
and chicken salad, with curry dressing, 117
and chicken salad, with Parmesan dressing, 116–117
with fried eggs and feta, 51
soup
in bacon and egg drop, 211
and chorizo, 245
miso, with scallops, soba, and, 234–235
miso, with shrimp, soba, and, 235
peanut, spicy curried, with chicken and, 243
in tortilla lasagna, 467
and turkey meat loaf, 699
and white bean frittata, 494–495
Split pea soup, 267
Spring rain noodles, 333
Squash
au gratin with toasted nuts, 430–431
cider-braised turkey and, 703
Squid
black pepper, and bok choy, 551
and cauliflower, stir-fried, with rustic romesco, 591
fideos with tomatoes, corn, and, 309
pasta with tomatoes and, 310–311
salad, Greek, with orzo and, 111
salad, warm escarole and white bean, with, 99
scampi, smoky, 547
seared, in tomato sauce, 593
soup, Provençal tomato, with fennel and, 217
soup, Thai coconut, with, 253

timing doneness, 551
and tomato paella, 379
Sriracha shrimp salad roll, 160–161
Staple ingredients
freezer staples, 19–20
fridge staples, 18–19
interchangeable, 21
pantry staples, 15–17
shopping for speed, 14
Steak (beef)
flank
chipotle-marinated and asparagus, 723
mustard-marinated and cherry tomatoes, 723
soy-marinated and cherry tomatoes, 722–723
soy-marinated and green beans, 723
pan-seared corn and, 455
and potato enchiladas, 744–745
salad
bacon steakhouse, 55
green, with orzo and, 111
Spanish steakhouse, 55
steak fajita, 97
steakhouse, 54–55
sandwich
and black bean burrito with fresh salsa, 171
with charred onions, 192–193
with charred scallions and soy mayo, 193
Italian-style wrap with lettuce and herbs, 711
Mexican-style wrap with lettuce and herbs, 711
tacos with lots of options, 182–183
Thai-style wrap with lettuce and herbs, 710–711
with warm horseradish mayo, 193
seared
with creamy spinach, 709
with garlicky chard, 709
with lemon spinach, 709
with mustard spinach, 708–709
and vegetables with chimichurri, 718–719
Steak (fish). *See* Fish, steaks
Steak (ham)
BBQ-glazed, with collards, 765
honey-mustard-glazed with kale, 765
maple-glazed, with collards, 764–765
Steamed
broccoli rabe with shrimp, 113
chicken, 684–685
clams, 552–553
fish, recipe-free, *556–557*
poached eggs, 325
salmon, 554–555
tender vegetables, 954
Steaming racks, rigging, 685
Stews. *See also* Braising; Chili
broccoli rabe with garlic, 269
chicken
and dumplings, 694–695, 779
and mushroom, 264–265
Provençal, 644–645
quick-stewed green beans with, 451
in white chili, 273
chickpea and couscous, 228–229
cod or fish fillets
and chickpea, 566–567
and fava bean, 567
and white bean, 567
collard greens with smoked pork, 268–269
eggs sukiyaki, 524–525
green beans
with bacon, 450–451
with chicken, 451
with ham, 451
with sausage, 451
with shrimp, 451
with tomatoes, olives, and almonds, 255
kale and white bean, with vegetable flatbread, 463–464
lamb, with tomatoes, 254–255
lentil and mushroom, 506–507
mushroom and chicken, 264–265
pork
basic recipe, 745
with black beans and collards, 783
and dumplings, 778–779
Provençal, and fennel, 784
in white bean chili, 783
with white beans and kale, 782–783
saag
mushroom and spinach, 439
potato and spinach, 438–439
tofu and spinach, 439
stewed greens and tomatoes, salmon with, 555
vegetables, heartier braised, 423
white beans
chili, 783
and cod, 567
and kale, stewed, with Parmesan toast, 483
and kale, with vegetable flatbread, 463–464
and tomatoes, stewed, with Parmesan toast, 482–483
Sticky rice, 352, 355
Stir-fry
about, 731
beef
and broccoli with scallions and ginger, 730–731
caramel, 716–717
with skillet kimchi, 712–713
bok choy, 927
chicken
and broccoli with black bean sauce, 634–635
and broccoli with tomato-soy sauce, 635
with collards and dried chiles, 632–633
with corn and red onion, 641
with edamame, 501
and kale, 632–633
chickpeas, curried, 486–487
lamb and green peppers, 790–791
noodles with beef and celery, 344–345
noodles with tofu and celery, 345
pork
and broccoli with chiles, 731
caramel, with green beans, 717
with edamame, 501, 748–749
with skillet sauerkraut, 713
and white beans, with cabbage, kimchi style, 500–501
recipe-free, *636–637*
shrimp
and cauliflower with rustic romesco, 590–591
with shitakes, eggs, and cilantro, 589
with tomato, eggs, and basil, 589
with tomato, eggs, and scallions, 588–589
squid and cauliflower with rustic romesco, 591
tofu and green beans, 516–517
veal with shallots and peas, 735
Stocks
about
cooking in, 385
storing, 19
substituting ingredients, 21
beef, 212
chicken, 213
dashi, 213, 234–235
fish, 213
master recipes, 212–213
quinoa cooked in, 945
vegetable, 212
Stone fruit, prep shortcuts, *32*
Stove, eating around, 449
Strawberry(ies)
and almond smoothie, 811

Strawberry(ies) *(cont.)*
toast with almond butter and, 814–815
tomato and strawberry panzanella, 47
tomato salad with feta, balsamic, and, 46–47
Striped bass
about, 587
and cucumber ribbons, 565
and fennel, 565
and zucchini ribbons, 564–565
Stroganoff
beef, 647
chicken, 646–647
pork, 647
Stuffing
flavoring variations, 701
sage sausage, 700–701
skillet, 952
Substituting ingredients, 21–22
Succotash, 933
Sugar, 17, 978
Sukiyaki, eggs, 524–525
Sundaes, 976
Sushi grade fish, 541
Sustainable seafood, 395, 587
Swedish meatballs, 891
Sweet and sour bok choy, salmon with, 555
Sweet peppers. *See* Bell pepper(s)
Sweet potato(es)
about, 21
beef tenderloin, pan-roasted, with, 741
and black-eyed pea burgers, BBQ, 153
breakfast burritos, with chorizo and, 857
and chicken adobo, 692–693
chickpeas, spicy, stir-fried with, 487
and crab cakes, 601
and fish fillets, teriyaki-glazed, 575
flautas, 436–437
fries, 963
hash, 860–861
lamb chops, miso, with, 793
and lamb fundido, 659
and pork enchiladas, 745
purée, with pork tenderloin, 773
rösti with orange sauce, 427
sautéed, 964
soup with pears and bacon, 221
warm three-bean salad and, 103
Swiss cheese in Reuben sandwich, 186
Swordfish
about, 586
broiled, 562–563

T

Tabbouleh
broccoli, with charred tomato and lemon, 124–125
cauliflower, with charred tomato and lemon, 125
fennel and radish, with charred tomato and lime, 125
warm, with mussels, 396–397
warm, with tuna, 397
Tacos
about, 183
charred chicken and tortillas with taco fixings, 649
chicken, crisp, and watermelon, 185
filling variations, 183
pork, crisp, and apple, 185
pork, crisp, and peach, 185
pork, crisp, and watermelon, 184–185
steak, with lots of options, 182–183
Tahini
chickpea and cucumber salad with parsley and, 63
chickpeas with fried eggs, 846–847
in cold sesame noodles, 331
creamed spinach, 936
-lemon potato salad, 962
in peanut vinaigrette, 953
in salad dressing, 86–87, 89
in sesame chicken tenders, 675
in slaw, 923
in yogurt-tahini sauce, 691
Tamale(s)
masa harina in, 241
soup, chicken, 240–241
soup, pork, 241
Tapas on skewers, no-cook, 878
Tapenade
-crusted chicken with eggplant, 622–623
warm, broiled swordfish or fish steaks with, 563
Tarka, 372–373
Tarragon
about, 21
clams, steamed, with cream and, 553
lemon-tarragon aïoli, 161
lobster and egg salad with cucumber and, 105
in mayonnaise, 159, 161
peach and blue cheese salad with, 922
scrambled eggs with ham and, 839
shrimp and egg salad with cucumber and, 105
shrimp simmered in lentils with, 599
in vinaigrettes, 115
Tartar sauce
curried, 69
fish and chips with, 594–595
herby, 68–69
Tempura, celery root, 448–449
Tenderloin
beef, pan-roasted, with chile sweet potatoes, 741
beef, pan-roasted, with potatoes, 740–741
pork
about, 773
with butternut purée, 772–773
grilled or broiled, sauerkraut and apple salad with, 123
homemade cold cuts, master recipe, 775
pan-roasted, with celery root, 741
with Parmesan mashed potatoes, 773
spice-rubbed with pineapple salsa, 756–757
with sweet potato purée, 773
Teriyaki
beef cocktail meatballs, 890
beef, udon with, 337
chicken, udon with, 337
-glazed fish fillets and shitakes, 575
pork, udon with, 337
tofu, udon with, 336–337
Thai peppers, 456
Thai-style
coconut lentils, shrimp simmered in, 599
coconut soup, 252–253
curry-braised beef and eggplant, 738–739
peanut chicken with crisp cabbage and bean sprouts, 654–655
roasted nuts, sweet and salty, 895
steak, lettuce, and herb wrap, 710–711
steamed clams with spinach, 553
sticky rice with meaty vegetable sauce, 374–375
sticky rice with pork and mustard greens, 375
vinaigrette, 75
Thin ribbons, *35*
Three-bean salad
warm, with potatoes, 102–103
warm, with sweet potatoes, 103
Thyme
chicken salad sandwich with olives and, 165
panfried olives with shallots and, 879
Tikka, cauliflower, with boiled eggs, 470–471
Time-texture continuum, 215
Tiramisu, 991

Toasted bread
for bread salad, 119
breakfast, 814–817, 830–833
for sandwiches, 137
Toasted nuts
beet gratin with, 431
broccoli and, 926
celery root gratin with, 431
squash au gratin with, 430–431
Tofu, 516–531
about
marinades and rubs, 796–797
nonstick cookware, 519
pressing, 519
seasoning, 89
storing, 519
substituting for chicken, 93
types of, 518–519
BBQ, and cauliflower, 523
braised
with tomatoes and broccoli, 530–531
with tomatoes and cauliflower, 531
with tomatoes and peas, 531
chili
with black beans, 526–527
with black-eyed peas and collards, 527
with white beans, 527
chipotle-orange, and cauliflower, 523
deep-fried, with peanut sauce and scallions, 520–521
deep-fried, with pistachio sauce and cilantro, 521
in eggs sukiyaki, 524–525
hash, sweet potato and, 861
Manchurian, and cauliflower, 522–523
noodles
with celery and, 345
with chile oil, edamame, and, 335
cold cashew, with, 331
cold peanut, with, 330–331
cold sesame, with, 331
udon with teriyaki, 336–337
pressed
and celery salad with sesame-chile vinaigrette, 91
and cucumber salad with hoisin vinaigrette, 90–91
and tomato salad with soy vinaigrette, 91
roasted, with sesame drizzle, 528–529
saag, spinach and, 439
salad
chipotle, with pepitas and raisins, 93
crisp, with cabbage and coconut-lime dressing, 88–89
crisp, with cabbage and peanut-lime dressing, 88–89
curried, and cabbage with coconut-lime dressing, 89
curried, with pecans and golden raisins, 92–93
green bean, with avocado and, 75
pressed, and celery salad with sesame-chile vinaigrette, 91
pressed, and cucumber salad with hoisin vinaigrette, 90–91
pressed, and tomato salad with soy vinaigrette, 91
sandwich
Buffalo, 143
with cucumber and hoisin mayo, 142–143
with pickles and Dijon mayo, 143
with red onions and chipotle mayo, 143
seared, 529
smoothie, blueberry and, 811
soup
gumbo, 261
hot and sour, with Asian greens and, 271
miso, with soba, bok choy, and, 235
peanut, Chinese-style, with bok choy and, 243
stir-fried, and green beans, 516–517
Tomatillo(s)
in salsas, 562–563
in sauces, 421
tomato salad with queso fresco and, 47
Tomato(es). *See also* Cherry tomato(es)
about
canned, 16, 227, 295
prep shortcuts, *30*
seasoning with, 943
substituting ingredients, 21
types of, 294–295
-braised lentils and potatoes, 510–511
with bread crumbs, 930
bulgur, shrimp kebabs over, 577
and chicken packages, 680–681
in dipping sauce, 176
dried. *See* Dried tomatoes
fideos with, 308–309
-garlic couscous, 821
pasta with seafood and, 310–311
pie, deconstructed, with spinach, ricotta, and, 469
prosciutto-wrapped, 886
salad
in BLT salad with rosemary-mayo dressing, 120–121
broccoli tabbouleh with lemon and, 124–125
and broiled eggplant, with peanut-soy dressing, 87
cauliflower tabbouleh with lemon and, 125
and chicken, with basic vinaigrette, 114–115
and chicken, with Parmesan dressing, 117
crab, curried, with coconut and, 93
fennel and radish tabbouleh with lime and, 125
kale with pine nuts, Parmesan, and, 45
with olive oil and yogurt, 913
with sesame and soy, 913
with strawberries, feta, and balsamic, 46–47
and strawberry panzanella, 47
and tofu, pressed, with soy vinaigrette, 91
with tomatillos and queso fresco, 47
with watermelon, feta, and balsamic, 47
sandwich
and broccoli rabe hero with mozzarella and lemon zest, 173
chicken, bacon, and avocado wrap with, 166–167
chicken, bacon, and blue cheese wrap with, 167
turkey and Brie, broiled, with, 151
and seafood paella, 378–379
with shrimp, 588–589, 855
soup
and bread, 224–225
peach gazpacho with crisp bacon and, 203
Provençal, with fennel, 216–217
stew
and beans, 482–483
green bean, with olives, almonds, and, 255
and greens, stewed, with salmon, 555
lamb, with, 254–255
tofu, braised, with, 530–531
in tomato-paprika mayo, 161
in vinaigrettes, 73
Tomato paste
in rubs, 797
seasoning with, 295
storing, 16
in tomato broth, 581
in tomato rice with corn and shrimp, 367

Tomato salsa
burrito with, 170–171
fish fillets or steaks with, 539, 563
master recipe, 145
with peaches, 757
picante rojo, 563
salmon with, 538–539
Tomato sauce
about, 20
with basil, 592–593
buttery, 490–491
chipotle, 801
coconutty, 491
eggs poached in, 851
fresh, 296
-garlic, 420–421
lamb and bulgur meatballs in, 800–801
with lots of garlic, 296
master recipe, 296–297
pasta with spicy eggplant and, 292–293
Provençal, 801
puttanesca, 293
smashed peas and, 935
spaghetti with, 290–291, 320–321
tomato-soy, 635
with wine, 296
-yogurt, 739
Tortilla(s)
black bean and cabbage gratin with tortilla crumbs and Jack, 493
charred, 907
and charred chicken, with taco fixings, 649
cheesy, 483
and chicken salad, 119
flautas, potato and chorizo, 437
flautas, sweet potato, 436–437
French toast, 832–833
fried, 907
lasagna, 466–467
masa harina in, 241
microwaved, 907
scramble, 842–843
soup, chicken, 241
Spanish, 460–461
warm flour, 907
Tortillas rojas, 894
Trout
panfried
with bacon and Brussels sprouts, 583
with bacon and leeks, 582–583
with chorizo and red onions, 583
and rice cakes, with cucumber salsa, 377
smoked, scrambled eggs with dill and, 839
Truffles, goat cheese, 885
Tuna
about, 395, 586
farro with white beans and, 394–395
pan-seared, with ginger-scallion snow peas, 540–541
pasta with dried tomatoes and, 304–305
poke
with daikon and peanuts, 544–545
with kohlrabi and, 545
with kohlrabi and cashews, 545
salad
and celery root rémoulade, 67
and egg, with radishes and dill, 104–105
and green beans, with avocado and, 74–75
and green beans, with mango and, 75
Niçoise style, 75
sandwich
with avocado and cilantro, 147
with cucumbers and feta, 147
with fennel, capers, and lemon, 147
melt with pickles and mustard, 147
with olives, 147
with pickles and mustard, 146–147
seared, Niçoise, 163
seared, with bok choy and soy mayo, 162–163
tabbouleh, warm, with, 397
Turkey
about, 703
in cabbage, unstuffed, with ground meat, 425
homemade cold cuts, master recipe, 774
meat loaf with spinach, 699
meatballs and spaghetti with tomato sauce, 321
roasted, with sage sausage stuffing, 700–701
sandwich
with Brie and tomatoes, broiled, 151
and broccoli rabe hero, 172–173
burgers, 666–667
and kale hero with Gruyère, 173
salad, with apples and sage, 165
and spinach hero with fontina and lemon zest, 173
wine-braised, 702–703
Turnip greens in andouille, black-eyed pea, and Southern greens soup, 247

U

Udon
about, 333
miso soup with chicken, snow peas, and, 235
in noodles
with chicken and cilantro-scallion pesto, 340–341
with chile oil and edamame, 335
with chile oil and snow peas, 334–335
with chile oil and spinach, 335
panfried, 951
with teriyaki beef, 337
with teriyaki chicken, 337
with teriyaki pork, 337
with teriyaki tofu, 336–337

V

Vanilla custard sauce, 989, 992
Vanilla extract, 979
Veal
about, 733
braised
with edamame, 735
with garlic and white beans, 735
with peas, 734–735
Marsala, 733
and mushroom sauté with mustard and cream, 683
scaloppini with lemon and capers, 732–733
scaloppini with peas and white wine, 733
stir-fried, with shallots and peas, 735
Vegetable(s), 410–471. *See also* Salad(s); *specific vegetables*
about
cooking in one pot, 103
marinades and rubs, 796–797
prep shortcuts, *28–32*
salting, 91
storing, 19
braised, heartier, 423
caprese, bubbling, 414–415
charred. *See* Charred vegetables
and chicken cutlets, with chimichurri, 719
and chicken pancakes, Korean-style, 662–663
and chicken, split whole, 686–687
cobbler, cherry tomato, 464–465
fattoush, 440–441
noodles
in broth with chicken and vegetables, 670–671
cold cashew, with vegetables, 331
cold peanut, with vegetables, 330–331
cold sesame, with vegetables, 331

pan roast
with mussels and coconut curry, 605
with mussels and saffron aïoli, 604–605
with mussels and tomato broth, 605
with shrimp and saffron aïoli, 605
pan sauce, 631
pickled. *See* Pickled vegetables
and pork chops, with chimichurri, 719
queso fundido, sweet pepper, 418–419
raw, in pinzimonio, 884
raw, with romesco, 882
roasted, master recipe, 416–417
root, 57, 147
sandwich
egg salad, classic, with lots of, 155
egg salad, curried, with lots of, 155
egg salad, with lots of, 154–155
and hummus pita pockets, 140–141
skillet spanakopita, 468–469
soup
and chicken, with rice, 262–263
frozen, 214–215
frozen, creamy, 215
stock, master recipe, 212
and steak, with chimichurri, 718–719
tender, 954
tortilla lasagna, 466–467
tortilla, Spanish, 460–461
Vegetarian
couscous helper, 401
vegetarian sauce sub, 189
Vietnamese-style
bánh mì, 180–181
Brussels sprouts, glazed, with Vietnamese flavors, 422–423
caramel-cooked cod, 568–569
scallops, 569
shrimp, 569
stir-fried beef and green beans, 716–717
stir-fried beef and peppers, 717
stir-fried pork and green beans, 717
pho, fast, 236–237
Vinaigrette(s)
about, 45
additions to, 70
bacon, 52–53
basil, 114–115
curry, 953
dill, 115
hoisin, 90–91
marinating in, 47, 57
master recipe, 70–71
mustard, 115
peanut, 158–159, 953
sesame, 953
sesame-chile, 91
shallots in, 70
soy, 91
tarragon, 115
Thai, 75
tomato, 73
warm, 53
Vinegar
about, 21
-shallot sauce, 595

W

Waffles
cheddar, with bacon maple syrup, 870–871
corn, with blueberry maple syrup, 871
molasses, with ginger maple syrup, 871
Walnut(s)
caramelized, in maple-ginger oatmeal, 825
charred Brussels sprout salad with figs and, 127
charred Brussels sprout salad, with Gorgonzola and, 126–127
chicken and chard gratin with blue cheese and, 657
in honey-walnut johnnycakes, 865
roasted spaghetti squash with brown butter and, 458–459
roasted spaghetti squash with rosemary-garlic oil and, 459
spinach with apples, goat cheese, and, 45
Walnut butter, toast with apples and, 815
Watercress
about, 49
garlicky, pan-seared halibut with, 541
with peaches, pecans, and blue cheese, 44–45
Watermelon
gazpacho, melon with crisp prosciutto, 202–203
Malaysian-style BBQ fish with, 579
salad with feta and mint, 922
in salsa, 613
soup with fresh herbs, 973
tacos, crisp chicken and, 185
tacos, crisp pork and, 184–185
tomato salad with feta, balsamic, and, 47
Wheat
cracked. *See* Cracked wheat
puffed, with dried apricots and pistachios, 61
in wheaty oven-fried chicken with roasted corn, 677
White bean(s)
with bacon, greens, and garlic, 481
chicken cutlets, smoked paprika-spiced, with dried tomatoes, 627
chili, 783
chili, tofu and, 527
and farro
with arugula and Parmesan, 395
Greek-style, 395
with tomato and fennel, 395
with tuna, 394–395
fideos with chorizo, tomatoes, and, 309
and ham gratin, 502–503
with Italian sausage, 763
pasta with fennel and, 288–289
with pork and cabbage, kimchi style, 500–501
with prosciutto and escarole, 515
refried, with rosemary, 938
in rice, beans, and broccoli, 350–351
salad
and corn salad with garlic chicken, 109
and cucumber salad with yogurt and dill, 62–63
and fish salad with tomato vinaigrette, 73
and warm escarole salad with poached eggs, 98–99
and warm escarole salad with squid, 99
in salad dressing, 97
with sausage, greens, and garlic, 480–481
and shrimp burrito with corn salsa, 171
and smoked fish gratin, 503
soups and stews
chili, 783
cod or fish fillet stew, 567
and kale stew with vegetable flatbread, 463–464
and kale, stewed, with Parmesan toast, 483
pork stew with kale and, 782–783
soup with rosemary and lemon, 209
tomato and bread soup with, 224–225
and tomatoes, stewed, with Parmesan toast, 482–483
and spinach frittata, 494–495
stuffed poblanos with mozzarella and, 435

White bean(s) *(cont.)*
on toast with Parmesan and sage, 477
veal, braised, with garlic and, 735
wine-braised, with cherry tomatoes and Parmesan, 499
and zucchini burgers, 153
and zucchini with fried eggs, 846–847
White chili, 273
White chocolate
molten cake, 987
-orange pudding, 990
White rice, 941
Whole wheat
bread, 136
couscous, 910
Whoopie pies, molasses, 981
Wine
braised pork with cabbage and, 767
braised pork with celery and, 767
-braised turkey, 702–703
-braised white beans with cherry tomatoes and Parmesan, 499
in cauliflower "polenta" with mushrooms, 432–433
in cranberry-port sundaes, 976
linguine with clams, cream, and, 303
in marinades, 796
pasta with chicken, mushrooms, and, 314–315
quinoa with rosemary and, 945
tomato sauce with, 296
veal scallopini with peas and, 733
Woks, 731
Wonton skins, 327
Wonton soup, broken, 248–249
Wraps
about, 167
BLT, chipotle, 167
chicken, bacon, avocado, and tomato, 166–167
chicken, bacon, tomato, and blue cheese, 167
chicken, Greek, 167
Italian-style steak, lettuce, and herb, 711
Mexican-style steak, lettuce, and herb, 711
Thai-style steak, lettuce, and herb, 710–711

Y

Yellow lentils with charred broccoli, 509
Yogurt
about
flavoring, 819
storing, 18
varieties of, 809
beet and cabbage salad with dill and, 57
in fruit, yogurt, and graham cracker parfait, 808–809
pound cupcakes, 985
in rubs, 797
in sauces
curried yogurt, 595
honey-yogurt, 818–819
tomato-yogurt, 739
yogurt, 891
yogurt raita, 916
yogurt-blue cheese, 691
yogurt-harissa sauce, 690–691
yogurt-tahini, 691
tomato salad with olive oil and, 913
white bean and cucumber salad with dill and, 62–63

Z

Za'atar
about, 690
chicken and onions, 651
chicken wings and eggplant with yogurt-harissa sauce, 690–691
Ziti
broiled, 298–299
with olives and feta, 283, 299
Zucchini
bulgur, lemony, with olives, ricotta salata, and, 387
burgers, white bean, and, 153
couscous paella with chicken and, 406–407
fish fillets or steaks with toasted bread crumbs and, 537
pork souvlaki with, 754–755
ribbons, striped bass and, 564–565
salad
and broiled eggplant, 86–87
fattoush, 440–441
raw, with warm lima beans, 101
slaw with chopped spicy chicken, 106–107
slaw with chopped spicy shrimp, 107
slaw with crisp ground lamb, 107
soup, tomato and bread, with, 225
stew. chicken and, 265
warm-pickled, 896
and white bean burgers, 153
and white beans with fried eggs, 846–847

Converting Measurements

Essential Conversions

VOLUME TO VOLUME

3 teaspoons	1 tablespoon
4 tablespoons	¼ cup
5 tablespoons plus 1 teaspoon	⅓ cup
4 ounces	½ cup
8 ounces	1 cup
1 cup	½ pint
2 pints	1 quart
4 quarts	1 gallon

VOLUME TO WEIGHT

¼ cup liquid or fat	2 ounces
½ cup liquid or fat	4 ounces
1 cup liquid or fat	8 ounces
2 cups liquid or fat	1 pound
1 cup sugar	7 ounces
1 cup flour	5 ounces

Metric Approximations

MEASUREMENTS

¼ teaspoon	1.25 milliliters
½ teaspoon	2.5 milliliters
1 teaspoon	5 milliliters
1 tablespoon	15 milliliters
1 fluid ounce	30 milliliters
¼ cup	60 milliliters
⅓ cup	80 milliliters
½ cup	120 milliliters
1 cup	240 milliliters
1 pint (2 cups)	480 milliliters
1 quart (4 cups)	960 milliliters (0.96 liters)
1 gallon (4 quarts)	3.84 liters
1 ounce (weight)	28 grams
¼ pound (4 ounces)	114 grams
1 pound (16 ounces)	454 grams
2.2 pounds	1 kilogram (1,000 grams)
1 inch	2.5 centimeters

OVEN TEMPERATURES

Description	°Fahrenheit	°Celsius
Cool	200	90
Very slow	250	120
Slow	300–325	150–160
Moderately slow	325–350	160–180
Moderate	350–375	180–190
Moderately hot	375–400	190–200
Hot	400–450	200–230
Very hot	450–500	230–260